AI Risk and Resolution in Higher Education and Academic Integrity

Nuzhat Younis
The University of West of the England, UK

Yasmine Rosunally
The University of West of the England, UK

Mazhar Hussain Malik
https://orcid.org/0000-0001-8890-1310
University of the West of England, UK

IGI Global
Scientific Publishing
Publishing Tomorrow's Research Today

Vice President of Editorial	Melissa Wagner
Director of Acquisitions	Mikaela Felty
Director of Book Development	Jocelynn Hessler
Production Manager	Mike Brehm
Cover Design	Jose Rosado

Published in the United States of America by
IGI Global Scientific Publishing
701 East Chocolate Avenue
Hershey, PA, 17033, USA
Tel: 717-533-8845 | Fax: 717-533-7115
Website: https://www.igi-global.com E-mail: cust@igi-global.com

Library of Congress Cataloging-in-Publication Data

LCCN: 2025033188 (CIP Data Pending)
ISBN13: 9798337355863
Isbn13Softcover: 9798337355870
EISBN13: 9798337355887
British Cataloguing in Publication Data
A Cataloguing in Publication record for this book is available from the British Library.

Table of Contents

Detailed Table of Contents

This study investigates the transformative potential of Generative AI (GenAI) in education, emphasizing its role in improving instructional efficiency, grading accuracy, and personalization, while addressing ethical concerns. Using a systematic literature review of 71 articles, the study categorizes GenAI integration into traditional (no AI), GenAI-assisted, and GenAI-empowered assignments. The analysis reveal that GenAI reduces educator workload by 60%, aligns 86% with human grading, and supports personalized tutoring, adaptive learning, multilingual content creation, exam design, and multimodal assessments. The study incorporates ChatGPT case studies and proposes phased implementation starting with AI-assisted methods. It urges institutions to provide AI literacy training and develop ethical guidelines to ensure responsible use. This research offers comprehensive framework analyzing GenAI in both teaching and assessment, delivering actionable insights for educators, institutions, and policymakers aiming to integrate AI effectively and ethically. Ask ChatGPT

Digital technologies are transforming higher education by reshaping teaching, research, and administration. While they enhance efficiency and access, they also pose ethical and governance challenges involving fairness, privacy, and academic integrity. This chapter explores how responsible digital governance can ensure inclusive and ethical transformation. Focusing on pedagogical, governance, and operational dimensions, it emphasizes transparency, accountability, and institutional capacity building. Drawing from global practices, it highlights ethics committees, policy frameworks, and literacy programs that foster trust. A value-driven, multi-

The integration of AI in education opens new horizons to enhance the management of classroom and assist teachers with learning aids. The study will focus on the application of popular machine learning algorithm, XGBoost model for analyzing students' data. The target is to predict student's engagement, detect which learners are at risk with the goal of prescribing a targeted intervention. The authors selected XGBoost because of its capability to handle complex and nonlinear data as well as its encouraging predictive power in offering teachers the possibility to identify problem areas early on and cater for individual learning needs. Student attendance, participation, submitted homework on time and previous academic performance were all significant predictors of risk. These learnings provide important guidance for teachers to adjust both instruction and classroom strategies, as well as underscore the critical nature of intuitive AI tools, data security and ethics in education.

Artificial Intelligence (AI) has brought a new age of innovation to every industry, especially to education. Schools are making an effort to meet the changing and diverse needs of a dynamic society. AI is a powerful tool for revolutionizing traditional education. This technology has an impact on education in the following ways: personalized learning, the creation of intelligent tutoring systems, better administrative functions, and higher student engagement. This study highlights how AI could potentially revolutionize the experience of learning for higher education students but, at the same time, indicates a divergence problem. The chapter reviews the role and application of artificial intelligence (AI) in higher education and the difficulties encountered in the process of implementation. The paper also presents examples of how educational institutions have incorporated AI in the field of education to ensure that everyone receives quality and equitable education. Last, the paper examines the limitations and challenges to the implementation of AI in educational settings.

The artificial intelligence (AI) sector is reshaping higher education through the teaching, learning, and administration. However, many institutions experience resistance toward AI-based applications owing to the threat of job losses, insufficient digital skills, and the conflict of ethics. The chapter elaborates on the human and organizational factors which hamper AI in higher education organizations and suggests effective change management strategies to resolve them. It emphasizes the role of the top management, communication, and the professional development programs in reducing the uncertainty and building trust in AI systems. The chapter constructs practical models that use well-established theories such as Kotter's, ADKAR, and Lewin's to guide the institutions through the process of technological change. The discussion emphasizes that successful AI adoption depends not only on technology but also on people-centered change processes.

Equity, accountability, and capacity gaps have become increasingly significant with the rapid advancement of artificial intelligence in higher education, particularly in resource-constrained institutions across Asia, Africa, and Latin America. This chapter examines how universities in these contexts navigate the dual challenge of pursuing digital transformation while ensuring fairness in learning and assessment. It analyzes the interplay between institutional readiness, infrastructural limitations, and cultural diversity that influence technology adoption. A conceptual framework is proposed to guide responsible and equitable AI integration, emphasizing that sustainable digital transformation requires technological preparedness, human capacity, ethical governance, and culturally responsive pedagogy.

The quick use of AI in schools has changed the duties of teachers in a big way. They now need to be good at digital literacy, data analytics, and technology-enabled teaching. Training and professional development for AI are important for teachers to learn how to use intelligent systems in teaching, research, and institutional innovation. This chapter talks about why teachers should be AI literate, how teaching roles are changing, and ways to build capability that will last. It looks at the institutional frameworks for AI training, such as programs for ongoing professional development, partnerships between business and academia, and AI-powered learning platforms. By showing the finest practices from across the world and where things are going in the future, it stresses the importance of ongoing, cross-disciplinary, and inclusive professional development to make teachers leaders in the AI-driven education ecosystem.

Artificial Intelligence (AI) is a transformational technology that provides opportunities in the fields of teaching and research. Its adoption to success greatly relies on how the faculty is ready and the Professional Development opportunities the faculty. This paper provides a systematic literature review of 44 studies to examine faculty

Artificial intelligence micro-credentials are discussed as a lever for reshaping higher education towards more flexible, learner-centred and inclusive lifelong learning. The chapter first clarifies how micro-credentials are defined, designed and classified, with a particular focus on AI-focused and AI-supported offerings. It then considers how learning analytics, adaptive platforms and digital credential infrastructures can be used to strengthen quality assurance, personalisation, recognition and cross-border portability of modular learning. Equity, accessibility and ethical risks and opportunities for disadvantaged, non-traditional and disabled learners are examined throughout. Finally, a human-centred, multi-stakeholder model is outlined for linking AI micro-credentials to national qualification systems, institutional strategies and labour-market needs, so that they complement rather than replace traditional degrees while broadening meaningful opportunities for learning and work.

This chapter explores the evolving landscape of AI-driven research misconduct, highlighting how artificial intelligence technologies have transformed traditional notions of academic integrity. It examines emerging forms of misconduct such as AI-generated plagiarism, data fabrication, deepfake research outputs, and citation manipulation, emphasizing their detection challenges and institutional implications. The discussion integrates ethical literacy, prevention frameworks, and policy responses aimed at safeguarding scholarly credibility in the digital era. By addressing detection methodologies, prevention strategies, and governance reforms, the chapter underscores the urgent need for transparency, accountability, and adaptive institutional policies to preserve the integrity of scientific research in the age of AI.

Generative Artificial Intelligence (AI) disrupts not only textual production but also the epistemic foundations of authorship, originality, and academic integrity in higher education. This chapter critically examines the erosion of authorship as an ethical and subjective practice under linguistic automation. Drawing on philosophy of technology, epistemology, and pedagogy, it shows how detection-first responses risk inequity and due-process failures, while international guidance now prioritises assessment redesign and transparency. We introduce the EROS framework (Ethics, Reflexivity, Originality, Situatedness) to re-conceptualise integrity through accountability, process evidence, and contextualised originality. The chapter details a 12-point blueprint, rubrics, and governance mechanisms, illustrating with vignettes and decision trees how integrity can be safeguarded without punitive overreach. Ultimately, it argues for reclaiming authorship as an existential and creative act, fostering critical co-authorship with machines and hermeneutic responsibility in an AI-saturated academy.

Preface

Artificial intelligence has rapidly emerged as one of the most transformative forces shaping the future of higher education. From personalized learning environments and intelligent tutoring systems to institutional governance and academic research, AI technologies are redefining how knowledge is created, delivered, assessed, and managed. While these advancements offer unprecedented opportunities to enhance educational quality, accessibility, and efficiency, they also introduce complex challenges surrounding academic integrity, ethical governance, transparency, privacy, and institutional accountability. As universities continue integrating AI into teaching, learning, research, and administration, the need for responsible implementation has become increasingly critical.

AI Risk and Resolution in Higher Education and Academic Integrity brings together an interdisciplinary collection of scholarly contributions that examine both the opportunities and challenges associated with artificial intelligence in higher education. The chapters explore how institutions can leverage AI to improve educational outcomes while preserving the fundamental principles of academic honesty, fairness, inclusivity, and ethical responsibility. Through a combination of theoretical discussions, systematic literature reviews, conceptual frameworks, case studies, and practical applications, this volume offers readers a comprehensive understanding of how AI is reshaping higher education across diverse institutional and cultural contexts.

The research presented throughout this book extends beyond technological innovation to address the human, organizational, and policy dimensions of AI adoption. Contributors examine institutional governance, faculty development, student experiences, responsible assessment practices, digital transformation, research ethics, and emerging models for lifelong learning. Collectively, these perspectives demonstrate that the successful integration of artificial intelligence depends not only on technological capability but also on thoughtful leadership, ethical decision-making, stakeholder engagement, and sustainable educational policies. As institutions worldwide navigate this period of rapid technological change, the insights presented in this volume provide valuable guidance for educators, researchers, administrators, and policymakers seeking to maximize the benefits of AI while minimizing its associated risks.

CHAPTER OVERVIEW

Chapter 1 examines the evolution of teaching and assessment through the integration of generative artificial intelligence. It explores how AI enhances instructional efficiency, grading accuracy, personalized learning, and assessment design while emphasizing the importance of ethical implementation, AI literacy, and institutional guidelines for responsible educational practice.

Chapter 2 investigates the role of responsible AI governance in higher education by examining ethical, operational, and institutional considerations surrounding digital transformation. The chapter proposes a value-driven governance framework that promotes transparency, accountability, fairness, and trust while supporting sustainable technological innovation across academic institutions.

Chapter 3 explores the principles of responsible artificial intelligence adoption within higher education, emphasizing that successful implementation requires balancing technological advancement with inclusivity, transparency, privacy, and student well-being. The discussion highlights collaborative approaches that involve educators, students, technologists, and policymakers.

Chapter 4 focuses on responsible artificial intelligence in relation to academic integrity by examining issues surrounding fairness, transparency, accountability, and ethical literacy. The chapter presents a framework that encourages institutions to utilize AI as a tool that complements rather than replaces human judgment while preserving scholarly honesty.

Chapter 5 presents an artificial intelligence-driven approach for identifying students at academic risk through predictive analytics. Using machine learning techniques, the study demonstrates how institutions can leverage educational data to improve student engagement, personalize interventions, and strengthen learning outcomes while maintaining ethical standards in educational analytics.

Chapter 6 reviews the applications and challenges associated with artificial intelligence adoption across higher education institutions. The authors examine AI's potential to transform teaching, learning, administration, and student engagement while addressing implementation barriers related to equity, infrastructure, and institutional readiness.

Chapter 7 investigates organizational resistance to artificial intelligence adoption within higher education and proposes change management strategies that facilitate successful technological transformation. Drawing upon established organizational models, the chapter emphasizes leadership, communication, and professional development as key drivers of institutional acceptance.

Chapter 8 explores responsible artificial intelligence implementation within resource-constrained higher education environments. The chapter examines how institutions can promote equitable and inclusive digital transformation through educator empowerment, ethical governance, culturally responsive pedagogy, and fair assessment practices despite limited technological resources.

Chapter 9 examines the growing importance of faculty training and professional development in preparing educators for artificial intelligence integration. The discussion highlights institutional strategies that strengthen AI literacy, instructional innovation, interdisciplinary collaboration, and long-term professional growth.

Chapter 10 presents a systematic literature review investigating faculty preparedness for artificial intelligence adoption in higher education. The review synthesizes global research on barriers, enabling factors, digital literacy, and professional development while providing recommendations for sustainable institutional capacity building.

Chapter 11 investigates students' perceptions, experiences, and ethical expectations regarding artificial intelligence within higher education. The findings illustrate how students view AI as a valuable academic resource while expressing concerns regarding misinformation, overreliance, and academic honesty, emphasizing the importance of institutional guidance and ethical frameworks.

Chapter 12 explores the emergence of artificial intelligence microcredentials as flexible learning pathways that complement traditional higher education. The chapter discusses quality assurance, personalized learning, digital credentialing, accessibility, and workforce alignment while proposing a human-centered framework for lifelong learning.

Chapter 13 examines the growing challenges associated with AI-driven research misconduct, including plagiarism, fabricated data, citation manipulation, and synthetic research outputs. The authors discuss detection methods, prevention strategies, institutional governance, and ethical policies designed to preserve research integrity in an increasingly AI-enabled scholarly environment.

Chapter 14 concludes the volume by critically examining the philosophical and ethical implications of authorship in the era of generative artificial intelligence. The chapter challenges conventional understandings of originality and plagiarism while proposing new frameworks that promote responsible AI-assisted scholarship through transparency, accountability, and reflective academic practice.

We hope that this volume will serve as a valuable resource for researchers, educators, institutional leaders, policymakers, graduate students, and practitioners seeking to better understand the opportunities and challenges associated with artificial intelligence in higher education. By bringing together diverse perspectives on responsible AI adoption, academic integrity, governance, faculty development, student engagement, and research ethics, this collection contributes to the ongoing conversation surrounding the future of education in an increasingly intelligent digital world. It is our hope that the research presented throughout these chapters will inspire continued innovation, thoughtful policy development, interdisciplinary collaboration, and ethical leadership that ensures artificial intelligence enhances rather than compromises the core values of higher education.

Nuzhat Younis
The University of the West of England, UK

Yasmine Rosunally
The University of the West of England, UK

Mazhar Malik
The University of the West of England, UK

Chapter 1
From Traditional to AI-Enhanced:
The Evolution of Teaching and Assessment in Higher Education Through Generative AI

Amandeep Dhaliwal
http://orcid.org/0000-0002-6545-1449
Manav Rachna International Institute of Research and Studies, India

ABSTRACT

This study investigates the transformative potential of Generative AI (GenAI) in education, emphasizing its role in improving instructional efficiency, grading accuracy, and personalization, while addressing ethical concerns. Using a systematic literature review of 71 articles, the study categorizes GenAI integration into traditional (no AI), GenAI-assisted, and GenAI-empowered assignments. The analysis reveal that GenAI reduces educator workload by 60%, aligns 86% with human grading, and supports personalized tutoring, adaptive learning, multilingual content creation, exam design, and multimodal assessments. The study incorporates ChatGPT case studies and proposes phased implementation starting with AI-assisted methods. It urges institutions to provide AI literacy training and develop ethical guidelines to ensure responsible use. This research offers comprehensive framework analyzing GenAI in both teaching and assessment, delivering actionable insights for educators, institutions, and policymakers aiming to integrate AI effectively and ethically. Ask ChatGPT

DOI: 10.4018/979-8-3373-5586-3.ch001

1. INTRODUCTION

Artificial Intelligence (AI) encompasses technologies that mimic human-like abilities such as problem-solving, interpretation, and self-directed learning (Sheikh, Prins & Schrijvers, 2023). Unlike traditional AI, which is primarily focused on data analysis and interpretation, generative AI goes a step further by generating novel content in response to prompts, including text, code, and images (Feuerriegel, et al., 2024). This distinction has made generative AI a powerful tool in education, particularly in areas like writing, where systems like ChatGPT and Gemini (formerly Bard) have demonstrated an ability to produce human-like responses on a variety of topics. As a result, educators' interest in these tools has surged, especially since their release, as they present opportunities and challenges for teaching, learning, and assessment (Cotton et al., 2024; Owan et al., 2023).

The rapid advancement of generative artificial intelligence (Gen AI) technologies has generated significant interest among educators regarding their potential applications in higher education, particularly in the areas of both student assessment and learning. The supporting proponents highlight the benefits of Gen AI, emphasizing its ability to enhance student engagement, provide timely feedback, and reduce instructor workloads, thereby fostering a more personalized and accessible learning environment (Jaime-Vargas, 2025; Porter & Grippa, 2020; Smith & Vickers 2024). In the context of learning, AI can support students by offering tailored resources, facilitating adaptive learning paths, and enabling immediate responses to queries, all of which can significantly enhance the learning experience (Clark, 2024).

However, the rapid adoption of generative AI by faculty and students, particularly for writing tasks, has raised concerns about its potential impact the integration of Gen AI tools into educational practices. Critics argue that the use of AI in assessments could compromise academic integrity, potentially increasing instances of plagiarism and undermining the reliability of assessment outcomes (Smith & Green, 2018). As generative AI tools generate text that can be difficult to distinguish from human-written work, questions about plagiarism and the authenticity of student submissions have become central to academic debates (Cotton et al., 2024; Moorhouse et al., 2025). Moreover, there are concerns that heavy reliance on Gen AI could impair students' development of critical thinking and writing skills, which are fundamental to higher education, ultimately leading to a decline in the quality of instruction and learning outcomes (Davis. A, 2024; Walker, 2025). Over-dependence on these tools may hinder students' ability to engage deeply with their learning.

Furthermore, educators have expressed concerns that automated content generation could diminish the quality of learning outcomes and disrupt the traditional roles of teachers and students in the classroom (Lee & Kwon, 2024). These concerns are compounded by the increasing capabilities of large language models (LLMs), such as OpenAI's Generative Pre-trained Transformers (GPT), Google's XLNet, and Meta's LLaMA. These models, developed by major organizations like Google, Meta, and Microsoft/OpenAI, have become central to the debate about the future of education, particularly in the context of student assessments and the role of AI in supporting learning (Zawacki-Richter et al., 2019). However, despite these concerns, many academics believe that generative AI can be leveraged positively in education (Clark, 2024; Jaime-Vargas, 2025). For instance, AI can enhance student participation by providing instant feedback, fostering collaboration, and offering personalized learning experiences (Porter & Grippa, 2020; Smith & Vickers, 2024; Zhai & Nehm, 2023).

In this context, the ongoing debate about the integration of generative AI into educational systems revolves not only around its potential risks but also its opportunities. Many scholars have recommended that instead of focusing on whether to use AI in education, the conversation should shift to how these tools can be effectively incorporated into teaching and assessment practices (Zhai & Nehm, 2023).

In current times it is crucial to understand the broader impact of GenAI on the educational experience, particularly as it pertains to how these tools will alter learning dynamics, foster critical thinking, and affect student outcomes. The growing body of research into the use of GenAI in higher education reflects a significant interest in understanding its potential and limitations, as educators and policymakers alike seek to navigate the opportunities and challenges posed by these technologies (Rahman & Watanobe, 2023).

However, the process of adoption of generative AI in tertiary education is far from uniform and is not even predetermined. Using the framework of the Technology Acceptance Model developed by Davis (1989), one may speak of educators who find GenAI useful for alleviating their workload and of others who find its implementation epistemologically dangerous for basic educational tenets. In addition to this, Rogers's (2003) Theory of Diffusion of Innovations provides insight into the context of changes that have occurred in terms of the penetration of technology into the domain of education as determined both by the technology itself and by organizational context.

As more and more educators are adopting AI for educational assignments and assessments and to assist in personalized learning, it is critical to explore the factors influencing instructors' decisions to adopt or reject AI in higher. This study aims to investigate the factors that influence higher education instructors' adoption of generative AI tools, with a focus on how these technologies are reshaping assessment methods and educational practices.

2. RESEARCH METHODOLOGY

This study aims to explore how generative artificial intelligence (GenAI) can transform higher education by examining its impact on two major educational domains: Teaching and assessment. In this chapter, the narrative synthesis method is adopted to conduct a critical analysis of the existing literature on generative AI within higher education research, based on two thematic areas. For its theoretical foundation, the chapter builds upon an earlier systematic review by Chiu et al. (2023), who explored 71 papers extracted from such scholarly databases as SCOPUS, EBSCO, Web of Science, and ProQuest for the period between 2018 and 2024. Nevertheless, unlike Chiu et al. (2023), this chapter not only maps out the existing literature but seeks to question its underlying assumptions, evaluate the dimensions of governance that have remained under examined, and incorporate voices from both the Global North and Global South. The chapter's analytic structure will be guided by Rogers' (2003) model of diffusion.

This framework serves as a foundational tool for data collection and analysis in the current study, offering a structured approach to understanding how GenAI might shape the future of higher education. By focusing on these two domains, the study will provide valuable insights into the transformative potential of GenAI in enhancing educational practices and outcomes.

3. AI AND GEN AI EVOLUTION INTO EDUCATION

The release of ChatGPT on November 30, 2022 marked a pivotal moment in the field, further accelerating the wave of innovation driven by generative AI. These developments in generative models, such as the Generative Pre-trained Transformer (GPT) series, have brought unprecedented capabilities in text generation. The rapid evolution of artificial intelligence (AI) has sparked a significant shift in various sectors, particularly in education. Generative AI (GenAI), a subset of AI technology, is capable of generating new and unique outputs, such as images, text, audio, video, and 3D models, which resemble human creativity (Feuerriegel et al., 2024). The advent of tools like ChatGPT, GPT-4, and other generative models has revolutionized content creation, enabling industries such as education, entertainment, and product design to benefit from AI's potential (Castelli & Manzoni, 2022). These models produce highly sophisticated and realistic content, providing valuable applications in higher education, from personalized learning experiences to the creation of teaching materials and even automating responses to student inquiries (Chiu et al., 2023). As technology continues to evolve, generative AI applications like MidJourney, GitHub Copilot, and others are now integral to the academic landscape, assisting in everything from course content creation to code generation for research (Chiu et al., 2023).

The proponents of GenAI highlight its potential benefits, including enhancing student engagement, providing timely feedback, and reducing the workload of educators, which could make learning more personalized and accessible (Jaime-Vargas, 2025; Smith & Vickers, 2024). These tools can create tailored learning paths, offer real-time responses, and improve the overall educational experience by providing instant feedback and individualized support (Clark, 2024; Porter & Grippa, 2020). As a result, GenAI is viewed as a transformative tool capable of reshaping how both teaching and assessment are approached in higher education.

-Gen AI significantly reduces the time and effort required for designing, administering, and grading assessments. Automated processes enable educators to manage large volumes of assessments without compromising quality. For instance, AI tools can grade thousands of essays in a fraction of the time it would take a human grader, ensuring timely feedback for students (Porter & Grippa, 2020; Smith et al., 2024). It enables personalized assessments tailored to individual student needs. Adaptive assessments, powered by AI, can dynamically adjust question difficulty based on a student's performance, ensuring that the evaluation remains challenging yet achievable. This adaptability promotes a more equitable learning environment by addressing diverse proficiency levels (Crompton & Burke, 2024).

AI-driven assessments minimize human biases that can influence grading. By relying on pre-set criteria and algorithms, Gen AI ensures consistency and fairness in evaluation. This objectivity is particularly critical in high-stakes assessments, such as college admissions or certification exams, where subjective judgments can have significant consequences (Zhao, Chapman & Sabet, 2024).The integration of Gen AI in assessments encourages educators to adopt innovative pedagogical approaches. For example, using AI-generated scenarios or simulations as part of assignments allows students to engage in experiential learning. These approaches foster creativity, critical thinking, and problem-solving skills, aligning with the demands of modern workplaces (Garcia et al.,2026).

The uptake of GenAI, however, is deeply influenced by geopolitical and infrastructural inequalities that need to be recognized. As US, UK, and Australian educational institutions continue at pace to incorporate platforms such as ChatGPT into teaching and assessment practices, institutions within Sub-Saharan Africa, South Asia, and Latin America suffer from several obstacles, such as poor internet connectivity, software licensing fees, and lack of relevant policies of governing AI technology that fit their educational context. The notion of decolonial AI coined by Mohamed, Png & Isaac (2020), where it is emphasized that development of AI technology has been predominantly guided by Western knowledge systems, poses crucial questions concerning who the users of those technologies are and what cultural values underpin them. Similarly, invoking Ubuntu ethics in relation to artificial intelligence, as argued by Mhlambi (2020), challenges the individualistic paradigm that is central to the design of AI and proposes to reconsider relations between people and machines and their nature in a community-based setting.

4. GEN AI IN TEACHING

Generative artificial intelligence (GenAI) is increasingly recognized as a transformative force in the field of education, particularly in teaching. By leveraging advanced algorithms and machine learning capabilities, GenAI can generate human-like text, multimedia content, and adaptive learning resources, offering unprecedented opportunities to enhance teaching methodologies and outcomes. This technology has the potential to revolutionize instructional practices by enabling educators to create personalized, engaging, and effective teaching materials tailored to the diverse needs of learners (Feuerriegel et al., 2024; Moturu & Nethi, 2022).Some of the prominent areas where Gen Ai can be instrumental in supporting teaching include:

(a) **Content Creation** - One of the most impactful contributions of GenAI in teaching is its ability to streamline and enhance content creation. Tools such as ChatGPT, Bard, and GitHub Copilot enable educators to develop lesson plans, generate quizzes, design interactive teaching aids, and even draft assessment rubrics. These capabilities reduce the time spent on administrative tasks, allowing teachers to dedicate more effort to higher-order activities, such as facilitating critical discussions and addressing individual student needs (Chiu et al., 2023; Rahman & Watanobe, 2023). Additionally, GenAI can dynamically adapt content to suit different learning levels, offering foundational scaffolding for beginners while challenging advanced learners with complex materials, thereby fostering differentiated instruction (Castelli & Manzoni, 2022).

(b) **Enhancing Teaching Efficiency**-AI technologies streamline classroom administration by automating tasks such as uploading, assigning, and distributing learning materials, and reading aloud text-based problems (Zawacki-Richter et al., 2019). While these tools simplify teaching processes, many educators remain skeptical about fully trusting AI-driven systems, limiting their widespread adoption.

(c) **Providing Adaptive Teaching Strategies**- AI systems leverage multimodal sensor data to assess students' affective states, enabling teachers to tailor subject matter, instructional strategies, and communication techniques accordingly (Lampos, Mintz & Qu, 2021; Luo & Yusuf, 2026). However, significant challenges remain, such as developing robust evaluation techniques and efficient algorithms to optimize these adaptive systems.

(d) **Supporting Teacher Professional Development-**AI can analyze real-time classroom data to provide feedback on teachers' instructional practices, including their behavior, discourse, and questioning techniques (Hu, 2024; Li & Su, 2020). By offering neutral and data-driven evaluations, AI promotes reflection and reduces potential resentment among instructors. However, the limited research in this area indicates that such applications are still in their early stages.

(e) **Intelligent learning Systems-** AI-based learning systems, such as intelligent laboratories and intelligent tutors, have emerged as transformative tools in education by personalizing learning tasks based on student competence (Hirankerd & Kittisunthonphisarn, 2020; Murtaza et al., 2022). However, the lack of adequate learning resources poses a significant obstacle, limiting the potential of these systems. Additionally, students often adopt a passive role in the learning process, relying heavily on the system's efficiency to facilitate their progress.

(f) **Human-Machine Interaction in Learning -** AI technologies also facilitate human-machine conversations through tools like AI chatbots and interactive books, enabling students to engage in ongoing dialogue that enhances communication skills (Chew & Chua, 2020; Kim, Murai & Chang, 2021; Miller, 2024; Vazquez-Cano et al., 2021). Despite their potential, these interactions are currently limited in depth and scope, restricting their effectiveness. AI systems also analyze student work and learning processes to deliver timely feedback. For example, an AI-powered notebook app has been used to evaluate kindergarten students' handwriting by recognizing and analyzing the shape, order, and direction of writing segments (Bonneton-Botte et al., 2023).

(g) **Faculty Development and AI Literacy** - Without any ongoing investment in faculty development initiatives, it would be impossible to leverage the pedagogical potential of GenAI within teaching. According to Holmes et al. (2022), AI literacy can be described as a combination of skills, knowledge, and abilities to assess the output provided by artificial intelligence algorithms, recognize the limitations involved, and use the technology ethically. Nevertheless, such provision is currently insufficient. Alasadi & Baiz (2026) have pointed out a considerable disparity in terms of the speed at which AI technologies become incorporated into the curriculum and that at which faculty members receive training. In effect, institutions risk adopting these systems in a manner which could be described as 'performative,' failing to reconceive pedagogical practice as a result. Institutions should consider creating programs that will encourage faculty members to engage with AI from an epistemological perspective.

(h) **Adaptability and Interactivity-**AI technologies capture extensive student learning data to create more adaptive and interactive digital environments

(Anderson et al., 2025; Westera et al., 2020). However, the challenge of identifying suitable evaluation methods persists, impacting the effectiveness of these technologies. Generative AI (GenAI) advances these roles by offering enhanced capabilities, such as generating new learning content, facilitating more natural and meaningful conversations with students, and providing detailed feedback. Nonetheless, the integration of GenAI introduces the need for students to develop new competencies, including prompt engineering, digital and AI literacy, and ethical awareness.

(i) **In creating simulations and interactive models-** In STEM education, GenAI is particularly effective in creating simulations and interactive models that help students grasp abstract concepts. For instance, tools like MATLAB's AI-integrated features and GitHub Copilot can generate code snippets and debug solutions, providing real-time support to educators teaching programming and computational thinking (Moturu & Nethi, 2022). In subjects such as physics and biology, AI-powered simulations allow students to visualize complex phenomena, bridging the gap between theoretical knowledge and practical understanding (Smith & Vickers, 2024). These applications make learning more engaging and tangible, thereby improving comprehension and retention.

(j) **Fostering inclusivity-** Generative AI also plays a crucial role in fostering inclusivity in education. By supporting multilingual content generation, AI tools like ChatGPT enable educators to create teaching materials for linguistically diverse classrooms. Moreover, GenAI facilitates the development of accessible content, such as text-to-speech conversions, visually enhanced materials, and alternative formats for students with disabilities (Clark, 2024). These features ensure that educational resources are equitable and cater to a broader range of learning needs.

5. GEN AI IN ASSIGNMENTS

The latest studies research in domain of education resonates with emphasizing the transformative potential of Gen AI in crafting multimodal educational resources (Garcia et al., 2026). They highlight the versatility of Gen AI in creating diverse assignments incorporating multimedia elements. Gen AI's ability to generate diverse forms of content, such as text, images, audio, and video, supports the creation of multimodal assessments. For example, educators can design assignments that require students to create podcasts, videos, or infographics, integrating creativity and digital literacy into the evaluation process. Tools like DALL-E and Synthesia enable the generation of high-quality visuals and interactive content, enriching the assessment experience (Garcia et. al., 2026). These multimodal assessments cater to diverse learning preferences and promote the development of 21st-century skills, including communication, collaboration, and technological fluency. As noted by Perkins et al. (2024), "Integrating multimodal tasks in assessments prepares students for real-world challenges by fostering interdisciplinary competencies."

The evolving role of generative artificial intelligence (Gen AI) in education has prompted researchers to classify assignments into distinct categories based on its integration. This study identifies three primary categories: assignments without Gen AI, Gen AI-assisted assignments, and Gen AI-empowered assignments. These classifications emerge from the diverse applications of Gen AI in teaching and learning, as consistently highlighted by participant responses. Each category represents a specific pedagogical approach reflecting educators' perceptions of the benefits and challenges associated with Gen AI adoption.

Assignments without Gen AI - Assignments without Gen AI represent traditional forms of assessment where students are explicitly prohibited from using generative AI tools. According to participant responses, such assessments include in-person exams, oral presentations, practical applications, and final project presentations. The rationale behind this restriction is to maintain academic integrity and ensure that students demonstrate their independent understanding and mastery of subject matter.

A nursing professor sharing his experience elaborated, "In the course description, I informed my students where they can use Gen AI and where they cannot use it. So already they know in exams and oral presentations they are not allowed to use it." This aligns with existing literature that emphasizes the importance of maintaining non-AI-dependent assessments for specific learning objectives (Heidari & Ekström, 2025). The intent is to encourage original thought and prevent overreliance on external tools during critical evaluations.

Gen AI-Assisted Assignments - The second category, Gen AI-assisted assignments, allows students to utilize generative AI tools as aids rather than primary creators of their submissions. Participants reported that students could leverage Gen AI for brainstorming, generating initial ideas, or enhancing teamwork projects, but they were required to compose the final submission independently. This approach seeks to balance innovation with skill building by fostering critical thinking and encouraging students to critique AI-generated content.

A computer-engineering professor noted, "Allowing students to use ChatGPT or any generative application enhances the learning ethics of AI and its literacy. My students were not allowed to copy and paste the ideas; I requested that they critique and develop the materials, and also include the generated text as an appendix in the final project." This reflects pedagogical strategies emphasizing reflective AI use and aligns with studies suggesting that guided exposure to AI tools can improve digital literacy (Haroud & Saqri,2025).

Additionally, some faculty members have adopted Gen AI for designing assignments. An assistant professor in social sciences shared, "I used generative AI to create project-based assignments, saving time by providing the tool with criteria and the final outcome." This dual-purpose use of AI highlights its utility for both students and educators, enabling the efficient creation of tailored, innovative assessments.

Gen AI-Empowered Assignments - Gen AI-empowered assignments represent the highest level of AI integration, wherein students are granted full autonomy to incorporate Gen AI tools throughout their projects. This approach emphasizes advanced skills such as critical thinking, problem-solving, and self-reflection. As a requirement, students were often asked to write reflective essays detailing their experiences and evaluating the AI's contribution to their work.

An IT professor observed, "Students are allowed to fully integrate Gen AI into their assignments, but they are also required to write a reflection paper on their experience using it." However, this practice remains contentious. A humanities professor argued, "Using Gen AI to empower students in the assignment will make them lazy and depend on it in the future. I do not like to use it in this way; my idea is that educators use it only for assessment, teaching, and scientific research." These contrasting perspectives echo broader debates within academia regarding the ethical implications and long-term effects of unrestricted AI use in education (Zhao, Chapman & Sabet, 2024).

The regulation of assignment categories within GenAI-enhanced classes can no longer be left to personal discretion alone by the teachers. In their UNESCO (2024) Global Report on Ethical AI in Education, UNESCO calls for policies at the institutional level that outline acceptable applications of AI in various courses to ensure uniformity, clarity, and fairness in how AI is encountered by students regardless of discipline. In its OECD (2023) AI Framework, the OECD, while highlighting the need for clear communication of these norms, goes further to explain that these norms should be established not only for purposes of maintaining academic integrity but also as a means of fostering the development of ethical decision-making in regard to the use of AI. These three categories described in this chapter can be considered a starting point for institutional policies on this subject, provided that criteria for each are clear and updated accordingly.

6. GEN AI IN ASSESSMENT

Assessment plays a pivotal role in education by providing essential data for tracking progress, guiding instructional efforts, and supporting informed decision-making for students, parents, educators, and policymakers (Davis, Bush & Wood 2024; Kim, Murai & Chang 2021). It serves as a critical tool for evaluating student achievement, showcasing educational value, and influencing learning outcomes (Jones & Carter, 2019). However, challenges such as inaccuracies in data collection and contested interpretations of results can undermine the efficacy of assessments (Taylor & Taylor, 2021). Assessment frameworks in higher education—such as norm-referenced and criterion-referenced systems—facilitate the formal recording of achievements and promote learning outcomes (Sternberg et al., 2022). The development of robust assessment systems, aligned policies, and international standards underscores their importance in enhancing educational quality and student outcomes. Thoughtfully designed assessments not only reflect current capabilities but also shape students' future opportunities and professional success (Sutherland-Smith & Dawson, 2022).

The incorporation of generative artificial intelligence (AI) tools into higher education assessment practices has prompted significant discourse on the evolution of traditional assessment strategies. Educators and students exhibit differing attitudes toward the use of AI in assessments. Educators tend to support the integration of AI tools to develop tailored assessments that foster critical thinking and analytical questioning, while students often voice concerns about the potential erosion of creativity in such processes (Zhao, Chapman & Sabet, 2024). Furthermore, research highlights the challenges posed by AI-generated content, such as that produced by GPT-4, in detecting academic misconduct, thereby emphasizing the need for robust AI detection tools and increased awareness among faculty and students (Smith et al., 2024). Addressing these challenges necessitates a shift in assessment strategies to include AI-resistant mechanisms, AI-inclusive evaluation methods, and comprehensive training for educators and learners (Chen et al., 2020).

a) **Generating Exam Questions -** One of the primary uses of Gen AI in assessment is the generation of exam questions. Educators can use AI tools to create a wide range of questions, including multiple-choice, true/false, and essay questions. For instance, ChatGPT-4 has been utilized to generate questions aligned with course objectives, ensuring relevance and reducing the time required for manual preparation. According to Smith et al. (2024), "Generative AI tools enable educators to rapidly produce diverse and adaptive question banks, catering to varying levels of difficulty." AI tools can also adapt questions to different cognitive levels, adhering to frameworks such as Bloom's Taxonomy. For example, they can generate questions that assess basic recall (e.g., multiple-choice questions) or higher-order thinking (e.g., case studies and problem-solving tasks). This adaptability ensures that assessments address a range of learning outcomes, enhancing their overall validity (Patel, 2025).
b) **Automated Grading and Feedback -** Gen AI facilitates automated grading and personalized feedback, especially for written assignments and projects. Tools like ChatGPT-4 and GradeScope can assess essays, research papers, and even

handwritten submissions. By employing pre-defined rubrics, these tools can evaluate grammar, coherence, critical thinking, and alignment with assignment objectives. For example, a study by Heidari & Ekström (2025) found that AI-assisted grading systems reduced grading time by up to 60%, allowing educators to focus on more strategic aspects of teaching. Moreover, Gen AI-generated feedback can be tailored to individual students. By analyzing the strengths and weaknesses in submissions, the AI provides actionable insights for improvement. This personalization has been shown to increase student engagement and foster self-regulated learning (Francis, Jones & Smith, 2025).

c) **Utilizing Gen AI for Rubric Design -** Another significant application of Gen AI identified in the study involves the design of assignments and grading rubrics. Faculty members reported that AI tools facilitated the creation of equitable and precise assessment criteria. A computer engineering professor stated, "I used these tools to generate ideas for my assignments to ensure fairness and make sure my students complete the assignment without Gen AI assistance." This underscores the potential of Gen AI to enhance efficiency and consistency in assessment design while maintaining academic standards (Lee et al., 2022).For instance, Gen AI can propose project ideas, case scenarios, or problem-solving tasks based on specific criteria provided by instructors. This capability is particularly beneficial for large classes or interdisciplinary courses where generating varied and contextually relevant assignments can be challenging (Zhao, Chapman & Sabet, 2024). Additionally, Gen AI can assist in designing rubrics that outline clear and measurable evaluation criteria. Rubrics generated by AI tools help ensure transparency and consistency in grading, reducing potential biases and enhancing the reliability of assessments (Lee et al., 2022).

d) **Ethics of Governing Assessment through AI-** The use of GenAI in the context of formal assessment prompts issues relating to governance that go beyond decisions made by individual tutors. From an institutional perspective, the adoption of tools based on GenAI for assessment purposes needs to involve open disclosure to students, robust testing of algorithmic accuracy by demographic groups, and means of human supervision and appeal. The principles laid out by the Council of Europe (2024) in its AI Governance Convention are directly relevant to educational assessment settings; institutions using GenAI-powered grading tools have to make sure they comply with these principles, especially in high-stakes assessment scenarios involving degrees and professional qualifications. Data privacy presents yet another important governance issue. Given the involvement of commercial large language models in processing of student content, there arise issues related to data retention, re-use, and cross-border data flows, which are regulated by frameworks like the EU General Data Protection Regulation (GDPR) among others. According to Cotton et al. (2024), most teachers who employ the use of AI in assessments do so without adequate understanding of the data agreements they enter into on behalf of their learners. Moreover, according to Kasneci et al. (2023), the very nature of LLMs, which entails the inability to explain their reasoning processes, creates major difficulties with the notions of justification and transparency associated with valid assessment processes.

e) **Automated Grading and Feedback -** Gen AI facilitates automated grading and personalized feedback, especially for written assignments and projects. Tools like ChatGPT-4 and GradeScope can assess essays, research papers, and even handwritten submissions. By employing pre-defined rubrics, these tools can evaluate grammar, coherence, critical thinking, and alignment with assignment objectives. AI-assisted grading systems reduced grading time by up to 60%, allowing educators to focus on more strategic aspects of teaching (Heidari & Ekström 2025). Moreover, Gen AI-generated feedback can be tailored to individual students. By analyzing the strengths and weaknesses in submissions, the AI provides actionable insights for improvement. This personalization has been shown to increase student engagement and foster self-regulated learning (Francis, Jones & Smith, 2025).

7. CASE STUDY - CHATGPT IN LEARNING, TEACHING & ASSESSMENT

ChatGPT, a large language model developed by OpenAI, is increasingly being recognized as a transformative tool in education. Its diverse capabilities provide opportunities to enhance learning experiences and support teaching in various ways. Below are specific applications of ChatGPT in education, supported by research evidence.

a) **Personalized Tutoring-**ChatGPT can deliver personalized tutoring and feedback tailored to individual learning needs. Chen et al. (2024) demonstrated the effectiveness of a generative model-based conversational agent in providing math tutoring to students. The study revealed that the agent offered explanations customized to students' misconceptions and adapted to their comprehension levels, resulting in improved learning outcomes. Such personalized support enhances students' engagement and conceptual understanding.

b) **Automated Essay Grading-**ChatGPT can automate the grading of student essays, enabling teachers to allocate more time to instructional tasks. Mizumoto, & Eguchi (2023) conducted a study where a generative model trained on human-graded essays achieved a grading correlation of 0.86 with human assessors. The model effectively identified key features of well-written essays and provided feedback comparable to that of human graders. This capability holds potential for reducing teachers' workloads while maintaining grading accuracy.

c) **Language Translation-**ChatGPT can make educational materials more accessible by translating them into multiple languages. Johnson & Kathirvel (2025) found that a generative model trained on bilingual sentence pairs achieved state-of-the-art performance on translation benchmarks. The model demonstrated an understanding of sentence meanings in one language and generated accurate translations in another, expanding access to educational content for linguistically diverse audiences.

d) **Interactive Learning-** Interactive learning experiences can be enriched through ChatGPT's conversational capabilities. Peng, Zhou & Liu (2022) highlighted the benefits of a conversational agent based on a generative model in supporting English as a Second Language (ESL) learners. The study showed that the agent effectively responded to students' questions, facilitating improved language proficiency and creating a dynamic learning environment.

e) **Adaptive Learning-** ChatGPT can support adaptive learning systems by tailoring teaching methods based on a student's progress. Chiang, Chang & Chen (2024) demonstrated that a generative model could enhance programming education by generating problems of appropriate difficulty based on students' knowledge levels. The study found that this adaptive approach significantly improved students' performance on programming assessments, underscoring ChatGPT's potential in creating personalized learning pathways.

ChatGPT has the potential to revolutionize education through its applications in personalized tutoring, automated grading, language translation, interactive learning, and adaptive learning systems. By leveraging its generative capabilities, educators can create more inclusive, efficient, and engaging learning experiences, ultimately transforming the educational landscape.

8. CHALLENGES OF AI IN EDUCATION

However, the integration of GenAI in teaching is not without challenges. Concerns about data privacy, ethical implications of AI-generated content, and the potential over-reliance on AI tools are critical issues that require careful consideration (Rahman & Watanobe, 2023). Educators must understand the limitations of GenAI, ensuring it serves as a complementary tool rather than a substitute for traditional teaching practices. For instance, while AI can automate grading and feedback, the nuanced understanding and empathetic guidance provided by human educators remain irreplaceable (Davis, 2024; Walker, 2025). Some of the other challenges include"

a) **Accuracy and Reliability-** Despite its advantages, Gen AI tools are not infallible. Issues such as inaccuracies in content generation, redundancy in questions, and errors in grading have been reported. For example, Heidari, & Ekström (2025) observed that AI-generated multiple-choice questions often contained factual errors or ambiguous phrasing, undermining their validity. It is equally important to recognize the limitations of AI tools, such as their propensity to produce erroneous or misleading information ("hallucinations"). An IT assistant professor stated, "When I use Gemini to generate multiple-choice and true/false questions, I notice high similarity in questions. These tools are not professional enough to generate exams." Such observations align with research highlighting the limitations of Gen AI in producing contextually nuanced or error-free content (Crompton & Burke, 2024; Memarian & Doleck, 2023).
b) **Ethical Concerns-** The use of AI in assessments raises ethical questions regarding data privacy, fairness, and academic integrity. For instance, there is a risk of students misusing Gen AI tools to generate assignments, bypassing the learning process. Educators must establish clear guidelines to prevent overreliance on AI and ensure its ethical use (Smith et al., 2024).
c) **Accessibility and Equity-** Not all educational institutions have equal access to advanced AI tools due to cost or technological limitations. This disparity can exacerbate existing inequalities in education, particularly in under-resourced schools. Efforts must be made to democratize access to Gen AI technologies to ensure inclusive education (Perkins et al., 2024).
d) **Resistance to Change-**The adoption of Gen AI in assessments may face resistance from educators and institutions accustomed to traditional methods. Concerns about reliability, loss of human touch, and potential job displacement contribute to skepticism. Addressing these concerns requires robust training programs and evidence-based practices demonstrating the benefits of Gen AI (Francis, Jones & Smith, 2025).
e) **Limited Professional development** - While GenAI has the potential to influence adaptive teaching strategies significantly, its impact on teacher professional development and efficiency enhancement remains limited. For instance, GenAI can persuade educators to adopt adaptive learning approaches but may not address deeper concerns, such as trust in AI systems or algorithmic transparency. Nonetheless, the evolving capabilities of GenAI underscore its promise as a transformative tool in education, capable of bridging gaps in both learning and teaching domains.

f) **Undermining of traditional evaluation methods -** Generative AI offers several advantages in educational assessments. However, concerns persist about the potential undermining of traditional evaluation methods, such as essay writing, due to the ability of AI tools to generate high-quality written content that excels in standardized assessments (Smith et al., 2024).

When evaluated from the perspective of Rogers's (2003) Diffusion of Innovations Theory, much of the issues stated above are not simply coincidental rather they are predictable elements of the adoption process when a technology bumps into the institutional resistance to change. In other words, the hesitation expressed by some faculty members who are uneasy about AI-driven assessment can be considered one of the compatibility barriers defined by Rogers. This notion applies to the concerns about accuracy and reliability – the inability of GenAI applications to produce hallucinations or inappropriate exam questions leads to their decreased usefulness and prevents the adoption process. The identification of the issues in the framework provided by the Diffusion of Innovations Theory is not only about putting the information into categories. It is also about recognizing the key factors that should be addressed in order for GenAI to make a difference in different educational institutions.

9. CONCLUSION

Despite these challenges, the potential of GenAI to transform teaching practices is undeniable. When integrated thoughtfully, GenAI can enhance creativity, efficiency, and inclusivity in education, paving the way for innovative pedagogical strategies that align with the needs of 21st-century learners. Its ability to adapt to diverse educational contexts and provide scalable solutions underscores its value as a critical resource in modern education (Jaime-Vargas, 2025; Zawacki-Richter et al., 2019).

This research demonstrates that generative AI represents a transformative force in higher education, offering significant opportunities to revolutionize both teaching and assessment practices. The study reveals three distinct categories of AI integration in assignments: traditional non-AI assignments that maintain academic integrity through direct evaluation, AI-assisted assignments where students use AI as a supportive brainstorming and enhancement tool while maintaining independent composition, and AI-empowered assignments allowing full integration with mandatory reflective components to develop critical AI literacy skills.

In the teaching domain, generative AI proves particularly valuable across multiple dimensions. Content creation capabilities enable educators to streamline lesson planning, generate diverse quiz materials, and develop interactive teaching aids, significantly reducing administrative burden. The technology's adaptive teaching strategies leverage multimodal data to personalize instruction based on individual student needs and learning states. Enhanced teaching efficiency through automated administrative tasks allows educators to focus on higher-order pedagogical activities, while intelligent learning systems and human-machine interaction tools create more engaging and responsive educational environments. Particularly noteworthy is AI's role in fostering inclusivity through multilingual content generation and accessibility features for diverse learner populations.

The assessment domain shows equally promising applications, including automated essay grading achieving 86% correlation with human assessors, sophisticated personalized feedback generation, and efficient rubric design processes. Tools like ChatGPT demonstrate remarkable effectiveness in personalized tutoring, real-time language translation, and adaptive learning systems, with AI-assisted grading reducing educator workload by up to 60% while maintaining quality standards.

However, significant challenges persist that require careful consideration. Accuracy and reliability concerns include AI hallucinations and content redundancy, while ethical considerations encompass academic integrity preservation, data privacy protection, and preventing over-dependence on AI tools. Accessibility disparities threaten to exacerbate educational inequalities, and institutional resistance to technological change remains a barrier to widespread adoption. The study emphasizes that successful AI integration requires viewing these tools as complementary resources rather than replacements for human expertise, ensuring thoughtful implementation that maintains academic standards while embracing technological advancement for 21st-century educational excellence.

Instructors must design assessments that leverage the strengths of AI while challenging students to apply their knowledge in innovative and critical ways. This approach is particularly significant in disciplines such as language and literature, where creativity and subjectivity are central to learning outcomes. Integrating AI tools effectively in assessments ensures that they supplement rather than replace the teaching process, thereby enriching educational experiences without compromising academic integrity (Zhou and Kim, 2024).

Translating these ideas into practice involves a concerted, collaborative effort on multiple fronts. Universities should abandon piecemeal experiments and begin developing AI governance policies outlining acceptable applications of AI, mechanisms for supervision, and equal access to AI for all students. The policy community should develop AI-friendly regulatory frameworks; otherwise, there is a high likelihood that any excessive regulation might lead to the adoption of AI technologies "underground." Technology creators must develop technologies that are transparent and auditable and adhere to the principles of education as opposed to business efficiency. Finally, faculty members cannot simply receive training on the effective use of AI technology, but must engage with these technologies intellectually in order to understand their value for education and their impact on students. The three-fold taxonomy developed in this chapter - non-AI, AI-assisted, and AI-empowered assignments - serves as an excellent foundation for discussions of institutional policy around AI. Yet such discussions must take into account the significant inequities in AI-readiness worldwide, meaning that the GenAI story will not be a uniform one going forward but instead many different stories determined by geography, economic capacity, and educational philosophy.

10. IMPLICATIONS FOR THE FUTURE OF EDUCATION

The integration of Gen AI into assessment practices has profound implications for the future of education. By streamlining processes, enhancing personalization, and fostering innovation, Gen AI has the potential to redefine how learning is evaluated. However, its successful implementation depends on addressing challenges such as accuracy, equity, and ethical considerations.

Educational institutions must prioritize professional development programs to equip educators with the skills needed to effectively use AI tools. Collaboration between educators, policymakers, and technology developers is essential to establish best practices and ethical guidelines. Furthermore, ongoing research is needed to evaluate the long-term impact of Gen AI on learning outcomes and student development (Smith et al., 2024).

The future of education will require strategic adaptation to maximize generative AI's transformative potential while addressing inherent challenges. Educational institutions must prioritize comprehensive professional development programs to equip educators with AI literacy skills and ethical frameworks for responsible implementation. Policymakers need to establish clear guidelines balancing innovation with academic integrity, ensuring equitable access across diverse institutional contexts.

Future research should focus on longitudinal studies examining AI's impact on student learning outcomes, critical thinking development, and digital literacy skills. The development of more sophisticated AI detection tools and transparent algorithms will be crucial for maintaining assessment validity. Collaboration between educators, technologists, and policymakers is essential to create standardized best practices and ethical guidelines.

Institutions should invest in infrastructure supporting AI integration while addressing accessibility concerns to prevent educational inequalities. The evolution toward AI-augmented education requires careful consideration of human-AI collaboration models, ensuring that technology enhances rather than replaces the irreplaceable elements of human guidance, empathy, and nuanced understanding in educational contexts.

REFERENCES

Alasadi, E. A., & Baiz, C. R. (2026). Generative artificial intelligence in higher education: A systematic review of perceptions, implementation and pedagogical transformation. *Education and Information Technologies*, *31*, 1553–1580. DOI: 10.1007/s10639-025-13867-0

Anderson, J., Nguyen, C. A., & Ucok Hughes, M. (2025). Mapping theory to practice: AI-enhanced teaching theories for fostering diverse perspectives in business education. *Journal of International Education in Business*. DOI: 10.1108/JIEB-07-2024-0081

Bonneton-Botté, N., Miramand, L., Bailly, R., & Pons, C. (2023). Teaching and rehabilitation of handwriting for children in the digital age: Issues and challenges. *Children (Basel, Switzerland)*, *10*(7), 1096. DOI: 10.3390/children10071096

Castelli, M., & Manzoni, L. (2022). Generative models in artificial intelligence and their applications. *Applied Sciences (Basel, Switzerland)*, *12*(9), 4127. DOI: 10.3390/app12094127

Chen, A., Wei, Y., Le, H., & Zhang, Y. (2024). Learning-by-teaching with ChatGPT: The effect of teachable ChatGPT agent on programming education. *ArXiv, abs/2412.15226.*

Chen, L., Chen, P., & Lin, Z. (2020). Artificial Intelligence in Education: A Review. *IEEE Access : Practical Innovations, Open Solutions*, *8*, 75264–75278. DOI: 10.1109/ACCESS.2020.2988510

Chew, E., & Chua, X. N. (2020). Robotic Chinese language tutor: Personalising progress assessment and feedback or taking over your job? *On the Horizon*, *28*(3), 113–124. DOI: 10.1108/OTH-04-2020-0015

Chiang, Y. H. V., Chang, M., & Chen, N. S. (2024). Can generative AI help realize the shift from an outcome-oriented to a process-outcome-balanced educational practice? *Journal of Educational Technology & Society*, *27*(2), 347–385. https://www.jstor.org/stable/48766179

Chiu, T. K., Xia, Q., Zhou, X., Chai, C. S., & Cheng, M. (2023). Systematic literature review on opportunities, challenges, and future research recommendations of artificial intelligence in education. *Computers and Education: Artificial Intelligence*, *4*, 100118. DOI: 10.1016/j.caeai.2022.100118

Clark, D. (2024). *Artificial intelligence for learning: Using AI and generative AI to support learner development*. Kogan Page Publishers.

Cotton, D. R. E., Cotton, P. A., & Shipway, J. R. (2024). Chatting and cheating: Ensuring academic integrity in the era of ChatGPT. *Innovations in Education and Teaching International, 61*(2), 228–239. DOI: 10.1080/14703297.2023.2190148

Council of Europe. (2024). Framework convention on artificial intelligence and human rights, democracy and the rule of law (CETS No. 225). https://www.coe.int/en/web/conventions/full-list?module=treaty-detail&treatynum=225

Crompton, H., & Burke, D. (2024). The educational affordances and challenges of ChatGPT: State of the field. *TechTrends, 68*(2), 380–392. DOI: 10.1007/s11528-024-00939-0

Davis, A. J. (2024). AI rising in higher education: Opportunities, risks and limitations. *Asian Education and Development Studies, 13*(4), 307–319. DOI: 10.1108/AEDS-01-2024-0017

Davis, C., Bush, T., & Wood, S. (2024). Artificial intelligence in education: Enhancing learning experiences through personalized adaptation. [IJCITSM]. *International Journal of Cyber and IT Service Management, 4*(1), 26–32. DOI: 10.34306/ijcitsm.v4i1.146

Davis, F. D. (1989). Perceived usefulness, perceived ease of use, and user acceptance of information technology. *Management Information Systems Quarterly, 13*(3), 319–340. DOI: 10.2307/249008

Feuerriegel, S., Hartmann, J., Janiesch, C., & Zschech, P. (2024). Generative AI. *Business & Information Systems Engineering, 66*(1), 111–126. DOI: 10.1007/s12599-023-00834-7

Francis, N. J., Jones, S., & Smith, D. P. (2025). Generative AI in higher education: Balancing innovation and integrity. *British Journal of Biomedical Science, 81*, 14048. DOI: 10.3389/bjbs.2024.14048

Garcia-Ruiz, M. A., Lin, R., Nam, S., Hu, S., Nasir, M., & Santana-Mancilla, P. C. (2026). Integrating AI and XR for Smarter Learning in Computer Science Education: Teaching in the Age of Intelligence and Immersion. In *New Media Applications in Digital Education* (pp. 33-72). IGI Global Scientific Publishing. https://doi.org/ DOI: 10.4018/979-8-3373-5157-5.ch002

Haroud, S., & Saqri, N. (2025). Generative AI in higher education: Teachers' and students' perspectives on support, replacement, and digital literacy. *Education Sciences, 15*(4), 396. DOI: 10.3390/educsci15040396

Heidari, E., & Ekström, J. (2025). From Paper to Algorithm: A Qualitative Study on Teachers' Perspectives on AI in English Literature Education. https://urn.kb.se/resolve?urn=urn%3Anbn%3Ase%3Ahv%3Adiva-23341

Hirankerd, K., & Kittisunthonphisarn, N. (2020). E-learning management system based on reality technology with AI. *International Journal of Information and Education Technology, 10*(4), 259-264. doi: https://doi.org/DOI: 10.18178/ijiet.2020.10.4.1373

Holmes, W., Porayska-Pomsta, K., Holstein, K., Sutherland, E., Baker, T., Shum, S. B., Santos, O. C., Rodrigo, M. T., Cukurova, M., Bittencourt, I. I., & Koedinger, K. R. (2022). Ethics of AI in education: Towards a community-wide framework. *International Journal of Artificial Intelligence in Education*, *32*(3), 504–526. DOI: 10.1007/s40593-021-00239-1

Hu, S. (2024). The effect of artificial intelligence-assisted personalized learning on student learning outcomes: A meta-analysis based on 31 empirical research papers. *Science Insights Education Frontiers*, *24*(1), 3873–3894. DOI: 10.15354/sief.24.re395

Jaime-Vargas, J. A. (2025). Generative AI for enhancing accessibility and inclusion in higher education: A systematic review. *HighTech and Innovation Journal*, *6*(2), 723–734. DOI: 10.28991/HIJ-2025-06-02-022

Johnson, J. W., & Kathirvel, K. (2025). Evaluating the effectiveness of ChatGPT in language translation and cross-lingual communication. In *Applications of Mathematics in Science and Technology* (pp. 434–439). CRC Press., DOI: 10.1201/9781003606659-82

Jones, B., & Carter, D. (2019). Relationships between students' course perceptions, engagement, and learning. *Social Psychology of Education*, *22*(4), 819–839. DOI: 10.1007/s11218-019-09500-x

Kasneci, E., Seßler, K., Küchemann, S., Bannert, M., Dementieva, D., Fischer, F., Gasser, U., Groh, G., Günnemann, S., Hüllermeier, E., Krusche, S., Kutyniok, G., Michaeli, T., Nerdel, C., Pfeffer, J., Poquet, O., Sailer, M., Schmidt, A., Seidel, T., & Kasneci, G. (2023). ChatGPT for good? On opportunities and challenges of large language models for education. *Learning and Individual Differences*, *103*, 102274. Advance online publication. DOI: 10.1016/j.lindif.2023.102274

Kim, Y. J., Murai, Y., & Chang, S. (2021). Implementation of embedded assessment in maker classrooms: Challenges and opportunities. *Information and Learning Science*, *122*(3-4), 292–314. DOI: 10.1108/ILS-08-2020-0188

Lampos, V., Mintz, J., & Qu, X. (2021). An artificial intelligence approach for selecting effective teacher communication strategies in autism education. *npj Science of Learning, 6*(1), 25. https://doi.org/DOI: 10.1038/s41539-021-00102-x

Lee, D., & Kwon, H. (2024). Meta-analysis on effects of artificial intelligence education in K-12 South Korean classrooms. *Education and Information Technologies, 29*(17), 22859–22894. DOI: 10.1007/s10639-024-12738-4

Lee, I., Zhang, H., Moore, K., Zhou, X., Perret, B., Cheng, Y., & Pu, G. (2022, February). AI book club: An innovative professional development model for AI education. In *Proceedings of the 53rd ACM Technical Symposium on Computer Science Education-Volume 1* (pp. 202-208). https://doi.org/DOI: 10.1145/3478431.3499318

Li, M., & Su, Y. (2020). Evaluation of online teaching quality of basic education based on artificial intelligence. [iJET]. *International Journal of Emerging Technologies in Learning, 15*(16), 147–161. https://www.learntechlib.org/p/217942/. DOI: 10.3991/ijet.v15i16.15937

Luo, L., & Yusuf, A. (2026). Bridging AI and pedagogy: How AI-adaptive feedback shapes Chinese EFL students' writing engagement, metacognitive writing strategies, and writing performance. *Assessment & Evaluation in Higher Education, 51*(3), 508–531. DOI: 10.1080/02602938.2025.2548919

Memarian, B., & Doleck, T. (2023). ChatGPT in education: Methods, potentials, and limitations. *Computers in Human Behavior: Artificial Humans, 1*(2), 100022. DOI: 10.1016/j.chbah.2023.100022

Mhlambi, S. (2020). From rationality to relationality: Ubuntu as an ethical and human rights framework for artificial intelligence governance. *Carr Center for Human Rights Policy Discussion Paper Series*, 2020-009. Harvard Kennedy School. https://carrcenter.hks.harvard.edu/files/cchr/files/ccdp_2020-009_sabelo_b.pdf

Miller, W. (2024). Adapting to AI: Reimagining the Role of Assessment Professionals. *Intersection: A Journal at the Intersection of Assessment and Learning, 5*(4), 99-113. https://aalhe.scholasticahq.com/article/121439-adapting-to-ai-reimagining-the-role-of-assessment-professionals

Mizumoto, A., & Eguchi, M. (2023). Exploring the potential of using an AI language model for automated essay scoring. *Research Methods in Applied Linguistics, 2*(2), 100050. DOI: 10.1016/j.rmal.2023.100050

Mohamed, S., Png, M. T., & Isaac, W. (2020). Decolonial AI: Decolonial theory as sociotechnical foresight in artificial intelligence. *Philosophy & Technology, 33*(4), 659–684. DOI: 10.1007/s13347-020-00405-8

Moorhouse, B. L., Wan, Y., Wu, C., Wu, M., & Ho, T. Y. (2025). Generative AI tools and empowerment in L2 academic writing. *System, 103779*, 103779. Advance online publication. DOI: 10.1016/j.system.2025.103779

Moturu, V. R., & Nethi, S. D. (2022). Artificial intelligence in education. In *Emerging IT/ICT and AI technologies affecting society* (pp. 233–244). Springer Nature Singapore., DOI: 10.1007/978-981-19-2940-3_16

Murtaza, M., Ahmed, Y., Shamsi, J. A., Sherwani, F., & Usman, M. (2022). AI-based personalized e-learning systems: Issues, challenges, and solutions. *IEEE Access : Practical Innovations, Open Solutions*, *10*, 81323–81342. DOI: 10.1109/ACCESS.2022.3193938

OECD. (2023). *OECD framework for the classification of AI systems*. OECD Publishing., DOI: 10.1787/cb6d9eca-

Owan, V. J., Abang, K. B., Idika, D. O., Etta, E. O., & Bassey, B. A. (2023). Exploring the potential of artificial intelligence tools in educational measurement and assessment. *Eurasia Journal of Mathematics, Science and Technology Education*, *19*(8), em2307. Advance online publication. DOI: 10.29333/ejmste/13428

Patel, A. (2025). Artificial Intelligence-Driven Personalized Learning: Application, Challenges, and Future Directions in Digital Education. *Digital Education and Future Learning, 1*(1), 1-18. https://journals.cypedia.net/defl/article/view/97

Peng, C., Zhou, X., & Liu, S. (2022). An introduction to artificial intelligence and machine learning for online education. *Mobile Networks and Applications*, *27*(3), 1147–1150. DOI: 10.1007/s11036-022-01953-3

Perkins, M., Furze, L., Roe, J., & MacVaugh, J. (2024). The AI Assessment Scale (AIAS): A framework for ethical integration of generative AI in educational assessment. *Assessment & Evaluation in Higher Education*, *49*(8), 1223–1237. DOI: 10.1080/02602938.2023.2290283

Porter, B., & Grippa, F. (2020). A platform for AI-enabled real-time feedback to promote digital collaboration. *Sustainability (Basel)*, *12*(24), 10243. DOI: 10.3390/su122410243

Rahman, M. M., & Watanobe, Y. (2023). ChatGPT for education and research: Opportunities, threats, and strategies. *Applied Sciences (Basel, Switzerland)*, *13*(9), 5783. DOI: 10.3390/app13095783

Rogers, E. M. (2003). *Diffusion of innovations* (5th ed.). Free Press., https://teddykw2.wordpress.com/wp-content/uploads/2012/07/everett-m-rogers-diffusion-of-innovations.pdf

Sheikh, H., Prins, C., & Schrijvers, E. (2023). Artificial intelligence: Definition and background. In *Mission AI* (pp. 15–41). Springer., DOI: 10.1007/978-3-031-21448-6_2

Smith, A. M., & Green, M. (2018). Artificial intelligence and the role of leadership. *Journal of Leadership Studies, 12*(3), 85–87. DOI: 10.1002/jls.21605

Smith, N., & Vickers, D. (2024). Living well with AI: Virtue, education, and artificial intelligence. *Theory and Research in Education, 22*(1), 19–44. DOI: 10.1177/14778785241231561

Smith, S. J., Rowland, A., Goldman, S., & Carreon, A. (2024). A Guide for Special Education Leaders to Utilize Artificial Intelligence: Students' Perspectives for Future Consideration. *Journal of Special Education Leadership, 37*(2), 77–92. https://files.eric.ed.gov/fulltext/EJ1441807.pdf

Sternberg, R. J., Chowkase, A., Parra-Martinez, F. A., & Landy, J. (2022). Criterion-referenced assessment of intelligence as adaptation to the environment: Is it possible, plausible, or practical? *Journal of Intelligence, 10*(3), 57. DOI: 10.3390/jintelligence10030057

Sutherland-Smith, W., & Dawson, P. (2022). Higher education assessment design. In *Contract cheating in higher education: Global perspectives on theory, practice, and policy* (pp. 91–105). Springer International Publishing., DOI: 10.1007/978-3-031-12680-2_7

Taylor, J. E. T., & Taylor, G. W. (2021). Artificial cognition: How experimental psychology can help generate explainable artificial intelligence. *Psychonomic Bulletin & Review, 28*(2), 454–475. DOI: 10.3758/s13423-020-01825-5

UNESCO. (2024). Global report on AI in education: Ethics and governance. UNESCO Publishing. https://www.unesco.org/en/artificial-intelligence/recommendation-ethics

Vázquez-Cano, E., Mengual-Andrés, S., & López-Meneses, E. (2021). Chatbot to improve learning punctuation in Spanish and to enhance open and flexible learning environments. *International Journal of Educational Technology in Higher Education, 18*(1), 33. DOI: 10.1186/s41239-021-00269-8

Walker, L. (2025). Artificial intelligence in medical education: Potential and pitfalls. *Australian Journal of General Practice, 54*(10), 743–746. https://search.informit.org/doi/10.3316/informit.T2025101800002790791144166. DOI: 10.31128/AJGP-02-25-7559

Westera, W., Prada, R., Mascarenhas, S., Santos, P. A., Dias, J., Guimarães, M., Georgiadis, K., Nyamsuren, E., Bahreini, K., Yumak, Z., Christyowidiasmoro, C., Dascalu, M., Gutu-Robu, G., & Ruseti, S. (2020). Artificial intelligence moving serious gaming: Presenting reusable game AI components. *Education and Information Technologies*, *25*(1), 351–380. DOI: 10.1007/s10639-019-09968-2

Zawacki-Richter, O., Marín, V. I., Bond, M., & Gouverneur, F. (2019). Systematic review of research on artificial intelligence applications in higher education — Where are the educators? *International Journal of Educational Technology in Higher Education*, *16*(1), 39. Advance online publication. DOI: 10.1186/s41239-019-0171-0

Zhai, X., & Nehm, R. H. (2023). AI and formative assessment: The train has left the station. *Journal of Research in Science Teaching*, *60*(6), 1390–1398. DOI: 10.1002/tea.21885

Zhao, J., Chapman, E., & Sabet, P. G. (2024). Generative AI and educational assessments: A systematic review. *Education Research and Perspectives*, *51*, 124–155. https://search.informit.org/doi/10.3316/informit.T2025061800005500592641426. DOI: 10.70953/ERPv51.2412006

Zhou, W., & Kim, Y. (2024). Innovative music education: An empirical assessment of ChatGPT-4's impact on student learning experiences. *Education and Information Technologies*, *29*(16), 20855–20881. DOI: 10.1007/s10639-024-12705-z

Chapter 2
Responsible AI and Governance in Higher Education:
Building Ethical Foundations for Digital Transformation

Gurpreet Singh
http://orcid.org/0009-0000-4011-8626
Guru Kashi University, India

Vakil Singh
http://orcid.org/0009-0007-1198-0250
Faculty of Computing, Guru Kashi University, Talwandi Sabo, India

ABSTRACT

Digital technologies are transforming higher education by reshaping teaching, research, and administration. While they enhance efficiency and access, they also pose ethical and governance challenges involving fairness, privacy, and academic integrity. This chapter explores how responsible digital governance can ensure inclusive and ethical transformation. Focusing on pedagogical, governance, and operational dimensions, it emphasizes transparency, accountability, and institutional capacity building. Drawing from global practices, it highlights ethics committees, policy frameworks, and literacy programs that foster trust. A value-driven, multi-level governance model is proposed to guide institutions in embedding ethics into technological adoption, turning digital innovation into a force for equity, integrity, and sustainable academic progress.

DOI: 10.4018/979-8-3373-5586-3.ch002

1. INTRODUCTION

Artificial Intelligence (AI) is now widely recognized as a transformative force shaping the future of higher education. In the last decade, the swift advancement of machine learning algorithms, natural language processing models, predictive analytics systems, and generative AI tools has revolutionized the way universities teach, learn, assess, research, and manage administration (Crompton & Burke, 2023). AI is no longer a futuristic concept but has become an integral part of the modern academic landscape, where data-driven insights, intelligent automation, and personalized systems are woven into the fabric of institutional operations. This AI-powered academic landscape presents a dual narrative, with its potential for innovation, efficiency, and accessibility on one side, and the pressing concerns of fairness, ethics, privacy, accountability and the threat to academic integrity on the other (Barus et al., 2025).

While there is an increasing body of literature on the use of AI in higher education, the literature so far focuses on either the opportunities of AI or the ethical issues of its use. Although there has been a lot of research on adaptive learning, predictive analytics, generative AI, and academic integrity, there has been little research on how to combine governance, ethics, and operational readiness in a single framework for higher education institutions. In addition, much of the current debate is influenced by experiences in technologically advanced areas, and there is relatively little consideration of governance realities in low-resource and emerging educational contexts. This leaves a major knowledge gap on how universities can responsibly embrace AI while considering innovation, institutional responsibility, inclusivity, and contextual issues. This gap needs to be filled in order to create ethically informed and practically implementable governance pathways in various higher education contexts.

The swift adoption of AI in higher education has outpaced the creation of institutional governance frameworks to guarantee ethical, transparent, and accountable use. While AI presents significant potential in learning, assessment, research, and administration, issues of algorithmic bias, data privacy, academic integrity, and institutional readiness remain as obstacles to responsible implementation. The absence of context-sensitive governance frameworks creates uncertainty regarding how universities can balance technological innovation with ethical responsibility and institutional trust.

Based on the identified gap and problem, this chapter is guided by the following research questions:

RQ1: What are the opportunities and challenges of AI in higher education?

RQ2: What are the ethical, governance, and operational frameworks that facilitate the responsible use of AI in higher education institutions?
RQ3: What are the governance models for responsible integration of AI in higher education institutions that are inclusive, transparent, and context-sensitive?

This chapter takes a conceptual and narrative review approach to explore opportunities, ethical risks, governance challenges, and responsible use of artificial intelligence in higher education. Recent developments in generative AI, governance frameworks, ethics and institutional implementation practices were captured by reviewing relevant literature published between 2023 and 2025. The discussion synthesizes evidence from peer-reviewed journal articles, policy reports, institutional case studies, and international governance frameworks related to higher education and AI. Specific focus is placed on the concepts of transparency, accountability, inclusivity, academic integrity, and readiness to operate in various educational settings. The chapter builds a structured understanding of responsible AI governance by incorporating global perspectives and emerging practices, and outlines pathways for ethical and context-sensitive institutional adoption.

2. THE EXPANDING ROLE OF AI IN CONTEMPORARY HIGHER EDUCATION

The use of AI technologies in higher education is growing in a variety of ways and becoming more sophisticated (Chan, 2023). Adaptive learning platforms tailor learning experiences, analytics dashboards provide real-time insights for timely interventions, and predictive models help identify learners at risk. Automated grading and plagiarism detection improve efficiency and integrity in assessment, while research applications speed up discovery and foster interdisciplinary collaboration. From an administrative perspective, chatbots and predictive analytics optimize processes, enhancing resource allocation and student services (Oncioiu & Bularca, 2025). These advancements underscore the potential of AI in enhancing the accessibility, inclusivity, and effectiveness of higher education. Table 1 provides an overview of the key uses of AI in teaching, assessment, research, student support, and institutional administration in higher education.

Table 1. Applications of AI Across the Higher Education Ecosystem

Domain	Examples of AI Applications	Benefits
Teaching & Learning	Intelligent tutoring systems, adaptive learning platforms, learning analytics dashboards, recommender systems	Personalized instruction, immediate feedback, data-driven instructional design, improved retention
Assessment	Automated essay scoring, AI-assisted grading of assignments, plagiarism detection, proctoring tools	Reduced grading workload, consistency in evaluation, timely and formative feedback
Research	Machine learning-based simulations, AI-driven literature review systems, large-scale data mining tools	Discovery acceleration, advanced pattern recognition, cross disciplinary collaborations
Student Support	Conversational AI chatbots for FAQs, enrollment assistants, personalized academic planning	24/7 student support, more efficient access to services
Administration	Predictive analytics for student recruitment and retention, resource optimization algorithms	Streamlined operations, better decision-making, cost-effectiveness

3. EMERGING RISKS AND EARLY POLICY RESPONSES

AI has great potential but also poses great risks (Khan et al., 2025). Algorithmic bias can exacerbate inequalities, data-driven systems can raise privacy concerns, and "black box" models can decrease accountability. Generative AI can be used to plagiarize or generate false work, which is a new challenge to academic integrity (Michel-Villarreal et al., 2023). In response, advanced economies like the European Union have developed regulatory frameworks, such as the AI Act, which categorizes educational tools as "high risk," necessitating transparency, risk assessments, and human oversight (Selvaratnam & Venaruzzo, 2024). To enhance internal governance and build trust, universities around the world are creating ethics boards, advisory committees, and privacy task forces (Batool et al., 2025). Table 2 provides an overview of the key risks of AI use in higher education and their potential institutional implications.

Table 2. Key Risks of AI in Higher Education

Risk Type	Description	Potential Consequences
Algorithmic Bias	AI systems trained on biased datasets can perpetuate existing inequalities	Unfair grading, biased admissions, systemic discrimination
Privacy and Data Security	AI systems often rely on sensitive student and faculty data	Data breaches, surveillance, erosion of trust
Lack of Transparency	Complex AI algorithms act as "black boxes," making decisions difficult to interpret	Reduced accountability and trust in AI-driven decisions
Generative AI Misuse	AI-generated text or images used unethically (e.g., plagiarism, fake outputs)	Decline in academic integrity and credibility

4. GOVERNANCE GAPS AND THE NEED FOR RESPONSIBLE AI

AI adoption in emerging economies is not always accompanied by governance maturity (Mangundu, 2025). Many institutions do not have formal policies, funding, expertise, or oversight mechanisms, resulting in a "governance gap" between technology adoption and risk management. This mismatch can lead to the importation of models that were developed in Western contexts and may not be applicable to local cultural and institutional contexts (Birkstedt et al., 2023). Higher education institutions need to adopt responsible governance frameworks that are based on values of transparency, accountability and inclusivity (Dafoe, 2018) to ensure equitable, fair and trustworthy adoption of AI. These frameworks should be multidisciplinary and context-sensitive, incorporating knowledge from computer science, law, ethics, and educational policy (Ghimire & Edwards, 2024). To overcome these governance constraints, a systematic grasp of responsible AI principles and their practical implications in higher education is needed.

5. RESPONSIBLE AI PRINCIPLES AND DIMENSIONS

Artificial Intelligence is no longer a nascent technology but has become an integral part of academic systems all over the world. AI has become a vital asset for universities, supporting their learning, research, and administrative processes and boosting the quality and efficiency of their operations. But this fast uptake has also brought with it ethical and operational risks of bias, opacity, data misuse and diminished accountability. The need to address these risks has led to the rise of the concept of Responsible AI, which provides a framework for integrating AI in ways that are ethical, transparent, and aligned with human values (Batool et al., 2025).

Responsible AI in higher education is the deliberate and responsible design, implementation, and oversight of AI systems to ensure that technology enhances educational outcomes while promoting fairness, transparency, and inclusivity (Chan, 2023). It highlights the intricate interplay between students, teachers, policymakers, and developers, each of whom plays a crucial role in shaping the responsible use of AI for the betterment of humanity. This strategy promotes the view of AI as a socio-technical system, urging universities to ensure that AI aligns with the ethical standards of the academic community (Selvaratnam & Venaruzzo, 2024).

Objectives of Responsible AI

The objectives of Responsible AI in higher education are to foster the ethical application of AI and to maximize its potential to improve the quality of education and institutional trust.

Enhancing teaching and learning without compromising integrity: Responsible AI aims to personalize learning experiences, assist educators with feedback, and improve accessibility while ensuring that AI tools are not used for plagiarism or academic dishonesty (Batool et al., 2025).

Minimizing algorithmic bias: Algorithms that are used in admission, grading, or resource allocation can be biased if trained on biased data. To ensure that all students are treated fairly and equitably, regular audits of datasets and models are necessary for responsible AI (Mangundu, 2025).

Enhancing transparency in decision-making: Complex AI models can make decisions that are hard to explain. Transparent systems enhance the understanding of educators and students regarding the AI-based judgments, fostering confidence and accountability (Chan, 2023).

Ensuring data privacy and security: Universities must ensure that AI systems comply with privacy regulations and have clear consent mechanisms for data collection, given that they often handle sensitive academic and personal information (Selvaratnam & Venaruzzo, 2024).

Fostering accountability: Responsible AI requires human oversight to be at the heart of all decisions made with the help of AI tools. Clear policies should be established regarding who is responsible for outcomes and that accountability is not fully delegated to automated systems (Wu et al., 2024).

These objectives are the cornerstones of ethical stewardship in AI-driven education. They make sure that technological advancement is consistent with academic honesty, social justice and human dignity.

Dimensions of Responsible AI

Responsible AI in higher education can be explored in three key areas: pedagogical, governance, and operational. Table 3 summarizes these dimensions and their associated focus areas and practices. These dimensions collectively contribute to the effective and ethical use of AI in education.

Table 3. Dimensions of Responsible AI in Higher Education

Dimension	Focus Areas	Example Practices
Pedagogical	Enhancing learning outcomes and integrity	Adaptive learning systems, intelligent tutoring, formative feedback
Governance	Policies, ethics, and oversight	AI ethics boards, codes of conduct, risk assessments
Operational	Infrastructure, training, auditing	AI literacy, algorithm audits, cybersecurity protocols

Pedagogical Dimension: AI should complement, not supplant, the human aspect of teaching. Adaptive learning platforms, virtual tutors, and intelligent feedback tools can assist educators in identifying student needs and providing timely interventions (Chan, 2023). Institutions should establish clear guidelines regarding the use of generative AI, verify AI-generated content with human oversight, and maintain transparency when AI is used to inform assessments or recommendations (Batool et al., 2025). The emphasis should continue to be on human creativity, critical thinking and personalized learning experiences.

Governance Dimension: Trust and accountability in the use of AI requires effective governance frameworks. Universities should establish ethics committees and task forces to assess risks, oversee the use of AI, and develop codes of conduct for staff and students (Mangundu, 2025). Transparent reporting mechanisms can inform users about the involvement of AI systems in academic processes and when it occurs (Wu et al., 2024). These structures also facilitate alignment of institutional policies with the wider legal framework, which ensures that higher education continues to meet national and international standards.

Operational Dimension: Operational readiness is a key element to the successful implementation of Responsible AI. There is a need for institutions to invest in training programs to enhance AI literacy among students, teachers, and administrators (Chan, 2023). Ethical awareness, responsible use of generative AI, data privacy literacy, and critical evaluation of AI-generated outputs should be part of a baseline AI literacy framework. These skills enable responsible and informed interactions with AI technologies. AI models should be regularly audited to identify errors, ensure fairness, and uphold ethical standards (Selvaratnam & Venaruzzo, 2024). Security, consent, and equitable access to technology should be at the forefront of data governance practices, with the aim of ensuring that all stakeholders in the academic ecosystem are treated fairly (Batool et al., 2025).

International Practices in Responsible AI

The adoption of responsible AI practices differs from region to region around the world, influenced by factors such as policy, technology, and culture. Several examples are provided to show how universities are applying these principles in various settings.

In the United States, universities like those in the Big Ten network have established AI governance boards with faculty, IT specialists, legal experts, and student representatives. These boards are responsible for approving and monitoring the use of AI tools and providing ongoing AI literacy training for educators to guide students in using AI responsibly and ethically (Wu et al., 2024).

The AI Act defines educational technologies as high-risk systems, which must undergo comprehensive risk assessments and human oversight in the European Union. In other countries, like Germany and the Netherlands, universities have established AI impact assessments and ethics review boards, providing students with more transparency about the use of their data, which promotes institutional transparency (Dafoe, 2018).

AI adoption in South Africa is growing, with governance still in its infancy. The study underscores the importance of formal policy frameworks, faculty training, and robust oversight mechanisms to ensure responsible integration of AI (Mangundu, 2025).

In Asia, especially in Hong Kong, Singapore and India, institutions are developing codes of conduct that reconcile innovation with ethical responsibility. For instance, the University of Hong Kong mandates that students identify the use of generative AI in their assignments, and universities in Singapore have introduced AI ethics courses in general education to raise awareness early on (Chan, 2023).

As these examples illustrate, Responsible AI is a global and context-sensitive practice. Universities with a pedagogical, governance and operational focus can develop sustainable systems that promote innovation while maintaining ethics and equity (Selvaratnam & Venaruzzo, 2024).

There are also sustainability issues to take into account, as large-scale AI systems consume more energy and require more computing power. Therefore, responsible AI governance should encourage environmentally friendly digital practices.

6. OPPORTUNITIES AND BENEFITS OF AI IN HIGHER EDUCATION

AI is a key innovation in the field of higher education. AI, when used responsibly, has the potential to greatly enhance teaching, learning, research, and institutional administration. It also improves inclusion and access, helping universities to better serve diverse populations. The subsequent subsections explore the impact of AI in higher education in six areas, including case studies of its practical applications. The key benefits of AI across teaching, assessment, research, student support, administration, and inclusion are mapped in Figure 1, highlighting the interconnections among these domains.

Figure 1. AI-Driven Benefits in Higher Education

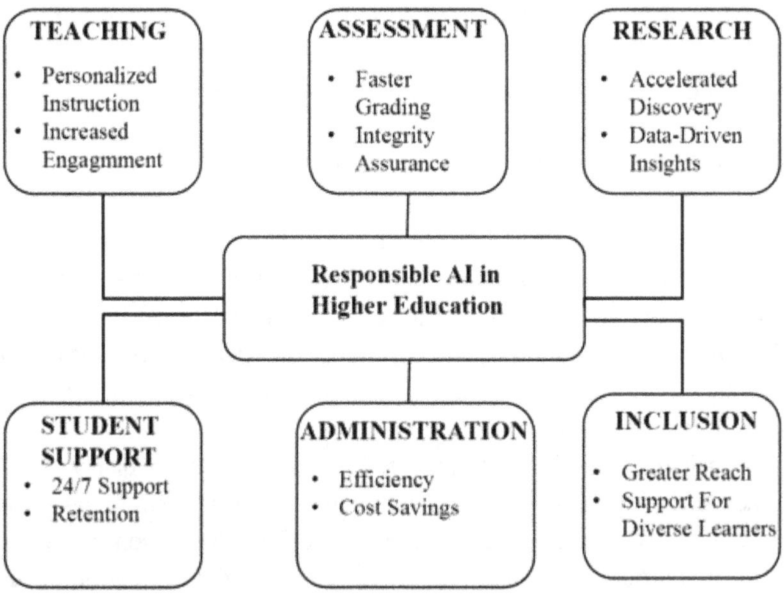

Enhancing Teaching and Learning

The use of AI in adaptive learning systems has revolutionized the personalization of teaching and learning by leveraging detailed student behavior, performance metrics, and engagement patterns. These systems can create personalized learning paths that adapt to student needs in real time, offering specific recommendations and resources based on student performance. These platforms streamline the time-consuming aspects of teaching, freeing up educators to focus on mentorship, critical thinking facilitation, and creativity in the classroom. In a practical example at the National University of Singapore, the use of adaptive learning systems (ALS) resulted in about 12 percent improvement in student outcomes in STEM fields (Chan, 2023). The use of AI in higher education also poses pedagogical questions about the design of learning, the values of education, and the role of human agency in learning and teaching in AI-supported learning environments (Holmes & Porayska-Pomsta, 2022).

Intelligent Tutoring Systems (ITS) take these benefits one step further by emulating one-to-one tutoring interactions. ITS platforms adjust to students' answers, provide immediate feedback, interactive problem-solving activities, and step-by-step guidance on complex concepts. ITS can be deployed at scale to effectively support large cohorts without compromising the quality of personalized support, increase engagement, improve retention rates and meet the learning needs of a diverse student population. Adaptive learning and ITS platforms are examples of how AI can be used to provide a responsive, student-centred learning environment and allow teachers to focus on higher-order learning goals (Batool et al., 2025).

Improving Assessment and Feedback

Traditional assessment processes have always been subjective, prone to human bias, time-consuming, and labor-intensive. With the advent of AI, essay, short answer, and other qualitative assessments can now be automated using natural language processing and semantic analysis. These systems give detailed, real-time feedback, which encourages students to learn in an iterative fashion and make continuous progress over the course of the school year.

Plagiarism detection tools and AI-powered content verification platforms also help maintain academic integrity by detecting plagiarism, paraphrasing, or AI-generated content. These technologies give teachers insightful information, allowing them to check for plagiarism while retaining the final say in the evaluation of the work for fairness. Schools that have implemented such AI systems have seen significant decreases in grading time, greater consistency in evaluations, and more time for teachers to dedicate to higher-value educational activities (Wu et al., 2024).

Transforming Research and Knowledge Creation

AI technologies have proven to be valuable tools for speeding up research processes, from data analysis to literature review and predictive modeling. Machine learning algorithms can identify complex patterns in large and diverse datasets, revealing insights that might not be apparent. NLP tools can quickly analyze thousands of research papers to find new research trends, research gaps, and potential interdisciplinary research opportunities.

Furthermore, AI-powered simulations can be used to simulate experiments in different fields, including climate science, material science, economics, and healthcare. These simulations decrease research cycles, offer cost-effective alternatives to conventional laboratory experiments, and promote cross-disciplinary collaboration by enabling researchers to test hypotheses in silico prior to real-world implementation. In this way, AI is not just a tool for efficiency; it's a catalyst for innovation. But the increasing adoption of generative AI in research has led to concerns about fabricated citations, hallucinated findings, plagiarism, and AI-assisted paper mills. It is therefore essential for universities to have clear governance frameworks to ensure transparency, responsible disclosure, and verification of AI-generated content in academic publications (Qadhi et al., 2024).

Enhancing Student Support

AI also plays a crucial role in student support and engagement, offering predictive analytics and ongoing digital assistance. Conversational agents, like chatbots, can guide students through enrollment procedures, financial aid applications, and campus services around the clock, enhancing accessibility and convenience. Predictive models are used to identify students who are at risk of underperforming or dropping out based on their academic performance, attendance, and engagement data, allowing for timely and targeted intervention by academic advisors.

One such example is Arizona State University, which saw a 15 percent drop in student dropouts over five years thanks to predictive analytics tools. This shows the ability of AI to improve student retention, but also to improve the overall effectiveness of the institution by enabling teachers to intervene proactively and support students better (Dafoe, 2018).

Optimizing Institutional Administration

AI can streamline administrative processes by improving decision-making in enrollment forecasting, scheduling, and resource allocation. Decision-support dashboards enable university leaders to gain insight into their institution's performance, pinpoint operational inefficiencies, and make informed decisions based on data.

AI-driven scheduling and resource management systems led to a 40 percent decrease in administrative tasks, freeing up time for Dutch researchers to focus on research, student engagement, and strategic planning. This case demonstrates the role of AI in enhancing not just efficiency but also agility and sustainability within institutions (Mangundu, 2025).

Expanding Access and Inclusion

AI is also a great facilitator of inclusivity and equitable access to education. Multilingual classrooms are supported by real-time translation technologies, which allow students with different language backgrounds to fully access content. While accessibility tools such as speech-to-text systems and screen readers can help students with disabilities, AI-powered grading and proctoring systems can inadvertently disadvantage neurodivergent learners if accessibility and accommodation needs are not taken into account.

AI-powered online learning platforms also help to reach underserved and remote populations, reducing the geographical and socio-economic barriers to learning. These efforts are in line with the United Nations Sustainable Development Goal 4, which seeks to ensure inclusive and equitable quality education and promote lifelong learning opportunities for all (Chan, 2023). AI can be used in the teaching, assessment, and support of students to create a more equitable, inclusive, and participatory learning environment.

While the advantages of AI in teaching, assessment, research, student support, administration, and inclusion are interdependent, their sustainable implementation requires strong governance structures (Batool et al., 2025).

7. ETHICAL RISKS AND GOVERNANCE CHALLENGES IN HIGHER EDUCATION

AI holds tremendous promise in revolutionizing higher education, with its potential applications in teaching, learning, research, and administration. But the swift and widespread adoption of AI also presents institutions with a host of ethical, social and legal issues. These risks impact fundamental academic values such as fairness, privacy, transparency, accountability and trust. In the absence of strong governance frameworks, technologies designed to enhance efficiency and personalisation can have the unintended side effect of exacerbating inequalities, reinforcing biases and compromising academic integrity (Dafoe, 2018). To fulfill its role responsibly in the digital era, HEIs need to establish ethical governance models that tackle risks at the local level while acknowledging the transnational character of AI implementation. Figure 2 shows the main ethical concerns of AI use in higher education and their impact on institutional governance.

Figure 2. Key Ethical Risks of AI in Higher Education

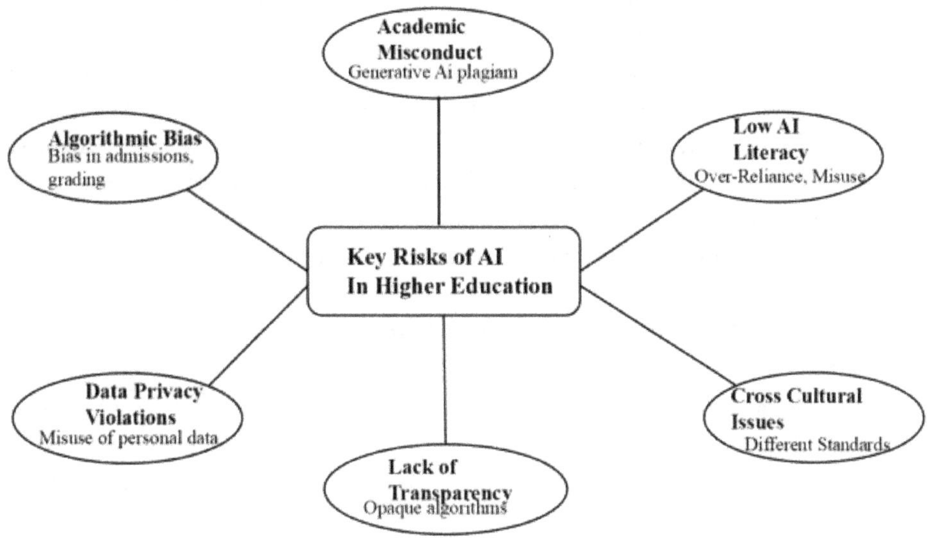

Algorithmic Bias and Inequality

AI systems use past data to make predictions, recommendations, and automated decisions. If these datasets are biased towards certain groups in society, AI models will inevitably replicate and even exacerbate these biases. Admissions algorithms can inadvertently discriminate against marginalized groups, grading systems can undervalue nontraditional language styles, and course recommendation engines can channel students into limited pathways based on biased assumptions (Mangundu, 2025). While AI-driven education systems can enhance personalization and accessibility, it is crucial to also address the needs of neurodiverse learners and students with disabilities. The consequences are subtle but significant, resulting in systemic inequalities under the guise of objectivity. Despite the progress in higher education settings to support neurodivergent students, there are still challenges to address, and poorly designed AI systems can inadvertently perpetuate exclusion if accessibility, adaptive learning needs, and inclusive practices are not considered (Clouder et al., 2020; Pierrès et al., 2024). AI systems in education can also inadvertently harm students with disabilities or neurodivergent learners if accessibility and inclusive design are not taken into account. Thus, there is a need to pay more attention to ethical issues of bias, usability, privacy, and accessibility in responsible AI governance frameworks (Morris, 2020; Fitas, 2025). The use of AI in higher education also brings up general issues of social harm, differential effects on groups of learners, and environmental sustainability of widespread AI use. Scholars also warn against the idea of AI being a neutral educational tool, and the need for critical and context-sensitive governance approaches (Selwyn, 2022).

Algorithmic bias is not just a technical issue, it is a moral hazard. Predictive analytics or learning technologies that continue to discriminate pose reputational and ethical risks for universities that are dedicated to equity and inclusion. It is therefore essential for institutions to conduct bias audits, create diverse and representative training datasets, and establish oversight mechanisms to ensure that AI is used to promote fairness and inclusion, not perpetuate inequality.

Privacy, Security, and Data Protection

The implementation of AI relies on extensive data, such as demographic information, academic records, engagement metrics, and biometric identifiers for online proctoring systems, all of which are sensitive and must be protected. Mismanagement of this data can result in unauthorized access, surveillance, reputational damage, and legal liabilities. While there are frameworks like the European General Data Protection Regulation (GDPR) that offer good protection, implementation varies from university to university (Dafoe, 2018).

Ethical responsibility goes beyond legal compliance, it means that students must feel confident that their personal information is protected. To ensure trust and protect privacy, institutions need to have robust data governance practices, such as encryption, informed consent procedures, anonymization methods, and independent audits. One data breach can have lasting effects, eroding institutional trust and deterring the use of new AI technologies. In addition to immediate risks, institutions need to take into account long-term privacy implications of AI-enabled systems. Ongoing learner profiling and extended data storage can raise issues of surveillance, autonomy and informed consent.

Transparency and Accountability

Many advanced AI models, especially deep learning systems, operate as "black boxes" that are difficult to interpret even by the developers (Chan, 2023). This opacity poses challenges in higher education, as students might not grasp the rationale behind their "at risk" status, instructors might have trouble challenging AI-generated grades, and administrators might have trouble justifying AI-generated policy suggestions.

The absence of explainability jeopardizes accountability. When an AI system generates discriminatory or harmful results, it is difficult to determine who is responsible. Who is responsible: the developer, the vendor, the university or faculty? To address this risk, universities should focus on explainable AI solutions and implement accountability frameworks with clear lines of responsibility and appeal and oversight mechanisms.

Academic Integrity and Generative AI Misuse

The use of generative AI tools such as ChatGPT, Bard, and Claude has challenged traditional academic practices. These systems can be used to improve creativity and facilitate learning, but they can also be used to plagiarize, ghostwrite, provide false references, and fake datasets (Batool et al., 2025; Wu et al., 2024).

In response, universities in the United States are implementing new integrity codes, detection tools, and awareness campaigns, while European universities are incorporating generative AI guidelines into formal academic policies (Dafoe, 2018). But punitive measures are not enough. Institutions must foster digital literacy, ensuring that students and faculty are knowledgeable about the responsible use of AI and its limitations.

Faculty and Student Readiness

AI's impact is contingent upon human preparedness and digital literacy. There is a wide range of familiarity with AI tools among faculty and students. Some teachers might embrace AI with too much enthusiasm, using the automated results without fully comprehending them, while others may be hesitant to use AI because they lack the training or understanding of its capabilities (Chan, 2023). Recent bibliometric evidence further highlights institutional barriers, ethical concerns, and governance-related challenges that continue to affect responsible AI adoption in higher education (Elamrani Elhassani et al., 2025). Likewise, students might misunderstand the AI-generated results and interpret them as absolute facts.

Capacity building is thus crucial, given the growing burden on faculty members in terms of hidden workloads for curriculum redesign, AI literacy development, and monitoring academic integrity in AI-supported settings.

Cross-Cultural and Global Governance Challenges

AI in higher education is used in a variety of legal, cultural, and infrastructural settings. International programs at universities face a quilt of regulations, ethical norms, and resource constraints. The AI Act in the European Union (EU) categorizes educational AI applications as "high risk," requiring transparency, explainability, and human oversight (Dafoe, 2018). Many African institutions, including those in South Africa, have quickly embraced AI without robust governance structures, resulting in faculty members lacking adequate training and policies being underdeveloped

(Mangundu, 2025). Similar findings across African higher education systems indicate persistent challenges related to governance maturity, institutional readiness, and policy development for responsible AI implementation (Jacobs-Basadien & Pather, 2026). While some universities in Asia have taken proactive steps to establish codes of conduct and AI literacy requirements, there are still gaps in access and digital readiness (Chan, 2023).

This is an uneven terrain that makes global governance difficult. What works in one area may not work in another, both in terms of policy and ethics. If there is no coordination, gaps may grow, with some institutions having strong safeguards and others having only basic safeguards.

Institutional Trust and Reputation

Trust is a key element of higher education, in the relationship between students and teachers, between the institution and the public, and between the university and the regulators. This trust can be lost if AI is poorly governed. Institutional reputation can be harmed by data breaches, algorithmic bias, or high-profile instances of AI-generated plagiarism, potentially leading to legal consequences (Batool et al., 2025). On the other hand, universities with transparent and ethically based governance models can improve their credibility as responsible leaders in digital transformation. Once lost, trust is hard to earn back, and principled, proactive AI adoption helps institutions to be seen as forward-thinking and reliable.

The ethical and governance issues of AI in higher education are deep. Bias compromises equity, privacy breaches erode trust, opacity undermines accountability, and generative AI poses threats to academic integrity. The adoption is further complicated by the fact that there are different levels of literacy among faculty and students, and there are differences in regulation around the world, which leads to gaps in governance. To ensure the responsible use of AI, universities need to shift from reactive to proactive governance. It is important to incorporate ethical, legal and cultural protection measures into institutional strategies. Responsible AI and governance frameworks are essential to safely innovate, uphold academic integrity, and foster trust in higher education (Dafoe, 2018). The ethical and operational risks of AI in higher education highlight that the mere use of technology is not enough to guarantee equitable and trustworthy outcomes. Issues like algorithmic bias, privacy concerns, academic misconduct, and varying institutional readiness necessitate governance frameworks that can transform ethical principles into tangible safeguards. The next section thus explores governance models, policy instruments and stakeholder roles that facilitate responsible AI implementation. Table 4 provides an overview of the key ethical concerns and governance issues related to the use of AI in higher education.

Table 4. Key Ethical Risks and Challenges in AI for Higher Education

Risk/Challenge	Description	Potential Consequences
Algorithmic Bias	Models trained on biased data perpetuate inequality	Discriminatory admissions, unfair grading
Data Privacy Violations	Misuse of sensitive data	Legal consequences, erosion of trust
Lack of Transparency	AI decisions lack explainability	Reduced accountability, difficulty contesting outcomes
Academic Misconduct	Use of generative AI for plagiarism or fabricated research	Erosion of academic integrity
Uneven Governance	Regulatory variations across borders	Difficulty in policy enforcement
Low AI Literacy	Limited awareness among faculty/students	Over-reliance, misinterpretation of AI recommendations

8. GOVERNANCE MODELS, POLICY TOOLS, AND STAKEHOLDER ROLES IN AI FOR HIGHER EDUCATION

AI in higher education is not just a technological shift, but a sociotechnical transformation. The successful integration of AI is not just about the excitement of innovation, but also about a well-designed governance framework, effective policy tools, and defined roles for various stakeholders. Good governance guarantees that AI systems improve learning, research, and administration while maintaining ethical standards, fairness, transparency, accountability, and the integrity of academic practices (Dafoe, 2018). In the absence of robust frameworks, institutions may be tempted to implement AI technologies in a disjointed and vendor-centric way, which can lead to issues of algorithmic bias, reputational damage, legal liability, and a loss of academic integrity (Batool et al., 2025).

Multi-Layered Governance Models

Recent research suggests that universities are moving towards a multi-layered governance model that combines strategic oversight, operational management, and discipline-specific adaptations. Governance models define the decision-making process for AI tools, specify who is accountable, and uphold ethical principles, transparency, and accountability throughout all levels (Mangundu, 2025).

Institutional ethics boards are the first line of defense at the highest level. These boards are usually made up of faculty members from a variety of disciplines, legal professionals, student representatives, IT professionals, and sometimes outside advisors. They are responsible for establishing institutional values, formulating general principles, creating codes of conduct, and giving the final approval before AI systems are implemented. A survey of Big Ten universities in the United States found that such boards are now commonplace, and that decisions on the deployment of AI are now made not only for technical feasibility, but also for social impact and alignment with academic and institutional values (Wu et al., 2024).

In addition to this central oversight, there are cross-functional task forces, which are frequently ad hoc groups that are established to review a particular tool, test a new initiative, or assess a policy. These teams include representatives from teaching and learning units, legal and compliance offices, research administration, and information technology services. They perform thorough AI impact assessments, analyze data privacy and security concerns, and suggest measures to minimize potential harms. These multidisciplinary structures are essential for European universities, especially for high-risk AI systems, like those that affect grading, admissions, or academic recommendations, that need human oversight, careful documentation, and continuous evaluation (Dafoe, 2018).

Many institutions have decentralized governance in addition to the centralized and cross-functional layers, which are organized in the form of departmental committees. These committees work very near to the realities of the academic disciplines. For instance, a medical school committee could evaluate the impact of AI decision-support systems on clinical student training, while an engineering faculty committee could examine AI-based code-generation tools. Departmental committees interpret and tailor institutional policies to the specific needs of their disciplines and provide results and recommendations to the central ethics committee. This multi-layered approach ensures that AI governance is grounded in ethical principles, legally compliant, and attuned to the specific needs of each discipline, fostering consistency, transparency, and contextual relevance throughout the institution (Selvaratnam & Venaruzzo, 2024). Table 5 provides a comparative overview of governance structures commonly used for AI implementation in higher education institutions.

Table 5. Comparative Overview of Governance Structures for AI Implementation in Higher Education

Governance Structure	Typical Composition	Strengths	Limitations
Institutional Ethics Boards	Faculty, legal counsel, students, IT experts	Centralized oversight, consistent policy development	May be slow, high-level perspective
Cross-Functional Task Forces	Representatives from multiple departments	Multidisciplinary evaluation, responsive to emerging risks	Requires active coordination
Departmental Committees	Domain-specific faculty and specialists	Contextualized decisions, closer to field requirements	Risk of inconsistency without coordination

The governance process typically involves four steps: policy development, risk analysis, implementation monitoring, and ongoing evaluation. Policy formation is the process of creating and regularly revising institutional policies that establish guidelines for responsible use of AI. For example, some Big Ten schools have issued official AI ethics guidelines that establish guidelines for the use of AI throughout the campus. Algorithmic impact assessments (AI Impact Assessments, AIIAs) are used to assess potential bias, fairness, and data risks prior to procurement of an AI system. After deployment, AI systems are monitored, audited for performance, and subject to feedback from stakeholders to identify model drift or unforeseen risks. Lastly, governance frameworks are dynamic, adapting to technological advancements and regulatory shifts, making AI governance an ongoing and evolving process.

There are different governance models around the world. Models in the United States are very participatory, and student representatives are frequently members of oversight committees. European institutions are subject to regulatory frameworks like GDPR and the EU AI Act, which mandate a lot of documentation and structured risk assessment processes. South African universities are at the beginning stages of developing maturity models, with pilot committees and AI literacy initiatives, but with capacity gaps (Mangundu, 2025). In Asian universities, especially in Hong Kong and Singapore, codes of conduct for the use of generative AI and strict transparency guidelines are emphasized.

For governance to be effective, it needs to be human-centred, meaning that decisions are made in a participatory way and not just by technologists. Research shows that involving students, teachers, and other stakeholders in decision-making processes enhances the acceptance of governance policies and fosters a respect for cultural and disciplinary diversity (Selvaratnam & Venaruzzo, 2024). Figure 3 shows a multi-layered governance model that depicts the interplay between institutional oversight, task forces, and departmental structures in responsible AI governance.

Figure 3. Multi-Layered AI Governance Model for Higher Education

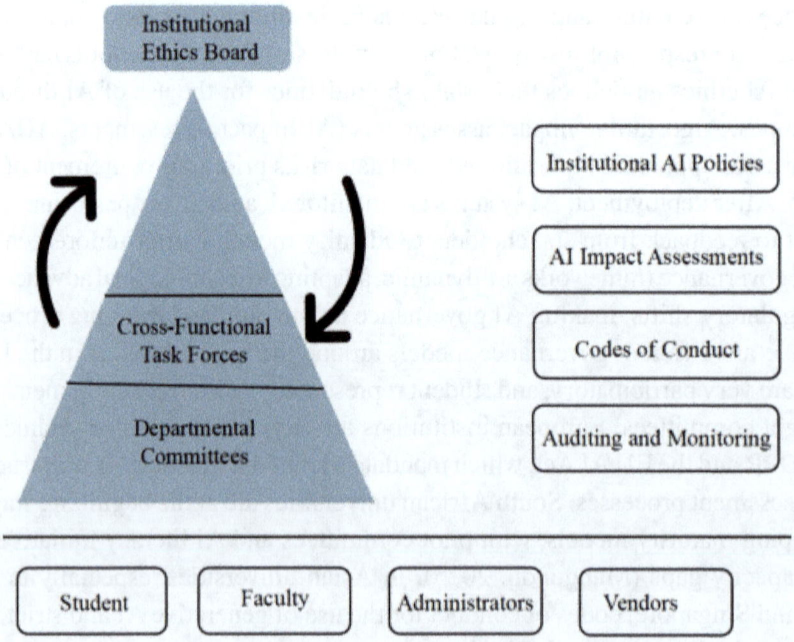

Policy Tools and Accountability Mechanisms

Policy tools and accountability mechanisms are the means by which the principles of effective governance in higher education are put into practice. The most frequently used instruments are:

Institutional AI policies that establish acceptable uses of AI and responsibilities for faculty, students, and vendors. These policies frequently incorporate academic integrity guidelines and are applicable to AI-powered assignments, grading systems, plagiarism detection tools, and predictive analytics platforms (Wu, Zhang, & Carroll, 2024).

AI Impact Assessments (AIIAs) to assess the potential risks and benefits of new AI applications. Evaluations take into account the quality of the datasets, bias, human oversight, adherence to legal regulations (e.g., GDPR and the EU AI Act), and unintended discrimination. In Europe, AIIAs are mandatory for high-risk AI systems before deployment (Batool et al., 2025).

Codes of conduct that set behavioral standards for faculty and students. They explain what is expected of responsible use of AI, such as disclosing the use of generative AI, conducting ethical research, and not relying too heavily on automated systems (Chan, 2023).

Training and literacy programs aimed at developing competencies in AI ethics, practical application, and responsible use. In many Asian universities, including in Hong Kong and Singapore, students are required to attend AI literacy workshops (Chan, 2023).

Auditing and monitoring systems to continuously assess deployed AI systems for accuracy, fairness, and performance. Regular audits can identify bias, errors, or model drift before it becomes problematic (Selvaratnam & Venaruzzo, 2024).

Consent and transparency mechanisms that safeguard data privacy, empower users, and offer insights into how AI systems collect and process data. Some institutions provide dashboard-type portals that allow students to view the information held about them and request corrections (Selvaratnam & Venaruzzo, 2024).

These policy instruments are stacked, with several checks and balances. For instance, an AI-enabled grading platform is first evaluated via an AIIA, then deployed with clear codes of conduct, monitored through regular audits, and continuously assessed using stakeholder feedback. This multi-layered accountability ensures that AI systems augment human judgment and uphold academic values (Batool et al., 2025; Wu, Zhang, & Carroll, 2024). Figure 4 shows the accountability framework that enables governance mechanisms, policies, and monitoring systems to support responsible AI implementation.

Figure 4. Accountability Framework for AI in Higher Education

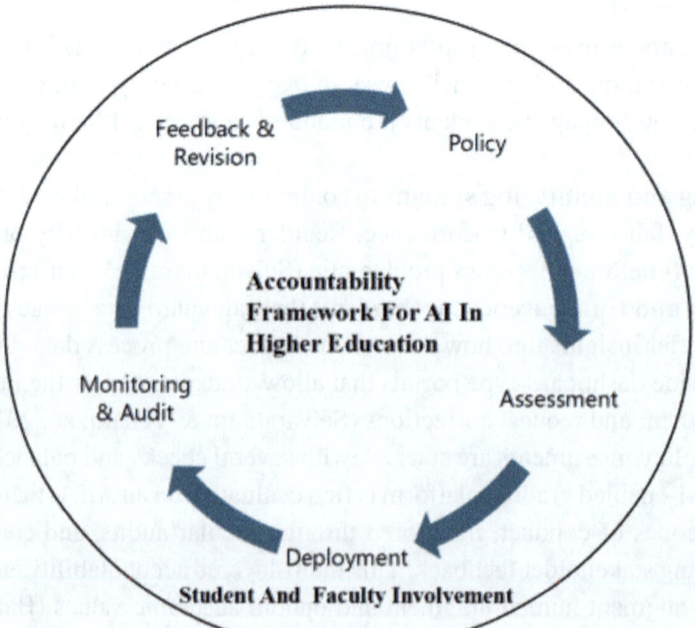

Stakeholder Roles in Responsible AI Governance

AI governance in higher education is a shared responsibility that involves everyone in the academic community. Responsibility needs to be shared among stakeholders, with each stakeholder bringing unique expertise and responsibility to the process. Collaboration between students, faculty, administrators, technical teams, legal experts, and external vendors is crucial to ensure the ethical and effective deployment of AI (Batool et al., 2025).

The role of students in AI governance becomes more and more prominent. They interact with AI-powered learning analytics dashboards, adaptive learning platforms, automated grading systems, and AI advisory chatbots. Students are not passive recipients; they are actively involved in governance, giving feedback on AI systems, following disclosure guidelines for using generative AI, and helping to refine policies. Their involvement guarantees that AI tools are aligned with learning outcomes, ensuring transparency and trust (Chan, 2023).

The faculty members serve as mediators between technology and pedagogy. They identify the role of AI in curricula, teaching and assessment practices, and demonstrate responsible use of AI in research. Additionally, faculty members keep an eye on algorithmic bias, maintain the importance of human judgment in decisions impacting student evaluation, and help students navigate ethical interactions with AI technologies (Selvaratnam & Venaruzzo, 2024).

Academic leaders, such as provosts, deans, and vice-chancellors, set strategic priorities, allocate resources, and incorporate AI governance into institutional quality assurance frameworks. Their choices determine whether AI is a tool for academic success or an uncontrolled risk. Leadership commitment plays a vital role in the integration of ethical values in institutional practices and in the creation of a culture of accountability (Dafoe, 2018).

IT professionals and data specialists are tasked with implementing, maintaining, and monitoring AI systems to guarantee security, explainability, and performance. They work closely with ethics boards to ensure compliance with institutional standards. More and more, institutions are bringing in ethicists and social scientists to technical teams to help drive home the point that AI development is not just technical, but also social and ethical (Selvaratnam & Venaruzzo, 2024).

Legal advisors, compliance officers, and ethicists ensure compliance with legal and regulatory requirements, interpret institutional policies, and audit AI systems for fairness and compliance. They also make sure that contracts with external vendors contain clauses that enforce ethical procurement, transparency, and accountability (Wu, Zhang, & Carroll, 2024).

External vendors and partners are held accountable through contractual obligations to provide transparent and auditable AI tools, respect institutional policies, and deliver guarantees regarding fairness, explainability, and reliability. Their engagement is essential for sustaining trust and guaranteeing that AI systems are aligned with the educational mission and do not detract from it (Batool et al., 2025). Figure 5 illustrates the interdependent web of stakeholders that are engaged in responsible AI governance in higher education institutions.

Figure 5. Collaborative Network of Stakeholders in AI Governance

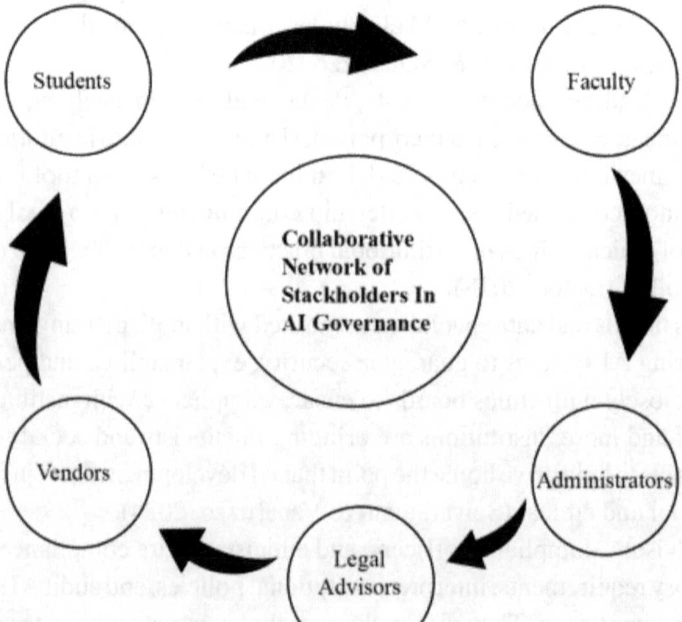

International experience shows that good governance requires consultative processes, including public forums, interdisciplinary workshops, annual impact reports and advisory panels. Faculty–student–IT panels have been established at Big Ten universities to assess AI tools before they are rolled out across the campus (Wu, Zhang, & Carroll, 2024). European institutions institutionalize stakeholder involvement in compliance with the EU AI Act, with documentation of decision-making and human oversight. Asian universities emphasize AI literacy training to empower stakeholders to participate meaningfully in governance (Chan, 2023).

The multi-layered governance models, policy tools, and stakeholder collaboration enable universities to move beyond a technical exercise to a living, participatory culture of AI governance. This way, AI systems can stay effective, trustworthy, and aligned with academic values, and ethical standards can evolve in tandem with technological advancements (Selvaratnam & Venaruzzo, 2024).

9. GOVERNANCE FRAMEWORK AND PATHWAYS TOWARD ETHICAL AND INCLUSIVE DIGITAL TRANSFORMATION

AI in higher education is not just a technological upgrade; it's a transformative shift in the institution. AI systems are reshaping the landscape of decision-making, accountability, and knowledge generation in universities. Institutions need to implement a holistic, values-based, and adaptive governance model to fully leverage the potential of AI while upholding the ethical standards of academic institutions. This will mean that innovation will continue in line with the university's mission of fairness, transparency and human dignity (Dafoe, 2018).

Building a Value-Driven and Integrated Governance Model

The core of responsible AI governance is to adopt AI at the speed of values, not technology. Universities need to establish a common set of principles, such as equity, accountability, transparency, privacy, and academic integrity, and integrate them throughout the AI lifecycle, from design to procurement, deployment, monitoring, and decommissioning. These principles are not fixed, but rather continuously develop based on institutional experience, feedback from stakeholders, and shifts in global society (Selvaratnam & Venaruzzo, 2024).

To make these values operational, governance needs to shift from isolated or departmental to multi-level and integrated governance. AI Ethics and Oversight Councils at the institutional level can help shape strategy, interpret new laws like the EU AI Act, and harmonize academic and administrative activities. Cross-functional task forces assess and test AI tools, conduct impact assessments, and oversee implementation below this level. These guidelines are then further tailored to the needs of the discipline by departmental or faculty committees, making them relevant to a variety of academic settings.

This vertically integrated system of governance, with a central authority and local autonomy, can bring together moral leadership and technical expertise. Crucially, this integration moves AI governance beyond mere compliance to a strategic tool for institutional trust and academic innovation.

Embedding Risk Assessment, Capacity Building, and Transparency

Institutionalizing AI Impact Assessments (AIIAs) is a key part of responsible governance. These evaluations, which are now being implemented in some European and American countries, are crucial for addressing issues of bias, explainability, privacy, and potential effects on academic integrity (Wu, Zhang, & Carroll, 2024).

AIIAs are required before AI is used, which means that universities can assess the fairness, reliability, and ethical integrity of new technologies before they impact students or staff.

AIIAs outcomes should be shared throughout the institution, promoting transparency and shared responsibility. After deployment, there should be continuous monitoring and periodic audits to ensure that systems continue to be aligned with institutional principles and meet changing societal and regulatory expectations.

But without AI literacy and institutional capacity, there can be no robust governance. It is essential for faculty, administrators, and students to be aware of the capabilities and limitations of AI. Thus, universities should have a holistic AI literacy initiative, add ethics courses to the curriculum, and provide continuous training for teachers and staff (Chan, 2023). This capacity building fosters a culture of critical engagement, challenging AI systems instead of taking them on faith.

There should also be transparency and accountability in the procurement and use of AI systems. Vendors should be mandated to give detailed information on data sources, algorithmic design, and system limitations. Explainability dashboards can be used internally to help users understand how AI systems are producing outputs or classifications, which can help to reinforce institutional accountability. Furthermore, there should be mechanisms for appeal and review to allow for the possibility of challenging AI-assisted decisions by human authority (Selvaratnam & Venaruzzo, 2024).

In a globalized academic environment, institutions need to be aware of the transnational dimension of governance as well. Universities with international campuses or partnerships need to create hybrid models that are sensitive to local legal and cultural requirements while remaining ethically consistent on a global scale. Ensuring internal policies are consistent with UNESCO's Recommendation on the Ethics of AI and the OECD AI Principles helps to align with international norms while also allowing for regional diversity (Mangundu, 2025).

This interconnection of mechanisms, such as risk assessment, literacy, transparency, and global adaptation, provides a basis for universities to establish trustworthy and sustainable AI ecosystems. Table 6 provides a summary of the major dimensions of governance and the recommendations.

Table 6. Governance Dimensions and Key Recommendations

Governance Dimension	Key Recommendations
Structures and Oversight	Establish multi-level councils, task forces, and departmental committees with clear mandates
Risk Assessment	Make AI Impact Assessments compulsory; integrate continuous audits and transparent reporting
Capacity Building	Implement AI literacy programs for faculty and students; embed responsible AI education
Transparency and Accountability	Require vendor documentation, explainability dashboards, and appeal mechanisms
Global Adaptation	Develop hybrid governance models for multi-campus institutions; align with UNESCO and OECD standards

Toward Continuous, Ethical, and Inclusive Digital Transformation

The governance of AI in higher education should be a dynamic and cyclical process that adapts to technological and social change. Structures, policies, stakeholder roles and international collaborations are built on the foundation of institutional values. Feedback loops are used to periodically review governance decisions based on new technologies, regulatory changes, and stakeholder experiences. Adaptively applied responsible AI governance can be a tool to foster innovation based on integrity, equity and inclusion. While AI can improve learning outcomes, streamline administration, and increase access to education globally, there are potential issues of algorithmic bias, opacity, and a loss of trust in the academic system. The use of AI in education is not just about technology; it's about governance, and whether it is used to enhance or hinder the educational mission (Batool et al., 2025; Selvaratnam & Venaruzzo, 2024).

Structural support comes from institutional ethics councils, cross-functional task forces, and departmental committees, while tools like AI Impact Assessments, audit cycles, codes of conduct, and transparency dashboards bring governance to life. Governance is continually monitored, stakeholders are consulted and governance is continually updated. Capacity building and AI literacy initiatives integrate ethical considerations across the academic landscape, promoting equity, inclusivity, and innovation in research. By adopting adaptive governance models, universities can not only establish their credibility as institutions but also shape the future direction of higher education's digital transformation, ensuring that AI progress is aligned with knowledge, equity, and human judgment (Birkstedt, Minkkinen, Tandon, & Mäntymäki, 2023).

10. CONCLUSION

AI is reshaping higher education, enhancing teaching, research, administration and inclusion while posing ethical, social, and legal challenges. The need for value-driven frameworks is underscored by algorithmic bias, privacy risks, lack of transparency, misuse of generative AI, and uneven governance. While technology can't ensure success, responsible AI governance is crucial to ensure that AI use in education is aligned with academic integrity, fairness, and human-centred learning.

The successful integration of AI involves a balance of governance, pedagogy, faculty readiness, student engagement, and institutional responsibility. With the help of AI literacy and capacity-building efforts, these structures enable stakeholders to interact with AI systems in a critical and responsible manner. Case studies from around the world, including the United States, Europe, South Africa, and Asia, highlight the need for context-specific, participatory approaches that prioritize innovation while upholding ethical principles. By implementing adaptive, values-driven AI governance, universities can unlock the transformative potential of AI while maintaining credibility, trust, and integrity, thereby fostering sustainable and equitable digital education ecosystems

REFERENCES

Barus, O. P., Hidayanto, A. N., Handri, E. Y., Sensuse, D. I., & Yaiprasert, C. (2025). Shaping generative AI governance in higher education: Insights from student perception. *International Journal of Educational Research Open*, *8*, 100452. DOI: 10.1016/j.ijedro.2025.100452

Batool, A., Zowghi, D., & Bano, M. (2025). AI governance: A systematic literature review. *AI and Ethics*, *5*(3), 3265–3279. DOI: 10.1007/s43681-024-00653-w

Birkstedt, T., Minkkinen, M., Tandon, A., & Mäntymäki, M. (2023). AI governance: Themes, knowledge gaps and future agendas. *Internet Research*, *33*(7), 133–167. DOI: 10.1108/INTR-01-2022-0042

Chan, C. K. Y. (2023). A comprehensive AI policy education framework for university teaching and learning. *International Journal of Educational Technology in Higher Education*, *20*(1), 38. DOI: 10.1186/s41239-023-00408-3

Clouder, L., Karakus, M., Cinotti, A., Ferreyra, M. V., Fierros, G. A., & Rojo, P. (2020). Neurodiversity in higher education: A narrative synthesis. *Higher Education*, *80*(4), 757–778. DOI: 10.1007/s10734-020-00513-6

Crompton, H., & Burke, D. (2023). Artificial intelligence in higher education: The state of the field. *International Journal of Educational Technology in Higher Education*, *20*(1), 22. DOI: 10.1186/s41239-023-00392-8

Dafoe, A. (2018). *AI governance: A research agenda.* Centre for the Governance of AI, Future of Humanity Institute, University of Oxford. https://www.governance.ai/research-paper/agenda

Elamrani Elhassani, A., Oulamine, A., & Elbarhoumi, F. (2025). Rethinking the adoption of artificial intelligence in higher education: A bibliometric study of barriers, ethical issues, and governance challenges. *IJDAM: International Journal of Digitalization and Applied Management*, *2*(2), 97–116. DOI: 10.23882/ijdam.25216

Fitas, R. (2025). Inclusive education with AI: Supporting special needs and tackling language barriers. *AI and Ethics*, *5*(6), 5729–5757. DOI: 10.1007/s43681-025-00824-3

Ghimire, A., & Edwards, J. (2024). From guidelines to governance: A study of AI policies in education. In Olney, A. M., Chounta, I.-A., Liu, Z., Santos, O. C., & Bittencourt, I. I. (Eds.), *Artificial intelligence in education: Posters and late breaking results, workshops and tutorials, industry and innovation tracks, practitioners, doctoral consortium and blue sky* (pp. 299–307). Springer Nature Switzerland., DOI: 10.1007/978-3-031-64312-5_36

Holmes, W., & Porayska-Pomsta, K. (2022). *The ethics of artificial intelligence in education: Practices, challenges, and debates*. Routledge., DOI: 10.4324/9780429329067

Jacobs-Basadien, M., & Pather, S. (2026). Assessing AI policy and guideline progress within the South African public higher education system: Insights from documented policies. *Universal Access in the Information Society*, *25*(2), 71. DOI: 10.1007/s10209-026-01340-9

Khan, S., Mazhar, T., Shahzad, T., Khan, M. A., Rehman, A. U., Saeed, M. M., & Hamam, H. (2025). Harnessing AI for sustainable higher education: Ethical considerations, operational efficiency, and future directions. *Discover Sustainability*, *6*(1), 23. DOI: 10.1007/s43621-025-00809-6

Mangundu, J. (2025). Navigating artificial intelligence governance: Insights from South African higher education IT decision-makers. *The African Journal of Information Systems*, *17*(1), 1–20.

Michel-Villarreal, R., Vilalta-Perdomo, E., Salinas-Navarro, D. E., Thierry-Aguilera, R., & Gerardou, F. S. (2023). Challenges and opportunities of generative AI for higher education as explained by ChatGPT. *Education Sciences*, *13*(9), 856. DOI: 10.3390/educsci13090856

Morris, M. R. (2020). AI and accessibility. *Communications of the ACM*, *63*(6), 35–37. DOI: 10.1145/3356727

Oncioiu, I., & Bularca, A. R. (2025). Artificial intelligence governance in higher education: The role of knowledge-based strategies in fostering legal awareness and ethical artificial intelligence literacy. *Societies (Basel, Switzerland)*, *15*(6), 144. DOI: 10.3390/soc15060144

Pierrès, O., Christen, M., Schmitt-Koopmann, F. M., & Darvishy, A. (2024). Could the use of AI in higher education hinder students with disabilities? A scoping review. *IEEE Access : Practical Innovations, Open Solutions*, *12*, 27810–27828. DOI: 10.1109/ACCESS.2024.3365368

Qadhi, S. M., Alduais, A., Chaaban, Y., & Khraisheh, M. (2024). Generative AI, research ethics, and higher education research: Insights from a scientometric analysis. *Information (Basel)*, *15*(6), 325. DOI: 10.3390/info15060325

Selvaratnam, R., & Venaruzzo, L. (2024). Human-centered approach to the governance of AI in higher education: Principles of international practice. *Journal of Ethics in Higher Education*, *5*(5), 79–102. DOI: 10.26034/fr.jehe.2024.6864

Selwyn, N. (2022). The future of AI and education: Some cautionary notes. *European Journal of Education*, *57*(4), 620–631. DOI: 10.1111/ejed.12532

Wu, C., Zhang, H., & Carroll, J. M. (2024). AI governance in higher education: Case studies of guidance at Big Ten universities. *Future Internet*, *16*(10), 354. DOI: 10.3390/fi16100354

Chapter 3
Using Responsible Artificial Intelligence to Revolutionize Higher Education

Olivia Jana
http://orcid.org/0009-0009-2101-9513
Brainware University, India

Shivnath Ghosh
http://orcid.org/0000-0001-7368-7139
Brainware University, India

ABSTRACT

This chapter explores the idea of responsible AI adoption in higher education, emphasizing the frameworks, values, and principles that must govern this adoption in addition to the technological potential. Educational institutions are under increasing pressure to innovate, but they must do so without sacrificing the core principles of inclusivity, academic integrity, and student welfare. The concept of "responsibility" in the application of AI suggests a methodical and careful approach—one that considers the social and cultural diversity of learners, foresees outcomes, maintains transparency, and safeguards privacy. Such a strategy calls for active communication between students, educators, technologists, and legislators in order to create an ecosystem where AI is not only used but also deeply ingrained in higher education.

DOI: 10.4018/979-8-3373-5586-3.ch003

1 LITERATURE REVIEW

Over the course of more than 50 years, the discussion surrounding artificial intelligence (AI) and higher education has become more complex, multidisciplinary, and significant. This discussion, which began with pedagogical experimentation and technological optimism, has developed into a critical investigation of the social, ethical, and educational ramifications of AI adoption. What started out as a straightforward investigation into whether machines could enhance education has developed into a sophisticated analysis of how artificial intelligence (AI) transforms classroom settings, organizational frameworks, and student experiences.

1.1. The Foundations: Computer-Assisted Instruction in the 1960s and 1970s

The foundation for artificial intelligence (AI) in education was established in the late 1960s and early 1970s by groundbreaking work in computer-assisted instruction (CAI). Computers could be used to deliver repetitive drill-and-practice exercises more effectively than traditional classroom methods, as demonstrated by platforms like PLATO (Programmed Logic for Automated Teaching Operations). By today's standards, these early systems were primitive, frequently emphasizing rote memorization and the reinforcement of fundamental skills. However, they marked a revolutionary change: the automation and personalization of learning processes through the use of digital tools. At this point, the value proposition was obvious: teachers could focus on more difficult work while machines took care of the tedious, repetitive parts of teaching (Baker & Inventado, 2014; Bender et al., 2021).

1.2. Rise of Intelligent Tutoring Systems in the 1980s

Driven by developments in cognitive science and symbolic AI, the 1980s saw a significant shift in emphasis from basic CAI to Intelligent Tutoring Systems (ITS). In contrast to their predecessors, ITS aimed to replicate tutoring that was human-like by simulating both the subject matter and the cognitive state of the learner. Rule-based expert systems that could modify feedback and direction based on the learner's responses were introduced during this time. Individualized learning pathways were a key component of these systems, enabling students to advance at their own speed with tailored assistance. ITS established the groundwork for the development of adaptive learning technologies, despite the fact that the technology was constrained by the requirement for substantial manual programming and rule-coding (Holmes et al., 2022).

1.3. Constructivist Learning and Pedagogical Advances in the 1990s

The landscape changed once more in the 1990s, this time as a result of constructivist teaching methods. Learner-centered approaches that prioritized active engagement, exploration, and reflection were promoted by educational theorists and technologists. Learner modeling, self-explanation prompts, and domain-independent tutoring shells—modular software that could be modified for use in a variety of subjects and contexts—were the main features of this era. During this time, research acknowledged that promoting deeper cognitive processes like metacognition and conceptual understanding was just as important to effective learning as providing the appropriate content. In an effort to promote critical thinking as opposed to memorization, AI systems started implementing these components (Cotton et al., 2024).

1.4. The Millennium Shift: From Rule-Based AI to Machine Learning

Two revolutionary paradigm shifts occurred at the turn of the millennium. The emergence of data-driven machine learning came first. In contrast to symbolic AI, this method used statistical algorithms and sizable datasets to find patterns, forecast outcomes, and adjust in real time. Businesses that provide individualized content at scale, such as Knewton, ALEKS, and Carnegie Learning, have become leaders in adaptive learning platforms. These platforms could forecast problem areas, suggest specialized learning activities, and continuously evaluate student performance. Increased scalability was made possible by machine learning, but it also brought forth new difficulties with explainability and transparency (OECD, 2019; Bender et al., 2021).

1.5. Platformization and the Big Data Turn in Higher Education

The second significant change was the platformization of higher education, which was marked by the growth of micro-credential ecosystems, Massive Open Online Courses (MOOCs), and Learning Management Systems (LMS). Large volumes of "digital exhaust"—data trails left by students' online interactions—were produced by these digital environments. Predictive analytics, learning analytics, and algorithmic decision-making were developed using this data and are currently applied to everything from curriculum design to student retention. To direct educational interventions, track student progress, and improve learning environments, institutions started depending on data dashboards and AI-powered recommendation engines (Page & Gehlbach, 2020; Selwyn, 2019).

1.6. Interdisciplinary Growth: 2015–2024

Systematic mapping reviews showed that the amount of research on AI in education increased exponentially between 2015 and 2024. The field's development into a strong interdisciplinary field that includes computer science, cognitive psychology, critical data studies, education theory, and digital sociology is reflected in this boom. Researchers are now investigating the social, ethical, psychological, and institutional effects of AI in learning rather than just the technical viability of the technology. Cross-disciplinary viewpoints are becoming more and more valued in academic journals, conferences, and international consortia as they realize that AI in education cannot be approached solely from a technical standpoint (Holmes et al., 2022; Siemens & Long, 2011).

1.7. Ethics Takes Center Stage

The ethical shift in AI and education research has been one of the biggest trends in recent years. Academics started to raise concerns about the wider political economy of EdTech, the consequences of surveillance capitalism in educational technologies, and the algorithmic biases present in AI systems. These criticisms focus on how institutional and commercial incentives influence the development and application of AI tools, frequently at the price of student agency, equity, and transparency. In educational contexts, the emphasis has moved from "what AI can do" to "what AI should do."

1.8. Equity, Transparency, and Student Agency

The educational community started insisting that AI systems be held to strict standards of fairness, explainability, and respect for autonomy as ethical concerns gained traction. Innovations are no longer praised only for their originality or effectiveness. Rather, their legitimacy is assessed based on whether they respect the agency of educators and students, provide transparent decision-making processes, and encourage equitable outcomes. In the era of artificial intelligence, these principles are the new yardstick for evaluating educational technology (Tlili et al., 2023; Ouyang et al., 2022).

1.9. The Socio-Technical Convergence

The literature has finally come to a socio-technical conclusion: AI is a cultural artifact influenced by the beliefs, values, and power dynamics of both its developers and users, rather than just being a neutral or objective tool. Every step of the development of AI is impacted by social contexts and human choices, from the selection of training data to interface design and institutional policy. In order to enable educators, legislators, and students to critically analyze, evaluate, and influence AI technologies in morally sound ways, this convergence necessitates a critical AI literacy (Holmes et al., 2019; Zhao & Watterston, 2021).

2 INTRODUCTION

This chapter's introduction attempts to familiarize readers with the significant and rapidly growing influence of artificial intelligence (AI) in higher education, a development that has completely changed teaching, learning, and institutional operations during the previous 20 years. The discussion has moved from theoretical curiosity to practical urgency as universities increasingly incorporate AI-driven tools, such as intelligent tutoring systems, predictive analytics, administrative automation, and personalized learning platforms. In higher education, artificial intelligence (AI) has two sides: on the one hand, it offers previously unheard-of possibilities for expanding personalized instruction, improving student outcomes, and streamlining institutional decision-making; on the other hand, it presents serious problems with regard to algorithmic bias, data privacy, academic integrity, ethical governance, and the decline of human-centered pedagogy. This chapter starts by dissecting that dichotomy, emphasizing both the sociocultural conflicts and the technological benefits of artificial intelligence. This balance is reflected in the chapter's structure, which starts with a conceptual and historical overview of AI's introduction in higher education before moving on to an investigation of responsible AI frameworks, ethical issues, implementation difficulties, and institutional preparedness. It ends with a contemplation of the future of ethical, inclusive, and fair AI systems in scholarly settings. When taken as a whole, these sections offer a thorough basis for comprehending the potential and risks of artificial intelligence in influencing higher education.

Artificial intelligence (AI) in higher education has developed in three interconnected and overlapping waves rather than linearly. Each wave denotes a different stage of AI's technological development, characterized by the technology's increasing integration with academic procedures and the expansion of its educational institution stakeholder base.

Wave 1: Automation

When the early stages of AI adoption in academia first emerged in the late 20th century, automation was the primary focus. During this wave, rule-based systems and simple machine logic were used to streamline repetitive and time-consuming administrative tasks. Optical mark readers (OMRs) revolutionized exam scoring by processing thousands of student responses in a few minutes, removing the need for hours of manual grading. Expert systems began automating scheduling processes, including faculty assignment, timetable creation, and library cataloging, increasing operational efficiency across the campus. These tools created institutional trust in AI's capacity to manage complexity and reduce human labor in predictable, rule-governed tasks, even though they were not pedagogical in nature (Ifenthaler & Yau, 2020).

Wave 2: Augmentation

When AI started to support the actual teaching and learning processes, the second wave signaled a dramatic change. Machine learning algorithms have made it possible for educational tools to learn from data and get better over time, going beyond rule-based logic. This made it possible to create platforms for adaptive learning, which modify course material according to a student's performance and level of engagement. Data-driven models were used by homework platforms like ALEKS and Carnegie Learning to modify the level of difficulty, offer immediate feedback, and suggest practice tasks based on each student's needs. In the meantime, Turnitin and other AI-powered tools have become commonplace for identifying plagiarism, protecting academic integrity. Additionally, schools implemented early warning systems that use predictive analytics to identify students who might be at risk of dropping out or failing academically. These dashboards used demographic data, attendance, grades, and LMS activity to initiate prompt interventions. AI in this wave supported better decision-making and more individualized instruction by acting as a potent augmentation tool rather than replacing teachers (Luckin et al., 2016; UNESCO, 2021).

Wave 3: Co-Creation

From automation and augmentation to cooperation and co-creation, the third and current wave signifies a revolutionary change. AI tools now actively participate in creative and cognitive processes alongside students and educators thanks to the development of large language models (LLMs) like GPT and multimodal generative AI (e.g., DALL·E, Synthesia, Sora). AI is now an active participant in the educational process rather than merely a supporting system or tool in this wave. Students can write code, create graphics, simulate experiments, write essays, and even collaborate to make presentations or videos using generative models. Faculty use LLMs to create feedback, design assessments, and develop curricula. The distinction between human and machine authorship has become more hazy as a result of this wave, which has led to serious concerns regarding originality, intellectual property, and the very nature of learning (Luckin et al., 2016).

Furthermore, a wider range of stakeholders have become involved in the discussion of AI in education as a result of the ripple effects of this co-creative capacity. The way transcripts represent AI-assisted work is being reassessed by registrars. AI is being incorporated into course architectures by instructional designers. New frameworks are being developed by quality assurance organizations and accreditors to assess the legitimacy of AI-mediated learning. As concerns over liability, content authenticity, and data ownership become more complicated, even insurers and legal counsel are getting involved.

Each of these three waves expands and diversifies the use of AI in education, rather than making earlier technologies obsolete. Back-office automation gave way to a complex ecosystem where AI now co-authors, supports, and improves the educational process. This trajectory highlights the potential and challenges of AI in higher education, necessitating updated policies, new competencies, and a broader ethical imagination (UNESCO, 2023; Williamson & Eynon, 2020).

2.1 Opportunities and Challenges

There are many opportunities and challenges associated with integrating artificial intelligence (AI) into higher education. On one end of the spectrum are opportunities for transformation that hold promise for improving learning outcomes, increasing the effectiveness of institutions, and democratizing access to high-quality education. On the other hand, if not handled carefully and strategically, a number of issues—technical, organizational, pedagogical, and ethical—threaten to negate these advantages.

There are numerous and substantial opportunities in AI-enabled education. The ability to design individualized learning pathways is arguably the most notable. Real-time analysis of a student's performance, behavior, and preferences by AI systems enables the provision of individualized pacing, customized assessments, and content. Students with disabilities or those who have historically been underserved by traditional educational models are among the diverse learning needs that this personalization holds particular promise for supporting.

Data-informed advising is another significant opportunity. In order to facilitate more accurate and proactive academic advising, artificial intelligence (AI) can synthesize enormous amounts of data, including attendance and course performance records as well as behavioral patterns on learning platforms. This facilitates the early identification of at-risk students, the creation of suitable interventions, and the more efficient tracking of progress by faculty and support staff. Scalable feedback systems are also advantageous to institutions, as natural language processing

(NLP) tools can help with formative feedback on peer reviews, discussion boards, and assignments. AI can also help optimize resources by optimizing administrative processes like staffing, facility usage, and course scheduling. This allows institutions to concentrate human resources where they can have the biggest impact.

But these developments are offset by a wide range of difficult problems. Ethical opacity is one of the main issues. Many AI systems operate as "black boxes," providing little insight into the decision-making process, particularly those that rely on deep learning. In educational settings, where fairness, accountability, and trust are crucial, this poses important questions. This is accompanied by the constant risk of algorithmic bias. AI systems run the risk of sustaining or even escalating biases in student evaluations, admissions procedures, or predictive analytics when they are trained on biased historical data, such as unequal grading practices, gender disparities, or socioeconomic inequalities.

Another urgent concern is data governance. There are serious privacy and security issues with the gathering, storing, and using of private student information—often across several platforms and vendors. Another level of complexity is added by adhering to laws like FERPA and GDPR, particularly for organizations that conduct business internationally. Furthermore, a growing concern is pedagogical displacement. There is concern that the humanistic and dialogic components of education may be undermined as AI systems take on duties that are typically performed by teachers, such as giving lectures, grading student work, or even facilitating discussions. Efficiency may take precedence over critical thinking and reflective inquiry in this depersonalized and instrumental approach to education.

A more complex understanding of these tensions is offered by the insights gathered from stakeholder interviews that were carried out on six continents. Even though many academics are aware of how AI could improve their instruction, their excitement is frequently dampened by underlying concerns. The worry that an excessive dependence on automation may de-skill educators and reduce their function to that of content managers is known as de-skilling. Others worry about unfair surveillance, arguing that AI-powered monitoring systems might unfairly single out underprivileged pupils, escalating their sense of estrangement and mistrust. The fear that higher education may stray from its core values of civic engagement, critical thinking, and holistic development and instead become narrowly focused on workforce development and productivity metrics is known as "mission drift."

These difficulties show that there are significant socio-institutional as well as technical obstacles to the adoption of AI. More than just infrastructure or algorithms are needed to implement AI in higher education; careful consideration of ethical frameworks, policy reform, interdisciplinary discussion, and inclusive governance structures are also necessary. Accordingly, implementing AI responsibly is a negotiated process involving institutional priorities, cultural values, and a shared vision rather than a technical one. It is a path that needs to be taken with prudence, compassion, and a steadfast dedication to the public purpose of education (Luckin et al., 2016; Mittelstadt, 2019; OECD, 2019).

3 UNDERSTANDING RESPONSIBLE AI IN EDUCATION

This section clarifies conceptual underpinnings before translating them into design heuristics.

3.1 Ethical Foundations

Artificial intelligence (AI) in education must be based on a strong ethical framework that puts the rights, welfare, and dignity of all stakeholders first. This means that it cannot be implemented purely for the sake of innovation or technical efficiency. Five fundamental ethical principles—beneficence, non-maleficence, autonomy, justice, and explicability—form the basis of responsible AI in education. These guidelines are useful standards for developing, assessing, and overseeing AI systems in higher education in addition to acting as moral compass points. Their application in academic institutions necessitates a nuanced and context-specific interpretation, despite their close alignment with international guidelines like the UNESCO Recommendation on the Ethics of Artificial Intelligence and the OECD AI Principles.

Figure 1. Pillars of Responsible AI

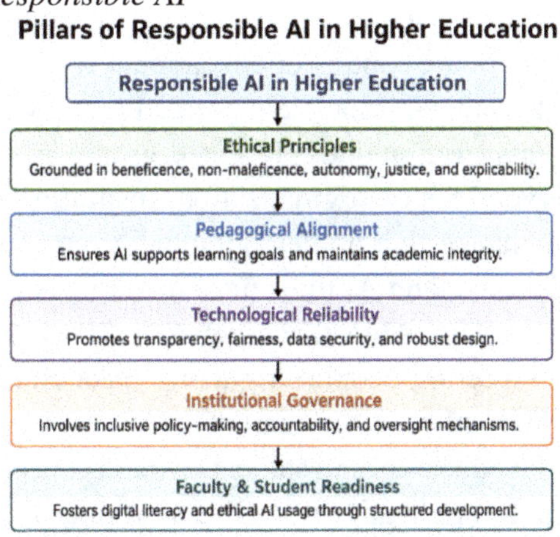

The Pillars of Responsible AI in Education are depicted in the diagram above. It arranges the five essential elements visually:

- **Ethical Principles**
- **Pedagogical Alignment**
- **Technological Reliability**
- **Institutional Governance**
- **Faculty & Student Readiness**

Each element contributes to a holistic and responsible approach to integrating AI in higher education.

1. **Beneficence** Fundamentally, beneficence is the duty to do good—to produce favorable, significant results for students and organizations. This principle requires that the use of AI in education result in measurable gains in student achievement, engagement, and learning outcomes. In order to demonstrate that AI systems improve pedagogical efficacy, facilitate differentiated instruction, or support more general institutional missions like access and retention, they should be empirically validated. Crucially, beneficence is a quantifiable objective rather than a theoretical ideal: if an AI system does not clearly aid in the learning process, its implementation ought to be re-examined (Baker & Inventado, 2014; Mittelstadt, 2019; Tlili et al., 2023; UNESCO, 2021).
2. **Non-Maleficence** The ethical commitment to refrain from harming others, known as the principle of non-maleficence, is closely related to beneficence. This includes more subtle risks like data breaches, biased evaluations, or a decline in confidence in academic systems, in addition to physical or psychological harm in the context of educational AI. For instance, the system transgresses this ethical principle if predictive analytics disproportionately identify students from underrepresented groups as "at-risk," resulting in needless interventions or stigmatization. Institutions must put safeguards in place to guarantee that no demographic group is systematically disadvantaged or harmed, and AI tools must undergo extensive testing for bias, dependability, and unintended consequences (Page & Gehlbach, 2020).
3. **Autonomy** Respecting people's rights to make educated decisions about their educational paths is at the heart of the autonomy principle. In actuality, this implies that educators and students should continue to have significant influence over the application of AI in classrooms. Faculty should maintain agency in interpreting and applying AI-generated insights, and learners should have the choice to accept or reject specific AI-based recommendations or interventions. Additionally, students need to know exactly how their data

is gathered, used, and analyzed. Transparency and user empowerment are essential components of respecting autonomy, which makes sure AI complements human decision-making rather than replaces it (UNESCO, 2021).

4. **Justice** Justice, which calls for fairness in both the process and the result, is arguably the most urgent issue in modern AI ethics. This entails aggressively tackling systemic injustices in academia that data-driven systems may make worse. For example, an AI platform may reproduce and reinforce inequality if it primarily uses historical data (like standardized test scores) that reflects current achievement gaps. For a system to be considered just, it must be designed with equity in mind. This means that diverse populations must be taken into account during development, datasets must be inclusive, and the system's effects must be routinely audited to identify and address unfair trends. Justice also entails more extensive dedication to the rights of education, accessibility, and inclusivity (Holmes et al., 2022).
5. **Explicability** The last principle is explicability, also known as explainability or transparency, which refers to the duty to make sure AI operations and decisions are intelligible to human users. Explaining how an algorithm came to a conclusion—for example, why a student was flagged for support or which content was recommended—is crucial in educational settings where trust is crucial and decisions frequently have long-term effects. Because stakeholders need to be able to track, challenge, and even dispute AI outputs, explainability makes accountability possible. Additionally, it upholds pedagogical integrity by enabling teachers to incorporate AI suggestions into their professional judgment as opposed to depending solely on ambiguous "black-box" forecasts (Selwyn, 2019; Siemens & Long, 2011).

The foundation of responsible AI governance in education is made up of these five ethical pillars taken together. High-level guidance is provided by global frameworks such as those published by the OECD and UNESCO, but their application in educational institutions needs to be contextually calibrated—sensitive to local cultures, regulatory environments, institutional missions, and student populations. Higher education is a place of critical thinking, democratic participation, and knowledge creation; it is not just a service sector. As a result, ethical frameworks for AI in this field need to take into account both technical proficiency and educational principles. Universities can guarantee that technology acts as a catalyst for inclusive and moral academic progress by establishing AI on the principles of beneficence, non-maleficence, autonomy, justice, and explicability (Ouyang et al., 2022).

3.2 Pedagogical Alignment

While efficiency, personalization, and scalability are frequently used to assess the promise of artificial intelligence (AI) in higher education, pedagogical alignment is a more fundamental criterion that must ultimately be used to determine the true value of AI. That is, rather than changing pedagogy to fit technological limitations, AI systems must be developed and applied in ways that further predetermined educational objectives. The question is no longer whether a tool works, but rather whether it supports students' learning processes and motivations as AI integration becomes more widespread.

Instructional integrity must come before technological innovation, according to pedagogical alignment. This entails examining AI tools closely to determine how they contribute to learning rather than giving in to the urge to use them merely because they are novel or economical. Instead of replacing critical pedagogy, subject-matter expertise, or meaningful human interaction, a well-aligned AI tool should function as an open and flexible extension of the educator's intent.

Four fundamental alignment checks are suggested to help organizations and teachers assess the pedagogical soundness of AI systems:

Epistemic Fit

Whether the AI system is in line with the epistemological underpinnings of the field to which it is being applied is the first and most fundamental factor to take into account. The norms, procedures, and standards of evidence used by various academic disciplines vary. For instance, whereas literary studies frequently place a higher value on ambiguity, interpretive nuance, and voice, engineering knowledge construction places more emphasis on procedural correctness and logical consistency. Because each requires a different set of evaluation criteria, an AI tool that assesses student writing must be able to discern whether the writing is promoting technical clarity, persuasive argumentation, or creative expression. AI systems run the risk of applying a one-size-fits-all logic in the absence of such epistemic sensitivity, which could unintentionally diminish intellectual diversity and flatten disciplinary richness.

Cognitive Load Appropriateness

The learner's cognitive load—the amount of mental work necessary to interact with a task or interface—is the subject of the second check. By breaking down difficult tasks into manageable steps, providing guidance, or visualizing abstract ideas, a well-aligned AI tool should serve as a scaffold, promoting students' cognitive development. However, by providing students with an excessive amount of data, feedback, or complicated dashboards that require excessive multitasking, many AI systems unintentionally increase cognitive load. Confusion, annoyance, and disengagement may follow from this. Usability and learner psychology must be taken into consideration when designing pedagogically responsible AI to make sure that the system facilitates rather than hinders students' cognitive processing.

Formative Feedback Quality

The learner's cognitive load—the amount of mental work necessary to interact with a task or interface—is the subject of the second check. By breaking down difficult tasks into manageable steps, providing guidance, or visualizing abstract ideas, a well-aligned AI tool should serve as a scaffold, promoting students' cognitive development. However, by providing students with an excessive amount of data, feedback, or complicated dashboards that require excessive multitasking, many AI systems unintentionally increase cognitive load. Confusion, annoyance, and disengagement may follow from this. Usability and learner psychology must be taken into consideration when designing pedagogically responsible AI to make sure that the system facilitates rather than hinders students' cognitive processing.

Motivational Resonance

Lastly, in order to sustain students' intrinsic interest, sense of agency, and academic curiosity, effective AI in education must promote motivational alignment. In higher education, where motivation is strongly linked to intellectual identity and personal relevance, this is particularly crucial. An artificial intelligence tool that only gamifies learning to increase engagement might produce momentary activity but fall short in fostering longer-term inquiry or a stronger bond with the material. According to self-determination theory, tools should be evaluated based on whether they improve motivation by promoting autonomy, competence, and relatedness. When AI systems trivialize complexity, simplify tasks into easy rewards, or deprive learning of its real-world context, motivation may be compromised.

Misalignment can manifest itself in subtle yet important ways, even when it is not immediately apparent. A natural language processing (NLP)-powered writing tutor that effectively improves grammar and sentence structure is a powerful example. Although technically impressive, such a system might overlook important elements of successful academic writing, such as argumentative coherence, audience awareness, and rhetorical purpose. Because of this, students might learn to write in ways that are mechanically correct but intellectually deficient, which would limit their expressive possibilities and inhibit critical or creative thinking.

Therefore, pedagogical alignment is a moral and educational requirement rather than an optional feature. AI systems must be assessed for their contributions to human development, disciplinary integrity, and meaningful learning in addition to their accuracy and functionality (Bender et al., 2021; Buckingham Shum & Ferguson, 2012; OECD, 2019).

3.3 Technological Considerations

The successful application of responsible AI in education depends on equally rigorous technological considerations, even though ethical and pedagogical alignment are essential. Transparency, inclusivity, security, and dependability must all be considered when designing and implementing AI systems in educational settings. Model interpretability, dataset representativeness, edge case resilience, and privacy by design are four crucial technical factors that are particularly important in assessing whether AI systems can be relied upon to fairly and successfully support educational objectives (Cotton et al., 2024).

The degree to which human users can comprehend and explain the outputs of a machine learning model is known as model interpretability. Interpretability is crucial for guaranteeing accountability and permitting significant human oversight in educational settings where AI is utilized to evaluate student work, offer learning recommendations, or forecast dropout risk. Both teachers and students need to be able to comprehend the reasoning behind a model's recommendations or decisions, particularly if those decisions have an impact on academic pathways, grading schemes, or institutional interventions. When applied in high-stakes situations like admissions, financial aid eligibility, or disciplinary procedures, tools that rely on "black-box" algorithms—like deep neural networks without explainability layers—present significant difficulties in this area (UNESCO, 2023).

The problem of dataset representativeness is closely related to interpretability. The effectiveness and fairness of AI systems depend on the quality of the data they are trained on. In the context of education, this implies that training data needs to reflect the variety of student populations that the AI system is anticipated to support. The resulting model may produce biased or invalid results if datasets are skewed, underrepresenting particular socioeconomic classes, genders, ethnic groups, or neurodiverse learners. An AI writing tutor that has been trained primarily on English essays written by native speakers from prestigious universities, for instance, might unintentionally penalize students from non-traditional academic backgrounds or non-native English speakers. Curating inclusive datasets is only one aspect of addressing representativeness; another is integrating bias detection and correction tools into every step of the AI process, from model creation to post-deployment auditing (Buckingham Shum & Ferguson, 2012).

The issue of edge case resilience, or the AI system's capacity to operate dependably in the face of unusual or unexpected inputs, goes beyond these worries. Students frequently act creatively, experimentally, or in unique ways in learning environments, which might not match the patterns found in training data. These edge cases must be handled gracefully by a resilient AI system—without producing inaccurate feedback, unfair evaluations, or sudden system failures. This is particularly important in fields where responses frequently defy strict categorization, such as the arts, humanities, or interdisciplinary studies. In order to prevent brittleness and create systems that permit flexibility, ambiguity, and open-ended exploration when necessary, developers must account for a broad range of user behaviors (Williamson & Eynon, 2020).

Lastly, privacy by design is a crucial component of any technological considerations discussion. Concerns regarding data security and user consent have become crucial as AI systems depend more and more on detailed user data, including click patterns, keystroke dynamics, biometric inputs, and even emotional cues. Institutions must make sure that privacy is built into AI systems' architecture from the ground up rather than being added later. Particularly in jurisdictions subject to strict data protection laws like the General Data Protection Regulation (GDPR) in Europe or India's Digital Personal Data Protection Act (DPDP), techniques like federated learning—which allows models to train across decentralized data sources without sharing raw data—and homomorphic encryption—which permits computation on encrypted data—are no longer futuristic ideals but rather standard expectations. These techniques maintain the usefulness of large-scale learning analytics while reducing the risks associated with data exposure (Page & Gehlbach, 2020).

In conclusion, the ethical and pedagogical legitimacy of AI in education is inextricably linked to its technical robustness. To guarantee that educational AI systems are interpretable, inclusive, resilient, and secure by design, institutions and developers must work together. Only then will these technologies be able to protect the principles that characterize human-centered and responsible education while also genuinely improving learning (Bender et al., 2021).

4 SAFEGUARDING ACADEMIC INTEGRITY

4.1 AI and Plagiarism

The field of academic integrity has changed, especially with regard to plagiarism, as a result of the introduction of generative AI tools like ChatGPT, GrammarlyGO, Jasper, and other large language models (LLMs). Generative AI presents new, more intricate forms of plagiarism that defy accepted definitions, whereas traditional forms involved the direct copying of text or ideas without attribution. For instance, students who use artificial intelligence (AI) to rewrite preexisting content in a way that avoids plagiarism software detection but adds minimal original thought are engaging in synthetic paraphrasing. When students use artificial intelligence (AI) to produce significant portions of their work—essays, code, or design elements—without giving credit, it's known as "stealth co-authoring," which makes it difficult to distinguish between authorship and assistance. Prompt laundering, in which students feed extremely specific prompts into AI systems to replicate academic outputs without referencing the original intellectual sources of the ideas, is another new issue. These procedures make it more difficult for the teacher to assess whether a submission accurately captures a student's independent work and academic development (Cotton et al., 2024; Holmes et al., 2019)..

Educational institutions are responding by starting to move away from detection-only models, which mainly rely on plagiarism detection programs like Turnitin or Copyleaks, and toward more proactive, pedagogy-driven strategies that are based on ethics and openness. This changing paradigm promotes candid discussion about when and how AI assistance might be suitable rather than portraying AI use as fundamentally dishonest. In order to teach students how to properly acknowledge AI involvement, cite AI-generated content, and differentiate between acceptable support and academic dishonesty, universities are increasingly incorporating "ethicist pedagogy" into their writing and research curricula. In addition to outlining institutional expectations, this kind of training promotes critical thinking, ethical reasoning, and technological literacy (Tlili et al., 2023).

The efficacy of this strategy is supported by empirical research. Clear, transparent AI-use policies are linked to lower rates of academic misconduct, according to studies done in a variety of higher education contexts. Through workshops, orientation modules, or course-integrated instruction, students who comprehend the ethical implications of AI tools report higher levels of metacognitive awareness during their learning experiences. They are more likely to ask for human input, consider how and why they use AI, and see academic integrity as a shared duty rather than a duty based on surveillance. In the end, schools can adopt a culture of responsible, thoughtful, and knowledgeable use of emerging technologies by establishing AI literacy as a component of ethical academic citizenship (Ouyang et al., 2022; Zawacki-Richter et al., 2019).

4.2 Assessment Integrity in AI-Enriched Settings

Traditional assessment models, especially those that use multiple-choice, short-answer, or standard essay formats, are becoming more susceptible to automated cheating and shallow engagement as generative AI technologies become more widely available to students. Maintaining the integrity of assessment necessitates a fundamental redesign of how learning is measured and evaluated in this changing educational environment, where AI tools can generate grammatically correct, factually plausible, and stylistically coherent content in seconds. Teachers and organizations are realizing that reevaluating the type of work we give students is a better way to find the solution than relying just on monitoring or detection.

The move toward authentic assessments—tasks that reflect real-world issues, demand critical thinking, and involve students in applied learning—is one of the best ways to maintain academic integrity in AI-enriched environments. Examples are oral defences, where students must present and defend their ideas in a live, dialogic setting; design thinking sprints, which promote creativity and iterative problem-solving; and case analyses, where students analyze and react to intricate, real-life scenarios. Because they require contextual awareness, individual viewpoint, and impromptu reasoning—skills that present AI systems find difficult to replicate effectively—these formats are resistant to automation. Authentic assessments inherently encourage deeper learning and lessen the likelihood of academic dishonesty by emphasizing how students think rather than just what they produce (Selwyn, 2019; Holmes et al., 2022).

Additionally, when rubrics move the focus from finished products to the learning process itself, assessment integrity is reinforced. Teachers are now urged to reward process documentation, such as brainstorming logs, revision histories, reflections on tool use (including AI), and feedback integration, rather than just assessing well-written essays or completed projects. This method makes it harder to outsource or fabricate work by emphasizing the student's intellectual journey. It also promotes teamwork, metacognition, and iterative development. Pupils are more likely to absorb academic values and interact with the content in a meaningful way if they are aware that they need to justify and consider their approaches. In this sense, the evaluation serves as a tool for measurement as well as a teaching tactic, promoting the values of creativity, responsibility, and moral education (OECD, 2019).

In conclusion, maintaining the integrity of assessments in the era of artificial intelligence necessitates a comprehensive pedagogical change rather than merely technical barriers. Teachers can lower the risk of AI-enabled misconduct and foster the very abilities that characterize deep, human-centered learning—creativity, critical thinking, communication, and ethical reflection—by adopting authentic, process-oriented, and context-rich assessments (Bender et al., 2021; Mittelstadt, 2019).

4.3 Detection and Deterrence Strategies

Academic integrity cannot be ensured by detection alone as generative AI tools become more complex. However, detection is still a crucial component of the larger integrity ecosystem, and recent initiatives have shifted from conventional plagiarism checks to hybrid detection techniques. These use a variety of technical techniques to detect instances in which student work may have been improperly created or aided by artificial intelligence. Semantic fingerprinting, process forensics, and stylometry are some of the most promising methods.

The computational study of a writer's distinct stylistic signature, including sentence structure, word choice, syntax complexity, punctuation usage, and rhythm, is known as stylistometry. Instructors or automated systems may become suspicious when a student submits work that is radically different from their previous submissions in terms of style. This method, which has its origins in authorship attribution research, has shown promise in identifying AI-assisted outputs and ghost writing.

Semantic fingerprinting is more in-depth, concentrating on the structure and pattern of ideas rather than the style of writing. This approach examines the coherence, uniqueness, and conceptual flow of student submissions using natural language processing (NLP). Semantic fingerprinting aids in identifying work that lacks nuanced insight or personalized reasoning, especially in open-ended tasks, as generative AI tools often generate contextually accurate but semantically generic content.

By looking at the creation process as opposed to just the finished product, process forensics adds another level of scrutiny. One way to determine whether text was created naturally or copied from another source is to examine keystroke dynamics, such as typing speed, rhythm, and pauses. Version histories, like those found in LMS-integrated tools or collaborative writing platforms like Google Docs, can also show how a document changed over time, revealing information about student effort, revision patterns, and possible use of AI tools. The lack of a developmental writing trail or abrupt, extensive insertions may be signs of outside help (UNESCO, 2021; Ifenthaler & Yau, 2020).

However, deterrence alone cannot be the long-term solution to upholding academic integrity, even though these hybrid strategies can aid in the detection of anomalies. The development of an academic trust culture is equally important. This entails creating an educational setting where ethical scholarship is valued, taught, and modeled rather than just enforced. In order to clearly communicate scholarly norms like appropriate citation, originality, collaborative boundaries, and the responsible use of tools—including artificial intelligence—faculty and institutional leaders are essential. Students are more likely to internalize these values and behave appropriately when they comprehend not only what is expected of them but also why academic integrity is important.

It takes constant communication, not just one-time warnings, to establish this culture of trust. It entails integrating conversations about academic ethics into the curriculum, promoting introspection about the use of tools, working with students to create honor codes, and recognizing creative thinking. By bringing students' intrinsic motivations into line with institutional expectations, such initiatives lessen the likelihood of misconduct. Even in the presence of potent new technologies, students are more likely to interact honestly in settings where trust is the norm and integrity is viewed as an essential component of intellectual identity rather than a compliance issue (Holmes et al., 2019).

5 INSTITUTIONAL AND FACULTY READINESS

5.1 Change Management

Artificial intelligence integration in higher education is a transformative process that reflects the intricacy of significant organizational change, not just a matter of acquiring new technologies. Curriculum design, pedagogy, assessment, administration, student services, data governance, and institutional identity are all impacted by the use of AI in education. As a result, adopting AI successfully requires a systemic, strategic approach supported by a well-organized change management framework.

John Kotter's Eight-Step Change Framework is one of the most well-known models for directing these kinds of changes, and it is still particularly applicable in educational environments that are battling digital transformation. When navigating the cultural, ethical, and pedagogical shifts necessary for AI integration, the framework highlights a series of strategic actions that build momentum, foster stakeholder buy-in, and reduce resistance.

One of the best-known models for guiding these kinds of changes is John Kotter's Eight-Step Change Framework, which is still especially relevant in educational settings struggling with digital transformation. The framework outlines a number of tactical steps that increase momentum, encourage stakeholder buy-in, and lessen resistance when negotiating the cultural, ethical, and pedagogical changes required for AI integration.

Developing and sharing a compelling vision for how AI will support the institution's overarching mission are the next steps. Institutions must tie the adoption of AI to fundamental objectives like increasing student success, advancing equity and inclusion, boosting teaching effectiveness, and guaranteeing long-term financial sustainability rather than portraying it as a cost-cutting strategy or a technological fad. AI could be used, for instance, to increase access to individualized education, identify and assist students who are at risk, or automate repetitive administrative work to free up faculty time for mentoring and research (Zawacki-Richter et al., 2019; Zhao & Watterston, 2021).

Importantly, the vision needs to be realized through tangible steps and quick victories that boost self-esteem and show advancement. These could be AI-supported advising platforms, course redesign projects, faculty training programs, or pilot projects. Institutions can build on these early successes and broaden their efforts by integrating AI into governance frameworks, quality assurance procedures, and strategic planning. Lastly, integrating new methods into the institutional culture through updated curricula, promotion standards, policies, and acknowledgment of teaching and service innovation ensures long-lasting change.

In conclusion, good change management is a fundamental component that facilitates responsible and sustainable. incorporating AI into higher education. In order to succeed in an academic future enhanced by artificial intelligence, institutions that embrace a methodical, inclusive, and mission-driven approach—like Kotter's—will be better equipped to manage the risks, seize the opportunities, and foster the trust necessary (Mittelstadt, 2019).

5.2 Faculty Training and Development

How well faculty members are assisted in gaining technical proficiency and pedagogical confidence is a major factor in an institution's ability to responsibly implement artificial intelligence (AI) in higher education. Professional development for faculty members must be both flexible and structured, moving from fundamental awareness to active leadership. Faculty should first acquire a conceptual grasp of what AI can and cannot do, dispelling myths and investigating its possible uses in administration, teaching, and assessment. This knowledge develops the critical literacy required for ethical engagement and encourages a spirit of informed curiosity. Building on that, faculty should be able to experiment with AI tools, like writing assistants, adaptive tests, or analytics dashboards, in low-risk settings through practical workshops, design studios, and sandbox environments as part of professional development. In addition to using AI, this hands-on experience teaches educators how to interpret results, identify algorithmic constraints, and match technological affordances with learning objectives. Institutions must enable faculty to assume leadership positions in forming institutional AI strategy and policy, in addition to providing skill development.

Faculty leaders can mentor colleagues, take part in governance, co-develop guidelines, and make sure AI deployment stays rooted in academic principles. Universities should fund peer mentoring circles and provide micro-credential pathways that acknowledge and reward professional development, like digital badges or AI teaching certificates, in order to promote the diffusion of expertise beyond early adopters. In addition to indicating a faculty member's preparedness to take the lead in an academic setting enhanced by technology, these mechanisms support a collaborative learning culture. In the end, AI professional development should be viewed as an ongoing process that combines academic goals, ethical responsibility, and technical proficiency rather than as a one-time course (UNESCO, 2021; Selwyn, 2019)v.

5.3 Infrastructure and Policy Gaps

Any institution hoping to implement AI-enhanced learning on a large scale must have a strong digital infrastructure. Data interoperability is crucial at the technical level: learning activities, evaluation outcomes, and engagement metrics must all flow naturally between analytics dashboards, adaptive platforms, and learning management systems (LMSs). The common vocabularies and event models made possible by open standards like IMS Caliper and Experience API (xAPI) enable click-stream events, competency statements, and portfolio artifacts to be recorded once and reused across tools. Adopting these standards helps institutions avoid vendor lock-in, streamline system integrations, and produce more comprehensive longitudinal datasets for student success interventions and research.

Secure identity management is equally important. As AI services proliferate, from virtual labs and writing tutors to intelligent chatbots that offer advice, each one needs to securely authenticate users while safeguarding personal information. Federated identity solutions that integrate attribute-based access controls, multi-factor authentication (MFA), and single sign-on (SSO) are becoming more and more common in contemporary higher education settings. While limiting each service to the bare minimum of privileges needed, protocols like SAML 2.0, OAuth 2.0, and OpenID Connect allow staff and students to navigate an expanding ecosystem of AI applications without getting tired of passwords. Zero-trust networking concepts and ongoing monitoring, when layered on top of authentication, aid in identifying unusual activity. This is especially important since AI systems have the ability to initiate automated processes that impact financial aid, enrolment status, or grades (Page & Gehlbach, 2020; Tlili et al., 2023).

High-performance computing (HPC) resources are required to support these front-end services. It can take thousands of GPU hours and petabytes of fast storage to train or fine-tune large language models, run computer-vision pipelines for remote proctoring, or perform real-time learning analytics at campus scale. Universities must choose between using cloud-based AI platforms that provide elastic capacity and managed services or investing in on-premise GPU clusters, which are advantageous for sensitive data and research customization. In hybrid configurations, bulk training jobs run in the cloud, optimizing both cost and performance, while edge computing appliances can handle latency-sensitive inference (e.g., classroom speech-to-text) (Zhao & Watterston, 2021).

However, technical capabilities are only half of the infrastructure equation; the other half consists of the governance and policy framework that establishes the ownership, use, and sharing of data and AI-generated artifacts. Questions about data ownership come up frequently: after an AI system logs a student's click-stream or biometric data, who is in charge of it? When is it possible for outside vendors to mine those data in order to enhance their algorithms? Similarly, when students use generative AI to co-produce essays, code, or designs, the rights to intellectual property (IP) become unclear. Who is the author—the student, the model provider, or a composite? A collaborative policy-making process involving legal counsel, privacy officers, faculty governance bodies, and—most importantly—student representatives, whose data and creative outputs are most directly impacted, is necessary to resolve such ambiguities.

A thorough governance charter ought to state:

- Well-defined retention periods and data classification tiers;
- Terms of licencing for student work mediated by AI (such as Creative Commons with attribution clauses for model assistance);
- Provisions in vendor contracts requiring algorithmic-bias disclosures, audit rights, and GDPR/DPDP compliance;
- Student-led oversight committees with the authority to examine and challenge AI-driven decisions.

By pairing standards-based technical infrastructure with inclusive, forward-looking policy, institutions can create an environment where AI tools interoperate securely, perform at scale, and respect the rights and expectations of all academic stakeholders (Siemens & Long, 2011; UNESCO, 2021).

6 DESIGNING INCLUSIVE AI SYSTEMS

6.1 Addressing Bias and Discrimination

The potential for bias and discrimination to be reinforced or amplified—two issues that can jeopardize inclusion, fairness, and trust—is one of the most urgent worries surrounding the use of AI in higher education. AI systems can inherit and even worsen societal inequalities that are ingrained in training data, institutional procedures, or model design, despite the fact that they are frequently seen as objective and data-driven. Therefore, tackling bias in AI requires a multi-layered, ongoing process that is integrated into the entire AI development and deployment pipeline rather than being a one-time fix.

Careful consideration of data sampling is the first step in the bias mitigation process. The student populations that training datasets are intended to serve must be represented in both diversity and quality. In order to capture differences in language use, learning styles, cultural contexts, socioeconomic status, and educational backgrounds, it is necessary to go beyond demographic quotas. When applied to underrepresented groups, a predictive model that was primarily trained on data from elite or majority-privileged institutions may perform poorly or unfairly. Institutions must thus make a concerted effort to curate inclusive datasets that include the experiences of first-generation students, students from rural areas, students with disabilities, and neurodiverse people (Buckingham Shum & Ferguson, 2012).

In addition to data, algorithmic auditing is essential for detecting and reducing bias in AI systems. To assess whether results are dispersed fairly among various demographic groups, these audits usually employ quantitative fairness metrics. Common metrics include disparate impact (which measures indirect discriminatory effects), demographic parity (which guarantees equal prediction rates regardless of group membership), and equalized odds (which determines whether error rates are comparable across groups). With the use of these tools, developers and institutions can systematically assess whether a model is biased against particular groups, such as when it persistently and unjustifiably flags female students or students from minority communities as "at-risk."

But using fairness metrics requires more than just one-dimensional classifications. When overlapping identities (such as race, gender, and disability) interact in ways that exacerbate disadvantage, AI systems may display intersectional bias. For instance, discrimination against female students with learning disabilities may persist even in a model that treats male and female students equally. In order to ensure that fairness is measured across attribute combinations rather than isolated traits, auditing practices must be intersectional in design. To evaluate AI system outputs and identify unexpected consequences, institutions should also think about enlisting the help of diverse stakeholder panels or outside evaluators, such as ethicists, disability advocates, and student representatives (Ouyang et al., 2022).

Institutional accountability systems must also be in place in conjunction with technical audits. This entails setting up review boards for AI ethics, creating clear reporting guidelines, and providing grievance redressal channels for students who feel that algorithmic decisions have harmed them. Instead of being tokenistic or reactive, bias mitigation needs to be proactive and inclusive. By doing this, organizations demonstrate their dedication to equity in the development, implementation, and day-to-day operations of their AI systems as well as in policy declarations (Mittelstadt, 2019; OECD, 2019).

6.2 Accessibility and Universal Design

Unprecedented opportunities to promote accessibility and inclusion are presented by the incorporation of artificial intelligence (AI) into educational systems, especially when based on the ideas of Universal Design for Learning (UDL). UDL is a framework that encourages the development of adaptable learning environments by offering a variety of engagement, representation, and expression channels. This guarantees that all students, irrespective of their background or ability, have fair access to educational experiences and materials. These guidelines oppose one-size-fits-all strategies and support customization and diversity from the outset of instructional design (Cotton et al., 2024).

When inclusivity is ingrained from the beginning of system development, AI can greatly improve each of these UDL dimensions. Artificial intelligence (AI) algorithms can track student interaction patterns and dynamically modify the way content is delivered to keep students interested and motivated. Examples of this include providing timely reminders, changing formats, or proposing alternate routes. In terms of representation, AI can automatically create real-time video captions, translate text into speech, and provide language localization features that translate or culturally adapt educational materials. It can also modify the readability of content to match a learner's literacy level. For students who struggle with language processing, hearing, or vision, these features are especially important. In order to ensure that assessments are inclusive and unrestricted by a learner's particular abilities or preferences, AI-powered platforms enable students to demonstrate understanding in a variety of formats, including typed text, voice recordings, digital drawings, and even video presentations.

These advantages are not always present, though. From the beginning of the development of AI systems, they necessitate a conscious dedication to inclusive design. When accessibility features are added after a platform has been developed, the results are frequently insufficient or incomplete. Instead, to identify potential barriers and integrate universal access from the ground up, development teams must work with disability advocates, accessibility experts, and diverse student groups throughout the design process. In order to prevent perpetuating current disparities, AI models should be trained on datasets that represent linguistically, culturally, and neurodiverse populations. In this sense, artificial intelligence (AI) transforms education into a transformative tool that affirms the worth and dignity of every student, rather than merely being a tool for efficiency or personalization (UNESCO, 2021; Zawacki-Richter et al., 2019).

Figure 2. AI-driven accessibility features and Universal Design for Learning (UDL)

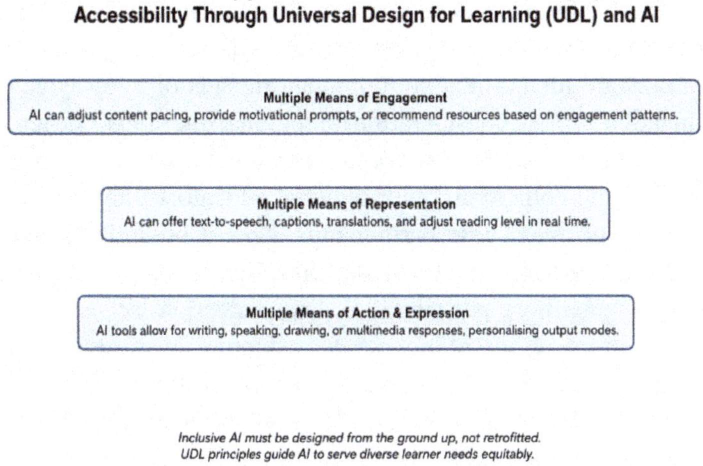

The visual diagram above shows how AI-driven accessibility features and Universal Design for Learning (UDL) principles complement each other. It emphasizes:

- **Multiple Means of Engagement**
- **Multiple Means of Representation**
- **Multiple Means of Action & Expression**

6.3 Cultural Sensitivity in TNE Contexts

Artificial intelligence's role in transnational education (TNE) deserves special attention as it becomes more and more integrated into the global higher education architecture. TNE describes educational programs that are offered by institutions across national borders, including online courses, offshore campuses, and dual-degree offerings. Diverse student populations studying in wildly disparate cultural, linguistic, and regulatory contexts are frequently involved in these initiatives. Designing and implementing AI-powered educational technologies in these kinds of situations requires a high level of contextual awareness and cultural sensitivity.

Given its increasing integration into the global higher education architecture, the role of artificial intelligence in transnational education (TNE) merits particular attention. TNE refers to educational programs, such as online courses, offshore campuses, and dual-degree offerings, that are provided by institutions across national borders. These initiatives often involve diverse student populations studying in highly disparate cultural, linguistic, and regulatory contexts. It takes a high degree of contextual awareness and cultural sensitivity to design and implement AI-powered educational technologies in these kinds of scenarios (Mittelstadt, 2019; OECD, 2019).

Such technologies run the risk of promoting a type of pedagogical imperialism in which learners are forced to adopt dominant models of knowledge production and communication without consideration for regional traditions, epistemologies, or educational values if deliberate design changes are not made. Institutions involved in TNE must actively collaborate with regional educators, linguists, and cultural specialists to prevent this. These partnerships make it possible to guarantee that AI systems are tailored to local linguistic diversity, learning norms, and policy environments, such as those pertaining to data protection, accessibility, and ethics. Localization strategies could include, for example, adapting language models to comprehend regional dialects, adjusting AI grading systems to take culturally sensitive communication styles into consideration, or creating interfaces that both aesthetically and functionally appeal to local user preferences.

In the end, cultural sensitivity in AI for TNE is about respecting the autonomy and identity of global learners, not just about preventing misunderstandings. As institutions broaden their digital presence, they should embrace co-design principles that respect the diversity of regional customs and knowledge systems rather than implementing uniform AI solutions in all contexts. This method promotes a more egalitarian and decolonized model of global education in addition to increasing the efficacy of AI-supported learning (Holmes et al., 2022).

7 POLICY, PRIVACY, AND GOVERNANCE

7.1 Legal Frameworks and Consent

Institutions of higher learning must negotiate a quickly changing legal environment that regulates data privacy, algorithmic accountability, and student rights as artificial intelligence (AI) systems become essential to teaching, assessment, advising, and administrative tasks. These frameworks, which specify how educational data can be gathered, processed, shared, and preserved, are legally required and not optional. Present-day global compliance expectations are based on a number of important laws and proposals, such as the General Data Protection Regulation (GDPR) in the European Union, the Family Educational Rights and Privacy Act (FERPA) in the United States, the Digital Personal Data Protection Act (DPDP) in India, and proposed AI-specific laws like the EU Artificial Intelligence Act. When taken as a whole, these laws aim to set precise guidelines for the moral and lawful application of AI in educational settings (Williamson & Eynon, 2020).

Under GDPR and similar laws, students are not just passive data subjects—they are rights-bearing individuals entitled to control over their personal information. This includes the right to access their data, correct inaccuracies, object to certain types of processing, and request deletion. When applied to AI in education, these rights raise critical issues: students must be informed if AI is being used to assess their learning, flag them as at-risk, monitor behaviour, or personalize content. More importantly, they must be able to understand what data is being collected, how it will be used, and who has access to it.

The idea of informed and revocable consent is essential to these regulations. Institutions need to get rid of the generic, one-time acceptance forms that are buried in enrolment or platform onboarding paperwork. Granular consent should be used instead, enabling students to choose which kinds of data collection or AI-driven interventions to participate in. For example, sharing behavioural analytics for tailored feedback but not for predictive risk scoring. Additionally, consent ought to be revocable, allowing students to opt out of data-sharing contracts or AI tools without facing disciplinary action, losing access, or other negative outcomes. In situations where there is an imbalance of power, such as in education, where students might feel pressured to comply without fully comprehending their rights, this principle is especially important (UNESCO, 2023).

The institutional duty to put in place transparent procedures and easily navigable privacy dashboards that let students monitor and control their data-sharing preferences is equally crucial. By enabling students to see what information has been gathered, where it has been used, and why, these tools can help put the concepts of abstract consent into real-world situations. As sector-specific frameworks like the proposed EU AI Act, which categorizes educational AI systems as "high-risk" and subjects them to strict audits and documentation requirements, emerge, legal teams and data protection officers within universities must simultaneously create data governance policies that align institutional AI practices with national and international compliance standards (Cotton et al., 2024; Holmes et al., 2019).

In conclusion, adhering to the law in AI-enhanced education is an ethical requirement based on student autonomy, accountability, and transparency rather than just being a box-ticking exercise. Incorporating granular, informed, and revocable consent into data practices allows institutions to meet legal requirements while simultaneously promoting a culture of trust and digital dignity where students are valued members of the AI-enhanced learning ecosystem.

7.2 Institutional Governance Models

Institutions of higher learning must create strong governance models to guarantee the moral, responsible, and context-sensitive use of artificial intelligence as it becomes more and more integrated into the academic, administrative, and operational tiers of higher education. Developing the principles, standards, and decision-making procedures that direct the integration of AI into institutional life is the essence of effective AI governance, which goes beyond simple compliance and risk management. Universities must implement systems that support supervision, diversity, interdisciplinary cooperation, and adaptability to new issues in order to accomplish this. Centralized oversight committees, federated departmental stewards, and hybrid governance councils are currently the three most common forms of governance in higher education settings.

Large or research-intensive institutions, where a cohesive approach is crucial, frequently use the centralized oversight model. A specialized AI ethics or digital governance committee made up of senior administrators, legal professionals, IT officers, and academic representatives is usually a part of this model. This model's strength is its coherence and consistency: data security is easier to manage, policies can be applied consistently across departments, and institutional goals—like equity, transparency, or innovation—can be advanced through coordinated action. Centralized models, however, run the risk of losing touch with discipline-specific contexts or failing to account for the variety of needs of faculty and students across programs (Williamson & Eynon, 2020; Zhao & Watterston, 2021).

The federated model, on the other hand, gives departments, faculties, or academic units the authority to designate their own AI stewards or advisory boards. These local stewards are able to modify technical guidelines, pedagogical approaches, and policies to fit their particular disciplinary practices. An AI tool used in an engineering lab, for example, might cause quite different issues than one used in a law school or humanities seminar. More faculty ownership, contextual sensitivity, and bottom-up innovation are all encouraged by the federated model. But in the absence of effective coordination, this model may lead to disarray, disparate standards, and unequal ethical protections throughout the organization.

Many universities are now implementing a hybrid governance model that combines the advantages of departmental autonomy and centralized oversight in recognition of the shortcomings of both approaches. A university-wide digital governance council creates baseline policies, compliance guidelines, and institutional frameworks under this arrangement. It also collaborates with departmental AI leads to support local innovation and contextual adaptation. Frequently functioning as two-tiered structures, these hybrid councils distribute implementation and experimentation while centralizing strategic vision and ethical standards. In order to make governance more responsive and dynamic, this model also permits feedback loops between faculty or student users and central governance bodies.

No matter which model is selected, inclusive participation is a must. Since students are frequently the subjects of data collection and the users of AI-enhanced platforms, their voices must be included in any effective AI governance. It must also include technologists who are aware of the limitations and system architectures, as well as ethicists who can foresee the ethical ramifications of new technologies. Furthermore, there should be clear channels for grievances, policy revision, and continuous evaluation of the AI tools being used, as well as transparent, iterative, and accountable governance.

Regardless of the model chosen, inclusive participation is essential. Any effective AI governance must include the voices of students, who are often the users of AI-enhanced platforms and the subjects of data collection. It must also comprise ethicists who can anticipate the ethical implications of emerging technologies and technologists who understand system architectures and limitations. In addition, there should be transparent, iterative, and accountable governance, as well as clear channels for grievances, policy revision, and ongoing assessment of the AI tools being used (Siemens & Long, 2011).

7.3 Collaboration with EdTech Providers

Universities rely more and more on outside educational technology (EdTech) providers to supply AI-enabled teaching, assessment, advising, and administrative tools in the rapidly changing higher education ecosystem. Although these collaborations have a lot of potential for innovation and growth, they also raise important issues with institutional autonomy, data privacy, accountability, and ethical alignment. Therefore, a strategic, values-driven approach that prioritizes co-creation, transparency, and long-term trust is necessary for successful collaboration with EdTech providers; it cannot be limited to licensing and procurement.

A foundational component of this relationship is the vendor contract, which must move beyond standard service-level agreements to include detailed clauses governing data handling, algorithmic operations, and shared responsibility for potential harm. Data handling clauses should clearly specify what data is being collected, for what purposes, who owns it, where it is stored, how long it is retained, and under what conditions it may be shared or sold. These agreements should also include student data rights in line with national privacy regulations (e.g., GDPR, FERPA, or India's DPDP Act), and should prevent unauthorized repurposing of educational data for commercial or non-educational aims (Page & Gehlbach, 2020; Selwyn, 2019).

A contractual focus on algorithmic transparency is equally important. AI systems' decision-making processes must be transparent to institutions, particularly when those decisions have an impact on student achievement, retention, or disciplinary measures. This includes having access to documentation regarding the model's decision-making process, training data, and error rates for various demographic groups. In addition to right-to-explanation clauses that enable organizations and students to comprehend and contest algorithmic outputs, contracts should contain provisions for third-party audits, bias testing, and impact assessments. Universities can start to reduce the risks associated with "black-box" systems that function without supervision or accountability by incorporating such requirements into procurement procedures.

But control and compliance are insufficient on their own. Institutions and EdTech providers must adopt a co-design mindset in order to promote the truly meaningful and responsible use of AI in education. This entails switching to a collaborative innovation model from a "vendor-client" dynamic. Co-design hubs or innovation studios are being established by many progressive universities, where academics, students, developers, and instructional designers collaborate to develop, test, and improve AI tools prior to their widespread use. These hubs enable iterative development cycles that take into account local pedagogical practices, accessibility standards, cultural contexts, and actual classroom feedback. This ensures that tools support the institution's educational philosophy and social mission in addition to functionality requirements (Holmes et al., 2022).

There are several advantages to such participatory approaches: vendors gain a deeper understanding of the lived realities of teaching and learning environments; students are treated as active stakeholders rather than passive users; and faculty feel more ownership over the tools they use. Furthermore, because institutions are not limited by strict vendor roadmaps, co-design allows for greater flexibility and sustainability as they can modify technology to meet changing pedagogical needs.

In summary, working with EdTech providers should be viewed as a strategic partnership based on openness, equity, and shared responsibility rather than merely a service contract. Institutions can contribute to ensuring that AI technologies not only satisfy functional needs but also preserve the principles that characterize inclusive and responsible higher education by establishing participatory design cultures and enshrining ethical standards in vendor contracts (Page & Gehlbach, 2020; Selwyn, 2019; UNESCO, 2023).

8 CASE STUDIES AND BEST PRACTICES

8.1 Real-World Implementations

The effective use of AI in higher education is already happening in a variety of institutional settings worldwide; it is no longer merely a theoretical concept. Universities can learn not only which tools work but also how to use them ethically, contextually, and pedagogically to achieve significant results by examining real-world implementations. The following illustrations show how AI is being applied to address urgent issues in academic advising, student retention, enrolment management, and administrative effectiveness.

One of the most frequently cited success stories is from Georgia State University (GSU) in the US, which used an AI-powered chatbot named Pounce to lessen "summer melt," a phenomenon where admitted students drop out of school because of organizational, financial, or psychological difficulties. The chatbot, which was programmed with thousands of frequently asked questions and was accessible by SMS around-the-clock, provided prompt answers to student inquiries regarding deadlines, housing, financial aid, and registration. Importantly, Pounce escalated unresolved issues to human advisors and personalized interactions using natural language processing (NLP). GSU experienced a 21% decrease in summer melt within a year of implementation, which resulted in noticeably higher first-generation and low-income student enrolment and retention rates. This example shows how strategically and sympathetically implementing AI can improve student support and equity (Williamson & Eynon, 2020).

The Open University, a leader in online and remote learning in the UK, used predictive learning analytics to increase student retention among its widely scattered and diverse student body. The predictive models found patterns associated with student disengagement and dropout risk by examining both historical and current data from the university's learning management system (LMS). Metrics like quiz performance, forum participation, assignment submission delays, and login frequency were among these indicators. Tutors were notified and able to step in with tailored messages or extra help after at-risk students were identified. The Open University consequently noted significant gains in module completion and progression rates, particularly for adult learners who are juggling work and family obligations with their studies (Selwyn, 2019).

A third striking example is provided by Deakin University in Australia, which collaborated with IBM to incorporate Watson, a cutting-edge AI virtual assistant, into its ecosystem of student services. Under the alias Deakin Genie, the assistant provided prompt answers to questions about academic policies, assignment due dates, campus navigation, and schedules. Crucially, it was integrated into the university's mobile application, enabling on-demand access. Genie allowed university staff to focus their time and energy on more complicated advising tasks, like academic appeals or mental health referrals, by automating high-volume, low-complexity queries. A strong argument for intelligent automation in administrative tasks was made by the implementation, which not only raised student satisfaction but also showed how AI can supplement human ability rather than replace it (Zawacki-Richter et al., 2019).

Several characteristics of successful AI integration in higher education are demonstrated by these case studies:

- A precise determination of the institutional pain points, such as staff overload, student retention, and summer melt
- Using AI as a tool to enhance rather than replace
- Tight coordination between student services, academic staff, and technical teams
- Iterative improvement based on outcome tracking and user input
- A dedication to openness, accessibility, and moral data use

They also demonstrate the importance of localized adaptation. What works in one context may not translate well to another if the institutional mission, student demographics, infrastructure capacity, and regulatory obligations are not taken into consideration. Universities considering similar deployments are advised to co-design processes, ensure strong governance, and prepare faculty and staff through professional development programs.

All things considered, these practical applications offer both motivational and admonishing examples. AI has the potential to address long-standing issues and improve the caliber and equity of higher education when it is properly regulated and in line with educational objectives. However, how the technology is implemented, maintained, and regularly assessed within the institutional ecosystem is just as important to its success as the technology itself (Selwyn, 2019; Tlili et al., 2023; Williamson & Eynon, 2020; Zawacki-Richter et al., 2019).

8.2 Lessons Learned from Diverse Institutions

As educational institutions around the world experiment with integrating AI into their curricula, a multitude of cross-case insights have begun to emerge. Implementations ranging from student-interaction chatbots to predictive analytics and intelligent tutoring systems demonstrate that thoughtful planning, inclusive design, and adaptable leadership—rather than merely cutting-edge technology—produce the best outcomes. A synthesis of lessons learned from different institutional contexts has led to the development of four critical success factors that consistently distinguish high-impact AI initiatives from those that perform poorly or face resistance.

1. **Stakeholder Co-Creation** The significance of inclusive, stakeholder-driven design processes is among the most obvious lessons. Higher levels of buy-in, usability, and pedagogical relevance are reported by institutions that include students, faculty, administrators, IT personnel, and even outside partners in the early phases of developing AI tools. Instead of imposing generic technological solutions, co-creation guarantees that the final tools reflect actual user needs, local values, and contextual challenges. Additionally, this participatory approach promotes trust and transparency, especially with users who might be initially dubious about AI's potential in education. Institutions can better align AI solutions with strategic priorities and lived academic realities by incorporating stakeholder voices from the beginning (Holmes et al., 2019).
2. **Phased Pilots with Clear KPIs** The importance of phased implementation through pilot projects, each with clearly defined key performance indicators (KPIs), is another important lesson. Successful universities start with controlled pilots—within a single course, department, or support service—instead of implementing AI systems across the entire institution without validation. Metrics like student engagement, satisfaction, retention, efficiency, or learning gains are used to evaluate these pilots. This method minimizes disruption and maximizes learning by enabling institutions to measure results, test hypotheses, and identify risks early. Additionally, it fosters a culture of experimentation and ongoing development where decisions regarding investment and scaling are guided by facts rather than conjecture (Ifenthaler & Yau, 2020). .
3. **Ethical Impact Assessments** Another characteristic of mature AI implementations is ethical foresight. Formal ethical impact assessments, or EIAs, are being used by institutions more frequently to assess the psychological, social, and cultural effects of AI tools prior to their implementation. These tests look at how technology may change pedagogical relationships, increase bias, or impact student autonomy. In order to identify risks and suggest safeguards, EIAs frequently entail cross-disciplinary panels that include ethicists, legal experts, data scientists, and students. Universities show their dedication to responsible innovation and prevent reputational, legal, and educational harms before they arise by instituting these assessments (Mittelstadt, 2019).
4. **Iterative Feedback Loops Linking Analytics to Curriculum Redesign** Lastly, iterative feedback loops that link learning analytics to curriculum and instructional improvement are a hallmark of successful AI projects. Leading universities utilize the information obtained from AI systems to improve course content, update pedagogical approaches, and inform student support services

rather than using analytics as a monitoring tool. For instance, teachers can update the course materials, change the tempo, or add scaffolding activities if analytics show that a sizable percentage of students have trouble understanding a given concept. AI thus turns into a diagnostic and developmental partner in the learning ecosystem, supporting the continuous improvement of academic relevance and quality (OECD, 2019).

In conclusion, these four lessons—curricular feedback loops, ethical impact assessment, phased piloting with KPIs, and stakeholder co-creation—represent best practices that cut across institutional or technological boundaries. They provide a tactical guide for academic institutions looking to leverage AI's potential while preserving the efficacy, inclusivity, and integrity of education. Organizations can guarantee that AI supports higher education's long-term goals of promoting human development, knowledge creation, and social responsibility by approaching AI implementation as an iterative, collaborative process as opposed to a top-down technology deployment.

9 FUTURE DIRECTIONS

9.1 Generative AI and Large Language Models

The next generation of large language models (LLMs) will act as Socratic learning partners rather than just "answer engines." Advanced LLMs will be trained to probe a learner's reasoning, uncover misconceptions, and scaffold higher-order thinking through open-ended dialogue rather than providing prepackaged facts. Ragged context windows that preserve long-term learning histories will improve their conversational depth by enabling the model to remember past conversations and create continuity between semesters.

Prompt engineering, which was formerly a specialized skill, will develop into a complete academic literacy similar to research methodology or rhetoric as this transition takes place. Students will learn from faculty how to create prompts that generate counterarguments, elicit nuanced viewpoints, and synthesize interdisciplinary evidence. The final product as well as the prompt-design justification and ethical considerations (such as bias checks and source verification) will be assessed using rubrics. In order to strengthen metacognitive abilities, curricula may incorporate "dialogic AI clinics," where students engage in iterative questioning, reflection, and self-explanation with an AI counterpart. Additionally, future LLMs will work with domain-specific models (for design, math, code, etc.), allowing for multi-modal co-creation of simulations, data visualizations, text, and even lab protocols. When humans and LLMs collaborate to create academic artifacts, institutions will require policies that make co-authorship standards and intellectual property ownership clear (UNESCO, 2021).

9.2 Predictive Analytics and Learning Analytics

Textual discussion posts, click-path behaviors, biometric wearables, speech emotion cues, and even eye-tracking patterns are among the multi-modal data streams that are being integrated into holistic learner dashboards by emerging analytics platforms. Next-generation systems will offer precision advising by combining these signals in real-time, which will include adaptive pacing that is in line with cognitive load, personalized study-skill recommendations, and early warnings about disengagement.

Streaming data architectures and cross-model ensembles that can interpret heterogeneous inputs will be the foundation of the analytical backbone. A micro-intervention, such as a soothing video, a quick conversation with an AI mentor, or outreach from a human tutor, may be triggered, for instance, by an increase in heart-rate variability during an online test coupled with slowed navigation in follow-up materials. By revealing hidden struggles before traditional assessments notice them, such fine-grained insight promises to close equity gaps.

However, the stakes for privacy rise proportionately. GDPR and similar laws classify physiological or affective data as special-category information, requiring strict purpose limitation and explicit, revocable consent. Important protections will include algorithmic-explainability layers, federated-learning pipelines, differential privacy, and transparent data-governance dashboards. Institutions run the risk of regulatory penalties and harm to their reputation if they don't combine strong privacy design with analytical capabilities (UNESCO, 2023; Zawacki-Richter et al., 2019; Zhao & Watterston, 2021).

9.3 Preparing for Rapid Innovation

AI developments are currently happening faster than traditional academic planning cycles. Therefore, universities require organized technological-foresight mechanisms that maintain strategy in line with new threats and opportunities. Three methods are becoming more popular:

1. Scenario Planning: Multidisciplinary groups create best-, worst-, and wildcard scenarios (such as AI tutors passing important tests, laws prohibiting black-box grading, or quantum-accelerated model training). Contingency budgeting and policy stress tests are informed by these narratives.

2. Regulatory Horizon Scanning: These units keep a close eye on legislative developments, such as the EU AI Act's vertical requirements, India's DPDP regulations, and U.S. state statutes on algorithmic decision-making. They also notify leadership of any gaps in compliance or opportunities for advocacy.
3. Sandbox Experimentation: Under "safe-to-fail" innovation sandboxes, students and faculty can test beta AI tools in a controlled setting while results are tracked by ethical review boards. Agile procurement guidelines and curriculum refresh cycles are informed by insights.

Institutions will support these frameworks by developing staff micro-credential pathways, faculty AI-fluency fellowships, and student innovation hubs that incentivize quick prototyping. Review cadences (such as yearly model-risk audits) and sunset clauses that retire legacy tools that no longer satisfy pedagogical or ethical standards will be incorporated into governance charters. Agility ultimately depends on a culture that views AI as a dynamic socio-technical ecosystem that necessitates ongoing learning, iteration, and shared stewardship rather than as a one-off project (Ouyang et al., 2022; Page & Gehlbach, 2020).

10 CONCLUSION

10.1. Reaffirming Educational Values

As artificial intelligence (AI) becomes more and more integrated into higher education in this age of rapid technological advancement, institutions must consider the following important question: What aspects of the learning process should remain essentially human? The core principles that define higher education—not as a commodity, but as a profoundly human and transformative experience—need to be reaffirmed in light of the expanding capabilities of generative models, predictive analytics, and intelligent tutoring systems.

Fundamentally, the promise of AI in education does not lie in automating students, replacing teachers, or maximizing efficiency at all costs. Instead, its greatest promise is to enhance human potential, allowing students to think more critically, express themselves more creatively, and delve deeper into the material. AI ought to be a tool that encourages the pursuit of ethical reasoning, civic duty, and intellectual curiosity rather than a crutch. These are the characteristics of education that go beyond the simple dissemination of knowledge. They demonstrate universities' dedication to developing not only highly qualified professionals but also considerate citizens and lifelong learners.

Rethinking how AI is applied in the classroom, in assessments, and in institutional policy is necessary to reorient education around these ideals. For example, teachers can use AI to scaffold feedback instead of using it to grade essays without context, which frees up time for more in-depth discussions and mentoring. Faculty can use AI's insights to spark thought-provoking conversations that encourage metacognition and self-directed learning, rather than depending on it to monitor engagement through passive metrics. Institutions can make sure that technology enhances rather than lessens the social mission of education by coordinating AI tools with values like equity, autonomy, inclusivity, and critical inquiry.

Furthermore, ethical stewardship is required to reaffirm educational values in an AI-rich environment. It is imperative that students learn not only how to use AI tools but also how to critically evaluate them, taking into account their limitations, potential biases, and the effects of automation on society. Teachers must also be encouraged to become ethical facilitators of AI integration rather than merely users of the technology. To preserve a human-centered approach to learning, governance models, curriculum design, and assessment techniques must all be adjusted.

In the end, higher education has a special duty as AI becomes more widespread: to set an example for ethical, values-driven, and responsible innovation. This entails bucking the urge to embrace technology for its own sake and instead considering whether it furthers our goals of empowerment, inspiration, and education. Institutions can guarantee that AI continues to benefit humanity by carefully addressing that question—improving rather than replacing our best instincts (Cotton et al., 2024; UNESCO, 2021; Zawacki-Richter et al., 2019).

10.2. Strategic Recommendations

Higher education institutions must go beyond experimentation and embrace a strategic, values-driven approach to governance, implementation, and ongoing improvement as artificial intelligence becomes a permanent fixture in the institution's architecture. In addition to utilizing AI's potential, the objective is to make sure that its incorporation advances education's long-term objectives of human flourishing, quality, equity, and integrity. Four strategic recommendations—governance, capacity building, equity prioritization, and continuous evaluation—are put forth in light of best practices and cross-institutional insights (Ifenthaler & Yau, 2020).

10.3. Governance: Establish Multi-Stakeholder Ethics Boards

The foundation of adopting AI responsibly is effective governance. Institutions should set up digital governance councils or AI ethics boards made up of a variety of stakeholders, such as students, faculty, legal professionals, ethicists, technologists, and advocates for accessibility. These bodies must have the authority to audit, postpone, or veto deployments that raise moral, educational, or legal issues in addition to reviewing proposals. Procurement criteria approval, algorithmic bias reports, consent mechanism supervision, and post-deployment impact monitoring should all be part of their duties.

Crucially, in order to preserve confidence in the academic community, these boards must function with accountability, transparency, and procedural fairness. Their presence indicates that the organization is taking responsibility for the moral aspects of educational innovation rather than contracting out ethical judgment to outside parties or technology (Zawacki-Richter et al., 2019).

10.4. Capacity Building: Embed AI Literacy Across Curricula and Staff Development

AI integration necessitates capacity building at all institutional levels in addition to governance. The first step in doing this is incorporating AI literacy into graduate and undergraduate programs so that students can comprehend the tools they use, challenge their presumptions, and investigate the societal ramifications of their choices. In addition to computer science, courses on data ethics, algorithmic bias, machine learning fundamentals, and responsible AI design ought to be available in the fields of education, the humanities, business, and law.

Structured professional development pathways, such as workshops, peer mentoring circles, and micro-credentials, must also be used to support faculty and staff. Technical fluency, pedagogical integration, and ethical awareness should be the main goals of these programs so that teachers can make well-informed decisions about incorporating AI into their lessons (Zhao & Watterston, 2021).

10.5. Equity Lens: Prioritize Underserved Learners

The expansion of already-existing disparities is one of the biggest dangers of AI in education. Due to socioeconomic status, geography, language, or disability, students from marginalized backgrounds frequently encounter the biggest obstacles to digital access and might be the last to take advantage of new technology. Institutions must adopt AI with an equity-first perspective in order to buck this trend.

This entails allocating funds to guarantee that underprivileged students are given priority rather than being marginalized. For instance, foundational courses with high first-generation student dropout rates ought to test adaptive learning technologies. Learners in remote or low-connectivity areas should be assisted by AI tutors, and predictive models need to be audited to avoid perpetuating systemic bias. In order to ensure AI systems are inclusive and accessible, equity also entails universal design, multilingual interfaces, and cultural sensitivity (Williamson & Eynon, 2020).

10.6. Continuous Evaluation: Adopt Lifecycle Assessments

Artificial intelligence (AI) systems are dynamic instruments that change with time and are applied in dynamic contexts. Institutions must therefore embrace lifecycle-based assessment models that extend beyond initial procurement and deployment. This involves putting in place procedures for routinely reevaluating AI tools in light of new information, user input, potential hazards, and evolving learning objectives.

Every AI system in use should undergo an annual risk-benefit analysis that addresses performance indicators, moral considerations, and unforeseen consequences. Sunsetting criteria, which state that a tool should be updated or retired if it no longer satisfies equity benchmarks or pedagogical standards, should also be included in lifetime evaluations. By incorporating these ongoing feedback loops, AI is kept in line with institutional values and prevents from becoming misused or obsolete (UNESCO, 2023).

10.7. Final Thought

The four strategic pillars of inclusive governance, strong capacity building, equity prioritization, and ongoing evaluation work together to create a comprehensive roadmap for the adoption of AI that is not only creative but also inclusive, sustainable, and responsible. Instead of reshaping education to fit the capabilities of machines, they reflect the institutional will to mould technology around human values. Universities can successfully navigate the AI era while upholding their dedication to students, scholarship, and society by institutionalizing these practices (Siemens & Long, 2011; UNESCO, 2023)

REFERENCES

Baker, R. S., & Inventado, P. S. (2014). Educational data mining and learning analytics. In Larusson, J. A., & White, B. (Eds.), *Learning analytics: From research to practice* (pp. 61–75). Springer. DOI: 10.1007/978-1-4614-3305-7_4

Bender, E. M., Gebru, T., McMillan-Major, A., & Shmitchell, S. (2021). On the dangers of stochastic parrots: Can language models be too big? *Proceedings of the 2021 ACM Conference on Fairness, Accountability, and Transparency*, 610–623. DOI: 10.1145/3442188.3445922

Buckingham Shum, S., & Ferguson, R. (2012). Social learning analytics. *Journal of Educational Technology & Society*, *15*(3), 3–26.

Cotton, D. R. E., Cotton, P. A., & Shipway, J. R. (2024). Chatting and cheating? Ensuring academic integrity in the era of ChatGPT. *Innovations in Education and Teaching International*, *61*(2), 228–239. DOI: 10.1080/14703297.2023.2190148

Holmes, W., Bialik, M., & Fadel, C. (2019). *Artificial intelligence in education: Promises and implications for teaching and learning*. Center for Curriculum Redesign.

Holmes, W., Persson, J., Chounta, I.-A., Wasson, B., & Dimitrova, V. (2022). Ethics of AI in education: Towards a community-wide framework. *International Journal of Artificial Intelligence in Education*, *32*(3), 504–526. DOI: 10.1007/s40593-021-00239-1

Ifenthaler, D., & Yau, J. Y.-K. (2020). Utilising learning analytics for study success: Reflections on current empirical findings. *Research and Practice in Technology Enhanced Learning*, *15*(1), 1–17.

Luckin, R., Holmes, W., Griffiths, M., & Forcier, L. B. (2016). *Intelligence unleashed: An argument for AI in education*. Pearson Education.

Mittelstadt, B. D. (2019). Principles alone cannot guarantee ethical AI. *Nature Machine Intelligence*, *1*(11), 501–507. DOI: 10.1038/s42256-019-0114-4

OECD. (2019). *Recommendation of the Council on Artificial Intelligence*. Organisation for Economic Co-operation and Development.

Ouyang, F., Zheng, L., Jiao, P., & Moore, G. D. (2022). Artificial intelligence in online higher education: A systematic review of empirical research. *Computers and Education: Artificial Intelligence*, *3*, 100088.

Page, L. C., & Gehlbach, H. (2020). How an artificially intelligent virtual assistant helps students navigate the road to college. *AERA Open*, *6*(4), 1–12.

Selwyn, N. (2019). *Should robots replace teachers? AI and the future of education.* Polity Press.

Siemens, G., & Long, P. (2011). Penetrating the fog: Analytics in learning and education. *EDUCAUSE Review*, *46*(5), 30–40.

Tlili, A., Shehata, B., Adarkwah, M. A., Bozkurt, A., Hickey, D. T., Huang, R., & Agyemang, B. (2023). What if the devil is my guardian angel? ChatGPT as a case study of using chatbots in education. *Smart Learning Environments*, *10*(1), 1–24. DOI: 10.1186/s40561-023-00237-x

UNESCO. (2021). *Recommendation on the ethics of artificial intelligence.* United Nations Educational, Scientific and Cultural Organization.

UNESCO. (2023). *Guidance for generative AI in education and research.* UNESCO.

Williamson, B., & Eynon, R. (2020). Historical threads, missing links, and future directions in AI in education. *Learning, Media and Technology*, *45*(3), 223–235. DOI: 10.1080/17439884.2020.1798995

Zawacki-Richter, O., Marín, V. I., Bond, M., & Gouverneur, F. (2019). Systematic review of research on artificial intelligence applications in higher education. *International Journal of Educational Technology in Higher Education*, *16*(39), 1–27. DOI: 10.1186/s41239-019-0171-0

Zhao, Y., & Watterston, J. (2021). The changes we need: Education post COVID-19 and the opportunities of AI. *Journal of Educational Change*, *22*(1), 3–12. DOI: 10.1007/s10833-021-09417-3

Chapter 4
Defining Responsible AI in the Context of Higher Education:
AI and Academic Integrity

Sumiksha Shetty
http://orcid.org/0009-0005-4427-8332
NMAM institute of Technology(NMAMIT), NITTE (Deemed to be) University, India

A. B. Smitha
Sahyadri College of Engineering and Management, India

ABSTRACT

AI is transforming the world of higher education by providing an individualized learning experience, automated evaluation, and effective administration. Although AI has advantages, such as the ability to ensure better engagement and prompt feedback, it also creates the issues of bias, transparency, and academic integrity. The chapter suggests a model of responsible use of AI with the main principles of transparency, accountability, and ethical literacy. Institutions should make sure that AI can assist other people, but not to substitute human judgment without enhancing fairness and honesty. Incorporating ethics into AI is a way of creating trust and maintaining scholarly integrity.

INTRODUCTION

The Artificial Intelligence (AI) is already a force of change in the field of higher education to transform it how knowledge is being provided, evaluated, and controlled

DOI: 10.4018/979-8-3373-5586-3.ch004

AI-based systems of tutoring and individualized learning tools to administrative aids simplifying the enrollment and grading processes, use of AI is increasing rapidly in learning institutions. These technologies promise such advantages as increased interaction with students, instant feedback, adaptive. curricula, and efficiency in operations. Nonetheless, AI implementation into such a serious field. is not without consequences. It brings complicated ethical issues, especially in upholding academic integrity- a pillar of education practice(Moya et al., 2024)(Oh). Sanfilippo, 2024) As algorithms start to determine the results of assessment and the direction of studying, There is the concern of transparency, accountability and misuse that might be possible, e.g. generated bias or enables plagiarism with the help of generative tools. Besides these ethical Another group of critical problems related to the increased application of AI in higher education has been issues to do with equity and access. There will be less-privileged institutions and minority groups of students are less likely to access more advanced AI systems due to the institutions possessing more financial and they are better placed to be implemented by technological assets. These inequalities have the potential to increase the already existing socioeconomic differences in education and, more so, when AI-based assessments, advising, or learning analytics become the center of academic decisions. Unless the use of AI is actively policy-intervened, it can simply encourage structural inequalities instead of alleviating them.

Although the adoption of AI in educational settings has been done with acute excitement, most higher education institutions have practical issues of implementing AI, such as inadequate faculty readiness, inconsistent institutional regulations and absence of well-defined governance structures. Technological progress has usually been faster than ethical standards and control measures, resulting in asymmetrical and even unthoughtful implementation of AI applications in the learning environment. This chapter is based on these opportunities and challenge ssuggests a practical and comprehensive model of accountable AI application in higher education which incorporates the ethical management, safeguarding of academic honesty, lifecycle-conscious. AI use, and equity-associated institutional policies This will be aimed at creating a delicate balance between the exploitation of the possibilities of AI and the principles of intellectual honesty, fairness, and equity The framework does not think of AI as an alternative to human judgement underlines the fact that it is more a supportive tool, which must work within better-established ethical and pedagogical boundaries It presents principles of responsible implementation, including transparency based on algorithms, engagement of stakeholders, ongoing monitoring and ethical literacy. Lastly, the chapter proposes to both teachers and learners(Oh & Sanfilippo, 2024) institutions should adopt AI in a conscious, values-based strategy that will make the technology making is not detrimental to but makes education more honest and meaningful.

The other crucial component of responsible adoption of AI is that the ethical awareness must be formulated (a) through the whole stakeholder of students, the faculty and institutional administrators Users with the adoption of AI systems as a teaching, learning and assessment process can be seen as benefiting must not only understand how these technologies function but also learn how ethical is the use of such technologies. Colleges need to thus implement policies, which are clear-cut training courses, and ever-present support structures that will delineate what the acceptable use of AI is, and will inspire persons to make responsible decisions. Simultaneously, they should change the institutional governance to ensure that they remain in tune with changes in technology that ought to ensure accountability, openness and compliance with the university values. It is important to ensure significant collaboration between educators, technologists, ethicists, and policymakers to ensure there is no replacement of institutional missions by AI integration and harm them.

1.1The AI in Higher Education

AI has emerged as a revolutionizing aspect in the field of higher education, with all the levels of the academic setting being influenced by it, both the manner the learners study and interact with the information and the data-driven decisions made by the institution. Even though AI could be confined to research laboratories and technical spaces, it is the core and the very spirit of the university activities, as well as education. Its applications are in predictive analysis of student performance and intelligent tutoring, AI-mediated grading, and applicant selection. These instruments are evolving, hence, they are still having more influence on how students go about knowledge, how educators encourage learning, as well as how institutions can more efficiently utilize their resources. In the chapter, the author delves into the multi-faceted nature of the AI role in the context of higher education where the specified subject matter restructures the education process of a student and the academic administration (Diagram 1: AI Touchpoints in Higher Education).(Barus et al., 2025) Although the opportunities presented by AI in terms of efficiency and tailoring approaches to individuals have never been higher, it also leads to critical concerns of academic integrity, authorship, fairness, and re-definition of teaching and learning. According to the viewpoint of responsible AI, these changes require a more in-depth analysis of AI systems design, implementation, and regulation in colleges and universities. Fairness, accountability and transparency are directly impacted by decisions involved in sourcing of data, choice of algorithms and system management. In the absence of institutional-level governance mechanisms, the growing importance of AI threatens to make efficiency instead of being ethically responsible a priority, undermining the fundamental academic values.

1.2 Student learning path

The evolution of the student learning path via AI is one of the most effective changes in contemporary higher learning. The norm traditionally utilized in teaching was the linear, standardized model with lecturing and evaluation system prescribed and monotonous. Often this model could not take into consideration the difference in learning need and speed in students. Educational experiences, however, are also becoming more and more personalized with the introduction of AI. Smart educational systems can manipulate up to date information e.g. performance in assessments like quizzes, frequency of interaction, areas of interest, and they can even track emotional stimulus to condense the delivery of content. Such data-personalized delivery aids in the early warning of learning gaps, reinforces the learner at areas of strength and provides suitable challenges that makes it an adaptive learning experience that tailors itself with the learner. It therefore means that the students cannot be thought of anymore as mere recipients of knowledge but rather active participants in a process of dynamic education leading by technology. In addition, AI-enhanced personalization goes beyond the delivery of the content to smart tutoring system, interactive simulation, and prediction tools to recognize and help solve the problems before students experience issues. Indicatively, AI tutors help academically by 24/7 provision of hints, answering questions, and adjusting feedback according to the performance of the students. Predictive analytics has the capacity to identify, at the onset of any semester or course, learners who will have problems and intervene before it is too late by either the faculty or the support staff. Such systems not only spur superior learning outcomes, but also enhance involvement and memorization of the students and they feel more assisted and comprehended. These tools are ever-changing with the advancement of the students in their curriculums and is increasingly becoming customized with better strategy and, therefore, better experience and education. This transformation of the curriculum based teaching to a more flexible and learner centered instruction is what defines the rational shift of philosophy and practice of higher education. Although AI-based personalization can be observed to improve the outcomes of learning among a considerable number of students, the concept also elicits issues of equity and inclusivity. Depending on their access to a digital infrastructure, access to dependable internet connectivity, or sophisticated AI-based platforms, learners may not be equally served by such adaptive systems. Moreover, any personalization algorithms that have been trained on small or biased datasets can be insufficient to generate representatives of various learning styles, cultural experience, or language. To overcome these issues, institutions need to be based on the principles of inclusive design and regularly consider the effects the systems of AI have on various categories of students.

1.2.1 Predictive Analytics

Predictive analytics is already one of the most influential AI-based tools in the area of higher education as universities can now spot those students who might be at the risk of failing or becoming out of the game long before classical warning signs will appear. Predictive models that can identify subtle trends in student behavior, attendance, course performance and even online engagement can be made through utilizing massive data sets of historical data as well as real-time data. Specifically, the decrease in the number of students engaging in online studies or unstable logins to education services or declining submission quality of assignments may be the indicators of the possible struggles. The insights enable universities to step in before the problems grow to course withdrawal and failures by providing the necessary support to students so that they can perform accordingly.

The possibility to facilitate personalized interventions is one of the most important advantages of predictive analytics. Institutions are in a position to design strategies specific in their approach to the needs of individual students instead of using blanket strategies to address the needs of students. As an example, the students identified by the system can be referred to academic advisors who can suggest tutoring sessions, study workshops, or renewed learning plans. In the rest of the cases, predictive analytics may indicate the necessity of peer mentoring programs, mental health services, or financial support. With that amount of special attention, relationships between the learners and their institutions become much stronger, making the retention rates and overall performance much better. Although these benefits are present, the application of predictive analytics also brings in some ethical issues associated with data privacy, autonomy of students, and algorithmic determinism. Yet, when students are already labeled as at risk based on only the predictive models, it will be possible to stigmatize the students or even cause them to fulfill their own academic path. Making the model design transparent, informed consent on how the data will be used, and the involvement of human judgment in the interpretation of the predictions are all necessary parts of responsible deployment. Predictive analytics can be viewed as a decision-support tool and not as a determinate power during student evaluation.

1.2.2 Generative AI and ChatGPT

The generative AI (including ChatGPT) has essentially transformed the way students are interacting with academic material, researching it, and conducting the learning process in general. These newer language models have the capability of doing a broad variety of tasks such as brainstorming on project ideas, providing summaries on larger articles or research papers, translating complicated academic materials into easier understandable language and even writing a skeletal version of an essay or report. By providing such features, ChatGPT serves as an effective productivity tool that allows students to better structure their ideas and concentrate on learning assignments of a higher caliber instead of being blocked by some harmful creativity block like writer block.(Oh & Sanfilippo, 2024) This conversational way of such tools also enables learners to discuss issues in a much more interactive way with posing multiple follow-up questions and getting immediate feedback on them, similar to that of working with an academic tutor. Nevertheless, this trend of increased use of generative AI comes with added problems in the world of academia, especially on the aspect of academic integrity.(Neumann et al., 2023) Due to the fact that these tools are capable of producing coherent and contextually responsive pieces with very little effort, they are setting educators at an increasing disadvantage since the distinction between original student work and AI-generated content becomes hard to ascertain. Such blurring of the distinction between authorship begs serious concern as to how finer matters of knowledge and skill acquisition should be gauged in the AI era.(Evangelista, 2025) do we set assignments that would minimize the use of generative tools, or do we want to teach students to be transparent in their use as products of their academic toolbox. It is necessary to produce institutional policies that will establish the foundation on how the technologies must be utilized with specific attention to the way the technologies may be applied in a solemn style without coming between intellectual integrity and the other. It will entail change of culture in the higher education, where it is not regarded as a means of cut corners not to learn, generative AI could be incorporated on board as a helper that could be knowledge-building with ethical application and brood creativity To make responsible use operational, the institutions are supposed to develop clear codes of what should be termed as acceptable assistance and what qualifies as an academic violation. These policies should be underpinned by policies of redesign assessment, which is more significant emphasize on critical thinking, reflective learning and process based evaluation Professional educators should also be transformed to change teaching experience and evaluation with training methods in line with AI generative abilities. Generative AI can be used to bolster academic dishonesty and not weaken it by formal governing and integrity literacy campaigns.

1.2.3 AI-Based Evaluation Resources

In understanding the structure, coherence, originality, and knowledge of the subject in a piece of work, AI tools can offer feedback to student in details and on time. Such immediacy grants learners the freedom to correct and amend in subsequent drafts enabling the creation of a culture of iterative learning. Moreover, such systems are also scalable, meaning that a teacher could handle increased school classes with no loss of quality of the given feedback, which is another shoving concern especially in higher education. In addition to efficiency, there are also opportunities to provide more analytics and individualized insights, due to AI-assisted assessment instruments. The trends in student performance in different assignments and courses can be detected with the help of these systems, and educators will be able to detect areas of excellence and weakness in a particular student, as well as within the cohort. As an example, when many students have problems with a certain concept, the instructors may go over the learning content again or may offer additional learning materials. Likewise, learners will be able to take advantage of individualized learning suggestions in accordance with their examination grades resulting in more tailored and conducive learning environment. Such insights may also aid departments in improving over time in terms of curricula design to suit the students learning needs. Nonetheless, it is not an easy task to adopt AI-enhanced assessment scales.(Wan Nailah, Abdullah Syahiza et al., 2023) This further affects the reliability of such systems based on the quality of the training data and the range and variety of the data on which they are trained, and also the structure of the algorithms. It is possible to have unfair assessment because of biases in the training datasets, especially in cases where learners have different linguistics or cultural affiliations. Moreover, the reliability of creativity or unusual answers to a question, which do not coincide with the norm, can also work against the rewards of originality by AI tools. In this regard, institutions should see AI-based assessments as complementary and not the main form of assessment, meaning that human supervision should continue to be included in the evaluation process. Periodic auditing, making grading algorithms transparent and giving students the chance to appeal AI-based scores are parts of the necessary measures to uphold level-ground to level-ground relative equity and academic integrity.(Crompton & Burke, 2023) In a lifecycle view, AI-based assessment systems will have to be constantly monitored and validated after being deployed in the first place. The bias needs to be audited on a regular basis, models need to be recalibrated and human review should be periodically checked to maintain a high level of fairness and accuracy. Integrating the practices into institutional evaluation policies contributes to accountability and ensures the AI-enhanced evaluation is in line with the idea of responsible AI governance.

1.3 Academic Administration: Optimizing Institutional Processes

AI is transforming the very fabric of a higher education establishment and internalizes a broad sweep of admissions to administration tasks. AI is also driving quicker, evidence-based decisions on all aspects of admissions, curriculum management and other aspects contributing to the efficiency of institutions. As an example,

AI-driven admission systems are able to process large amounts of data about the applicants' academic records, personal statements, recommendation letters - within a few minutes and show the patterns and the most promising applicants to the human assessment. On the same note, technology-based scheduling will be able to come up with timetables free of conflict as they might be able to consider the availability of faculty members, course preferences of students, and room assignments more efficiently than manual scheduling. These improvements minimize the load on the administration and provide personnel with the possibility to concentrate on tactical planning and student interaction, as opposed to being engrossed in the predictable, logistical processes(Birks & Clare, 2023). Nonetheless, the growing automation of administrative processes also brings up the question of transparency, explainability and accountability of institutional decision-making. When AI systems get involved in determining admissions, scheduling, or grading results, stakeholders should know how they are made and how errors or biases may be mitigated. Careful administrative AI means that it is well documented, audited, and supervised with a well-structured oversight that oversight ensures that it is in line with institutional values and regulatory requirements.

Besides efficiency, such responsive and more accurate academic planning becomes achieved with the help of AI. Among them, predictive models utilize past and live data to build on courses, or enrolment patterns, and resource planning. AI would help plan the curriculum by highlighting the curriculum gaps or overlap and offering curriculum that fits the needs of the industry or the interests of the students. There is also the less controversial automated grading tools, which are making their way in- This is particularly evident when an instructor has to evaluate a large enrollment course and final evaluation contacts are of paramount importance.(Collins et al., 2021) Although such tools can be effective in quickening the feedback and grading activities, there are significant issues of fairness, bias, and over-using automation to be pointed out amid their usage. However, with the incorporation of reasonable use, AI can reinvent academic administration and drive it towards it becoming a more interactive and responsive as well as student-oriented environment.

1.3.1 The Power of AI Curriculum Planning: Strategic Change in Education Design

The inclusion of AI in the academic planning evolves a strategy of the development and maintenance of educational programs. Curriculum design was traditionally imprecise and cumbersome and dependent on manual input into a review cycle and more often than not anecdotal feedback. A.I. disrupts this relationship by facilitating the possibility of decision-making with data by means of analyzing current market trends, employment opportunities, alumni performance indicators, student success metrics, and course evaluations in real time.(Saaida, 2023) Such AI systems can predict the emergence of new sets of skills in areas such as data science, green technology, or even digital marketing, meaning that it is possible to foresee these skills sets within human committees, requiring several months. Subsequently, educational institutions will have a chance to rethink course curriculums and upgrade them or add new courses or even remove obsolete courses to align with student interests and the profile of the labor market. In addition to determining new focal areas, curriculum planning tools driven through AI can be used to sharpen existing school curricula to make them more efficient and effective. AI can identify overlaps, underperforming courses, or the lack of alignment in the academical progress by analyzing the enrolment patterns, dropout rates, predictive scores, and feedbacks. This can enable instructors and administrators to shift resources in more strategic ways, such as stemming the many electives that are hardly popular, or reprioritizing prerequisites, or assigning faculty.(Birks & Clare, 2023) Moreover, AI-enabling curriculum simulations could model the ripple consequences of curricular reforms on the student workload and graduation schedules so that reforms not only have pedagogical quality but also are pragmatic. In such a manner, AI contributes to the development of dynamic, future-concerned academic environments that could be current in the dynamic and transforming reality of the globe.

1.3.2 Higher Education Scheduling Algorithms

The practice of designing efficient class schedules in institutions of higher education is by all means a very complicated undertaking which demands a compromise of a large number of competing interests. The limited availability of faculty, varying course requirements of students, classroom space and the sequencing of laboratory-based curriculum all have a high degree of interrelating needs that are most frequently conflicting. According to tradition, administrative personnel make use of manual planning or very simple software systems that are hectic and subject to numerous errors. The manual process cannot effectively manage last-minute changes, employee absences, or growths in student enrollment and so on. The academic institutions that become larger and more complex present an even stronger case that traditional scheduling methods cannot adequately address the situations that arise, all the way to learning arbitration due to misalignment of the time line. Scheduling can be an effective solution to this old administrative problem since AI-based scheduling algorithms provide an effective solution to it.(Moya et al., 2024) Such systems are based on an extreme optimization model and machine learning to consider thousands of possible scheduling options on-the-fly. At the same time AI can take a large collection of data such as the workload limits a faculty member can handle simultaneously, the degree progression needs by a student, classroom availability, even the co-curricular schedules in degree progression and identify the possibilities that work, free of any conflict of interest. In contrast to traditional tools of scheduling, the AI-powered solutions will be able to adapt according to the real-time input dynamically. As an example, the algorithm can develop alternative arrangements immediately in the event of unavailability of faculty member or a course becomes full. Other systems even add historical data to estimate bottleneck values and self-correct in relation to them so that over the years, they receive a more efficient efficiency.

The inclusion and personalization of the academic planning are another substantial advantage of the scheduled tools based on AI. They may also be programmed to consider special accommodation arrangements, including teaching classes in day time in case of visual impaired students or that of not giving consecutive lectures to a learner with mobility difficulties. They can also consider limitations of part-time students or they can do scheduling of senior courses where the senior level courses will take place on the last semester in order to promote timely graduation. Thanks to the adaptability of the scheduling logistics to personal needs and the institutional objectives, AI creates a more student-centered learning landscape. Moreover, it decreases the organizational workload on employees, and reduces the attention towards the teaching quality and students.(Birks & Clare, 2023)(E, 2022) Finally, scheduling based on artificial intelligence is a major move towards academic administration modernization and equal treatment of people in providing access to educational opportunities.

1.3.3 AI Grading: Increasing Efficiency and Uniformity of Grading

Grading has been known to be one of the most tedious and routine items of an educators workload taking time that could be used in preparing curriculum or student mentorship, or innovation in pedagogical practices. Another solution to this problem is the usage of AI-assisted grading tools giving rise to the notion of scalable systems that can score huge amounts of student work in a very short period. These programs are particularly successful when used to grade standardized tests, multiple choice and short answer tests, with rules clearly established and distribute keys permitting the high speed, high accuracy evaluation.(Birks & Clare, 2023) In the recent past, however, artificial intelligence has grown to handle more complex tasks (evaluation of essays, open-ended responses, and even creative or analytical assignments) through natural language processing (NLP) and machine learning. These systems read into structure, coherence, grammar, strength of arguments among other characteristics and come up with usable scores or feedback. The potential of AI-supported grading to increase consistency and fairness is considered as one of the strongest benefits of its use in the process. The human grading is still beneficial but largely vulnerable to unconscious bias, fatigue, and inter- or intra-instructor or inter- or intra-time variations. With a more balanced input and calibration by human experts, the AI tools may provide a more consistent application of the grading criteria. This can be also very useful in big classes or in online courses - multiple instructors can grade the same kind of assignments. In addition, AI-powered systems will be able to give immediate feedback to students, which will allow them to learn the correct way by correcting their mistakes literally, instead of waiting days or weeks to get the results. This fast turnaround is used in formative assessment where active learning is encouraged and the academic environment is more engaging and responsive.

1.3.4 Admissions Screening

AI may also improve the speed and data-driven nature of decision in patterns and even correlations of successful applicants to admissions teams, which would increase candidate selection with efficiency and objectivity. Nonetheless, the ethical and social implications related to unfairness, transparency, and bias are also very significant in terms of AI usage in the admission process. When the training data that was used to make AI models are skewed in a certain way like in the past as in the way admissions were made to the school that favored the applicants that had privileged backgrounds whose training data are used then the system can indirectly recreate or even increase those biases. As an illustration, individuals who themselves belong to underrepresented groups, or went to underfunded schools, can suffer discrimination in case the algorithm used in AI puts too much stress on elite education levels or specific extra-curriculum classes that may not be affordable or accessible to all students. Also, privacy, consent and effectiveness of non-academic measures of student potential are raised by the implementation of personality or behavioral profiling tools.

To reduce such risks, it is paramount that admissions systems based on AI should be implemented and designed in such a way that they embody transparency, accountability, and fairness. The use of AI tools in the evaluation process will be a transparency issue to be reported by institutions and applicants should have a chance to appeal or argue decisions based on the algorithms. Proper auditing on a regular basis against bias, having a mix of various data sets to train the model, and final human intervention in decision making are all critical practices. Moreover, it is important that universities involve ethicists, legal professionals, teachers, and community members to design the policies of governing these systems and to make sure that AI is a tool that will provide more inclusion and opportunities, instead of a black box that will only contribute to social inequalities.All these administrative applications show that although AI has the potential to dramatically make institutional activities more efficient and responsive, its ethical implementation requires an open governance system, data practices, and a long-lasting human intervention to avoid exacerbation of existing disparities in the higher education framework.

1.4 Effects of Learning Experience and Teaching

With the introduction of AI to the higher education setting, educational practices are undergoing a paradigm shift towards new roles of pedagogies and the process of instruction. Conventional once where a student was merely receiving information being imparted to him by the instructor in a larger degree through lecture, is transforming to progressively learner centered nature. Adaptive learning This can be done through AI-driven site-based learning platforms, which enable real-time flexibility of content based on the performance of individual students, their rate of learning, and their interests. This has enabled the instructors to get out of the content transmission category as facilitators, guides, and learning designers. Teachers are also free to guide students on the skills of solving puzzling problems, thinking across disciplines or developing soft skills that are human and contextually oriented tasks that machines will not learn. This transition requires not only a technical literacy on the part of faculty but also a re-imagination of pedagogical paradigms that involve the infusion of data-informed practice into the very lifeblood of academic learning. Blended learning model, flipped classrooms, and hybrid pedagogies can be supported significantly in the classroom format and instructional strategy, and these models have also been revolutionized with AI. As an example in case of a flipped classroom, students receive lectures or lessons pre-recorded or machine-selected before materials, and the in-person instruction can be used to discuss in more depth, undertake collaborative tasks, or project-based learning. The Learning analytics dashboard gives educators the kind of detailed information regarding the engagement patterns of students, like the number of hours per module, quiz performance statistics, or modules with elevated dropout rates. Such insights can be used to identify struggling students early and, through them, the faculty can adjust content delivery or suggest tailored resources to address their issues before it is too late. Furthermore, AI aids in Universal Design of Learning (UDL) by providing information in a multimodal format that students with cognitive disabilities or students with a language barrier or various learning styles can easily access by listening to audio narration or reading a text-based resource or walkthrough analysis or even by participating in a simulation. In general, AI-based pedagogical frameworks can increase the efficiency of learning by transforming the process of instructional delivery to responsiveness to learners and refinement of the instructions through feedback. By applying AI sensibly, it can assist instructors to determine areas of weaknesses in learning, create instructional methods that are inclusive, and develop cognitive skills that are not rote memorized. The success of such models is, however, based on the willingness of the faculty, the ethical application of learner data, and the institutional support systems that make AI the supplement of pedagogical autonomy, not a limitation. Although identifying the reasons for the job vacancy is difficult, one can infer that the employer seeks skilled personnel to work across various sectors of the hotel industry.Even though it is hard to determine the causes of the vacancy, it can be assumed that the employer needs qualified individuals who can work in different areas of the hotel sector.

1.5 Ethical and Operational Governance of AI in Higher Education

As AI technologies continue to penetrate the sphere of academic decisions, universities should develop well-defined ethical and working governance systems. Such mechanisms can be used to safeguard the academic integrity, fairness, and trust of the stakeholders through the establishment of the acceptable scope, limitations, and accountability frameworks when using AI in education. Devoid of such governance, the swift introduction of AI poses a threat to strengthen inequities, blur the decision-making procedures, and diminish trust in the institutional practice. (Fowler, 2023; Oh & Sanfilippo, 2024)

With the growing integration of Artificial Intelligence (AI) technologies in virtually all aspects of the teaching and running of institutions of higher learning, ethical and functional considerations have come to take center stage in academic discussions.. Such guidelines should not only dictate what constitutes ethical or unethical use of AI in academic work but should also give an outline of how far AI systems can and should be allowed to make or influence important decisions of the institution, such as grading, course recommendation, or status. Without this set of ethical and operational standards, the universities run the risk of creating a culture of confusion, disparity, and the loss of trust. Institutions should therefore be proactive in the formulation of blanketed policies which keep at par with the trend in technology and the practicality of the age-old principles of higher learning.

The universities should design the policies of using the AI, which stipulate:

- **Which kinds of AI apps can be used in an assignment?**

There are now more options than ever before with the introduction of generative AI tools such as ChatGPT, DALL·E, and GitHub Copilot, which allow students to get help in accomplishing school assignments. This leads to an ethical issue of supreme importance: are there possible AI helpers that do not undermine academic integrity? Colleges have to make their boundaries with regard to what constitutes support and what amounts to unethical behavior. To put it into perspective, such pursuits as brainstorming outlines or rephrasing difficult text with the help of an AI tool may be permissible, but another behavior, such as handing in an AI-generated text without proper acknowledgement, may fall under the label of academic dishonesty. Policies must differentiate between the following: assistive and substitute use of AI as one involves the improvement of the thinking process of a student, and the latter, the replacement of the thought process all together. Moreover, guidelines should be subject specific; that is, application of AI to creative writing can be vastly different as compared to coding or mathematics. Setting clear rules and examples allows institutions to prevent confusion and make sure that students use AI tools in a responsible way and in a transparent manner.

- **The application of AI in grading and assessment How AI is used in grading and assessment**

The grading tools built on AI have such large-scale benefits in terms of speed, repetition, and consistency. Yet, they should be strictly controlled not to provide unjust results and maintain the educational standards. Institutions need to explain the use of AI in grading and in what areas and how, a way that involves using AI in grading objective items and not on assignments and papers that need initial marking. More to the point, they should be informed when learning is assessed by another AI program, and one should provide feedback on the assessment so that individual students know how marking is performed. When it comes to high-stakes situations, like final exams or thesis evaluation, AI should not substitute the human judgment as a whole. Where assessment is based on the collaboration of artificial intelligence but not controlled by it, so-called hybrid models are more ethical and productive. Faculty must be prepared to give AI-generated insights a critical look and not take them at face value. Openness, explainability, and the right to challenge the assessments grounded in AI should be primary characteristics of the grading policy schemes.

- **Rationality of AI choice in admissions or academic result**

AI tools have become prominent in the automation of screening admission cases, screening scholarship applications, and even student progression toward degree accomplishment. Although such systems make work more efficient, they conceal the process of decision-making, particularly in instances when algorithms are viewed as the unintelligible black boxes. Universities must have transparency rules revealing the means and timing of the role of AI in admissions or academic status so that fairness and trust can be maintained. A person should have the right to an explanation and to challenge decision makers, and applicants must be told whether their material is to be scored by algorithms and have the inability to see the result. Likewise, the learners with academic risk identified by predictive models must be informed about the terms of reference and given human mediated remedies as opposed to authenticated punishments.

1.6 Collaborative Human–AI Ecosystems in Higher Education

The emphasis in no case should be made on how to incorporate AI into the current frameworks, but rather how to reinvent the academic community as a co-evolutionary zone. In this case, AI and human actors are in a continuous cycle of learning about each other, improve the processes, and co-create learning value. Ideal New Ecosystems such as these must be planned, interdisciplinary, ethically minded, and they promise a more individualized, inclusive, and progressive future landscape of higher education altogether. Facilities engaging in it are not just safeguarding themselves against the future, they are shaping it actively.

1.6.1 AI Literacy for Educators and Staff

Literacy in AI is becoming a valuable skill in the changing situation in higher education. faculty and other personnel in the institutions. Introduced with the aid of artificial intelligence, it is possible the evaluation procedure, the curriculum structure, assessment systems and even student analytics engagement, and it is also imperative that academic staff are not just in possession of working knowledge. The conceptual level of literacy must contain a far deeper level of probable knowing what the artificial intelligence systems would be like, and what their limitations would be the application in schools and education issues in general and the ethics of their application. those endeavor's. The redesign of the faculty development programs should be in this way to provide holistic, interdisciplinary education that will allow teachers to accept AI as securely and efficiently as possible. Some of the primary foundational elements, which such programs ought to have, including explanations of how and why these are crucial, are provided below:

- **Get to know Machine Learning and Generative AI Models:** Teacher's ought to be exposed to the fundamental context of a machine learning (ML) and generative AI, i.e. the technologies that underpin systems like ChatGPT, Grammarly, and automatic assessment tools. This includes learning how such models are trained using the large datasets to find similarities and draw conclusions on them or produce texts and similar output. The significance of this fact is that, in the absence of specialized knowledge in this area, teachers can blindly trust the insides of the AI and not realize that it is being done on a provisional basis, on the quality of the information used. Let us say, a generative AI could work out grammatically correct but factually wrong papers that could be misleading not only the instructors but also the students. Being aware of what the difference between supervised, unsupervised, and reinforcement learning entails, also empowers an educator to inculcate the difference between the AI use cases (e.g., personalized learning vs. predictive analytics).

- **Algorithm and Data Representation Bias:** Algorithmic bias is one of the most urgent problems in AI and it may arise due to biased training sets, faulty assumptions, or the lack of representation. The teachers have to educate themselves on how bias can exist within the AI systems employed in the classrooms either as a biased grading system, unfair predictive model of student grades, biased natural language tools, etc. What is important: Faculty who are ignorant about ways in which biases are embedded in algorithms can perpetuate educational disparities without actually intending to do so. The example that can be given is a writing assessment tool that disadvantages students who do not write in English as their first language or a predictive risk model that targets students because of their socioeconomic background. Unethical not only that it is unfair. AI literacy should assist educators with identifying, challenging, and preventing such risks both in the selection of a tool and its use in the classroom.
- **Appraising AI Outputs in terms of Accuracy and Relevance**: Not everything produced by AI is truthful, in its context, or edifying. Teachers are going to have to be prepared to take a critical approach to the quality of the AI outputs and to know the difference between deceiving, or over generic content and results with pedagogical relevance. Why it matters: A lot of AI generators prioritize consistency or eloquence rather than accuracy or teaching, and, therefore, it is likely that the things they will say are lies. It will be possible that an AI raises plausible-sounding yet false information, particularly in areas where it is important to know precise information (such as in medicine, law, or history). Faculty should be the informed assessors who make sure that students are not confused by AI tools, and that the materials developed on the basis of AI or the assessment produced by it are adequate to the learning goals.

AI literacy among teachers empowers them to be more critical with automated recommendations, create assessments to maintain academic integrity and teach students to use AI responsibly. As soon as faculty is given both technical knowledge and ethical sensibility, AI will be a pedagogical tool and not a disruptor. Continuous professional development as an institutional investment in higher education is thus the focus of sustainable AI adoption in higher education. Through understanding how other businesses work, one can understand how they will operate Teachers will be at an advantage of being able to make assessment forms that are effective and, simultaneously, are scholarly. They will also be placed in a better position not to blindly follow AI-suggestions and not be dependent on automated systems.

1.6.2 Student Dual Literacy Technical and Ethical

In the age of generative AI, students must also be equipped not only with the way to work with AI tools effectively; they must also understand what are the ethical consequences of its use. This blend of skills referred to as dual literacy is what is required to survive in a climate of higher education started to be dominated by the advent of intelligent systems. Technical literacy allows students can make good use of AI technologies, and ethical judgment can enable them to make a choice of how to operate tools in pertinent and correct manners that are accountable. Lacking the capacity to The development of either of the 2 facets of literacy can be abused, overused or even cheated Therefore, it is not just a matter of competencies when it comes to developing two literacies establishment, and yet one of the basic plans of making responsible students and future practice professionals. There are five critical dimensions of dual literacy which are discussed below.

subpoints:

- Robotical reliance on AI-driven technologies, such as ChatGPT, Grammarly and GitHub Copilot must not be confused with the successful usage of such tools. in the course of learning; rather, it amounts to intelligent and judicious assimilation. Despite the fact that these tools produce immense benefits such as the backing of the language. structure, syntax and conciseness, and assistance in the code process, it is not to be. deemed as a final instrument that suits all. Students have to know all the details of the purpose and the restrictions of each tool: e.g. Grammarly, is capable of correcting syntax and the fineness of style, but incapable of verifying the logical soundness and deepness of the argument. In the same manner, GitHub Copilot can automate the code snippets, which are not necessarily aligned with best practices without critical review of the user. The effective exploitation of such tools includes the involvement with their products as recommendations, but not definitive responses. That is editing, polishing, and situating AI-written material to suit academic requirements and personal styles of expression and learning. By not being taken as weapons used to avoid the intellectual process but instead being viewed as supplements to the brainstorming, revision, or debugging processes, the tools will help us to learn the material better and to take charge of our own educational progress without undermining the originality of our work.

- When AI-generated response is trivial or biased or wrong, being able to recognize it is one of the central ideas of responsible and successful academic AI use. Even when AI tools will deliver content organized in a well-structured and grammatically correct format, it will most likely not have the depth, contextual sensitivity as well as the factual reliability of the content that is being delivered in higher education. Their constraints can be attributed to the fact that they were trained using large but flawed datasets that can contain either outdated data, implicit biases, or incomplete viewpoints. Consequently, they should be instructed to develop the habit of interrogating AI output when this is required where the assignments need to appeal to facts or critical thinking. This will involve fact-checking assertions stated by AI with the use of credible sources using academic research, checking to see whether the content created actually makes use of the specific requirements of the prompt, and being cautious of the slightest instrence of bias- such as stereotypical language, or cultural insensitivity- especially in the fields that are related to history, ethics, or social justice. Developing such critical appraisal skills would make students less pussy in front of AI as a person in charge, but rather using it as a mere device with its recommendations that should be investigated, improved, or even discarded in case they are inferior to the academic quality. Refusal means not only a failure to achieve academic results but also the imposition of warped worldviews by-passing criticism, hence a dilution of the role of education in being a producer of informed ethical thinkers.
- We are aware that I do not in any real sense perceive context or meanings, but only guesses likely streeweries of words or consequences, basing its guesses on past experience. AI is good at pattern recognition, predictive text and summarizing, but not as good at human values in an emotional context, in subtle judgment and in profound creativity. Although AI can be used to produce a well-formatted essay or present solution that can be used to solve a problem within a certain timeframe, such practice cannot be used in disciplines like philosophy, literature, or social work among others, since humans have the crucial understanding that cannot be replaced by a machine. It is necessary that the students should know that: We know that AI does not in any real sense understand context or meaning, it merely predicts probable sequences of words or outcomes based upon past evidence. It is best left to humans to carry out the tasks that require empathy (e.g., writing a reflective journal), moral-ethical judgment (e.g., case analysis), or an innovative form of synthesis (e.g., development of a unique theory). Excessive use of AI in this regard can result in hollow and boilerplate entries and lost opportunities to develop

intellectually. By being aware of such constraints, learners will be able to make instrumental choices concerning when the use of AI might be useful in their work and when they need to abandon abstractions in favor of actual human thought.

- Blind reliance on AI recommendations, failing to interrogate or edit such advice, may stimulate the degradation of the integrity of a submissive, even jeopardizing the superficial of academic compliances. To eliminate this, the students ought to be advised or even be compelled to reveal the manner in which AI tools were applied when learning or writing in an institution that observes strict transparency rates. This could be in the form of written statements about AI use or the presence of drafts with revision notes and short reflections on assignments with an explanation of how the student interacted with AI-generated text. These practices should not only help students to build ownership over their work and acquire skills of metacognition but also help to preserve the academic integrity. Through such reflective activity, teachers enable students to get over their passive consumption of machine-produced products.
- In order to successfully teach dual literacy to students, teaching AI has to become an intrinsic part of the curriculum and needs to be introduced already at the first year of study. This integration would eliminate a situation where students who study the sciences, humanities, business, and the arts receive differing knowledge and ethical standards to help them survive in an AI-powered world, both within and outside the classroom. Institutions can integrate AI literacy into foundational courses like first-year seminars, general education requirements, or online workshops in digital competencies and in this way make responsible AI engagement a more normal practice. Some of the fundamental elements of such curricular integration can consist of practical workshops that would help students learn to ethically use such tools as ChatGPT, Grammarly, or Copilot, assignments that would have students evaluate the work of a human being and AI-generated one critically, and the case-based discussions that would focus on an actual ethical dilemma related to AI and education or the work sphere. Moreover, exercises that would ask the challenge students to enhance or explain some of the AI results so that they can work on them understanding of the functioning of AI and its limitations. By inculcating these into the early studies of a student, one brings in a culture of critical reflection, introspection and culpability. More importantly, it places students to continue with their academic thinking of their future professional life where the Full understanding of AI, both technical and ethical is already reaching the status of an occupational standard.

Learning to be dual literate would also assist students to strain through AI learning environments developments in critical reflexivity, responsibility, and intellectual autonomy. Instead of discouraging AI implementation, colleges should train students to use that equipment in a critical and receptive approach, ensuring that the human judgment is central to the academic research and career development.

1.6.3 Engagement and the Inclusion of Stakeholders

This is because the effective application of AI tools in universities is not limited to advanced technology but it must also be relevant, its tasks should be easily used, and adhere to ethical standards of the university. Participatory design can be one of the best ways to make certain these qualities owing to its approach of involving key stakeholders, such as educators, students, administrators, and technologists, in the design, testing, and deployment activities of AI systems. This is in contrast to a top-down approach to implementation whereby the implementation team makes decisions unilaterally, in a vacuum, leading to the placement of tools in the environment that do not reflect the real needs or processes end-users encounter in their day-to-day operations. Participatory design makes contextual appropriateness, greater adoption, and a sense of co-ownership and responsibility possible. The main benefits of participatory design during the implementation of AI are provided below with further details on each point explained after them

- It is said that AI tools that are not developed with the in-depth knowledge of the practical aspects of life in educational institutions are destined to lack much-needed functionality or generate meaningless information output. Because teachers will encounter varied challenges based on the size of the classroom, the topic or subject teaches, the teaching method, and the demography of learners, the work is a challenging one. Faculty involvement in designing AI tools will make them sensitive to such variables. As the example of the AI grading assistant that works on humanities subject can show, any given system needs to understand the value of subtle argument and language tonality, which may not be felt by the developers who may be more familiar with the sciences. By allowing teachers to participate in the design of tools, designers have the ability to shape the characteristics and aspects of how the tool can feedback a student, the grading rubric or the line of questioning in an assignment; thus focusing on making the technology truly assist in the learning process as opposed to making things more complex.
- Artificial intelligence in education cannot be introverted and innervated in the vacuum of education objectives; they need to be created as an aid to support and bridge learning outputs of the institution. The use of AI tools can be

embedded into larger pedagogical structures and accreditation guidelines, by engaging the curriculum designers, departmental heads, and academic governance institutions with the development process. As an example, an AI-based assessment system should make sure that it would evaluate such competences as critical thinking or problem-solving, or ethical reasoning, the results that are usually highlighted in the institutional mission statements. In the absence of alignment, there exists a danger that the AI will place more importance on superficial measures of success (e.g., speed or correctness) as opposed to more fundamental educational goals. Through participatory design, a deliberate alignment of AI measures with what institutions seek to educate in the first place becomes possible.

- Make sure that on LBC-Surveillance, Fairness, Personalization Student Concerns are put in On the part of the student, there may be grave concerns over the issue of privacy, fairness, and biasness of the algorithms with regards to AI tools particularly those that are used in the activities of behavior monitoring and performance evaluation. In the example above, attendance monitoring, keystroke monitoring, or emotional cues through learning analytics platforms can be viewed as intrusive, particularly when the learning analytics is introduced without the consent or even without an appropriate description. Such concerns can be expressed through participatory design in which students have a say on the implementation and, shape the collection, storage and utilization of data. Examples of features that can be advocated by students include data dashboards that spell out how their behavior is analyzed, or options to opt in or out of tracking options of certain kinds. How the developers can determine what can be considered personalization, and what might be intrusive or even manipulative can also be determined by including students.
- Build Trust in it Making it Open and Having the Responsibilities Shared Possibly, the greatest result of participatory design is trust between institutions and their scholarly societies, which it creates. By engaging stakeholders in AI design, it is more likely that they will know the purpose of the tool and how it can operate and what precautions are in that area. This openness minimizes distrust and concerns which are ambient in situations involving AI based grading, plagiarism scanning, or admission screening. Responsibility also implies shared responsibility such that in case of failings or judgement could be managed as opposed to defensively. In the case of a predictive analytics tool incorrectly labeling a student as being at risk, the involvement of the students and the faculty in its design will give them the outlet that they need to give it feedback and adjustments. An outsider can come to effectively

trust an insider not by his (or her) perfection, but by his (or her) openness and accountability which are the central principles of participatory design.

1.7 Future Prospects and Problems

The future of AI in higher education is on the verge of redefining itself, and here the multimodal nature of the AI systems that have the potential to interpret and react to the text, voice, images, and flows of information simultaneously, are at the center of the development. Such breakthroughs will allow the establishment of the most immersing and adaptive learning environments, which will include simulation-based activities like virtual laboratories, intelligent examples, and emotionally responsive AI tutors. (Aler Tubella et al., 2024). of utmost importance, the ongoing trend toward AI in education and evaluation should not bring harm to academic freedom or the choice of students. AI was to be used in education to support, not to substitute, human judgment, creativity, and inquiry. Proactive action against such issues can help institutions to develop an academic future that is driven by the presence of AI helping to improve the learning process without disrupting the ethics of equity, freedom, and sustainability.

CONCLUSION

The role of AI in higher education is improving by leaps and bounds and is being applied to the whole academic life, including the involvement of the learners with the knowledge and the organization of the operation of the institutions.(Neumann et al., 2023) At least on one hand, AI gives teachers tools of individualized teaching, immediate response and dispensable evaluation that accommodate personal learning style and requirements. On the one hand, it provides support in improving administrative tasks that are time-consuming, including scheduling, screening of admissions, and grading, thereby making key institutional decisions available to support and nurture students. Although it has such opportunity to transform higher education, the implementation of AI in the field should be treated with hesitation and considerations. Institutions should place particular emphasis on the values that underlie academic work: equity, so that no student is left behind during the digital transition, transparency, so that the AI systems have been made understandable and their decisions explicable, and responsibility, where the developers and the users of such systems remain accountable to the ethical use of such systems. Universities thus need to formulate review committees or ethics boards which will be tasked with periodically evaluating the effects of AI tools on the teaching, learning and assessment practices. These institutions are possible to play an important role in overseeing unintended consequences, responding to the emergent biases, and providing timely adjustments to institutional guidelines. Moreover, the cooperation between the institutions, both domestically and internationally, may aid the formulation of common norms and best practices in using responsible AI. This sort of group work can serve to make them less fragmented, more interoperable, and to make sure that the ethical considerations take center stage as AI technologies continue to evolve. With a flexible, accountable, and collaborative approach to AI governance frameworks, institutions of higher learning will be able to improve the alignment between technological innovation and enduring academic goals and social obligations.

REFERENCES

Aler Tubella, A., Mora-Cantallops, M., & Nieves, J. C. (2024). How to teach responsible AI in Higher Education: Challenges and opportunities. *Ethics and Information Technology, 26*(1), 1–14. DOI: 10.1007/s10676-023-09733-7

. Barus, O. P., Hidayanto, A. N., Handri, E. Y., Sensuse, D. I., & Yaiprasert, C. (2025). Shaping generative AI governance in higher education: Insights from student perception. *International Journal of Educational Research Open, 8*(December 2024), 100452. DOI: 10.1016/j.ijedro.2025.100452

Birks, D., & Clare, J. (2023). Linking artificial intelligence facilitated academic misconduct to existing prevention frameworks. *International Journal for Educational Integrity, 19*(1), 1–10. DOI: 10.1007/s40979-023-00142-3

Crompton, H., & Burke, D. (2023). Artificial intelligence in higher education: The state of the field. *International Journal of Educational Technology in Higher Education, 20*(1), 22. Advance online publication. DOI: 10.1186/s41239-023-00392-8

. E, V. O. L. U. M. (2022). Research Trends in Multidisciplinary Research. In *Research Trends in Multidisciplinary Research*. DOI: 10.22271/ed.book.2005

Evangelista, E. D. L. (2025). Ensuring academic integrity in the age of ChatGPT: Rethinking exam design, assessment strategies, and ethical AI policies in higher education. *Contemporary Educational Technology, 17*(1), 1–19. DOI: 10.30935/cedtech/15775

Fowler, D. S. (2023). AI in Higher Education. *Journal of Ethics in Higher Education, 3*(3), 127–143. DOI: 10.26034/fr.jehe.2023.4657

Moya, B., Eaton, S., Pethrick, H., Hayden, A., Brennan, R., Wiens, J., & McDermott, B. (2024). Academic Integrity and Artificial Intelligence in Higher Education (HE) Contexts: A Rapid Scoping Review. *Canadian Perspectives on Academic Integrity, 7*(3), 59–75. DOI: 10.55016/ojs/cpai.v7i3.78123

Nailah, W., & Syahiza, A. (2023). Influence of Psychological Well-Being and School Factors on Delinquency, During the Covid-19 Period Among Secondary School Students in Selected Schools in Nakuru County : Kenya. [IJRISS]. *International Journal of Research and Innovation in Social Science, VII*(2454), 1175–1189. DOI: 10.47772/IJRISS

Neumann, M., Rauschenberger, M., & Schon, E. M. (2023). "We Need To Talk About ChatGPT": The Future of AI and Higher Education. *Proceedings - 2023 IEEE/ACM 5th International Workshop on Software Engineering Education for the Next Generation, SEENG 2023*, 29–32. DOI: 10.1109/SEENG59157.2023.00010

Oh, S. H., & Sanfilippo, M. (2024). University Governance for Responsible AI. *Proceedings of the ALISE Annual Conference*. DOI: 10.21900/j.alise.2024.1706

Saaida, M. B. E. (2023). AI-Driven transformations in higher education: Opportunities and challenges. *International Journal of Educational Research and Studies*, *5*(1), 29–36. www.multidisciplinaryarticle.org

Chapter 5
AI Risk and Resolution in Higher Education and Academic Integrity

Karthik Srinivasan
http://orcid.org/0000-0002-9822-2060
Saudi Electronic University, Saudi Arabia

M. Azhagiri
http://orcid.org/0000-0002-6124-3773
SRM Institute of Science and Technology, India

A. Rajesh
http://orcid.org/0000-0002-8812-5697
FET, Jain (Deemed to be) University, Bangalore, India

ABSTRACT

The integration of AI in education opens new horizons to enhance the management of classroom and assist teachers with learning aids. The study will focus on the application of popular machine learning algorithm, XGBoost model for analyzing students' data. The target is to predict student's engagement, detect which learners are at risk with the goal of prescribing a targeted intervention. The authors selected XGBoost because of its capability to handle complex and nonlinear data as well as its encouraging predictive power in offering teachers the possibility to identify problem areas early on and cater for individual learning needs. Student attendance, participation, submitted homework on time and previous academic performance were all significant predictors of risk. These learnings provide important guidance for teachers to adjust both instruction and classroom strategies, as well as underscore the critical nature of intuitive AI tools, data security and ethics in education.

DOI: 10.4018/979-8-3373-5586-3.ch005

INTRODUCTION

AI in Education

Artificial Intelligence (AI) has become an influential technology in education, shaping both learning and teaching practices. Many educators believe AI opens the door to provide personalized learning options based on the content, speed, spread, and level of challenge depending on how a student is performing and how able they are. For example, Duolingo and Khan Academy incorporate learning theories to recommend exercises and lessons that best suit individual students. Another significant contribution is that both platforms function as Intelligent Tutoring Systems (ITS), when designed appropriately, they can function as virtual tutors since it can provide students with instant feedback, explanations and hints when the learner hits a wall (Zhai et al, 2021).

Educational institutions have increasingly adopted AI through automated grading and assessment where AI uses algorithms to grade assessments so teachers can save time and educators are provided more rapid responses to quizzes, essays and coding assignments. Educational institutions have also adopted AI-powered chatbots and virtual assistants to support students with 24/7 support, respond to students' questions, prompt students of deadlines, and collect and provide study materials for students to support their ongoing learning out of the classroom. Finally, AI is also positively influencing accessibility and inclusivity with its use for real-time language translation, converting text to speech functions for blind and visually impaired learners, or immersive readers for students with dyslexia.

AI-driven gamification enhances learning by transforming lessons into engaging game-based activities. Also, with all of the benefits AI has for education, there come challenges with AI in education such as data privacy risks, expensive implementations, and the potential for students becoming too reliant on technology (Kurni et al, 2023). However, if used purposefully, AI has the potential to change the landscape of education by making learning more efficient, engaging, and available to all people. Additionally, AI not only helps teachers in their tasks but also grants students the ability to learn at their own pace, which can make education more effective and future-ready (Schiff, 2022).

Figure 1 illustrates how interaction and personalization enabled by artificial intelligence can enhance classroom learning. Artificial intelligence in education employs several important practices to enhance learning. Machine learning helps analyze student achievement in order to appropriately adjust lessons and content. When it comes to individualized learning, each student can engage with instruction designed around their learning style, obstacles and pace. Natural language processing supports AI's ability to understand and respond to student questions in natural language which improves interactions. Lastly, Intelligent tutoring systems provide real-time support and feedback by simulating one-on-one instruction. Together, they provide a more efficient, tailored and engaging learning environment.

Figure 1. AI in Education (Author's own illustration)

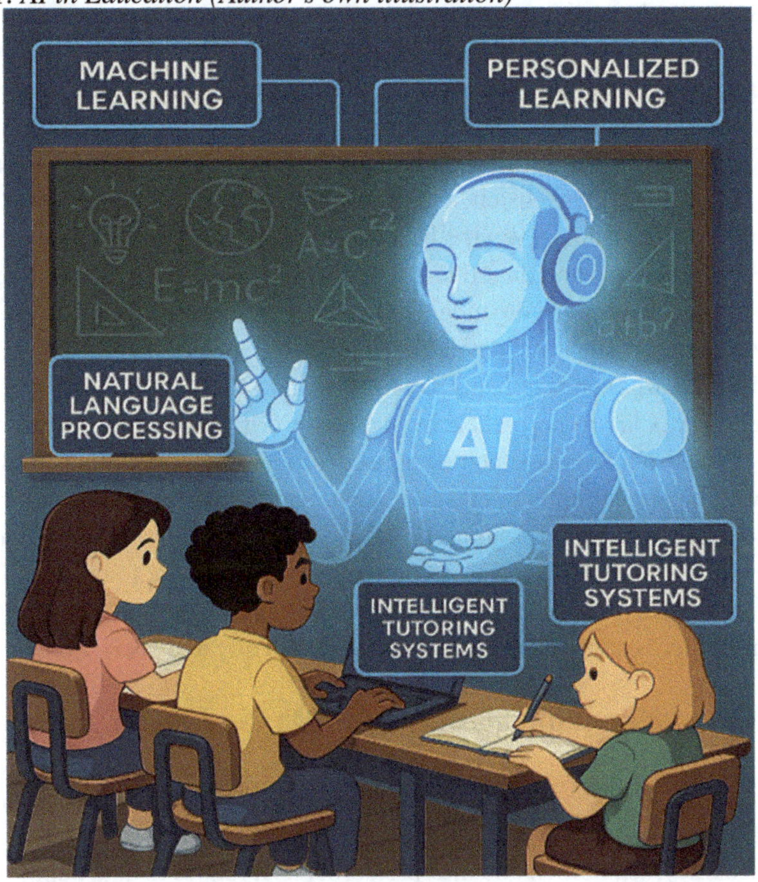

Why Classroom Management Matters?

Classroom management is one of the key components of effective teaching because it shapes how much students learn and how well the classroom runs. A well-structured and organized classroom provides a positive learning environment for students and allows them to learn in a safe environment. Clear rules, routines, and expectations help students understand acceptable behaviour and can help minimize distractions and disruptions. This maximizes the time spent on actual teaching and learning activities compared to managing discipline.

Effective classroom management also establishes fairness and equity, ensuring that all students, regardless of background or ability, have a chance to learn without interruption. Classroom management aids in the establishment of productive teacher-student relationships based on trust and respect. Students are more likely to be engaged and responsible if a strong relationship with the instructor is developed. Classroom management also supports students in their social and emotional development by promoting values such as teamwork, self-control, and accountability. Effective classroom management allows lesson plans to be implemented successfully because students can focus, listen, and follow directions. Poor management, on the other hand, can undermine even the best lesson plans and cause students to reflect on their personal focus and directives. A well-organized, managed classroom provides structure and support for students to gain academically, sensitizes students to encourage positive behavioral development, diminishes teacher and student stress, and cultivates learner engagement (Kunter et al, 2007).

In summary, Classroom management plays a critical role in educational success. Good classroom management enhances the learning environment and overall educational experience for students, who can benefit from the structure, support, and anticipation provided through effective, strategic, and intentional classroom management approaches. Good classroom management is the foundation for a rewarding, constructive, beneficial, and fun learning experience for all students while establishing success with their peers, both academically and socially.

Why XGBoost specifically for Class Management?

Extreme Gradient Boosting (XGBoost) has emerged as an effective machine learning algorithm for addressing complex classroom management challenges because of its high accuracy, scalability, and interpretability as it relates to data being handled. The complexity around classroom management and prediction problems such as predicting student behaviors, performance, and engagement patterns, often include large, imbalanced datasets involving many students from different and vulnerable groups (e.g., special education students, minimum/lower-income students), among other contextual factors (Asselman et al, 2023). XGBoost is particularly suitable for educational predictive analytics because it performs effectively on structured educational data. Also, it provides new insights to structured educational data, handle missing and null values, and regularization to minimize overfitting all in the consideration of educational ontology. Recent studies have shown that XGBoost often outperforms traditional models (logistic regression, random forest, etc.) in predicting student performance and risk of dropout (Chen, & Guestrin, 2016).

XGBoost is a particularly effective tool for classroom management because of its versatility, combining multiple variables—attendance, participation, assessment scores, and behavioral indicators—when creating an early warning system (Altabrawee et al., 2019). In addition, XGBoost produces feature importance outputs, which educators are able to use to pinpoint features related to classroom management, such as, the number of times a student participates or whether a student is submitting assignments (Al Luhaybi, 2021). This level of interpretability is important for teachers so they can take action rather than relying on a black-box model. Because of its parallel processing and scalability, XGBoost also makes sense to suit large datasets as education moves toward digitized classrooms (Oyedotun et al., 2025). Overall, we argue that XGBoost is especially useful for classroom management because it provides not only much larger predictive powers than its peer models, but also is able to provide information that teachers can use to modify their teaching practices (and hence students' classroom outcomes).

Scope and objectives

The scope of AI-Powered Classroom Management and Teaching Support system with XGBoost encompasses the transformation of traditional teaching practices into data-driven, adaptive and efficient practices. This includes predictive analytics on student performance, early detection of learning difficulties, real-time analyses of student engagement, and automated feedback. Utilizing XGBoost's high accuracy and interpretability, the system can work with the variety of educational information available, such as attendance patterns, participation sequences, assessments, and behavior patterns, to provide educators with meaningful feedback. The scope also focuses on inclusion, scalability of solution for educators, and evidence-based decision making for both teachers and students. The objectives are listed as below,

1. Predict Student Performance - Leverage XGBoost predictive capabilities to provide educators information on how to forecast academic performance and provide early warning on students that are at-risk of not meeting academic outcomes.
2. Increase Classroom Engagement - Analyze participants in classroom activities pedagogically, while persona based data can encourage personalized and best next actions to support student learning.
3. Automate Routine Administrative Tasks - Mitigate educators administrative hardships by automating grading, feedback, and attendance data in classroom activities.

4. Provide Educators Actionable Insights - Provide easily interpret reports that identify most important of attributes that influence student success.
5. Support Inclusive Education - The AI-Powered Classroom Management and Teaching Support system with XGBoost will provide robust automated recommendations designed to support accessibility to students with an array of learning tasks and needs.
6. Empower Educators - Enable educators the ability to make informed and data-driven decisions to improve their approach to teaching methodologies and pedagogies.

LITERATURE REVIEW

Classroom Management Systems

A Classroom Management System is a platform or set of tools that an instructor can use to build, observe, and organize classroom activities. It privileges technology and methodology in an effort to engage students, improve student behavior, foster collaboration, and impact student learning.

The study of Chung, C., & Ackerman, D. (2015) established a few parameters for how students with different learning styles reacted to the use of Moodle, a classroom management technology. The study examined students' dispositions towards an organizational tool in support of their coursework, to access learning resources, and to support their learning. The findings show that although many students felt flexible and convenient using Moodle, their satisfaction and engagement with learning within the platform might have depended on their preferred learning styles and prior experiences with technology. The findings do emphasize that findings are tethered to Moodle and may not translate with the same effectiveness were the educational experiences to be recreated with Google Classroom or Blackboard.

Another study of Chicioreanu, T. D., & Cosma, I. (2017) provides a comparison between Google Classroom and Moodle as a classroom management and learning environment. The authors' aim is to describe, differentiate, and identify features, usability, and whether or not the platforms work appropriately for teachers in this digital age. The comparison between the two systems highlighted the strengths of both. For instance, Google Classroom's usability and integration with Google tools versus Moodle's flexibility, one-of-a-kind customizability, range of learning system functionally, and features such as communication between teacher to student. This study is beneficial to educators by helping them think through the system (if any) that meets their teaching needs.

Further the study conducted by Lima, D. A., & Isotani, S. (2021) offers a systematic literature review on the use of Google Classroom as a Learning Management System (LMS) in online education during the period of the Covid-19 pandemic. The authors review multiple research studies to assess the challenges, constraints, effectiveness and solutions of Google Classroom used in an online or blended learning environment. The focus of the study on the challenges faced during the pandemic limits the study of the long-term use of the platform.

The study conducted by Gumasing et al, (2023) investigates and evaluates the usability of three Learning Management Systems (LMSs): Blackboard, Google Classroom and Canvas using a systematic usability assessment. The authors assessed how learners and instructors utilized the learning platforms in terms of four attributes: ease of use, efficiency, learnability and satisfaction. The results of the research demonstrate the strengths and weaknesses of each LMS and highlight which LMS's are most suited for online teaching and learning. One limitation of the study is that it only assessed the usability factors of LMSs and did not take into consideration more salient factors such as cost, scalability, and integration with other platforms.

Machine Learning Approaches to Classroom Analytics

Machine Learning (ML) in Classroom Analytics is characterized by the continued use of data-based algorithms to analyze, predict, and utilize student data to help improve teaching and ensure better student learning outcomes. This can be achieved by collecting all available data from Learning Management Systems (LMS), assessments, attendance, participation, and student behaviors to analyze classroom interactions. Machine Learning is a valuable way to conduct data-driven classroom analytics, which is based on predicting performance, clustering learners, personalizing content, and enhancing teaching approaches for better efficiency in student-centred learning.

This study (Moubayed, 2018) assessed how ML and Data Analytics could help with assessing some of the viable challenges of e-learning. The authors considered challenges such as student engagement, personalization of content, assessment of outcomes, and student dropout prediction. Within this work they utilized a range of methods, including Decision Trees, SVM, Random Forest, and Logistic Regression, in order to predict performance and successful course completion. They reviewed a variety of ML and data analytics methods that have been used to enhance some e-learning platforms, including methods such as predictive modelling, clustering learners, recommending, and real-time analytics. They noticed that this work principally focused on technical ML solutions and less on realistic implementation challenges within different education contexts. Importantly to note, the work primarily presents studies already conducted in the field rather than new experimental work.

Another study conducted by Virvou (2019) delivered an overview of machine learning paradigms utilized in learning analytics. Specifically, the study examined how machine learning techniques facilitated, managed, and analyzed educational data, to inform teaching and learning practices, personalize learning experiences for students as well as predicted student outcomes based on that data. The authors discussed various ways to implement machine learning procedures including supervised learning, unsupervised learning, and reinforcement learning and how these processes provide educators, learners, and policymakers with in-depth data-driven analysis. This body of work illuminated the application(s) of machine learning in education and learning analytics, as well as trends and future directions of research.

Guo (2021) developed a classroom teaching model used in a university level course teaching model utilizing decision tree analysis as derived learning patterns on teaching with decision tree analysis and machine learning with collected classroom data. Decision tree analysis conducted on the data found key factors affecting student performance as well as predicted outcomes. The model served to expand classroom teachers understanding of data, which lead them to selective teaching strategies and informed classroom management decisions. Albeit this study concentrated mainly on decision tree analysis as model it did little to compare the machine learning model with other machine learning models.

The research (Baran, 2023) delineated the design and execution of an automated classroom analytics system. It was mostly about getting teachers, students, and administrators involved in figuring out what the most important metrics were and how to map classroom activities. The system gathered and looked at data to give ideas on how to make teaching more effective and get students more involved. The research employed Decision Trees and Random Forest to forecast student engagement and performance. It was only about one implementation, so it wasn't easy to apply to other schools. It was hard to get enough labeled data for supervised learning in real classrooms.

While many Artificial Intelligence (AI) and machine learning models have been utilized to support classrooms and teaching, there are limitations in the approaches related to accuracy, scalability, and interpretability or explainability. For example, deep learning models usually achieve high accuracy of prediction with low explainability, and traditional machine learning models, such as support vector machine (SVM) or Decision Trees, are poor-performing models when educational dataset are large and imbalanced. Similarly, there has been very little research using gradient boosting methods, such as XGBoost, to fill the gap in the literature.

METHODOLOGY

This research uses an AI-led approach, enabled by the XGBoost algorithm to conceptualize a predictive model that focuses on managing classrooms, while being able to monitor student performance and the early identification of potential at-risk students. The complete system architecture is depicted in Figure 2. The proposed framework utilizes a publicly available educational dataset, then preprocessing the data, initially applying dimensionality reduction techniques for feature selection, training the final model based on partitioned data, making predictions regarding student outcomes, and subsequently evaluating the performance of the model based on key metrics. This clearly defined action plan included all components necessary to support educators with a robust model that yields actionable insights to allow them to support ultimately differentiate for at-risk students.

Figure 2. Proposed Machine Learning System Architecture (Author's own creation)

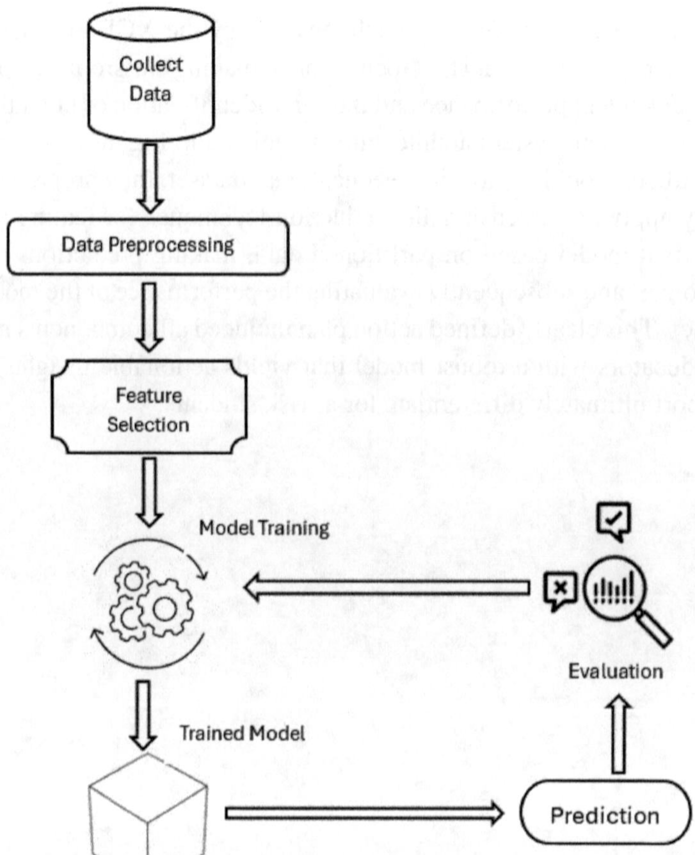

Data Collection

The research in this paper will be based on the Open University Learning Analytics Dataset (OULAD), an open educational dataset (Kuzilek et al. 2017). OULAD contains anonymous personal data of 32, 593 students studying 22 Open University in United Kingdom courses, which was collected from 7 delivered academic presentations between February 2013 and October 2014.

It consists of student demographic data, assessments grades, students' interaction with Virtual Learning Environment (VLE), and final grades. For this research, a subset of 5,000 student records was used which was randomly selected after data pre-processing and cleaning by discarding the samples where the learning activity pattern was undefined as well as the samples where the outcome label was missing in the original data set. The final samples selected were representative of three academic terms and were used for constructing the student risk prediction model.

Data Preprocessing

Preprocessing is an essential step to ensure that OULAD was clean and in a suitable format for use in machine learning algorithms.

Data Cleaning

Data cleaning is the process of correcting or dealing with missing or incorrect values in datasets. Any missing values, such as students interacting with the VLE or demographic information, are replaced through imputation. For example, missing numeric values can be replaced with the mean or median for that column. Outliers that may bias the model's results, such as unusually high or low counts of VLE clicks, were also removed, transformed, or flagged using logarithmic transformation.

Data Transformation

Data transformation is necessary to prepare the features for model training.

1. Normalization/Standardization:

All numerical features were scaled to ensure consistent contribution during model training. It is a good idea to standardize the values because it is robust to outliers. This process transforms the features to have a mean of 0 and a standard deviation of 1. The formula is:

$$X_{standardized} = \frac{x - \mu}{\sigma} \tag{1}$$

where X is the original feature value, μ is the mean, and σ is the standard deviation.

2. Encoding:

Encoding converts categorical features which are generally in string format to a numerical format in my case. One-Hot Encoding can be used for categorical variables that have more than one category. For binary features like gender on the other hand, Label Encoding which I have done in this case (i.e. Male=0, Female=1) is usually sufficient.

Feature Selection

Feature selection is a necessary step towards improving machine learning models to retain feature values that are the most informative while minimizing processing time, which ultimately improves predictive performance. In this case, Principal Component Analysis (PCA) was chosen as the main method for statistical dimensionality reduction. PCA allows high-dimensional data to be transformed into a unique set of orthogonal components that account for the maximum variance in a dataset.

In order to meet an acceptable tradeoff of efficiency and predictive performance, the top ten principal components were kept based on explained variance ratio. The principal components and their explained variance ratios were recorded, and cumulative explained variance ratio was over 92.7% of total variance. This was done in order to retain the important, informational content of the dataset but greatly reduce dimensionality. PCA has been shown to improve computational efficiency while retaining predictive accuracy.

In addition to universal numerical transformation, feature selection also covered domain-specific feature engineering to pick up pedagogically significant patterns of student learning activity. Three complementary measures were developed:

1. LMS Usage Statistics: The composite score is calculated on the basis of online learning management system activities that include logins, time spent, and the resources that are accessed.
2. Instructor-Annotated Behavioral Flags: Qualitative characteristics that are defined by teachers to describe behavioral trends, e.g. inconsistent work on assignments or participation.
3. Activity Consistency Measure: Quantitative version of activity consistency in terms of the occurrence of activity in the student (i.e. behaviour) and timing of activity (i.e. daily vs. non-daily).

The framework was efficient in computation and was relevant to the domain by combining both statistical techniques of dimensionality reduction and feature engineering by domain. Moreover, the feature set was tailored to not only support the standard data transformations to support the predictive modelling process but also to detect pedagogical patterns and predict future contexts.

PCA transforms original features into a new feature set (principal components), which are uncorrelated with each other, and we can choose the most important ones in order to decrease the dimensions. The features that are chosen in this model are:

attendance, engagement score, assignment submission time, behavior flags, week activity variance, final exam score, gender, and socioeconomic status. Table 1 shows that summary of input features used in the model.

Table 1. Summary of input features used in the model.

Feature	Description	Type
Attendance	A measure of a student's presence and participation.	Numerical (Normalized)
Engagement Score	A composite score based on student interaction with the VLE.	Numerical (Normalized)
Assignment Submission Time	The time difference (in days) between the due date and submission.	Binary (0 = Late, 1 = On-time)
Behavior Flags	Indicators for unusual student behavior (e.g., late submissions).	Categorical (one-hot encoded)
Weekly Activity Variance	The standard deviation of a student's weekly VLE activity.	Numerical
Final Exam Score	The student's score on the final examination.	Categorical (Pass/Fail)
Gender	The student's gender.	Categorical (one-hot encoded)
Socioeconomic Status	A categorical variable representing a student's socioeconomic background.	Ordinal (low, medium, high)

Model Training

The preprocessed and selected data is divided into two parts: training and testing. An 80–20 ratio is a common practice, where 80% of the data is used in training while the rest (20%) is used in testing. During the training phase, the algorithm identifies patterns and relationships between the extracted features and student outcomes.

Prediction

The model is then used to predict student outcomes, such as the probability of passing or the risk of dropping out. The primary goal is to identify and flag students who are at risk of poor educational outcomes based on their academic and behavioral data. This early identification allows the educators to implement timely interventions.

Evaluation

The model's performance is assessed on the test set using various metrics to ensure the model is reliable and effective.

1. **Accuracy:** Accuracy looks at how many of the model's predictions were right. It shows how often the model gets the classifications right for both at-risk and successful students.

$$Accuracy = \frac{TP + TN}{TP + TN + FP + FN} \quad (2)$$

   TP: Students correctly identified as at-risk.
   TN: Students correctly identified as successful.
   FP: Successful students incorrectly flagged as at-risk.
   FN: At-risk students misclassified as successful.

2. **Precision:** Precision tells how accurate the positive predictions are. It shows what percentage of the students that the model thought were at risk were actually at risk. A high precision score means that the model doesn't often make false alarms.

$$Precision = \frac{TP}{TP + FP} \quad (3)$$

3. **Recall (Sensitivity):** Recall is a measure of how well the model can find all the positive cases. It shows what percentage of the students who were really at risk the model got right. It is very important to have a high recall rate so that students who really need help are not missed.

$$Recall = \frac{TP}{TP + FN} \quad (4)$$

4. **Specificity:** Specificity tells how correct the negative predictions are. It shows what percentage of the students who really did well the model correctly identified as successful. To avoid mistakenly identifying successful students, which could lead to unnecessary interventions, it is important to have a high specificity score.

$$Specificity = \frac{TN}{TN + FP} \quad (5)$$

5. **F1-Score:** The F1-Score is a single measure that balances precision and recall. It's the harmonic mean of the two, and it's especially helpful when working

with datasets that aren't balanced (like when there are fewer at-risk students than successful students).

$$F1 - Score = 2\,x\,\frac{Precision\ x\ Recall}{Precison + Recall} \tag{6}$$

EXPERIMENTAL SETUP

This study utilized an integrated dataset that combined academic, engagement and behavioral data of 5000 students across three academic terms in virtual learning environments, from the Open University Learning Analytics Dataset (OULAD). Preprocessing of the data included cleaning and normalization and a principal components analysis for feature selection. The dataset was partitioned into 80% training, 10% validation and 10% test sets using stratified sampling to guarantee the balanced distribution of each class. The model was tested using 5-fold cross-validation and evaluated by several metrics: accuracy, precision, recall, F1-score, ROC-AUC and confusion matrix. We tested baseline algorithms - logistic regression (LR), support vector machine (SVM) and Random Forest model for model comparison.

Grid search was used for hyperparameter tuning in order to optimize parameters such as regularization, batch size, filter sizes, and learning rate. Educators qualitatively assessed the interpretable decision rules provided by the rough set component. The generalizability of the model was evaluated using a second batch of external student data from a different term. The ROC curve and confusion matrix indicated balanced classification performance, and the XGBoost model demonstrated high predictive accuracy, interpretability, and robustness across cohorts. Table 2 describes the specifics of the experimental setup. Subgroup evaluations based on demographic information from the OULAD dataset, with gender and socioeconomic status categories serving as the main variables, were necessary for the analysis of model bias. For each research group, the analysts separately computed prediction accuracy, precision, and recall.

Table 2. Experimental setup details

Parameter	Details
Dataset	5000 student records from virtual learning environments across three terms
Attributes	Academic scores, behavioral metrics, engagement levels
Data split	80% training, 10% testing, 10% validation
Validation method	5-fold cross validation

continued on following page

Table 2. Continued

Parameter	Details
Baseline models	Logistic regression, support vector machine, random forest
Evaluation metrics	Accuracy, precision, recall, Specificity, F1 score, confusion matrix
Hyperparameters	Learning_rate (0.05 – 0.3), n_estimators (500–1000), max_depth (3–6)

RESULTS

In this section, the performance of the proposed XGBoost method is evaluated on the Open University Learning Analytics Dataset (OULAD). Empirical results show that the framework demonstrates strong potential for accurate prediction of academic performance thus validating its efficacy. And the method further works well to predict high-risk students, providing an opportunity for early intervention. Crucially, the results also highlight opportunities for data-driven approaches to inform student management and school decision making.

Model Performance on Evaluation Metrics

Table 3. Results of performance metrics

Metric	Accuracy	Precision	Recall (Sensitivity)	Specificity	F1 Score	ROC-AUC
XGBoost	97.0%	96.2%	98.6%	95.0%	97.4%	0.96
Random Forest	94.0%	93.3%	96.0%	91.5%	94.6%	0.93
SVM	90.0%	87.7%	94.3%	85.1%	90.9%	0.89
Logistic Regression	88.0%	86.0%	92.5%	83.0%	89.1%	0.87

Utilizing the Open University Learning Analytics Dataset (OULAD), we have systematically compared four machine learning models – XGBoost, Random Forests, Support Vector Machine (SVM) and Logistic Regression – as tools for technology-enhanced learning. Accuracy, Precision, Recall Specificity, F1 Score and ROC-AUC of the compared approaches are reported in Table 3. Together, these measures give a global overview of the models' ability to classify as-03: being able to put students into risk classification. As expected, the performance of XGBoost was better than any other models. In particular, XGBoost achieved an accuracy of 97%, which means that a good pointwise correctness is reached. Its 98.6% recall is a sign of the model's very high sensitivity in identifying high-risk students; almost no eligible at risk students would remain undetected. The model also included a specificity of 95%, thus validating its capacity to make the accurate classification of those students who are not at risk. In addition, XGBoost achieves a strong balance between precision and recall (the F1 Score is 97.4%) and it shows excellent discriminative power between positive and negative classes (0.96 in terms of the ROC-AUC).

XGBoost consistently outperformed in comparison to other models. Though classification performance of Random forest and SVM was competitive, recall and specificity values of these models were lower than that of the other three models indicating tendency to miss some at-risk students (lower recall) or misclassify non-risk students (low specificity). Logistic Regression, as a basic linear model, performed the most poorly overall, indicating that it is not suitable for processing the complex non-linear relationships found in learning analytics data. The superior performance of XGBoost may also be due to its property as a gradient boosting framework that constructs an ensemble set of trees step-by-step, recovering mistakes from prior trees and accounting for complex feature interactions. In addition, XGBoost also makes use of regularization methods to help with overfitting and increase the generalisation capability of model for unseen data. We expect this to be especially useful in the context of a variety of educational datasets, which are often highly dimensional and imbalanced.

Confusion Matrix Analysis

Figure 3 presents the confusion matrix generated from the OULAD dataset and it shows the classification results using the XGBoost model. The matrix records the distribution of true and predicted outcome values for 500 student data points, which are a mixture of students who are not at risk (negative class) and students are at-risk (positive class).

Figure 3. Confusion Matrix of the Proposed XGBoost Model (Generated by the authors using OULAD experimental results)

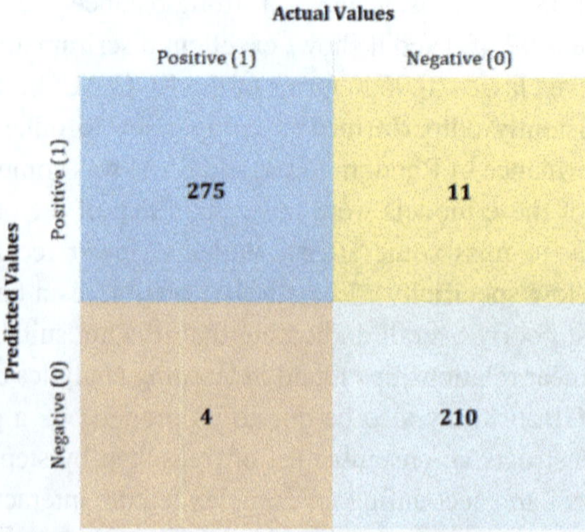

The matrix values are as follows:

- True Positives (TP): 275 Students correctly identified as at-risk
- False Positives (FP): 11 Successful students incorrectly flagged as at-risk.
- False Negatives (FN): 4 At-risk students misclassified as successful.
- True Negatives (TN): 210 Students correctly identified as successful.

Based on these values, a series of performance metrics could be calculated. The model displayed a high sensitivity (recall) of 98.6%, correctly capturing 275 out of the at-risk-for-failure students. This finding is of special importance in educational scenarios, where the failure to identify students at risk (false negatives) might result in academic failure or dropout. The false negative rate of 1.4% is an encouraging indication that the model is dependable in identifying students who need help (i.e., identifying them for intervention).

Furthermore, the model achieved 96.2% precision rate which indicated that if a student was predicted to be at-risk, it had a 96.2% chance of actually being true. This worst case misses 11 students flagged out of 286 unnecessarily intervened upon. The specificity of 95.0% further supports that the student success localization model is good not to predict successful students erroneously, without keeping fair in both groups.

Overall, In general, the result of confusion matrix analysis indicates that XGBoost model is sensitive and distressing with respect to positive and negative classes. The trade-off between the recall (for finding at-risk students) and precision (for making good predictions) puts it as a robust decision-support instrument for schools. This equitable classification of offenses allows for interventions to be both precise and effective, in order to best influence student support initiatives and institutional success.

Comparative Analysis with Baseline Models

Figure 4 presents an accuracy and precision performance of all four machine learning models in student outcome prediction and risk identification. XGBoost achieved the highest accuracy (97.0%) and precision (96.2%), showing its better performance in terms of the capability to predict students outcomes correctly and to minimize the number of false positives. This is the most effective and reliable model for identifying at-risk students. Random Forest also established good performance, with accuracy 94.0% and precision 93.3%, and is a solid candidate for educational risk prediction. However, it is marginally inferior to XGBoost in both aspects. SVM and Logistic Regression are somewhat competitive. Although their accuracy and precision are greater than 85%, much lower results compared to the XGBoost and Random Forest. These may be good models for exploratory analysis or to use as reference/baseline models that would not support high-stakes decision making.

Figure 4. Accuracy and Precision Comparison of Machine Learning Models (Author-generated from experimental results)

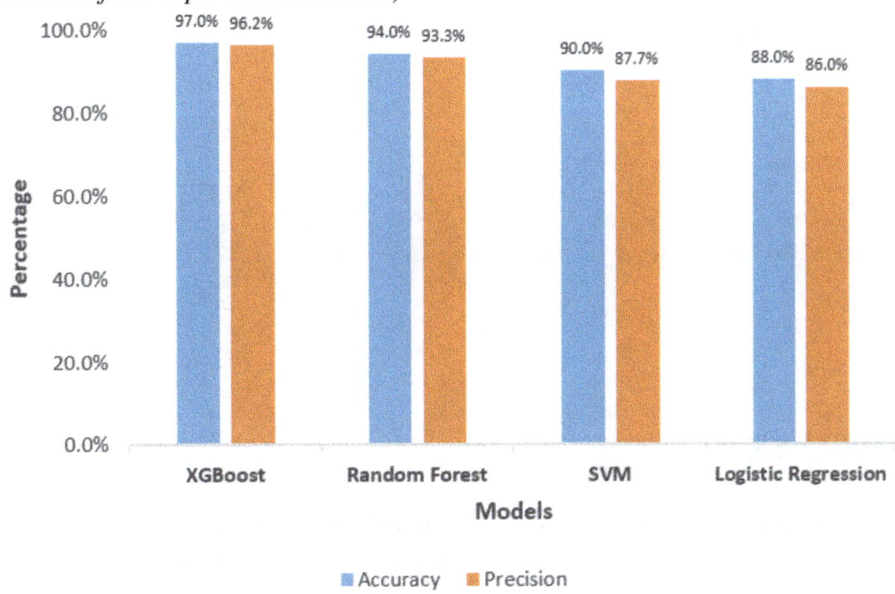

Figure 5 shows a comparison of the four machine learning models based on their AUC-ROC scores from confusion matrix data. The AUC-ROC measure is one of the most common metrics for quantifying a model's discriminative ability (i.e., to discriminate between at-risk students (positive class) and not-at risk students (negative class)). Of the fitted models, XGBoost obtained the highest AUC-ROC with a value of 0.96 (the steepest line). This indicates superior classification performance and discriminative capability of its ability to identify at-risk students with less tradeoff between sensitivity and specificity. Random Forest came in at a close second with an AUC-ROC of 0.93 indicating good predictability but a bit of high false positives to XGBoost. Flatter curves were found for SVM (0.89) and Logistic Regression (0.87), which indicated lower discrimination between two classes. These findings firmly confirm XGBoost is the most dependable model for student risk prediction, with significantly more confident early predictions of at-risk students compared to other approaches.

Figure 5. AUC-ROC Comparison of Machine Learning Models (Author-generated from experimental results)

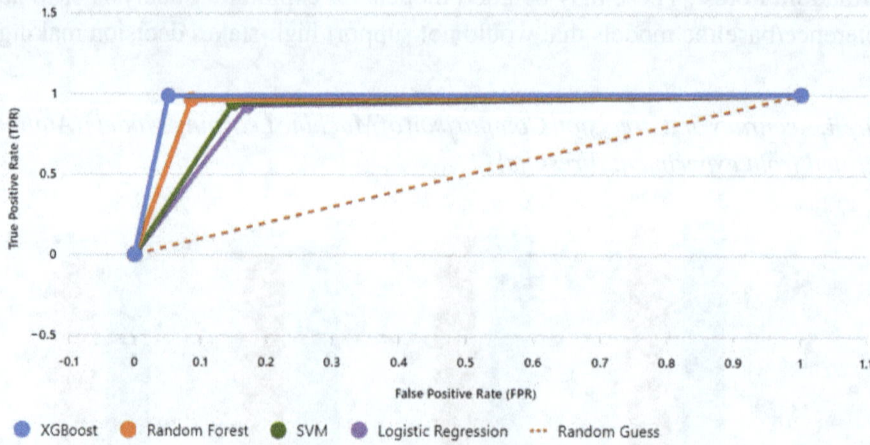

CONCLUSION

This research shows that the XGBoost model works well in improving student support by predicting their academic progress and recognizing at-risk students in time. Trained with Open University Learning Analytics Dataset (OULAD), the model achieved superior accuracy. (97%) and precision (96.2%) compared to traditional machine learning methods, effectively handling the complexity of educational data.

The results have important practical implications for educational organizations. The model allows early identification of at-risk students, so that interventions may be implemented in a timely manner to prevent dropout, supports personalized learning, and enables proactive measures to identify and support at-risk students. The inclusion of the rough-set component improves model interpretability so that outputs of our model are easy to understand for educators, facilitating trustworthy results and practical use in a real life environment.

For future work, it would be interesting to look into extending the model by leveraging different learning analytics datasets and other student attributes such as emotional, social and behavioral aspects in order to improve predictive power and personalization. Furthermore, the incorporation of state-of-the-art methods such as deep learning and reinforcement learning could allow the framework to adapt to changes in student behavior and academic patterns. These developments could bring about major improvement to educational data analytics, resulting in responsive, supportive and inclusive learning environments that are capable of serving individual students effectively.

REFERENCES

Al Luhaybi, M. (2021). *Explainable machine learning for educational data* (Doctoral dissertation, Brunel University London).

Altabrawee, H., Ali, O. A. J., & Ajmi, S. Q. (2019). Predicting students' performance using machine learning techniques. *JOURNAL OF UNIVERSITY OF BABYLON for pure and applied sciences, 27*(1), 194-205.

Asselman, A., Khaldi, M., & Aammou, S. (2023). Enhancing the prediction of student performance based on the machine learning XGBoost algorithm. *Interactive Learning Environments, 31*(6), 3360–3379. DOI: 10.1080/10494820.2021.1928235

Baran, E., AlZoubi, D., & Morales, A. S. (2023). Design and implementation of an automated classroom analytics system: Stakeholder engagement and mapping. *TechTrends, 67*(6), 945–954. DOI: 10.1007/s11528-023-00905-2

Chen, T., & Guestrin, C. (2016, August). Xgboost: A scalable tree boosting system. In *Proceedings of the 22nd acm sigkdd international conference on knowledge discovery and data mining* (pp. 785-794).

Chicioreanu, T. D., & Cosma, I. (2017). I Am a Teacher in the Digital Era. What to Choose: Google Classroom or Moodle?. *eLearning & Software for Education, 2.*

Chung, C., & Ackerman, D. (2015). Student reactions to classroom management technology: Learning styles and attitudes toward Moodle. *Journal of Education for Business, 90*(4), 217–223. DOI: 10.1080/08832323.2015.1019818

Gumasing, M. J. J., Endozo, E. K., Laingo, J. C. C., & Tapucar, W. H. (2023, March). Usability evaluation of online learning management system: Blackboard, Google Classroom and Canvas. In *2023 11th International Conference on Information and Education Technology (ICIET)* (pp. 92-97). IEEE.

Guo, Y. (2021). University classroom teaching model based on decision tree analysis and machine learning. *Mobile Information Systems, 2021*(1), 6926013. DOI: 10.1155/2021/6926013

Kunter, M., Baumert, J., & Köller, O. (2007). Effective classroom management and the development of subject-related interest. *Learning and Instruction, 17*(5), 494–509. DOI: 10.1016/j.learninstruc.2007.09.002

Kurni, M., Mohammed, M. S., & Srinivasa, K. G. (2023). AI-enabled gamification in education. In *A Beginner's Guide to Introduce Artificial Intelligence in Teaching and Learning* (pp. 105–114). Springer International Publishing.

Kuzilek, J., Hlosta, M., & Zdrahal, Z. (2017). Open university learning analytics dataset. *Scientific Data*, *4*(1), 1–8. DOI: 10.1038/sdata.2017.171 PMID: 29182599

Lima, D. A., & Isotani, S. (2021, October). Constraints, effectiveness and solutions in using Google Classroom as a Learning Management System during Covid-19 pandemic: a systematic literature review. In *2021 XVI Latin American Conference on Learning Technologies (LACLO)* (pp. 38-43). IEEE. DOI: 10.1109/LACLO54177.2021.00012

Moubayed, A., Injadat, M., Nassif, A. B., Lutfiyya, H., & Shami, A. (2018). E-learning: Challenges and research opportunities using machine learning & data analytics. *IEEE Access : Practical Innovations, Open Solutions*, *6*, 39117–39138. DOI: 10.1109/ACCESS.2018.2851790

Oyedotun, S. A., Ejenarhome, O. P., & Oise, G. P. (2025). Learning Analytics and Predictive Modeling: Enhancing Student Success through Data-Driven Insights. *Journal of Scientific Research and Reports*, *2*(3), 42–51.

Schiff, D. (2022). Education for AI, not AI for education: The role of education and ethics in national AI policy strategies. *International Journal of Artificial Intelligence in Education*, *32*(3), 527–563. DOI: 10.1007/s40593-021-00270-2

Virvou, M., Alepis, E., Tsihrintzis, G. A., & Jain, L. C. (2019). Machine learning paradigms: advances in learning analytics. In *Machine learning paradigms: Advances in learning analytics* (pp. 1–5). Springer International Publishing.

Zhai, X., Chu, X., Chai, C. S., Jong, M. S. Y., Istenic, A., Spector, M., Liu, J.-B., Yuan, J., & Li, Y. (2021). A Review of Artificial Intelligence (AI) in Education from 2010 to 2020. *Complexity*, *2021*(1), 8812542. DOI: 10.1155/2021/8812542

Chapter 6
Assessing the Applications and Challenges of Artificial Intelligence Adoption in Higher Education Institutions

Garima
http://orcid.org/0000-0002-1793-8084
Maharishi Markandeswar (Deemed to be) University, India

Komal Bhardwaj
http://orcid.org/0000-0002-9378-5542
Maharishi Markandeswar (Deemed to be) University, India

Dalip Kumar Bishnoi
Chaudhary Charan Singh Haryana Agricultural University, Hisar, India

ABSTRACT

Artificial Intelligence (AI) has brought a new age of innovation to every industry, especially to education. Schools are making an effort to meet the changing and diverse needs of a dynamic society. AI is a powerful tool for revolutionizing traditional education. This technology has an impact on education in the following ways: personalized learning, the creation of intelligent tutoring systems, better administrative functions, and higher student engagement. This study highlights how AI could potentially revolutionize the experience of learning for higher education students

DOI: 10.4018/979-8-3373-5586-3.ch006

but, at the same time, indicates a divergence problem. The chapter reviews the role and application of artificial intelligence (AI) in higher education and the difficulties encountered in the process of implementation. The paper also presents examples of how educational institutions have incorporated AI in the field of education to ensure that everyone receives quality and equitable education. Last, the paper examines the limitations and challenges to the implementation of AI in educational settings.

1. INTRODUCTION

In recent decades, a technological revolution has transformed society from one based on traditional living conditions to one focused on information, with progress driven by innovation and invention. Artificial Intelligence (AI) is rapidly changing many industries and education is no exception. Learning personalization can be achieved through AI as it adjusts educational data to suit the specific needs of every individual student (Hennekeuser et al., 2024). In the field of education, Artificial intelligence (AI) holds promise for many facets of learning, such as personalization, learning speed adaptation, iteration to improve students subject matter knowledge. Educators therefore envision a future where a benefit of AI will be that it "evaluate students, provide feedback, and generate and test scientific hypotheses at least as well as humans can" (Syukri et al., 2025). Students in well-designed learning environments have greater self-efficacy and are more positive toward their schooling (Doe et al., 2025). Artificial intelligence is an integral factor in general and higher education affecting students' academic progression in a myriad of avenues and challenges (Vieriu & Petrea, 2025). The implications of artificial intelligence in education are revolutionary as well as complicated. AI-powered tools are making experiences such as these possible by searching through mass data for gaps in knowledge, then strategically providing interventions (Baker, 2021). An increase in student engagement and performance is found when learning occurs via adaptive learning systems, which use AI-powered technologies to provide immediate feedback and customized learning paths (Luckin & Holmes, 2016; Zawacki-Richter et al., 2019). As such, AI is used in education for many purposes, from embedding the technologies within other educational software applications like chatbots, intelligent tutoring and automated grading systems. Opportunities abound for all stakeholders to benefit from these AI-based resources during the teaching-learning process (Celik et al., 2022). The implementation of AI in educational settings raises crucial ethical concerns for areas like accessibility, equity and the evolving nature of conventional teaching methods.

Traditional education encourages students to become active in their learning process as they build abilities in investigation, analysis and problem solving. Students' general learning experiences are based on critical thinking skills. Educators commonly use questioning strategies, group discussion, and assignments to help students become more adept at evaluating material and developing their own viewpoints (Zahid & Nawab, 2025). Moreover, higher educational institutions invest a significant amount of time and energy on the admission, education, and achievement of each and every one of their students, resulting in the waste of data and energy on unnecessary repetition (Solanki, 2025). They are now under a lot of strain to invest more in data processing and attracting and retaining teachers. If they rely significantly on manual work, it will increase operating expenses and increases errors. Higher education relies mostly on manual work which raises operating expenses and increases the possibility of errors as well as slow processing in the field results (Agarwal & Vij, 2024). As a result, the rapid processing of information and intelligent reactions of AI challenge the traditional ways of learning and raise questions regarding differences between human learning and machine learning.

In contrast, Artificial Intelligence (AI) has the ability to completely transform education by improving its effectiveness, personalization, and engagement. AI can be utilized to create customized learning programs that adjust to each learner's requirements and skills. AI systems fall into one of two categories: thinking-intelligent or mechanically-intelligent. Whereas thinking-intelligent systems can learn from data and modify their performance accordingly, mechanically-intelligent systems are skilled at effectively completing repeated tasks. AI systems rely on a massive collection of big data, which includes text, audio, and video, in order to reach this degree of intelligence and can learn and improve their performance by employing computational techniques like machine learning and deep learning on this vast dataset (Jaiswal & Arun, 2021). Moreover, implementing artificial intelligence can help the higher education sector adopt a more cost-effective and responsive strategy while minimizing both monetary and tangible losses. For example, as per the study conducted on teachers and students, in Kuwait by Qadir (2023) stated an increasing interest in incorporating AI into the educational system. ChatGPT has rapidly become a useful tool that benefits both students and teachers. ChatGPT acts as a 24/7 virtual assistant for students, helping them comprehend complex subjects and improve their writing abilities. At the same time, it helps teachers create engaging lesson plans, instructional materials, and engaging classroom activities (Buabbas et al., 2023). It is open and easy to access, easy to use and has powerful conversational AI features that can boost teaching and learning. Furthermore, for broader and more extensive transmission of information, it is necessary to understand that AI technology has created an incredible number of chances and strategies for educational implementation. (Zobel et al., 2023).

The fact that AI can better our teaching and learning, not only makes it possible to revolutionize our teaching and learning environment but it is also responsible for bringing grave problems, which are worth thorough research and regulation. Therefore, our usage of AI should be a careful balance, where it complements human interaction and development of critical thinking rather than substitute for them (Wu, 2023). In order for AI to work in education, understanding of technology and education needs to be acquired. Complexity of AI increased further due to the new ethical issues, with growing usage of generative artificial intelligence. Even though AI can analyze and process data very fast, it is limited with creativity and understanding of details that represent human thinking processes (Luckin & Holmes, 2016). As pointed out by Qadir (2023), "the potential for academic dishonesty with student's use of AI is a serious concern and, in many cases, an inevitable consequence with students producing AI-generated work and claiming it as their own with no citation". In order to solve the problem institutions of higher education needs to establish what the limits and boundaries of AI usage and scope should be in the teaching of students (Holmes & Tuomi, 2022).

Similarly, the benefits and problems that can occur with the application of AI is in the Indian context, which thrives on education for upward socio-economic mobility. Traditional education promotes active learning by developing analytical, research-oriented and problem-solving capabilities. Critical thinking is essential to the entire development of students' learning experiences. Facione (2020) states that instructors often employ questioning tactics, group projects, and assignments to assist students grow better at assessing evidence and establishing their own judgments. AI's rapid processing of information and intuitive responses, however, threaten traditional learning methods and make it impossible to separate machine learning from humans. For example, AI may not have the higher-order understanding and creativity that human cognition provides, even while it can efficiently process and analyze data (Luckin & Holmes, 2016). This indicates that AI needs to be applied comprehensively and carefully so that it can reinforce the interaction and critical thinking development rather than weaken it (Wu, 2023). There are many issues when applying AI in classrooms. To use artificial intelligence effectively, understanding of learning and technology processes are needed. This complexity can further increase due to the ethics issue, in relation to its use of generative artificial intelligence (Qadir, 2023). It must be understood that when to accept or reject the generated knowledge so that equality is not prejudiced (Akinwalere & Ivanov, 2022). This research aims to explore the integration of artificial intelligence into the Indian education system, challenges to adoption and learning enhancements.

2. IMPLICATION OF ARTIFICIAL INTELLIGENCE IN HIGHER EDUCATION

Since the emergence of Artificial Intelligence in Education (AIED) AI strategies are being investigated to enhance creative ways of teaching and learning, offering opportunities that might have been unachievable (McCalla, 2023). AI gives machines reasoning abilities to allow machines to mimic humans, learn to respond to novel input and even learn from their own errors. Identifying patterns and generating predictions by using labeled (supervised learning) and unlabelled data (unsupervised learning) is one of the initial applications of AI, as many other AI applications (Duan, et al., 2019). There are various AIED techniques to consider such as deep learning, machine learning, neural networks, natural language processing, genetic algorithms, to mention only a few of them, the most talked about are deep learning and machine learning. There are numerous techniques such as deep learning, machine learning, neural networks, natural language processing, genetic algorithms to mention only a few, and these techniques are machine learning and deep learning which are the most commonly discussed in education. AI today revolutionises the use of technology, providing intelligent tutoring, customizable interfaces and analytics, automating content creation and feedback to allow teaching and learning in various areas of learning including in schools and universities (Gobert, 2023). The way we learn and the institutions assisting them has changed significantly recently due to the advent of AI (Zawacki-Richter et al., 2019). More specifically, an output from GenAI technologies would be synthesis of speech and audio, independent generation of text, graphics, and raw video content and datasets, which often rely on deep learning architectures, NNs, and large training datasets (Nirala et al., 2022). It has certainly been a revolution in this aspect but what brought it into mainstream was when ChatGPT (generative pre-trained transformer), a chatbot, was introduced by OpenAI in November 2022. A generative conversational AI interface, ChatGPT acknowledges "its mistakes, challenges incorrect premises, and rejects inappropriate requests" using natural language to interact in a realistic way and can even respond to follow-up questions. Although the primary function of ChatGPT is to simulate human conversation and produce desired responses, it can also be used for teaching and learning activities such as solving questions, writing essays, stories, poetry, or role playing any character it is capable of. It has been the driving force for other GenAI tools and particularly LLMs that are similar to ChatGPT to be designed and released with significant success after ChatGPT's launch. As a consequence, the development and popularity of GenAI applications like ChatGPT and GitHub Copilot increased the interest to use AI powered systems in teaching and learning. Particularly, ChatGPT use is showing a lot of interest in education, as seen by the fact that practically all educational institutions have created their own policies on its use. Some nations have created "sandboxes" where both public and private organizations can test LLMs without taking any risks. They have also created their own LLM versions that solve possible privacy and security issues or better support specific languages. However, in context of usage, the United Nations Educational, Scientific and Cultural Organization (UNESCO) has stepped in by publishing the document "Guidance for Generative AI in Education and Research" (UNESCO, 2023), by researchers Holmes & Miao, (2023). While some companies, like Turnitin, have created plagiarism detection tools for LLMs, others, like Magic School and Eduaide, have created student and teacher aides based on OpenAI's LLM technology. Recent LLM research has shown intriguing applications, including creating feedback and support messages. Moreover, Tapalova and Zhiyenbayeva (2022) assert that the integration of AIED technologies in higher education offers numerous advantages for developing personalized educational pathways, including enhanced engagement and interest in learning, customization of educational content to individual requirements, expedited educational processes, cognitive stimulation, exploration of psychological dimensions in virtual environments, continuous access to academic progress, and prompt feedback.

3. ARTIFICIAL INTELLIGENCE CASES IN HIGHER EDUCATION

Over the past few years, the development of AI interfaces has been another aspect which can be said as innovation (Bayne, 2015). They went beyond keyboards and mice to allow even beginners to utilize an AI through voice recognition or image recognition. It can increase the clearness of a communication between complicated systems and users and allow even the weakest to benefit. Intelligence artificial (AI) can benefit greatly in terms of education, it can achieve the individualized learning and meet every student's need and knowledge. Students can work with their own speed to perfect themselves. University administrators state that one of the main benefits is AI's ability to "assess students, provide feedback, and formulate and test hypotheses at levels comparable to those achieved by human subjects" (Alexander et al., 2019). Several examples about AI usage in universities have been illustrated in the section.

MIP Politecnico di Milano Graduate School of Business

The MIP Politecnico di Milano Graduate School of Business collaborated with Microsoft to create FLEXA. It operates on Microsoft Azure and employs artificial intelligence as well. Students can assess their competencies and receive guidance to align with the requirements for employment and academic courses. FLEXA furthermore creates customized strategies according to your level of busyness. It aligns with the concept of lifelong learning, as articulated by Alexander et al. (2019).

Washington State University

Washington State University joined forces with edtech firm Cialfo to boost its recruiting efforts. They aim to connect with more than 250,000 international high school students through Cialfo's AI-powered Explore platform. Cialfo is useful to universities, such as WSU, because it helps to connect counselors, students and parents. It is adopted in 100 countries. This partnership will ensure that WSU not only reaches more students, but will also make it to its goals for the year, despite the challenges that lie before it.

IIT Madras

The school of engineering at IIT-Madras offers an online BSc in Data Science and Applications with artificial intelligence embedded in the curriculum. Students receive AI-powered tools such as an AI Teaching Assistant and an AI Interview Companion to provide them with continuous support. It's a sign of a significant shift towards personalized learning in India's higher education, although it may not be completely uniform across all institutions. So, it advances educational tech and innovative teaching methods.

Pearson Group

Pearson Group employs artificial intelligence to enhance foreign language education. In January 2018, Microsoft Asia Research formed a strategic alliance with Pearson Group to improve the integration of artificial intelligence in English education. The two businesses previously partnered to develop "Long Wen Xiaoying," an interactive English learning application utilizing artificial intelligence. Achieving competency in foreign languages is crucial across all age demographics and educational levels, from Key Stage 12 to Higher Education and Lifelong Learning (Achieng, 2023).

Reducing assessment activities markedly saves time for educators, exemplified by the partnership with Microsoft's associate Gama Learn, an AI solution adept at authoring, proctoring, and grading to enable automation, self-directed, and tailored tests. This AI-Cyber program assists higher education institute in preserving the integrity of extensive examination sessions by documenting numerous compromising incidents, consequently detecting issues during the session and providing forensic dashboards, among other capabilities (Lukin & Bagshaw, 2025).

4. LITERATURE REVIEW

With the resurgence of machine intelligence, deep learning, and cognitive architectures over the last few years, many experts believe that the future for AI is bright across all aspects of society (Kaku, 2019; Kelly, 2026). Tan (2020) maintains that we have not achieved Artificial General Intelligence when computer processing capabilities are at the same level as the human capacity for understanding and processing knowledge. According to Bostrom (2017), there has been an 'AI Winter' which has led to less trust in AI protagonists. However, Artificial Intelligence arrival has transformed the research in every discipline causing many methodological and paradigm shift. Use of AIEd technologies in higher education provided various valuable advantages for individualized learning paths such as enhanced learner involvement and interest, content personalized to individual learner, rapid learning, cognitive stimulation, access to psychological research in virtual environments, and constant round the clock access to student performance and immediate feedback. AI is going to elevate the level of education. In discussing the rise of artificial intelligence "no other technology is positioned to impact higher education as significantly as artificial intelligence". An et al., (2018) set out the following objectives for the use of AI in higher education: enhanced learning outcomes, increased access, improved retention rates, reduced costs, and time to completion. The proposed pedagogical model that the study examined took into account the increasing influence of AI on our society and its economy, the potential for morality and social challenges faced by humans and the role of AI in transforming education, particularly the way it provides customized and individualized learning (Tapalova & Zhiyenbayeva, 2022). The 1950s was when research on AI-related solutions started to take place. The notion of AI coined by McCarthy (1956) still continues to serve as guidance for contemporary AI researchers: "The conviction upon which study of artificial intelligence must proceed is that any part of learning or any other feature of intelligence can be spelled out in a way so precise that a computer can be programmed to mimic it". In addition, machine learning can perform advanced text analysis to find patterns and even to identify gaps in research papers (Burger et al., 2023). Those can enable the researchers to drill down to their respective study problems further and pay attention to their works' concepts and theories. Literature reviews have greatly benefited from the capacity of AI to analyse natural language. According to Muller & Mønsted (2025) it can handle large amounts of information, summarise it for researchers, and suggest further research. One of the most impressive examples of how AI is driving forward interdisciplinary research is its ability to analyze and interpret vast amounts of scientific data. One of its most impressive uses is the analysis and interpretation of large volumes of scientific data, making interdisciplinary research much easier. AI can sift through a huge amount of data in various subject areas and help researchers find linkages that were never noticed before. This results in innovative projects and collaborations across disciplines, as stated by (Beretta et al., 2021). This is not just changing the way everyday research is done, it's also changing the very way science is conceptualized. It allows for a much more detailed analysis of data that would not otherwise be practical in a period of time, and thus can help in the understanding of the environment we live in (Russell, 2010). Artificial Intelligence is already being used by segments of society. However, there is a great deal of potential but not a lot of concrete results with respect to its direct impact on education (Tuomi, 2018). Artificial Intelligence (AI) is making a profound impact on education, changing the learning experiences of students and the way they are taught (Rahayu, 2023). Research has shown that AI can improve classroom inclusivity by making learning resources accessible to every learner and their preferred speed (Hoque et al., 2021). The use of AI in education has several other ways of improving teaching. It helps you to create individual programs that adjust to fit your level. AI can either accelerate or decelerate the difficulty level based on how fast you are and how fast you learn (Grace et al., 2023). Furthermore, AI allows students to get feedback right away, they don't have to wait until a teacher has graded the work, they get instant feedback. In addition, there are intelligent teaching systems and adaptive software that make use of your data to tailor lessons just for you (Bimba, 2021). This means the end of boring, same class! In addition to assisting children, AI significantly conserves time for educators as well. With the help of tools, it is now possible to automate the class scheduling process (Lee et al., 2019), which enables the teacher to focus more on teaching than administration. In conclusion, AI's goal in education is to generate the most efficient, faster, and personalized learning experience for every student. The immediate feedback also makes the learning process becomes more engaging and efficient due to the application of AI-based tools such as intelligent systems and virtual coaches. Furthermore, AI may handle administrative tasks such as record-keeping and attendance tracking and also allow more extensive engagement with students (Kumar et al., 2023). But in a research Pratama et al. (2023) stated no replacement of professors with AI. Holmes et al. (2018) discussed some of the difficulties in implementing evidence-based teaching in classrooms and a framework for identifying and helping teachers in implementing the effectiveness of technology enhanced personalized learning material, as well as the effect size concept for effectiveness in this case. The artificial intelligence based personalized assistive devices are developed by Barua et al. (2022) which aims to support students with learning difficulty, such as dyslexia, attention deficit hyperactivity disorder, and autism spectrum disorder with neurodevelopmental problems through an assistive device. Hoque et al., (2021) also pointed out the problems that education may face with respect to cost, dependency on technology, and so on. Special care should be taken in the application of AI in education in terms of economic issues as well as the technical needs for devices, particularly in less developed countries. As described by Ahmad et al., (2023) it is very hard to ensure that the accuracy and reliability of AI. There are several issues that studies mention that cause concerns when it comes to AI in education such as it is expensive and the user is too dependent on technology; and it has serious privacy concerns and may be unreliable and/or not valid, it can also affect students' behavior during exams. Author thinks this tool should be implemented in careful consideration. Challenges with AI are vast, multifaceted and complicated. It goes beyond legal regulations and ethics; it is also very important to ensure that all individuals have the opportunity to access quality education on a fair and equal footing. While AI holds great promise, there are many hurdles to be overcome in the field of education. One significant aspect is Ethics of using AI in education. These technologies raise significant concerns about privacy and information security in collecting and using student data (Ma & Jiang, 2023). Another significant obstacle is supporting international students to adapt to processes using AI Some aspects of the culture are hard to deal with and sometimes hinders their assimilation and learning in technologically rich environments. This can affect their level of comfort and participation, and may result in a feeling of being left out (Kamak et al., 2024).

5. RESEARCH METHODOLOGY

This research uses the qualitative descriptive research with secondary data. Qualitative research is preferred when there is a need for a detailed understanding of a topic or situation. The data sources are compiled by library research methodologies utilizing both offline and online resources, including news articles, books, and scholarly papers produced by reputable organizations. Data are evaluated, and conclusions are drawn in relation to the study's objectives.

Objectives of the study:

- To explore the role and applications of AI in enhancing higher education practices.
- To investigate the challenges faced by the educators in adopting AI in higher education.

6. ROLE AND APPLICATION OF AI IN HIGHER EDUCATION

Artificial intelligence (AI) in education provides a number of possibilities made possible by classroom AI. Adaptive tutoring, intelligent test scoring, and learning analytics are examples of technology that can tweak lessons and reduce administrative tasks (Faisal, 2024; Francis et al., 2025). Tutoring systems now adapt to pupils' real-time performance (Doe et al., 2025). This piques their attention and motivates them to improve. Plus, the majority of people are fine with these technologies, therefore AI is quickly becoming a part of classroom instruction. As an example, the field is constantly progressing, as seen in Chart GPT (Beckingham et al., 2024). But you need tech-savvy individuals to work on the tech in order to receive these benefits. According to Pavlik (2023), AI simplifies the process of achieving excellent outcomes.

1. **Adaptive learning and personalization:** Adaptive learning systems can change the way they teach based on what each student needs. This makes learning and the experience better for all of them (Raj & Renumol, 2022). Based on how well students do, these systems look at data to change the types of lessons and how hard they are. Not only do they figure out where students might be having trouble, but they also tailor their help to those problems (Latif et al., 2026; Gligorea et al., 2023). However, Lin et al. (2023) said that this human touch makes learning a lot more interesting. AI has made a huge difference in the way things are taught by making them very specific to each student. Every child's background, likes, and skills should be taken into account when lessons are personalized. According to Murtaza et al. (2022), and Hashim et al. (2022), this is an instance of technology being used to assist each student to learn at their own level and pace.
2. **AI in grading and assessment process:** AI-powered automated assessment gives teachers quick feedback on how well their students is doing, so they don't have to grade things like homework, essays, and tests by hand. Grading can be as easy as going through a bunch of multiple-choice questions or as hard as going through a mountain of written work. Hooda et al. (2022), Hahn et al. (2021), and González- Calatayud et al. (2021) stated that this AI in higher education helps both students and teachers so that they can see what went wrong and how to fix it. Also, when AI does the marking, teachers have more time to plan lessons preparing for class and mentoring students—when automated assessment takes the monotony out of grading. By comparing student work to that of other students at different schools and to publicly available internet content, certain AI systems are able to identify instances of plagiarism.
3. **Intelligent tutoring systems:** ITS employs robust algorithms and machine learning methodologies to comprehend students' learning requirements and tailor their training (Bates et al., 2020). ITS evaluates student actions, interests, and answers to tailor content and feedback, thereby personalizing the learning experience for each individual student. It emulates individualized tutoring designed to provide students with tailored, one-on-one instruction that replicates

the experience of being taught by a human tutor, potentially accelerated by AI technology (Harry & Sayudin, 2023). With the help of AI, ITS can merge class-based and individual tutoring to provide personalized training and feedback, like having a superstar assistant for each student (Dandachi, 2024). For the science subject it is quite an issue since these systems offers tailored assistance with hints, explanations and tests matching individual's learning style (Kamalov et al., 2023). Moreover, ITS utilize the machine learning aspect to predict user's behavior such as when the student is about to learn and when the student will be losing attention. However, in many cases the students have very specific input using a variant of ML known as NLP (Natural Language Processing). An added benefit of these intelligent systems is their combination of pedagogical and domain knowledge with the actual requirements of the student as well as established methods of teaching.

4. **Behavioural prediction and profiling:** AI technologies analyze student data to predict their academic performance, engagement, or probability of dropping out. It is helpful for the instructors to provide an early intervention and support students (Rastrollo-Guerrero et al., 2020). Moreover, they assist in advising and designing activities where students are directed towards appropriate courses and learning materials, suitable choices of study or career and relevant guidance (Zawacki-Richter et al., 2019). These models process large data set like quiz scores, attendance data, and interaction with an online platform. Using these data sets, they can find trends and predictions. In one of the studies, Berens et al. (2019) were able to identify the at-risk students in German universities with a precision ranging from 79% to 95%. Although it's only one among a few studies on the issue and does not address the varied needs of diverse or disadvantaged learners.
5. **Administrative efficiency:** In terms of administrative tasks, AI is used to handle scheduling, resources, student information, communication and to answer straightforward questions. By helping the teachers with administration, they will have more time for more valuable contact with the students, such as to teach, guide, and observe them (Chen et al., 2020; Ge and Hu, 2020; Khosravi et al., 2022; Celik et al., 2022). It can be used in administrative tasks like assessment, scheduling, and managing registration. The automated marking systems are already able to mark multiple choice exams, and even some essay exams, which frees up teachers for interactions with the students and the education process (Zhang & Aslan, 2021; Seo et al., 2021). AI is applied within the educational institutions in order to increase the student experience, and minimize the costs.
6. **Online learning and distance education:** AI improves online learning through personalized learning paths, quick feedback, and better interactions. To tackle challenges the AI adaptive learning algorithms for async content provide for

remote learning at one's own speed. Additionally automated feedback systems and AI chatbots provide round-the-clock help, saving teachers from always being online. With data analytics, AI watches how students behave in courses and spots disengagement early, then steps in to help. This all happens thanks to AI, making online education more effective (St-Hilaire et al., 2022; Tonbuloğlu, 2023; Manuel, 2025).

7. LIMITATION AND CHALLENGES OF AI IN HIGHER EDUCATION

In the tangled world of information, business, innovation and legislation all in constant flux, lies AI. The problem that surrounds AI is that "AI is playing an increasingly critical role in today's technological era... With increasing numbers of people relying on AI to accelerate the learning process" (Jain and Jain, 2019). One of the challenges lies in using AI to augment, and not replace, human relationships. While AI is skilled in automatizing and finding patterns within information, it does not offer the human-centred skills of emotional intelligence and creativity, that a human tutor can provide (Holmes and Tuomi, 2022). The over reliance upon the automation of feedback can limit the development of deep learning conversations, needed for the acquisition of advanced cognitive skills (Facione, 2020). However, AI can offer significant changes through personalised lessons and tailored learning trajectories; the application needs to be treated carefully, and with full understanding of the pedagogy, ethics, and institutional structures that surround its implementation. Solutions need to be sought as a whole, where a fair, accessibly, human-centric, balanced solution may serve to both complement and enhance the learning environment (Vieriu & Petrea, 2025). The following questions issues that surround the implementation of AI in higher education.

1. **Negative consequences:** However, there are drawbacks to integrating AI into higher education. This includes potential adverse consequences: Those designing and implementing the systems may have good intentions; however, unintentional negative outcomes and even backfire could occur. When applying to a learning system, several elements should be considered. Data might not be consistently of high quality, could be outdated, or may have been compiled using a particular sector of the youth population-not the entire population we are interested in: For example, AI learning systems may have different accuracy and results when tested on students from one type of community college or university in California, as compared to tests with students from a particular institution in

other parts of the country. An AI system for Gen X, for example, could underperform for the digital generation (Akinwalere & Ivanov, 2022).

2. **Security and privacy of data:** Data security and privacy present an additional challenge for AI in education. Extensive quantities of student data are essential for the operation of AI systems, prompting inquiries about data accessibility and utilization. Consequently, it is imperative to establish explicit guidelines and protocols for the collection, utilization, and distribution of student data. (Grace et al., 2023).
3. **Potential problems and damage:** There are worries about the possible issues and harm this extensive use could cause to higher education. The most concerning element is probably how it will affect academic research, which could have a negative impact on researchers' motivation and innovative thinking, taint the spirit of academic study, and even foster unhealthy rivalry (Cui et al.,2024)
4. **The discrepancy factor:** The reason AI hasn't had much of an influence on teaching and learning in higher education up to this point is that education typically lags behind new technology. In many areas of education, learning, and development, resistance to using new technology stems from a lack of desire to take chances or embrace novel ideas as well as a lack of funding for anything other than conventional teaching techniques (Wheeler, 2019). Many educators must be persuaded that a novel concept may enhance or expand learning experiences and outcomes, which is why the education sector is still quite cautious about new technologies.
5. **Inclusiveness:** A further aspect of data is comprehensiveness. Stated differently, does the data provide details about a range of students? Recently, this has become a hot topic in the context of facial recognition. According to academics examining the usage of face recognition by businesses like Google, IBM, Microsoft, and Face++, these tools were frequently created using internal employee data or proprietary data. (Perera & Aboal, 2020) Light-skinned men can use the instruments with significantly more accuracy than either light-skinned women or men with darker skin tones. In one study, for instance, the facial recognition software had an accuracy of almost 100% for men with light complexion, but only 65% for women with dark skin. (Perera & Aboal, 2019)
6. **Execution:** In order to use these systems appropriately, staff members and teachers need to be aware of both their advantages and disadvantages. However, when algorithmic evaluations or recommendations conflict with professional judgment, schools must establish very clear procedures for what staff members should do. To avoid unfair disparities, they must have explicit guidelines for when applying or disregarding computer-generated insights is appropriate (Akinwalere & Ivanov, 2022).

7. **Accuracy:** The problem of accuracy comes up again. AI tools are not infallible and may yield erroneous or deceptive outcomes and models are not indicative of causality; rather, they are based on correlation. Less obvious, weaker correlations and patterns are what AI tools and models are meant to demonstrate. Erroneous feedback or evaluations can adversely affect students' educational experiences (Sharma & Rani, 2025). It might be challenging to discern between patterns and correlations that are true and those that are just noise.
8. **Algorithmic Bias:** The training datasets contribute to bias and discriminatory effects. Training on data is a fundamental requirement for most Artificial Intelligence (AI). If training data is limited to certain socio-economic groups, instead of capturing the general community, the systems can be biased and thus favour only a part of society, thereby exacerbating the social divide (Holstein & Doroudi, 2021). There are chances for education as well which are impacted by such bias (Chen et al., 2024).

8. CONCLUSION

This study highlights how AI could potentially revolutionize the experience of learning for higher education students but at the same time, indicates a divergence problem. From smart learning systems, analysis on student performance to systems which adapt to learning styles of pupils, higher institutions are increasingly utilizing more AI at present with an aim of improving operational efficiency and personalizing courses. This brings with it more benefits like improved student performance and engagement, personal courses. There are multiple other benefits like adaptive learning, intelligent tutoring, AI grading and assessment, behavior prediction, efficiency in higher institutions, as well as support for online and distance learning, as shown above. At the same time, there are some issues that have to be dealt with simultaneously. Schools and institutions of learning should review advantages of using AI tools in education alongside its disadvantages while ensuring student data is kept confidential, and also removing bias among others. With a more thorough evaluation of the pros and cons of AI, the educational experience of everyone will improve; creating a more efficient and personalized form of education. A thorough study should also be undertaken to identify opportunities presented by artificial intelligence in the domain of education as well as explore associated ethical concerns. The potential dangers and challenges presented by artificial intelligence are important in the educational institutions as it is becoming a popular trend. This covers privacy, bias in algorithms, effect on employees in an institution. For young children the complexity of learning environment increases as these children are unable to legally consent to collection and use of their personal information. Without a doubt, privacy of personal data has been continuously broadening across international, national, and regional levels. In practice and policy, residents still receive fewer rights in many systems compared to other entities in both developed countries as well as countries undergoing development. More research must be done to enhance understanding of the ethical and social impacts of AI in education.

REFERENCES

Achieng, S. A. (2023). Intercultural competence in foreign language teaching and learning. Strategies and challenges. In *17th International conference for Language, Individual & Society* (Vol. 17, pp. 19-26). International Scientific Publications. DOI: 10.62991/LIS1996073068

Agarwal, P., & Vij, A. (2024). Assessing the challenges and opportunities of artificial intelligence in Indian education. *International Journal for Global Academic & Scientific Research, 3*(1), 36–44. DOI: 10.55938/ijgasr.v3i1.71

Ahmad, S. F., Han, H., Alam, M. M., Rehmat, M., Irshad, M., Arraño-Muñoz, M., & Ariza-Montes, A. (2023). Impact of artificial intelligence on human loss in decision making, laziness and safety in education. *Humanities & Social Sciences Communications, 10*(1), 311. DOI: 10.1057/s41599-023-01787-8

Akinwalere, S. N., & Ivanov, V. (2022). Artificial intelligence in higher education: Challenges and opportunities. *Border Crossing, 12*(1), 1–15. DOI: 10.33182/bc.v12i1.2015

Alexander, B., Ashford-Rowe, K., Barajas-Murph, N., Dobbin, G., Knott, J., McCormack, M., & Weber, N. (2019). *Horizon report 2019 higher education edition* (pp. 3-41). EDU19.

An, S., Bates, R., Hammock, J., Rugaber, S., & Goel, A. (2018). VERA: popularizing science through AI. In *International Conference on Artificial Intelligence in Education* (pp. 31-35). Cham: Springer International Publishing.

Baker, J. A. (2021). Artificial intelligence in education: Bringing it all together. In *OECD digital education outlook 2021: Pushing the frontiers with AI, blockchain, and robotics* (pp. 43–56).

Barua, P. D., Vicnesh, J., Gururajan, R., Oh, S. L., Palmer, E., Azizan, M. M., Kadri, N. A., & Acharya, U. R. (2022). Artificial intelligence enabled personalised assistive tools to enhance education of children with neurodevelopmental disorders—A review. *International Journal of Environmental Research and Public Health, 19*(3), 1192. DOI: 10.3390/ijerph19031192

Bates, T., Cobo, C., Mariño, O., & Wheeler, S. (2020). Can artificial intelligence transform higher education? *International Journal of Educational Technology in Higher Education, 17*(1), 42. DOI: 10.1186/s41239-020-00218-x

Bayne, S. (2015). Teacherbot: Interventions in automated teaching. *Teaching in Higher Education, 20*(4), 455–467. DOI: 10.1080/13562517.2015.1020783

Beckingham, S., Lawrence, J., Powell, S., & Hartley, P. (2024). Using generative AI effectively in higher education. *London: Routledge, 10*, 9781003482918.

Berens, J., Schneider, K., Gortz, S., Oster, S., & Burghoff, J. (2019). Early detection of students at risk—Predicting student dropouts using administrative student data and machine learning methods. *Journal of Educational Data Mining, 11*(3), 1–41.

Beretta, V., Calandra, D., Cho, C. H., Demartini, C., & Biancone, P. (2021) Sustainability Education: Preparing Future Leaders for a Sustainable Economy.

Bimba, A. T., Idris, N., Al-Hunaiyyan, A., Ibrahim, S. U., Mustafa, N., Supa'at, I., & Ahmad, M. Y. (2021). The effects of adaptive feedback on student's learning gains. *International Journal of Advanced Computer Science and Applications, 12*(7), 68–80. DOI: 10.14569/IJACSA.2021.0120709

Bostrom, N. (2017). Strategic implications of openness in AI development. *Global Policy, 8*(2), 135–148. DOI: 10.1111/1758-5899.12403

Buabbas, A. J., Miskin, B., Alnaqi, A. A., Ayed, A. K., Shehab, A. A., Syed-Abdul, S., & Uddin, M. (2023). Investigating students' perceptions towards artificial intelligence in medical education. []. MD]. *Health Care, 11*(9), 1298.

Burger, B., Kanbach, D. K., Kraus, S., Breier, M., & Corvello, V. (2023). On the use of AI-based tools like ChatGPT to support management research. *European Journal of Innovation Management, 26*(7), 233–241. DOI: 10.1108/EJIM-02-2023-0156

Celik, I., Dindar, M., Muukkonen, H., & Järvelä, S. (2022). The promises and challenges of artificial intelligence for teachers: A systematic review of research. *TechTrends, 66*(4), 616–630. DOI: 10.1007/s11528-022-00715-y

Chen, L., Chen, P., & Lin, Z. (2020). Artificial intelligence in education: A review. *IEEE Access : Practical Innovations, Open Solutions, 8*, 75264–75278. DOI: 10.1109/ACCESS.2020.2988510

Chen, Z., Chen, C., Yang, G., He, X., Chi, X., Zeng, Z., & Chen, X. (2024). Research integrity in the era of artificial intelligence: Challenges and responses. *Medicine, 103*(27), e38811. DOI: 10.1097/MD.0000000000038811

Cui, R., Xie, X., Fan, L., & Yang, X. (2024, August). The Application and Challenges of Artificial Intelligence in Supporting Educational Innovation. In *2024 4th International Conference on Big Data Engineering and Education (BDEE)* (pp. 38-42). IEEE. DOI: 10.1109/BDEE63226.2024.00014

Dandachi, I. E. (2024). AI-powered personalized learning: Toward sustainable education. In *Navigating the intersection of business, sustainability and technology* (pp. 109–118). Springer Nature Singapore.

Doe, J., Smith, J., Brown, R., Green, A., White, M., Johnson, E., & Carter, E. (2025). Leveraging deep and reinforcement learning to optimize academic performance in higher education: A comprehensive scoping review. *AI*, *6*(2), 40. DOI: 10.3390/ai6020040

Duan, Y., Edwards, J. S., & Dwivedi, Y. K. (2019). Artificial Intelligence for Decision Making in the era of Big Data–Evolution, Challenges and Research Agenda. *International Journal of Information Management*, *48*, 63–71. DOI: 10.1016/j.ijinfomgt.2019.01.021

Facione, P. A. (2020). *Critical thinking: What it is and why it counts.* Insight Assessment.

Faisal, E. (2024). Unlock the potential for Saudi Arabian higher education: A systematic review of the benefits of ChatGPT. []. Frontiers Media SA.]. *Frontiers in Education*, *9*, 1325601. DOI: 10.3389/feduc.2024.1325601

Francis, N. J., Jones, S., & Smith, D. P. (2025). Generative AI in higher education: Balancing innovation and integrity. *British Journal of Biomedical Science*, *81*, 14048. DOI: 10.3389/bjbs.2024.14048

Ge, Z., & Hu, Y. (2020). Innovative application of artificial intelligence (AI) in the management of higher education and teaching. *Journal of Physics: Conference Series*, *1533*(3), 32089. DOI: 10.1088/1742-6596/1533/3/032089

Gligorea, I., Cioca, M., Oancea, R., Gorski, A. T., Gorski, H., & Tudorache, P. (2023). Adaptive learning using artificial intelligence in e-learning: A literature review. *Education Sciences*, *13*(12), 1216. DOI: 10.3390/educsci13121216

Gobert, J. D. (2023). Inq-ITS: Creating rigorous assessment and real-time support of science learning. *XRDS: Crossroads. The ACM Magazine for Students*, *29*(3), 36–40. DOI: 10.1145/3589647

González-Calatayud, V., Prendes-Espinosa, P., & Roig-Vila, R. (2021). Artificial intelligence for student assessment: A systematic review. *Applied Sciences (Basel, Switzerland)*, *11*(12), 5467. DOI: 10.3390/app11125467

Grace, E. G., Vidhyavathi, P., & Malathi, P. (2023). A study on" AI in education: Opportunities and challenges for personalized learning. *Industrial Engineering Journal*, *52*(05), 750–759. DOI: 10.36893/IEJ.2023.V52I05.750-759

Hahn, M. G., Navarro, S. M. B., Valentín, L. D. L. F., & Burgos, D. (2021). A systematic review of the effects of automatic scoring and automatic feedback in educational settings. *IEEE Access : Practical Innovations, Open Solutions*, *9*, 108190–108198. DOI: 10.1109/ACCESS.2021.3100890

Harry, A., & Sayudin, S. (2023). Role of AI in Education. [INJURITY]. *Interdiciplinary Journal and Hummanity*, *2*(3), 260–268.

Hashim, S., Omar, M. K., Ab Jalil, H., & Sharef, N. M. (2022). Trends on technologies and artificial intelligence in education for personalized learning: Systematic literature. *Journal of Academic Research in Progressive Education and Development*, *12*(1), 884–903. DOI: 10.6007/IJARPED/v11-i1/12230

Hennekeuser, D., Vaziri, D. D., Golchinfar, D., Schreiber, D., & Stevens, G. (2024). Enlarged education—Exploring the use of generative AI to support lecturing in higher education. *International Journal of Artificial Intelligence in Education*, •••, 1–33.

Holmes, W., Anastopoulou, S., Schaumburg, H., & Mavrikis, M. (2018). Technology-enhanced personalised learning: Untangling the evidence.

Holmes, W., & Miao, F. (2023). *Guidance for generative AI in education and research*. Unesco Publishing.

Holmes, W., & Tuomi, I. (2022). State of the art and practice in AI in education. *European Journal of Education*, *57*(4), 542–570. DOI: 10.1111/ejed.12533

Holstein, K., & Doroudi, S. (2021). Equity and artificial intelligence in education: will" aied" amplify or alleviate inequities in education? *arXiv preprint arXiv:2104.12920*.

Hooda, M., Rana, C., Dahiya, O., Rizwan, A., & Hossain, M. S. (2022). Artificial intelligence for assessment and feedback to enhance student success in higher education. *Mathematical Problems in Engineering*, *2022*(1), 5215722. DOI: 10.1155/2022/5215722

Hoque, R., Sorwar, G., & Alzoubi, M. (2021). A Comprehensive Review of the Use of Artificial Intelligence in Education: Opportunities and Challenges. *Journal of Educational Technology & Society*, *24*(2), 110–123.

Jain, S., & Jain, R. (2019). Role of artificial intelligence in higher education—An empirical investigation. *IJRAR-International Journal of Research and Analytical Reviews*, *6*(2), 144–150.

Jaiswal, A., & Arun, C. J. (2021). Potential of artificial intelligence for transformation of the education system in India. *International Journal of Education and Development Using Information and Communication Technology*, *17*(1), 142–158.

Kaku, M. (2019). 10 Robots, artificial intelligence, and the future of work. *Environmental Health and the US Federal System: Sustainably Managing Health Hazards*, 254.

Kamak, R., Debo, D., & Saaida, M. (2024). *Challenges of AI in higher education. LVR Center.* Libra Academy.

Kamalov, F., Santandreu Calonge, D., & Gurrib, I. (2023). New era of artificial intelligence in education: Towards a sustainable multifaceted revolution. *Sustainability (Basel), 15*(16), 12451. DOI: 10.3390/su151612451

Kelly, A. E. (2026). AI-Supported Knowledge-Building Action Networks (KBANs) for Education. In *Third International Handbook of Educational Change* (pp. 1–19). Springer Nature Switzerland. DOI: 10.1007/978-3-031-88898-4_13-1

. Khosravi, H., Shum, S. B., Chen, G., Conati, C., Tsai, Y. S., Kay, J., ... & Gašević, D. (2022). Explainable artificial intelligence in education. *Computers and education: artificial intelligence, 3*, 100074.

Kumar, D., Haque, A., Mishra, K., Islam, F., Mishra, B. K., & Ahmad, S. (2023). Exploring the transformative role of artificial intelligence and metaverse in education: A comprehensive review. *Metaverse Basic and Applied Research, 2*, 21. DOI: 10.56294/mr202355

Latif, E., Liu, V., & Zhai, X. (2026). A systematic review of intelligent and robot tutoring systems: Evolution, pedagogical design, and AI-driven classification. *Smart Learning Environments, 13*(1), 1. DOI: 10.1186/s40561-025-00427-9

Lee, J., Suh, T., Roy, D., & Baucus, M. (2019). Emerging technology and business model innovation: The case of artificial intelligence. *Journal of Open Innovation, 5*(3), 44. DOI: 10.3390/joitmc5030044

Lin, Y., Luo, Q., & Qian, Y. (2023). Investigation of Artificial Intelligence algorithms in education. *Applied and Computational Engineering, 16*(1), 180–184. DOI: 10.54254/2755-2721/16/20230886

Luckin, R., & Holmes, W. (2016). Intelligence unleashed: An argument for AI in education.

Ma, X., & Jiang, C. (2023). On the ethical risks of artificial intelligence applications in education and its avoidance strategies. *Journal of Education. Humanities and Social Sciences, 14*, 354–359.

Manuel, C. C. J. (2025). The impact of AI on inclusivity in higher education: A rapid review. *Education Sciences, 15*(9), 1255. DOI: 10.3390/educsci15091255

McCalla, G. (2023). The History of Artificial Intelligence in Education – the First Quarter Century. In B. du Boulay, T. Mitrovic, & K. Yacef (Eds.), Handbook of Artificial Intelligence in Education. Edward Elgar Publishing., Retrieved February 13, 2024, from. DOI: 10.4337/9781800375413.00010

McCarthy, J. (1956). Measures of the value of information. *Proceedings of the National Academy of Sciences of the United States of America*, *42*(9), 654–655. DOI: 10.1073/pnas.42.9.654

Müller, S. D., & Mønsted, T. S. (2025). AI-enhanced learning: Exploring the use of generative AI as a study tutor.

Murtaza, M., Ahmed, Y., Shamsi, J. A., Sherwani, F., & Usman, M. (2022). AI-based personalized e-learning systems: Issues, challenges, and solutions. *IEEE Access : Practical Innovations, Open Solutions*, *10*, 81323–81342. DOI: 10.1109/ACCESS.2022.3193938

Nirala, K. K., Singh, N. K., & Purani, V. S. (2022). A survey on providing customer and public administration based services using AI: Chatbot. *Multimedia Tools and Applications*, *81*(16), 22215–22246. DOI: 10.1007/s11042-021-11458-y

Pavlik, J. V. (2023). Collaborating with ChatGPT: Considering the implications of generative artificial intelligence for journalism and media education. *Journalism & mass communication educator, 78*(1), 84-93.

Perera, M., & Aboal, D. (2019). The impact of a mathematics computer-assisted learning platform on students' mathematics test scores: The case of the automotive industry in turkey.

Pratama, M. P., Sampelolo, R., & Lura, H. (2023). Revolutionizing education: harnessing the power of artificial intelligence for personalized learning. *Klasikal: Journal of education, language teaching and science, 5*(2), 350-357.

Qadir, J. (2023). Engineering education in the era of ChatGPT: Promise and pitfalls of generative AI for education. In *2023 IEEE global engineering education conference (EDUCON)* (pp. 1-9). IEEE.

Rahayu, S. (2023). The impact of artificial intelligence on education: Opportunities and challenges. *Jurnal Educatio FKIP UNMA*, *9*(4), 2132–2140.

Raj, N. S., & Renumol, V. G. (2022). A systematic literature review on adaptive content recommenders in personalized learning environments from 2015 to 2020. *Journal of Computers in Education*, *9*(1), 113–148. DOI: 10.1007/s40692-021-00199-4

Rastrollo-Guerrero, J. L., Gómez-Pulido, J. A., & Durán-Domínguez, A. (2020). Analyzing and Predicting Students' Performance by Means of Machine Learning: A Review. *Applied Sciences (Basel, Switzerland)*, *10*(3), 1042. DOI: 10.3390/app10031042

Russell, S. J. (2010). *Artificial intelligence a modern approach*. Pearson Education, Inc.

Seo, K., Tang, J., Roll, I., Fels, S., & Yoon, D. (2021). The impact of artificial intelligence on learner–instructor interaction in online learning. *International Journal of Educational Technology in Higher Education*, *18*(1), 54. DOI: 10.1186/s41239-021-00292-9

Sharma, A., & Rani, R. (2025). *Artificial Intelligence and Speech Technology*.

Solanki, M. (2025). Exploring the factors affecting dropout rates in higher education institutions in India. *International journal of applied*, *2*(01), 43-49.

St-Hilaire, F., Vu, D. D., Frau, A., Burns, N., Faraji, F., Potochny, J., . . . Kochmar, E. (2022). A new era: Intelligent tutoring systems will transform online learning for millions. *arXiv preprint arXiv:2203.03724*.

Syukri, M., Basri, M., Halim, A., & Maghfirah, S. (2025). Improving Students Ability to Evaluate and Conclude Through a Scientific Approach. *Current STEAM and Education Research*, *3*(1), 1–12. DOI: 10.58797/cser.030101

Tan, S. (2020). Artificial intelligence in education: Rise of the machines. *Journal of Applied Learning & Teaching*, *3*(1), 129–133. DOI: 10.37074/jalt.2020.3.1.17

Tapalova, O., & Zhiyenbayeva, N. (2022). Artificial intelligence in education: AIEd for personalised learning pathways. *Electronic Journal of e-Learning*, *20*(5), 639–653. DOI: 10.34190/ejel.20.5.2597

Tonbuloğlu, B. (2023). An evaluation of the use of artificial intelligence applications in online education. *Journal of Educational Technology and Online Learning*, *6*(4), 866–884. DOI: 10.31681/jetol.1335906

Tuomi, I. (2018). *The impact of artificial intelligence on learning, teaching, and education*. Publications Office of the European Union.

Vieriu, A. M., & Petrea, G. (2025). The impact of artificial intelligence (AI) on students' academic development. *Education Sciences*, *15*(3), 343. DOI: 10.3390/educsci15030343

Wheeler, S. (2019). *Digital learning in organizations: Help your workforce capitalize on technology*. Kogan Page Publishers.

Wu, Y. (2023). Integrating generative AI in education: How ChatGPT brings challenges for future learning and teaching. *Journal of Advanced Research in Education*, *2*(4), 6–10. DOI: 10.56397/JARE.2023.07.02

Zahid, A., & Nawab, A. (2025). Teaching strategies influencing learning strategies: Exploration of teaching and learning practices in a higher education context in Pakistan. *Social Sciences & Humanities Open*, *11*, 101442. DOI: 10.1016/j.ssaho.2025.101442

Zawacki-Richter, O., Marín, V. I., Bond, M., & Gouverneur, F. (2019). Systematic review of research on artificial intelligence applications in higher education—Where are the educators? *International Journal of Educational Technology in Higher Education*, *16*(1), 39. DOI: 10.1186/s41239-019-0171-0

Zhang, K., & Aslan, A. B. (2021). AI technologies for education: Recent research & future directions. *Computers and education. Artificial Intelligence*, 2, 100025.

Zobel, T., Staubitz, T., & Meinel, C. (2023) Introducing a Smart Learning Assistant on a MOOC Platform: Enhancing Personalized Learning Experiences. In *2023 IEEE 2nd German Education Conference (GECon)* (pp. 1-6). IEEE.PI.

Chapter 7

Overcoming Resistance to AI Adoption Using Change Management Strategies in Higher Education Institutions

Sushil Bhardwaj
http://orcid.org/0000-0001-5184-3866
RIMT University, Punjab, India

Harpominder Jit Kaur
http://orcid.org/0009-0000-3821-9057
Chandigarh University, Punjab, India

Vinod Kumar
http://orcid.org/0000-0002-1123-9389
Guru Kashi University, Talwandi Sabo, India

Vandita
RIMT University, Punjab, India

Meentu Grover
Guru Kashi University, Talwandi Sabo, India

ABSTRACT

The artificial intelligence (AI) sector is reshaping higher education through the teaching, learning, and administration. However, many institutions experience resistance toward AI-based applications owing to the threat of job losses, insufficient digital

DOI: 10.4018/979-8-3373-5586-3.ch007

skills, and the conflict of ethics. The chapter elaborates on the human and organizational factors which hamper AI in higher education organizations and suggests effective change management strategies to resolve them. It emphasizes the role of the top management, communication, and the professional development programs in reducing the uncertainty and building trust in AI systems. The chapter constructs practical models that use well-established theories such as Kotter's, ADKAR, and Lewin's to guide the institutions through the process of technological change. The discussion emphasizes that successful AI adoption depends not only on technology but also on people-centered change processes.

1. INTRODUCTION

As one of the most transformative, artificial intelligence has now become an integral part of modern education. It has resulted in a change of teaching, assessing, and learning management in universities. AI takes the place of the technological tools used by a tutor, auto grading, and assessments based on predictive analytics. These changes in the academic setting are not merely promises but are being realized through technological advancements that are being utilized by the students of today (Tarisayi, 2023). Nevertheless, the journey to of adoption AI has not been without pitfalls. The ability to incorporate it at many universities is contested. Teachers, administrators, and support staff often question it, its place, and its overall effect. Concerns are not because of reluctance towards technology but they come with more fundamental issues, details about control, values, and identity.

Education mostly relies on personal connections, creative thinking, and the ability to decide for yourself. Automation, however, is the entry of a challenger to this particular environment, as it contradicts the long-held beliefs. A lot of teachers are in the opinion that AI will actually as intelligent machines take decision for human beings. The concern of some others is that systems which drive are likely to ignore students' social and emotional learning aspects (Chimpiri, 2025). These problems are one of the main sources of tension in the digitization of education.

The adoption of AI is therefore not a technical problem but a human one. It comes from feelings, perceptions, and experiences. Faculty members, who have spent many years adjusting their teaching style, could find such systems different and less personal. Caretakers may think along the lines of fairness, cost, and the long-term aspect. Students would have the same question concerning whether the decisions from an AI can be trusted or they are transparent. Besides changing the perspective these also complicate the change process (Yuan, 2024). The pace of change in higher education has always been slow. The universities are known for their value of thought process, discussion, and arriving at a consensus. Nevertheless, the increasing speed of technological development engenders a feeling of urgency that collides with the culture of academia (Doan Erlangga et al., 2025). The leaders have to do a balancing act of introduction of innovation while also keeping the institutional values intact. If the conflict is not managed properly tensions will rise, and people will become confused and fragmented.

The deployment of artificial intelligence implies a clear-cut promise and a certain suspension of the status quo. On the one side, it may mean easing administrative burdens, recognizing learning deficiencies, and tailor-making teaching. Conversely, it gives rise to ethical and psychological issues. Whose data is it anyway? How do we assure equality and privacy? What is the situation when a robot does not coincide with the views of a teacher? If educational institutions are to correctly utilize AI, these matters ought to be addressed with utmost seriousness.

The management of change gives a framework to go through this state of affairs. This approach basically focuses on guiding the people through the transition process rather than imposing consent. The effective management of change is based on the acknowledgment of feelings, the building of trust, and the communication of objectives. It changes passive resistance into active involvement by partnering technology with human needs (Tsarkos, 2024). For these reasons, the institutions must make sure to treat the faculty and staff not as subjects of change but as partners in innovation with AI adoption processes. The encouragement is participation in ownership. When teachers are made to see the role played by AI in the improvement of their work, it will lessen their fear. They will experience a shift in addressing the topics because of the new possibilities rather than defending the old routines. Therefore, engagement should start before the implementation, and durable throughout the transformation process.

Leadership is key in this venture. The leaders with vision paint a picture of AI that is a necessity and what the technology drives. They build a sense of shared purpose beyond technology. The successful leaders do not dictate change; they manage it with empathy and transparency. Their trustworthiness gives birth to faith that in turn results in credible communication. Trust is the absolute basis of change within the academic circle. Faculty members have trust in administrators that they would keep academic integrity whole, similarly, students trust their teachers in fairness. AI has to fit well into this structure. If the technology turns out to be a distrustful entity, it might even bring down the most advanced systems. Hence, wise governance and accountability must be present in every facet of AI integration (Hojeij, 2025). Schools are also to actively recognize the difference in readiness levels among their faculties. There are some instructors who are keen on being first with digital innovations and try them out. Others adopt a delay strategy until there are results that they can rely on (Magrill et al., 2024). A smaller number of them will not have anything to do with it because of fear, uncertainty, or even issues like the lack of backing. It is vital that all three categories are supported in the process of change management through communication, training, and recognition.

Training and professional development are essential for overcoming resistance. Many educators resist not because they oppose technology, but because they feel unprepared. Practical workshops, mentoring programs, and peer learning reduce anxiety. When people feel competent, they participate more willingly (Torrisi-Steele, 2025). Continuous learning ensures that technological transformation strengthens rather than disrupts teaching quality.

Another equally significant factor in the process of AI implementation in universities is ethical considerations. They are not only about increasing productivity: universities should also be morally accountable. They have to ensure that they are fair with privacy and respect for intellectual freedom. On the other hand, ethical reflection for the implementation of AI is needed to protect the principles that education is after. Transparent data policies, bias audits, and the role of a human are the main tools with which to demonstrate accountability and win trust.

Another important issue is the culture fit. Each institution has its own traditions, power structures, and shared beliefs. What works well in one environment may have a different outcome in another. Strategies must be adjusted to local cultures and the leadership must respect the values that are already there, while at the same time push for innovation. Adoption of AI should be understood as a natural evolutionary process rather than a disruption.

The communication is the sewing thread of change that links all things together. Without a clear and comprehensive communication strategy, even the best laydown plans will not work. It is necessary for institutions to communicate what AI is, its significance, and how it will be used. Frequent announcements, open discussions, and sincere conversations will help avoiding rumors and problems. Communication has also to be two-sided; for this, the leaders should keep the balance between talking and listening. People’s fear of not being included or not being asked is often the reason of resistance. The aims turn the lack of understanding into a common action (Sejdiu et al., 2025). When individuals witness that their thoughts are taken into account, they feel acknowledged. The feeling of belonging in the community then has a transforming effect on the lack of clarity turning it into interest. Consequently, AI becomes a joined venture instead of just a top-down prescription. The emotional factor in change must be taken into account. Transition brings out emotions such as fear, confusion, and fatigue which are normal. The recognition of these feelings creates psychological safety. Therefore, the leaders should provide spaces for talk, be empathetic, and celebrate even the small achievements. The act of recognition is a sign of one's commitment and reminds the people of the significance of their contributions.

AI must be regarded not just as a tool but rather as a vehicle for the renewal of learning processes at higher education institutions. AI can help by streamlining data management, improving usability, and increasing the reach of the curriculum. That said, AI's success will hinge on maintaining people's humanity. AI should complement teaching rather than substitute it. In decision-making, it should assist, but not override human judgment. AI’s long-term inclusion in the school system is a way to transform the main goal of education. By doing so, universities will be able to prioritize and concentrate more on creativity, ethics, and critical thinking. The routine tasks being handled by technology, the educators will have more time to mentor and inspire their students. Therefore, AI is being a great support for the cause of education that is not only mere learning but wisdom development.

This chapter comprises the scan of the strategies of strict change management for the shift towards AI in universities (Westover, 2024). Readings will encounter anecdotes about what the decision-making process can trigger, the leaders' role in trust uplifting, and what are the structures that help in the change process. Moreover, this paper is going to cite case studies and types of plans that show how human-centric practices pave the way for sustained success. People at the end of the chapter will recognize promotion of AI, not a technical event, rather a cultural procedure. This evolution is based on vision, discipline, and empathy. The path of change management is clear and guarantees that innovation builds up and not breaks down.

The effect of artificial intelligence on the field of education cannot be underestimated going forward. The institutions that will cope with the ups and downs will not only just survive but also excel. They will then give rise to a new kind of learning that is smart, inclusive, and ethical. Their major achievement will be the demonstration of the feasibility of coexistence of progress with the benefits of humanity. The upcoming change will not be about machines taking over from humans. Rather, it will be empowering the teachers to learn and teach in new and impactful ways. When the direction is provided with intentionality, the result is the fading of resistance and the thriving of innovation (Qiu et al., 2023). The educational context of being in a state of balanced technology with trust lies on the way of true education.

Understanding Resistance to AI in Academic Settings

The resistance that is faced by the artificial intelligence in higher education is a natural phenomenon and it is also complex. It does not refer to the simple rejection by technology, but to the expression of beliefs, habits, and values. The evolution of universities is slow and comes through the social dialogue and reflection. The outcome of this dilemma is mistrust and resistance when the innovation is faster than the comprehension. Understanding the reasons for this resistance helps institutions design strategies that are inclusive, ethical, and sustainable. The challenge of AI in education occurs in various domains such as the way of teaching, evaluating, and interacting. It is an introduction of an uncertain aspect about their role, authority, and purpose to many educators (Kazimova et al., 2025).

Within these situations, the AI is considered to be both a helpful tool and a danger to human creativity and professional independence. On the other hand, the AI is seen as a tool that can assist the work of other professionals and a possible danger to the autonomy of these people. The next part covers the key areas of resistance - psychological, structural, ethical, communicative, and human - which are the factors that construct the different forms of people's reactions to technological advances.

Psychological and Cultural Barriers

The first layer of the wall is the psyche. The cycle of any change begins with the brain, and new and strange machines trigger fears, worries, and anxiety. There is a group of educators who think that AI should not be their game because AI can be better than them in making judgments or it may be seen the AI is taking their independence. They may imagine that the AI will eliminate the human interaction that is part of the teaching process. The cultural barriers increase this fear. Teaching and learning value academic culture independence, resistance, and individual interpretation very much. But artificial intelligence is an environment that makes use of patterns, data, and predictions, which are, of course, opposite to that of AI. This difference in viewpoint generates tension. Faculty members may feel that data-driven systems challenge their autonomy or question their expertise (Nithya, 2025).

The lack of the right knowledge about how the programs such as AI work usually exacerbates challenges. Deep machine-learning algorithms and technical jargon give the impression that AI is a black box or that it cannot be trusted. This results in distrust of the technology. The assurance of transparency and the form of an open dialogue are therefore the key in persuading people to believe and use the technology. The scope of confusion in the culture of readiness can be widely felt in the institutions. Engineering and computer science sectors may be more than happy with automation than humanities and other social sciences that may take a positive but conservative stand against it. The acknowledgement of this diversity empowers leaders to be able to modify communication and training (Farid, 2025). Empathy and education are the driving forces for the removal of psychological and cultural barriers. Educators' anxiety about the integration of technology is reduced when they are educated, supported, and given time to adapt. The embrace of knowing instead of turning a blind eye from it makes all the difference to a feeling of fear overcoming that of involvement.

Structural and Institutional Challenges

The resistance also comes from the institutional structures. Many universities are rooted in traditional governance systems that are slow to change. Decision-making is often along with unyielding hierarchies, which do not let faculty get much say in technological executions. When the decision for change is made by management, it is going to be an act of self-defence to that change.

The bureaucratic complexity that it brings is an additional difficulty factor. The introduction of AI involves a web of different steps such as approvals, policy formulation, and redistribution of resources. Such activities might cause delays in progress and serve as impediments for the innovators. Dealing with the slow mechanisms leads to the loss of interest. Resource limitations also pose another difficulty. The adoption of AI requires a technical infrastructure, human specialists, and an initial investment. These are resources that most institutions, especially small and publicly funded ones, lack. When the technology breaks down due to poor support, it serves as a concrete fuel for distrust.

Policy inconsistency is also a factor that can fuel resistance. If the AI utilization guidelines are unclear, it is very probable that faculty members will feel insecure about accountability or data misuse. Uncertainty of the consequences creates fear. To cut through the structural barriers, the administrative bodies must be flexible. Universities should undergo the participatory governance process where the faculty and students have their distinct input in decision-making. Trial projects could help with gradual introduction and testing before the whole system is up and running (Chadha, 2024). Clear communication of duties and results means that there is transparency. When institutions reorient their structures to be built around cooperation and shared responsibility, technology turns from a thing that is imposed from the outside to a collaborative goal. As the community starts to deliver what it stands for, so the force weakens.

Ethical and Pedagogical Concerns

Ethical and pedagogical problems are the major sources of resistance. Education is a type of moral profession. Faculty members are concerned fairplay, integrity, and student growth. They resist when they see technology as a factor that can threaten those values.

Data protection is indeed a very ethical problem. Artificial intelligence systems frequently consider astrophysics of huge data loads of student information—academic records, attendance, and behaviour data. If insufficient protections are in place, this data can be used for purposes other than intended or released to unauthorized parties. Concerned about the use of this information and the way it is applied tutors are faced with a dilemma.

Bias in algorithms is quite another serious concern. AI systems which are fed with data that already contain inequalities, will learn from this data. Thus, uncorrected algorithms can show these biases again. For instance, some programs for grading or admissions could, by chance, prefer some backgrounds over others.

Pedagogical issues impact the resistance, too. The majority of the teachers want to automate the process of learning rather than computers taking over the whole process. They highlight the role of personal relationships, discussion, and creativity that are not comparable with machines. Faculty members wonder that AI might save time at the expense of sympathy (Farooq et al., 2024).

Taking the right steps to address these worries, institutions must build ethics into all stages of AI implementation. The policies should clearly set the boundaries for data use, and teachers must be given the final say over any academic decisions. Ethical committees are responsible to watch the systems to be fair and to hold accountability. AI is to teach in an enhanced way, but not in a dictated way. Trusting in the knowledge that technology is a partner for improving learners' performance, teachers start to believe in its potential. Ethical assurances turn moral doubts into professional curiosity.

Communication and Perception Gaps

As the communication is breaking down, the resistance is increasing. A number of institutions set up new technologies with a very short explanation or hint hoping that users will naturally adapt. What happens in reality is that improper communication creates misunderstanding, and fear. If the information is not clear, people will imagine the worst possible outcomes. Perceptual misfits are outstanding between the tech teams, the boards, and the teachers. Technological teams are usually preoccupied with performance and modernity, while the majority of teachers are dedicated to student welfare and pedagogy (Al Daraai et al., 2024). Due to such a misalignment, the two different targets emerge. When educators think their opinions matter little, they become very defensive.

Language is in itself an obstacle. The technical words make artificial intelligence look like an exotic and hidden space place which is hard to access. The teachers who aren't competent in keeping up with the mechanics of complex discourse could completely tune out. This communication has to be inclusive which means that it should use simple and relatable language. Openness lies at the core of it all. The institutions ought to be transparent both in sharing their achievements and the problems openly. When people perceive the institutions as straightforward, their confidence improves. Overlooking issues damages the credibility of the person. Channels of feedback are also significant. A two-way communication flow ensures that the teachers will get a chance to communicate their views and accordingly influence the decisions. Regular meetings, forums, and surveys create a sense of engagement. The institutions that are responsive and treat everyone equally are the ones which listen. Communication evolves to become a bridge that connects not persuades. People trust one another when they feel they are being listened to and valued.

The Human Element of Change

The main reason for AI resistance not being technology, but it is the people. So, it is a symbol of emotion, identity, and belonging. Teachers regard their activities as part of their personalities or even the whole selves. When around are new devices that could seem to challenge that self, then resistance happens as means to keep the self-esteem intact.

Realizing this emotional layer is crucial for effective change processes. In educational institutions, faculties should not be seen as obstacles, but as partners in the navigation process through the times of uncertainty (Salmon et al., 2024). Changes in the environment typically lead to insecurity and reduced motivation, which, in turn, affect professional pride. For that reason, leaders must be empathetic. The engagement process has to be continuous rather than episodic. Frequent communication, acknowledgement, and reassurance build the trust. When educators realize that their opinions significantly contribute to the outcomes, they become more willing to try new methods. Training and mentoring enhance knowledge, while emotional support helps build self-confidence. Schools should promote peer networks in which teachers can talk about their experiences, successes, and challenges. The communities provide a sense of comradeship and lessen solitude.

The leaders should also personify the humane side of change. By being truthful about the challenges and saying thank you, they create a commitment. Transparent leadership levies commitment and builds resilience. Change has a dual character: it is not only selecting the right tools for a job but also the development of the proper frame of mind. When people feel they are in a safe haven and are one supported, they are inclined to think technological novelties with interest instead of apprehension. The resistance is not raised when the change process is operated keeping the human dignity.

Emotional intelligence is the way for artificial intelligence to come true in education. Empathy, equity, and honor have stayed the only means of change. When educational institutions entwine these personal assets with creativity, technology becomes a legitimate partner in education. The resistance by the higher education institutions to the AI is due to various causes-inherent fears, conservative institutions, ethical concerns, and communication barriers (Kayyali, 2025). Nonetheless, none of the barriers are here to stay. Through purposeful leadership and people-centric change management, the ground can be prepared for the transition from resistance to readiness.

Learning why people are resistant is the crucial first step to the success of any technological march. It gives institutions the opportunity to create not only practical but also compassionate strategies. When fear gives way to understanding and exclusion makes place for participation, then the shift becomes rapid. AI is bound to promote learning but only in case it serves the purpose of humans. Hence, such changes should be implemented in a manner that is empathic, clear, and respectful. The institutions are getting ready for the era of coexisting while addressing the roots of resistance through technology and humanity moving forward collectively in harmony.

THE ROLE OF INSTITUTIONAL LEADERSHIP IN AI CHANGE MANAGEMENT

Leadership determines how smoothly higher education institutions adopt artificial intelligence (Katsamakas et al., 2024). While technology provides the tools, leadership provides the direction, trust, and motivation needed for transformation. When institutional leaders approach AI with clarity, empathy, and strategy, resistance decreases naturally. Successful AI adoption depends less on technical skill and more on leadership that inspires confidence and shared purpose.

Vision Building and Strategic Alignment

In most cases, a successful transformation starts with a clear and mutual vision. The leaders need to state their position on AI and what good it will do for the institution. With no such clarity, academic staff and faculty may think of technology as a featured part of the journey rather than the end, of the result. An effective vision is one that presents AI projects as part and parcel of institutional values and educational missions. It tells how AI improves teaching quality, research productivity, and administrative visibility. When the goal is clear, people tend to join voluntarily.

Strategic alignment is the principle that makes sure that all departments target the same outcome. The leaders need to tie AI projects to student outcomes, institutional growth, and academic quality. This coordination avoids confusion and keeps the resources intact. Involving persons is the basic step for the creation of a shared vision. At all stages, the leaders need to get the input of faculty, IT staff, and students. If people are part of the planning process, they become the owners of the change. Collaborative goal-setting encourages commitment and trust, which helps to reduce resistance at initial stages. Besides, the overall vision should be achievable. Unrealistic targets can only lead to disappointment. Leaders should communicate attainable milestones, underlining the fact that the digital change is a process of time and learning. A clear, inclusive, and achievable vision is the basis for the construction of long-termed transformations.

Transparent Communication and Trust Building

Trust is the basis of every change initiative. In the case of implementing AI, trust must be developed at different levels- between leaders and faculty, among faculty, and between humans and machines. Without trust even the most sophisticated technology is difficult to accept.

Communication should be clear and thus a priority for any leader who wishes to shift the paradigms of trust. Leaders should be transparent and share their goals, outline processes, and discuss the potential impact of AI integration. Ignoring the issues or uncertainties can invite fear and mistrust. On the contrary, being honest encourages people to work together. A communicative platform can be established through a two-way contact, where workers give inquiries, announce concerns, and offer suggestions (Martins, 2023). Public forums, workshops, and one-on-one conversations are great platforms for dialogue creation. When leaders hear and react to people’s views with empathy, they manifest respect for individual perspectives (Singh et al., 2024).

Unity in communication is another vital factor. Wrong signals from different administrators may create ambiguity among the employees. It is the duty of leaders to make sure that all communication follows the same, all-inclusive institutional vision. Consistent and clear messages indicate that the leadership is coordinated and self-assured. Trust develops also by leaders who practice ethics (AL-Alosi, 2025). They have to show the right handling of technology, protection of privacy, and security of academic integrity. If the faculty see these actions, they are going to be more likely to act in the same manner. Trust cannot be introduced on demand; it has to be achieved through transparency and exemplification.

Leading by Example and Encouraging Participation

Modeling the behavior is one of the best strategies for managing change in the technology. When the leaders utilize AI applications and participate in training courses, they demonstrate a strong commitment to the cause. Faculty and staff are more likely to involve themselves in the process when they see leaders learning together with them. Inclusion is one of the strongest forms of understanding. When the leading figures in the organization take part in training programs, meetings and assessments, they openly express their faith in the program. Their presence dissipates doubts and entices others to follow suit.

Leaders should also mentor those who are quick to introduce new practices and are creative. AI tools can be used by the faculty members who are the chief innovators; they can teach their colleagues how to use the tools. The recognition and rewards for such individuals will help foster the collaborative culture of the institute. The other crucial task is to eliminate the obstacles that stand in the way of experimentation. Bureaucratic systems and rigid structures can hinder creativity. Leaders should streamline processes while providing the means for testing and validating. Openness helps to remove obstacles to the original growth of ideas (Kabir, 2023). To promote participation also means to acknowledge the contribution of others. By telling the success stories—no matter how small—build up workers moral and show them that they make progress. Individuals when they feel grateful, their enthusiasm spreads to others. In the long term, participation will create a flow that changes resistance into common accomplishment.

Governance and Ethical Oversight

Ethical rules have to guide the educational technological change. Institutional heads should ensure that the use of AI conforms with the standards of academic knowledge, fairness and privacy. Even the well-intentioned initiatives unduly can create ethical risks without governance and oversight.

The foundation of governance is laid with policies. Data should be collected, used, and protected as disclosed by the institutions. The transparency of these processes decreases fears and confidence is built in the faculty and students. Policies should address issues of consent, the prevention of bias, and the appropriate usage of AI-derived knowledge. Ethical committees must be created by the leaders to oversee the related projects. These committees will analyze the fairness and the visibility of the algorithms that power the technology in ways that are consistent with the institutional principles. Prevention of unethical behaviors and strengthening obligation are done through ethical oversight. Inclusivity is a part of governance too. Ethical deliberation should have the representatives of the teaching, research, administration, and student associations. The sharing of responsibility in this way will bring a diverse set of views to the policy-making process.

Strong governance systems make it possible to manage the balance between innovation and accountability. They are signals that the institution means it when it comes to responsible AI usage. Leadership, thus, makes the unknown turn into trust and gives technology the purpose of marketing education, thus, human flourishing, and collective learning.

CHANGE MANAGEMENT MODELS FOR AI INTEGRATION

Change management provides a systematic approach for guiding institutions through digital transformation. In higher education, it ensures that the adoption of artificial intelligence aligns with academic goals and human values. Institutions that follow structured models reduce confusion, build confidence, and sustain progress during technological change (Jin et al., 2024). The most effective frameworks combine communication, participation, and continuous learning.

Kotter's 8-Step Model in Academic Contexts

Kotter's 8-stepped procedure is a very convenient route for managing transformation. Its regulations-creating urgency, forming coalitions, and anchoring change-fit educational settings conjointly. The model enhances the performance of universities by steering them in the direction of the cooperation of the students and the administration through the well-structured engagement.

The first thing is to create a state of urgency. The responsible individuals have to illustrate the reasons why the adoption of Artificial Intelligence has to be immediately conducted. By showing the students and the staff how technology facilitates the teaching, research, and managing processes, they are encouraged to join the implementation. When individuals recognize the necessity of change, they take the first step. Secondly, the collaboration coalition has to be formed. The coalition has to consist of academic leaders, faculty innovators, and technical experts. Together, they provide credibility and support for transformation. A diverse team also ensures that every perspective is represented. The next thing Kotter's model contemplates to do is presenting a crisp vision and strategy. Institutions must emphasize how AI serves their mission and values. The vision should both be plain and sufficient to build trust. Fourth, communication is the channel. The vision should be shared via meetings, workshops, and open discussions. Continuous communication keeps staff in the loop and let them feel involved. Addressing concerns is the way to develop mutual respect and turn down resistance. The next steps are the empowerment of employees and the generation of short-term wins. Academic departments and supervisors should be persuaded to assess AI instruments through pilot programs. The early achievements breathe the momentum and demonstrate the pros of the participation.

Finally, the change should be consoled and embedded in the culture of the organization. The policies, training programs, and acknowledgment system are the tools for keeping the progress on track. In education, Kotter's model is largely effective because it marries organization with motivation. It reshapes vague objectives into concrete, human-oriented tasks.

ADKAR Framework for Individual Transformation

While Kotter's model focuses on institutional change, the ADKAR framework targets personal transformation. Developed around five elements—Awareness, Desire, Knowledge, Ability, and Reinforcement—it explains how individuals accept and adapt to change. Awareness begins when faculty understand why AI is needed. Clear communication about benefits and risks helps create awareness. Without understanding, resistance continues. Desire develops when individuals see how AI enhances their professional lives. Leaders can foster this desire by connecting technology with personal goals, such as reduced workload or improved teaching outcomes. Knowledge follows awareness and desire. Training programs, workshops, and peer learning provide the information required to use AI tools effectively. Knowledge empowers people to act with confidence.

Ability represents the stage when individuals can practically apply new skills. Institutions must provide access to technical support, mentoring, and hands-on opportunities. Ability turns learning into capability. Reinforcement ensures that adoption becomes permanent. Recognition, rewards, and regular feedback encourage continued engagement. When educators see consistent support and appreciation, their motivation remains strong.

The ADKAR model is especially useful in universities because it focuses on personal growth. It recognises that transformation is emotional as much as procedural (Abou Adel et al., 2025). Faculty members adapt more easily when their individual needs are understood and addressed.

Lewin's Change Theory and Organisational Stability

The Change Theory by Kurt Lewin presents a different yet majorly important lens for the management of technological shifts in education. It sees the total transformation as a three-stage model: Unfreeze, Change, and Refreeze. The model's uncomplicated design is a natural fit for extensive organizations with intricate formations. The stage of Unfreeze is the preparatory one for recent innovations and transformations. Schools must discover and challenge existing beliefs or practices that keep them stuck in the situation (George et al., 2023). For this stage, it is necessary to both express the necessity of AI observance and diminish fear of unexplored topics.

The Change stage involves the introduction of new processes and equipment. Professors are trained, pilot projects are conducted, and evaluations are made. During this phase, the dialogue held openly is very crucial. Errors should be interpreted as a kind of learning rather than a fault. The Refreeze phase is the final step to solidifying the transformation. The formal declaration of new regulations, job descriptions, and employee evaluation systems is crucial. The main aim is to have

AI use on a daily basis in all academic practice. Refreezing of the changes ensures that old paths do not come back.

According to Lewin's model, the central point of flexibility and stability is the balance between them. Universities usually are having problems with the extremes-either moving very quickly or very slowly. The three-step approach is the one that holds steady progress without the risk of overwhelming the entire institution. Applied to AI acceptance, the theory of Lewin turns into a reminder that the minds of the people should be prepared first before bringing any new system and commitment should be secured before moving forward. By bringing a systematic problem into action, it is about turning the resistance of people into the readiness of them for change through the suitable interval and communication.

Integrative Model for Higher Education

Every change management model has its specific advantages. But a higher education institution is looking for a single approach that consists of structure, empathy, and inclusivity altogether. An integrative model, designed purposely for the academy, fuses the best of existing models while treating human beings as the primary drivers of technology change.

It starts with the shared vision that Kotter has proposed and involves the process of establishing the identity. Schools have to rally around a single that is easily understood sentence, which presents AI as a priority for Education. A shared vision unifies the departments and prevents the misinterpretations. Then comes personal preparedness, inspired by the ADKAR model. The change has to surround the individual knowledge, motivation, and ability to get things done. Professors and staff should be trained in such a way that no one is left behind. Rigorous support, as in the case of mentorships and peer networks, not only creates a foundation for informal sessions of learning, but it also allows for the progression of learning outside of the classroom.

The last stage synthesizes Lewin's law of stability. Once the AI practices are effectively embraced, they will be sustained through the policies and the culture. Regular meetings and feedbacks will help in evaluating the effect and maintain commitment.

The integrated model also puts emotional intelligence in the first place as a priority leadership aspect. Change leaders should realize the fact that they are anxious, they should commend the advancements, and they should respond with consciousness to the hesitation. The empathy is the building block of the trust which is built faster than guidance by instruction. The more respect the teacher gets the more willing he or she becomes to engage. Another element that is equally important is the ethical alignment of the AI practices. The past actions of the individuals always have a say in trust either building or breaking it. Ethical governance gives the members of the academic community reassurance that the integrity of the institution will not be compromised.

The inscape of the integrative model is through the cycles of planning, participation, and reflection in practical use. The understanding that each cycle deepens and the commitment that it strengthens are the main features. It is through the joining of the structure and heart that resistance turns into readiness. The integration of AI in higher education is a multi-faceted activity since it requires both learning at the organizational and individual levels. Indeed, management of change serves as the roadmap for this expedition. The effectiveness of Kotter's model, the human-centeredness focus of ADKAR, and the abiding principles in Lewin have contributed to providing a holistic perspective on the change process.

It is only when joined into one comprehensive method that these models become a real support for universities to evolve within the ethical legacy of technological advancement. Innovation in the classroom is ensured by these practices which are rooted in tradition and in which human beings are the fabric of education. To not only promote the use of new techniques but also to change the mindset to one that thrives on flexibility, collaborative work, and trust among all staff, is the final target.

FACULTY ENGAGEMENT, TRAINING, AND PARTICIPATION

Faculty members are the foundation of every higher education institution. Their engagement determines whether innovation succeeds or fails. In the case of artificial intelligence adoption, their participation is even more critical. AI directly influences teaching practices, evaluation methods, and the overall learning environment. Without faculty support, institutional transformation remains incomplete. Engagement, training, and participation form the three pillars of successful adoption. When faculty are included in decision-making, equipped with the right skills, and appreciated for their contributions, their resistance declines. They begin to view technology not as an external imposition but as a personal and collective opportunity for growth.

This section explores four key elements of faculty engagement—co-creation, capacity building, recognition, and peer collaboration. Each component strengthens trust, builds confidence, and cultivates long-term commitment to responsible AI integration.

Co-Creation and Participatory Design

The process of co-creation wherein the educators are the driving force of transformation is a good thing. It makes sure the technology aids only the people who are using it. The professors taking part in the first steps of AI design creates proprietary and trust. When the educators participate in the shaping of the system, they are not so likely to resist it. Co-creation starts with listening. Institutions must allow faculty members to speak about their expectations, concerns, and needs. These dialogues give rise to the AI strategies that are realistic and inclusive. For instance, when professors convey the difficulties they face in teaching their subject matter, it opens up the way for the developers to align AI tools with actual requirements in the classroom.

Participatory design makes the theoretical plan collaborative by making it an experiment. Workshops, focus groups, and pilot projects are platforms for teachers and technologists to work in pairs. This interactive teamwork helps everyone to know the viewpoint of the other side. Educators share their teaching strategies and practices, whereas technical experts describe AI's capabilities and limitations.

Joint testing periods often produce practical understandings which planners might miss. For instance, faculty can detect usability irregularities that engineers overlook. Likewise, data scientists can illustrate how AI might add to grading fairness or boost student engagement. As a result, these interactions form the groundwork for mutual regard. The engagement of the faculty helps to ensure that ethical issues are recognized. When teachers join in, they can talk about privacy standards or fairness questions before any operations begin. The proactive participation that this entails prevents issues arising later and also makes the institution more trustworthy.

Participation rightly should not be ensured only by a small group of innovators. Each department should have its own representative in decision-making committees. The larger the involvement the greater the sense of property. Over time, co-creation continues building a community of trust and common objective.

Capacity Building and Digital Literacy

A system however well it is designed, will not work without a capable user. Capacity building gives the facility to teachers to learn, use, and improve AI tools at their own pace. It results in an increase of uncertainty being transformed into disempowerment and curiosity being changed into abilities. Digital literacy really begins with getting to be acquainted with it. A big number of teachers do not know about artificial intelligence. The first step is to have introductory sessions that define AI, describe its operations and reason its importance for education. These gatherings should avoid technical terms and rather use straightforward illustrations and practical demonstrations.

After getting introduced to new technologies, the next step is the application of the hands-on principle. Institutions should set up training programs that will expose the faculty to theoretical and practical experience. Teachers should work with AI-powered platforms such as grading systems, chat-based tutoring tools, or research analytics dashboards. Practical experience is a much quicker form of building confidence than lectures or manuals. Mentorship can give a boost to this process. Associating digital specialists with assistants allows peer learning. Mentors present guidelines, respond to queries, and model the best practices. This relationship makes a safe psychological environment for all to learn at their own pace.

Continuous assistance is not optional. Digital abilities may become weak if they are not applied. Institutions should provide follow-up workshops, online tutorials, and help desks for any technical assistance needed. This ongoing service demonstrates the commitment to long-term academic staff development. Training should also focus on ethics. Faculty should have the knowledge about the way AI handles data, where it can be biased, and how to protect the privacy of students. When teachers are informed about both the advantages and the dangers, they can be responsible when using technology.

Teaching people how to build is not just a one-off battle. Instead, it should be embedded in the identity of the institution. Further training and upskilling are necessary to keep instructors up to speed with the arrival of new technology. This culture of learning should be cultivated in a landscape where consistency in creation takes place. Once the faculty runs digital confidence, they become the change of agents. Whether through inspiring their colleagues, guiding students, or submitting ideas, they play their part. Therefore, digital literacy is more than just being competent; it is about leading through knowledge.

Incentives and Recognition

Human motivation survives and achieves great things through the power of appreciation. Change efforts increase their support massively when people become aware that their contributions are solid. Financial and honorary rewards are necessary means to induce collective faculty to AI integration. Institutions mostly tend to be focused on infrastructure, but a lot of motivation is usually missed. The faculty teachers are under constant pressure to perform and the acquisition of new technology is just one more problem to solve. Recognition is the vehicle which instead of extra burdens, makes feelings for one's work a happy and healthy one.

Incentives can take many forms. One of the most typical and understood is that of tangible things such as funding for special teaching projects, travel money for conferences, or bonuses related to one's performance. The fact that these are rewards granted for alternative forms of teaching/learning and it shows that the institution values innovation is some of the evident of these among others. Yet, there are other, less materialistic symbols of gratitude, like simple certificates, and awards or publications in the institution's newspaper, that can also do as much as the concrete ones. Presenting awards to faculty in public during meetings or at annual events can add fire to a peer-to-peer motivating environment.

What stands out is the acknowledgment of leaders. When the administrators show their respect and thank teachers for their hard work directly, they build an emotional bond. Even a simple small note of thanks or a quick mention in the official speech can have a great effect. The acknowledgement from the peers is another great motivator. Some institutes stress the system where teachers elect and proclaim the contributions of each other. Recognition from colleagues evokes a strong sense of community. Learning has to be rewarded alongside success through recognition. A number of teachers are usually hesitant to implement AI applications in their lectures out of the fear of not being successful. Institutions must reiterate that trial and error are both equally important. The atmosphere of gratitude encourages students to take risks and make learning more fun. Last but not least, the rewards should connect with the aims of the organization. The granting of teamwork, ethical behavior, and inventiveness as a reward is the only way to say it right. Recognition, which is rooted in the shared values of the institution, will then become more significant. The strategic implementation of incentives generates a continuous movement in the veins of the organization. They convert autonomous actions into collective реформs and guarantee that the reform spirit never dies.

Peer Support and Communities of Practice

Change becomes sustainable when supported by community. The faculty members who work together, share experiences, and learn jointly are the ones who are able to face the changes better. These are the communities of practice. They constitute platforms for connecting, reflecting, and innovating. A community of practice comprises teachers who are enthusiastic about the use of Artificial Intelligence (AI) in the learning process. They schedule regular meetings to talk about the obstacles that they meet in teaching, to try the new tools, and to exchange the lessons that they have learned. At the end of the process, all this results in the growth of their collective knowledge.

Peer collaboration is a key strategy for teachers to deal with the anxiety of uncertainty. When people encounter problems with the technological devices, instead of inviting external consultants, they ask their colleagues for help. This connection among peers leads to the establishment of trust and reliance on informal structures rather than formal ones. The communities also provide a platform for open discussion. Faculty can speak out their concerns freely and investigate ethical issues together. Issues such as fairness, prejudice, and data privacy, if discussed extensively, promote understanding and build self-confidence. The group, gradually, comes up with common principles that govern the use of AI.

These communities must get the full support of the institutions. The provision of time, space, and digital platforms should be the priority, with a view to stimulating participation. Leaders can, from time to time, be present in the sessions, not just to listen but also to appreciate the progress made. The active engagement of the time would imply an acknowledgment given by the institution of respecting the voices of the faculty. Mentorship is the driver of these networks. The experienced faculty gives guidance to the newcomers, providing them with both reassurance and direction. The bridge of mentorship is built across the gaps of the generations, and it also creates a sense of continuity in the departments. Communities of practice drive innovation as well. Many of the joint projects that stem from these groups, such as collaborative research or pilot programs, are born out of the synergy and shared learning that develop into inventive solutions benefiting the complete institution.

The regular display of work, along with feedback sessions from fellow faculty, serves as a constant source of energy that keeps motivation high. Faculty can arrange the presentation of their work, the celebration of achievements, and the discussion of the lessons learned from challenges. These events are where feelings of pride are raised as well as where people are inspired to take part. The communities, as they become mature, start running the course of their own. Instead of being part of a formal initiative, peer collaboration mostly becomes a part of the daily culture. This independence not only guarantees the continuation of innovation even if the administration is focused elsewhere but also shows that the teachers can exert their influence outside the normal structures. Thanks to the consistent support from their peers, the institutions gain two results - the development of their staff and mental resilience. The faculty members understand that the integration of AI tools is not an individual's responsibility, but rather a combined effort of exploration and improvement.

The active engagement of the faculty is the lifeblood of digital transformation in the learning process. Without their playful participation, neither any plan, nor any technological resource can be successful. The elements of co-creation, building of capacity, recognition through public accountability, and community as a network create ownership, confidence, motivation, and belonging. The teachers, who are ploughed into innovation, become the frontliners of responsible innovation. They cultivate the AI systems that are in line with ethical teaching, academic freedom, and student growth. Because of their contribution, the technology gets to serve its right purpose, that is, to create minds and not machines.

The institutions, by putting in money in the engagement of teachers, assure their future. Engaged teachers will always discover new avenues, ways to inspire, ways to adapt, and ways to lead. The AI tools may augment their capacities, but the human power of inventiveness and emotional intelligence are one of a kind. In this collaboration where technology is the driver of change and people are the facilitators, the academic institutions find a straightforward route to their sustainability.

CASE STUDIES: SUCCESSFUL CHANGE MANAGEMENT IN AI INTEGRATION

Learning from real experiences helps institutions understand how artificial intelligence can be introduced effectively in higher education. Case studies provide evidence of how change management transforms resistance into participation. Each example demonstrates that success depends on leadership, communication, collaboration, and ethical commitment. AI adoption becomes meaningful only when people feel involved, supported, and valued.

The following case studies highlight institutions that implemented AI responsibly and achieved sustainable change. They show that thoughtful leadership, faculty engagement, and inclusive governance are the true drivers of technological progress in academia.

Case 1 – AI in Teaching and Assessment

A mid-sized university introduced AI to address growing workloads in student evaluation and feedback. Faculty members, on the other hand, were grading excessively which was adversely affecting their time for mentoring. The administration proposed the idea of an AI-based grading system to reduce the workload and bring about consistency. Early responses from the faculty were divided. Some were for the motion, while a few were against it, out of the concern of being deprived of the power of academic discretion. Disputes about equity and bias were the most significant matters during the early conversations. Instead of hurrying into the project, they chose a participatory approach.

The first step they took was ensuring transparency. The leadership team arranged workshops to present how the AI system worked, what data it used, and how teachers would still be in charge even with the use of it. Faculty had the opportunity to assess the baseline model's design and also engage in the pilot tests. Every department was instructed to nominate individuals to react to the conduct of the tests. Instructors compared the scores generated by artificial intelligence with those by human evaluators and then reported their findings deviating from the norm. The outcomes showed that AI was able to utilize speed for grading better while keeping it fair when people supervised it.

Then the institution established clear rules to make it clear that AI was to be a tool and not a replacement. Final grading decisions were with educators, as always. This was a clear statement that helped restore trust and advance the great shift (Osman et al., 2024). Training sessions were conducted to help faculty with the system's interface and features of interpretation which they could learn. Over time teachers progressed to not only employ the technology for grading but also for personalized feedback. AI assisted in recognizing revisions in learning that were apparent which consequently concluded that instructors could focus on introducing new concepts rather than making similar corrections. In a period of one academic year, the satisfaction of all departments increased. Students not only got feedback fast but also, faculty had less workload. The university's all-encompassing, careful approach turned a concerned situation into collaboration. The case showed that sustainability in AI adoption requires transparency, gradual implementation, and human oversight.

Case 2 – Building Trust through Storytelling and Data

Another organization, which is a big public university, met the resistance expressed by teaching and administrative staff to the idea of using AI in academic advising. Many believed that the machines that are programmed to give advice via automated algorithms were not capable of feeling or actually understanding the students and their unique circumstances. To answer these worries, the university introduced narrating and data-driven communication to be trusted. Leaders started collecting the aforementioned success stories by other universities that had already been practicing them. They distributed these stories through the newsletters, open meetings, and faculty seminars. Real examples of improved student involvement and less dropout rates were effective in reducing scepticism.

Subsequently, the institution collected internal data concerning existing advising systems' inefficiencies. The reports mentioned that many students were left waiting for appointments for weeks and were provided with limited not feedback. Visual representations of the data in simpler formats made it much easier for the faculty to understand the need for the changes. Afterward the leadership team started a pilot program, an AI-assisted advising system that dealt with queries at the basic level like course selection and attendance tracking. Personal and emotional issues were left to the discretion of human advisors alone. This hybrid model was based on the principle that automation would support the staff rather than replace them. A weekly review session was conducted during the pilot run. The faculty, advisors, and administrators assessed the performance of the tool and exchange experiences with one another. The recommendations, in addition to addressing the interface that was causing the most problem, also included adding the manual override option. The communication plan was kept open at all times. The vice-chancellor often provided the staff with the updates and the outcomes which were clear and were held responsible for them. The building of trust between them, in turn, led to the rise of faculty involvement.

Only after a year, the advising system was used in all the departments. The level of student satisfaction rose, and the workload on the faculty's part decreased significantly. And, perhaps, the most important, the culture of conversation and the feeling of being included were factors that made the relationship between the leadership and the staff more solid.

This case demonstrates the power of storytelling, data transparency, and empathy in overcoming resistance. Technology is more often embraced when people realize its true purpose and the benefits it brings to human life.

Case 3 – Policy and Ethics Task Force

A research-focused university in another region faced challenges introducing AI for plagiarism detection and academic integrity management. Although the top management regards the use of AI as the most important way to ensure fairness, the faculty members were seriously worried about surveillance and privacy. A number of people pointed out that automated systems might wrongly accuse students or misuse data. Hence, the university issued the Policy and Ethics Task Force. The committee was comprised of faculty members with different fields of specialization, legal professionals, students, and IT staff. Their plan was to form ethical guidelines that had to be followed even before any action was taken.

The task force commenced by bringing up principles like fairness, transparency, and accountability. It proceeded to investigate how data would be handled from collection, to storage, and to analysis. Each algorithm's structure was examined by the members to make sure that the AI tools were compatible with the institutional values.

The academic staffs were invited to decide on the steps to be taken. The public had the opportunity to receive reports and express their opinions in the discussion forums that were held regularly. This collaboration helped combat the technology myths and pointed out the protective features.

After the launch of the plagiarism detection system, faculty was the one authorized to interpret it. AI-generated reports were merely pieces of advice rather than final judgments. Professors had the option to go through the flagged content and determine if it was intentional wrongdoing or a misleading match.

The university did not only stop there; it also promoted programs aimed at raising awareness among students. Workshops were organized to inform them about the functioning of the system, the reasons for its introduction, and the steps to protect academic integrity. This transparency fostered confidence throughout the community.

Bias and performance audits were issued periodically to assess the situation. The results were publicly disclosed, proving accountability, and frankness. The system was promptly and generally regarded as a just and efficient supporting tool.

This particular case can be summed up as ethical governance is not an obstacle to innovation but rather a cornerstone for it. By focusing on fairness and collaborative decision-making, the university turned opposition into involvement. The Policy and Ethics Task Force found a permanent place in the overall digital governance structure of the institution and continued responsible monitoring and trust.

Cross-Case Insights and Lessons Learned

The three case studies reveal several common themes. Although each institution faced unique challenges, their success depended on similar principles—transparency, inclusion, communication, and ethical alignment.

An important finding is that transparency leads to trust. In fact, as pointed out by Robinson (2025), it is the faculty and staff that are more willing to back the introduction of AI technologies when they are aware of the way in which it works as well as its limitations. Thus, data use, decision-making algorithms, and oversight, that are openly presented, act as a reassurance for the stakeholders that their authority or integrity will not be compromised by technology.

The second lesson is the importance of involving people. Participation of faculty members in all successful scenarios was direct, including participation in planning, testing, evaluation, and refinement. For example, when teachers are presented with the opportunity to decide on the design and policy, they, in turn, feel ownership of it. Involvement of teachers that way is a transforming factor changing passive resistance into active support.

The third point illustrates that leaders' communication is crucial. Clear communication strategies, in every case, have brought clarity instead of uncertainty. Leaders were able to create mutual respect by being honest about their goals and listening to the feedback. Regular updates, open discussions, and being accessible reinforced commitment.

On the other hand, the ethical aspect in governance is paramount for being successful in the long run. Ethical issues largely neglected by the institutions have borne them the consequences (i.e., rebuff and a loss of trust). The people that have founded the rules and established boards survived the previous condition keeping their respect. Proper data management, fairness tests, and human oversight are shields for the institutional image and the social bond.

Moreover, a significant insight that has been mentioned is that implementing things step by step has great importance. The aforementioned institutions made none of their AI systems the main course all at once. They began with pilot projects, gauged success, and then gradually expanded. Such a measured approach gave room for ongoing learning and adjustments. In addition, the time span allowed cultural adaptation.

Training and support were recognized as another determinant. Faculty members who are given training continuously will feel more assured when dealing with AI tools. The committed professional development was a good antidote to early burnouts and kept the spirit of enthusiasm alive in the faculties.

Finally, those were the universities whose chief focus was culture, not just the technology that was the most successful. Instead of simply seeing the keeping of AI technology as the adoption of an innovation strategy, they considered this a broader cultural transformation based on a collaborative and ethical approach. The adoption of these values in their daily life was the guarantee for the sustainability of the organizational change.

The lessons taken collectively create a scheme for other universities that intend to go through a similar transformation. They illustrate that the key to the successful implementation of AI is not the shortage of a technical problem but the lack of human one. More often than not, while technology is a catalyst, humans are the driving force.

When the institutions create workplaces where innovation is inseparable from empathy, the resistance quickly dissolves. Teachers start to see AI as their partner rather than a rival. Learning systems are further benefited by the students getting accustomed to them, while the school staff accomplishes more. Most notably, the mutual trust in the academic community becomes deep-rooted.

The above experiences prove that the successful change management is capable of changing fear to trust. The institutions that balance a visionary leadership approach with a human factor are the ones that will continue to lead the education sector in a responsible way. The lessons of the journey can be interpreted as a symbiosis with technology, ethics, and empathy in higher education.

CHALLENGES, RISKS, AND MITIGATION STRATEGIES

Artificial intelligence promises to transform higher education, but its adoption introduces complex challenges. These challenges are not limited to technology; they extend to ethics, culture, infrastructure, and governance. Institutions must recognise these risks early and develop proactive strategies to mitigate them. Effective change management requires foresight, resilience, and a commitment to responsible innovation.

This section explores the primary risks that institutions face when integrating AI and provides practical ways to address them. Successful transformation depends on balancing innovation with accountability and human well-being.

Managing Ethical Risks and Data Governance

Ethics and data governance are the cornerstones of reliable AI systems. Universities gather a significant amount of data from students, faculty members, and administrative operations. When the AI uses this data, privacy and fairness become crucial issues. The persistence of these ethical safeguards, along with the innovative ideas, cannot be intrusive.

Data misuse is one big problem here. AI systems usually require sensitive information such as academic performance, attendance, or financial records. The manipulation of inappropriate access to this information can lead to damaged reputations and violations of privacy laws. Therefore, institutions must have rigorous data management policies. The access must be limited, encryption should be compulsory, and data-sharing agreements must be disclosed.

Another ethical concern is algorithmic bias. The AI models are trained from historical datasets, which might have certain societal or cultural imbalances. If they are not addressed, algorithms can duplicate or accentuate these biases. For instance, automated exam scoring or job application systems could, by mistake, endorse a specific group. Accordingly, schools must assess their algorithms systematically and admit wider datasets in the process of training.

One other thing essential for transparency is a means for users to understand how decisions are made by AI systems. Colleges and universities could begin with explainable AI protocols so that the outputs are delicate and reviewable. The presence of signs leads to increased trust in the community.

The institutions also need to make sure that the ethical risks are not overlooked by the formation of special AI Ethics Committees that are dedicated to project work. The committees should incorporate instructors, technical experts, attorneys, and students. Their mission is to inspect the rules, track adherence, and advise on ethical use. Such scrutiny creates a balance between innovation and responsibility.

Ethical governance can also be realized through training. Faculty and staff should be instructed on data privacy and responsible AI practices. Upon everyone else's awareness of their ethical accountability, the institutional culture gains a sort of self-regulation.

Strong data governance, together with ethical frameworks, ultimately safeguards people and organizations alike. They convey the message that the technology in education is not merely about efficiency but also driven by integrity.

Change Fatigue and Psychological Resistance

Technological advancements have a major impact on stress and health problems, including insomnia, anxiety, and depression. The feeling of fatigue that professors and personnel often have is the result of change of technology such as bringing new systems before they have fully adopted them to the old systems. Frustration, passive resistance, and disconnection are some of the consequences of this feeling.

The primary fatigue trigger is information overload. The pressure of mental strain due to constant updates, new programs, and ceaseless communication makes an employee feel that they are always behind schedule. But communication that is clear helps. The leaders should only give out brief updates and put clarity above volume.

Another factor is emotional exhaustion. Learning to use new digital instruments needs brain power. The faculty can feel insecure whether they will be able to carry out their duties or they might lose their jobs. Change management has to deal with these feelings through compassion and assurance.

Making an environment for open dialogue is another step in decreasing stress. Repeated meetings make the faculty approve and air their worries. Showing that one is listening to the feedback builds trust and solidifies the relationship.

Also, recognition is effective in fighting fatigue. The small parties of achievements are reminders of the people that their work is important. The positive endorsement reinvigorates staff and increases motivation.

A more profound form of resistance springs from identity conflict. The teachers may see it that way, but AI is not taking away my work with machines taking over from people. There are concerns about the machine replacing creativity with the automation of processes. The officials need to make it clear to the staff that AI is just a tool to improve human intelligence and not the other way around.

Emotional intelligence is the mainstay of transitioning that is psychological. Peaceful paced learning and schedules for adjusting that are flexible are the factors that reduce stress. The individuals regain their confidence when they feel that they are getting the right support.

Colleges can coordinate well-being schemes with technical training. Workshops on stress management, cooperation, and balancing will help mental resilience. Dealing with emotional health means that the innovation is for the good and not for the bad.

Change fatigue, the complex norm that awakens the ethical issue of an essentially humane transformation. Fan the passion of the spirit and not the sternness of the disciplinarian to your institutional success.

Strategic Mitigation and Sustainable Adaptation

Effective mitigation strategies combine technology, communication, and human development. They transform potential risks into opportunities for learning and improvement. Sustainable adaptation ensures that AI integration remains stable and beneficial in the long term (Khan et al., 2025). The initial phase is careful planning. Organizations should assess potential risks beforehand. The risk assessment instruments categorize the issues as moral, technical, or operational.

Effective communication strategies are crucial for offsetting any effects. Clear communications and open sessions prevent misinformation. When people know the causes of the changes, the resistance is minimal. Communication should be two-way so that teachers and students can share their feelings and ideas.

Testing in small batches diminishes large risks. The phased introduction of artificial intelligence systems gives us a chance to discover issues early on. The feedback from the pilot users is the main source of the improvement-related changes. The actual scaling of a system is easier and safer if the scale is stable at the start. Building cross-functional teams is a good way to enhance oversight. The joint work of the branches within the academic, administrative, and technical fields makes it possible to achieve equitable decisions. Different views lead to the foreseeing of the negative results before they arise.

Continuous monitoring systems can also be adopted by the institutions. The ongoing assessment of AI's performance and compliance with ethics will help to maintain trust. Measures like effectiveness, equity, and the level of users' contentment are indicators of necessary adaptations.

Flexibility is a key to sustainability as well. The AI systems should be adjusted based on new rules, academic priorities, and technological innovations. Flexible institutions are able to react more promptly to inventions.

The lasting success relies on the consistency of leadership. Regular shuffling of administration can be a hindrance to progress. It is not merely the desires of the leaders but the establishment of institutional frameworks in the first place, which is the best determinant of adherence to norms into the future.

The campaigns for education and awareness propagate shared accountability. When everyone at the institution has good knowledge; understanding their tasks in ethical AI use, accountability becomes the whole community's (Gunder et al., 2025) task.

Moreover, sustainability calls for learning lessons. Institutions should keep track of what they learn from both their successes and failures. Such an organizational memory is a handbook for future projects and a means to prevent errors from being repeated.

Adaptive sustainability is not a process but an event where you reflect and renew continually. Through the transformation of culture, universities create resilience that ensures the technology adoption does not affect ethics or well-being.

Artificial intelligence is a double-edged sword in higher education. While ignoring the risks can lead to ethical failures and disorder, those institutions recognizing those challenges early will be able to make obstacles into opportunities.

Proper planning, empathy, and adaptability are the things that one needs. Ethical governance is a way of promoting justice, willingness is a way of ensuring stability, emotional care is a way of ensuring engagement, and remediation is a way to make sure the system goes on.

AI is not simply a tool; it is a transformative force that demands responsibility. By addressing its challenges thoughtfully, institutions build systems that are intelligent, transparent, and deeply human. The future of higher education depends not on avoiding risks but on managing them with integrity and foresight.

CONCLUSION AND FUTURE DIRECTIONS

Artificial intelligence has begun reshaping higher education, not as a passing trend but as a lasting force of transformation. Yet, its true success depends less on technology and more on people. Throughout this chapter, the focus has remained on one central idea—change management. It is the bridge that connects innovation with human understanding, allowing institutions to adopt AI responsibly and confidently.

Despite the visions of efficiency, accuracy, and insight, the respect of academic values and cultural diversity should be strictly adhered to in the introduction of AI in education. Institutions think they want to quickly adopt it without dealing with the issues on human side but may encounter resistance, confusion, and ethical risks anyway. In comparison, those firms that blend careful planning with empathy discover the truth that change is more often collaborative than disruptive. The heartfelt issue with the connection of AI is that it is people who guide it not by automation but by empowerment upward.

Unwillingness to embrace AI often stems from the fear—fear of losing control, relevance, or identity. The transformation of long-held positions may well bring these feelings. The most effective change management practices include recognizing their fears, reframing them, and allowing the people to express their opinions. When teachers are well aware of the art of technology, they become collaborators in development instead of barriers. Inclusion in communication decreases doubts and fosters a mutual concern for the transition.

The leadership factor in this progress remains crucial. Leaders in institutions should not only be at the forefront of change but should also be open, patient, and provide moral clarity. They should demonstrate the values they want to promote and show that technology is a tool, not a replacement for human judgment. Forward-thinking leadership brings digital transformation into alignment with the mission of the institution, which in turn ensures trust and integrity are solidified.

Faculty involvement is as equally important. The main communicators of technology in a class of learning are the instructors. Their role guarantees that the AI is integrated with real teaching and learning, not mechanical instructions. Workshops, brainstorming, and awards turn the doubts of the faculty into constructive drive. When teachers feel recognized and equipped with the necessary resources, they become the first movers in the process of innovation. A participatory culture not only brings skills but also brings self-confidence.

The framework for governance and ethics lays out the pathway to sustainable and long-term achievements. Ethical AI systems should be clear, just, and accountable. The institutions are to devise explicit policies to safeguard privacy and delineate responsibilities. Correct governance is in the Stetson thematic, prevents wrongful use, and avails to the project a dignified definition of the topics covered by the problem.

Around the world, the Case studies seek to prove that one constant runs through all this: the successful implementation of AI is starting with trust. Institutions that are direct in their communication get their stakeholders involved, and stick to its ethics will have long-lasting transformation. The ones that are committed to viewing the process of change as a joint journey create the most resilient, high-motivated, and far-sighted environments. It is not the machines that build trust, it is not one or another, it is the people through accountability and open communication that earn trust.

The reality of scarcity of resources, data risks, and psychological fatigue is still there. But they can be handled with good and compassionate planning. The institutions must make hardware and software investments and also in the human development sector. Programs of training, ethical committees and mental programs keep the culture of well-being balanced and humanity-focused. The innovation that the people feel they are respected, are supported, and are informed about grows sustainably.

The statement is unequivocal—artificial intelligence is doing away with old traditional ways while higher education keeps on evolving amidst its presence. The human factor will not be wiped out but rather enhanced in the future of learning. While AI does its routine tasks, teachers can spend their time and energy on creative projects, mentorship, and critical thinking. And those institutions that will encourage being adaptive, cooperating, and being ethical throughout will be the ones that prevail over time.

The advice is straightforward: AI in usefully is not only a technically driven project; but it also transforms human lives. Change management is a guiding force for this transformation that provides it with direction, stability, and empathy. Only when leadership, the communication path converges, and ethics are the fulcrum, technology will ally in the broader mission of education-increment the knowledge of the people and thus help societies in their development.

The journey toward intelligent, inclusive, and ethical AI integration is only beginning. Its success will depend on the courage to lead, the willingness to learn, and the wisdom to balance progress with purpose. In this balance lies the future of higher education—a future where intelligence, integrity, and innovation grow together in harmony.

REFERENCES

Abou Adel, M. A., Abouelnour, M. M., Alhourani, M. I., & Awad, A. (2025). Towards intelligent universities enhanced with artificial intelligence (AI). Journal of Infrastructure. *Policy and Development*, *9*(1), 10412. DOI: 10.24294/jipd10412

AL-ALosi. A. (2025). Navigating AI adaptation in organizational operations: Challenges, strategies, and ethical considerations. https://doi.org/DOI: 10.31219/osf.io/z78fu_v1

Al Daraai, S. B., Al Maqrashi, M., Al Zakwani, M., & Al Shaikh, Z. (2024). *Integrating AI in higher education*. IGI Global., DOI: 10.4018/979-8-3693-2145-4.ch008

Cabir, M. N. (n.d.). Artificial intelligence-based digital transformation strategy in higher education institutions. https://doi.org/DOI: 10.34190/eciair.19.014

Chadha, A. (2024). Transforming higher education for the digital age. *Journal of Interdisciplinary Studies in Education*, *13*(S1). Advance online publication. DOI: 10.32674/em2qsn46

Chimpiri, T. R. (2025). AI-augmented ERP systems in higher education: Pathways to digital transformation (pp. 1–7). DOI: 10.1109/ICCIT65724.2025.11167093

Doan Erlangga, A. P., & Magdalena, Y. (2025). AI-driven transformation of higher education. *Systematic Reviews*, •••, 1–7. DOI: 10.1109/ICCIT65724.2025.11167254

Farid, O. (2025). Strategies for leading institutional change in the age of digital transformation. DOI: 10.20944/preprints202504.1846.v1

Farooq, U., Malik, S., & Syed, A. S. (2024). Revolutionizing higher education: The transformative impact of artificial intelligence on teaching, learning, and career preparation. *ShodhKosh Journal of Visual and Performing Arts*, *5*(3). Advance online publication. DOI: 10.29121/shodhkosh.v5.i3.2024.3239

George, B., & Wooden, O. (2023). Managing the strategic transformation of higher education through artificial intelligence. *Administrative Sciences*, *13*(9), 196. Advance online publication. DOI: 10.3390/admsci13090196

Gunder, A., Vito, M., Ramírez, M., & Ford, C. (2025). Beyond AI awareness: How institutions are strategically and pedagogically embedding AI skills development. *Ubiquity Proceedings*, *14*, 14. Advance online publication. DOI: 10.5334/uproc.182

Hojeij, Z. (2025). Strategic leadership for AI integration in higher education. Advances in Computational Intelligence and Robotics Book Series, 329–348. DOI: 10.4018/979-8-3693-7332-3.ch020

Jin, Y., Yan, L., Echeverría, V., Gašević, D., & Martínez-Maldonado, R. (2024). Generative AI in higher education: A global perspective of institutional adoption policies and guidelines. https://doi.org//arxiv.2405.11800DOI: 10.48550

Kabir, M. N. (2023). Artificial intelligence-based digital transformation strategy in higher education institutions. https://doi.org/DOI: 10.34190/eciair.19.014

Katsamakas, E., Pavlov, O. V., & Saklad, R. (2024). Artificial intelligence and the transformation of higher education institutions. arXiv.Org, abs/2402.08143. https://doi.org//arxiv.2402.08143DOI: 10.48550

Katsamakas, E., Pavlov, O. V., & Saklad, R. (2024). Artificial intelligence and the transformation of higher education institutions: A systems approach. *Sustainability (Basel)*, *16*(14), 6118. DOI: 10.3390/su16146118

Kayyali, M. (2025). AI in higher education. Advances in Educational Technologies and Instructional Design Book Series, 31–62. DOI: 10.4018/979-8-3693-7949-3.ch002

Kazimova, D., Tazhigulova, G. O., Shraimanova, G., Zatyneyko, A. M., & Sharzadin, A. M. (2025). Transforming university education with AI: A systematic review of technologies, applications, and implications. [iJEP]. *International Journal of Engineering Pedagogy*, *15*(1), 4–24. DOI: 10.3991/ijep.v15i1.50773

Khan, A., Jehangir, M., & Wang, X. (2025). The rise of AI in academia: Adaptation strategies for transforming higher education. *American Journal of Smart Technology and Solutions*, *4*(2), 42–48. DOI: 10.54536/ajsts.v4i2.4892

Magrill, J., & Magrill, B. (2024). Preparing educators and students at higher education institutions for an AI-driven world. *Teaching & Learning Inquiry*, *12*. Advance online publication. DOI: 10.20343/teachlearninqu.12.16

Martins, M.Maicon Roberto Martins. (2023). Adapting change management strategies for the AI era: Lessons from large-scale IT integrations. *World Journal of Advanced Research and Reviews*, *19*(3), 1604–1629. DOI: 10.30574/wjarr.2023.19.3.1556

Nithya, A. (2025). *Faculty readiness and professional development for AI integration.*, DOI: 10.34293/9789361634437.ch.005

Osman, Z., & Yatam, M. (2024). *Enhancing artificial intelligence-enabled transformation acceptance among employees of higher education institutions*. International Journal of Academic Research in Accounting, Finance and Management Sciences., DOI: 10.6007/IJARAFMS/v14-i2/21322

Qiu, R., Xiao, Y., Kong, W. M., & Gao, X. (2023). *Empowering higher education: A comprehensive review of artificial intelligence integration*. Springer Nature., DOI: 10.1007/978-981-99-5961-7_21

Robinson, T. (2025). Generative artificial intelligence in higher education: Understanding faculty adoption through the technology acceptance model. *I-Manager's Journal of Education Technology, 22*(1), 18. DOI: 10.26634/jet.22.1.21796

Salmon, I., & Psarras, A. (2024). Facilitating change management of higher education institutions by integrating artificial intelligence tools in their balanced scorecards. DOI: 10.35629/3002-12102026

Sejdiu, N. P., & Sejdiu, S. (2025). The quiet transformation of higher education in the AI era. *Open Research Europe, 5*, 249. DOI: 10.12688/openreseurope.20715.1 PMID: 40963694

Singh, S., & Waoo, A. A. (2024). Exploring the transformative impact of artificial intelligence on higher education. *ShodhKosh Journal of Visual and Performing Arts, 5*(5). Advance online publication. DOI: 10.29121/shodhkosh.v5.i5.2024.1895

Tarisayi, K. S. (2023). Strategic leadership for responsible artificial intelligence adoption in higher education. DOI: 10.55056/cte.616

Torrisi-Steele, G. (2025). AI and the humans in higher education. Advances in Educational Technologies and Instructional Design Book Series, 209–230. DOI: 10.4018/979-8-3373-0502-8.ch009

Torrisi-Steele, G. (2025). AI in higher education. Advances in Computational Intelligence and Robotics Book Series, 171–198. DOI: 10.4018/979-8-3373-2397-8.ch007

Tsarkos, A. (2024). Navigating change in Education 5.0. Advances in Educational Marketing, Administration, and Leadership Book Series, 256–280. DOI: 10.4018/979-8-3693-3045-6.ch015

Westover, J. (2024). Embracing AI in change management. *Human Capital Leadership Review, 13*(1). Advance online publication. DOI: 10.70175/hclreview.2020.13.1.11

Yuan, Y. (2024). *A study of artificial intelligence-driven change in higher education in the age of digital intelligence*. Contemporary Education and Teaching Research., DOI: 10.61360/BoniCETR242016080306

KEY TERMS AND DEFINITIONS

Artificial Intelligence (AI): Artificial intelligence, also known as AI, is a type of technology that is designed to carry out tasks that require human intelligence by imitating human brain functions. AI, for example, is able to assist lecturers with teaching, assessment, and automation of tasks through data analysis in the higher education space. Some of the forms of AI that may be included in this are chatbots, predictive analytics, and adaptive learning platforms. AI is not only aimed at increasing efficiency and creating more personalised learning experiences but it is also a tool for teachers to manage their workloads with the help of real-time insights. Nevertheless, the key to the successful launching of AI in education by institutions is the ethical use of the technology, transparency, and human intervention to make sure that the decisions made by the machines are supported, not to say, substituted by, human skills and imagination but rather to be added on to them in the process of learning.

Change Management: Change management is nothing more than the formal method that is used to help people, groups, and organizations move through a transformation. The virtual (AI) angle is the one that helps universities to migrate from the traditional way of doing things to the technology-driven system, without losing the trust and the balance. Active changing management is all about communication, participation, educating people, and shining the leadership light. The model is driven by emotional intelligence that leads to addressing concerns and producing a shared vision. The collaborative approach that combines strategic action with empathy transmutes reluctance into readiness and ensures that the innovation matches the institutional culture and value systems.

Ethical Governance: Ethical governance promotes ethical use of AI in education through transparency, fairness, and accountability. This is the talking of policies that create a space where one is free to be to privacy violations, bias, and breaches of academic integrity. Ethical governance is aware that it is the human beings who should dictate the direction of technology and not the other way around. Institutions' ethical committees, data management frameworks, and application oversight are set up to monitor the use of AI. This governing practice leads to the creation of trust between faculty, students, and administrators and, in turn, helps to ensure that the innovation is scientifically moral and socially responsible.

Faculty Engagement: Faculty engagement is the process of letting teachers participate in initiation, planning, and monitoring of the technological circuit that is being formed. The faculty members who are interested in machine learning capacity feel also that they have been respected and they are no longer just being told what to do without being asked their opinions. Involving the teaching staff as part of the team in the process of AI adoption, together with facilitating professional development, and mentor-peer networking is what faculty engagement entails. The approach results in changing passive users into active innovators who shape technology in a way that results in significant improvements in teaching and learning outcomes. When the institution recognizes and encourages the engagement of faculty, they reinforce ownership, minimize resistance, and create a culture of collective commitment to advancement.

Institutional Leadership: Institutional leadership is the term that refers to the ability of academic leaders to ignite, explain, and bolster change in higher education. Functioning leaders are those who are not only showing the way but also building the trust and maintaining high moral standards through AI integration. They express themselves clearly, pay attention to what is being said, and are models for the behavior they want to see in others. Leadership in AI deployment is not firstly about power: it is mainly about empowerment. It creates an alignment between the innovation and the institutional mission and values, and formulates the way for both the teachers and students to progress while keeping the dignity of humans intact and disregarding control over the academic.

Resistance to Change: Resistance to change is a term that refers to the feelings of emotional, cognitive, or behavioral reactions that change followers have when they encounter the unknowns or insecurities of a new system. In higher academics, teachers may not endorse AI as a result of fear, ignorance, or their apprehension about academic autonomy. Resistance has its dimensions-negatives which mean that there is a need for dialogue, assistance, and friendship. In cases where it is managed empathetically and inclusively inclusive, resistance may provide important feedback which will be used to correct the design of technology adoption.

Chapter 8

Responsible AI Adoption in Resource-Constrained Higher Education by Empowering Educators and Ensuring Fair Assessment

Hajra Murtaza
http://orcid.org/0009-0005-6336-8691
University of Management and Technology (UMT), Pakistan

Amal Wahid
University of Management and Technology (UMT), Pakistan

Muhammad Ali
University of Management and Technology (UMT), Pakistan

Muhammad Nouman
http://orcid.org/0000-0001-5747-6518
Mahidol University, Thailand

Junaidy Suparman Rustam
Mohammad Natsir University Bukittinggi, Indonesia

DOI: 10.4018/979-8-3373-5586-3.ch008

ABSTRACT

Equity, accountability, and capacity gaps have become increasingly significant with the rapid advancement of artificial intelligence in higher education, particularly in resource-constrained institutions across Asia, Africa, and Latin America. This chapter examines how universities in these contexts navigate the dual challenge of pursuing digital transformation while ensuring fairness in learning and assessment. It analyzes the interplay between institutional readiness, infrastructural limitations, and cultural diversity that influence technology adoption. A conceptual framework is proposed to guide responsible and equitable AI integration, emphasizing that sustainable digital transformation requires technological preparedness, human capacity, ethical governance, and culturally responsive pedagogy.

1. BACKGROUND

The field of higher education has been saturated with both fears and hopes regarding the revolutionary power of artificial intelligence (AI) in the areas of teaching, evaluation, and learning. Despite AI's promises to enhance feedback accuracy, reduce administrative hassles, and personalize learning paths, its implementation at institutions with limited resources exposes fundamental structural inequities. Universities in the Global South, particularly in Asia, Latin America, and Africa, face the double-edged sword of trying to be globally competitive while dealing with high student-to-faculty ratios, inadequate institutional preparation, and poor digital infrastructure. In these contexts, ethical leadership, digital literacy, and cultural sensitivity are essential because AI is more than a technological advancement; it is a strategic adjustment. In the post-pandemic age, digital ecosystems are crucial for maintaining educational continuity. However, the digital transformation of institutions has not been uniform. As a result of problems with bandwidth, device accessibility, and faculty preparation, numerous southern colleges lagged behind their wealthier northern counterparts in implementing data-driven, AI-enabled assessment models. This disparity emphasizes the significance of not considering the adoption of AI as a universal technological trajectory but as a contextual process affected by local culture, infrastructure, and institutional policies. First, we provide a working definition of resource-constrained higher education, outlining its essential features such as physical infrastructure limits, pedagogical adaptation, and institutional capacity. The Resource-Constrained Higher Education Ecosystem Framework is a theoretical model that combines system-level readiness with student-centered education strategies, which are introduced in the next section. For AI inclusion to be fair and sustainable, the framework underlines the importance of teacher agency, governance structures, and technical competency aligning. Educational institutions in Latin America, Africa, and Asia are utilizing AI-enabled solutions to address structural barriers to equitable assessment and student inclusion, as demonstrated in this chapter's case studies. The talk concludes by portraying responsible AI deployment as an ethical and technological need. The report argues that AI-driven review should prioritize efficiency and accuracy while also embracing diversity, openness, and cultural relevance. In order to gain a better grasp of these characteristics, we will take a look at the ways in which institutions are getting ready for the AI revolution, the ways in which resource-constrained higher education is seen, and the potential pedagogical paths that could be found to encourage human-AI collaboration in different types of classrooms.

This chapter employs a critical conceptual synthesis approach, drawing on peer-reviewed empirical studies, policy reports, and theoretical frameworks published primarily between 2014 and 2025. Literature was identified through systematic searches of databases including Scopus, Web of Science, and Google Scholar, using search terms combining 'artificial intelligence', 'higher education', 'assessment', 'equity', 'resource-constrained', 'algorithmic bias', and 'Global South'. Inclusion criteria prioritized studies addressing AI adoption in educational contexts, with particular emphasis on low- and middle-income country settings. The review is guided by three overarching research questions: a) How do resource-constrained higher education institutions in Asia, Africa, and Latin America navigate the dual challenge of AI adoption and maintaining assessment equity? b) What specific risks and opportunities does AI-driven assessment present for marginalized student populations in low-resource educational settings? c) What practical implementation strategies offer viable and ethically responsible pathways for AI integration in institutions with limited financial, technological, and human capital?

A significant research gap motivates this chapter. Existing literature tends to address these dimensions in isolation: studies of AI in education in the Global South rarely foreground algorithmic bias; work on academic integrity seldom addresses implementation constraints; and infrastructure-focused analyses seldom engage with pedagogical equity. This chapter addresses that gap by synthesizing these three dimensions into an integrated conceptual framework — the Resource-Constrained Higher Education Ecosystem Framework that foregrounds cultural agency, ethical governance, and institutional readiness simultaneously.

Figure 1. Progression towards equitable implementation of artificial intelligence in resource-constrained higher education systems. Critical elements of sustainable AI deployment emphasized during this transition encompass cultural agency, diversity, and the synchronization of governance, competency, and transparency.

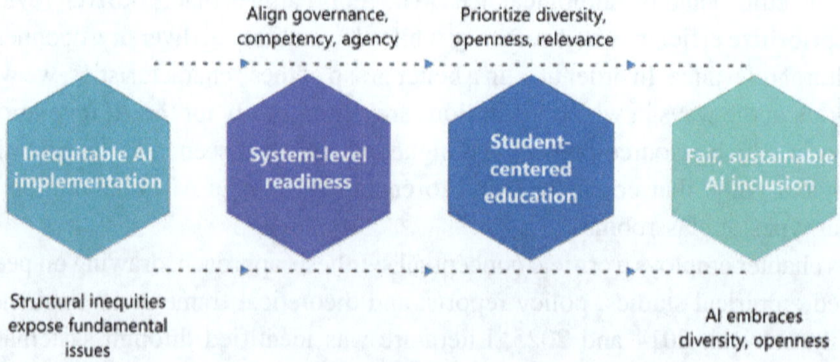

1.1 Resource-Constrained Higher Education: Context and Core Challenges

Resource-constrained higher education refers to institutions facing significant limitations in financial, technological, and human resources, which directly impact their ability to deliver quality education. This is especially prevalent in regions such as Asia, Africa, and Latin America, where universities often contend with limited bandwidth, outdated IT infrastructure, and insufficient faculty-to-student ratios. Resource constraints in higher education encompass restricted access to funding, inadequate physical infrastructure, limited digital connectivity, and shortages in qualified faculty. These limitations hinder the ability to provide quality education, conduct research, and support student engagement and success. For example, East African universities struggle with limited learning resources, outdated pedagogical approaches, and insufficient ICT skills among both students and staff, all of which are exacerbated by unreliable access to WiFi and electricity.

1.2 Digital Readiness and Institutional Capacity

Digital readiness in resource-constrained settings is shaped by both infrastructural and human factors. Students and faculty often rely on smartphones as primary learning tools due to limited access to computers and stable internet connections. Institutional capacity is further challenged by a lack of systematic frameworks for integrating digital technologies and by insufficient faculty development initiatives.

Successful digital transformation requires not only investment in technology but also participatory approaches that engage all stakeholders in understanding and adapting to existing practices. Faculty development and collaborative networks are critical for building institutional capacity and fostering innovation, especially in medical and interprofessional education contexts.

1.3 Cultural and Pedagogical Diversity in Technology Use

Cultural and pedagogical diversity significantly influence how technology is adopted and used in resource-constrained higher education. Students and educators develop adaptive strategies to navigate infrastructural limitations, often prioritizing community-oriented and career-driven goals. The acceptance and usability of digital technologies depend on factors such as student awareness, access, and the characteristics of lecturers, as well as the broader institutional culture. Additionally, strong social interactions among academic staff can help maintain commitment and morale despite poor physical working conditions.

Students from East Africa study practices are shaped by access to WiFi, electricity, and mobile devices, with collaboration and community care as key motivators 1. Institutions in South Africa face challenges in implementing interprofessional education due to limited human and financial resources, but faculty development and agreed conceptual frameworks can help overcome these barriers. Faculty development and professional networks in Sri Lanka are essential for advancing medical education careers in resource-constrained environments.

Table 1. Some of the key structural challenges influencing AI readiness in resource-constrained higher education systems.

Challenge Area	Description/Example	Region(s)	References
Digital Infrastructure	Limited WiFi, outdated IT, reliance on smartphones	East Africa	(Simiyu, 2021; Woldegiorgis)
Faculty-to-Student Ratios	Insufficient faculty, high teaching loads	Africa, Asia	(Bajwa et al., 2024; Machumu, 2014)
Institutional Capacity	Lack of frameworks, limited faculty development	Africa, Asia	(Chimbunde & Jakachira, 2025; Jowi, 2024)
Cultural/Pedagogical Diversity	Adaptive strategies, community focus, tech acceptance	Global South	(Medina Vásquez et al., 2025; Wimpenny et al., 2022)

2. OPPORTUNITIES AND RISKS OF AI IN ASSESSMENT

2.1 Efficiency and scalability versus fairness and transparency

Artificial intelligence is rapidly emerging as a technology that has the potential to alter the dynamics of higher education assessment, especially in resource constrained contexts. Most universities around the world are also experiencing growing student numbers, increased demands for immediate (timely), high-quality feedback, and staff shortages. Within these parameters, AI tends to reveal itself as a valuable proposition, particularly in terms of efficiency and scalability - the capacity to analyze large numbers of student work, produce personalized feedback instantly, and prognosticate possible future performance.

However, assessment is not simply a logistical problem; it is also an ethical and academic act of responsibility. Grades provide access to scholarships, postgraduate programs, and ultimately professional opportunities; if AI systems provide features that prioritize efficiency over fairness and transparency while providing educational institutions with efficiencies that further entrench inequities, then the role of assessment within higher education has in effect been undermined. Therefore, the real question is not whether AI can provide different efficiencies, but rather if it can provide efficiencies alongside justice, accountability, and trust. This section will explore the tension between efficacy and fairness, summarizing the potential benefits, risks, and methods of justifying these competing priorities.

Figure 2. **Conceptual framework for balancing efficiency and fairness in AI-enhanced higher education assessment.**

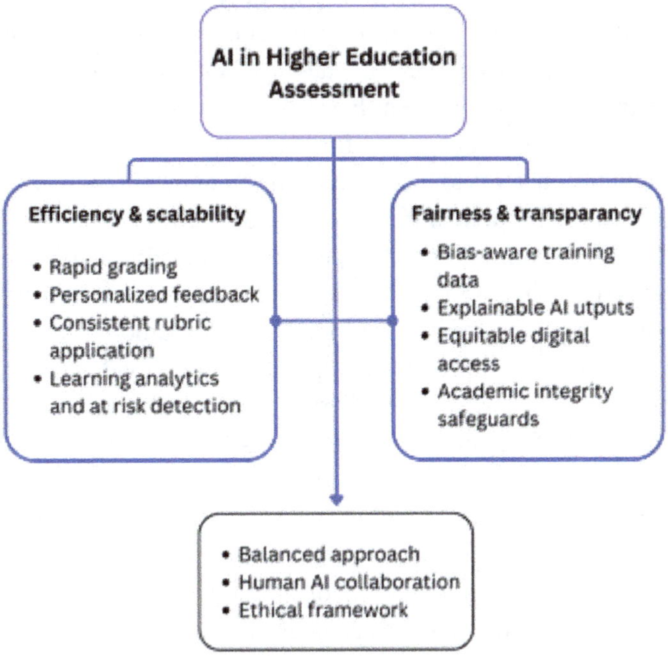

Figure 2 illustrates two dimensions of AI adoption in educational assessment: (a) efficiency and scalability, which emphasizes the capability of AI systems to generate grading outcomes more rapidly for larger cohorts, particularly in resource-constrained environments; and (b) fairness and transparency, which highlights concerns regarding algorithmic bias, unintended negative consequences, and limitations in explanation that impact student trust, academic integrity, and equitable access. The lower node, the balanced approach, signifies a reconciliation of competing interests via human-AI synergy, ethical and regulatory frameworks, and inclusive design that reflects diverse cultural, linguistic, and socio-economic contexts. The model indicates that efficiency must not compromise fairness, and fairness measures should not eliminate efficiency strategies that enhance scalability. A properly regulated middle path ensures that AI enhances rather than replaces human educators, thereby promoting a more responsible, equitable, and sustainable future in educational assessment.

2.2 The promise of efficiency and scalability

The most obvious benefit of AI in assessment is efficiency. Traditional grading takes up a lot of precious time for faculty, especially in institutions in which one instructor may be assessing hundreds of students. Automated grading systems, like ETS's e-rater, or Pearson's Intelligent Essay Assessor, can assess thousands of essays in much less time than a human. Efficiency is not just about saving time, it is also about allowing educators to focus their time on higher order teaching tasks like mentoring, innovating in curriculum and doing research (Luckin & Holmes, 2016).

Another benefit is ability to provide personalised feedback at scale. Intelligent tutoring systems (ITS), like ASSISTments, provide step by step tutoring for subjects like mathematics provides personalised feedback like tailored hints. The system explains students' progress through each question and provides an overall picture of student progress (Heffernan & Heffernan, 2014). There is no way that you could offer this level of personalised instructions to hundreds of students without the help of AI. For resource constrained universities, student to teacher ratios can be unmanageable for teaching, in these cases, scalability is not a luxury, it often becomes a necessity. AI also supports consistency in assessment. Grading can be subject to fatigue, unconscious bias, or inconsistency in application of the rubric for human graders. Furthermore, AI uses standardized criteria for every submission, thus limiting variability. This apparent objectivity can bolster student confidence in fairness of grading, particularly large classes where personal bias may go unnoticed.

Also, AI supports institutional scalability beyond grading. Learning analytics platforms can analyze massive amounts of student data to identify patterns of misunderstanding, identify students at-risk, and assist faculty to alter their strategies in real time. Analytics like these are critical in these massive-scale online courses (MOOCs) with tens of thousands of students. For smaller and underfunded universities, this technology may also be able to augment academic capacity and can address retention.

2.3 The imperative of fairness and transparency

However, being efficient is not sufficient to define good assessment. The fairness of AI tools is complicated by the data and algorithms. If there is bias in the training data, then the outcomes will be biased. For example, an automated essay scoring system may, without awareness, penalize students who compose in non-standard English, or write in imaginative and non-traditional forms that don't align with conventional templates (Balfour, 2013). Likely, this disproportionate effect may be particularly serious for non-native English speakers, students from linguistically marginalized perspectives, or students encouraged to think critically in ways that don't approximate the standard method.

The second issue is transparency. A number of AI models are "black boxes," producing grades or feedback without offering clear reasoning. If a student receives the grade of 62% on an essay, but this system does not explain why, the opportunity for learning is lost. As problematic, if an instructor wants to challenge, correct or amend algorithm outputs, this is impractical when it is a black box. This lack of interpretability affects trust and accountability. Fairness also applies to access and equity. Even though AI could improve learning in some contexts, the absence of necessary infrastructure would further isolate some students from learning, e.g., wide range of internet connectivity, site licenses, devices, the cost of high-speed Internet modem devices could create a barrier. Equipment purchases can create significant barriers to student access in developing regions or in low income communities, together creating a digital divide. Thus, the discussions around fairness extend beyond those who buy algorithms to include the broader social and economic factors that determine who can benefit from AI.

Finally, fairness and assessment are also tied to academic integrity. While AI can assist educators in identifying some cases of plagiarism or unusual patterns of responses, there are risks in overreliance on automated surveillance in this process at the expense of students' privacy and autonomy. Students may feel under surveillance instead of feeling supported, turning into a suspicious environment rather than an environment of trust.

2.4 Striking a balance

The main issue for educators and policy makers is to establish a sustainable balance between efficiency and equity in a way that they mutually support and improve each other, rather than detracting from each other. As educators and policy makers explore their next steps, some promising approaches are emerging to construct a balance of this type – a) *Explainable AI*: instead of providing opaque results explainable models highlight the criteria behind their decisions. For example, an AI grading an essay might cite weak thesis statements and unclear transitions by underlining them. This transparency enables the potential for developing students understanding, while ensuring a fairness monitoring tool to educators (Miller, 2019), b) *Human in the loop models*: Several academics suggest a hybrid approach to AI-assisted assessments where AI takes care of what is needed to grade assignments in further stages, while an educator steps in to be the 'decision-maker'. For example, an AI can handle grading for all the objective questions and flag for reviewing unusual responses while a piece of writing or creative project can still come to be reviewed by a human. This implied a balance between being efficient in assessments while still considering the nuanced professional judgement that only educators can provide (Beardsley et al., 2021), c) *Policy frameworks and accountability*: Institutions need to consider developing policies and protocols related to assessments with a clear parameter of guidelines for the use of AI. Ethical AI requires accountability, transparency, and upholding human rights. Universities should have institutional standards of when AI can be used, how results are verified, and how students appeal the decision made by an AI, d) *Inclusive design*: Developers and institutions should ensure whenever they create or test AI tools, inclusion should involve a wide variety of student populations to minimize buyers. That is, inclusion involves that these systems work for a greater range of varying cultural, linguistic, and socio-economic backgrounds.

Case examples demonstrate that different approaches lead to different outcomes. In the United States, some districts suspended the use of automated essay scoring after complaints that minority students were unfairly assessed. In contrast, infant land is part of national assessments with human evaluators, algorithms alerting potential issues, but the final authority belongs to the teachers (Williamson et al., 2023). Distinct cases are compared to highlight that technology is neither really fair nor unfair, it matters based on institutional decisions. AI has the capacity to redefine the assessment landscape of higher education, especially in resource constrained environments where improving efficiency and scalability is strongly desired. AI enabled tools offer the possibility of grading at scale, offering rapid feedback, and providing detailed, robust analysis of student's data will all offer tangible advantages to the quality of teaching and learning. There are also risks if put forward and not monitored appropriately, AI could reinforce human biases, remove transparency from the assessment process, and inadvertently exclude students from having equitable learning experiences away from university.

The sustainable future of responsible AI in the assessment of learning outcomes is balance. We must strive for efficiency, while ensuring that this does not incur a cost on fairness. We should seek fairness, until it makes efficiency impossible. Universities must insist that AI vendors provide transparency to reasonably use hybrid human AI designs and develop governance frameworks that establish equitable access and student trust. AI should not be seen as a replacement for human educators or a replacement for the work they have previously done. Using AI efficiently in resource constrained environments should involve educators working as partners with AI to support their efforts in the learning process. There is capacity for AI, used responsibly, to enhance access, improve quality and contribute to sustaining the ethical place of higher education assessment. We can reconcile the desire for efficiency and fairness, in fact, they should go hand in hand, as two complimentary pillars for an inclusive sustainable future in education.

3. HOW ALGORITHMIC BIAS MAY AFFECT MARGINALIZED STUDENTS

Whereas the previous section outlined the overall ethical commitment of fairness, this section describes a single particular and important threat which is algorithmic bias. In the environment of AI-based assessment, algorithmic bias can be defined as systematic and repeatable mistakes made by a computer system that produces unfair results, such as sampling a significantly skewed distribution of grades, or the inaccurate determination of student capabilities. Algorithmic biases tend to be disproportionately harmful to minority students, such as racial minorities, students who are not native English speakers, students who come from low socioeconomical backgrounds, and students with disabilities (Bird et al., 2025).

3.1 The Sources and Forms of Bias

In justifying its algorithmic behavior, bias is not an intentional unfairness in the AI program; rather, it reflects the biases embedded in the training data used to develop the model. This becomes particularly problematic for AI systems trained on historical datasets that often contain pre-existing human biases (Mehrabi et al., 2021). The primary source of the bias is the training data. For example, an automated essay grading system that is trained only from essays written by students of a dominant language culture. The automated grading system is likely to make greater assessments of writing style, word use, and grammar based on regulations from the other contexts and cultures (Williamson et al., 2020). One student who has a different English dialect could receive low scores, due to the automatic evaluation of their essay, even though their essay was quite good. Different forms of bias appear in the flow chart below.

Figure 3. **The pathways from biased training data to algorithmic bias in AI-based educational assessment.**

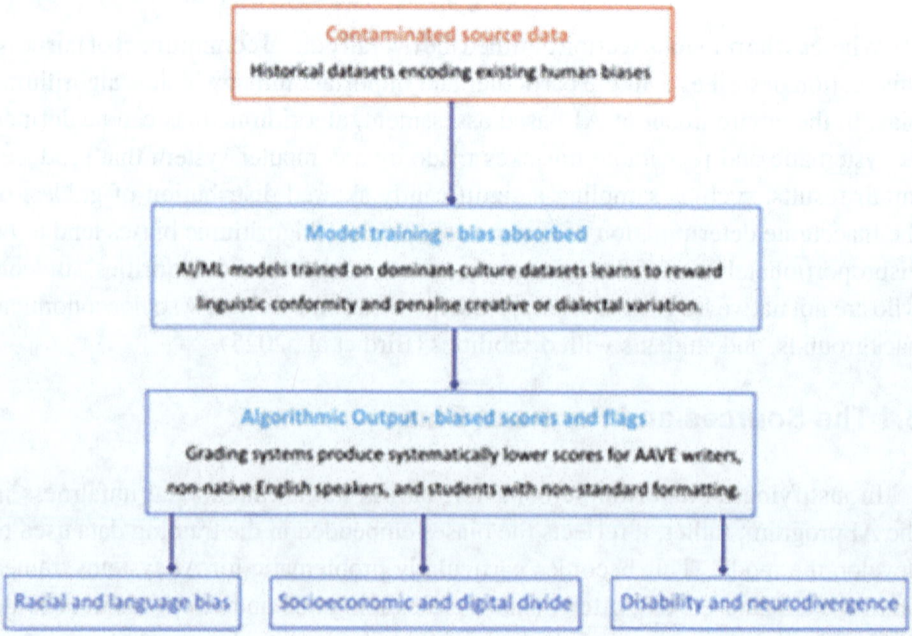

It suggests that AI and machine learning models will likely produce outputs that are even more biased than the historical, social or digital bias in the dataset from which it was trained. The chart identifies three key places for bias to manifest: Bias Against Disabled and Neurodivergent Students can result in systems that do not cater for inclusion or access; Socio-economic and the Digital Divide Bias can disadvantage people from lower-income backgrounds, or the people with poor access to technology are disadvantaged; and Racial and Language Bias can result in certain groups being fairly treated.

The influence of algorithmic bias manifests across multiple domains, as outlined below: 1) *Racial and Language Bias*: Research indicates that automatic grading programs have a track record of damaging the writing of students from minority groups. Certain AI graders awarded lower marks to African American Vernacular English (AAVE) essays than for Standard English essays of similar quality. These programs tend to be constructed to recognize patterns and rules shared by a dominant culture, and they penalize for diversity and creativity in the way ideas get expressed, 2) *Socioeconomic and Digital Divide Bias*: As mentioned before, AI systems often need internet connectivity and high-quality technology. Students from poorer households might not have the devices, reliable Wi-Fi, or software to utilize these platforms effectively, and they'll suffer correspondingly. Moreover, if such systems are applied in critical tests, scores may not reflect a student's real capability but how well they have access to resources. This maintains the socio-economic disparities that currently exist (Robinson et al., 2020), 3) *Bias Against Disabled and Neurodivergent Students*: AI evaluation software, particularly those involving timed responses or specific formats, may unintentionally disadvantage students with learning disabilities or other conditions of neurodivergence (Holstein et al., 2019). A system that includes typing speed or that rigidly follows a specific format may not appropriately represent the multiple ways a student perceives and realizes information. While there may be options to provide accommodations, if the AI evaluation systems were not initially programmed to support those needs, it could yield substantial issues with equitable assessment.

3.2 Mitigating Bias: A Way Forward

Alleviating algorithmic bias is not solely about rewriting the program, it is also ensuring the commitment to fairness within the design, application, and governance of such tools. A commitment requires multiple channels of action, as demonstrated in the flow chart below.

Figure 4. **A multidimensional framework for mitigating algorithmic bias in educational AI tools.**

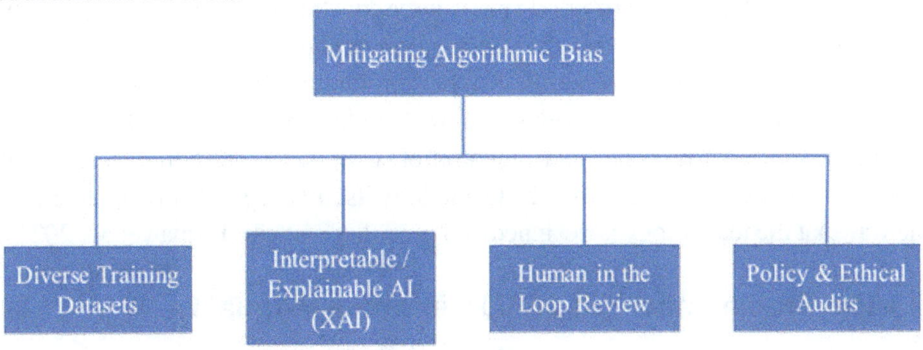

The chart highlights four important strategies: the first is developing representative training datasets, so models are trained on diverse data; the second is utilizing interpretable or explainable AI (XAI) to know how or why models arrive at decisions; the third is employing a human-in-the-loop review process to support human review and decision making on model generated outputs; the last is to ethically and through policy audits to verify where their systems comport with fair and just standards.

Each of these crucial tactics is covered in further detail in the section below: 1) *Diverse Data Sets*: The first step is using training data that reflects the different types of students the software will work with. You need to include examples of writings, response type, and data from various backgrounds, languages, and cultures (Buolamwini & Gebru, 2018), 2) *Interpretable Models*: The "black box" issue is a major contributor of bias. Explainable AI (XAI) models allow educators to observe how the AI reached its decision and locate biases. For example, if an AI identifies a student's essay as poor quality, the XAI will reveal how the score was lowered due to the absence of transition words. This enables the educator to provide precise commentary and feedback rather than a score [12], 3) *Human in the Loop Review*: As mentioned in previous section, that's a key approach. Human teachers need ultimate authority over grades and should have the right to modify AI-produced marks. This ensures that significant detail and background that a program may not see a student's imagination and unique life events demonstrated in their assignments matters. A good model employs AI as an aid to do, not substitute for human discretion, 4) Policy and Ethical Audits: Institutions should require regular checks of their AI assessment tools. These checks, done by outside groups, should look for biased results and negative impact to marginalized groups. Clear rules for student appeals and for checking the fairness of an AI system are important for keeping trust and accountability (Williamson et al., 2020).

AI can make things more efficient but deploying it without algorithmic bias knowledge makes entrenched inequalities more serious. For AI to be responsibly used in higher education, particularly in resource constrained spaces, effort needs to go into uncovering and mitigating bias. This needs to happen for everyone to have an equal opportunity to succeed regardless of background. While discussing efficiency and bias is one thing, the main thing is how that plays out in reality. The story of AI in education isn't just one story, but a set of successes and failures. What these case examples demonstrate is that the technology itself isn't good or bad, rather, it's the way that the technology is designed and used that matters (Litman et al., 2021).

3.3 The Problematic: When AI Reinforces Inequality

Many of the most concerning accounts regarding AI assessment systems take high-stakes forms that failed students, often from marginalized communities (Schaller et al., 2024). Automated essay scoring (AES) tools were adopted by several U.S. school districts and colleges in the hopes of providing faster scoring of writing. The promise was speed, but the reality was very different. Reports from teachers and educational researchers presented AES systems as easily gamed. AES systems would grant high scores to essays that employed complex vocabulary or consisted of long sentences but then appended few or no meaningful sentences. Conversely, AES systems would penalize students whose writing was straightforward and authentic or reflected a different cultural construction of writing (Wilson & Huang, 2024).

The greatest surprise was that both systems frequently gave lower grades to high-quality essays written by students who are represented by a minority group. The AI was not grading neutrally; it was grading based on historical bias in the data on which it was trained (Guo et al., 2025). The fallout was an extraordinary immediate public backlash, and, in some cases, the ceasing of use of these systems because they were being cast as a violation of equity in education. The lesson is clear here: when AI is a "black box" and its decisions are final, it can do greater harm than good, particularly when it is adjudicating something as complex as human thought and creativity (Jiang et al., 2024).

Figure 5. **Operational flow and equity risks in automated essay scoring (AES) systems.**

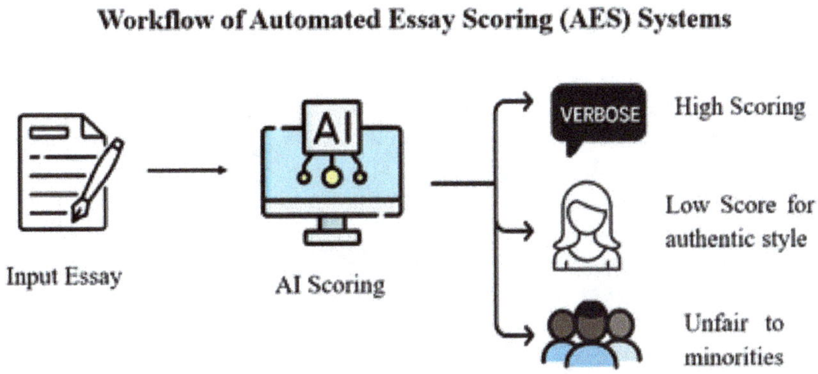

The AI scoring system uses algorithmic models to evaluate the quality of the writing. The results raise major questions: (1) excessively wordy writing, regardless of content, is systematically granted exertion levels that equal some sizeable form of reward system or lower levels of effort and possibly unjustified praise (2) authentic or shorter styles of writing that are reflective of individuality or being creative tend to be graded more unfavorably; and (3) the algorithm also contains biases that are identical to humans, therefore, students from minority backgrounds who are penalized for distinguishing cultural or linguistic elements. Collectively, this indicates that AES systems, while efficient, likely replicate inequities in educational assessment. The AES systems appear to reward conformity rather than authenticity and fairness.

Almost every university used AI-supported proctoring systems for online examinations during the pandemic. These systems monitored students with webcams and microphones to prevent cheating. While it was a good idea, it was poorly executed.

These systems misidentified many students due to bias. Students of color saw their integrity flagged due to inaccurate AI lighting detection since it never received training data for these features that was even remotely diverse. Students who wore headscarves or turbans or had messy hair, for whatever reason, were also flagged. The systems flagged students with disabilities who had to look away from their computers or take slightly longer breaks. Not only did these systems create distress for the students and also flagged students falsely that damaged trust and threatened some students' academic integrity. This is a classic case of technology, in this case designed primarily for convenience devoid completely of a need for fairness and human dignity (Paul et al., 2024).

Figure 6. **Discriminatory impact areas in AI-based automated proctoring tools.**

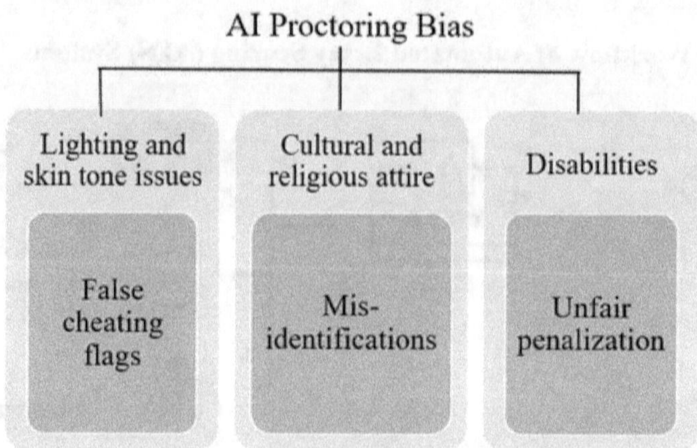

First, the technical limits from lighting conditions and differences in skin tones can lead to false cheating alerts against students with darker skin tones or inadequate lighting in their room. Second, clothing norms from different cultures and religious practices, such as headscarves, turbans, and face coverings can lead to misidentifications because the algorithms that are used don't see clothing differences as normal clothing styles and mark these students as suspicious. Finally, to include students with disabilities, including local (assistive devices) or those that act in non-standardized ways, where all systems will not have been designed with accessibility in mind and will be penalized for that. Overall, these examples have demonstrated how AI proctoring might reaffirm systemic inequalities which directly challenge the fairness and inclusiveness that should have accompanied the transition to digital exams.

3.4 The Successful: When AI Supports and Empowers

Not every story is cautionary. The use of AI as a tool to assist and enhance human work, rather than taking the place of human work, can result in much more positive success, especially in underresourced contexts. ASSISTments is an AI-based tutoring system for K-12 mathematics. It does not just give a final grade; it gives real-time, tailored feedback to students as they work through problems. When a student answers a question incorrectly, the AI will provide hints, and step-by-step instruction for correction. This is not about assigning a grade; this is about scaffolding the learning for the student in the moment. For a teacher, this means that an assignment can be made, and the teacher can be supplied instantaneously with insight as to where the class is struggling without the burden of having to mark student work. The teacher can then focus on the bigger picture - patterns and trends and can interactively engage with individual needy learners. This works for a teacher because the AI is not the ultimate arbiter; it is an instructional assistant (Feng et al., 2023).

Figure 7. **AI as an instructional mediator in the teaching-learning process.**

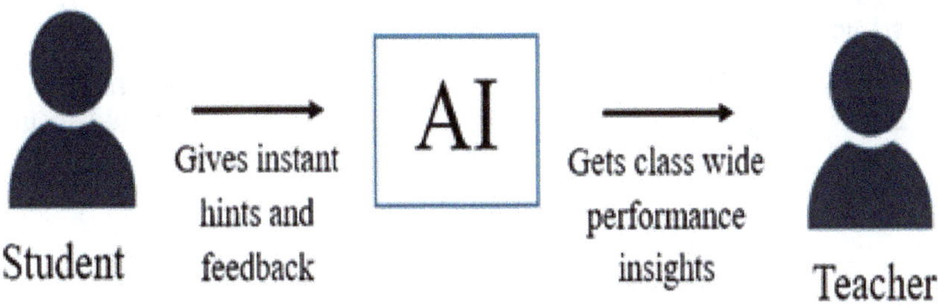

On one side, students interact with the system and receive immediate hints and feedback that are personalized, so they can correct any mistakes and better their understanding in real time. Conversely, teachers have access to reports about the performance of the whole class as well as ways to examine trends over time and next steps in terms of student development, curricular modifications, intervention, evaluation and assessment. The fact that AI serves both of these purposes supports individual learning for students, while simultaneously providing teachers with data they can act upon in their classrooms.

Finland has gained the rightly earned reputation for having a quality education system. Their national student assessments use AI for scoring student essays, but they are doing it in a thoughtful and human centered manner. Instead of letting the AI score essays and provide feedback, the system serves as a first layer of filtering. It flags potential problems, like essays that are missing a critical part or that seem too similar to a prior known source. However, the teacher ultimately determines their score and the entire set of comments. AI is a partner to the human teacher that helps the teacher to work more efficiently, by working on the easy stuff, and by presenting the hard problems. The best part of using this hybrid system is that it creates speed and consistency of grading, but still includes the human judgement that only an instructor can apply, along with geospatial considerations, etc. Using AI in Finland's national student assessments is a great example of technology helping to enhance the capacity of an educator, not the educator's jurisdiction.

Figure 8. **Comparison of fully automated AI grading and Finland's hybrid human-AI assessment model.**

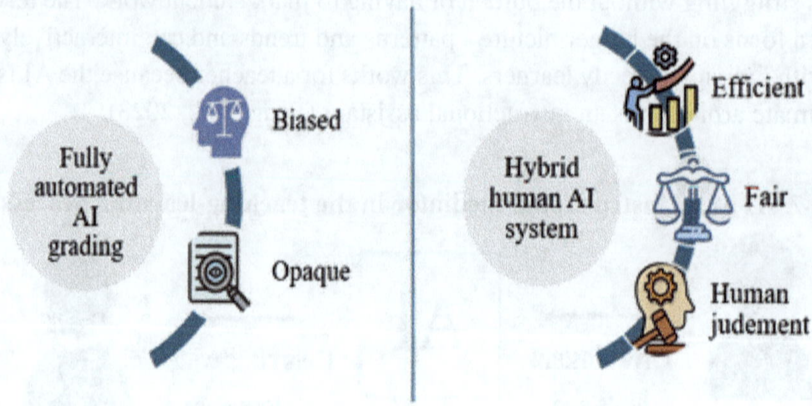

In figure 8, the left, fully automated AI grading comes with serious risks. Bias, where a decision may reflect biases lurking in the data; and opacity, when the grading decision process is never clear or open to explanation by either students or educators. On the right, Finland's hybrid human–AI model favors a more balanced fusion of human expertise and computational power. Efficiency is delivered through automation, fairness is moderated through algorithm bias limitations, and human judgment could accommodate contextual factors that machines do not underpin their grading decisions. These combined operational elements underscore the importance of thinking through the design of AI systems based on education that is anchored in performance and ethical considerations. These examples illustrate a fundamental conclusion, the debate isn't about whether to use AI, but how to use it responsibly. The scenarios that are troubling are the high stakes, "black box" situations where AI is given a silver bullet status that results in an ultimate "authority" that damages fairness and equity. The successful examples we draw from another conversation, where AI was framed as a partner in learning that was providing real-time assistance, while freeing up human educators to do what they are trained to do: educate, mentor, and provide human non-cognitive care as needed. This notion of a partnership model, particularly for resource-limited institutions, suggests an ideal way to scale capacity without sacrificing the core philosophy of a just and equitable education.

4. AI AND THE EROSION (OR PRESERVATION) OF ACADEMIC INTEGRITY

The basis of higher education is academic integrity with the assertion that a student's work belongs to a student. Artificial intelligence has presented a significant challenge to this. AI has the ability to both harm and help academic integrity. For example, it is easier for students than ever to cheat using tools like ChatGPT (Cotton et al., 2024). Nevertheless, this same AI can also help to flag dishonest behavior and create a more consistent process. The real question is whether AI will undermine the trust and integrity which education is premised on, or can we use AI to enhance and strengthen it.

4.1 The Threat: AI as a New Form of Cheating

The most apparent challenge we are dealing with in relation to academic integrity relates to generative AI. Students now have the ability to use software to write essays, solve complex math problems, or generate unique code with unrelated effort. This fundamentally alters cheating. A student copying their friend's homework does not involve any original work but even less when generative AI does their original work for them (Kasneci et al., 2023). Generative AI like ChatGPT can generate essays that are super coherent and organized in seconds. This makes it very difficult for educators to determine if a student comprehends the content or is simply a great prompter with generative AI. When a student generates the answer, however they can simply copy and paste it, they are not critically thinking or learning (Gamage et al., 2023). AI can quickly rewrite content to avoid detection with traditional plagiarism checkers. It can paraphrase an article's section or synthesize content from different sources to create content that is original and that the educator would not have recognized or labeled unoriginal. Consequently, this undermines the purpose of original writing assignments, which is to support students in developing their voice, arguments, and ideas (Cotton et al., 2024).

For resource constrained universities with large class sizes, this is a huge challenge. For one instructor to reflectively check the originality of hundreds of assignments is practically impossible, and many are struggling to figure out if their existing tools and policies can even respond to this cheating epidemic.

4.2 The Promise: AI as a Guardian of Integrity

Despite this challenge, AI can also be viewed as a legitimate collaborator to support academic integrity. Directly used, AI can support academic integrity by helping educators identify and mitigate cheating in new ways: 1) In addition to allowing cheating, AI can also be used to identify cheating. Advanced AI tools will examine writing styles to identify patterns. For example, if there is a dramatic change in writing style from basic, straight-forward language to complicated, sophisticated language, an AI could possibly catch the anomaly. This even applies where there are more subtle patterns of collusion between learners, or unlikely changes in the pattern of a learner's response during an exam (Oyedokun, 2025), and 2) Shifting Assessment Focus: The most effective way AI can assist is to prompt educators to rethink assessments. Rather than relying on the traditional take home essays that can be bypassed through AI, and by designing assessments to be authentic and less easily defeated by AI, educators can rethink their assessments – a) In-person timed assessments: This is the most direct way to guarantee that a student's work is their work, b) Process-based assignments: Rather than relying solely on the final output for grading, instructors can require their students to provide drafts, outlines, reflections on what their creative process looked like, etc. Even if an AI provided feedback or value on the drafts, the final submission remains a representation of the student's learning process (one that is more difficult to fake), c) Oral exams or presentations: The nature of these tasks requires students to share their knowledge with the instructor in real-time, so AI-written/assisted submissions will not be much of some help, and d) The Proactive Approach: Rather than merely being antagonistic, some institutions are using AI to educate their students on academic integrity. Utilizing tools in low stakes assessments to show students how their writing might be flagged helps teach students to know the rules of ethical citations or original work before engaging in a high stakes assessment (Kasneci et al., 2023).

The arrival of AI in education is another major turning point for academic integrity. AI represents an entirely new and significant threat to traditional assessment methodologies, and to see AI strictly as a force of erosion is simply short-sighted. If used well, AI will provide educators with new tools to identify academic misconduct, but more importantly, it will challenge us to redesign our assessments, so they are authentic and meaningful. In a world with resource-challenged institutions, the solution is not to ban AI, but rather, to understand the duality of it, and to think strategically. By avoiding easily-cheatable assignments and incorporating assessments that are more human-focused and process-based, we can position AI to be a partner in protecting the trust and value of higher education, rather than a destructor.

5. IMPLEMENTATION STRATEGIES FOR LOW-RESOURCE INSTITUTIONS

Artificial Intelligence (AI) in education may offer a significant improvement in learning processes. However, educational institutions still face limitations in integrating AI into learning due to low resources, such as inadequate digital infrastructure and educators' limited ability to use it in the teaching and learning (Boison, 2025). Institutions with limited resources to address the challenges of empowering AI technology in educational by setting an investment budgets for the development of digital technologies that support adequate learning facilities in the integration of AI (Owoc et al., 2021). In addition, institutions need to expand AI literacy through structured training programs and workshops that can help bridge the knowledge gap between educators and students in the use of AI in the learning process (Tan et al., 2025). Institutions also need to develop clear and targeted policies to effectively integrate AI into education using open-source AI tools (Kohnke et al., 2025). With this implementation strategy, educational institutions can optimally utilize AI to improve student learning outcomes, even with low resources.

This section explores three promising strategies for implementing AI-based education for low-source institutions in such contexts: open-source tools for automated feedback, offline-compatible AI tutors and chatbots, and peer-assessment supported by AI.

5.1 Open-Source Tools for Automated Feedback

Many students have a traditional view of feedback in learning, where they still expect passive feedback from educators rather than active feedback. AI technology can provide opens source tools for automatic feedback to improve learning outcomes in higher education (Kovari, 2025; Youn et al., 2025). Automatic feedback with AI not only improves students' academic performance but also serves as an efficient strategy for developing active feedback for students in large classrooms (Huskisson et al., 2024). Furthermore, the broader impact of open-source automated feedback with AI can affect student motivation, active engagement in learning, self-regulation, and curriculum design through real-time monitoring and adaptive learning environments because AI technology can empower educators to identify students who are experiencing difficulties early on and adjust teaching strategies according to the needs expected by students (Hooda et al., 2022).

The use of AI open source for automatic feedback systems has significant effectiveness in supporting the teaching and learning process through the provision of rapid feedback for each student in institutions (Youn et al., 2025). This open source system can increase student participation and learning outcomes, particularly in the context of formative assessment (Chen et al., 2025). Moreover, open-source for automated feedback in learning can be adapted to local needs, both in terms of curriculum and language, making it more accessible and beneficial for educational institutions in remote or rural areas, where standard learning materials often do not reflect the local cultural and linguistic context (Yang et al., 2023).

For low-resourced institutions, the use of open-source software for automated feedback in learning process is an attractive option because it does not require licensing fees and can be modified according to specific needs (Huskisson et al., 2024). Several open-source platforms such as Moodle and OpenEdX have adopted AI technology for automatic feedback in learning process. This tool enabling educators to provide broader learning support and active feedback on student assessment without significant additional costs (Oussous et al., 2023). Another example of open-source AI application in education is PapagAI, a hybrid system designed to provide automatic feedback on reflective essays that was developed based on didactic theory to support the teaching process by providing consistent, pedagogy-based feedback to prospective educators. Unlike general large language models, PapagAI focuses on the educational context, thereby improving learning outcomes while reducing the workload of educators (Solopova et al., 2023).

The use of AI technology in education is aligned with global trends, where automation processes are used to improve quality, timeliness, and personalization of learning feedback. Open-source platforms encourage community-based development, so that these tools can continue to evolve according to the real needs of the education sector. For example, platforms such as Moodle have contributed to shaping teacher professionalism in institutions, where educators play an active role in adapting and developing learning tools to suit their pedagogical approaches (Tierens et al., 2024). However, challenges such as scalability limitations and personal data protection, especially in low-resource institutions, remain a major concern (Hariyanto et al., 2025).

Although open source for automatic feedback systems based on AI technology may offer many benefits, their implementation still faces several significant challenges in education. One of the main obstacles is the limitations of AI in handling aspects that require deep understanding, such as sensitivity to cultural and religious contexts, assessment of creative writing, and analysis of higher-level thinking (Chen, 2025). To overcome these limitations, human involvement is still necessary to ensure that the feedback provided is truly relevant and contextually meaningful. A hybrid approach is a promising solution in implementing open source for automatic feedback by combining the speed and efficiency of AI in handling routine tasks, such as technical corrections or common errors, and combining it with the ability of educators to provide more in-depth and nuanced assessments. Thus, educators can focus more on the complex aspects of student writing, while AI helps reduce the administrative workload (Youn et al., 2025).

5.2 Offline-Compatible AI Tutors and Chatbots

Limited internet access is a major problem for low-resource institutions to apply AI in education, particularly in rural or remote areas (Sambuli, 2016). Additionally, low-resource institutions in rural areas often lack infrastructure, digital tools, and trained educators to integrate internet-based learning effectively. Consequently, students may face obstacles in implementing digital-based learning due to limited internet access and a lack of guidance in using technology, including low AI literacy (Dai, 2025).

In response to these challenges, AI tutors and chatbots that can be operated by offline allows students to continue learning and interacting with AI technology systems without a constant internet connection (Dai, 2025; Labadze et al., 2023). AI tutors and chatbots designed to work without a continuous internet connection offer viable alternatives that allows students to continue learning and interacting with intelligent systems even in environments with limited internet connectivity (Anitha, 2025). Advances in Natural Language Processing (NLP) have enabled the development of AI models that can run locally on devices with limited computing resources (Wibawa & Kurniawan, 2024). In the context of chatbots, NLP enables machines to understand, interpret, and generate human language and make it more natural and contextual conversations, as the system can recognize the user's intent, understand the context, analyze emotions, and provide coherent responses (Anitha, 2025).

The potential of offline-compatible AI tutors and chatbots can simulate one-on-one tutoring experiences, providing explanations, answering questions, and adapting to individual learning paces (Dong et al., 2023). For example, initiatives like Kolibri by Learning Equality offer offline-accessible educational content integrated with AI-driven analytics, allowing educators to monitor student progress effectively. This method is a transformative offline internet solution that aids learning in regions where internet access is scarce (Vesna, 2025). Therefore, by combining AI technology and the ability to operate offline, this solution has the potential to bridge the digital divide and expand access to quality education, particularly in rural areas.

However, offline-compatible AI tutors and chatbots in education may face limitations in terms of scalability and functionality. A review study by Castro et al. (2025) described the barrier of offline compatible AI in education including limited device capacity, lack of real-time updates, and reduced model accuracy. Educators may struggle to integrate these tools without proper training, and underserved regions may still lack the basic infrastructure needed to run offline AI effectively (Castro et al., 2025). The lack of real-time updates and limited access to cloud-based resources can restrict their ability to provide dynamic learning experiences (Brugliera, 2024; Mohsen & Munassar, 2025).

5.3 Peer-Assessment Supported by AI

Peer-assessment support by AI has been recognized as an effective pedagogical strategy for encouraging critical thinking and collaborative learning in educational institutions (Ortega-Ruipérez & Correa-Gorospe, 2024). This approach helps students understand assessment criteria, reflect on their work, and improve their self-regulated learning (SRL) skills. For institutions with limited resources, AI-based peer assessment can improve reliability and efficiency, making it easier to implement without requiring significant human resources. The algorithms of AI technology on peer-assessment can help educators in evaluate the accuracy of peer feedback, identify biases, and provide additional guidance for the students (Topping et al., 2025). Platforms such as Moodle, which are open-source and customizable, have integrated AI-based peer assessment features that support SRL development more effectively (Ortega-Ruipérez & Correa-Gorospe, 2024).

A study by Topping (2025) highlights that peer assessment can increase student independence and engagement. When reinforced by AI, these benefits are even greater because the system becomes more scalable and consistent. For example, the Peergrade platform uses machine learning algorithms to analyze peer reviews, maintain the quality of feedback, and reduce the workload of educators (Topping et al., 2025). This is particularly relevant for low-resource institutions with limited teaching staff, AI can take over some administrative and evaluative tasks. Moreover, AI-based peer assessment has the potential to democratize education by encouraging students to take an active role in the learning process. AI can transform assessment into more responsive and learner centered (Ortega-Ruipérez & Correa-Gorospe, 2024). However, to realize this potential, ethical, technical, and pedagogical challenges must be considered. It is important to ensure that the AI tools used are inclusive, transparent, and aligned with educational values (Memarian & Doleck, 2024).

AI-based education offers practical solutions for low-resource institutions which may face financial, technical, and infrastructure challenges. Open-source tools for automated feedback can be an effective strategy for low-source institutions that provide affordable customization in the learning system. Moreover, offline-compatible AI tutors and chatbots also offer a significant solution for low resource institutions to ensure access to AI tutors and chatbots in areas with poor internet connectivity. AI-supported peer-assessment also can be utilized in the low-resource institutions to promotes collaborative learning and reduces teacher workload. However, successful implementation requires addressing issues like limited technical skills, scalability, and ethical concerns. Future research should focus on developing sustainable models that leverage local resources and expertise to maximize the impact of AI technologies in underserved educational contexts. By prioritizing inclusivity and adaptability, these approaches can pave the way for equitable access to quality education globally.

6. CONCLUSION

This chapter has examined the complex landscape of responsible AI adoption in resource-constrained higher education, with a particular focus on institutions in Asia, Africa, and Latin America. The central argument advanced throughout is that AI in education is not a neutral technological trajectory but a deeply contextual process one that can either reproduce and amplify existing structural inequities or, if deployed thoughtfully, serve as a meaningful equalizer of educational opportunity. The chapter demonstrated that resource-constrained institutions face a compounded challenge: the structural barriers of limited bandwidth, outdated infrastructure, and unfavorable faculty-to-student ratios are not simply practical obstacles but are also sites where algorithmic bias operates with particular severity. Automated essay scoring tools, AI proctoring systems, and adaptive learning platforms designed predominantly in high-income contexts — carry embedded assumptions about language, learning behavior, and technological access that consistently disadvantage students from marginalized communities.

At the same time, the case evidence presented from ASSISTments in mathematics education to Finland's hybrid human-AI assessment model and offline-compatible tools such as Kolibri demonstrates that AI need not be exclusionary. When deployed as a partner to human educators rather than a replacement, and when designed with inclusive data, explainability, and human-in-the-loop governance, AI can extend educational capacity meaningfully even in under-resourced settings. The Resource-Constrained Higher Education Ecosystem Framework proposed in this chapter underscores that sustainable AI integration depends on the simultaneous alignment of three pillars: technological readiness and infrastructure investment; human capacity building and educator agency; and ethical governance characterized by cultural responsiveness, transparency, and institutional accountability. The absence of any one pillar undermines the transformative potential of the other two.

As AI capabilities continue to accelerate, the decisions made now about how to deploy these technologies in educational assessment will have consequences for generations of learners. This chapter has argued that equity, not efficiency alone, must serve as the primary metric of success. A future in which AI genuinely expands educational opportunity in the Global South is not only possible it is an ethical imperative.

7. IMPLICATIONS FOR PRACTICE AND POLICY

The findings of this chapter carry significant implications for several key stakeholders in higher education.

Institutions should adopt a phased AI integration strategy that begins with a thorough readiness assessment evaluating not only infrastructure but faculty digital literacy and existing cultural attitudes toward technology. Open-source platforms (e.g., Moodle, OpenEdX) should be prioritized over proprietary alternatives, as they allow customization for local linguistic and pedagogical contexts without prohibitive licensing costs. Governance structures must include clearly defined protocols for AI tool auditing, student appeal mechanisms, and bias reporting.

Educators should be equipped with training not only in how to operate AI tools but in how to critically evaluate their outputs. A human-in-the-loop approach should be institutionalized as standard practice for any high-stakes assessment involving AI. Educators in resource-constrained settings are encouraged to redesign assessments to be process-based and portfolio-oriented — forms that are inherently more resistant to AI-assisted academic misconduct and more reflective of diverse learning pathways.

National and regional education policy frameworks should establish minimum ethical standards for AI use in assessment, drawing on existing guidance from UNESCO and OECD. Funding agencies are encouraged to prioritise grants for locally-developed AI tools that are trained on culturally and linguistically diverse datasets from the Global South. International research partnerships linking high-resource and low-resource institutions offer a promising mechanism for building shared capacity without perpetuating epistemic dependency.

Developers are urged to incorporate inclusive design principles from the earliest stages of AI tool development including diverse training datasets, offline-compatible architectures for low-bandwidth environments, multilingual support, and accessibility features for neurodiversity and disabled learners. Transparency through explainable AI (XAI) interfaces should be treated as a non-negotiable design requirement rather than an optional feature.

Collectively, these implications point towards an ecosystem approach to responsible AI adoption one that is collaborative, culturally grounded, and committed to educational justice as its foundational value.

REFERENCES

Anitha, C. (2025). Applications of Natural Language Processing in Chatbot. *Journal of Information Systems Engineering & Management*, *10*(33s), 1099–1106. Advance online publication. DOI: 10.52783/jisem.v10i33s.5936

Bajwa, N., Tudor, T., Varela, O., & Leonard, K. (2024). Teaching in Higher Education after COVID-19: Optimizing Faculty Time and Effort Using a Proposed Model. *Education Sciences*, *14*(2), 121. DOI: 10.3390/educsci14020121

Balfour, S. (2013). Assessing Writing in MOOCs: Automated Essay Scoring and Calibrated Peer Review. *Research & Practice in Assessment*, *8*, 40–48.

Beardsley, M., Albó, L., Aragón, P., & Hernández-Leo, D. (2021). Emergency education effects on teacher abilities and motivation to use digital technologies. *British Journal of Educational Technology*, *52*(4), 1455–1477. 10.1111/bjet.13101. DOI: 10.1111/bjet.13101

Bird, K. A., Castleman, B. L., & Song, Y. (2025). Are algorithms biased in education? Exploring racial bias in predicting community college student success. *Journal of Policy Analysis and Management*, *44*(2), 379–402. 10.1002/pam.22569. DOI: 10.1002/pam.22569

Boison, R. B. (2025). Barriers and Enablers to Artificial Intelligence (AI) Adoption in Administrative Functions in Public Universities in Ghana: A Case Study of the University of Education, Winneba. *Canadian Journal of Educational and Social Studies*, *5*(4). Advance online publication. DOI: 10.53103/cjess.v5i4.377

Brugliera, P. (2024). The Effectiveness of Digital Learning Platforms in Enhancing Student Engagement and Academic Performance - Consensus. *Journal of Education, Humanities, and Social Research*, *1*(1), 26–36. Advance online publication. DOI: 10.70088/xq3gy756

Buolamwini, J., & Gebru, T. (2018). *Gender Shades: Intersectional Accuracy Disparities in Commercial Gender Classification* Proceedings of the 1st Conference on Fairness, Accountability and Transparency, Proceedings of Machine Learning Research. https://proceedings.mlr.press/v81/buolamwini18a.html

Castro, G. P. B., Chiappe, A., Ramírez-Montoya, M. S., Nieblas, C. A., Barrera Castro, G. P., Chiappe, A.,…Alcántar Nieblas, C. (2025). Key Barriers to Personalized Learning in Times of Artificial Intelligence: A Literature Review. *Applied Sciences, Vol. 15, Page 3103, 15*(6). DOI: 10.3390/app15063103

Chen, Q. (2025). Students' Perceptions of AI-Powered Feedback in English Writing: Benefits and Challenges in Higher Education. *International Journal of Changes in Education*. DOI: 10.47852/bonviewIJCE52025580

Chen, X., Zhou, Y., Chen, X., & Zhou, Y. (2025). Open-Source Collaboration and Technological Innovation in the Industrial Software Industry: A Multi-Case Study. *Systems, Vol. 13, Page 433, 13*(6). DOI: 10.3390/systems13060433

Chimbunde, P., & Jakachira, G. (2025). Threading through the needle of digital education in Sub-Saharan Africa: Understanding the concerns of university lecturers. *Interactive Learning Environments, 33*(1), 39–51. DOI: 10.1080/10494820.2024.2335479

Cotton, D. R. E., Cotton, P. A., & Shipway, J. R. (2024). Chatting and cheating: Ensuring academic integrity in the era of ChatGPT. *Innovations in Education and Teaching International, 61*(2), 228–239. DOI: 10.1080/14703297.2023.2190148

Dai, K. (2025). The Digital Divide and Rural Education — A Study Based on CFPS Data. *International Theory and Practice in Humanities and Social Sciences, 2*(9), 42–53. Advance online publication. DOI: 10.70693/itphss.v2i9.754

Dong, C., Zhang, F., & Dong, C. (2023, February). F. Z. (2023). Book Review: Machine Learning and Human Intelligence: The Future of Education for the 21st Century. *Policy Futures in Education, 21*(2), 239–240. Advance online publication. DOI: 10.1177/14782103221117655

Feng, M., Heffernan, N., Collins, K., Heffernan, C., & Murphy, R. (2023). Implementing and Evaluating ASSISTments Online Math Homework Support At large Scale over Two Years: Findings and Lessons Learned. In (pp. 28-40). DOI: 10.1007/978-3-031-36272-9_3

Gamage, K., Dehideniya, S., Zhiheng, X., & Tang, X. (2023). ChatGPT and higher education assessments: More opportunities than concerns? *Journal of Applied Learning & Teaching, 6*(2). Advance online publication. DOI: 10.37074/jalt.2023.6.2.32

Guo, S., Wang, Y., Yu, J., Wu, X., Ayik, B., Watts, F. M., & Zhai, X. (2025). Artificial Intelligence Bias on English Language Learners in Automatic Scoring. *International Conference on Artificial Intelligence in Education*; pp. 268–275. DOI: 10.1007/978-3-031-98462-4_34

Hariyanto, Kristianingsih, F. X. D., Maharani, R., Hariyanto, Kristianingsih, F. X. D., & Maharani, R. (2025). Artificial intelligence in adaptive education: a systematic review of techniques for personalized learning. *Discover Education; 4:1, 4*(1). DOI: 10.1007/s44217-025-00908-6

Heffernan, N. T., & Heffernan, C. L. (2014). The ASSISTments Ecosystem: Building a Platform that Brings Scientists and Teachers Together for Minimally Invasive Research on Human Learning and Teaching. *International Journal of Artificial Intelligence in Education, 24*(4), 470–497. DOI: 10.1007/s40593-014-0024-x

Holstein, K., Vaughan, J. W., Daumé, H., Dudik, M., & Wallach, H. (2019). Improving Fairness in Machine Learning Systems: What Do Industry Practitioners Need? *Proceedings of the 2019 CHI Conference on Human Factors in Computing Systems*, (pp. 1–16). DOI: 10.1145/3290605.3300830

Hooda, M., Rana, C., Dahiya, O., Rizwan, A., & Hossain, M. S. (2022). Artificial Intelligence for Assessment and Feedback to Enhance Student Success in Higher Education. *Mathematical Problems in Engineering, 2022*, 5215722–5215722. DOI: 10.1155/2022/5215722

Huskisson, S., O'Mahony, T., & Lacey, S. (2024). Improving student outcomes using automated feedback in a first-year economics class. *International Review of Economics Education, 47*, 100303–100303. DOI: 10.1016/j.iree.2024.100303

Jiang, Y., Hao, J., Fauss, M., & Li, C. (2024). Detecting ChatGPT-generated essays in a large-scale writing assessment: Is there a bias against non-native English speakers?, *217*(C %J Comput. Educ.), 14. DOI: 10.1016/j.compedu.2024.105070

Jowi, J. O. (2024). Recent developments in higher education in Africa: Partnerships for knowledge transformations. *Kokusai Kyoiku Kyoryoku Ronshu, 26*(1), 34–48. DOI: 10.1108/JICE-11-2023-0037

Kasneci, E., Seßler, K., Küchemann, S., Bannert, M., Dementieva, D., Fischer, F., Gasser, U., Groh, G., Günnemann, S., Hüllermeier, E., Krusche, S., Kutyniok, G., Michaeli, T., Nerdel, C., Pfeffer, J., Poquet, O., Sailer, M., Schmidt, A., Seidel, T., & Kasneci, G. (2023). ChatGPT for Good? On Opportunities and Challenges of Large Language Models for Education. *Learning and Individual Differences, 103*, 102274. DOI: 10.1016/j.lindif.2023.102274

Kohnke, L., Zou, D., Ou, A. W., & Gu, M. M. (2025). Preparing future educators for AI-enhanced classrooms: Insights into AI literacy and integration. *Computers and Education: Artificial Intelligence, 8*, 100398. Advance online publication. DOI: 10.1016/j.caeai.2025.100398

Kovari, A. (2025). A systematic review of AI-powered collaborative learning in higher education: Trends and outcomes from the last decade. *Social Sciences & Humanities Open, 11*, 101335. Advance online publication. DOI: 10.1016/j.ssaho.2025.101335

Labadze, L., Grigolia, M., Machaidze, L., Labadze, L., Grigolia, M., & Machaidze, L. (2023). Role of AI chatbots in education: systematic literature review. *International Journal of Educational Technology in Higher Education, 20:1, 20*(1). DOI: 10.1186/s41239-023-00426-1

Litman, D., Zhang, H., Correnti, R., Matsumura, L., & Wang, E. L. (2021). A Fairness Evaluation of Automated Methods for Scoring Text Evidence Usage in Writing. In (pp. 255-267). DOI: 10.1007/978-3-030-78292-4_21

Luckin, R., & Holmes, W. (2016). Intelligence Unleashed: An argument for AI in Education.

Machumu, H. (2014). Quality Assurance Practices in Higher Education Institutions: Lesson from Africa. *Journal of Education and Practice*, *5*, 144–156.

Medina Vásquez, M. L., Campos Ramírez, L. C., Yataco Bernaola, M. L., Yataco Torrealva, J. R., Ramos Torrealva, Z. M., Castro Cárdenas, D. M., & Altamirano, S. F. S. (2025). Inclusive pedagogy and active learning in higher education: Cluster and dimensional insights into teaching competency integration. *Social Sciences & Humanities Open*, *12*, 102060. 10.1016/j.ssaho.2025.102060. DOI: 10.1016/j.ssaho.2025.102060

Mehrabi, N., Morstatter, F., Saxena, N., Lerman, K., & Galstyan, A. (2021). A Survey on Bias and Fairness in Machine Learning. *54*(6%J ACM Comput. Surv.). *Article*, *115*. Advance online publication. DOI: 10.1145/3457607

Memarian, B., & Doleck, T. (2024). A review of assessment for learning with artificial intelligence. *Computers in Human Behavior: Artificial Humans*, *2*(1), 100040. Advance online publication. DOI: 10.1016/j.chbah.2023.100040

Miller, T. (2019). Explanation in artificial intelligence: Insights from the social sciences. *Artificial Intelligence*, *267*, 1–38. 10.1016/j.artint.2018.07.007. DOI: 10.1016/j.artint.2018.07.007

Mohsen, S. A., & Munassar, N. M. A. (2025). Combining Deep Learning with Edge Computing in Improving Accessibility and Performance of E-Learning. *Journal of Science and Technology*, *30*(8), 1–12. Advance online publication. DOI: 10.20428/jst.v30i7.2935

Ortega-Ruipérez, B., & Correa-Gorospe, J. M. (2024). Frontiers | Peer assessment to promote self-regulated learning with technology in higher education: Systematic review for improving course design. *Frontiers in Education*, *9*, 1376505. Advance online publication. DOI: 10.3389/feduc.2024.1376505

Oussous, A., Menyani, I., Srifi, M., Lahcen, A. A., Kheraz, S., Benjelloun, F.-Z.,… Benjelloun, F.-Z. (2023). An Evaluation of Open Source Adaptive Learning Solutions. *Information, Vol. 14, Page 57, 14*(2). DOI: 10.3390/info14020057

Owoc, M. L., Sawicka, A., & Weichbroth, P. (2021). Artificial Intelligence Technologies in Education: Benefits, Challenge. *IFIP Advances in Information and Communication Technology*, *599*, 37–58. Advance online publication. DOI: 10.1007/978-3-030-85001-2_4

Oyedokun, G. (2025). *AI and Ethics*. Academic Integrity and the Future of Quality Assurance in Higher Education.

Paul, J., Farhath, O., & Selvan, M. (2024). AI based Proctoring System –. *RE:view*, 1–5. Advance online publication. DOI: 10.1109/ICICT60155.2024.10544779

Robinson, L., Schulz, J., Khilnani, A., Ono, H., McClain, N., Levine, L., & Tolentino, N. (2020). Digital inequalities in time of pandemic: COVID-19 exposure risk profiles and new forms of vulnerability.

Sambuli, N. (2016). Challenges and opportunities for advancing Internet access in developing countries while upholding net neutrality. *Journal of Cyber Policy*, *1*(1), 61–74. Advance online publication. DOI: 10.1080/23738871.2016.1165715

Schaller, N.-J., Ding, Y., Horbach, A., Meyer, J., & Jansen, T. (2024). Fairness in Automated Essay Scoring: A Comparative Analysis of Algorithms on German Learner Essays from Secondary Education. In E. Kochmar, M. Bexte, J. Burstein, A. Horbach, R. Laarmann-Quante, A. Tack, V. Yaneva, & Z. Yuan, *Proceedings of the 19th Workshop on Innovative Use of NLP for Building Educational Applications*.

Simiyu, D. (2021). Blended Learning: The Post Covid-19 Solution for Higher Education in Kenya (A Case of KCA University). *International Journal of Research and Innovation in Social Science*, *05*(11), 815–819. DOI: 10.47772/IJRISS.2021.51145

Solopova, V., Gruszczynski, A., Rostom, E., Cremer, F., Witte, S., Zhang, C., & Landgraf, T. (2023). PapagAI:Automated Feedback for Reflective Essays. /arXiv.2307.07523DOI: 10.48550

Tan, X., Cheng, G., & Ling, M. H. (2025). Artificial intelligence in teaching and teacher professional development: A systematic review. *Computers and Education: Artificial Intelligence*, *8*, 100355. Advance online publication. DOI: 10.1016/j.caeai.2024.100355

Tierens, T., Decuypere, M., & Hartong, S. (2024). Navigating open-source platforms in schools: An inquiry into changing teacher professionality. *Learning, Media and Technology*. Advance online publication. DOI: 10.1080/17439884.2024.2392114

Topping, K. J., Gehringer, E., Khosravi, H., Gudipati, S., Jadhav, K., Susarla, S.,… Susarla, S. (2025). Enhancing peer assessment with artificial intelligence. *International Journal of Educational Technology in Higher Education, 22:1, 22*(1). DOI: 10.1186/s41239-024-00501-1

Vesna, L. (2025). Digital Divide in AI-Powered Education: Challenges and Solutions for Equitable Learning. *Journal of Information Systems Engineering & Management, 10*(21s), 300–308. Advance online publication. DOI: 10.52783/jisem.v10i21s.3327

Wibawa, A. P., & Kurniawan, F. (2024). Advancements in natural language processing: Implications, challenges, and future directions. *Telematics and Informatics Reports, 16*, 100173. Advance online publication. DOI: 10.1016/j.teler.2024.100173

Williamson, B., Bayne, S., & Shay, S. (2020). The datafication of teaching in Higher Education: Critical issues and perspectives. *Teaching in Higher Education, 25*(4), 351–365. DOI: 10.1080/13562517.2020.1748811

Williamson, B., Komljenovic, J., & Gulson, K. (2023). *World Yearbook of Education 2024: Digitalisation of Education in the Era of Algorithms*. Automation and Artificial Intelligence., DOI: 10.4324/9781003359722

Wilson, J., & Huang, Y. (2024). Validity of automated essay scores for elementary-age English language learners: Evidence of bias? *Assessing Writing, 60*, 100815. Advance online publication. DOI: 10.1016/j.asw.2024.100815

Wimpenny, K., Finardi, K., Orsini-Jones, M., & Jacobs, L. (2022). Knowing, Being, Relating and Expressing Through Third Space Global South-North COIL: Digital Inclusion and Equity in International Higher Education. *Journal of Studies in International Education, 26*(2), 279–296. DOI: 10.1177/10283153221094085

Woldegiorgis, E. T. Challenges of integrating technology in East African higher education systems in the post-pandemic era: emerging academic cultures. *Technology, Pedagogy and Education*, 1-19. DOI: 10.1080/1475939X.2025.2520589

Yang, H., Kim, J., Lee, W., Yang, H., Kim, J., & Lee, W. (2023). Analyzing the Alignment between AI Curriculum and AI Textbooks through Text Mining. *Applied Sciences, Vol. 13, Page 10011, 13*(18). DOI: 10.3390/app131810011

Youn, C. H., Salam, A. R., & Rahman, A. A. (2025). AI-Driven Tools in Providing Feedback on Students' Writing. *International Journal of Research and Innovation in Social Science, IX*(IIIS), 58-67. DOI: 10.47772/IJRISS.2025.903SEDU0006

Chapter 9
Faculty Training and Professional Development for AI

Deependra Nath Pathak
http://orcid.org/0000-0002-1318-3083
Amity Law School, Amity University, Patna, India

Abhijeet Rajan
Amity Law School, Amity University, Patna, India

Radha Ranjan
http://orcid.org/0009-0009-1550-7780
Amity Law School, Amity University, Patna, India

R. Retna Mony
http://orcid.org/0000-0003-3494-5582
Koneru Lakshmaiah Education Foundation (Deemed to be University), India

Shivendu Kumar Rai
http://orcid.org/0000-0001-8240-1884
Tecnia Institute of Advanced Studies, India

Beaulah David
Nehru Institute of Technology, India

V. Bhoopathy
http://orcid.org/0000-0003-2175-6328
Sree Rama Engineering College, India

ABSTRACT

The quick use of AI in schools has changed the duties of teachers in a big way. They now need to be good at digital literacy, data analytics, and technology-enabled teaching. Training and professional development for AI are important for teachers to learn how to use intelligent systems in teaching, research, and institutional innovation. This chapter talks about why teachers should be AI literate, how teaching roles are changing, and ways to build capability that will last. It looks at the institutional frameworks for AI training, such as programs for ongoing professional

DOI: 10.4018/979-8-3373-5586-3.ch009

development, partnerships between business and academia, and AI-powered learning platforms. By showing the finest practices from across the world and where things are going in the future, it stresses the importance of ongoing, cross-disciplinary, and inclusive professional development to make teachers leaders in the AI-driven education ecosystem.

1. INTRODUCTION

Acquiring knowledge and competencies that extend beyond disciplinary specialisation is essential for preparing to teach in the health professions today. Having extensive academic training as a teacher is now seen as crucial, in contrast to the previous belief that subject matter competence alone might qualify one to teach. In order for faculty members to excel as educators, it is crucial for them to directly improve their teaching abilities, in addition to their competence in their respective disciplines. In response to this requirement and in an effort to boost instructors' efficacy, numerous health-related fields have implemented faculty development programs. Nevertheless, there have been scant reports of faculty development initiatives in veterinary education, even though this need is receiving more and more attention. This article aims to draw on the literature on medical education with an emphasis on faculty development programs that aim to enhance the effectiveness of teaching (Steinert, 2023). To get there, we'll go over some standard operating procedures (such as the most popular educational formats and important subject areas), problems that people usually run into, and some guidelines for making good programs. In this context, it shall refer to the wide variety of strategies employed by institutions to refresh and support professors as faculty development, or staff development.

The rapid advancement of Artificial Intelligence (AI), particularly Generative AI technologies such as ChatGPT, Gemini, and Copilot, is transforming higher education worldwide. AI is reshaping teaching methodologies, curriculum design, assessment practices, academic research, and student engagement. While these technologies offer significant opportunities for personalized learning, automated feedback, and enhanced academic productivity, they also introduce substantial risks, including algorithmic bias, misinformation, data privacy concerns, academic integrity violations, and overreliance on automated systems.

In this evolving educational landscape, faculty members play a critical role in ensuring that AI technologies are used responsibly, ethically, and effectively. However, many educators lack the necessary AI literacy, technical competencies, and ethical understanding required to integrate AI into teaching and learning processes. Consequently, faculty development programs have emerged as a strategic mechanism for preparing educators to navigate the opportunities and risks associated with AI-enabled education.

This chapter examines the importance of faculty training and professional development in the age of AI. Specifically, it addresses the following questions: (1) What AI competencies are essential for higher education faculty? (2) How can institutions design effective AI-focused professional development programs? (3) What challenges and risks are associated with AI adoption in higher education? and (4) What strategies can promote responsible and ethical AI integration in teaching and learning? The chapter contributes to the growing discourse on AI risk management in higher education by presenting a comprehensive overview of AI literacy, faculty preparedness, institutional strategies, and future directions for sustainable AI-enabled academic development.

One definition of faculty development is a program or series of programs aimed at preparing institutions and faculty members for their various roles, with the overarching objective of enhancing instructors' expertise in the classroom, the lab, and the office. The overarching goal of faculty development programs is to ensure that faculty members are able to fulfil their current and future roles effectively within their respective institutions and departments by providing them with opportunities to learn and grow professionally. Additionally, it is imperative that they tackle the ever-evolving educational institutions. In particular, professional development opportunities for educators should focus on improving participants' attitudes and beliefs, educating them about effective teaching and learning strategies grounded in research, and encouraging them to hone their abilities in the areas of lesson planning, student evaluation, and reflective practice. The mechanisms that impact faculty members' instructional roles should be the primary focus of faculty development at the organisational level. The necessity to empower teachers and recognise and reward outstanding teaching and learning is one overarching goal. Another is to provide faculty with opportunities to learn collaboratively in intra- and inter-professional groups. Lastly, it must address contextual issues that impact the efficacy of teaching and learning (Ali, Muhammad Yousuf, Richardson, 2025).

2. THE IMPORTANCE OF AI LITERACY IN ACADEMIA

An individual's ability to critically evaluate AI technologies; communicate and collaborate effectively with AI; and use AI as a tool online, at home, and in the workplace is what's meant by AI literay. There is talk of it being a newly, emerging concept. A literature analysis served as the basis for their framework, which outlines the four main components of AI literacy: knowledge and comprehension of AI, its application, evaluation and creation of AI, and knowledge and ethical use of

AI. Given the importance of users having a solid grasp of AI, put up a conceptual framework that includes essential competences for AI literacy. To further aid AI researchers, teachers, and entrepreneurs in building learner-centred AI they have also offered design considerations. Library professionals are talking a lot about AI lately since AI-based apps and software are becoming more integrated into library services. Librarians and patrons alike will need to undergo ongoing professional development to keep up with the rapid pace of technological change in the library industry. It is, therefore, not unexpected that knowledge of AI is now essential in many fields, such as the library and information science, information and communications technology, healthcare, academia, business, and marketing. Library patrons may be underserved if staff lack knowledge about AI.

The capacity to recognise AI, understand how to interact with it, be aware of its limits, and perceive its potential is crucial. The study conducted by on AI awareness among academic libraries in Indonesia has provided valuable insights into the perceived benefits of AI and the different competences needed for AI literacy. It is important for librarians to be knowledgeable with the tools that libraries use to support AI. These tools can range from semantic web and augmented/virtual reality to robotic operations, interactive websites, inference engines, development engines, and camera facilities for behavioural mapping analysis. Observed that university libraries in Pakistan were gradually implementing AI techniques. Comparing the AI strategies of the top UK and top Chinese institutions, found limited academic library engagement with AI. Libraries play a crucial role in promoting AI literacy, they say, because of the widespread use of AI and associated technologies in educational institutions. Academic libraries can play an enabling role by serving as mentors to teach university students AI literacy, which contributes to the advancement of AI (Stes et al., 2021). A solid understanding of AI fundamentals among Zambian librarians and positive attitudes towards AI's potential benefits in library services were the findings of a recent study on AI literacy among academic librarians. A more comprehensive proficiency level has not been achieved by this cohort due to a number of obstacles. In his survey of US academic librarians, found that 3.58% of LIS professionals had high AI literacy, while 45.39 percent had a moderate level.

The results show that people have a moderate level of self-rated knowledge of AI principles, but they have little practical experience with AI tools and there are significant gaps when it comes to talking about the ethical implications and working together on, project, he says. Participants appear to be unprepared for implementation, even though they recognise the benefits. Medical head librarians' perceived AI literacy and its potential impact on work performance is the subject of the study published by (Morselli & Schumacher, 2025). The Pakistani respondents' work performance was positively affected by AI literacy, leading to improved library services. This influence was determined to be statistically significant. It detailed a program at the University of New Mexico's College of University Libraries and Learning Sciences that makes GPT-4, a paid, more advanced version of ChatGPT, available to teachers and staff. Integrating AI into library services and operations, ultimately ensuring that libraries continue to be indispensable centres of knowledge, learning, and innovation in the digital age is the goal that Lo has been advocating for, building on previous work that promoted collaborative problem-solving and hands-on experimentation with AI.

Despite its transformative potential, AI presents several risks that educational institutions must address. Generative AI systems may produce inaccurate or fabricated information, commonly referred to as hallucinations, which can negatively affect teaching quality and student learning outcomes. Algorithmic bias embedded within AI models may reinforce existing inequalities and lead to unfair educational decisions. Furthermore, concerns regarding data privacy, cybersecurity, intellectual property rights, and academic integrity have become increasingly significant as AI tools are integrated into educational environments. Faculty members must therefore develop not only technical AI competencies but also a strong understanding of ethical, legal, and societal implications to ensure responsible AI adoption in higher education.

3. THE CHANGING ROLE OF FACULTY IN THE AGE OF AI

3.1 Faculty Advancement

Faculty development has been widely defined as including a vast variety of efforts aiming at improving faculty performance across all facets of their professional roles. It was initiated by medical education. All of their roles and duties as faculty members, including teaching, researching, advising, and leading the academic community, fall under this umbrella. There were several different phases in the development of faculty development. During the first stage, called the Scholar Age, people focused on becoming really good at what they studied. One of the most important skills for a successful educator to have in the 1970s was the ability to convey complex ideas clearly and concisely to students (Allen, 2021). During the 1980s, known as the Age of the Developer, there was a surge in interest in using student evaluations of teachers to gauge the success of educational institutions. Educators shifted from being the sage on the stage delivering content to more of a guide on the side who supported active knowledge construction through collaborative engagement in the 1990s, marking a paradigm shift away from traditional teaching methods and towards student-centered learning. A similar shift from rubies to oak was proposed by (Hadidi & George, 2023). This metaphor illustrates the transformation of education from a top-down, exclusive system (represented by the oak tree) to a bottom-up, collaborative one (represented by rubies, a static but valuable stone).

This shift from knowledge-based to competence-based education has been the most significant change in faculty development. The current Age of the Network is characterised by a number of changes, including increased expectations for lifelong learning on the part of individuals and institutions, new student demographics, and different approaches to teaching and scholarship. Academic institutions are confronted with a more diverse and uncertain workforce, as well as ageing cohorts of faculty, as they embark on a new phase of faculty development. Concurrently, new competencies are required to meet the needs of a diverse student body that includes first-generation immigrants and under-represented groups, as well as to adapt to external forces such as MOOCs, data analytics, and alternative providers. In addition, a professional learning community is essential for faculty development rather than an isolated event. Argues that in order to reflect, learn, diversify, rethink, envisage, and be intentional about their own pedagogies, interdisciplinary and collaborative approaches are crucial. Ultimately, self-reporting is more commonly used in faculty development assessment studies than objective measures connected to external observation or measurement (Aljemely, 2024). Research must shift towards post-positivist, interpretivist, and critical theory frameworks in order to effectively contextualise and solve complex educational dynamics; otherwise, the risk of relying too much on a positivist research paradigm will persist.

3.2 AI in Higher Education for Instruction and Learning

AI is still in its infancy. In light of these difficulties, this part takes into account the most current literature studies that have been conducted since 2024. AI techniques were utilised to aid in the search process. Deep searches were carried out using Perplexity, while consensus and elicit were also employed. Reviews on the use of AI for faculty development in higher education was the question that started the co-constructed searches (Youmei Wang, 2021). The majority of the reviewed literature discusses the pros and downsides of generative AI in educational settings. Its ability to improve accessibility, equity, and quality while decreasing the gap between educational outcomes and labour demand is a strength that could help advance Sustainable Development Goal 4 (SDG 4). The adaptability, student-acceptance, and educational advancement of AI are emphasised by used a textual narrative synthesis method to determine that emotional intelligence, personalised learning, mentoring, and higher-order thinking were the most common themes. All of these ideas highlight how important it is to find a middle ground between generative AI's many potentials and human-centered educational techniques. How to improve DL and creativity are two more major topics (Jianzheng & Xuwei, 2023).

Furthermore, researchers concur that AI improves education in three areas: assessment, by automating and enhancing assessment processes; intelligent tutoring systems and personalised learning, by improving the teaching and learning experience for students through the provision of tailored interventions and the matching of their needs and interests; and profiling and prediction, by deploying data-driven approaches for making informed decisions and forecasts, for example, to assist at-risk students. A more inclusive and responsive education system can be achieved through the use of data-driven personalised educational interventions that are designed to meet the unique needs of each learner (Leo S. Lo, 2024). These technologies also play a significant role in preventing students from dropping out of school. Although there are numerous benefits to generative AI in the classroom, researchers have also pointed up some problems, such as with data fabrication, evaluation methods, and academic honesty. Data privacy and algorithmic biases are two areas that think could cause problems, while think that ethics has to be more of a priority. Universities should establish rules for the use of AI tools and encourage students and teachers to act ethically when using these tools. There has been a dearth of research on the use of AI in teacher professional development, with the majority of studies concentrating on AI applications for classroom instruction. Finding out what kinds of things teachers can do to learn more about AI and find ways to incorporate it into their lessons is crucial (Amaewhule, 2025).

4. KEY AREAS OF FACULTY DEVELOPMENT FOR AI INTEGRATION

To determine if a machine is clever, Alan Turing proposed the Turing Test in a 1950 article. The test requires the machine to successfully imitate human behaviour. NN and learning algorithms, which were inspired by the human brain, were developed as a result of substantial research that began with the official genesis of AI. According to the first AI system was the logic theorist (Logic Theory LT) software that created that year to answer mathematical problems. Afterwards, from 1965 to 1970, there was a dark period in AI research and development since the technology couldn't manage large amounts of data and failed to develop into intelligent computers. Research and development in AI has progressed through both stalemates and breakthroughs (Raptopoulou, 2025). Some progress was made in the years 1970 and 1980 in AI. AI nowadays is based on AI technology that emerged from advances in disease diagnosis. They state that the 1980s saw the incorporation of AI into bigger initiatives and its adaptation to address real-world issues. The Fifth Generation Project, which aimed to build a machine that could communicate, translate languages, recognise pictures, and argue like a human and received funding from the Japanese government, was one of many AI-related initiatives in the late 1980s. Many Japanese businesses also invested heavily in this field. Expert systems proved that AI could make specialised decisions at the end of the twentieth century, which improved its use in healthcare and finance. The subsequent renaissance of DL AI technology in 2015 was exemplified by the triumph of Google's AlphaGo computer over the global Go champion. The majority of current AI applications are built around this new type of machine learning. The transition from AI's theoretical foundations to its practical applications exemplifies the technology's influence on society and its promise for the future of teaching (Chigwada, 2024).

4.1 AL and Customised Education

New AL and PL methodologies emerged from the initial AI applications as technology progressed. Personalised learning takes place when teachers tailor lessons to each student's unique strengths and weaknesses (Norberg, 2025). In the realm of higher education, one example of an AL tool is Pearson Interactive Labs. Online microbiology and biology labs with guided feedback and real-world scenarios are available on this platform. Students' requirements and ability levels are taken into account when this application generates personalised assignments. In order to tailor the learning experience to each student's unique requirements, activities, and results, it collects data from their tool interactions as well. With the present capabilities of AL technologies, it is possible to determine what students need and then create personalised learning plans to meet those needs. Due to the ever-changing nature of both the concept and the technology used to adjust learning, it can be more difficult to define AL (Al-Mughairi & Bhaskar, 2024). The data-driven—and, in some cases, nonlinear—approach to instruction and remediation remains a key component of AL system (Al-Zyoud, 2020). With the use of feedback and material, these systems determine what students already know and what they need to improve upon. Assume, for the sake of argument, that a student is making use of Duolingo to acquire a new language. As a result, it can adjust the lesson plan depending on the student's performance, adjusting the complexity of the questions accordingly. By tracking how well students are doing in class, AL systems can tailor their lessons to each individual's needs (Ngan & Hastie, 2025). At the moment, AI is at the heart of most AL systems capacity to tailor content to individual students' requirements. For the most part, these ideas and frameworks overlap, and their educational potential is currently growing.

4.2 Faculty Perceptions of AI in Higher Education

The use of AI in academic settings is not without its pros and cons. It found that instructors who use these technologies in the classroom use them for scenario-based examples, personalised learning, tutoring, and resource supplementation. Automated feedback systems, test creation, and collaboration tools for brainstorming are some of the AI applications. There are still issues with correctness, reliability, and plagiarism (Helen Crompton, 2023). There are also other obstacles. Different professors have different views on the use of AI. Research using social media content analysis found that early adopters had conflicting opinions on the topics of efficiency, ethics, and productivity among other things. Academic honour code transgressions and the absence of defined policies and mechanisms for detection are a source of concern for many. Some people think that more people will use AI to help them finish their schoolwork, while others think that limits should be lifted. Professors still don't trust AI and don't know how to effectively integrate it, even though they're familiar with the concept (Frederico Peres, 2023).

4.3 Education Using AI

Efforts to automate teaching tasks and free teachers from mundane work date back to the 19th century. This was the original goal of programmed education. Several methods have helped bring technology into the classroom, such as Computer-Supported Collaborative Learning (CSCL), Intelligent Tutoring Systems (ITS), programming languages like LOGO, and Computer-Assisted Instruction (CAI) (Sajja et al., 2024)v. Given their importance to ongoing AI initiatives in the field of education, CAI and ITS are the primary foci of this research. Behaviorally-based learning including exercises for rote memorisation has been a hallmark of CAI since the dawn of computers. The ITS use a cognitivist approach to mimic the way learners' minds work and help them go from beginner to expert. Its structure allowed for collaborative learning by mimicking the brain's semantic network. Tools driven by AI have progressed and improved since then. Leading AI-powered writing aid products like QuillBot and Grammarly are examples of AI-powered tools utilised in education. Students can benefit from using Grammarly when writing since it can catch and fix typos, misspellings, and irregularities in style and grammar (Irfan & Ali, 2023). In addition to its many features that boost writing efficiency and quality, QuillBot also has a plagiarism detector that can help students stay true to their academic standards. QuillBot calls attention to possible cases of plagiarism and calls on users to be ethical by properly citing their sources. According to QuillBot's personalised writing support and powerful language processing capabilities helped users be more productive. Grammarly and other similar tools have helped students become more confident writers and improve their writing fluency. AI is transforming student writing by making it easier to produce high-quality writing with less effort. It should be emphasised that these tools, if not utilised properly, can hinder students' capacity to improve their writing, creativity, and critical thinking (Pendidikan & Sangadji, 2025).

5. INSTITUTIONAL STRATEGIES FOR FACULTY TRAINING

The program's intended participants were assistant professors and other faculty members with less than five years of experience in the classroom. Since this program had never been used before, assistant and associate professors with moderate teaching experience (>5 but ≤10 years) could also apply. There was no pressure to participate. In an effort to encourage more participation, the group was small (20 people) and diverse in terms of academic background. The program's stated goal was to improve student-centered education by elevating teachers' professional practices. The eight modules examined various aspects of the didactic paradigm outlined by (Muhammad et al., 2025):

- Beginning with the didactic situation (module 1).
- Objectives covered in a course (section 4).
- Focussing on the students' learning process (module 3), the teaching and learning environment (module 8) are important.
- Subject matter, pedagogical approaches, student grouping methods, and supplementary materials were the subject of other parts (module 5).

By taking on the role of student in the exercise, participants were able to see the following student-centered teaching strategies in action and weigh their pros and cons (Evangelos Katsamakas, 2024):

- Discussions centred on video segments (modules 1 and 8).
- Problem-Based Learning (Module 2).
- Facilitated self-directed learning (module 3).
- Virtual dialogues (module 4).
- Collaborative tasks (modules 5 and 7).
- Case analyses (module 6).

Only one day a month was allowed for contact. While some of these were more focused on specific tasks, others encouraged participants to think critically about their own classroom practices. Competencies and ideas were both pushed for additional development in this manner (Zhou et al., 2023). Participants' learning and participants' behavioural change were the levels of impact that it focused on, according to as mentioned before. Participants' own teaching practice served as a springboard for the assignments given to them outside of class, which served to supplement the in-person instruction. It wants over the following homework tasks in further detail:

- A delineation of the participant's perspective on pedagogy and education (modules 1 and 8).
- A preliminary design for a valid and reliable evaluation (module 2).
- An examination of a pedagogical setting (module 3).
- A delineation of the participant's course objectives in connection to the curriculum goals (module 4).
- An examination of an electronic platform deemed effective in enhancing students' learning processes module 5).
- A preliminary design for an alternate evaluation (module 6).
- A preliminary proposal for enhancing curriculum quality and a summary of the techniques employed by the participant to assess their teaching efficacy (module 7).

It took half a day of study every week for a year to complete the assignments and attend the contact moments. In addition to other (conflicting) academic responsibilities, participating in the program required a substantial time commitment. The many modules made use of a wide range of written, visual, and technological resources. A guidebook with content-related information and practical guidance was distributed to each participant. The course was conducted in an online learning environment where students may communicate with each other in real-time, submit homework using email, and access supplementary materials (Zakir, 2025). Two requirements were established for participants to be eligible for a certificate upon completion of the training program: first, they were expected to actively participate in 80% of the contact moments; and second, they were required to qualitatively elaborate on the assignments for a minimum of six modules. The purpose of this was to make the certificate more valuable so that it might be considered when the participant came up for a promotion (Brown et al., 2025).

6. TOOLS AND PLATFORMS FOR AI-BASED FACULTY TRAINING

In the thirty years following Netscape's launch in October 1994, the Internet and the World Wide Web had a profound effect on the way schools taught their courses.

There has been a meteoric rise in the use of technology to provide programs and courses since then. Especially in light of the events of the last several years during the pandemic, it must ask what would have transpired if the means to disseminate knowledge had been unavailable on a global scale through the Internet, the World Wide Web, and associated technologies (Alamäki et al., 2024) (Husayn et al., 2025). Now that AI-based platforms are more accessible than ever before, the next step is to figure out how to use them in a sustainable and ethical manner to help students, teachers, and schools. Regardless of the technology used in the classroom, it must ensure that students continue to receive a high-quality education while also addressing concerns about the moral implications of these tools.

Naturally, it should address the reservations and queries that arise regarding the correct uses of newly introduced technologies, as is customary whenever such innovations are made public. Having said that, it shouldn't ignore their abilities completely. According to certain authors generative AI-based technologies have the ability to both alter and eliminate certain types of jobs. As everyone knows, some people were worried about the future of phone line operators in the main offices of the phone company when the automated telephone first came out (Tine Wirenfeldt Jensen, 2025). The number of persons required to handle phone line and IP address switching now would be exponentially higher if the phones hadn't been automated due to job losses. Countless times greater than the full human population. When the World Wide Web was first created, people had similar concerns. There has also been an influx of AI into the realm of education. Concerning its ethical application, several problems must be addressed. Students, teachers, and schools can all use AI in an ethical way if certain precautions are taken. Faculty, students, and the future of AI in educational institutions will be the primary topics of the sections that follow (Stephen Atlas, 2023).

6.1 How Faculty Could Use AI-Based Platforms Ethically

Teachers should use AI tools in the classroom. They can enhance student engagement and involvement by utilising these technologies. They can make instructional content and use these technologies. It would be beneficial for faculty to make an effort to provide students with the necessary skills and practical experiences using novel technologies that are currently and will be used in many sectors in the near future. In this way, students can find their unique imagination and fresh concepts. Their usage can enhance pupils' compositional abilities (Peláez-sánchez et al., 2024) v. Before instructors can accomplish these things, they must become acquainted with the features of the platform. and dangers. Several authors have already stated that platforms like these will alter the way it educates that our students learn. Faculty members should take the initiative to create a policy outlining the proper and ethical usage of AI platforms in the submission of course work (Bećirović et al., 2025). Teachers should make it clear in their lesson plans how students are to properly reference material found on these sites. In order for teachers to gauge their students' proficiency in writing, they should offer tasks throughout class. There may be a requirement to modify the type of course assignments in some locations. Teachers can have students use these sites for homework and then provide feedback on the quality of the generated answer. Many helpful pointers regarding the correct application of AI in the classroom can be found on the website of the University of Calgary's resources for AI in education. Teaching staff have the opportunity to showcase the tools' potential for sparking new ideas. For instance, by checking the precision of the produced codes, they can utilise these instruments to enhance the efficacy of the assessment process. Teachers can show their pupils how to use these resources to their advantage and promote habits of continuous learning (Bleikher et al., 2025).

6.2 How Could AI-Based Platforms Be Used Ethically by Educational Institutions

Institutions of higher learning would do well to form a small committee comprised of instructors, staff, representatives from student groups, IT experts, and administrators to investigate the viability of implementing AI-based platforms in the classroom. Housing, academic advising, counselling, admission, registration, financial aid, student affairs, facilities, libraries, business and financial operations, advancement, teaching and learning, and scholarship are among the potential areas of use to think about. Because technology is advancing at a dizzying rate, it is imperative that all students not only learn the fundamentals of AI but also how to responsibly apply these tools in the workplace and in their personal lives (Ko Chun Ru and Rong Tang, 2025). Institutions of higher learning should formulate policies about the acceptable and moral use of campus resources. Many organisations are aiming to use these tools to help close educational disparities. These tools have the ability to boost efficiency, which in turn could lower operational expenses. Before deciding to employ these tools, campuses should be prepared by knowing what risks they may pose and putting safeguards in place. Rising cyber security threats are one example of these dangers. Additionally, there is a risk of data leakage and the dissemination of inaccurate, incomplete, or misleading information while using these technologies (Ramsey et al., 2025).

6.3 How Can Students Use AI-Based Platforms Like ChatGPT Ethically

Using ChatGPT or similar technologies by students can lead to serious plagiarism problems, as seen in the cases given above. Tasks such as this include creating essays, writing programming, analysing finances, marketing, and business plans. The use of generative AI systems in educational settings is often met with grave concerns. It conducted tests with ChatGPT to determine if it can identify essays and/or programs created by AI platforms; unfortunately, it cannot (Hamdy, 2025). On the other hand, pupils may benefit from these technologies being more widely available. By giving students, the opportunity to try out various systems, it can boost their engagement with the material. Ethical usage of AI is possible with the right protections in place. In order to reduce instances of plagiarism, it may be necessary to make adjustments to course homework and other tasks. Not only should these systems not be banned, but according to certain writers they represent the future of learning (Alejandro Acuyo Cespedes Nazarbayev, 2025). These systems' real-time translation capabilities facilitate the rapid acquisition of new languages by pupils in fields like language learning. The same holds true for learning how to generate codes in other languages; students could utilise these tools to do just that while learning a new programming language. In order to supplement, rather than substitute for, students' individual written assignments, other possible course subjects include business and marketing plan development. The platform may produce plans, and students can compare and contrast them with their own ideas before submitting both to teachers for evaluation (Karataş et al., 2025).

7. DISCUSSION

The literature reviewed in this chapter demonstrates that AI literacy has become a fundamental competency for higher education faculty. The findings indicate that educators generally acknowledge the potential of AI to enhance teaching effectiveness, personalize learning experiences, automate administrative tasks, and support academic research (Alqawasmi et al., 2025). However, significant challenges remain regarding AI readiness, ethical awareness, and institutional support.

A recurring theme across the reviewed studies is the gap between faculty awareness of AI technologies and their ability to effectively integrate these tools into teaching practices. While many educators recognize the benefits of AI-enabled learning environments, limited technical expertise and insufficient training opportunities often hinder implementation. This finding highlights the necessity of structured faculty development programs that combine technical skill development with pedagogical and ethical training.

The literature also reveals growing concerns regarding academic integrity, data privacy, algorithmic bias, and overdependence on AI-generated content. These risks reinforce the importance of responsible AI governance within higher education institutions. Faculty development initiatives should therefore emphasize critical AI literacy, ethical decision-making, and risk management alongside practical AI applications.

Institutional commitment emerged as another key success factor. Universities that provide dedicated training resources, policy frameworks, technical support, and collaborative learning communities are more likely to achieve successful AI adoption among faculty members. Consequently, faculty development should be viewed as a continuous professional learning process rather than a one-time training activity.

Overall, the reviewed evidence suggests that AI-focused faculty development programs can significantly improve educators' preparedness to utilize AI technologies responsibly while mitigating associated risks. Such programs are essential for ensuring that AI enhances, rather than replaces, human-centered teaching and learning.

8. CHALLENGES AND BEST PRACTICES IN FACULTY TRAINING FOR AI

Innovative educational paths are not the only thing that teachers create; they are also the ones that bring innovation to their classrooms (Qureshi, 2019). It is necessary to analyse the issues faced by them in addition to revealing their opinions and attitudes concerning AI utilisation. Motive is the driving force behind AI adoption in the classroom. They can collect data on AI adoption and use if they're really interested. The second component that can result in the use of AI is the skill component. Teachers have a rudimentary understanding of computers and the internet, but they aren't well-versed in AI (Kashif et al., 2024). Trainers can focus on improving instructors' abilities and expanding their understanding of AI, but they won't be able to adequately inspire them because intrinsic motivation is a human quality. But there might be some inspirational appeals in the training materials to get the teachers excited about using AI.

8.1 Best Techniques

The research that was considered showed that educational institutions should give teachers the right conditions to use AI, and that there should be a balance between education technology and human instruction. Furthermore, educators should be aware of how technology is changing society so that they can be motivated to use AI in the classroom (Ronald R. Danault, 2025). In order to embrace AI and conquer the obstacles it presents, educators must not only the necessary motivation, but also comprehensive training. When educators have adequate training in AI and its applications, they are better able to facilitate effective learning processes. Prior to training, however, students must form an attitude towards AI so that they can embrace this novel with the help of technology, they can take the initiative to study. Only 25% of teachers actually used AI in the classroom, despite widespread positive sentiment towards the technology(Bower et al., 2024). Hence, regardless of the generally used ChatGPT, they should receive training at every level that will give them with a variety of AI tools (Jeyakarthic & Karthic, 2025). Training programs should cover the fundamentals of AI's operation before diving into the technical aspects and discussing the social and ethical implications. In order to encourage educators to use ChatGPT, an AI tool outlined four viewpoints. Innovative educational technology, theme-based learning, professional development, and time-saving strategies are all part of these broader viewpoints.

Privacy, reliability, and less human interaction are just a few of the limiting concerns that they brought up. They went on to say that teachers' difficulties explain why they don't use ChatGPT more. Some of these obstacles include university constraints, a lack of direction, and a general absence of institutional support (Mcgrath et al., 2023). Teachers must be adequately trained in order to incorporate ChatGPT into their lessons. So, trainers may train teachers by identifying what helps and what hinders. In addition, the results showed that AI-using educators will be able to outperform their robotic counterparts in the long run and that AI adoption can boost educators' efficiency in the classroom (Kallunki et al., 2024). Consequently, educators need AI training, but program designers should bear in account the difficulties educators may have when crafting the curriculum. The research also showed that there are knowledge factors, motivational factors and will, skill, and tool variables that influence instructors' use of AI. Trainers creating AI utilisation programs for educators would do well to keep all of these points in mind (Buele & Llerena-aguirre, 2025).

9. FUTURE DIRECTIONS

- Development of AI competency frameworks for faculty.
- Establishment of institutional AI governance policies.
- Continuous professional development in Generative AI tools.
- Training on AI ethics, bias mitigation, and data privacy.
- Integration of AI literacy into faculty promotion and appraisal systems.

- Creation of interdisciplinary AI learning communities.
- Research on the long-term impact of AI-enabled faculty development programs.
- Adoption of adaptive and personalized faculty training platforms powered by AI.

10. CONCLUSION

It is anticipated that they will teach students to utilise generative AI, and they are already learning how to incorporate it into their activities. While they are concerned that students may use it for academic misconduct, they should encourage students to use it because of its added value. But students will keep utilising AI regardless of how teachers feel about it. Sometimes students will use DL to help them study better and other times they will use surface learning to cheat, save time, and get things done. The importance of evaluation in shaping students' perspectives and encouraging in-depth learning has been well-documented. Instructors may only guarantee a DL strategy when evaluation aligns with the planned learning outcomes (Okunade, 2024). Thus, evaluation can be a tool to incorporate AI critically, using it as a valid component when needed in a lawful way. A potential chasm between evaluation methods and learning could be created by outright prohibiting generative AI or by tacitly accepting its use without changing academic procedures. In addition, assessment should no longer be seen as a static tool for summative purposes, but rather as an ongoing process for formative learning. Overall, it is important to teach both students and teachers to think critically about AI. In order to make sure that AI is used ethically and responsibly, it is important to have both internal alignment and external oversight. As it enters the Age of AI, faculty development is set to see a major transformation. To accomplish this, faculty members can join a professional learning community and work together in an interdisciplinary setting to brainstorm new ways to incorporate AI into their lessons, all the while encouraging students to think critically and ethically.

Furthermore, educators may improve teaching techniques and better prepare students for a world driven by AI by adopting digital tools and generative AI to build inclusive, adaptive, and future-proof learning environments. Therefore, it is of the utmost importance to integrate AI in an ethical manner, finding a middle ground between utilising AI's capabilities and maintaining the human aspects of education. For educational systems to be prepared for the future, faculty training and professional growth in AI must be prioritised. Intelligent, technology-driven learning settings and more conventional methods of instruction can be effectively combined when teachers are given the autonomy to do so. Businesses and other organisations may boost their competitiveness and help prepare the next generation of workers for the digital age by investing in AI capacity building. Faculty members have the opportunity to spearhead the AI-powered educational revolution by demonstrating unwavering institutional commitment, aligning policies, and fostering a culture of lifelong learning (Yapay Zekânın, Üniversitedeki Öğretim, 2025).

REFERENCES

Al-Mughairi, H., & Bhaskar, P. (2024). Exploring the factors affecting the adoption AI techniques in higher education: insights from teachers' perspectives on ChatGPT. *Journal of Research in Innovative Teaching and Learning*. DOI: 10.1108/JRIT-09-2023-0129

Alamäki, A., Nyberg, C., Kimberley, A., & Salonen, A. O. (2024). *Artificial intelligence literacy in sustainable development : A learning experiment in higher education*. Issue March., DOI: 10.3389/feduc.2024.1343406

Alejandro, A. C. N. (2025). Pedagogical shifts in the age of GenAI : Faculty perspectives from a higher education context. *Journal of Pedagogical Sociology and Psychology*, *7*(3).

Ali, M. Y., & Richardson, J. (2025). *AI literacy guidelines and policies for academic libraries : A scoping review*. DOI: 10.1177/03400352251321192

Aljemely, Y. (2024). *Challenges and best practices in training teachers to utilize artificial intelligence : a systematic review*. Issue October., DOI: 10.3389/feduc.2024.1470853

Al-Zyoud, H. M. M. (2020). The role of artificial intelligence in teacher professional development. Universal Journal of Educational Research, 8(11B), 6263-6272.

Allen, B., McGough, A. S., & Devlin, M. (2021). Toward a framework for teaching artificial intelligence to a higher education audience. ACM Transactions on Computing Education (TOCE), 22(2), 1-29.

Alqawasmi, A. A., Alsalhi, N. R., Eltahir, M. E., Alakashee, B. A., Al-barakat, A. A., & Al, S. M. (2025). Artificial Intelligence : Faculty Awareness and Impact on Digital Transformation Skills and Technological Trends. *Research Article Cite, 17.*

Amaewhule, E. C. (2025). Literacy Level and Attitude of Academics towards the Adoption of Artificial Intelligence (AI) in Public Universities in Rivers State. *International Journal of Educational Management, Rivers State University., 1*(1), 73-86.

Atlas, S. (2023). *ChatGPT for Higher Education and Professional Development: A Guide.*

Bećirović, S., Polz, E., & Tinkel, I. (2025). Exploring students ' AI literacy and its effects on their AI output quality, self - efficacy, and academic performance. *Smart Learning Environments*, *3*(1), 29. Advance online publication. DOI: 10.1186/s40561-025-00384-3

Bleikher, O., Snegurova, V., Rvanova, A., Gotskaya, I., & Nakonechnaya, O. (2025). *ARTIFICIAL INTELLIGENCE (AI) LITERACY AMONG TEACHERS : THE CASE OF ITMO UNI- VERSITY LA ALFABETIZACIÓN EN INTELIGENCIA ARTIFICIAL (IA) EN LOS DOCEN- TES : EL CASO DE LA UNIVERSIDAD ITMO* (Vol. 21, Issue 106).

Bower, M., Torrington, J., Lai, J. W. M., Petocz, P., & Alfano, M. (2024). How should we change teaching and assessment in response to increasingly powerful generative Artificial Intelligence? Outcomes of the ChatGPT teacher survey. In *Education and Information Technologies* (Vol. 29, Issue 12). Springer US. DOI: 10.1007/s10639-023-12405-0

Brown, R., Sillence, E., & Branley-bell, D. (2025). *AcademAI : Investigating AI Usage*. Attitudes, and Literacy in Higher Education and Research., DOI: 10.1177/00472395251347304

Buele, J., & Llerena-aguirre, L. (2025). *Transformations in academic work and faculty perceptions of artificial intelligence in higher education*. Issue July., DOI: 10.3389/feduc.2025.1603763

Chigwada, J. (2024). A proposed framework for a digital literacy course for artificial intelligence in academic libraries (Vol. 90, Issue 2). DOI: 10.7553/90-2-2388

Crompton, H., & Burke, D. (2023). Artificial intelligence in higher education : The state of the field. *International Journal of Educational Technology in Higher Education, 20*(1), 22. Advance online publication. DOI: 10.1186/s41239-023-00392-8

Danault, R. R. (2025). *University of New Hampshire Scholars Repository Adapting to AI : The Evolving Role of Faculty in Higher Education*. University of New Hampshire Scholars Repository Faculty.

Hadidi, R., & George, J. F. (2023). Potential Uses of AI-Based Platforms in Teaching and Learning. *Journal of the Midwest Association for Information Systems, 2023*(2), 1–8. DOI: 10.17705/3jmwa.000081

Hamdy, S. M. (2025). Universities Devoid of Teaching Staff " Can AI Replace the Role of Professors in the Near Future? *Arab Journal of Administration, 45*(6), 451–464. DOI: 10.21608/aja.2024.308915.1687

Husayn, E., Alrumayh, S., Kasheem, M., Ibrahim, D., Alouzi, K., Shalghoum, N., & Almajri, S. (2025). The Impact of Artificial Intelligence on Knowledge Management : Faculty Perspectives from the University of Zawia ' s Faculties of Economics, Management, and Law. *Journal of Education and Teacher Training Innovation, 3*(1), 52–66. DOI: 10.61227/jetti.v3i1.163

Irfan, M., & Ali, S. (2023). Integration of Artificial Intelligence in Academia : A Case Study of Critical Teaching and Learning in Higher Education. *Global Social Sciences Review, VIII*(I), 352–364. DOI: 10.31703/gssr.2023(VIII-I).32

Jensen, T. W. (2025). AI literacy in the context of working with sources : Pitfalls and possibilities of generative AI models in academic writing. *Journal of Academic Writing, 14*(S2), 1–12. DOI: 10.18552/joaw.v15iS2.1224

Jeyakarthic, M., & Karthic, K. (2025). *Artificial Intelligence and Society* (Issue May).

Jianzheng, S., & Xuwei, Z. (2023). Integration of AI with Higher Education Innovation : Reforming Future Educational Directions. *International Journal of Science and Research (Raipur, India), 12*(10), 1727–1731. DOI: 10.21275/SR231023183401

Kallunki, V., Kinnunen, P., Pyörälä, E., Haarala-muhonen, A., Katajavuori, N., & Myyry, L. (2024). Navigating the Evolving Landscape of Teaching and Learning: University Faculty and Staff Perceptions of the Artificial Intelligence-Altered Terrain. *Education Sciences, 14*(7), 727. DOI: 10.3390/educsci14070727

Karataş, F., Eriçok, B., & Tanrikulu, L. (2025). *Reshaping curriculum adaptation in the age of artificial intelligence : Mapping teachers ' driven curriculum adaptation patterns* (Issue August 2024). DOI: 10.1002/berj.4068

Kashif, H., Alamdar, R., & Naseer, F. (2024). REDEFINING FACULTY ROLES IN AN AI-DRIVEN EDUCATIONAL ECOSYSTEM WITH IMPLICATIONS FOR TEACHING AND CURRICULUM DEVELOPMENT. *Joural of Media Horizons, November.*

Katsamakas, E. (2024). Artificial Intelligence and the Transformation of Higher Education Institutions : A Systems Approach. *Sustainability Article*, 1–21.

Lo Leo, S. (2024). *Evaluating AI Literacy in Academic Libraries : A Survey Study with a Focus on U. S. Employees*. Academic Department Resources., DOI: 10.5860/crl.85.5.635.This

Mcgrath, C., Cerratto, T., Juth, N., & Palmgren, P. J. (2023). Computers and Education : Artificial Intelligence University teachers ' perceptions of responsibility and artificial intelligence in higher education - An experimental philosophical study. *Computers and Education: Artificial Intelligence, 4*(April), 100139. DOI: 10.1016/j.caeai.2023.100139

Morselli, D., & Schumacher, S. (2025). The Age of AI in faculty development. Survey insights on integration of digital tools and AI. *AI Nel Faculty Development, 1*, 99–106. DOI: 10.7346/PO-012025-12

Muhammad, A. F., Astiana, N., Ardi, H., Nitswat, N., Nur, S. H., Razak, A. Z., Tajuddin, F. N., Aquil, A., Nur, M., Syahbana, S., Padjadjaran, U., Makassar, U. N., & Hasanuddin, U. (2025). *Impact of Artificial Intelligence on Academic Literacy among University Students in Indonesia : A Case Study* (Vol. 5, Issue 1).

Ngan, T., & Hastie, D. (2025). Artificial Intelligence for Academic Purposes (AIAP): Integrating AI literacy into an EAP module. *English for Specific Purposes, 77*, 20–38. DOI: 10.1016/j.esp.2024.09.001

Norberg, M. (2025). *PERCEPTIONS OF AI IN HIGHER EDUCATION : AFFORDANCES AND RISKS FOR STUDENTS WITH SWEDISH AS A SECOND* (Issue March).

Okunade, A. I. (2024). The Role of Artificial Intelligence in Teaching of Science Education in Secondary Schools in Nigeria. *European Journal of Computer Science and Information Technology, 12*(1), 57–67. DOI: 10.37745/ejcsit2013/vol12n15767

Peláez-sánchez, I. C., Velarde-camaqui, D., Glasserman-morales, L. D., & Peláez-sánchez, I. C. (2024). *The impact of large language models on higher education : exploring the connection between AI and Education 4. 0.* Issue June., DOI: 10.3389/feduc.2024.1392091

Pendidikan, J. T., & Sangadji, K. (2025). AI-Assisted Academic Writing : Evaluating Postgraduate Students ' AI Literacy and Skills. *Journal Teknologi Pendidikan, 27*(April), 45–55.

Peres, F. (2023). *Health literacy in ChatGPT: exploring the potential of the use of artificial intelligence to produce academic text.* https://doi.org/DOI: 10.1590/1413-81232024291.02412023EN

Qureshi, I. (2019). The Impact of AI on Teacher Roles : Towards a Collaborative Human-AI Pedagogy. *AI Edify Journal*, 1–11.

Ramsey, E., Fazio, P., Smith, M., Antoniou, G., Wallberg, W., Migliano, K., Peroni, M., Muckridge, B., Solomon, G., Qian, L., & Wolf, D. (2025). Artificial Intelligence in Higher Education : A Case Study of Faculty Teaching Methodologies at a Private University. [IJASSE]. *International Journal of Academic Studies in Science and Education, 3*(1), 1–30. DOI: 10.55549/ijasse.43

Raptopoulou, A. (2025). ChatGPT in Higher Education : Supporting Academic Literacy Through ChatGPT- Based Activities. *European Journal of Education, 60*(2), e70131. Advance online publication. DOI: 10.1111/ejed.70131

Ru, K. C., & Tang, R. (2025). Promoting AI literacy through U. S. academic libraries : An analysis of LibGuides from ARL and Oberlin group libraries using the EDUCAUSE AI literacy framework. *Information Research, 30*(iConf), 847–865. DOI: 10.47989/ir30iConf47182

Sajja, R., Sermet, Y., Cikmaz, M., Cwiertny, D., & Demir, I. (2024). Artificial Intelligence-Enabled Intelligent Assistant for Personalized and Adaptive Learning in Higher Education. *Information (Basel), 15*(10), 1–23. DOI: 10.3390/info15100596

Steinert, Y. (2023). *Faculty Development : Principles and Practices.* Featured Article Faculty.

Stes, A., Clement, M., & Van Petegem, P. (2021). The Effectiveness of a Faculty Training Programme: Long-term and institutional impact. *International Journal for Academic Development ISSN, 1324*(November). Advance online publication. DOI: 10.1080/13601440701604898

Wang, Y. (2021). Factors Affecting the Adoption of AI-Based Applications in Higher Education: An Analysis of Teachers' Perspectives Using Structural Equation Modeling. *Journal of Educational Technology & Society, 24*, 116–129.

Zakir, H. O. S. S. A. I. N. (2025). Exploring EFL Students ' AI Literacy in Academic Writing : Insights into Familiarity, Knowledge and Ethical Perceptions İngilizceyi Yabancı Dil Olarak Öğrenen Öğrencilerin Akademik Yazımda Yapay Zekâ Okuryazarlığını Keşfetmek : Aşinalık, Bilgi ve In rec. *Journal of Theoretical Educational Science, 18*(January), 157–181.

Zekânın, Y., & Öğretim, Ü. (2024, October). S. (2025). The Impact of Artificial Intelligence on University Teaching Processes. *Kastamonu Education Journal, 33*, 448–468. DOI: 10.24106/kefdergi.1748350

Zhou, X., Fang, L., & Schofield, L. (2023). Assessing AI literacy among academic staff: Insights from a higher education survey. *Research Article, 18*(1), 138–159.

Chapter 10
Faculty Training and Professional Development for AI Adoption:
A Systematic Literature Review

Nosheen Qamar
http://orcid.org/0000-0001-7560-208X
University of Management and Technology, Pakistan

Nabeel Ali Khan
University of Management and Technology, Pakistan

Mahreen Zaib
Beaconhouse National University, Pakistan

Nosheen Sabahat
http://orcid.org/0000-0002-1249-5552
Forman Christian College University, Lahore, Pakistan

Norsaremah Salleh
http://orcid.org/0000-0001-5625-7014
Kulliyyah of Information and Communication Technology, International Islamic University, Malaysia

ABSTRACT

Artificial Intelligence (AI) is a transformational technology that provides opportunities in the fields of teaching and research. Its adoption to success greatly relies on

DOI: 10.4018/979-8-3373-5586-3.ch010

how the faculty is ready and the Professional Development opportunities the faculty. This paper provides a systematic literature review of 44 studies to examine faculty training and other professional development towards AI adoption in higher education. The review will answer four research questions about publication trends, faculty preparedness, barriers and enablers, and the impact of prior digital literacy PD on adoption. The results indicate that faculty preparedness is not aligned regionally. This research adds value by identifying global research trends, conceptualizing a synthesis of the evidence on barriers and enablers, and re-emphasizing the critical importance of training PD, or digital literacy PD. The findings offer practical implications to higher education establishments and policy makers in preparation of viable, sustainable faculty development approaches to AI adoption.

INTRODUCTION

Artificial Intelligence (AI) is profoundly transforming the terrain of higher education, and it is altering teaching, learning, and research. The ability to improve faculty efficiency and student collaboration has been identified, and its potential application is wide-ranging (Mah and Groß, 2024; Shata and Hartley, 2025), including intelligent tutoring systems, automated assessment, and generative AI tools. These technologies can be successful only if the faculty is ready to incorporate them into pedagogical practices and is willing to do so (Liu, 2025). Faculty training and professional development (PD) are important features in this context, as they can determine sustainable adoption of AI. The wider field of AI in education discusses how smart systems can assist in decision-making, personalization of the learning experience, and institutional effectiveness (Okumu & Kenei, 2024; Qamar et al., 2020; Morales-Cevallos et al., 2025). The studies reveal that AI may cut the administrative workload, offer real-time feedback, and feedback-based teaching insights (Islam & Laughter et al., 2022). However, the adoption process cannot only be supported by the availability of technology, but also by investment in human competencies.

In this area, there is an emerging subfield to analyze faculty preparedness and professional development as a facilitator of adoption. According to the literature, professional growth enhances digital literacy and ethical awareness and pedagogical creativity *(Abdullah, 2025; Waddington, 2022).* The experienced faculty have been observed to be higher in confidence and positive outlook toward AI as compared to a lack of training, which leads to doubts, ethical issues, and objections *(Festus & Emmanuel, 2025).* Although there have been increments in scholarly attention, there are still gaps. Much of this literature has also been region-focused, with most working towards either the infrastructural or attitudinal factors, whereas leaving out much to be discussed about the systematic relationship between faculty training, digital literacy, and AI adoption outcomes *(*Gârdan *et al., 2025)*. Moreover, data in areas that are underrepresented, such as in Latin America and parts of Africa, are not abundant.

The issue of inconsistent cognition about the impacts of faculty training and PD on AI adoption is the focus of this paper. Absent a structured synthesis, institutions may build up improvised solutions that do not support the demands of the faculty or address other barriers present on the ground. This review combines evidence from 44 studies (2021-2025) to determine the patterns of faculty preparedness, inhibitors and facilitators, and the impact of digital literacy PD on AI adoption. This paper addresses the overall need to understand general trends in the field of AI education, regional peculiarities, and implications that could be seen as the guiding evidence for the PD frameworks development. This paper is a contribution to both scholarship and institutional practice, providing a systematic framework on which universities and policymakers could comprehend how they can enhance the role of faculty development in the context of AI integration. The research questions, methodology, and process of systematic synthesis that were used to guide this review are discussed below.

Integrating Artificial Intelligence into higher education isn't just a new trend in technology; it's a new cultural transformation in higher education, teaching, and educational management. Globally, the pressure on universities has dramatically increased, and align themselves with the Fourth Industrial Revolution, providing digital competency training for both students and faculty to address labor market availability and skills gaps. AI in education has been marked globally by initiatives such as UNESCO's "AI and Education: Guidance for Policy-makers" and the OECD's "AI in the Classroom Framework." Integration depends on the willingness and ability of educators to incorporate AI tools in a thoughtful, ethical, and impactful manner. This makes faculty training and professional development a priority on the strategic agenda to ensure that the adoption of AI promotes educational innovation, educational value, and human dignity.

Throughout the globe, there has been growing momentum. However, there are still signs of a lack of readiness and opportunity when it comes to how some regions of the world and the developing nations of the world are prepared. With the developing regions of the world, including Africa, there are challenges such as inadequate resources, poor development of technology, and a lack of institutional policies on AI. Even in the most developed regions of the world, educators are still faced with ethical and legal questions, concerns around data privacy, and the heightened workloads that AI threatens to bring. Hence, the emphasis on the need to understand the impact of professional development on attitudes, skills, and behaviors around adoption to close the gaps.

The professional development that literature has worked on to provide a more thorough approach to understanding the elements that prepare faculty, the institutional help they receive, and the AI adoption that they implement in their work to provide a more thorough understanding of the academic and functional AI adoption that they implement in their work, they intertwine to deepen the understanding of the adoption of AI technology and JoG excellence. By understanding the challenges that educators face in the work environment, this review will provide a more user-friendly and aligned approach to studies that have been done to create more streamlined and contextually appropriate faculty development programs that aim to support educators and help them to be fully engaged in the AI adoption process in the higher education system.

RELATED STUDIES

As Artificial Intelligence (AI) in higher education becomes more widespread, the training of the faculty and their PD has gained prominence as the factors that can facilitate its successful integration. Proposed studies consistently demonstrated a few common themes, namely the willingness and attitudes of educators when it comes to adopting AI (Eke, 2024), the effect structural support, policies, and infrastructure have on teacher willingness to adopt AI (Alnasib, 2023), and the need to develop digital literacies and confidence in teachers (Liu, 2025). Moreover, the study revealed that educators appreciate the pedagogical merits of AI tools, but they tend to face some barriers linked to mistrust, ethical issues, the increased workload, and the absence of systematic PD (Shata & Hartley, 2025; Baeten, 2025). Modern-day research has pointed more to how the perceptions of a teacher, as well as teacher professional development, play in an optimization of the educational management strategies (Gârdan et al., 2025). Overall, these works reinforce the necessity to have more holistic approaches to professional development that will encompass quality assessment models, research-based adoption models, teaching and learning instruments, and content-based approaches to optimize the role of faculty in the use of AI in the best way possible, as shown in Table 1.

Table 1. Most Relevant Papers on Faculty Training and Professional Development for AI Adoption

Sr.	References	Paper Title	Focus of Survey	Survey Approach	Research Framework	Teaching & Learning Tools	Content	Database
1	(Liu, 2025)	Exploring the Factors Influencing the Adoption of AI Technology by University Teachers: The Mediating Role of Confidence and AI Readiness	University teachers' AI readiness and PD needs	Survey + Mediation Analysis	✓		✓	Springer Link
2	(Shata & Hartley, 2025)	Artificial Intelligence and Communication Technologies in Academia: Faculty Perceptions and the Adoption of Generative AI	Faculty perceptions, trust, and adoption of generative AI in teaching	Survey + SEM	✓	✓	✓	Science Direct
3	(Gârdan et al., 2025)	Adopting AI in Education: Optimizing Human Resource Management Considering Teacher Perceptions	Teachers' perceptions shaping adoption and HRM optimization	Survey + Empirical Modelling	✓	✓		Web of Science
4	(Eke, 2024)	Assessing the Readiness and Attitudes of Nigerian Teacher Educators Towards the Adoption of AI in Educational Settings	Teacher educators' readiness for AI PD	Survey	✓		✓	Research Gate
5	(Alnasib, 2023)	Factors Affecting Faculty Members' Readiness to Integrate AI into Their Teaching Practices: A Study from Saudi Higher Education	Faculty readiness, attitudes, and PD enablers	Survey	✓	✓	✓	Web of Science
6	(Baeten, 2025)	The Influence of Artificial Intelligence Adoption on Educator Perceptions	Faculty's lived experiences of AI adoption in teaching	Phenomenological Interviews	✓	✓		Research Gate

METHODOLOGY

This study uses a Systematic Literature Review (SLR) as its research method. The review examines studies related to faculty training and professional development for AI adoption. A structured and objective approach to selecting and analyzing evidence is illustrated in **Figure 1**.

Figure 1. Systematic Literature Review (SLR) Process Steps and Outcomes

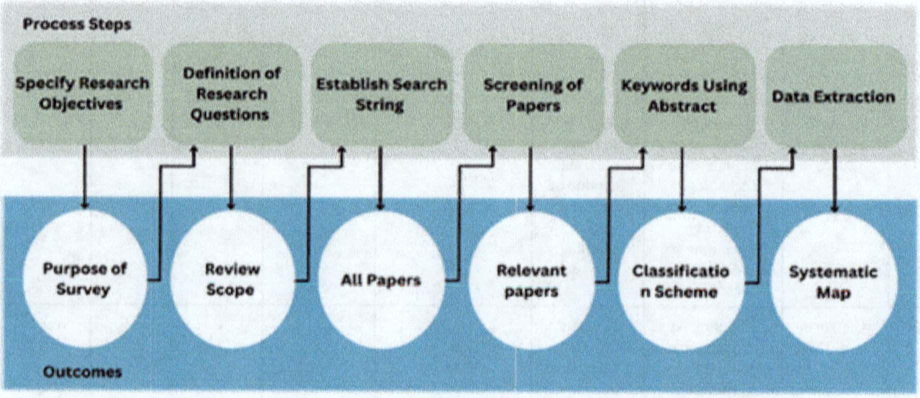

Research Questions & Objectives

Phase 1 of the proposed systematic literature review (SLR) will be an outline of the research questions and the evaluation of the existing research on the topic of faculty training and professional development for AI adoption. This SLR study attempts to answer four research questions as outlined in Table 2.

Table 2. Research Objectives and Motivations for Faculty Training and Professional Development in AI Adoption

RQ Statement	Objective	Motivation
RQ1: What are the publication channels of research on faculty Training and Professional Development for AI Adoption and how are the selected research papers distributed by publication year and geographical areas targeting this research over the years?	To name trustworthy publication sources, locate the distribution in time, and the spatial research pattern.	Makes the review of the literature systematic, comprehensive, and identifies global and time research trends.
RQ2: How prepared are faculty members in higher education for the integration of AI technologies into their teaching and research practices?	To determine faculty readiness measures, incorporating readiness levels of faculty as attitudes/awareness/ institutional support.	Assists in identifying areas of training and professional growth programs required with AI embracement.
RQ3: What are the key barriers and enablers to AI adoption among faculty in academic institutions?	To determine challenges (e.g., ethics, infrastructure, workload), and drivers (e.g., training, support, trust).	Offers groundwork for the creation of an intervention that can address the obstacles and leverage the facilitators.
RQ4: How does prior professional development in digital literacy influence faculty attitudes toward AI adoption?	To test the correlation of digital literacy training with perceptions of faculty of AI.	Motivates expenditure on specific professional training to encourage favorable attitudes towards the adoption of AI.

Search String

A systematic search was conducted using several academic databases with carefully designed search strings. The databases included Google Scholar, IEEE Xplore, ScienceDirect, MDPI, and Springer Link, as shown in Table 3. The search terms were selected to identify studies focused on faculty training, development, and preparation for AI adoption in educational institutions. Boolean operators, truncation, and proximity operators were applied where appropriate to refine the results and include only high-quality articles. Using multiple databases allowed for a broad and comprehensive review, ensuring diverse scholarly perspectives and a holistic understanding of AI-based faculty training and development.

Table 3. Search Strings Used Across Selected Databases for Identifying Relevant Studies

Sources	Search String
Google Scholar, ACM Digital Library, WoS, IEEE Xplore, Science Direct, MDPI, Springer Link	(Faculty Training OR Professional Development) AND (AI Adoption OR Artificial Intelligence Integration) AND (Higher Education OR Universities OR Academic Institutions)

Selection based on Inclusion/Exclusion criteria

In the initial search step, where the search protocol was used in the identified repositories, the initial identified papers were 11,132 papers. According to the exclusion criteria, 4,940 records were discarded as out of scope. At the second stage, 1,980 articles were examined on the basis of their title, and 1,250 were excluded because they were found to be irrelevant, leaving 980 records. During the eligibility phase, 1,030 articles were reviewed by their introductory and conclusion segments, and 481 articles were discarded as they were not on the primary focus of the faculty training or AI adoption. The PRISMA 2020 flow diagram was adapted from (Page et al.,2021) to illustrate the screening and inclusion process of this systematic review. This led to the identification of 44 studies that fitted all inclusion criteria and were synthesized in the systematic review displayed in Figure 2.

Duplicate titles and articles that were considered irrelevant were examined closely to ensure that they were removed from the screening process, which, as mentioned, was essential for screening reliability. Cohen's Kappa coefficient to compare the interdependence of two different authors' measures for the independent assessment of the same cases was 0.91, an excellent kappa. Such systematic filtering also ensured the highest degree of relevance and quality of included studies, which can provide a strong basis for analysis of training and professional development of teaching faculty involved in AI adoption.

Figure 2. Inclusion/Exclusion Criteria for Selected Studies Based on Prisma Model

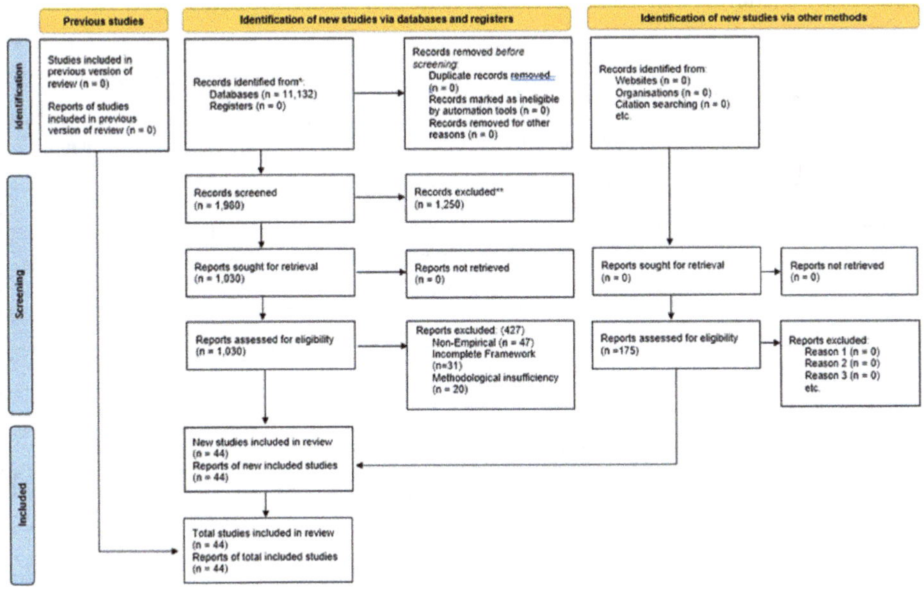

RESULTS

This Section describes the findings of this review based on the evidence extracted from existing studies. The answers to the research questions are presented in the following.

> RQ1: What are the publication channels of research on Faculty Training and Professional Development for AI Adoption, and how are the selected research papers distributed by publication year and geographical areas targeting this research over the years?

The identification of the publication channel is an important aspect of ensuring the rigor and credibility of any systematic literature review. In pursuing the current study, which is focused on the domain of Faculty Training and Professional Development for AI Adoption, it was necessary to consider venues where the relevant literature appears in order to determine the quality and quantity of the same. The review has considered journals, conferences, and other established sources to ensure that only relevant and good quality contributions constitute the evidence base. The global engagement and levels of maturity to deal with faculty training and professional development to use AI are highlighted in such mapping. The list of publication venue are summarized in Table 4.

Table 4. Publication Channel for Selected Studies

Sr No	Journal/Conference Name	No of Publication
1	International Journal of Educational Technology in Higher Education	2
2	Journal of Development and Social Sciences (JDSS)	2
3	Amfiteatru Economic	1
4	Applied Computing and Informatics	1
5	ArtsEduca	1
6	Australian Journal of Applied Linguistics	1
7	BMC Psychology	1
8	Bachelor's Thesis (Turku University of Applied Sciences)	1
9	CTE Workshop Proceedings	1
10	Caribbean Journal of Education and Development	1
11	Computers (MDPI)	1
12	Discover Education	1
13	Doctoral Dissertation (Athabasca University)	1
14	Doctoral Dissertation (University of Wisconsin-Stout)	1
15	E-Learn 2024 Conference Proceedings (AACE)	1
16	Education and Information Technologies	1
17	Behavioral Sciences	1
18	Frontiers in Education	1
19	Instructional Systems Design Book (ODU Digital Commons)	1
20	International Journal for Infonomics (IJI)	1
21	International Journal of Advanced Research in Education and Society	1
22	International Journal of Learning, Teaching and Educational Research	1
23	International Journal of Research and Innovation in Social Science (IJRISS)	1
24	International Journal of Science and Mathematics Education	1
25	International Journal of Science and Research (IJSR)	1
26	Journal of AI	1
27	Journal of Accounting and Organizational Change (Emerald)	1
28	Journal of Dental Education	1
29	Journal of Educational Technology & Online Learning	1
30	Journal of Research in Innovative Teaching & Learning (Emerald)	1

continued on following page

Table 4. Continued

Sr No	Journal/Conference Name	No of Publication
31	Journal of Science and Technology (UST, Aden)	1
32	Kenya Journal of Technical and Vocational Education and Training (KJ-TVET)	1
33	LAK22 Conference (ACM)	1
34	Language, Technology, and Social Media	1
35	Methodička Teorija i Praksa	1
36	New Horizons in Adult Education and Human Resource Development	1
37	Proceedings of the International Conference of Artificial Intelligence in Education (AIED)	1
38	ResearchGate Preprint	1
39	Scientific Reports (Nature)	1
40	Social Sciences (MDPI)	1
41	The Eurasia Proceedings of Educational & Social Sciences (EPESS)	1
42	Journal of Computer Assisted Learning	1
Total		44

Table 5 and Figure 3 show the geographical dissemination of the 44 publications reviewed in this study. It reveals a strong global interest in the integration of Artificial Intelligence within education. Asia accounted for the largest share, contributing 14 studies, reflecting the region's growing focus on leveraging AI for curriculum enhancement and classroom management. Africa followed with 11 publications, signifying an emerging recognition of AI's potential to address educational challenges across the continent. Europe contributed 10 studies, indicating steady engagement from academic institutions exploring systematic and policy-driven approaches to AI adoption. North America produced 9 publications, showcasing a vibrant research culture centered on faculty perceptions, generative AI tools, and professional development trends in higher education.

Generally speaking, the statistics show that the development of Faculty Training and Professional Development of AI Adoption is a global trend, mainly contributed by the developed and developing world. While the challenges and enablers may vary across applications, the geographical distribution speaks to the unquestioning embrace of the future potential of faculty readiness and AI-oriented professional development across all areas of the globe.

Table 5. Geographical Distribution of Selected Studies

Sr No	Continent	Country	No of Publication	Total
1	Asia	China	2	14
		India	2	
		Israel	1	
		Malaysia & Yemen	1	
		Oman	1	
		Pakistan	2	
		Philippines	1	
		Saudi Arabia	2	
		Turkey	2	
2	Africa	Egypt	2	11
		Ghana	2	
		Kenya	1	
		Nigeria	3	
		Nigeria	1	
		South Africa	1	
		Tunisia	1	
3	Europe	Albania	1	10
		Finland	2	
		Germany	1	
		Romania	1	
		Romania	1	
		Serbia	1	
		Spain	1	
		United Kingdom	2	
4	North America	United States	6	9
		Barbados (Caribbean)	1	
		Canada	1	
		Mexico & Colombia	1	
Total				**44**

Figure 3. Geographical Representation of Publications

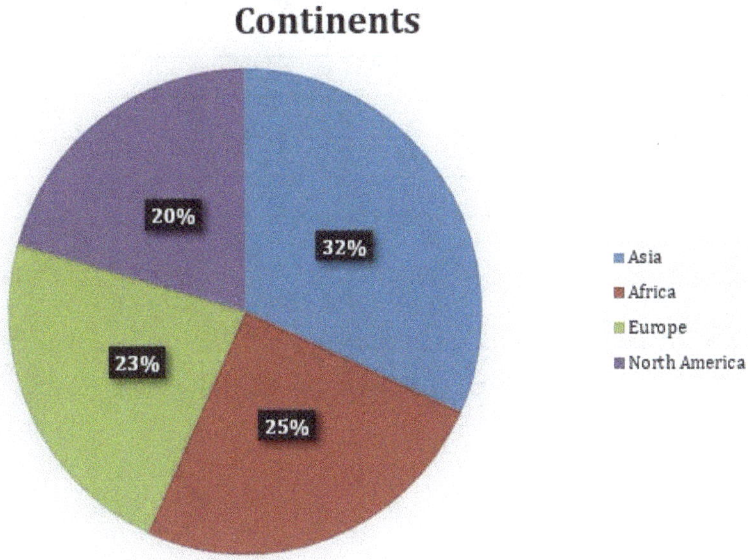

Understanding the distribution of research in terms of temporal and geographical coverage points would be crucial in understanding trends, gaps, and emerging points of interest in *the area of Faculty Training and Professional Development for AI Adoption*. The analysis for the year of publication will be useful for us; it will demonstrate the growth curve of the scholarly interest, indicating the year when there was an increased research interest in the area, and also provide an indication of the maturity of the field. The spatial distribution of contributions would also disclose the AI adoption priorities and strategies for different regions in higher education (both contextual challenges and readiness of the institutional dimension). The distribution of the reviewed studies is truly continental in nature, covering Asia, Africa, Europe, and North America, but certain countries, namely the United States, Nigeria, Pakistan, and China, are particularly prolific in the number of studies. Furthermore, the lowest publication levels are projected for 2023 and 2024, but the number of publications increases dramatically between 2025 and 2026, as shown in Table 6.

Table 6. Year-wise Distribution of Publications

Year	No of Publications
2021	1
2022	3
2023	6
2024	20
2025	14

Figure 4. Trends in Year-wise Publications

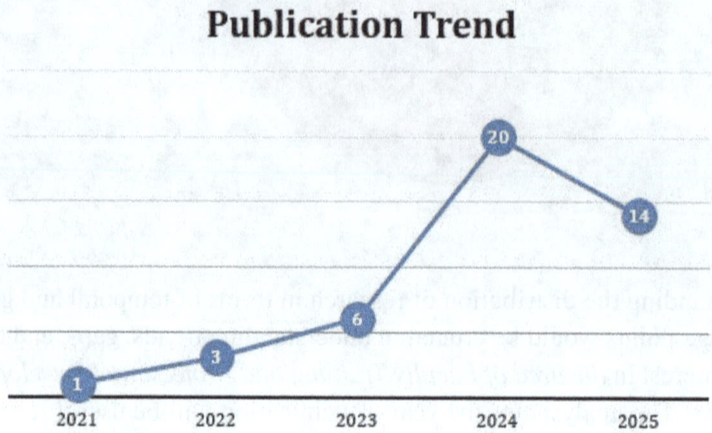

RQ2: How prepared are faculty members in higher education for the integration of AI technologies into their teaching and research practices?

Ans: Preparedness by faculty is a key parameter in establishing the level to which Artificial Intelligence (AI) can be successfully embedded within higher education. Whereas the teaching and research domains are discussing the incorporation of AI technologies like intelligent tutoring systems, automated grading tools, and generative AI platforms, the willingness of the faculty to incorporate and adapt to them is heterogeneous across settings. Some studies confirm a multi-dimensional construct of the faculty ready composed of technological literacy, flexibility, support of the institution, and sensitivities to ethics (Eke, 2024; Alnasib, 2023). As an example, the studies conducted in Saudi Arabia revealed that although the faculty members display moderate AI readiness, the barriers to its active implementation are quite high and include insufficient training and existing policy environments (Alnasib,

2023). In a similar vein, research in both Nigeria and Ghana accentuates that AI use by faculty requires greater facilities and professional development to become a reality (Eke, 2024; Festus & Emmanuel, 2025).

Besides, the readiness of faculty is frequently determined by their previous experience in encounters with professional training in the context of digital literacy. As a result of research, it is revealed that more confident and liberal feelings towards the utilization of AI are demonstrated by instructors who received their training in an organized way concerning the application of digital tools and pedagogical technologies (Liu, 2025). Conversely, the lack of specific training causes unease, reluctance, and ethical apprehensions, especially regarding questions pertaining to both academic integrity and workload (Shata & Hartley, 2025). Regional variation is also present: where the United States and European countries would underline faculty self-efficacy and confidence in AI systems, Asian and African environments depict structural enablers, i.e., readiness of institutions, infrastructure, and policy adjustment (Baeten, 2025; Gârdan et al., 2025).

All of the above findings evince that faculty preparedness cannot be regarded or conceived as something bound to the personal level of skills, but, in fact, it is a complex conjuncture of professional development opportunities, institutional support, and situational difficulties. The consideration of faculty readiness is thus important in determining how AI can be injected into teaching and research activities in higher institutions. Table 7 shows Faculty Preparedness to adopt AI in higher education.

1. Technological and Digital Literacy

Faculty readiness is based on digital competence. Educators with some preliminary experience of using digital solutions become more confident in working with AI. As an example, it was identified by Liu (2025) that digital literacy training had a significant mediating effect on the faculty's confidence and preparedness to adopt AI. Conversely, training brings about a certain amount of boldness and an urge to abandon the classical methods of teaching (Eke, 2024)

2. Institutional and Infrastructural Support

Preparedness is highly dependent on policies and the ability to access facilities at the institution. Research in Nigeria and Ghana found that even inspired teachers had a hard time adopting AI because of low connectivity, unavailability of AI software, and little administrative help (Festus & Emmanuel, 2025; Eke, 2024). However, compared to faculty in Saudi Arabia, a higher level of readiness had been shown in the presence of institutional policies and resources (Alnasib, 2023).

3. Pedagogical and Ethical Readiness

Preparedness is more than mere technical discernment of the morality and pedagogical coherence. Faculty argue that AI tools may raise issues such as plagiarism and the lack of academic integrity, and dehumanize teaching. Further, the factors trust and ethical assurance were shown to have a stronger relation to adoption than ease of use (Hata and Hartley 2025). These findings could also be juxtaposed with highlights from Baeten's (2025) work, who stressed that the ability to adopt AI as a teacher was one of balancing innovation with a concern for professionalism.

4. Regional Variations in Preparedness

Regional factors can also be considered as contextual forces. While the most significant obstacles in African and Asian iterations of the study appear to be infrastructural and funding-related, professional development and self-efficacy are more common in North America and Europe (Gârdan et al., 2025). Such contrasts indicate that AI adoption strategies should not be based on a single strategy but should be deliberated in the context and appended to a particular institutional reality.

A qualitative synthesis of the studies reviewed illustrates the variations in the level of preparedness of the faculty. Each study varied in detail regarding the awareness of faculty members, accessibility of AI tools, participation in professional development (PD) activities, and the readiness of the institutions. These observations guided the classification of preparedness into three broad levels:

- Low: Studies citing negligible AI exposure, little to no training, poorly developed support structures, or faculty awareness and training.
- Moderate: Studies citing partial AI familiarity, some training or initiatives from the institution under still prevailing challenges like persistent ethical issues, lack of support, or disarrayed institutional policy.
- High / Moderate–High: Studies reporting a high degree of initiative from the institution, functional PD training, or faculty confidence in using AI for teaching and research.

This categorization considers the qualitative descriptions contextualized in each study, rather than a numerical approach. For example, evidence citing anxieties of faculty, lack of exposure, or absence of policy structures resulted in a classification of "Low" or "Moderate" as opposed to institutional support, reflective teaching PD, or integrated training which were classified as "Moderate–High."

Table 7. Faculty Preparedness for AI Adoption in Higher Education

Sr No	Reference	Country	Faculty Preparedness Level	Key Barriers	Key Enablers
1	(Eke,2024)	Nigeria	Low–Moderate	Poor infrastructure, lack of PD, limited resources	Energy of the faculty, knowledge of the benefits of AI
2	(Festus & Emmanuel,2025)	Nigeria	Low	Funding gaps, cultural/linguistic challenges	Companies adaptive to the culture of AI tools, PD initiatives
3	(Alnasib,2023)	Saudi Arabia	Moderate	Lack of structured policies and training	Institutional, favorable attitudes
4	(Liu,2025)	China	Moderate–High	Anxiety, lack of exposure	Digitally literate training, self-assurance
5	(Shata & Hartley, 2025)	USA	Moderate–High	Trust and ethical concerns	Social reinforcing, institutional support
6	(Baeten,2025)	USA	Moderate	Ethical responsibility, workload	Reflective teaching/PD programs
7	(Gârdan et al., 2025)	Romania	Moderate	Limited policy integration	Faculty openness, PD-related to HRM

RQ3: What are the key barriers and enablers to AI adoption among faculty in academic institutions?

Ans: The barriers to and the enabling factors related to the faculty adoption of AI in higher education are a combination of factors that limit or facilitate the adoption process. There are still infrastructural and resource limits to some areas in Africa and Asia, unreliable connectivity, abilities to access tools, and funding defined in some parts as negative attitudes towards AI (Okumu & Kenei, 2024; Reuben & Kabilan, 2024). In addition to infrastructure, contextual frictions that include language mismatches and various local communication norms are also complicating classroom implementations of AI, even in teacher-training settings (Festus & Emmanuel, 2025). Europe and North America-based studies point to psychological and ethical inhibition to skepticism, the danger of workload, the possibility of plagiarism, and the risks of professional deskilling as the main barriers to hardware (Mah & Groß,

2024; Woodruff & Hutson, 2023). Cross-national studies contribute to explaining why faculty might lack clarity on how to use them, even in motivational cases, due to the lack of transparency in the institutional frameworks (policies, incentives, assessment guidelines et cetera) (Vazquez-Parra and Henao-Rodriguez et al., 2024; Karimov and Saarela et al., 2024).

On enabling perspective, there are three levers that are found across regions. Second, PD that specifically addresses digital competence skills, ethical use, and classroom integration shows promising results by raising confidence levels and increasing intention to integrate the use of AI into the classroom (Abdullah, 2025; Morales-Cevallos et al., 2025). Second, to move attitudes to practice, institutional support and leadership, which also includes formal strategies, resourcing, recognition, and governance, are needed (Jackman & Marshall et al., 2025; Islam & Laughter et al., 2022). Third, technology, organization, and environment fit-for-purpose frameworks unravel where to invest, and how an adoption decision is made (Abulail & Badran et al., 2025). Collectively, these studies indicate that barriers are infrastructure/policy gaps in the Global South, ethics/trust/workload in the Global North, whereas enablers are far more consistent: PD that is specific, institutional frameworks of explicitness, and leadership that equates incentives with the pedagogical goal. Table 8 depicts the Inhibitors and Promoters of AI Adoption by the Faculty.

1. Infrastructural and resource barriers

In environments where there is limited connectivity and equipment, AI can be lazy even when the faculty is interested. Answers to surveys in Kenyan TVET and North-East Nigeria universities show that bandwidth and access to devices and basic ICT resourcing are criterion bottlenecks (Okumu & Kenei, 2024; Reuben & Kabilan, 2024). The communication in the classrooms may also be deficient in instances where the AI tools are misaligned to the local instructional contexts in terms of culture and language (Festus & Emmanuel, 2025).

2. Ethical, trust, and workload concerns

The friction, in developed systems, is pulled onto the side of professional identity and assurance. The German faculty groupings consist of a critical and neutral profile with references to the threats of plagiarism, dehumanization, and workload carry-overs (Mah & Groß, 2024). The American educators also mention the absence of preparation and fears of extra workload with no noticeable advantages (Woodruff & Hutson, 2023).

3. Institutional frameworks and leadership

When attitudes are positive but there is unclear policy guidance and assessment, there is less adoption. The facilitating nature of both governance and incentives, as well as norms of assessment, is brought up by cross-regional evidence (Vazquez-Parra & Henao-Rodriguez et al., 2024; Jackman & Marshall et al., 2025). The driving force of leadership within professional schools is another example of how strategic framing results in the accelerated uptake (Islam & Laughter et al., 2022).

4. Professional development as a catalyst

The tentative interest refers to those who are interested but have not used more than mentioned yet, and are unlikely to continue to use; The sustainable development of digital competence and its applications in classrooms is likely to continue use. Results in adopter profiles by Finland indicate PD can help change faculty, who are wary or even opposed to new implementations, into active experimenters (Abdullah, 2025), and Spanish trainee-teacher findings illustrate how content-development capabilities can lead to positive AI implementation (Morales-Cevallos et al., 2025). The integrated decision frameworks (e.g., DOI/TOE/TAM) identify the points where PD and resources can be the most powerful (Abulail & Badran et al., 2025).

Table 8. Barriers and Enablers of AI Adoption among Faculty

Sr No	Reference	Country/Region	Key Barriers	Key Enablers
1	(Okumu & Kenei, 2024)	Kenya	Connectivity, ICT resourcing gaps	Policy-backed infrastructure investment
2	(Reuben & Kabilan, 2024)	Nigeria	Limited training, weak readiness	Targeted PD, institutional support
3	(Festus & Emmanuel, 2025)	Nigeria	Sociocultural/linguistic mismatches	Localized tools, communication-aware PD
4	(Mah & Groß, 2024)	Germany	Ethical skepticism, workload	Profile-specific PD, guidance
5	(Woodruff & Hutson, 2023)	USA	Training deficits, time burden	Collaborative PD, resource access
6	(Vázquez-Parra & Henao-Rodríguez et al., 2024)	Mexico & Colombia	Policy/assessment ambiguity	Institutional frameworks, incentives
7	(Karimov & Saarela et al., 2024)	Multi-country	Skills gaps, bureaucracy, ethics	Practical PD, collaboration networks

continued on following page

Table 8. Continued

Sr No	Reference	Country/Region	Key Barriers	Key Enablers
8	(Jackman & Marshall et al., 2025)	Barbados	Attitudes are less predictive than context	Leadership, facilitating conditions
9	(Islam & Laughter et al., 2022)	USA (Dental Ed.)	Unclear leadership for change	Four-frame leadership model for AI
10	(Abdullah, 2025)	Finland	Uneven adopter profiles	Tailored PD, sustainability focus
11	(Morales-Cevallos et al., 2025)	Spain	Limited institutional scaffolds	Digital-competence PD, content creation
12	(Abulail et al., 2025)	Jordan & Turkey	Usability/pressure uncertainties	DOI-TOE-TAM guidance, training, support

RQ4: How does prior professional development in digital literacy influence faculty attitudes toward AI adoption?

Ans: Previous professional development (PD) on digital literacy is one of the most critical determinants that influence faculty attitudes towards the adoption of AI. The research findings are consistent: When a faculty has participated in well-organized PD programs that deal with digital skills and knowledge, their attitudes toward AI transform, moving their perceptions beyond suspicion and toward curiosity, openness, and even excitement. As an example, Abulail et al. (2025) reported that in Jordan and Turkey, PD programs based on usability training alone with policy support positively influenced perceptions of PD and adoption intentions among faculty. In the same manner, Tarisayi (2024) stated that strategic leadership, which is backed by the development of the literature of responsible AI, assisted universities in South Africa to avoid ethical anxieties and resistance.

The relation can also be traced by research in Europe. In Finland, Abdullah (2025) discovered that PD introduced clear adoption patterns: a group of enthusiastic adopters preferred people who had a digital literacy preparation, whereas cautious and resistant groups did not have such training. In Romania, Gârdan et al. (2025) stated that a training program that incorporated both digital competence and change management enhanced the perceptions of the utility of AI in human resource management. These findings are replicated by North American studies. As demonstrated by Waddington (2022), PD that was developed based on Appreciative Inquiry enabled Canadian faculty to use PD as a thinking tool in reformulating AI as an opportunity, rather than a threat, when it comes to professional growth. In a similar vein, Agathursamy (2024) found that Indian faculty members viewed PD as a critical element of overcoming workload issues and rebranding AI tools as tools that help facilitate pedagogical practices but not replace them.

Interestingly, former PD is not only the source of technical confidence, but also moral and thoughtfulness intensifies as well. Morales-Cevallos et al. (2025) found that Spanish trainees with high training on the production of digital content had low pro-activity values and values of accordance with the use of AI. Taken together, these results reaffirm one of the major findings of our first study: that digital literacy PD is much more than a skills-based experience; rather, it serves as an attitudinal fulcrum that can be used to turn faculty resistance into responsible use, particularly in hospitable institutional contexts. Table 9 shows the impact of Digital Literacy PD on faculty attitude for AI adoption.

1. Digital Literacy Training as a Confidence Builder

When PD limits anxiety and develops confidence, then the attitudes of the faculty will be enhanced. In Jordan and Turkey, the training in the PD framework emphasized usability so that faculty members would not see AI as something to resist (Abulail & Badran et al., 2025). In Finland, trained faculty used to take a cautious approach, but their views changed to enthusiastic adopters, which indicates the power of PD (Abdullah, 2025).

2. Shaping Ethical and Reflective Attitudes

In addition to teaching the technical skills, PD will promote moral reasoning. Morales-Cevallos et al. (2025) noted that content creation PD led to more proactive involvement and adoption of AI tools amongst trainee teachers in Spain, which was, nevertheless, responsible in its nature. Tarisayi (2024) added that South African faculty were able to strike a balance between innovation and ethical teaching practices due to responsible AI leadership training.

3. Professional Development as a Driver of Positive Perceptions

The implementation of the PD coping with AI management in Canada proved that AI can be seen as a place to redefine negative attitudes towards an optimistic one (Waddington, 2022). Similarly, in India, Agathursamy (2024) revealed that trained faculty saw the opportunity of AI tools to improve efficiency but not to be a threat to autonomy.

4. Institutional Integration of PD

Faculty attitudes improve the most where PD is integrated into more institution-wide policies. As per Gârdan et al. (2025), the PD integrated into the HRM was effective to make faculty see AI as a part of institutional resources instead of a standalone tool in Romania. This level of similarity strengthened their confidence and trust to follow.

Table 9. Influence of Digital Literacy PD on Faculty Attitudes toward AI Adoption

Sr No	Reference	Country/ Region	PD Focus	Impact on Faculty Attitudes
1	(Abulail et al., 2025)	Jordan & Turkey	Usability, TOE-TAM integrated training	Built confidence, reduced resistance
2	(Tarisayi, 2024)	South Africa	Responsible AI leadership PD	Mitigated ethical concerns, fostered openness
3	(Abdullah, 2025)	Finland	Digital literacy & adopter profiling	Enthusiastic adoption linked to PD exposure
4	(Gârdan et al., 2025)	Romania	HRM-linked PD	Positive perceptions of AI's institutional role
5	(Waddington, 2022)	Canada	Appreciative Inquiry PD model	Shifted attitudes from threat to growth
6	(Agathursamy, 2024)	India	Faculty PD in digital tools	Framed AI as pedagogical support
7	(Morales-Cevallos et al., 2025)	Spain	Digital content-creation training	Encouraged proactive, responsible use

CONCLUSION AND FUTURE WORK

Conclusion

The present systematic literature review has synthesized the current body of knowledge in the area of faculty training and subsequent professional development (PD) of AI in higher education. Through a synthesis of a review of 44 peer-reviewed studies published between 2021 and 2025, the article found that faculty preparedness, digital literacies, prior professional development, and barriers and enablers to adoption influenced the adoption outcomes. While AI is a global problem, our results show that the factors associated with readiness vary considerably across geocultural and institutional contexts.

This review finds that there is more than one aspect to faculty preparedness, and that such preparedness is not just a technical competency but a matter of pedagogical agility, moral awareness, and institutional support. It is not unusual to find willing faculty in development settings, particularly in Africa and Asia, who are without appropriate structures, funding, and training schemes. On the other hand, mature environments in North America and Europe face fewer infrastructural challenges for faculty, but more ethical dilemmas, work overload, and trust toward AI technologies.

Barrier/enabler analysis identified a geographical duality of regions, with more infrastructural and policy-based barriers being situated in the Global South and psychological/ethical/cultural barriers being situated in the Global North. However, institutional support, policy frameworks, and professional development are among the few shared enablers across settings because of an understanding that AI adoption can't just be a question of individual accountability.

It also adds that previous digital literacy training played an important role in shaping faculty attitudes. Research has found that PD programs provide confidence, alleviate fear, and provide ethical and responsible adoption. When faculty associated AI with a threat, it was assigned a more negative pedagogical role than when they associated gender with a threat. This further justifies the need for institutions to create long-term context-specific professional development programmes that transcend skill provision through understanding of reflective and ethical use of AI in teaching and research.

For anyone involved in faculty development who seeks to improve their practice, this review is worth reading for its mapping of trends in publication, regional emphases, and an overview of the evidence in relation to the potential for faculty development in the adoption of artificial intelligence. These findings suggest that successful adoption will occur within a multi-faceted model: the development of faculty digital competency, the development of institutional plans for adopting digital technologies, and the overcoming of context-specific adoption barriers. In the future, longitudinal and cross-regional studies can be used to capture how PD and institution-level interventions can be translated into longitudinal pedagogical change while ensuring that the work of AI innovation is complementary and not a substitute for the human aspect of teaching and learning.

Future Work

While the contributions of this review have provided valuable insights into faculty training and professional development (PD) regarding the adoption of AI in higher education, there are still gaps and opportunities for future research to exploit. Most of the papers reviewed are cross-sectional in nature and rely on surveys or self-reported impressions, which are useful as moment-in-time snapshots, but are insufficient for capturing the longitudinal shift in faculty preparedness and attitudes. As such, longitudinal designs are needed to understand the impact of professional development, institutional-level policies, and infrastructural investments on the adoption process in future research. Second, there was a substantial geographic disparity within the literature, with most studies being located in North America, Europe, and a few regions of Asia and Africa, whereas little coverage can be found in Latin America, the Middle East, and small island countries. Increasing the geographical scale of research will make views more inclusive in terms of global AI adoption.

Further, future studies need to move beyond reporting barriers and enablers to testing intervention-based models, including studying the influence of targeted faculty adoption interventions, i.e., evaluating the effectiveness of specific PD, leadership, or AI literacy curricula. Experimental and quasi-experimental studies will offer strong evidence about which strategies are the most effective to develop digital competence and transform faculty attitude. One more essential subject of future investigation is the relations between ethics and professional growth. Although there were mentions of the themes of trust, plagiarism, and privacy, additional research is required in PD programs in terms of how ethical frameworks, critical thinking, and responsible uses of AI can be implemented in faculty training.

Moreover, the question of the involvement of emerging technologies in the PD delivery should be investigated. Adaptive learning based on AI technologies, training based on simulations, and virtual reality environments could be involved to offer a personalized faculty training experience, but, at the same time, there is little research conducted on the potential of these tools. Lastly, it will be important to consider the student perspective when it comes to AI adoption by the faculty: how is better faculty preparedness associated with student learning and experience, attentiveness, and trust? Filling this gap would be more comprehensive in terms of the effect of AI on the teaching-learning system.

Overall, future studies require increased attention to longitudinal, experimental, and cross-regional studies and a renewed interest in the ethical, technological, and learner dimensions of the study. These interventions will not only help advance scholarship but can also serve as useful models for universities and policymakers that are interested in cultivating sustainable and equitable adoption of AI by faculty and staff through professional development.

REFERENCES

Abdullah, A. (2025). Integrating artificial intelligence in higher education: a study on adoption and application of AI by business teachers at Turku University of Applied Sciences.

Abulail, R. N., Badran, O. N., Shkoukani, M. A., & Omeish, F. (2025). Exploring the Factors Influencing AI Adoption Intentions in Higher Education: An Integrated Model of DOI, TOE, and TAM. *Computers, 14*(6), 230. DOI: 10.3390/computers14060230

Alnasib, B. N. (2023). Factors affecting faculty members' readiness to integrate artificial intelligence into their teaching practices: A study from the Saudi higher education context. *International Journal of Learning. Teaching and Educational Research, 22*(8), 465–491. DOI: 10.26803/ijlter.22.8.24

Baeten, T. (2025). *The Influence of Artificial Intelligence Adoption on Educator Perceptions* (Doctoral dissertation, University of Wisconsin--Stout).

Eke, E. O. (2024). Assessing the readiness and attitudes of Nigerian teacher educators towards adoption of artificial intelligence in educational settings. *Journal of Educational Technology and Online Learning, 7*(4-ICETOL 2024 Special Issue), 473-487.

Gârdan, I. P., Manu, M. B., Gârdan, D. A., Negoi ă, L. D. L., Pa tiu, C. A., Ghi ă, E., & Zaharia, A. (2025, February). Adopting AI in education: Optimizing human resource management considering teacher perceptions. [). Frontiers Media SA.]. *Frontiers in Education, 10*, 1488147. DOI: 10.3389/feduc.2025.1488147

Islam, N. M., Laughter, L., Sadid-Zadeh, R., Smith, C., Dolan, T. A., Crain, G., & Squarize, C. H. (2022). Adopting artificial intelligence in dental education: A model for academic leadership and innovation. *Journal of Dental Education, 86*(11), 1545–1551. DOI: 10.1002/jdd.13010 PMID: 35781809

Jackman, G. A., Marshall, I. A., & Carrington, T. (2025). Opportunity or Threat: Investigating Faculty Readiness to Adopt Artificial Intelligence in Higher Education. *Caribbean Journal of Education and Development, 1*(2), 4–27. DOI: 10.46425/cjed1201029055

Karimov, A., Saarela, M., & Kärkkäinen, T. (2024, October). Teachers' Adoption of AI Tools: Motivations, Challenges, and Skills Required. In *eLearn: World Conference on EdTech* (pp. 610-615). Association for the Advancement of Computing in Education (AACE).

Liu, N. (2025). Exploring the factors influencing the adoption of artificial intelligence technology by university teachers: The mediating role of confidence and AI readiness. *BMC Psychology, 13*(1), 311. DOI: 10.1186/s40359-025-02620-4 PMID: 40148913

Mah, D. K., & Groß, N. (2024). Artificial intelligence in higher education: Exploring faculty use, self-efficacy, distinct profiles, and professional development needs. *International Journal of Educational Technology in Higher Education, 21*(1), 58. DOI: 10.1186/s41239-024-00490-1

Milutinović, V., Đorđević, S., & Obradović, I. (2025). Factors shaping the adoption of artificial intelligence in education. *Metodička teorija i praksa, 28*(1).

Morales-Cevallos, M. B., Alonso-García, S., Martínez-Menéndez, A., & Victoria-Maldonado, J. J. (2025). Artificial Intelligence Adoption Amongst Digitally Proficient Trainee Teachers: A Structural Equation Modelling Approach. *Social Sciences (Basel, Switzerland), 14*(6), 355. DOI: 10.3390/socsci14060355

Okumu, G. J., & Kenei, J. K. (2024). Adoption of Artificial Intelligence in Technical and Vocational Education and Training Institutions in Kenya. *THE KENYA JOURNAL OF TECHNICAL AND VOCATIONAL EDUCATION AND TRAINING VOL, 7*, 2.

Page, M. J., McKenzie, J. E., Bossuyt, P. M., Boutron, I., Hoffmann, T. C., Mulrow, C. D., Shamseer, L., Tetzlaff, T., Akl, E., Brennan, S., Chou, D., & Glanville, J. (2021). The PRISMA 2020 statement: An updated guideline for reporting systematic reviews. *BMJ (Clinical Research Ed.), 372*(71), 1–9. PMID: 33782057

Qamar, N., Kiran, H. M., Ahmad, F., Saeed, S., & Abid, B. (2020). Software engineering fresh graduates career choices and software industry demands: An empirical analysis. *Int. J. Comput. Sci. Netw. Secur, 20*(12), 72.

Reuben, B., & Kabilan, M. K. (2024). Assessment of university lecturers' readiness to adopt artificial intelligence (AI) technology in North-East of Nigeria. *International Journal of Advanced Research in Education and Society, 6*(2), 482–490.

Shata, A., & Hartley, K. (2025). Artificial intelligence and communication technologies in academia: Faculty perceptions and the adoption of generative AI. *International Journal of Educational Technology in Higher Education, 22*(1), 14. DOI: 10.1186/s41239-025-00511-7

Tarisayi, K. S. (2024, March). Strategic leadership for responsible artificial intelligence adoption in higher education. In *CTE workshop proceedings* (Vol. 11, pp. 4-14). DOI: 10.55056/cte.616

Vázquez-Parra, J. C., Henao-Rodríguez, C., Lis-Gutiérrez, J. P., Palomino-Gámez, S., & Suárez-Brito, P. (2024). *Perception of AI tool adoption and training: initial validation using GSEM method*. Applied Computing and Informatics.

Waddington, L. (2022). Supporting faculty adoption of technology and online learning: pandemic inspired possibilities.

Woodruff, K., Hutson, J., & Arnone, K. (2023). Perceptions and barriers to adopting artificial intelligence in K-12 education: A survey of educators in fifty states.

Chapter 11
Students' Voice in the Era of AI:
Perceptions, Usage, and Ethical Expectations in Higher Education

Lydia A. Omar
http://orcid.org/0009-0000-5259-2739
Mindanao State University-Tawi-Tawi College of Technology and Oceanography, Philippines

Hana An L. Alvarado
http://orcid.org/0009-0006-6550-616X
Mindanao State University-Tawi-Tawi College of Technology and Oceanography, Philippines

Rayana E. Sehaban
Mindanao State University-Tawi-Tawi College of Technology and Oceanography, Philippines

Sherlyn A. Iralan
Mindanao State University-Tawi-Tawi College of Technology and Oceanography, Philippines

Potchong M. Jackaria
http://orcid.org/0009-0006-1678-4841
Mindanao State University-Tawi-Tawi College of Technology and Oceanography, Philippines

DOI: 10.4018/979-8-3373-5586-3.ch011

ABSTRACT

This study investigated students' perceptions, usage, and ethical expectations regarding Artificial Intelligence (AI) in higher education. Employing a phenomenological design, ten undergraduate students from a state university in the southern Philippines were interviewed to capture their actual use of AI tools such as ChatGPT and Grammarly. Results revealed that students perceive AI as a valuable academic partner that enhances productivity, confidence, and engagement in learning. However, they also expressed apprehensions about overreliance, misinformation, and threats to academic honesty. Participants emphasized the importance of institutional policies, ethical frameworks, and digital literacy initiatives to promote responsible AI use. The study concludes that while AI holds transformative potential in fostering learner autonomy and efficiency, its integration must be guided by fairness, accountability, and human oversight to safeguard authentic learning and uphold integrity in higher education.

INTRODUCTION

In this era, artificial intelligence (AI) has quickly made its way into college classrooms. From tools that check grammar and detect plagiarism to systems that help grade essays or answer students' questions. AI is changing how students learn and how teachers teach. These tools are often introduced with the promise of making education more efficient, personalized, and accessible. However, while the institution focuses on the benefits of AI, an important perspective is often left out: that of the students.

Students are not just users of AI; they are directly impacted by how it is used. Whether it's receiving automated feedback on their work or being monitored during online exams, students interact with AI in ways that shape their learning experiences. Yet, we still know very little about what students thinks about these tools. Do they trust AI system? Do they feel the tools are fair? Are they concerned about how their data is being used? These are questions that need to be asked and answered if we are to use AI responsibly in education. According to Zawacki-Richer et al. (2019), the integration of Artificial intelligence in higher education raised complex challenges related to fairness, transparency, and accountability, especially when learners' perspectives were not considered.

While, the current conversation around AI in education focuses on technical performance and institutional readiness, there is growing concern about ethical and social-dimension of this technology. Many teachers are already concerned that students are becoming reliant on AI tools that can potentially hinder their ability to think independently (Mhlanga, 2023). Some raise broader risks such as diminishing human interaction, bias, threats to academic integrity and over-reliance (Jackaria et al., 2025). Similarly, Vera et al. (2024) emphasized that universities must address ethical awareness and digital literacy when integrating AI in teaching and learning. Furthermore, Ali et al. (2025) found that students' trust in AI tools was influenced by perceived fairness and transparency, highlighting the need for institutional guidelines on ethical use of Artificial Intelligence.

Listening to students' perspectives is not just a matter of inclusion, it's a matter of quality and responsibility. When students are invited to into the conversation, we can better understand the real-world impact of AI in the classroom. Their experience offers practical insights that can help shape more thoughtful and fair approaches to educational technology. As Almalki et al. (2025) noted that students voices served as valuable feedback channels for developing inclusive and human-centered AI system in education.

This chapter takes a closer look at how students perceive AI in their academic lives. It highlights their thoughts, concerns, and hopes about how these technologies are shaping their learning experiences. By bringing students perspective forefront, the chapter aims to offer valuable insights that can help educators and institutions make more informed, thoughtful, and ethical decisions about how AI integrated into higher education.

Through an in-depth exploration of students' perceptions, experiences, and utilization of artificial intelligence (AI) in higher education, this study examines how learners engage with and make sense of AI tools in academic contexts. Specifically, it aims to answer the following questions: (1) How do students perceive the use of artificial intelligence (AI) tools in higher education? and (2) What are the students' expectations regarding the role of AI in teaching, assessment, and academic support?

By understanding how students perceive and experience AI technologies, this chapter seeks to contribute to the development of a more inclusive and ethically responsive framework for integrating AI in higher education. It also aims to provide valuable insights that can guide educators, institutions, and policymakers in promoting responsible and equitable use of AI, ensuring that its integration enhances learning outcomes and supports the holistic development of students in the digital age.

RELATED LITERATURE

AI in education

In today's world, artificial intelligence (AI) has significantly improved people's lives in education in numerous ways. It changed the way teachers teach, students learn, and the strategies of the institution (Chen et al., 2020). AI encompasses natural language processing, automated learning, and data-driven algorithms that allow educational systems to make learning more personalized, automate administrative tasks, and make lessons more interesting and engaging (Abbasi et al. 2025; Ahmed et al., 2024). Long ago, AI was once a theoretical concept and now has become a practical tool that informs curriculum design, classroom instruction, and policy-making to help educators make evidence-based decisions to enhance the quality teaching and institutional quality (Portilla et al., 2025; U.S. Department of Education, 2023; Walter, 2024).

Nowadays, modern AI tools include generative AI applications, adaptive learning systems, intelligent tutoring platforms, and automated grading software support personalized instruction and feedback to make educators focus on creativity and the development of the students (Abbasi et al., 2025; Denny et al., 2024; Fitria, 2021). AI has the ability to modifies or adjusts content delivery, pacing and recognizing individual needs to promote inclusive, learner-centered environment by just simply analyzing learner behavior, performance metrics and interaction pattern (Hwang et al., 2020; Liang et al., 2025).

ChatGPT is one of the generative AI that enhance and provide explanations, problem-solving guidance, and scenario-based exercises that is more like theoretical knowledge with practical application (Ahmed et al., 2024; Michel- Villarreal et al., 2023). Al has a system that can be used to assess, make some suggestions or offer broad concepts to ensure consistency that allows learners to recognize errors, modify strategies, and engage in reflective practices. (Tsai et Al., 2025; Denny et Al., 2024). The competence of AI enriches the ability in empowering students to take ownership of their academic success by learning at their own pace.

Studies showed that contribution of AI in education extend beyond content delivery and highlights its potential to foster adaptive learning, support diverse learning styles, and reduce repetitive administrative burdens on education (Bearman et al., 2023). The application ranges from intelligent tutoring systems to automated grading platforms, in order to enhance efficiency while providing educators with deeper insights into learning outcomes (Chen et al., 2020). When supporting evidence-based decision-making, analytical platforms should monitor engagement, evaluate the strategies of teaching, and improve resource aid (Abbasi et al., 2025; McDonald et al., 2025).

Additionally, generative AI bridges the gap between theoretical pedagogy and work place readiness by making interactive, scenario-based learning experiences (Irish et al., 2025). Moreover, Hennekeuser et al. (2024) highlighted the role of AI in supporting lecturers, demonstrating how generative AI can helps make lecture materials, answer students' questions or queries, and scaffold complex concepts.

Usage of AI In Education

The usage of AI in education and in related sectors extend research, management of different activities and programs, and operational optimization, proceeding beyond mere implementation to strategic and thoughtful adaptation. In research, AI assists and supports literature reviews, organizes the collections of data, and facilitates collaboration with the different disciplines, allowing more products and data driven inquiry (Chubb et al., 2022; Burger et al.,2023). When it comes to an institutional setting, AI improves decision-making, rationalizes procedures, and enables evidence-based policy implementation that improves service delivery and how well an institution is, achieving its mission and goals (Van Noorzdt & Misuraca, 2022). For students, AI generative chatbot tools and adaptive systems that personalize learning instruction, deliver timely feedback, and cater to or accommodate individual learner needs, to foster engagement and improve results (Stöhr et al., 2024).

Additionally, the integration of artificial intelligence (AI) in education has become a major transformative force that reshapes how students learn and how teachers teach. The study of Crompton and Burke (2023) emphasized that AI promotes personalized learning experiences, streamlines administrative tasks, and supports educators in providing data-driven feedback. Likewise, Dogan et al. (2023) found that AI tools in online and distance education enhance student engagement and improve accessibility by adapting content to learners' needs. Moreover, the study of Harry (2023) also highlighted that AI can significantly improve educational efficiency and innovation by fostering interactive and learner-centered environments. However, these studies also stress the importance of maintaining ethical standards, teacher guidance, and human interaction to prevent the misuse of AI in academic contexts.

Recent studies further demonstrate the growing role of artificial intelligence in supporting pre-service teacher development and instructional practices. In a study involving science pre-service teachers, Jackaria et al. (2026) found that AI tools were widely utilized to assist lesson preparation, instructional material development, and reflective teaching practices during practice teaching. The findings suggest that AI can enhance teaching efficiency and pedagogical preparedness when used as a supplementary educational resource. Similarly, Alvarado (2026) argued that the emergence of AI technologies requires educators to redefine traditional teaching roles, shifting from being primary knowledge transmitters toward facilitators of learning, critical thinking, and responsible technology use. These studies reinforce the view that AI integration extends beyond student learning and significantly influences teacher preparation and professional practice.

Furthermore, study of Martin et al. (2024) further explored how AI is being applied in K–12 education to promote individualized instruction and skill mastery, noting that the effectiveness of AI depends on how responsibly it is implemented. In addition, Takerngsaksiri et al. (2024) examined students' experiences with AI-assisted code completion tools, revealing both positive effects on learning productivity and potential risks of overdependence. Similarly, Wang et al. (2024) conducted a comprehensive review that reinforced the need for clear policies, educator training, and ethical awareness to ensure the proper use of AI in educational settings.

The use of Artificial Intelligence (AI) is not dependent on technological capabilities but rather on several factors-human, organizational, and environmental. Venkatesh (2022) highlights the benefits and adoption that are influenced by these factors individually. Using the so-called Unified Theory of Acceptance and Use of Technology (UTAUT), framework, the study demonstrates the differences in how each factor affects the adoption processes and their benefits. Awareness and literacy of these dimensions can further help institutions make strategies that AI can enhance the outcomes of research, operations, learning, and decision-making.

Further in parts of learning, AI introduction has significant importance in management and functional programming. An organized study of AI applied in general guidance displays that implementation is formed by detailed possibilities and vulnerability demanding factual, collaborative, and theoretically based inquiry to supervise accomplishment successfully (Zuiderwijk et al., 2021). Likewise, AI in utilization in developing organizations illustrates its function to improve potential usage while managing user satisfaction, presenting estimative and information-based selection in complicated settings (Ngarambe et al., 2020). Together, these learning emphasize that effective AI utilization needs systematic organizing, formulating coordination, and arrangement among innovation and individuals to increase influence throughout subjects (Burger et al., 2023; Van Noordt & Misuraca, 2022; Stöhr et al., 2024).

Risk of Artificial Intelligence

Given the many benefits of Artificial intelligence not just education but also in other aspects is mesmerizing however, there is also a risk of using AI especially when misused, under-governed, or poorly designed, generates new and amplified vulnerabilities. For instance, Federspiel et al. (2023) argue that the used incorrectly "narrow" AI can threaten human health and well-being via three main pathways: enhancing opportunities for mass surveillance and manipulation, enabling dehumanized lethal autonomous weapons, and rendering human labor no longer useful, they furthermore warn of the possible existential risk posed by self-improving artificial general intelligence (AGI). In the health-care domain specifically, this means AI might build on biased or incomplete data, make incorrect decisions such misdiagnoses or exacerbate inequities by being deployed in contexts with low digital or regulatory readiness.

Beyond healthcare, a broad review of AI-safety and risk literature detects systemic threats. For instance, Salhab et al. (2024) presents a systematic literature review on AI safety emphasizing the need for trustworthiness, robustness, interpretability, fairness, and bias mitigation throughout design, deployment and operational phases. Meanwhile, Uuk et al. (2024) propose a taxonomy of systemic risks from general-purpose AI that can affect whole societies or economies covering environmental harm, structural discrimination, governance failure, and loss of control.

Moreover, the ethical hazard study by Guan et al. (2022) finds that technological uncertainty, incomplete data, and management errors are major sources of ethical risk in AI decision-making. The paper underscores how the interplay of human decision-making, algorithmic design, and organizational management constitutes layered risk. On the deployment side, research on AI in education points out over-reliance on AI systems, algorithmic bias, plagiarism, privacy concerns, and transparency issues as contributory factors undermining decision-making, critical thinking, and analytical capacity.

Additionally, the adoption of artificial intelligence tools brings significant risks beyond the familiar issues of misuse. For instance, Bo (2025) observes that algorithmic decision-making in educational settings (such as identifying students for intervention or progression) carries the danger of reinforcing existing inequalities, because automated systems may rely on biased data and opaque governance structures. Similarly, a systematic review of Garzón et al. (2025) emphasize that AI systems in education introduce concerns about data privacy, algorithmic bias, transparency, accountability, and the erosion of human agency in learning processes. In the classroom context, studies note that student over-reliance on AI tools may undermine critical thinking, diminish teacher and student interaction, and limit pedagogical flexibility, thus posing a threat to the quality of instruction and learning outcomes. As Delello et al. (2025) said these risks become especially salient when relatively large classroom sizes or limited teacher time (as in your thesis topic) mean that AI might be introduced as a "quick fix" rather than as part of a thoughtfully designed instructional strategy which can increase vulnerabilities rather than mitigating them.

Ethical use of AI

Despite the capabilities and benefits, AI integration needed to observe ethical considerations, such as data privacy, logarithmic bias, AI and digital divide, and over reliance on technology. Forming strong policy guide, professional development, and continuous monitor are necessary to make sure that AI can complement humanistic teaching and preserves emotional and social support (Behera et al., 2025; Bond et al., 2024; Garzón et al., 2025; Holmes & Tuomi, 2022).

Ethical use of AI has appeared as a critical counterbalance to the numerous risks associated with AI deployment (Khan et al., 2022). Ethical frameworks emphasize principles such as transparency, accountability, fairness, privacy, human oversight, safety, and societal benefit (Al-Kfairy et al., 2024; Li et al., 2022). Transparency ensures that AI decisions can be explained and understood, reducing the likelihood of unintentional harm (Pant et al., 2024). Accountability mechanisms establish clear responsibility for AI outcomes, enabling corrective measures and enhancing trust in the system (Batool et al., 2023). Additionally, the fairness or non-discrimination, requires that AI systems do not perpetuate existing biases or exacerbate social inequalities, which is particularly important in sensitive sectors such as healthcare, law, and education (Guan et al., 2022; Li et al., 2022).

Furthermore, privacy and data protection are central to ethical AI use, as AI systems often rely on large datasets containing personal and sensitive information (Al-Kfairy et al., 2024; Li et al., 2022). In addition, ethical AI mandates that informed consent is obtained, data is stored securely, and usage adheres to legal and moral norms. Human oversight is another key principle, ensuring that humans remain involved in critical decision-making processes and can intervene in cases where AI may produce harmful outcomes (Li et al., 2022; Pant et al., 2024).

Ethical frameworks are operationalized differently across domains. In healthcare, studies emphasize context-specific ethical reflection, noting that generic principles may be insufficient to address domain-specific challenges such as patient autonomy, data sensitivity, and algorithmic bias (Li et al., 2022; Llerena-Izquierdo & Ayala-Carabajo, 2025). In academia, ethical AI use addresses issues such as authorship, plagiarism, and research integrity, highlighting that ethical considerations extend beyond commercial or public applications into knowledge production itself (Llerena-Izquierdo & Ayala-Carabajo, 2025). Research also underscores the importance of embedding ethics into organizational culture, including staff training, ethical auditing processes, and continual reflection to ensure AI aligns with societal and human-centered values (Batool et al., 2023; Pant et al., 2024).

Governance and regulation are indispensable components of ethical AI deployment. Studies highlight that voluntary principles alone are insufficient and must be complemented with enforceable standards, independent audits, monitoring mechanisms, and multi-stakeholder participation (Batool et al., 2023; Pant et al., 2024). For example, responsible AI governance frameworks specify *who* is accountable, *what* is governed, *when* governance occurs, and *how* it is implemented, providing clarity and operational effectiveness in real-world applications (Batool et al., 2023). Similarly, in global healthcare applications, ethical considerations must be tailored to diverse cultural, social, and regulatory contexts to ensure inclusivity, equity, and social benefit (Li et al., 2022; Llerena-Izquierdo & Ayala-Carabajo, 2025).

The importance of maintaining human agency in AI-supported learning environments is further emphasized by Alvarado (2026), who noted that the increasing presence of AI in education necessitates a reexamination of teacher and student responsibilities. Rather than replacing educators, AI should function as a tool that supports instructional decision-making while preserving the teacher's role in fostering critical thinking, ethical judgment, and meaningful learning experiences. This perspective supports ethical AI frameworks that prioritize human oversight, accountability, and the responsible integration of emerging technologies in educational settings.

Moreover, literatures consistently emphasizes that ethical use of AI is not merely about avoiding harm, but about actively promoting fairness, human dignity, privacy, transparency, and societal well-being (Al-Kfairy et al., 2024; Khan et al., 2022). Ethical AI frameworks serve as a critical mechanism to mitigate the risks identified in the previous section, including bias, inequity, misuse, and systemic harms (Federspiel et al., 2023; Uuk et al., 2024). Embedding ethical principles throughout the AI lifecycle from data collection to algorithm design, deployment, and governance ensures that AI technologies remain aligned with human values and societal priorities (Li et al., 2022; Pant et al., 2024).

AI-Driven Academic Integrity

The rapid adoption of generative artificial intelligence (AI) tools such as ChatGPT, Gemini, and other large language models has introduced both opportunities and challenges for academic integrity in educational settings. Academic integrity refers to the commitment to honesty, trust, fairness, respect, responsibility, and courage in academic practice and scholarly communities (Mejía & Garcés-Flórez, 2025). Within this context, generative AI technologies have reshaped academic work by supporting learning, research, and writing processes. However, their integration has also raised concerns related to plagiarism, unauthorized assistance, authorship ambiguity, and the authenticity of student outputs (Kasneci et al., 2023; Gruenhagen et al., 2024).

A growing body of literature indicates that generative AI presents a dual effect in higher education, functioning simultaneously as a learning enhancement tool and a potential source of academic misconduct. Systematic reviews highlight that while AI tools can improve productivity and support academic tasks, they also increase risks associated with reduced transparency in authorship and inappropriate use in assessments (Bittle & El-Gayar, 2025). In addition, empirical studies suggest that students' engagement with generative AI is often widespread but not always aligned with institutional academic integrity policies, creating challenges in distinguishing legitimate academic support from unethical academic practices (Gruenhagen et al., 2024). Consequently, the integration of AI in education necessitates institutional responses that include policy development, assessment redesign, and the strengthening of AI literacy among both educators and students (Kasneci et al., 2023; Tlili et al., 2023).

At the student level, recent empirical findings indicate that generative AI is commonly used for idea generation, summarization, language refinement, and assignment completion. Johnston et al. (2024) found that students generally perceive AI technologies as valuable academic support tools; however, they also express concerns regarding potential misconduct, dependency on AI-generated outputs, and uncertainty about acceptable usage boundaries. These findings underscore the need for clearer institutional guidelines to define appropriate and ethical AI-assisted learning practices.

Similarly, research examining educators' perspectives reveals both cautious acceptance and critical concern regarding AI-generated academic outputs. Gustilo et al. (2024) reported that faculty members recognize the pedagogical benefits of AI-assisted writing but remain concerned about issues of originality, authorship, and academic honesty. Educators emphasized the need for institutional policies and redesigned assessment strategies that can better account for AI use while maintaining academic rigor and integrity.

Beyond individual perceptions, evidence from diverse higher education contexts suggests that generative AI challenges traditional understandings of academic misconduct. Yusuf and Pervin (2024) found that although both students and educators acknowledge the educational potential of AI tools, concerns persist regarding plagiarism, reduced critical thinking, and inequities in academic advantage. These findings indicate that existing academic integrity frameworks may be insufficient in addressing AI-mediated academic practices, necessitating conceptual and policy-level re-examinations.

Another critical issue highlighted in the literature is the risk of overreliance on generative AI, which may negatively affect cognitive engagement and independent learning. Studies suggest that while students often view AI as a productivity-enhancing tool, excessive dependence may limit opportunities for problem-solving, critical thinking, and knowledge construction (Johnston et al., 2024; Yusuf et al., 2024). A broader review of AI in education further emphasizes the importance of AI literacy initiatives that encourage students to critically evaluate AI-generated outputs and engage responsibly with emerging technologies (Jackaria et al., 2024). The growing accessibility of AI tools has also prompted discussions regarding students' learning behaviors and classroom practices. Alvarado et al. (2026) emphasized that while AI-assisted learning can provide immediate support, personalized explanations, and enhanced access to information, excessive dependence on AI may reduce opportunities for independent problem-solving and mathematical reasoning. The authors highlighted the need for instructional approaches that encourage students to critically evaluate AI-generated outputs rather than passively accepting them. This perspective aligns with concerns regarding academic integrity and supports calls for the development of AI literacy programs that promote responsible and ethical use of generative AI technologies in educational settings.

In response to these challenges, institutions are increasingly exploring alternative assessment strategies that emphasize authentic learning and process-oriented evaluation. Because traditional plagiarism detection tools are not designed to identify AI-generated content, educators often face difficulties in distinguishing between legitimate assistance and academic dishonesty. As a result, approaches such as reflective writing, oral examinations, and performance-based assessments are being recommended to ensure that student work reflects genuine understanding and individual competence (Gustilo et al., 2024).

At the institutional level, recent systematic reviews emphasize the urgent need for comprehensive governance frameworks that define acceptable AI use in academic settings. These frameworks should include clear guidelines on disclosure, citation practices, and ethical responsibilities when engaging with generative AI tools (Bittle & El-Gayar, 2025; Bond et al., 2024). Scholars further argue that effective governance must be supported by institution-wide policies that balance innovation with integrity while providing clear boundaries for both students and educators (Bacalso et al., 2026; Chan, 2023). In addition, AI literacy programs are increasingly recognized as essential in equipping learners with the skills to critically evaluate AI outputs and engage in responsible academic practices (Bond et al., 2024; Chan, 2023).

Recent scholarship from the Philippine educational context further enriches the discourse on AI integration in education. Studies by Alvarado (2026) and Jackaria et al. (2026) highlight how AI technologies are reshaping both teaching and learning processes, particularly in teacher education and classroom instruction. Their findings suggest that while AI offers substantial opportunities for instructional support, professional development, and learner engagement, its effective implementation requires careful attention to ethical considerations, critical thinking development, and responsible use. These studies complement international literature by providing context-specific evidence that AI adoption in education must balance technological innovation with pedagogical integrity and human-centered learning.

Overall, the literature indicates that artificial intelligence has emerged as a significant transformative force in education, reshaping pedagogical practices, learning processes, and institutional operations. It facilitates personalized and adaptive learning, automates routine academic and administrative tasks, and strengthens data-driven decision-making that enhances instructional quality and organizational efficiency. Contemporary AI applications, including intelligent tutoring systems, generative chatbots, and adaptive learning platforms, further extend instructional support by enabling individualized feedback, promoting learner autonomy, and allowing educators to concentrate on higher-order pedagogical functions. However, despite these advantages, the literature consistently highlights critical concerns associated with AI integration, particularly issues of data privacy, algorithmic bias, diminished critical thinking, and reduced human interaction in learning environments. These challenges underscore the importance of ethical and responsible AI deployment anchored in principles of transparency, fairness, accountability, and human oversight.

METHODOLOGY

This section discusses the research design, research participants, research instruments, data collection, and statistical data analysis used in this study.

Research Design. This study employed a phenomenological research design to explore the lived experiences and perceptions of undergraduate students regarding artificial intelligence (AI) in higher education. The phenomenology is aligning for the inquiry of this study, as it seeks to understand how students perceived AI tools in academic contexts. This study position at the core the student voices, aiming to uncover how students interpret the presence of AI in their academic lives and how these technologies shape their sense of fairness, trust, and participation in learning.

Research Participants. The participants of this study composed of 10 undergraduate students of different programs in the College of Education in a state university in the southern Philippines. Diversity in the academic background, gender, and year level is intentionally considered to capture a range of experiences, disciplines, and demographic backgrounds. The inclusion criteria required participants to have used or encountered AI tools in their coursework (e.g., Grammarly, Quillbot, DeepSeek, CiCi, ChatGPT). Participation is entirely voluntary, with informed consent secured prior to data collection. All participant information is anonymized to uphold ethical research standards and ensure confidentiality.

Data Collection. The data were collected through one-on-one semi-structured interviews conducted in person. An interview guide is to investigate the student's perceptions in higher education towards Artificial Intelligence in terms of the students' insights, their usage of AI, and their ethical expectation. Each interview was audio-recorded with participants permission.

Data Analysis. This study employed a thematic analysis conforming to the analytical phases set by Braun and Clarke (2017) to identify recurring themes within the data collected. To carefully look into the details, the analysis was divided into three categories anchored on the research main themes: 1). Perceptions, 2). Usage and 3.) Ethical Expectation.

RESULT AND DISCUSSION

The results and discussion section is organized according to the statement of the problem, critically exploring how students perceive, used, and ethically evaluate the use of Artificial Intelligence (AI) in higher education. This section presents the students' collective voices drawn from the transcribed interviews, highlighting their insights on AI as a learning partner, their motivations and challenges in using it, and the balance they maintain between support and dependency. Furthermore, the discussion elaborates on the participants' ethical expectations regarding the responsible and institutionalized integration of AI in academic contexts. The themes that emerged from the data reflect both the opportunities and concerns that accompany AI in higher education, providing a deeper understanding of its pedagogical, social, and ethical implications for 21st-century learners.

Students' Usage and Perceptions of AI in Higher Education

The findings revealed that students viewed Artificial Intelligence (AI) not merely as a technological trend but as a valuable academic companion that supported their learning processes and enhanced their productivity. Their insights and lived experience of using AI emphasized that AI played a meaningful role in shaping how they study, complete academic tasks, and engage with information. The students' reflections highlighted three interconnected themes: AI as a learning companion for academic productivity, as a source of confidence and engagement in learning, and as a tool that creates tension between support and dependency.

Figure 1. Themes for the Students' Usage and Perceptions of Artificial Intelligence

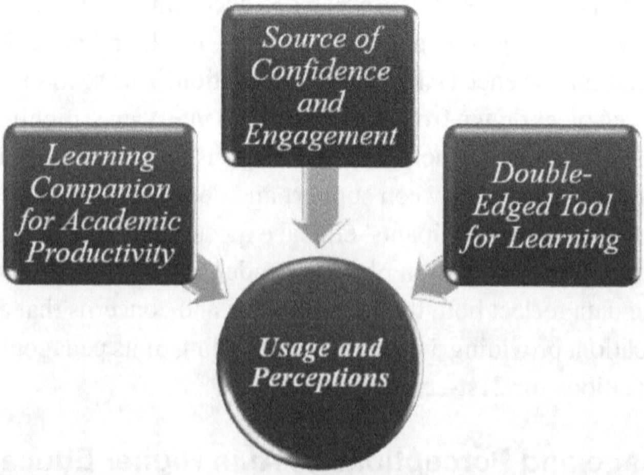

Theme 1. AI as a Learning Companion for Academic Productivity

The participants consistently perceived Artificial Intelligence (AI) as a valuable tool that supported their academic efficiency. It helped them generate ideas, improve writing, and clarify complex topics. Participant 1 described, *"AI is very helpful to the students because there are advantages and disadvantages... The advantage is that students have ideas in terms of academic writing."* Similarly, Participant 2 shared, *"I use AI to help me understand complex information."* Participant 3 added, *"AI is a big help, but using it should come with responsibility."* Other participants echoed similar experiences. Participant 4, a Statistics major, mentioned, *"I use AI for coding and manual interpretation...it makes my tasks easier."* Also, Participant 5 shared, *"It's easy to use and helpful in my studies."* Likewise, Participant 6 explained that AI helped her *"summarize long readings"* and *"organize notes,"* Same as Participant 10 said, *"AI helps summarize lessons and ideas quickly."* while Participant 7 noted that *"AI saves time because it helps produce content faster."* These reflections demonstrate that AI is perceived as a learning companion, a supportive, accessible, and time-saving tool that enhances productivity. However, students also emphasized that it must complement, not replace, human effort.

This insight aligns with the study Hartley et al. (2024) which revealed that ChatGPT serves as an effective learning aid that promotes independent learning, enhances problem-solving skills, and assists students in coding tasks by providing explanations and feedback that reduce cognitive load. Similarly, Kim et al. (2025)

found that students use generative AI tools to improve their academic writing through idea generation, organization of content, and refinement of drafts, leading to increased efficiency and confidence in completing academic tasks. Together, these studies suggest that AI functions not merely as a technological tool but as a collaborative learning partner that enhances students' productivity, supports self-directed learning, and complements human creativity and critical thinking in academic contexts.

Theme 2. AI as a Source of Confidence and Engagement in Learning

Participants also viewed AI as a motivator that built confidence and encouraged engagement in academic activities. Participant 3 expressed, *"I use AI academically, especially when I have quizzes or exams...it helps me review some things."* Similarly, Participants 2 shared that *"AI encourages me to learn new things since it can explain lessons in different ways."* Participant 8 explained that AI gave her *"confidence to express ideas more clearly,"* while Participant 9 said, *"When I use AI, I'm not afraid to make mistakes because I can always ask it again."* Participant 4 added that AI *"helps students who find it hard to communicate or study on their own."* These accounts show that AI fosters self-directed learning and academic confidence. It encourages exploration and reduces anxiety, especially in completing challenging tasks. For most participants, AI's accessibility and responsiveness transformed it into a safe space for inquiry and expression.

The insights same as Mohamed et al. (2025) which demonstrated that integrating AI tools in higher education enhances students' motivation, engagement, and self-directed learning by providing personalized feedback and interactive learning experiences. Their findings reveal that AI empowers students to take greater ownership of their learning, fostering curiosity and sustained academic interest. Similarly, Yavich et al. (2025) found a significant positive relationship between AI tool use and students' academic self-efficacy. The study showed that access to AI-assisted platforms increased learners' confidence in completing academic tasks, reduced anxiety, and encouraged active participation in learning activities. Collectively, these studies affirm that AI serves not only as an academic aid but also as a motivational partner that nurtures learners' confidence, autonomy, and enthusiasm for learning.

Theme 3. AI as a Double-Edged Tool for Learning

Although AI was praised for its benefits, participants also raised concerns about dependency. Participant 2 reflected, *"If we rely too much on AI, it can hinder our writing skills and critical thinking."* Participant 1 warned, *"Students' minds are controlled by AI when using it irresponsibly."* Similarly, Participant 3 admitted, *"If there's AI, some students become lazy...they just let it do their work."* Participant 7 stated, *"It helps, but sometimes it makes students too dependent."* Participant 6 noted *that "many students just copy outputs without understanding them,"* while Participant 5 added, *"Students expect too much from AI and don't trust their own ability to think."* These reflections reveal that while AI supports academic tasks, it also poses challenges to intellectual independence. The participants demonstrated awareness of this balance, viewing AI as both a tool for empowerment and a risk for dependency.

Students becoming overly dependent on Artificial Intelligence (AI) and how this reliance can weaken independent learning. Zhang et al. (2024) found that students with low academic self-efficacy and high academic stress are more likely to use AI problematically, depending on it to manage academic pressures. This behavior can negatively affect their critical thinking, creativity, and problem-solving abilities. In the same way, Revesai (2025) discovered that the excessive use of generative AI among university students in Zimbabwe led to an academic crisis where learners depended too much on AI-generated work, which reduced their performance and engagement in genuine learning. Together, these studies reveal that while AI can support academic success, irresponsible use may hinder intellectual growth and independent thinking.

Students' Ethical Expectations of Artificial Intelligence in Higher Education

The findings revealed that students regarded Artificial Intelligence (AI) not only as helpful academic tool but also as a technology that required ethical awareness, responsibility, and institutional guidance. Their perspectives underscored that while AI can enhance learning, its unregulated use may compromise integrity and fairness in education. The students' reflections and shared experiences highlighted three interconnected themes: awareness of ethical boundaries and academic integrity, the institutional role in promoting responsible AI practices, and the students' call for accountability and balanced utilization.

Figure 2. Themes for students' Ethical Expectations of Artificial Intelligence in Higher Education

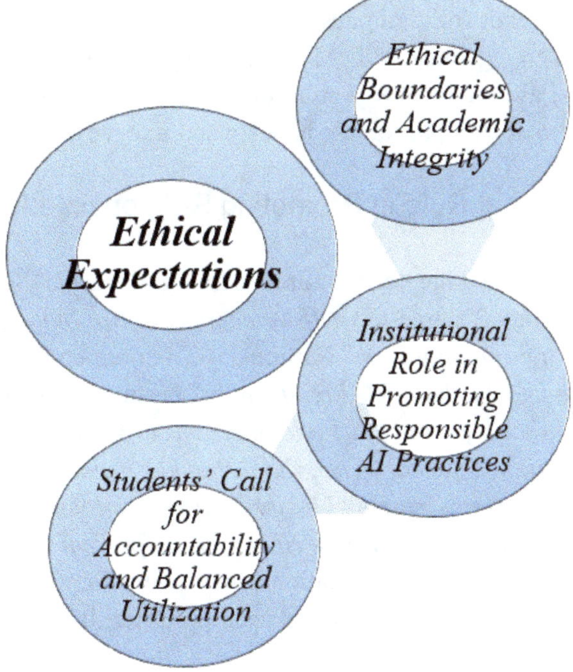

Theme 1. Awareness of Ethical Boundaries and Academic Integrity

All participants displayed awareness of ethical concerns related to AI use, including plagiarism, bias, and misinformation. Participant 1 admitted, *"It's very unethical because we didn't cite the source...plagiarism."* Participant 4 noted, *"Some students just copy and paste AI answers without verifying their reliability."* Similarly, Participant 6 emphasized, *"AI should only be used as a guide, not for copying."* Participant 8 added, *"If you use AI, you still need to understand what it gives you because sometimes it's wrong."* Participant 5 agreed, *"AI helps, but it doesn't mean you can claim its ideas as your own."* These reflections highlight that students understood academic honesty and the need to validate AI outputs. They recognized that AI's role is to support learning, not to replace personal effort.

Students' awareness of ethical boundaries and the importance of maintaining academic integrity when using Artificial Intelligence (AI) in educational contexts. Moya et al. (2023) conducted a scoping review that emphasizes the need for students to understand the ethical implications of AI use, particularly in relation to plagiarism, source attribution, and responsible application of AI-generated content. Similarly, Johnston et al. (2024) explored students' perspectives on generative AI and found that learners recognize the importance of using AI as a supportive tool rather than a substitute for their own work, emphasizing proper citation, verification of information, and critical engagement with AI outputs. Together, these studies reinforce the idea that ethical awareness is essential for ensuring that AI enhances learning while upholding principles of academic honesty and integrity.

Theme 2. Institutional Role in Promoting Responsible AI Practices

Participants emphasized the need for universities and teachers to guide responsible AI use. Participant 2 suggested, *"If we cannot control ourselves, the school should implement rules and policies."* Participant 3 recommended, *"Proper guidance and training on how to handle AI really help."* Participant 5 and Participant 4 both stated, *"There should be seminars and programs to teach students how to use AI properly."* Participant 6 added, *"The school should provide workshops for both teachers and students to understand AI better." Participant 9* echoed this, saying, *"AI can help in school, but there must be clear rules to prevent misuse."* These responses show that students believe educational institutions should foster AI literacy and ethical awareness. They want AI to be used purposefully, guided by training and accountability mechanisms.

This insight aligns with the study of Chan (2023) which emphasizes the need for universities to develop comprehensive AI policy frameworks that integrate ethical guidelines, training programs, and monitoring mechanisms to ensure AI supports teaching and learning effectively. Similarly, An et al. (2025) investigate how higher education institutions implement policies and guidelines for generative AI across teaching, research, and administrative functions, stressing the importance of clear rules, accountability, and capacity-building for both faculty and students. Over all, these studies reinforce the idea that institutions play a central role in fostering AI literacy, ethical awareness, and responsible practices to maximize the benefits of AI while mitigating risks.

Theme 3. Students' Call for Accountability and Balanced Utilization

Students expressed a shared call for ethical responsibility among all stakeholders. Participant 1 advised, *"Students should not depend on AI itself because some information there is not reliable."* Participant 3 emphasized that *"both teachers and students must be responsible and accountable in using AI academically."* Participant 2 added, *"There should be workshops to engage students in using AI the correct way."* Participant 7 noted *that "AI should not be banned but should be controlled through guidance,"* and Participant 8 concluded, *"We must balance our use of AI and our own effort."* These voices reveal that students advocate not for restriction but for ethical coexistence which is a partnership between human intelligence and artificial intelligence.

This insight aligns with the study of Johnston et al. (2024) which examined the students' perspectives on the use of generative artificial intelligence in higher education, highlighting the importance of responsible and transparent engagement with AI tools. Their findings revealed that students value AI as a learning support system but emphasize the need for personal accountability and critical evaluation of AI-generated content. Also, Al-Zahrani and Alasmari (2024) explored the ethical, social, and educational implications of AI in academic settings. They found that students and educators must work together to ensure that the use of AI remains balanced by promoting innovation while preserving integrity and human judgment. Both studies affirm that effective AI integration in education requires shared accountability and the cultivation of ethical awareness among all stakeholders.

CONCLUSION

This study explored students' perceptions, experiences, and reflections on the use of Artificial Intelligence (AI) in education. It examined how learners engage with AI tools as part of their academic journey and how these technologies influence their study habits, performance, and sense of responsibility. The findings revealed that students viewed AI as both a helpful guide and a powerful tool that enhances their learning experiences. They appreciated how AI could simplify complex ideas, assist in generating insights, and provide instant feedback. For them, AI served as a digital learning companion that supports their academic growth and makes studying more efficient and accessible.

The study also revealed the students' awareness of the ethical and institutional dimensions surrounding AI use. They recognized that while AI provides convenience, it must be guided by honesty, accountability, and proper regulation. The participants emphasized the role of schools and teachers in establishing clear guidelines, training, and seminars to promote responsible AI practices. They believed that universities should not prohibit AI use but instead teach students how to use it ethically and effectively. This sense of shared accountability between students, educators, and institutions highlights the importance of fostering AI literacy and moral awareness alongside technological advancement.

Altogether, this study reminds us that integrating AI into education is both an opportunity and a responsibility. It challenges educators and learners to maintain balance between innovation and integrity while embracing the potential of AI to transform learning. When used wisely, AI becomes a partner in developing critical thinking, creativity, and collaboration. However, when misused, it risks diminishing the authenticity of learning. For students, teachers, and institutions alike, the goal is not to replace human effort but to empower it, creating a learning environment that is both intelligent and human, where technology enhances education without compromising its values.

IMPLICATIONS

The findings of this study have important pedagogical, institutional, and ethical implications for the integration of artificial intelligence (AI) in higher education. First, the findings suggest that students perceive AI as a valuable learning companion that supports academic productivity, enhances confidence, and promotes engagement in learning. This implies that educators should recognize AI not merely as a technological tool but as a potential learning support system that can facilitate understanding, idea generation, and self-directed learning. Rather than prohibiting AI use, instructors may consider designing learning activities that encourage students to use AI critically and responsibly while maintaining opportunities for independent thinking, creativity, and problem-solving.

The findings also reveal students' concerns regarding overdependence on AI and its possible effects on critical thinking and intellectual independence. This highlights the need for pedagogical approaches that balance the benefits of AI-assisted learning with the development of higher-order thinking skills. Educators may need to redesign assessments and classroom activities that require students to analyze, evaluate, and reflect on AI-generated outputs rather than simply accepting them as accurate or complete. Such practices can help ensure that AI complements rather than replaces meaningful learning.

From an institutional perspective, the study underscores the important role of higher education institutions in promoting responsible AI use. Participants emphasized the need for clear policies, guidelines, training programs, and seminars that help students and faculty understand both the opportunities and limitations of AI technologies. Universities should therefore invest in AI literacy initiatives that equip stakeholders with the knowledge and skills needed to use AI effectively, ethically, and responsibly. Establishing institutional guidelines can also provide clarity regarding acceptable AI use in academic work, thereby reducing uncertainty and promoting academic integrity.

The findings further carry significant ethical implications. Students demonstrated awareness of issues related to plagiarism, misinformation, accountability, and responsible AI use. Their perspectives suggest that institutions should prioritize ethical AI education by emphasizing academic honesty, source verification, proper attribution, and critical evaluation of AI-generated content. In addition, concerns regarding fairness, transparency, and accountability indicate the need for universities to ensure that AI tools are implemented in ways that protect student privacy and uphold ethical standards. Students' call for balanced utilization highlights the importance of maintaining human judgment and responsibility in educational processes, ensuring that AI serves as a support mechanism rather than a substitute for human learning and decision-making.

Overall, the findings suggest that successful AI integration in higher education requires a collaborative effort among students, educators, and institutions. By fostering AI literacy, ethical awareness, and responsible use practices, higher education institutions can maximize the benefits of AI while safeguarding the values of academic integrity, critical thinking, and meaningful learning.

RECOMMENDATIONS

Based on the findings of this study, higher education institutions should develop comprehensive AI governance frameworks that provide clear guidelines on the acceptable and ethical use of artificial intelligence in academic settings. These frameworks should define the appropriate use of AI-generated content, establish standards for attribution and academic honesty, and outline procedures for addressing potential misuse. Clear institutional policies can help students and faculty navigate the opportunities and challenges associated with AI while maintaining academic integrity.

Universities should also invest in AI literacy programs, seminars, and workshops for both students and educators. The findings revealed that students value guidance and training in the responsible use of AI. Therefore, institutions should provide continuous professional development opportunities that equip faculty members with the knowledge and skills needed to integrate AI effectively into teaching, assessment, and research. Similarly, students should receive training on prompt design, source verification, critical evaluation of AI-generated outputs, and ethical AI practices.

Faculty members are encouraged to redesign assessments and learning activities that promote higher-order thinking skills and reduce overreliance on AI technologies. Assessment tasks that require reflection, analysis, problem-solving, and the application of knowledge can help ensure that students remain active participants in the learning process while using AI as a support tool rather than a substitute for their own thinking.

Higher education institutions should establish mechanisms that promote shared accountability among students, faculty, and administrators. Responsible AI use should be viewed as a collective responsibility that involves ethical awareness, transparency, and adherence to academic standards. Institutions may consider creating monitoring and support systems that encourage responsible AI practices while fostering a culture of integrity and trust. Finally, future researchers may expand this study by examining the perceptions and ethical expectations of students from different disciplines, institutions, and cultural contexts.

REFERENCES

Abbasi, B. N., Wu, Y., & Luo, Z. (2025). Exploring the impact of artificial intelligence on curriculum development in global higher education institutions. *Education and Information Technologies, 30*(1), 547–581. DOI: 10.1007/s10639-024-13113-z

Ahmed, Z., Shanto, S. S., & Jony, A. I. (2024). Potentiality of generative AI tools in higher education: Evaluating ChatGPT's viability as a teaching assistant for introductory programming courses. *STEM Education, 4*(3), 165–182. DOI: 10.3934/steme.2024011

Al-Kfairy, M., Mustafa, D., Kshetri, N., Insiew, M., & Alfandi, O. (2024, September). Ethical challenges and solutions of generative AI: An interdisciplinary perspective. In *Informatics* (Vol. 11, No. 3, p. 58). Multidisciplinary Digital Publishing Institute. https://doi.org/DOI: 10.3390/informatics11030058

Al-Zahrani, A. M., & Alasmari, T. M. (2024). Exploring the impact of artificial intelligence on higher education: The dynamics of ethical, social, and educational implications. *Humanities & Social Sciences Communications, 11*(1), 1–12. DOI: 10.1057/s41599-024-03432-4

Ali, I., Warraich, N. F., & Butt, K. (2025). Acceptance and use of artificial intelligence and AI-based applications in education: A meta-analysis and future direction. *Information Development, 41*(3), 859–874. DOI: 10.1177/02666669241257206

Almalki, M., Alkhamis, M. A., Khairallah, F. M., & Choukou, M. A. (2025). Perceived artificial intelligence readiness in medical and health sciences education: A survey study of students in Saudi Arabia. *BMC Medical Education, 25*(1), 439. DOI: 10.1186/s12909-025-06995-1 PMID: 40140763

Alvarado, H. A. L. (2026). Redefining Teaching in the Age of AI: A Reflective Autoethnography of Becoming a Mathematics Teacher. In *Redefining the Roles of Educators and Students in the AI Era* (pp. 77-98). IGI Global Scientific Publishing. https://doi.org/DOI: 10.4018/979-8-3373-8027-8.ch004

An, Y., Yu, J. H., & James, S. (2025). Investigating the higher education institutions' guidelines and policies regarding the use of generative AI in teaching, learning, research, and administration. *International Journal of Educational Technology in Higher Education, 22*(1), 10. DOI: 10.1186/s41239-025-00507-3

Bacalso, F. D., Villamor, F. E., Paclipan, C. P., Orquia, C. J. B., Rendon, I. P., Albiso, A. T., & Himang, C. M. (2026, May). Institutional approaches to generative AI management in higher education: a systematic review. In *Frontiers in Education* (Vol. 11, p. 1814426). Frontiers Media SA. https://doi.org/DOI: 10.3389/feduc.2026.1814426

Batool, A., Zowghi, D., & Bano, M. (2023). Responsible AI governance: a systematic literature review. *arXiv preprint arXiv:2401.10896*. https://doi.org//arXiv.2401.10896DOI: 10.48550

Bearman, M., Ryan, J., & Ajjawi, R. (2023). Discourses of artificial intelligence in higher education: A critical literature review. *Higher Education*, *86*(2), 369–385. DOI: 10.1007/s10734-022-00937-2

Behera, A., Trivedi, P., Patra, S. K., & Makeni, C. (2025). Artificial intelligence and higher education: A systematic review. *American Journal of STEM Education*, *11*, 27–52. DOI: 10.32674/0x43s107

Bittle, K., & El-Gayar, O. (2025). Generative AI and academic integrity in higher education: A systematic review and research agenda. *Information (Basel)*, *16*(4), 296. DOI: 10.3390/info16040296

Bo, N. S. W. (2025). OECD digital education outlook 2023: Towards an effective education ecosystem. *Hungarian Educational Research Journal*, *15*(2), 284–289. DOI: 10.1556/063.2024.00340

Bond, M., Khosravi, H., De Laat, M., Bergdahl, N., Negrea, V., Oxley, E., Pham, P., Chong, S. W., & Siemens, G. (2024). A meta systematic review of artificial intelligence in higher education: A call for increased ethics, collaboration, and rigour. *International Journal of Educational Technology in Higher Education*, *21*(1), 4. DOI: 10.1186/s41239-023-00436-z

Burger, B., Kanbach, D. K., Kraus, S., Breier, M., & Corvello, V. (2023). On the use of AI-based tools like ChatGPT to support management research. *European Journal of Innovation Management*, *26*(7), 233–241. DOI: 10.1108/EJIM-02-2023-0156

Chan, C. K. Y. (2023). A comprehensive AI policy education framework for university teaching and learning. *International Journal of Educational Technology in Higher Education*, *20*(1), 38. DOI: 10.1186/s41239-023-00408-3

Chen, L., Chen, P., & Lin, Z. (2020). Artificial intelligence in education: A review. *IEEE Access : Practical Innovations, Open Solutions*, *8*, 75264–75278. DOI: 10.1109/ACCESS.2020.2988510

Chen, X., Xie, H., & Hwang, G. J. (2020). A multi-perspective study on artificial intelligence in education: Grants, conferences, journals, software tools, institutions, and researchers. *Computers and Education: Artificial Intelligence*, *1*, 100005. DOI: 10.1016/j.caeai.2020.100005

Chubb, J., Cowling, P., & Reed, D. (2022). Speeding up to keep up: Exploring the use of AI in the research process. *AI & Society*, *37*(4), 1439–1457. DOI: 10.1007/s00146-021-01259-0 PMID: 34667374

Clarke, V., & Braun, V. (2017). Thematic analysis. *The Journal of Positive Psychology*, *12*(3), 297–298. DOI: 10.1080/17439760.2016.1262613

Crompton, H., & Burke, D. (2023). Artificial intelligence in higher education: The state of the field. *International Journal of Educational Technology in Higher Education*, *20*(1), 22. DOI: 10.1186/s41239-023-00392-8

Delello, J. A., Sung, W., Mokhtari, K., Hebert, J., Bronson, A., & De Giuseppe, T. (2025). AI in the classroom: Insights from educators on usage, challenges, and mental health. *Education Sciences*, *15*(2), 113. DOI: 10.3390/educsci15020113

Denny, P., Prather, J., Becker, B. A., Finnie-Ansley, J., Hellas, A., Leinonen, J., Luxton-Reilly, A., Reeves, B. N., Santos, E. A., & Sarsa, S. (2024). Computing education in the era of generative AI. *Communications of the ACM*, *67*(2), 56–67. DOI: 10.1145/3624720

Dogan, M. E., Goru Dogan, T., & Bozkurt, A. (2023). The use of artificial intelligence (AI) in online learning and distance education processes: A systematic review of empirical studies. *Applied Sciences (Basel, Switzerland)*, *13*(5), 3056. DOI: 10.3390/app13053056

Federspiel, F., Mitchell, R., Asokan, A., Umana, C., & McCoy, D. (2023). Threats by artificial intelligence to human health and human existence. *BMJ Global Health*, *8*(5), e010435. Advance online publication. DOI: 10.1136/bmjgh-2022-010435 PMID: 37160371

Fitria, T. N. (2021, December). Artificial intelligence (AI) in education: Using AI tools for teaching and learning process. In *Prosiding seminar nasional & call for paper STIE AAS* (pp. 134-147).

Garzón, J., Patiño, E., & Marulanda, C. (2025). Systematic review of artificial intelligence in education: Trends, Benefits, and challenges. *Multimodal Technologies and Interaction*, *9*(8), 84. DOI: 10.3390/mti9080084

Gruenhagen, J. H., Sinclair, P. M., Carroll, J. A., Baker, P. R., Wilson, A., & Demant, D. (2024). The rapid rise of generative AI and its implications for academic integrity: Students' perceptions and use of chatbots for assistance with assessments. *Computers and Education: Artificial Intelligence*, *7*, 100273. DOI: 10.1016/j.caeai.2024.100273

Guan, H., Dong, L., & Zhao, A. (2022). Ethical risk factors and mechanisms in artificial intelligence decision making. *Behavioral Sciences (Basel, Switzerland)*, *12*(9), 343. DOI: 10.3390/bs12090343 PMID: 36135147

Gustilo, L., Ong, E., & Lapinid, M. R. (2024). Algorithmically-driven writing and academic integrity: Exploring educators' practices, perceptions, and policies in AI era. *International Journal for Educational Integrity*, *20*(1), 3. DOI: 10.1007/s40979-024-00153-8

Harry, A. (2023). Role of AI in education. *Interdiciplinary Journal & Hummanity (INJURITY)*, *2*(3). https://radensa.ru/wp-content/uploads/2024/05/Role_of_AI_in_Education.pdf

Hartley, K., Hayak, M., & Ko, U. H. (2024). Artificial intelligence supporting independent student learning: An evaluative case study of ChatGPT and learning to code. *Education Sciences*, *14*(2), 120. DOI: 10.3390/educsci14020120

Hennekeuser, D., Vaziri, D. D., Golchinfar, D., Schreiber, D., & Stevens, G. (2024). Enlarged education–exploring the Use of Generative AI to support lecturing in Higher Education. *International Journal of Artificial Intelligence in Education*, •••, 1–33. DOI: 10.1007/s40593-024-00424-y

Holmes, W., & Tuomi, I. (2022). State of the art and practice in AI in education. *European Journal of Education*, *57*(4), 542–570. DOI: 10.1111/ejed.12533

Hwang, G. J., Xie, H., Wah, B. W., & Gašević, D. (2020). Vision, challenges, roles and research issues of Artificial Intelligence in Education. *Computers and Education: Artificial Intelligence*, *1*, 100001. DOI: 10.1016/j.caeai.2020.100001

Irish, A. L., Gazica, M. W., & Becerra, V. (2025). A qualitative descriptive analysis on generative artificial intelligence: Bridging the gap in pedagogy to prepare students for the workplace. *Discover Education*, *4*(1), 48. DOI: 10.1007/s44217-025-00435-4

Jackaria, P. M., Al-adzran, G. S., Alvarado, H. A. L., Jiripa, R. H. M., & Al-sabrie, Y. S. (2026). Students' Learning Math With the Aid of AI and the Need of Shifting Classroom Instructions. In *Generators, Bots, and Tutors: Creative Approaches to Human-AI Synergy in Classroom Instruction* (pp. 31-56). IGI Global Scientific Publishing. https://doi.org/DOI: 10.4018/979-8-3373-0847-0.ch002

Jackaria, P. M., Hajan, B. H., Mastul, A. H., & Sali, F. Z. (2024). Generation AI in a Reimagined Classroom: Challenges, Opportunities and Implications to Education. In Zaremohzzabieh, Z., Abdullah, R., & Ahrari, S. (Eds.), *Exploring Youth Studies in the Age of AI* (pp. 181–192). IGI Global Scientific Publishing., DOI: 10.4018/979-8-3693-3350-1.ch009

Jackaria, P. M., Pon, M. M. R., Eldani, N. A. S., Alvarado, H. A. L., & Iralan, S. A. (2026). Leveraging the Use of AI Tools in Practice Teaching: Insights from Science Pre-Service Teachers. In *Redefining the Roles of Educators and Students in the AI Era* (pp. 99-126). IGI Global Scientific Publishing. https://doi.org/DOI: 10.4018/979-8-3373-8027-8.ch005

Johnston, H., Wells, R. F., Shanks, E. M., Boey, T., & Parsons, B. N. (2024). Student perspectives on the use of generative artificial intelligence technologies in higher education. *International Journal for Educational Integrity*, *20*(1), 2. DOI: 10.1007/s40979-024-00149-4

Kasneci, E., Seßler, K., Küchemann, S., Bannert, M., Dementieva, D., Fischer, F., Gasser, U., Groh, G., Günnemann, S., Hüllermeier, E., Krusche, S., Kutyniok, G., Michaeli, T., Nerdel, C., Pfeffer, J., Poquet, O., Sailer, M., Schmidt, A., Seidel, T., & Kasneci, G. (2023). ChatGPT for good? On opportunities and challenges of large language models for education. *Learning and Individual Differences*, *103*, 102274. DOI: 10.1016/j.lindif.2023.102274

Khan, A. A., Badshah, S., Liang, P., Waseem, M., Khan, B., Ahmad, A., & Akbar, M. A. (2022, June). Ethics of AI: A systematic literature review of principles and challenges. In *Proceedings of the 26th international conference on evaluation and assessment in software engineering* (pp. 383-392). https://doi.org/DOI: 10.1145/3530019.3531329

Kim, J., Lee, S. S., Detrick, R., Wang, J., & Li, N. (2025). Students-Generative AI interaction patterns and its impact on academic writing. *Journal of Computing in Higher Education*, •••, 1–22. DOI: 10.1007/s12528-025-09444-6

Li, F., Ruijs, N., & Lu, Y. (2022). Ethics & AI: A systematic review on ethical concerns and related strategies for designing with AI in healthcare. *AI*, *4*(1), 28–53. DOI: 10.3390/ai4010003

Liang, J., Stephens, J. M., & Brown, G. T. (2025, April). A systematic review of the early impact of artificial intelligence on higher education curriculum, instruction, and assessment. In *Frontiers in Education* (Vol. 10, p. 1522841). Frontiers Media SA. https://doi.org/DOI: 10.3389/feduc.2025.1522841

Llerena-Izquierdo, J., & Ayala-Carabajo, R. (2025). Ethics of the Use of Artificial Intelligence in Academia and Research: The Most Relevant Approaches, Challenges and Topics. In *Informatics* (Vol. 12, No. 4, p. 111). MDPI. https://doi.org/DOI: 10.3390/informatics12040111

Martin, F., Zhuang, M., & Schaefer, D. (2024). Systematic review of research on artificial intelligence in K-12 education (2017–2022). *Computers and Education: Artificial Intelligence*, *6*, 100195. DOI: 10.1016/j.caeai.2023.100195

McDonald, N., Johri, A., Ali, A., & Collier, A. H. (2025). Generative artificial intelligence in higher education: Evidence from an analysis of institutional policies and guidelines. *Computers in Human Behavior: Artificial Humans*, *3*, 100121. DOI: 10.1016/j.chbah.2025.100121

Mejía, A., & Garcés-Flórez, M. F. (2025). What do we mean by academic integrity? *International Journal for Educational Integrity*, *21*(1), 1. DOI: 10.1007/s40979-024-00176-1

Mhlanga, D. (2023). Open AI in education, the responsible and ethical use of ChatGPT towards lifelong learning. In *FinTech and artificial intelligence for sustainable development: The role of smart technologies in achieving development goals* (pp. 387–409). Springer Nature Switzerland., DOI: 10.1007/978-3-031-37776-1_17

Michel-Villarreal, R., Vilalta-Perdomo, E., Salinas-Navarro, D. E., Thierry-Aguilera, R., & Gerardou, F. S. (2023). Challenges and opportunities of generative AI for higher education as explained by ChatGPT. *Education Sciences*, *13*(9), 856. DOI: 10.3390/educsci13090856

Mohamed, A. M., Shaaban, T. S., Bakry, S. H., Guillén-Gámez, F. D., & Strzelecki, A. (2025). Empowering the faculty of education students: Applying AI's potential for motivating and enhancing learning. *Innovative Higher Education*, *50*(2), 587–609. DOI: 10.1007/s10755-024-09747-z

Moya, B., Eaton, S. E., Pethrick, H., Hayden, K. A., Brennan, R., Wiens, J., & Lesage, J. (2023). Academic integrity and artificial intelligence in higher education contexts: A rapid scoping review protocol. *Canadian Perspectives on Academic Integrity, 5*(2), 59-75. https://doi.org/DOI: 10.11575/cpai.75990

Ngarambe, J., Yun, G. Y., & Santamouris, M. (2020). The use of artificial intelligence (AI) methods in the prediction of thermal comfort in buildings: Energy implications of AI-based thermal comfort controls. *Energy and Building*, *211*, 109807. DOI: 10.1016/j.enbuild.2020.109807

Pant, A., Hoda, R., Tantithamthavorn, C., & Turhan, B. (2024). Ethics in AI through the practitioner's view: A grounded theory literature review. *Empirical Software Engineering*, *29*(3), 67. DOI: 10.1007/s10664-024-10465-5

Portilla, J. E. N., Cedeño, J. K. Z., Jácome, G. O. L., & Gallegos, L. A. M. (2025). Systematic Review: Artificial Intelligence (AI) in Education 4.0. *The Journal of Educators Online*, *22*(3), n3. https://eric.ed.gov/?id=EJ1473947. DOI: 10.9743/JEO.2025.22.3.13

Revesai, Z. (2025). Generative AI dependency: The emerging academic crisis and its impact on student performance—a case study of a university in Zimbabwe. *Cogent Education*, *12*(1), 2549787. DOI: 10.1080/2331186X.2025.2549787

Salhab, W., Ameyed, D., Jaafar, F., & Mcheick, H. (2024). *A systematic literature review on ai safety: Identifying trends, challenges and future directions*. IEEE., DOI: 10.1109/ACCESS.2024.3440647

Stöhr, C., Ou, A. W., & Malmström, H. (2024). Perceptions and usage of AI chatbots among students in higher education across genders, academic levels and fields of study. *Computers and Education: Artificial Intelligence*, *7*, 100259. DOI: 10.1016/j.caeai.2024.100259

Takerngsaksiri, W., Warusavitarne, C., Yaacoub, C., Hou, M. H. K., & Tantithamthavorn, C. (2024, July). Students' perspectives on ai code completion: Benefits and challenges. In *2024 IEEE 48th Annual Computers, Software, and Applications Conference (COMPSAC)* (pp. 1606-1611). IEEE. https://doi.org/DOI: 10.1109/COMPSAC61105.2024.00252

Tlili, A., Shehata, B., Adarkwah, M. A., Bozkurt, A., Hickey, D. T., Huang, R., & Agyemang, B. (2023). What if the devil is my guardian angel: ChatGPT as a case study of using chatbots in education. Smart learning environments, 10(1), 15. https://doi.org/DOI: 10.1186/s40561-023-00237-x

Tsai, C. W., Lee, L., Lin, M. Y. C., Cheng, Y. P., Lin, C. H., & Tsai, M. C. (2025). Effects of integrating self-regulation scaffolding supported by chatbot and online collaborative reflection on students' learning in an artificial intelligence course. *Computers & Education*, *232*, 105305. DOI: 10.1016/j.compedu.2025.105305

US Department of Education. (2023). Artificial intelligence and the future of teaching and learning. *Washington, DC: Office of Educational Technology, U.S. Department of Education* https://files.eric.ed.gov/fulltext/ED631097.pdf

Uuk, R., Gutierrez, C. I., Guppy, D., Lauwaert, L., Kasirzadeh, A., Velasco, L., . . . Prunkl, C. (2024). A taxonomy of systemic risks from general-purpose AI. *arXiv preprint arXiv:2412.07780*. https://doi.org//arXiv.2412.07780DOI: 10.48550

Van Noordt, C., & Misuraca, G. (2022). Artificial intelligence for the public sector: Results of landscaping the use of AI in government across the European Union. *Government Information Quarterly, 39*(3), 101714. DOI: 10.1016/j.giq.2022.101714

Venkatesh, V. (2022). Adoption and use of AI tools: A research agenda grounded in UTAUT. *Annals of Operations Research, 308*(1), 641–652. DOI: 10.1007/s10479-020-03918-9

Vera, I. A. D., Briones, W. L., & Heredia, M. I. V. (2024). Ethical perspectives on the application of Artificial Intelligence in Higher Education. *Sinergias Educativas, 9*(1). Advance online publication. DOI: 10.37954/se.v9i1.438

Walter, Y. (2024). Embracing the future of Artificial Intelligence in the classroom: The relevance of AI literacy, prompt engineering, and critical thinking in modern education. *International Journal of Educational Technology in Higher Education, 21*(1), 15. DOI: 10.1186/s41239-024-00448-3

Wang, S., Wang, F., Zhu, Z., Wang, J., Tran, T., & Du, Z. (2024). Artificial intelligence in education: A systematic literature review. *Expert Systems with Applications, 252*, 124167. DOI: 10.1016/j.eswa.2024.124167

Yavich, R., Davidovitch, N., & Gerkerova, A. (2025). Exploring the Association between AI Tool Use and Academic Self-Efficacy among University Students in Israel. *African Educational Research Journal, 13*(3), 311–324. https://eric.ed.gov/?id=EJ1484697

Yusuf, A., Pervin, N., & Román-González, M. (2024). Generative AI and the future of higher education: A threat to academic integrity or reformation? Evidence from multicultural perspectives. *International Journal of Educational Technology in Higher Education, 21*(1), 21. DOI: 10.1186/s41239-024-00453-6

Zawacki-Richter, O., Marín, V. I., Bond, M., & Gouverneur, F. (2019). Systematic review of research on artificial intelligence applications in higher education–where are the educators? *International Journal of Educational Technology in Higher Education, 16*(1), 1–27. DOI: 10.1186/s41239-019-0171-0

Zhang, S., Zhao, X., Zhou, T., & Kim, J. H. (2024). Do you have AI dependency? The roles of academic self-efficacy, academic stress, and performance expectations on problematic AI usage behavior. *International Journal of Educational Technology in Higher Education, 21*(1), 34. DOI: 10.1186/s41239-024-00467-0

Zuiderwijk, A., Chen, Y. C., & Salem, F. (2021). Implications of the use of artificial intelligence in public governance: A systematic literature review and a research agenda. *Government Information Quarterly, 38*(3), 101577. DOI: 10.1016/j.giq.2021.101577

Chapter 12
Artificial Intelligence Microcredentials in Higher Education:
A New Paradigm for Quality, Personalization, and Inclusive Future-Oriented Learning

Ceren Ersoy
http://orcid.org/0000-0002-7168-744X
Gazi University, Turkey

ABSTRACT

Artificial intelligence micro-credentials are discussed as a lever for reshaping higher education towards more flexible, learner-centred and inclusive lifelong learning. The chapter first clarifies how micro-credentials are defined, designed and classified, with a particular focus on AI-focused and AI-supported offerings. It then considers how learning analytics, adaptive platforms and digital credential infrastructures can be used to strengthen quality assurance, personalisation, recognition and cross-border portability of modular learning. Equity, accessibility and ethical risks and opportunities for disadvantaged, non-traditional and disabled learners are examined throughout. Finally, a human-centred, multi-stakeholder model is outlined for linking AI micro-credentials to national qualification systems, institutional strategies and labour-market needs, so that they complement rather than replace traditional degrees while broadening meaningful opportunities for learning and work.

DOI: 10.4018/979-8-3373-5586-3.ch012

MAIN FOCUS OF THE CHAPTER

This chapter is structured around the fundamental assumption that education and skills policies must re-examine existing competency frameworks if education systems are to respond to rapidly changing skill requirements. In the face of changing social, technological and economic conditions, learning has become so dynamic that it can no longer be confined to long-term, singular competencies. In this context, micro-credentials, which are based on clearly defined learning outcomes and verifiable assessment processes, provide a framework for designing lifelong learning in a flexible and cumulative manner. However, the transformative potential of micro-credentials is contingent on the pedagogical and technological approaches used to design and manage these structures. In this chapter, AI-supported inclusive learning systems are addressed as a structural component in the personalisation, scaling, and quality assurance of micro-credentials. In addition, direct AI micro-credentials are positioned as a fundamental competency area for future education and employment ecosystems, not only in the context of imparting technical skills, but also in terms of ethics, responsible use, and critical literacy.

INTRODUCTION

The rapid increase in technology use following the emergence of the pandemic has led to significant momentum in the digital transformation of skill acquisition and development processes in education systems, through options such as distance learning and hybrid learning, etc. Furthermore, considering the changes in work practices across many employment sectors, it is evident that a new world order is emerging, in which learning, knowledge, and skill agility, collaboration, leadership, flexibility, and adaptability are of key importance. In the job market, the weight of complex cognitive tasks, that require a high level of social-emotional intelligence and cannot be reduced to routine, is increasing significantly. In this context, creative problem solving, innovation, collaboration, and teamwork have become fundamental expectations, while advanced skills and competencies are valued more highly than ever before. This situation puts higher education institutions under intense pressure to integrate more soft skills into their programs on the one hand, and to increase the depth and qualitative intensity of the programs they offer on the other (Murgatroyd, 2024). The need to meet learning needs at the highest level and the targeted skills approach arising from new employability needs are prompting stakeholders to collaborate on this common issue to establish global micro-credentials standards.

Aside from the potential benefits of micro-credentials, regional and global complexities also come into play. The conceptual confusion surrounding micro-credentials has become even more apparent with the numerous definitions and frameworks that have emerged in various regions and institutions worldwide in recent years. Different countries, regions, sectors, organizations, and higher education institutions are developing their own definitions of what micro-credentials are, proposing principles and standards that determine the core elements they should contain and how they should be designed and documented. However, it is not possible to say that all these initiatives are fully compatible with each other. What do we really mean by micro-credentials? There is still no single, globally agreed-upon definition of micro-credentials. This conceptual uncertainty makes it difficult for micro-credentials to be recognized and transferred across countries, regions, sectors, and institutions. Consequently, it also significantly limits the potential of micro-credentials to respond holistically and consistently to the global labor market needs and the global education ecosystem. In this context, it is necessary to clearly and consistently define not only what micro-credentials are, but also the areas of knowledge, skills, and competencies around which they are designed and the principles on which they are based. In the following sections, the main principles and concrete recommendations for designing micro-credential modules will be discussed, based on reference frameworks that can be used to structure digital competencies, particularly those focused on artificial intelligence.

Defining Microcredentials: Scope, Types, and Global Trends

Despite the numerous definitions used in different countries and institutions on micro-credentials in the literature, a "common language" is becoming increasingly visible. In a preliminary report prepared for UNESCO, Oliver (2022), using a Delphi-based process with a global panel of 50 experts, analyzed 15 different definitions found in policy documents and summarized the main characteristics of micro-credentials in the following dimensions: certification, relationship with other competencies, learning outcomes and assessment, standards and quality assurance, purpose, duration, ownership–portability–shareability, types of providers, security, and delivery format. Based on this analysis, the final definition proposed considers micro-credentials as a record of focused learning achievement that verifies what the learner knows, understands, or can do. The common points in definitions emphasize that it must include an assessment based on clearly defined standards, be issued by a reliable provider, have a meaningful and recognizable value in its own right, be able to be linked in a complementary manner with other micro and macro competencies, and be consistent with relevant quality assurance regulations (Loukkola & Cirlan, 2020; European Commission, 2020; ICDE, 2019; MicroHE, 2019; Oliver, 2022).

However, excluding critical and controversial dimensions such as duration, ownership, portability, shareability, and security from the definition indicates that conceptual consensus remains quite limited. The OECD's assessments also point to the relationship of micro-credentials with other short-term certified forms of learning in different education systems, the diversity in workload and certification processes, their position within national qualification frameworks and models, and their lack of a clear place in the ISCED classification as significant obstacles to global consensus and international portability (OECD, 2021). Nevertheless, when Oliver's work and the OECD's policy analyses are read together, it becomes apparent that a conceptual framework is emerging around the core of the micro-credential concept, with standard components such as focused learning outcomes, reliable assessment, quality assurance, and interoperability with other qualifications.

What are the regional and global benefits of micro-credentials? How can quality assurance and accreditation for micro-credentials be ensured? How should an effective and recognized micro-credential ecosystem be designed? What are the critical points to consider when using micro-credentials? It is observed that the answers to such questions also vary similarly (Steel, Louder & Drager, 2022). Should higher education prioritize the professional and economic needs of nations, or should it focus more independently on the individual as a whole and on personal development? In this context, it is essential to recognize that higher education aims to achieve objectives that extend beyond mere employability through micro-credentials. These credentials encompass a broader range of human, intellectual, and social objectives (Ralston, 2021; Wheelahan & Moodie, 2022). It is well known that short, outcome-focused courses have been an important part of adult, vocational, and professional education for decades (Brown et al., 2021). However, what are micro-credentials, and how do they differ? The answer to the question of why they have gained global momentum is quite important. At this point, the focus should be on how the risks and needs identified in traditional methods can be mitigated through micro-credentials. In this context, the fundamental goal of micro-credentials in higher education is not to reduce universities to merely "quick-response" technical actors in a market where numerous providers compete to meet employer demands; but to go beyond the discourse of employability and build structures that facilitate access to holistic qualities that are democratically and equitably open to all members of society, have meaningful value in both the labor market and social life, and serve as a bridge to lifelong learning. The purpose of education should be rethought in a way that broadens the vision of higher education, equipping individuals not only with the narrow technical requirements of specific jobs, but also with the knowledge, skills, and competencies that facilitate them to lead the lives they value. As illustrated in Figure 1, there are a number of micro-credentials that the institutions may use when designing the programmes.

Today's global narrative, centered on micro-credentials, is based on the assumption that these structures can address many long-standing problems of traditional education models, particularly from the perspectives of learners and employers. Indeed, traditional programs require long-term and high levels of commitment; are institution-centered and rigid, making them insufficiently flexible in responding to learner needs; have limited recognition of prior learning, slow progress in pedagogical innovation, inadequate support for students in terms of transparent and systematic career preparation, and often poor alignment with current and future labor market requirements. In contrast, micro-credentials offer flexible structures that can be adapted to the learner's time and pace with their shorter duration, modularity, and primarily online or hybrid formats, and are designed with "just-in-time" or "on-demand" reskilling opportunities. Furthermore, their openness to designs that enable the documentation and recognition of prior learning, their content that directly targets specific professional skills, knowledge, and competencies, and their support through digitized badging, identity verification, and achievement certification processes, make micro-credentials a learning format embedded in the digital ecosystem, rapidly adaptable, and more directly related to the labor market. Thus, there is a clear contrast between the heavy and cumbersome aspects of traditional education models and the agile, short-term, and needs-based structure of micro-credentials.

Figure 1. Micro-Credential Types

Furthermore, a significant aspect of the global interest in micro-credentials is related to the claim that they offer more equitable and accessible learning opportunities. To elaborate further, micro-credentials have the potential to broaden access to education, particularly for groups that have historically faced disadvantages in accessing traditional higher education (low-income individuals, adult learners, immigrants, caregivers, learners with special needs, gifted learners, etc.). The institutions that design micro-credentials have the capacity to enhance employability by offering more agile and personalized learning pathways, fostering a culture of lifelong learning that prioritizes inclusivity, and empowering individuals to reskill as needed. In summary, thanks to flexible entry and exit points, modular structures, and short-term learning designs, it creates a flexible and accessible alternative, often unattainable through traditional programs, especially for those who want to improve themselves while continuing their professional lives, as well as part-time students who are simultaneously working or taking on caregiving responsibilities.

WHY AI MICROCREDENTIALS FOR HIGHER EDUCATION?

The fundamental reason why AI-focused micro-credentials have become so important today is that they can be flexibly integrated into higher education systems in various ways, thereby supporting lifelong learning while also reshaping and strengthening employment and skills policies functionally. Governments and universities in OECD countries are making intensive efforts to develop micro-credential frameworks that are recognized both within higher education and in the labor market, with quality assurance in place. These efforts have the potential to make the micro-credential ecosystem, which appears fragmented and inconsistent, more coherent and consistent. However, it should not be forgotten that many of the issues currently debated around micro-credentials, particularly mutual recognition and equal opportunity, are actually structural problems that traditional diploma programs have also been grappling with for a long time. Therefore, policymakers and educators need to adopt a perspective shaped by long-term and sustainable goals that position micro-credentials in a way that is compatible and integrated with the overall architecture of higher education, rather than focusing on short-term structures.

Across Europe, strengthening student-centered teaching methods as a foundational strategy for enhancing the quality of education is emphasized, and the issue of positioning digital technologies as one of the primary tools enabling the pedagogical transformation is currently under discussion. The European University Association (EUA) also argues that digitalization is one of the most effective structures reshaping the field of higher education. Therefore, digital transformation and artificial intelligence are now considered a mandatory agenda item that determines the strategic orientation of universities, rather than an optional innovation. So, it is evident that universities are increasingly positioning themselves as innovative, student-centered, and digitally “pioneering” institutions. Institutional strategy documents define digital technologies and AI-based tools as a central element not only for transferring course content to an online environment but also for creating active and interactive learning environments, strengthening inter-campus collaboration, monitoring and evaluating student success, and raising the quality of education to the highest level (Elken et al., 2020). In this context, digitalization is viewed as a lever that accelerates the transition to student-centered pedagogies, aligning with national quality policies. Innovative assessment and evaluation applications developed in the age of artificial intelligence, digital exams, flexible and distance learning models, AI-supported learning analytics, and adaptive learning systems and also direct AI micro-credentials (AI literacy, ethics, data, and application-based competencies, model usage/adaptation etc.) are rapidly becoming key components of this transformation.

However, it is also emphasized that this ambitious vision cannot be consistently implemented with the same strength at the faculty, department, and program levels, and that a "strategy-implementation gap" exists between strategic discourse and classroom practices. In many institutions, digitalization is still limited to a "tool-oriented" approach, primarily focused on infrastructure provision (platforms, hardware, exam systems, etc.) and the digitalization of administrative processes. Using digital technologies to transform education, including artificial intelligence, into a genuine culture of quality in higher education, it is essential to provide systematic support for the digital and pedagogical competencies of teaching staff and academic leaders (Brown et al., 2023). Furthermore, creating institutional incentives (such as funds, awards, and professional development programs) for innovative teaching design is essential. These initiatives must be implemented through a multidimensional and dynamic process; they cannot be left solely to the enthusiastic efforts of individual actors. This perspective also highlights an important agenda for future research. It is necessary to examine in detail how national and institutional digitalization/artificial intelligence strategies are integrated into different layers of the organization (faculty, department, course level), as well as the costs, resistance, and learning processes that arise during this process.

Similarly, the interaction between digital and artificial intelligence-based solutions and different teaching strategies (active learning, flipped classroom, flexible/blended models, etc.) should be critically analyzed, along with the digital competency profiles of teaching staff and how these competencies are reflected in decision-making processes. However, with this multi-layered and critical perspective, digitalization and artificial intelligence can move beyond being a temporary "tool fad" in higher education and become a fundamental element of a lasting culture of quality and an inclusive learning ecosystem (Fossland & Tømte, 2020). In summary AI-focused restructuring has the potential to transform teaching processes and highlight the need for new types of learning units and flexible certification models. At this point micro-credentials emerge as a functional tool for producing, tracking, and certifying learning outcomes within digital and AI-supported learning ecosystems. It is now widely accepted that countries need learning systems that can quickly adapt to emerging new skill requirements and place greater emphasis on competencies rather than formal diplomas. Redesigning skills development, education, and lifelong learning policies to adopt flexible, competency-based, and rapidly updatable structures have started to gain prominence (Schwab & Zahidi, 2020; Valiente, 2014). Employers in the new era no longer view a formal university degree as a mandatory requirement for employment, but rather focus on the candidate's concrete skill portfolio and experience repertoire. However, it is essential to note that a diploma does not always align with the specific skill sets that employers are seeking. Even though diplomas typically represent more generalizable cognitive and academic competencies. Targeted structures, such as micro-credentials, are regarded as a more reliable indicator of specific skill sets.

Micro-credentials offer significant potential in responding to rapidly changing learner profiles and evolving labor market expectations (Cedefop, 2023). However, the increasing number of emerging new frameworks and standards leaves critical questions unanswered, such as how assessment, recognition, and quality assurance processes should be designed, and what level of detail and scalability is required. The solutions to be developed must be able to adapt to the dynamic and constantly evolving nature of micro-credentials; they must be scalable and cost-effective on the one hand, and proportionate, flexible, context-sensitive, and sustainable on the other. One of the most significant risks at this point is that micro-credentials may reproduce, or even deepen, existing inequalities in access to higher education. The social, technological, economic, environmental, and political trends highlighted in the EDUCAUSE Horizon Reports (Pelletier et al., 2022; Robert et al., 2025) demonstrate that digital transformation in higher education produces opportunities, as well as multi-layered risks. Political uncertainties and declining public funding are prompting universities to adopt more flexible and technology-intensive learning models. However, this shift poses new challenges related to quality assurance and equal access. The increasing use of learning analytics, big data, and artificial intelligence-based tools carries the risk of delegating pedagogical decisions to algorithmic systems. Data privacy, cybersecurity, and algorithmic biases are critical governance issues. In a professional context, the potential benefits of competency-based learning, micro-credentials, and hybrid teaching models in forging strong links with employment should not be overlooked. However, it is important to note that implementing these structures without adequate institutional support and ethical frameworks in place can increase the risk of fragmented learning and loss of quality.

While these challenges are significant, they do not preclude action, rather, they call for carefully designed interventions. Comprehensive information and guidance portals should be created, particularly for micro-credentials in the field of artificial intelligence, allowing learners to compare micro-credential options across different platforms, share their experiences, and access transparent information. Micro-credential providers should be encouraged to comply with a common standard and framework through targeted funding mechanisms and quality assurance processes. Inclusive and accessible micro-credential programs should be developed specifically for groups such as the NEET group (young people not in education, employment, or training), the long-term unemployed, young people who have dropped out of secondary education, and students at risk of dropping out of higher education. When such an approach is adopted, artificial intelligence micro-credentials will have the potential to become more than just "flexible short courses", they will become a strategic lever for quality, personalization, and inclusive future-oriented learning in higher education.

When integrated into higher education programs, micro-credentials emerge as a flexible model that both increases student engagement and graduation rates (McCartney & Rick, 2021; Sood et al., 2020) and offers individuals who have dropped out of education a second pathway to completion aligned with their prior learning such as The "Nexus" degrees developed by the University System of Georgia in the United States (University System of Georgia, 2021). Microcredentials can serve as a flexible bridge, designed both as "introductory" short courses and as credit-earning learning experiences to support the transition from upper secondary education to higher education. They enable students to explore their areas of interest with low risk, ease the transition process, and strengthen access to higher education, particularly for disadvantaged or gifted groups. Examples of this approach include converting undergraduate courses in a specific field into 3–6 ECTS "micro degrees" that count toward the undergraduate program upon successful completion, or designing dual enrollment models for gifted students in the US based on principles of inclusivity, thereby facilitating the transition to higher education for a broader student population at an earlier stage. (Colangelo, Assouline, & Gross, 2004; McCarthy, 1999; Mehl et al., 2020; Olszewski-Kubilius & Limburg-Weber, 2004; Olszewski-Kubilius, 2009).

Micro-credentials should be positioned as a flexible tool to support the return to employment of individuals who lost their jobs in the post-COVID-19 period by involving them in rapid reskilling and upskilling processes (Cedefop, 2024). They also serve as a strategic policy mechanism to reduce inequalities in education and labor markets, and expand access to higher education through programs designed for disadvantaged groups, such as NEET youth and the long-term unemployed. In some countries, the direct public funding of participation in free micro-credential programs, conditional on the provision of unemployment benefits or additional social transfers, has placed micro-credentials at the center of labor market revitalization policies (OECD, 2021a). It shows the importance of meeting the requirements of regulatory frameworks to ensure the recognition, comparability, and transparent documentation of micro-qualifications obtained through existing employer initiatives.

Microcredentials, which are currently predominantly chosen by individuals who have already completed higher education, are often held by socioeconomically advantaged individuals with strong support networks that have the potential to reproduce and even exacerbate inequalities in access to higher education and graduation rates. So the programs should be designed with the principles of inclusivity and fairness at their core, which can serve as a powerful policy tool that reduces access barriers for disadvantaged groups, offers alternative and flexible learning pathways, can be progressively integrated into a diploma, and thus increases participation in higher education (OECD, 2023). So it is so important to be positioned micro-credentials into policies not merely as "short courses" but as strategic intervention areas that strengthen equal opportunity, expand the right to learn, and transform the higher education system into a more inclusive structure (Van Damme, 2014). As exemplified by Kiron Open Higher Education, based in Germany, online micro-learning models that support refugees' transition to higher education, and the Multi-Campus Micro-Credentials (MC2) system initiative in Ireland, which includes a national framework, digital discovery platform, and strategic funding, provide strong examples of how micro-credentials can be positioned in line with both inclusivity and employability goals. At Kiron Open Higher Education, students can enroll in one of five different study tracks or take advantage of preparatory courses designed to develop foundational skills. Throughout this process, with various support services, the ultimate goal is for students to transition to an in-person program at one of Kiron's partner universities, where the credits they earned at Kiron will be recognized. Students can receive a maximum of 60 ECTS credits (equivalent to a full-time study year's workload) if they enroll in a Kiron partner university. The Irish MC2 initiative supports the delivery of over 500 modular courses across a wide range of subjects at 32 higher education institutions. It aims to create a new pathway to lifelong learning, enabling individuals to access reskilling and upskilling opportunities without severing their ties to the labor market. Concurrently, Ireland is implementing a strategic funding policy through the Human Capital Initiative, which supports various institutional micro-credential initiatives, primarily the MC2 initiative, to develop a national approach to micro-credentials. Furthermore, the impact analysis on micro-credentials indicates that short programs across Europe mostly cater to socio-economically advantaged groups who already hold higher education degrees. With their unique approach, the Nordic countries are among the few regions that utilize micro-credentials and short non-degree programs as a flexible pathway, where credits can be stacked and counted towards a degree, particularly for adults with relatively low access to higher education and "non-traditional" learners. (European Commission, 2021). At this point, it is critically important not only who micro-credentials reach, but also what common principles and standards they are designed according to. Therefore, good examples focused on inclusion need to be supported by scalable and interoperable standard frameworks.

To implement common micro-credential standards on a large scale in higher education systems, a core framework is needed that defines basic parameters, including workload, level, assessment, identity verification, and transcript. It is argued that other national/institutional regulations should be made compatible or interoperable with this framework (European MOOC Consortium, 2021). For the Common Microcredential Framework (CMF) to meet its requirements, micro-credentials offered by platforms included in this framework (FutureLearn, FUN, MiríadaX, EduOpen, and OpenupEd), as well as those from higher education institutions collaborating with them, must be designed according to a set of criteria. In this context, the CMF framework summarizes the requirements for micro-credentials as follows: having a specific and reasonable workload, being positioned at a level equivalent to the European Qualifications Framework (or national qualifications framework), being based on a reliable assessment process, identity verification in accordance with institutional standards, and documentation with a transcript that clearly shows learning outcomes, level, workload, and credit information. In this respect, the CMF serves as a reference framework offering simple yet scalable common standards that can be applied across a broad network of over 400 higher education institutions and businesses from different countries (OECD, 2021). The sustainability and systematization of these steps taken towards inclusiveness and quality in higher education largely depend on the creation of common and scalable standards for micro-credentials.

However, in most countries, there is currently no reliable and public information source that enables learners to systematically compare the basic characteristics of micro-credentials offered by higher education institutions and other providers. Developing public, reliable, and up-to-date information portals on micro-credentials is a critical infrastructure requirement that enables learners to compare options from different providers according to standard criteria, track the value and scope of their credentials, and manage all their diplomas, micro-credentials, and professional certificates within a single digital ecosystem throughout their lifelong learning process. At the same time, it is quite difficult to collect systematic and reliable data on the labor market outcomes of micro-credentials. This situation indicates the need for alternative indicators, such as verified learner feedback, when evaluating the value of programs (Iucu & Car i , 2025). For all these reasons, the micro-credential ecosystem must be supported not only by common standards but also by transparent information flow and data-driven monitoring mechanisms. Once such a comprehensive structure is established, micro-credentials will become a reliable system that includes institutionalized standards that both strengthen quality assurance in higher education and make concrete contributions to the goals of inclusivity and lifelong learning.

The Strategic Benefits of Micro-Credentials in Contemporary Education

Micro-credentials are not a replacement for existing education and employment policies aimed at supporting lifelong learning and employability, but flexible learning units that complement and strengthen these policies that play a complementary and reinforcing role to formal education and certified vocational training programs, while also functioning as independent qualifications that offer valid, recognizable, and valuable learning outcomes in their own right. While traditional diplomas remain the fundamental reference point for learning and employment, micro-credentials should be made sustainable as an effective way to support this structure, enabling individuals to continue their lifelong learning processes in a more flexible, modular, and needs-oriented manner (Brown et al., 2021; Brown & Nic-Giolla-Mhichil, 2022). To achieve this effectively, an ecosystem is needed where the meaning, scope, and recognition processes of micro-credentials are defined in a clear, consistent, and reliable manner. Making learning more effective and accessible will only be possible through multi-stakeholder collaboration involving higher education institutions, vocational training providers, employers, social partners, and policymakers. Researches highlight the key benefits of micro-credentials generally under the following headings:

1. *High alignment with the labor market:* By focusing on specific skills and competencies, they respond to concrete job needs, can react quickly to changing market conditions, and fill the gap between formal diplomas and the particular requirements of the sector.
2. *Supporting individual learning:* With their learner-centered, modular structure, they enable individuals to progress at their own pace, stack their learning over time to transform it into a competency, and facilitate the transition to formal education. Artificial intelligence can be used to design targeted and personalised learning experiences that take learners' readiness levels, prior experiences and career goals into account, and thereby introduce a degree of flexibility and adaptability that traditional programmes struggle to offer (Ersoy, 2025).
3. *Standalone value:* The ability to be recognized independently in the labor market as a meaningful part of a competency or as a complementary award that adds value to a formal competency.
4. *Making skills and competencies visible:* Contributing to the certification of knowledge, skills, and competencies acquired by individuals outside of formal

education, making them portable, visible in the digital environment, and representing more advanced levels of expertise. Responding to the need for upskilling/reskilling, it helps make the competencies of individuals who lack sufficient access to formal education visible, particularly through the recognition and certification of artificial intelligence skills acquired in informal and non-formal settings.

5. *Flexibility in educational design:* Offering structures that can be quickly implemented as needed at lower design costs and are compatible with the "learn on demand" approach.
6. *Time and cost advantages:* Being short-term, relatively low-cost, and producing accessible options for individuals who cover their own learning costs.
7. *Social justice:* Program designs for disadvantaged groups have the potential to reduce opportunity inequalities and broaden participation in lifelong learning, diversity in practices centered on inclusivity (EHEA, 2020; Gauthier, 2020; McGreal & Olcott, 2022)
8. *Supporting lifelong learning motivation and self-efficacy:* Their modular and short-term structures strengthen learners' sense of self-efficacy by providing visible and rapid feedback; they support learners' lifelong learning motivation through "small but meaningful successes."
9. *Career transitions and repositioning:* Particularly in the context of artificial intelligence and digital transformation, it enables employees to experiment with changing fields, trying new specializations, and gradually repositioning their careers with lower risk.
10. *Flexibility and innovation capacity of the program portfolio:* It enables higher education institutions to develop a multi-layered and modular program architecture rather than one focused solely on degrees, thereby increasing institutional innovation capacity and collaboration with external stakeholders.
11. *Deepening industry-university collaboration:* Particularly in the field of artificial intelligence, micro-credentials developed jointly with businesses serve as an interface that accelerates knowledge transfer and strengthens joint R&D and human resource development strategies.
12. *Contributing to data-driven policy development:* Thanks to their digital and traceable structures, they generate rich data on what types of skills are in demand in which areas and who benefits from these learning opportunities, paving the way for the design of data-driven skills policies.
13. *Interdisciplinary competencies and human–AI collaboration:* Micro-credentials designed for professionals in different fields bring together solid domain expertise with a practical level of AI understanding. In doing so, they help prepare learners for emerging roles in which people and AI systems work side by side and complement one another rather than compete.

14. *AI literacy and ethical awareness:* AI-focused micro-credentials do more than teach technical skills. They also provide small but crucial learning units on topics such as data ethics, algorithmic bias, privacy, transparency and human-centred design. Taken together, these elements support the growth of a more reflective, responsible and critically informed AI ecosystem (Ersoy, 2025).

Consequently, supporting ambitious national and institutional goals for digitalization and artificial intelligence with concrete, measurable, and recognizable learning outcomes at the local level makes micro-credentials a critical tool for higher education. From the perspective of teaching staff and education leaders, micro-credential programs focused on artificial intelligence and digital pedagogies offer structured learning paths that, on the one hand, question narrow "tool-based" approaches and focus on pedagogical design and digital competency development, while also enabling the institutional recognition and dissemination of innovative practices that have thus far been left mainly to the shoulders of "volunteers and enthusiastic individuals." From the students' perspective, micro-credentials focused on artificial intelligence, in particular, can strengthen both inclusivity and the concrete exercise of the right to learn by enabling learners with different socio-economic and academic profiles to acquire personalized, flexible, and professionally meaningful competencies through short, modular, and certifiable learning experiences, can strengthen both inclusivity and the concrete exercise of the right to learn. Consequently, digital and artificial intelligence micro-credentials should be positioned as a strategic mechanism that supports a culture of quality in higher education, partially bridges the "loosely coupled" structure between national strategies and daily practices at the department/course level, and enables both academic staff and students to participate in digital transformation as active subjects rather than observers.

CORE DESIGN PRINCIPLES FOR MICRO-CREDENTIALS

Micro-credentials should be designed within a consistent framework as a focused, assessment-based learning unit. In order to ensure quality and coherence, it is essential to adhere to common principles and standards, rather than allowing micro-credentials to be random and fragmented. In this context, skill sets and competency units within vocational education, as well as modularized components of higher education courses that include assessment and assessment-based industry/business certifications, can be considered micro-credentials. Conversely, courses based solely on participation without assessment, or activities that result in a "badge," as well as macro-qualifications (bachelor's, master's, diploma, etc.) already defined as degree/certificate programs within the national framework, should not be considered within the scope of micro-qualifications. The dividing line is the measurement and certification of learning and its ability to be linked to other qualifications when necessary. It is important that a minimum common knowledge set is provided for each micro-qualification at the design stage. Title, provider institution(s), brief description of content and learning outcomes; language of instruction, delivery format (face-to-face/online/hybrid; synchronous/asynchronous), duration and schedule; technical/program requirements for participation; fees and possible financial support; the type of assessment to be applied, the form of certification, and the nature of the credit or professional/academic recognition provided should be clearly stated. In addition, a brief explanation of quality assurance processes (relevant regulatory bodies, internal academic processes, etc.) and, if applicable, relationships with industry/professional organizations will enhance the credibility of micro-credentials (Pawilen, Tomida & Eugenio, 2024).

It is crucial that three key points are provided as standard. Learning outcomes should be defined clearly and measurably. In addition, it is necessary to have at least one valid assessment process that directly evaluates these outcomes. Finally, it is crucial to transparently express the volume of learning and position it at a level shorter than a full diploma program. Additionally, it should be clearly stated in which programs the micro-certificate is accepted as credit, which professional standards it complies with, or how it can be added to a larger certificate in a "stackable" manner. Micro-certificates should be designed not only as short courses but as quality-assured, transparent, and portable learning units. Within this framework, the fundamental principles for the design and delivery of micro-credentials can be summarized as follows (European Commission, 2021; MicroHE, 2019; UNESCO, 2018):

1. ***Quality:*** Micro-credentials should be integrated into national and institutional quality assurance systems, based on clear quality criteria that include instructional design, content, teaching staff competencies, and assessment processes.
2. ***Transparency:*** The objectives, learning outcomes, level, workload (e.g., ECTS credits), assessment method, and provider of each micro-credential should be clearly defined in a way that is easily accessible and understandable to learners and employers. Micro-credentials that are embedded in National Qualifications Frameworks (NQFs) are expected to make cross-border recognition easier, for example by using systems such as ECTS, and to encourage higher education institutions to treat them as part of a broader portfolio of qualifications that sit alongside traditional degrees. Yet for these certificates to be properly regulated and trusted and to function both as an accessible form of accreditation for learners and a reliable verification tool for employers and institutions, they need to be supported by a strong, interoperable digital infrastructure (Sanchez Barrioluengo, 2025).

3. ***Relevance:*** Micro-credentials should respond both to learners' needs and to the priorities of the labour market and society. They are expected to offer up-to-date, field-specific and context-sensitive content that reflects these evolving demands.
4. ***Valid assessment:*** The knowledge, skills, and competencies acquired within the scope of micro-credentials should be assessed and documented using reliable, valid, and evidence-based measurement tools; the assessment process should also be subject to quality assurance.
5. ***Learning pathways:*** Micro-credentials are designed in a modular way to support flexible learning pathways. Thanks to this modular structure, micro-credentials obtained from different providers can be combined over time to form a larger credential or part of a degree program. Which micro-credentials will be stacked or linked together is determined by the relevant institution (e.g., higher education institution, employer) within the framework of its own recognition and program design principles, considering the learner's goals. Furthermore, micro-credentials can be obtained not only by completing a specific course but also through the assessment of non-formal and informal learning outcomes (Kušić, Vrcelj, and Zovko, 2022). When an individual's knowledge, skills and competences gained through work experience, professional practice, project work or independent learning are assessed against clearly defined learning outcomes, they can be documented in the form of micro-credentials. In this way, learning that takes place outside formal education systems becomes officially visible and can be recognised (Cedefop, 2023).
6. ***Recognition:*** The integration of micro-credentials into national qualifications frameworks and inter-institutional recognition arrangements depends on clearly defining recognition routes in two directions: horizontally, between different institutions, and vertically, in terms of progression into higher-level programmes. The recognition of micro-credentials enables the outputs of small-scale learning units to be clearly "signaled," paving the way for such experiences to become a comparable and widespread learning option across the EU. Policy discussions increasingly converge on a simple idea: when micro-credentials are awarded by formal education providers, they should not sit outside existing recognition systems. Instead, they ought to be taken into account for academic progression and employment in much the same way as foreign qualifications or study periods completed abroad (Sanchez Barrioluengo, 2025). In this context, the difficulties in recognizing micro-credentials are no different from those encountered in general recognition processes; learning outcomes defined with consistent and common terminology emerge as a critical element facilitating this assessment.
7. ***Portability:*** Micro-credentials should be portable across different institutions, countries, and sectors, and should be transferable through certificates and dig-

ital badges supported by digital and reliable identity verification mechanisms (Lockley, Derryberry, & West, 2016). Micro-credentials are documents that are primarily and fundamentally owned by the learner; that is, the individual who earns the credential is the "owner," rather than the institution that awards it. Therefore, it is essential that micro-credentials can be stored in secure digital wallets (e.g., Europass) and easily shared at the learner's discretion. Under the General Data Protection Regulation (GDPR), learners get full control over which of their data are shared and with whom. For this model to function effectively, the underlying infrastructure needs to rely on open standards and common data models. This ensures interoperability between different institutions and countries, enables seamless data exchange, and allows for quick identity/authenticity checks. The Europass learning model and digital credentials infrastructure provide a common framework that supports the accumulation of micro-credentials across different institutions and periods "stackable" to form larger credentials, facilitating the processes of storage, sharing, and recognition. As a result, designing micro-credentials in digital format is no longer optional; it is a key condition that greatly facilitates their portability and recognition across learners, providers and employers.

8. ***Learner-centeredness:*** A design approach that is flexible in terms of time, pace, place, and format; facilitates the participation of learners of different ages, life cycles, and responsibilities; and focuses on individual needs and goals should be adopted (LeBlanc, 2021). Similarly, quality assurance processes for micro-credentials should also be designed with a learner-centered approach. Considering that learners with "non-traditional" profiles and individuals pursuing independent/individual micro-credentials may find it relatively more challenging to participate in these processes, flexible and accessible feedback mechanisms should be established to capture their views and experiences. Periodically collecting feedback from alumni and incorporating this data into the quality assurance plan for continuous improvement of micro-credentials will contribute to the institutionalization of the learner-centered design principle.
9. ***Authenticity:*** Micro-credentials should be structured around real-life problems, professional tasks, and authentic learning situations whenever possible, and should encourage the production of applied, project-based, and evidence-based products, particularly in the context of artificial intelligence. For micro-credentials to be reliably recognized, they must be clearly traceable and verifiable when, where, and by whom each credential was issued, and under what conditions it was awarded. Such metadata forms the basis of trust in both an individual micro-credential and the micro-credential system as a whole. Discussions about micro-credentials are at the heart of global debates on quality assurance and accreditation. While qualification and diploma systems are relatively well-established in traditional

education, micro-credentials occupy a much more uncertain and fragmented space. This situation raises critical questions such as: "How can learners be sure that the micro-credentials they obtain will be recognized by employers (at the regional, national, and international levels)?" and "Can these micro-credentials accumulate and become a meaningful learning pathway for future education?", "How can employers and institutions be confident that a given micro-credential genuinely carries a reliable credit value that reflects its level and workload?" Against this backdrop, the development of clear, verifiable and interoperable frameworks that safeguard the reliability and comparability of micro-credentials has emerged as one of the central policy and research priorities in this field. To meet this need, the European Commission launched the Europass Digital Credentials Infrastructure in 2020. This infrastructure provides institutions across the EU with free tools to issue diplomas, certificates, and micro-credentials at all levels in a forgery-resistant, automatically verifiable digital format. Europass digital credentials are legally recognised as authentic across the EU because they are signed with an e-Seal and treated as equivalent to paper documents containing the same information. This allows micro-credentials to be stored, shared and verified securely and almost instantly, and positions Europass as a key piece of infrastructure for enhancing transparency and trust within the wider credential ecosystem.

10. ***Digital Ecosystem and Technology Infrastructure for the Implementation of Micro-Credentials:*** The implementation of micro-credentials is a multi-layered process that requires not only pedagogical design or a policy framework, but also a robust and integrated digital ecosystem. The backbone of this ecosystem consists of a learning management system (LMS), a program/curriculum management system (CMS), digital badge and identity verification technologies, and an e-commerce and registration/accounting infrastructure that works in conjunction with these. When choosing such systems, institutions should follow global standards (for example Open Badges compatibility, secure and verifiable authentication, and quality assurance principles) not only as technical specifications, but as a minimum framework to ensure portability, interoperability and trustworthy certification. In this context, an LMS manages course content, interaction, assessment, and identity verification processes as the primary delivery platform for micro-credentials. Integration with a CMS enables courses and modules to be designed within a stackable program architecture, allowing for sustainable approval processes. Digital badging infrastructures should do more than generate a visual icon. They need to securely store rich metadata about the recipient, the issuing organisation, the criteria used to award the badge, its period of validity and the context in which the competencies were demonstrated. In this way, they provide a verifiable record of identity and

achievement that can, when required, be audited by third parties. Supporting these systems with blockchain or similar technologies, where possible, is also important for protecting ownership and data integrity. Finally, to increase the visibility of micro-credentials and ensure their implementation with a sustainable business model, an e-commerce/marketplace solution integrated with LMS and credentialing infrastructure is a critical component that incorporates registration, payment, marketing, and reporting processes into corporate operations. Throughout this technological ecosystem, data analytics, personal data protection, and cybersecurity issues must be defined from the outset with clear principles and internal policy documents; processes related to the collection, storage, and deletion of user data must be transparent and auditable. The main goal for organizations should be to position micro-credentialing technologies as part of a long-term, integrated transformation that is compatible with existing digital infrastructure and workflows, rather than treating them as a "temporary project" (Steel, Louder & Drager, 2022). Furthermore, the technology ecosystem supporting the development of micro-credentials emerges as a multi-layered structure fueled not only by internal LMS–CMS–badging infrastructures but also by digital learning platforms positioned at the global and national levels. From this perspective, the examples highlighted in policy documents can be broadly grouped as follows (OECD, 2021):

a. *MOOCs and global learning platforms:* Large-scale platforms such as Coursera, edX, FutureLearn and Udacity provide the digital infrastructure through which micro-credentials designed by universities and private companies can reach global audiences. The "specialization", "nanodegree", "professional certificate" and "MasterTrack" formats on these platforms illustrate how micro-credential–degree integration can work in practice, combining stand-alone certification with, in some cases, the recognition of micro-credential learning for credit in postgraduate programmes.
b. *State-supported national digital learning ecosystems:* Publicly supported initiatives such as France Université Numérique (FUN) in France, EduOpen in Italy and the national digital platform Campus IL in Israel make MOOC and micro-credential offerings available nationwide under a shared inter-university catalogue and set of standards. They offer flexible models in which short courses can be assembled into "pathways" and counted as credit towards certificates and degree programmes. At the same time, these platforms function as critical digital infrastructures: they strengthen open educational resources (OER) and OpenCourseWare initiatives and have helped to accelerate the digital transformation of higher education, particularly in times of crisis such as the COVID-19.

c. *Private sector "own-brand" learning and certification ecosystems:* Google's Career Certificates program, AWS's re/Start initiative, and platforms such as LinkedIn Learning offer micro-credential-like professional certifications in fields directly related to the labor market (cloud computing, data analytics, project management, UX design, etc.); subscription-based models provide learners with access to numerous short courses. These ecosystems help position micro-credentials within a digitally integrated technology environment that is closely tied to the labour market. Earned digital badges and certificates can be added to LinkedIn profiles, matched with employer talent pools and, in some countries, linked to public-sector hiring processes (for example, the use of Google Career Certificates as diploma equivalents in recruitment). Major technology companies such as Amazon, Microsoft, Amazon Web Services and IBM are also developing their own micro-credential programmes, often in collaboration with higher education institutions or other authorised providers. In this way, they create certified learning pathways that can be completed in a relatively short time and are directly aligned with sector-specific skill needs.

When these examples are considered together that micro-credentials should not be seen as isolated, stand-alone courses. They acquire their real significance within a multi-stakeholder, digitally mediated architecture shaped by platforms, open-source communities, government-backed national initiatives and the branded learning ecosystems of private companies.

11. ***Stakeholder Participation and Resource Management:*** The systematic involvement of various stakeholders (students, faculty, employers, professional associations, policymakers, etc.) in decision-making processes related to the design and delivery of new micro-credentials enhances the scope and depth of course content, ensuring that social needs are identified more accurately. The consensus that emerges from such processes can make micro-credentials more functional and sensitive to context, by bringing together the institutional strengths of higher education with feedback from a wide range of stakeholders. Across the EU, Member States have begun to use different strategies to place micro-credentials on their national agendas, for example by developing normative frameworks, drawing on EU funds and creating financial instruments that build on existing national financing systems. Start-up funds are important for getting micro-credential programmes off the ground, but periodic or project-based resources alone are not enough. To ensure their long-term viability, financial support for these programmes needs to be progressively anchored in core institutional budgets and mainstream education funding. This transition necessitates

establishing an inclusive financing architecture that ensures adequate enrollment levels through the identification of specific items allocated to micro-credentials within higher education budgets, the support of programs aligned with labor market needs through joint (co-financed) models with the business world, and the utilization of lifelong learning funds/learner subsidies.

12. ***Information and guidance:*** Strong information, counseling, and guidance services must be provided so that learners can meaningfully compare micro-competency options, plan their own learning paths, and understand how they can apply these competencies in an educational or employment context. Career guidance is a core support mechanism that helps individuals navigate their life-long careers and make more informed decisions about education, training and employment. Well-designed guidance practices involve systematic assessment of a person's interests, strengths and skills, providing a structured basis for exploring options and planning future pathways. In this process, guidance provided by employers, local and national employment offices, university career centers, Public Employment Services (PES), and other guidance services focused on education, employment, career development, and coaching offers an inclusive and widely accessible structure, making lifelong learning a force aligned with European values. Integrating information and guidance on micro-credentials into lifelong career guidance services can help learners make much better use of personalised learning pathways. It supports them in taking more informed, evidence-based and forward-looking decisions about their educational choices and career development over time. Thus, micro-credentials will become not just a certification tool, but an organic component of holistic career planning.

Micro-credentials have the potential to respond to both changing educational requirements and evolving labor market needs by offering flexible, targeted, and accessible learning opportunities. The fact that micro-credentials appeal to a broader audience, such as working professionals, lifelong learners, and "non-traditional" students, allows universities to diversify their student base, increase their social impact through teaching activities, and develop unique programs based on their areas of expertise. The online delivery of designed programs is quite widespread, with digital learning platforms becoming one of the leading distribution channels for these programs; the COVID-19 pandemic has accelerated this trend and paved the way for private companies whose main activity is not education to strengthen their online ecosystems, which have become their own brands (OECD, 2021b). However, learners who obtain micro-credentials from universities are generally groups with higher education levels and skill sets, stronger employer support, and greater financial resources. However, research shows that when not only universities' academic expertise but also other stakeholders, such as employers and professional organizations, are involved in decision-making processes regarding the design and diversification of new courses, the content range of micro-credentials becomes richer. A multi-stakeholder design approach allows employers to use micro-credentials as concrete instruments for bridging the gap between academic learning and workplace demands. When a range of actors take part in the design and recognition of micro-credentials, they are better able to shape them around real workplace needs. This, in turn, helps to narrow skills gaps and brings labour market expectations and higher education provision into closer alignment (Car i et al., 2022). In this context, it is evident that the micro-competency-focused ecosystem is not limited to internal program design; scalable online learning initiatives in the fields of digital skills and artificial intelligence also drive.

The spread of digital technologies is reshaping how work is organised and how labour markets are structured. While employment is shrinking in routine, easily automated roles, demand is growing for new types of jobs and more complex skill profiles. Recent research also makes it clear that technological change cannot be reduced to a simple “job-killing” narrative; its effects on employment are more differentiated and depend strongly on sector, occupation, and skill level. At the same time, it brings about labor-friendly innovations and new fields of endeavor, but it can also increase skill mismatches and labor turnover. For this reason, the European Commission defines digital skills as “the ability to use technology and digital tools effectively, critically, efficiently, and responsibly to perform tasks and solve problems” and has set ambitious targets for 2030, including ensuring that at least 80% of the population will have basic digital skills and reaching 20 million IT professionals.

Developed within this framework, DigComp 3.0, which is the fifth version of the framework, presents a structure consisting of five competence areas—information and data literacy, communication and collaboration, digital content creation, security, and problem solving—and 21 specific competences grouped under these areas, to define citizens' digital competencies and create a common language. The latest version of DigComp includes new content components that focus on artificial intelligence competence, cybersecurity competence, misinformation and disinformation, well-being in digital environments, and individuals' rights, choices, and responsibilities. DigComp 3.0 includes, for the first time, a learning outcomes approach. This is a well-established policy and practical tool that helps to ensure that the framework is easily and consistently interpreted and applied (Cosgrove & Cachia, 2025). The skill set required for digital transformation is not limited to the technical/digital dimension; cognitive, social, and managerial “non-digital” competencies, such as creative problem solving, analytical thinking, communication, teamwork, negotiation, leadership, project, and time management, remain important as complementary elements to advanced digital skills. The findings demonstrate that the adoption of artificial intelligence and other advanced digital technologies, in conjunction with offering continuous training opportunities for low-skilled workers, is conducive to the efficient and inclusive utilisation of digital technologies. Therefore, it appears critical that AI-focused micro-credentials designed for higher education serve not only to develop narrow technical skills but also to foster the holistic development of horizontal skills alongside DigComp-based digital competencies. In summary, DigComp 3.0 extends beyond being a normative framework that defines digital competencies; it also provides a functional roadmap for designing micro-competencies in the context of artificial intelligence.

FUTURE RESEARCH DIRECTIONS

Future research on AI-enabled micro-credentials in higher education should first generate robust empirical evidence about their actual impact on learning, employability, quality and equity. A key area for future research is to understand the practical impact of AI-focused micro-credentials on learners. To pursue this agenda, longitudinal and mixed-methods research is needed that tracks learners over time and compares those who follow AI-focused micro-credential routes with those who remain in purely traditional courses and degree programmes. Such studies should explore how stackable credentials shape educational and career paths in practice, and whether they genuinely open new opportunities for further study or employment. It is also important to look more closely at personalisation: to what extent recommendation engines and adaptive systems truly support diverse learners, and when they risk reproducing or amplifying existing inequalities. An additional priority is to ensure effective assessment and quality assurance. Researchers must explore how AI-supported analytics, automated scoring, and learning traces can be combined with expert human judgement in a valid way to produce credible, portable evidence of competence. They must also explore how that evidence is read and used by employers and professional bodies across different sectors.

A second group of questions focuses on governance, interoperability, and ethics. Future work should investigate how AI micro-credentials can be mapped into national and regional qualifications frameworks, credit systems and recognition procedures without compromising the flexibility that is supposed to be their key advantage. Making progress on these questions will require looking beyond single cases. On the one hand, there is a need for comparative policy work that examines how different countries and types of institutions approach micro-credentials. On the other hand, more design-centred research is needed on how to build interoperable credential systems in practice, including the underlying architectures, shared metadata conventions and digital wallets through which learners can manage their own credentials.

At the same time, issues of data protection, algorithmic transparency, and learner agency need to be examined in detail, with particular attention to non-traditional, marginalised, and disabled students. AI micro-credential ecosystems will only be successful if they are built with, rather than for, their users. AI micro-credential systems are unlikely to succeed if they are designed only from the top down. They need to be shaped together with the people who will actually use and govern them. Approaches that bring students, academic staff, quality assurance agencies and employers around the same table as co-design partners, rather than treating them as passive stakeholders to be consulted at the end, are crucial for building arrangements that are technically robust, socially trusted and genuinely worthwhile in educational terms.

CONCLUSION

Research on micro-credentials shows that despite the rapid proliferation of different initiatives, micro-credentials remain a "cloudy" concept for many students, academics, employers, and policymakers, and that the main barriers to their wider adoption are cultural and structural rather than technological. Nevertheless, there are notable expectations across all four stakeholder groups. Learners are looking for flexible, up-to-date learning opportunities, while higher education institutions are mainly concerned with having recognition processes that are efficient and reliable. Employers tend to favour more open, skill-focused designs, whereas policymakers place greater emphasis on transparency and trust, and expect new initiatives to be consistent with existing frameworks such as ECTS and EQF. This emerging "common language" provides a strong starting point for rethinking micro-credentials in an AI-supported higher education ecosystem.

In this ecosystem, AI-focused micro-credentials can be seen as compact, stackable and quality-assured records of learning that sit alongside data-driven, AI-supported learning processes. Existing studies suggest that a small set of conditions makes a real difference to the value of micro-credentials. Learning outcomes need to be expressed clearly enough for others to see what has been achieved; assessment has to be rigorous rather than symbolic; the issuing organisations must be trusted; learners' identities need to be checked in a secure way; and the information attached to each credential should be easy to read and compare, so that other institutions and employers can actually recognise and use it. Learning analytics, recommendation systems, natural language processing, and blockchain-based credentialing platforms such as Credentify offer concrete tools to implement these requirements in a scalable manner: These technologies have the potential to significantly contribute to micro-credential design in higher education by helping to track learning experiences spread across multiple providers, generate detailed evidence of competencies, and automate certain parts of recognition and credit transfer processes while preserving the value of human judgment.

On the other hand, it is also clear that microcredentials are not merely a technical tool, but also a kind of social contract established between students, universities, employers, and policymakers. Students find microcredentials valuable not only as digital badges, but when they are truly meaningful in terms of learning pathways and employability. Employers view microcredentials positively when they make profiles more transparent and "less complex"; however, they take a more cautious approach when they become an opaque layer that increases the burden of documentation. If AI-supported micro-credentials are to be genuinely useful, the surrounding ecosystem needs to give learners real agency, build content and purposes in close collaboration with industry, and be regulated in ways that protect privacy, curb algorithmic bias and prevent new certificates from reinforcing existing inequalities in whose learning is recognised.

In this chapter, under the title "Artificial Intelligence Microcredentials in Higher Education: A New Paradigm for Quality, Personalization, and Inclusive Future-Oriented Learning," it is argued that AI-enhanced microcredentials can address the fundamental challenges posed by MicroHE in at least four ways. As a starting point, those involved can look after quality in very concrete ways. For example, each credential can be required to carry a short, readable description of what the learner has achieved and how this was assessed. Assessment criteria can be set out in plain language and linked to agreed standards, and institutions can build in regular points at which learning outcomes are reviewed to see whether they are still being achieved in practice. Second, they can foster personalisation by drawing on learner data to recommend modular pathways that fit individual goals and prior learning, and by integrating AI support into the design, delivery and continuous adaptation of AI-focused micro-credentials. Third, they can strengthen inclusivity by recognizing learning that occurs in formal, non-formal, and informal contexts and offering flexible, small-scale learning opportunities that better fit the lives of non-traditional, working, and disadvantaged learners. Finally, they can prepare higher education for the future by enabling universities to move from one-time degrees to lifelong, stackable learning architectures that are responsive to rapidly changing skill requirements.

However, it should not be forgotten that the digital transformation targeted in higher education will be neither smooth nor linear. Policy frameworks, institutional regulations, and quality cultures are still largely shaped around "macro-competence"; many universities lack a consistent strategy for modularization and recognition; stakeholders have differing views on the extent to which decisions regarding learning and certification should be automated. For artificial intelligence micro-qualifications to move beyond a parallel and fragmented structure and become a truly transformative paradigm, national and European qualification frameworks must be updated, institutional recognition procedures must be redesigned, investments must be made in staff capacity for microlearning design and assessment, and students and employers must be involved in the process of jointly designing meaningful qualifications. AI-related micro-credentials bring higher education both an opportunity and a responsibility. They can open new routes into learning and recognition, but only if institutions pay close attention to how they are designed, governed and used in practice. If they are approached in this way, micro-credentials can help institutions deal with trade-offs that are otherwise hard to manage. In other words, it is possible to open more flexible and personalised routes into learning while keeping standards clear and comparable, and to innovate in credentials without jeopardising the trust on which recognition ultimately depends. Micro-credentials can make it possible to offer flexible routes without lowering standards, to personalise learning while still allowing fair comparison between learners, and to move quickly on innovation without losing reliable and trusted forms of recognition. However, their success will depend on whether universities and policymakers can move beyond the pilot project stage and establish learner-centered, collaborative, and ethically sound ecosystems. If micro-credentials can be made readable, recognisable and genuinely valuable across borders and sectors, AI-focused micro-credentials can move from the margins to the mainstream, helping to shape a more open, inclusive and forward-looking higher education system where every meaningful act of learning can be recognised, built on and used throughout life.

REFERENCES

Brown, M, McGreal, R and Peters, M. (2023). A Strategic Institutional Response to Micro-Credentials: Key Questions for Educational Leaders. *Journal of Interactive Media in Education*, 2023(1): 7, pp. 1–17. DOI: DOI: 10.5334/jime.801

Brown, M., Mhichil, M. N. G., Beirne, E., & Mac Lochlainn, C. (2021). The Global Micro-Credential Landscape: Charting a New Credential Ecology for Lifelong Learning. *Journal of Learning for Development*, *8*(2), 228–254. DOI: 10.56059/jl4d.v8i2.525

Brown, M., & Nic-Giolla-Mhichil, M. (2022). Unboxing micro-credentials: an inside, upside and downside view (Descifrando las microcredenciales: en qué consisten, ventajas e inconvenientes). *C&E, Cultura y Educación*, *34*(4), 938–973. DOI: 10.1080/11356405.2022.2102293

Car i , A., Leoste, J., Iucu, R., Kikkas, K., Tammemäe, K., & Männik, K. (2022). Conceptualizing micro-credentials in the higher education research landscape. A literature review. In *Conference on Smart Learning Ecosystems and Regional Development* (pp. 191-203). Singapore: Springer Nature Singapore.

Cedefop (2023). *Microcredentials for labor market education and training: microcredentials and evolving qualifications systems*. Luxembourg: Publications Office. Cedefop research paper, No 89. https://data.europa.eu/doi/10.2801/566352

Cedefop, (2024). *Microcredentials: striving to combine credibility and agility*. Publications Office of the European Union. https://data.europa.eu/doi/10.2801/966682

Colangelo, N., Assouline, S. G., & Gross, M. U. M. (Eds.). (2004). *A nation deceived. How schools hold back America's brightest students* (Vol. 2). University of Iowa.

Cosgrove, J., & Cachia, R. (2025). *DigComp 3.0: European Digital Competence Framework* (5th ed.). Publications Office of the European Union., https://publications.jrc.ec.europa.eu/repository/handle/JRC144121

EHEA (2020), *Rome Ministerial Communiqué,* European Higher Education Area (EHEA).

Elken, M., Maassen, P., Nerland, M., Prøitz, T. S., Stensaker, B., & Vabø, A. (2020). *Quality work in higher education*. Springer International Publishing. DOI: 10.1007/978-3-030-41757-4

Ersoy, C. (2025). Inclusive Transformation with Artificial Intelligence: Ethical Aspects, Policies, and Strategic Approaches for Equitable Education. *Pitfalls of AI Integration in Education: Skill Obsolescence, Misuse, and Bias: Skill Obsolescence, Misuse, and Bias*, 271-292

European Commission. (2020). *A European approach to micro-credentials – Output of the microcredentials higher education consultation group – Final report.* European Commission.

European Commission. (2021). *Commission Staff working document: Accompanying the proposal for a Council Recommendation on a European approach to micro-credentials for lifelong learning and employability (SWD(2021) 367),* Brussels. https://eur-lex.europa.eu/legalcontent/EN/TXT/?uri=CELEX:52021SC0367 (accessed on October 22, 2025).

Fossland, T., & Tømte, C. E. (2020). Technology as quality work? educational leaders and teachers' use of digital technology. In *Quality work in higher education: organizational and pedagogical dimensions* (pp. 57–77). Springer International Publishing. DOI: 10.1007/978-3-030-41757-4_4

Gauthier, T. (2020). The value of microcredentials: The employer's perspective. *The Journal of Competency-Based Education, 5*(2), 1–6. DOI: 10.1002/cbe2.1209

ICDE. (2019). *The Present and Future of Alternative Digital Credentials (ADCs),* International Council for Open and Distance Education (ICDE), Oslo.

Iucu, O., & Car i , A. (2025). Competency Profiles in Administrative Sciences. An Analysis of the Students' Perceptions and Possible Curricular Reshapes Through Micro-Credentials. *Transylvanian Review of Administrative Sciences, 21*(74), 5–29. DOI: 10.24193/tras.74E.1

Kušić, S., Vrcelj, S., & Zovko, A. (2022). Micro-credentials–Improvement or Fragmentation in Higher Education? *Journal in Education and New Developments, 2,* 152–156. DOI: 10.36315/2022v2end033

LeBlanc, P. (2021). *Students first: Equity, access, and opportunity in higher education.* Harvard Education Press.

Lockley, A., Derryberry, A., & West, D. (2016). Drivers, affordances and challenges of digital badges. In Ifenthaler, D., Bellin-Mularski, N., & Mah, D.-K. (Eds.), *Foundation of digital badges and micro-credentials. Demonstrating and Recognizing Knowledge and Competencies* (pp. 55–70). Springer., DOI: 10.1007/978-3-319-15425-1_4

Loukkola, T., & Cirlan, E. (2020). *Micro-credentials: What is behind all the buzz?* European University Association. https://www.eua.eu/our-work/expert-voices/micro-credentials-what-is-behind-all-the-buzz.html (accessed on December 9, 2025).

McCarthy, C. R. (1999). Dual-Enrollment Programs: Legislation Helps High School Students Enroll in College Courses. *Journal of Secondary Gifted Education, 11*(1), 24–32. DOI: 10.4219/jsge-1999-610

McCartney, M. L., & Rick, H. A. (2021). The adult student/consumer model: Micro-credentials as a solution for adult learners. In *Ensuring Adult and Non-Traditional Learners' Success With Technology, Design, and Structure* (pp. 244-261). IGI Global Scientific Publishing.

McGreal, R., & Olcott, D.Jr. (2022). A strategic reset: Micro-credentials for higher education leaders. *Smart Learning Environments*, *9*(1), 9. DOI: 10.1186/s40561-022-00190-1

Mehl, G.. (2020). *The Dual Enrollment Playbook: A Guide to Equitable Acceleration for Students*. Aspen Institute College Excellence Program.

Micro, H. E. (2019). Challenges and Opportunities of Micro-Credentials in Europe. Briefing Paper on the Award, Recognition, Portability and Accreditation of Micro-Credentials: an Investigation through Interviews with Key Stakeholders & Decision Makers. MicroHE Consortium. https://microcredentials.eu/wp-content/uploads/sites/20/2021/05/D3.1-Interviews-with-Key-Stakeholders-Decision-Makers-Overall-Summary-Report.pdf. (accessed on October 16, 2025).

Murgatroyd, S. (2024). *The future of higher education in an age of artificial intelligence*. Ethics International Press.

OECD. (2021a). *"Quality and value of micro-credentials in higher education: Preparing for the future", OECD Education Policy Perspectives, No. 40*. OECD Publishing., DOI: 10.1787/9c4ad26d-

OECD. (2021b). *"Micro-credential innovations in higher education: Who, What and Why?", OECD Education Policy Perspectives, No. 39*. OECD Publishing., DOI: 10.1787/f14ef041-

OECD. (2023). *"Micro-credentials for lifelong learning and employability: Uses and possibilities", OECD Education Policy Perspectives, No. 66*. OECD Publishing., DOI: 10.1787/9c4b7b68-

Oliver, B. (2022). *Towards a common definition of micro-credentials*. UNESCO Publishing., https://unesdoc.unesco.org/ark:/48223/pf0000381668

Olszewski-Kubilius, P. (2009). Special schools and other options for gifted STEM students. *Roeper Review, 32*(1), 61–70. DOI: 10.1080/02783190903386892

Olszewski-Kubilius, P., & Limburg-Weber, L. (2004). *Designs for excellence: A guide to educational programs for academically talented secondary students and their parents.* Northwestern University, Center for Talent Development.

Pawilen, G. T., Tomida, E., & Eugenio, D. O. (2024). Quality assurance framework for micro-credentials in Japan and in the Philippines: Micro-credentials in Japan and in the Philippines. *International Journal of Curriculum and Instruction, 16*(2), 401–421.

Pelletier, K., McCormack, M., Reeves, J., Robert, J., Arbino, N., Al-Freih, M., Dickson-Deane, C., Guevara, C., Koster, L., Sanchez-Mendiola, M., Skallerup Bessette, L., & Stine, J. (2022). *2022 EDUCAUSE Horizon Report Teaching and Learning Edition.* Boulder, CO: EDUC22. https://www.learntechlib.org/p/221033/ . (accessed on January 2, 2026).

Ralston, S. J. (2021). Higher Education's Microcredentialing Craze: A Postdigital-Deweyan Critique. *Postdigit Sci Educ, 3*(1), 83–101. DOI: 10.1007/s42438-020-00121-8 PMID: 40476912

Robert, J., Muscanell, N., McCormack, M., Pelletier, K., Arnold, K., Arbino, N., Young, K., & Reeves, J. (2025). *2025 EDUCAUSE Horizon Report: Teaching and Learning Edition.* Boulder, CO.

Sanchez Barrioluengo, M. (2025). *Micro-credentials in higher education,* Biagi, F. and Di Pietro, G. (editors), Publications Office of the European Union, Luxembourg, https://data.europa.eu/doi/10.2760/0157920, JRC142086.

Schwab, K., & Zahidi, S. (2020). The future of jobs report 2020. World Economic Forum, October 2020. https://www3.weforum.org/docs/WEF_Future_of_Jobs_2020 .pdf (accessed on October 21, 2025).

Sood, I.. (2020). *Future Impacts of Modularization and Micro-Credentials on European Higher Education and list of validated scenarios.* MicroHE Consortium.

Steel, C., Louder, J., & Drager, Y. (2022). A Global Perspective on the Potential and the Complexities of Micro-credentials. *Anthology White Paper, 3.*

UNESCO. (2018). Digital credentialing: Implications for the recognition of learning across borders. UNESCO Education Sector. https://unesdoc.unesco.org/ark:/48223/pf0000264428

University System of Georgia. (2025). Nexus Degree, https://www.usg.edu/academic_programs/nexus_degree (accessed on October 20, 2025).

Valiente, O. (2014). The OECD skills strategy and the education agenda for development. *International Journal of Educational Development*, *39*, 40–48. DOI: 10.1016/j.ijedudev.2014.08.008

Van Damme, D. (2014). Does lifelong learning perpetuate inequalities in educational opportunities? OECD., https://oecdedutoday.com/does-lifelong-learning-perpetuate-inequalities-in-educational-opportunities/, Retrieved October 20, 2025, from.

Wheelahan, L., & Moodie, G. (2022). Gig qualifications for the gig economy: Micro-credentials and the 'hungry mile'. *Higher Education*, *83*(6), 1279–1295. DOI: 10.1007/s10734-021-00742-3 PMID: 34366441

World Economic Forum. (2020). *The future of jobs report 2020*. World Economic Forum. https://www.weforum.org/publications/the-future-of-jobs-report-2020/ (accessed on October 18, 2025).

ADDITIONAL READING

Cedefop. (2025). *Preparing for 2040: Four AI-powered scenarios for the future of continuing skills development.* Cedefop research paper. Publications Office of the European Union. https://www.cedefop.europa.eu/en/publications/5614

Cosgrove, J., & Cachia, R. (2025). *DigComp 3.0: European Digital Competence Framework* (5th ed.). Publications Office of the European Union., https://publications.jrc.ec.europa.eu/repository/handle/JRC144121

EADTU. (2025). Personalisation of Education. Enhancing Equity, Learner Agency and Academic Success. *Zenodo*. https://doi.org/DOI: 10.5281/zenodo.17279059

Garcia, M. B., Rosak-Szyrocka, J., & Bozkurt, A. (Eds.). (2025). *Pitfalls of AI Integration in Education: Skill Obsolescence, Misuse, and Bias*. IGI Global. DOI: 10.4018/979-8-3373-0122-8

Hsu, Y. P. (2021). Technological Innovation and Massive Open Online Courses (MOOCs) in Taiwan Higher Education. In Hou, A. Y. C., Chiang, Tl., & Chan, S. J. (Eds.), *Higher Education in Taiwan. Higher Education in Asia: Quality, Excellence and Governance*. Springer., DOI: 10.1007/978-981-15-4554-2_10

Ifenthaler, D., Bellin-Mularski, N., & Mah, D. K. (2016). *Foundation of digital badges and micro-credentials: Demonstrating and Recognizing Knowledge and Competencies*. Springer International Publishing. DOI: 10.1007/978-3-319-15425-1

Lantero, L., Ferranti, L., Finocchietti, C., Gitto, E., Petrucci, E., Sanasi, F., & Spitalieri, S. (2023). *Artificial intelligence and recognition of qualifications: Opportunities and risks from an ENIC-NARIC perspective* (DOC CIMEA 141). CIMEA. https://www.cimea.it

Malik, M. H., Rosunally, Y., & Younis, N. (Eds.). (2026). *Digital frontiers of AI in transnational education*. IGI Global., DOI: 10.4018/979-8-3373-5403-3

OECD. (2024). *Reimagining Education, Realising Potential, International Summit on the Teaching Profession*. OECD Publishing., DOI: 10.1787/b44e2c39-

Orr, D., Pupinis, M., & Kirdulytė, G. (2020). *'Towards a European approach to micro-credentials: a study of practices and commonalities in offering micro-credentials in European higher education', NESET Report*. Publications Office of the European Union., DOI: 10.2766/7338

UNESCO. (2023). *Global Education Monitoring Report 2023: Technology in education–A tool on whose terms?* UNESCO., DOI: 10.54676/UZQV8501

KEY TERMS AND DEFINITIONS

Inclusive Future-Oriented Learning: Within the scope of the section, it is approached as a learning approach that combines the transformative potential of artificial intelligence and other digital technologies with the principles of *equality, access, and participation*; aiming to equip learners not only with their current competencies but also with the knowledge, skills, and attitudes that will meet the uncertain professional and social requirements of the future. This approach aims to support the effective participation of all learners from different backgrounds in a sustainable, equitable, and human-centered digital future by integrating AI-focused micro-competencies designed in higher education with horizontal skills such as DigComp-based digital competencies, creative problem solving, critical and ethical thinking, collaboration, adaptability, and lifelong learning.

Micro-credential: A micro-credential is a record of focused learning achievement that verifies what the learner knows, understands, or can do; based on clearly defined standards, provided by a reliable provider, possessing a meaningful and recognizable value on its own, while being complementary to other micro and macro competencies, and expected to be consistent with relevant quality assurance regulations.

Quality in Higher Education: It refers to the execution of learning-teaching processes, research activities, and social contribution efforts in line with a university's mission and vision, stakeholder expectations, and social requirements, based on the principles of *effectiveness, consistency, fairness, participation, and continuous improvement*, and the monitoring and development of these processes based on reliable evidence. In this context, quality is not only about program outcomes meeting predetermined standards, but also about students having meaningful and transformative learning experiences, graduates being able to adapt to changing workforce and societal needs, and the institution maintaining an accountable, transparent, and inclusive governance approach throughout all these processes.

The Common Micro-credential Framework (CMF): It is a framework that aims to define the minimum common elements for microcredentials in European higher education. It provides guiding principles in areas such as learning load (ECTS credits), level (EQF level), learning outcomes, assessment, quality assurance, and certification. The CMF's objective is to streamline the design, recognition, and portability of micro-credentials developed by various countries and institutions through the use of a uniform language and structure. This initiative aims to ensure that these credentials are more consistently aligned with national and international qualification frameworks.

Chapter 13
AI-Driven Research Misconduct:
Detection, Prevention, and Institutional Response

Debajit Karmakar
http://orcid.org/0000-0001-9272-0627
Lakshmibai National Institute of Physical Education, India

Anindita Das
http://orcid.org/0000-0002-6502-9619
Lakshmibai National Institute of Physical Education, India

Tashi Ongmu Bhutia
http://orcid.org/0009-0000-0127-5709
Sikkim Government B.Ed College, India

Karuppasamy Govindasamy
http://orcid.org/0000-0002-3019-5545
Symbiosis International University, India

Abhishek Kumar
http://orcid.org/0009-0009-6607-5375
Indira Gandhi Institute of Physical Education and Sports Sciences, India

ABSTRACT

This chapter explores the evolving landscape of AI-driven research misconduct, highlighting how artificial intelligence technologies have transformed traditional notions of academic integrity. It examines emerging forms of misconduct such as AI-generated plagiarism, data fabrication, deepfake research outputs, and citation

DOI: 10.4018/979-8-3373-5586-3.ch013

manipulation, emphasizing their detection challenges and institutional implications. The discussion integrates ethical literacy, prevention frameworks, and policy responses aimed at safeguarding scholarly credibility in the digital era. By addressing detection methodologies, prevention strategies, and governance reforms, the chapter underscores the urgent need for transparency, accountability, and adaptive institutional policies to preserve the integrity of scientific research in the age of AI.

1. INTRODUCTION

The proliferation of artificial intelligence technologies in academic research has fundamentally transformed the landscape of scholarly inquiry, bringing both unprecedented opportunities and novel challenges to research integrity. As generative AI systems become increasingly sophisticated and accessible, the academic community faces an emerging paradigm of research misconduct that extends far beyond traditional forms of plagiarism and data fabrication. This chapter examines the multifaceted phenomenon of AI-driven research misconduct, exploring its various manifestations, detection methodologies, prevention strategies, and institutional response frameworks necessary to maintain the integrity of scientific discourse in the digital age (Pennock, 2018).

The advent of large language models (LLMs) such as GPT-4, Claude, and specialized academic AI tools has created a watershed moment in scholarly communication. While these technologies offer legitimate benefits including enhanced writing assistance, literature synthesis, and data analysis capabilities, they have simultaneously opened new avenues for academic dishonesty that challenge established notions of authorship, originality, and intellectual contribution. The traditional triumvirate of research misconduct, fabrication, falsification, and plagiarism has evolved into a more complex taxonomy that encompasses AI-generated content manipulation, synthetic data creation, and algorithmic citation gaming (Resnik, 2014).

Contemporary research misconduct in the AI era is characterized by its technological sophistication, scalability, and the inherent difficulty in distinguishing between legitimate AI assistance and fraudulent AI exploitation. Unlike conventional misconduct, which typically required substantial human effort and knowledge, AI-driven misconduct can be perpetrated at unprecedented scale with minimal expertise, creating systemic risks to the reliability and trustworthiness of scientific literature. This shift necessitates a fundamental reconceptualization of research integrity frameworks, detection methodologies, and institutional governance structures (Powell, 2020). The implications of AI-driven research misconduct extend beyond individual cases of academic dishonesty to encompass broader epistemological questions about the nature of knowledge creation, the role of human cognition in scientific discovery, and the legitimacy of AI-assisted research practices. As academic institutions grapple with these challenges, the need for comprehensive, evidence-based approaches to detection, prevention, and response becomes increasingly critical. This chapter provides a systematic analysis of these emerging challenges while proposing practical solutions for maintaining research integrity in an AI-augmented academic environment (Pennock, 2018).

2. UNDERSTANDING AI-DRIVEN RESEARCH MISCONDUCT

- **AI-Generated Plagiarism**

AI-generated plagiarism represents a fundamental departure from traditional forms of textual appropriation, characterized by the use of artificial intelligence systems to create content that mimics existing scholarly work without proper attribution or that generates apparently original text through sophisticated paraphrasing and synthesis algorithms. This form of misconduct exploits the generative capabilities of modern language models to produce content that appears novel while drawing heavily from training data that may include copyrighted or previously published materials (Powell, 2020).

The mechanisms underlying AI-generated plagiarism are multifaceted and technically sophisticated. Large language models trained on vast corpora of academic literature can reproduce stylistic conventions, argumentative structures, and domain-specific terminology with remarkable fidelity. However, the stochastic nature of these systems often results in content that combines elements from multiple sources in ways that obscure direct textual similarity while maintaining conceptual and structural plagiarism (Resnik, 2014). This phenomenon, termed "mosaic plagiarism" in the context of AI generation, presents unique challenges for traditional plagiarism detection systems that rely primarily on string matching algorithms. Furthermore, AI-generated plagiarism can manifest through deliberate prompt engineering designed to circumvent detection systems. Sophisticated users may employ techniques such as iterative paraphrasing, cross-linguistic translation chains, and stylistic modulation to create content that maintains the intellectual substance of source materials while avoiding algorithmic detection. The emergence of specialized "anti-detection" AI tools that explicitly market themselves as plagiarism-evasion systems has exacerbated this challenge, creating an arms race between generation and detection technologies (Webster et al., 2013).

The temporal dimension of AI-generated plagiarism adds another layer of complexity. Unlike static plagiarism of existing texts, AI systems can generate new combinations and permutations of existing ideas in real-time, creating a continuously evolving landscape of potentially infringing content. This dynamic capability challenges traditional notions of textual fixity and raises fundamental questions about the boundaries between legitimate synthesis and illegitimate appropriation in AI-mediated research processes (Powell, 2020).

- **Fabrication and Falsification of Data**

The application of artificial intelligence to research data has opened unprecedented avenues for fabrication and falsification that leverage the synthetic capabilities of modern AI systems to create convincing but fraudulent datasets, experimental results, and statistical analyses. Unlike traditional data manipulation, which typically involved altering or selectively reporting actual experimental observations, AI-driven data fabrication can generate entirely synthetic datasets that exhibit realistic statistical properties while being completely disconnected from empirical reality. Generative adversarial networks (GANs) and other synthetic data generation techniques have become particularly problematic in this context. These systems can produce datasets that maintain complex statistical relationships, exhibit appropriate variance structures, and pass standard validity checks while being entirely artificial. The sophistication of these synthetic datasets often exceeds the detection capabilities of standard statistical auditing procedures, particularly when generated by individuals with sufficient technical expertise to ensure statistical plausibility (Watson II & Etzel, 2019).

The falsification of existing data through AI-assisted manipulation represents another significant concern. Machine learning algorithms can be employed to selectively modify datasets in ways that support predetermined hypotheses while maintaining superficial statistical coherence. These modifications can be subtle and sophisticated, involving techniques such as controlled noise injection, selective outlier removal, and systematic bias introduction that are difficult to detect through conventional statistical methods (Powell, 2020).

Particularly concerning is the emergence of AI-driven meta-analysis manipulation, where artificial intelligence is used to generate synthetic effect sizes, confidence intervals, and statistical measures that create the appearance of robust empirical support for particular theoretical positions. These synthetic meta-analyses can incorporate fabricated studies, manipulated effect sizes, and artificially generated heterogeneity measures that collectively present a convincing but entirely fraudulent picture of scientific consensus (Powell, 2020). The scalability of AI-driven data fabrication presents systemic risks to scientific integrity. Unlike manual data manipulation, which is constrained by human cognitive and temporal limitations, AI systems can generate vast quantities of fraudulent data with minimal human oversight. This capability enables the creation of entire fabricated research programs spanning multiple publications, datasets, and apparent research collaborations, creating complex webs of interconnected fraudulent scholarship that can be extremely difficult to unravel (Watson II & Etzel, 2019).

- **Deepfake Research Outputs**

The application of deepfake technology to academic research outputs represents an emerging frontier of research misconduct that exploits advanced AI capabilities to create convincing but fabricated visual evidence, experimental documentation, and multimedia research materials. This category of misconduct leverages the same underlying technologies used for entertainment and commercial deepfake applications but applies them specifically to the creation of fraudulent scholarly evidence (Webster et al., 2013).

Image-based deepfakes in academic contexts commonly involve the fabrication of experimental photographs, microscopy images, gel electrophoresis results, and other visual evidence that forms the empirical foundation of scientific claims. Advanced generative models can create images that exhibit appropriate technical characteristics, including proper lighting, resolution, and domain-specific visual markers, while depicting entirely fabricated experimental outcomes. These synthetic images often pass initial visual inspection and may require sophisticated forensic analysis to identify as artificially generated. Video deepfakes present particular challenges in fields that rely on behavioural observation, clinical documentation, or experimental process verification (Resnik, 2014). AI-generated videos can depict fabricated experimental procedures, falsified patient interactions, or non-existent research activities while maintaining sufficient visual fidelity to serve as apparently credible documentation of research processes. The temporal coherence and contextual appropriateness of modern video generation systems make these fabrications increasingly difficult to identify without specialized technical expertise. Data visualization deepfakes represent a subtle but significant category of research misconduct that involves the AI-assisted generation of fraudulent graphs, charts, and statistical visualizations. These synthetic visualizations can depict entirely fabricated experimental results while maintaining appropriate visual conventions, statistical relationships, and aesthetic qualities that make them indistinguishable from legitimate research outputs. The integration of AI-generated visualizations with fabricated datasets creates comprehensive packages of fraudulent evidence that can be extremely convincing to reviewers and readers (Watson II & Etzel, 2019).

The sophistication of contemporary deepfake technology enables the creation of multimedia research presentations that combine synthetic visual, audio, and textual elements into comprehensive fraudulent research narratives. These integrated deepfake packages can include fabricated conference presentations, synthetic interview recordings, and artificially generated documentation that collectively present a compelling but entirely fabricated account of research activities and findings (Resnik, 2014).

- **Automated Paper Mills and Fake Journal Submissions**

The industrialization of research misconduct through automated paper mills represents one of the most systematic and scalable forms of AI-driven academic fraud. These operations leverage artificial intelligence to mass-produce fake research papers, fabricated author profiles, and synthetic journal submissions that exploit vulnerabilities in the academic publishing ecosystem. The automation capabilities of modern AI systems enable these operations to function at unprecedented scale while maintaining sufficient quality to evade initial detection mechanisms. Contemporary paper mills employ sophisticated AI pipelines that integrate multiple generative technologies to create comprehensive fraudulent research packages. These systems typically combine large language models for text generation, synthetic data generation algorithms for fabricated results, AI-powered citation networks for reference manipulation, and automated submission systems for journal targeting. The integration of these technologies enables the production of hundreds or thousands of fraudulent papers with minimal human oversight (Rani & Sharma, 2012).

The AI-driven automation of author profile creation represents a particularly insidious aspect of modern paper mills. These systems generate synthetic researcher identities complete with fabricated publication histories, institutional affiliations, and even AI-generated photographs and biographical information. The sophistication of these synthetic profiles often includes cross-referencing with legitimate institutional websites, creation of corresponding social media presence, and generation of plausible research trajectories that can withstand superficial verification processes. Automated journal targeting systems represent another key component of AI-driven paper mills. These systems employ machine learning algorithms to analyze journal submission patterns, reviewer characteristics, and editorial preferences to optimize the placement of fraudulent papers in venues most likely to accept them. The sophistication of these targeting systems often exceeds that of legitimate researchers, creating unfair advantages in the publication process while simultaneously undermining journal quality control mechanisms (Powell, 2020).

The economic incentives driving automated paper mills have created a feedback loop that encourages continued technological sophistication and scale expansion. As detection mechanisms improve, these operations invest in more advanced AI technologies, creating an ongoing arms race that challenges the ability of academic institutions and publishers to maintain quality control. The global nature of these operations often places them beyond the reach of traditional academic governance mechanisms, requiring coordinated international responses to address effectively (Connelly, 2014).

- **Citation Manipulation through AI**

AI-driven citation manipulation represents a sophisticated form of research misconduct that exploits artificial intelligence capabilities to artificially inflate citation metrics, create fraudulent citation networks, and manipulate bibliometric indicators used for research evaluation. This category of misconduct leverages the scale and automation capabilities of AI systems to systematically distort the scholarly communication ecosystem in ways that can be extremely difficult to detect through conventional bibliometric analysis. Automated citation generation systems represent the most direct form of AI-driven citation manipulation. These systems employ natural language processing algorithms to identify opportunities for citation insertion in legitimate papers, generate contextually appropriate citation contexts, and create the appearance of genuine scholarly engagement while actually serving to artificially inflate target citation counts. The sophistication of these systems often enables them to create citations that appear naturally integrated into the text while serving primarily to boost bibliometric indicators (Rossouw et al., 2014).

AI-powered citation network creation involves the systematic generation of interconnected webs of fraudulent papers that cite each other in patterns designed to simulate legitimate scholarly discourse while actually serving to artificially inflate the visibility and apparent impact of target publications. These networks often exhibit statistical properties similar to legitimate citation patterns, including appropriate clustering coefficients, degree distributions, and temporal evolution patterns that can make them difficult to distinguish from organic scholarly communities. The manipulation of bibliometric databases through AI-driven techniques represents an advanced form of citation fraud that exploits automated systems to insert false citation records, modify existing bibliometric data, and create phantom publications that serve primarily to inflate citation metrics. These operations often target the lag periods between publication and database indexing to insert fraudulent citations that may persist undetected for extended periods (Connelly, 2014).

Cross-lingual citation manipulation has emerged as a particularly sophisticated form of AI-driven bibliometric fraud. These operations employ machine translation and cross-cultural adaptation algorithms to create citation networks that span multiple languages and cultural contexts, exploiting the limited cross-referencing capabilities of bibliometric databases and the practical difficulties of detecting fraudulent citations in unfamiliar linguistic contexts (Rossouw et al., 2014).

3. DETECTION OF AI-DRIVEN MISCONDUCT

- **Traditional Plagiarism Detection vs. AI-Generated Text**

The detection of AI-generated text presents fundamental challenges that expose the limitations of traditional plagiarism detection systems while necessitating the development of entirely new forensic methodologies. Conventional plagiarism detection relies primarily on textual similarity algorithms that compare submitted documents against databases of existing publications, identifying matches based on string overlap, syntactic similarity, and lexical correspondence. However, AI-generated text often exhibits superficial originality while incorporating substantial intellectual content from training data in ways that circumvent traditional detection mechanisms. The stochastic nature of modern language models creates a fundamental detection challenge by generating text that is statistically unique while potentially incorporating substantial amounts of existing intellectual content. Unlike traditional copy-paste plagiarism, which creates direct textual matches detectable through string comparison algorithms, AI-generated text typically exhibits novel surface features while potentially maintaining deeper structural, conceptual, or argumentative plagiarism that requires more sophisticated analysis methods (Rossouw et al., 2014).

Semantic plagiarism detection represents an emerging frontier in addressing AI-generated misconduct. These approaches employ natural language processing techniques to identify conceptual similarity, argumentative structure correspondence, and knowledge content overlap that may not be apparent through surface-level textual analysis. However, the computational complexity and interpretive ambiguity of semantic analysis create practical challenges for large-scale implementation in institutional settings (Panter & Sterba, 2011).

The temporal dynamics of AI-generated text detection add another layer of complexity to plagiarism identification. Unlike static traditional plagiarism, AI systems can generate multiple unique variations of the same underlying content, creating moving targets for detection systems. This capability enables sophisticated users to iteratively refine AI-generated content until it passes detection algorithms while maintaining the essential intellectual appropriation that constitutes plagiarism (Rhodes, 2005).

Statistical fingerprinting approaches have emerged as promising methods for identifying AI-generated text through analysis of linguistic patterns, stylometric features, and statistical regularities that differ between human and machine-generated content. These approaches analyze features such as sentence length distribution, syntactic complexity patterns, lexical diversity measures, and coherence metrics that often exhibit characteristic signatures in AI-generated text. However, the rapid evolution of AI systems and their increasing sophistication in mimicking human writing patterns creates ongoing challenges for maintaining detection accuracy (Connelly, 2014).

- **Emerging Tools for AI-Authorship Detection**

The development of AI-authorship detection tools represents a rapidly evolving field that combines advances in machine learning, natural language processing, and forensic linguistics to identify artificially generated content in academic settings. These tools employ diverse methodological approaches ranging from statistical analysis of linguistic features to neural network-based classification systems specifically trained to distinguish between human and AI-generated text (Rao et al., 2024).

GPT detectors and similar large language model identification systems represent the most prominent category of AI-authorship detection tools. These systems typically employ supervised machine learning approaches trained on datasets of known human and AI-generated text to identify statistical patterns and linguistic markers characteristic of artificial generation. Popular tools such as GPTZero, Originality. AI, and others have gained widespread adoption in academic settings, though their accuracy rates vary significantly depending on the specific AI system used for generation and the sophistication of attempts to evade detection. Stylometric analysis approaches to AI detection leverage computational linguistics techniques to identify subtle patterns in writing style, vocabulary usage, and syntactic structure that may distinguish human from machine-generated text. These approaches often employ features such as function word frequency, sentence structure complexity, lexical richness measures, and discourse coherence patterns that exhibit different statistical properties in human versus AI-generated content. Advanced stylometric systems may incorporate author attribution techniques adapted to distinguish between individual human authors and various AI systems (Palanski et al., 2021).

Perplexity-based detection methods exploit the predictive uncertainty characteristics of language models to identify text that exhibits statistical properties consistent with AI generation. These approaches analyze the predictability of word sequences, the distribution of rare versus common linguistic constructions, and the coherence patterns that differ between human cognitive processes and algorithmic text generation. Perplexity-based methods often demonstrate good performance in controlled conditions but may struggle with adversarial examples designed to evade detection (Steneck & Bulger, 2007).

Ensemble detection systems combine multiple methodological approaches to achieve more robust and accurate identification of AI-generated content. These systems typically integrate statistical analysis, neural network classification, stylometric features, and perplexity measures to create comprehensive profiles of textual characteristics that collectively indicate artificial generation. The diversity of detection methods in ensemble systems helps mitigate the limitations of individual approaches while providing more reliable identification across different types of AI-generated content.

- **Forensic Data Analysis in Spotting Fabricated Results**

Forensic data analysis for detecting fabricated research results requires sophisticated statistical and computational methodologies that can identify artificial patterns, impossible values, and statistical anomalies indicative of data manipulation or synthesis. Unlike traditional data validation, which focuses on accuracy and completeness, forensic analysis specifically searches for evidence of deliberate falsification, fabrication, or algorithmic generation of research data (Karmakar et al., 2025).

Benford's Law analysis represents one of the most established methods for detecting fabricated numerical data in research contexts. This approach examines the distribution of leading digits in datasets, which should follow predictable statistical patterns in naturally occurring data. Fabricated data often exhibits deviations from Benford's Law that can indicate artificial generation or manipulation, particularly when human intuition about "random" number generation creates unnatural digit distribution patterns. Statistical impossibility detection involves identifying combinations of statistical measures, effect sizes, and confidence intervals that could not realistically occur given the reported sample sizes and methodological constraints. Sophisticated forensic analysis can identify cases where reported standard deviations, correlation matrices, or significance levels exhibit mathematical relationships that indicate fabrication rather than empirical observation (Rao et al., 2024).

Duplicate data detection has become increasingly important as AI-enabled data fabrication systems may inadvertently create identical or near-identical observations within supposedly independent datasets. Advanced duplicate detection algorithms can identify subtle variations in fabricated data that maintain superficial uniqueness while exhibiting underlying systematic patterns characteristic of algorithmic generation. Time series analysis of research productivity and data generation patterns can reveal systematic anomalies indicative of AI-assisted data fabrication. These approaches examine the temporal distribution of data collection, the consistency of measurement precision across time periods, and the patterns of missing or outlier data that may indicate artificial generation rather than genuine empirical observation (Resnik, 2014).

- **Image and Figure Forensics**

Digital image forensics in academic contexts requires specialized techniques adapted to the specific characteristics and manipulation methods commonly employed in research misconduct. Unlike general-purpose image authentication, academic image forensics must address domain-specific manipulation types including gel electrophoresis band duplication, microscopy image enhancement, graph manipulation, and figure assembly fraud that exploit the technical nature of scientific imagery.

Pixel-level analysis techniques examine the statistical properties of image data to identify evidence of digital manipulation, including cloning, splicing, and synthetic generation. These approaches analyze characteristics such as noise patterns, compression artifacts, color distribution anomalies, and statistical regularities that differ between authentic and manipulated images. Advanced pixel-level analysis can identify subtle manipulations that maintain visual coherence while exhibiting forensic signatures detectable through computational analysis. Compression history analysis exploits the artifacts created by repeated image compression to identify evidence of manipulation between original capture and final submission. Scientific images that have undergone multiple editing cycles often exhibit characteristic compression artifacts that can indicate the extent and nature of post-processing, helping to distinguish between legitimate image preparation and fraudulent manipulation (Rao et al., 2024).

- **Limitations and False Positives in AI-Detection Methods**

The practical implementation of AI-detection technologies in academic settings faces significant challenges related to accuracy, reliability, and the potential for false accusations that can have serious consequences for researchers and students. Understanding these limitations is crucial for developing appropriate institutional policies and procedures that balance the need for integrity enforcement with protection against unjust accusations of misconduct.

False positive rates in AI detection systems remain a primary concern for institutional implementation. Studies of commercial AI detection tools have reported false positive rates ranging from 5% to 15%, meaning that a significant proportion of human-written text may be incorrectly identified as AI-generated. These false positives can disproportionately affect non-native English speakers, students with certain writing styles, and content in specialized domains where linguistic patterns may deviate from the training data used to develop detection algorithms (Steneck & Bulger, 2007).

The adversarial robustness of detection systems presents another significant limitation. Sophisticated users can employ various techniques to evade detection, including iterative paraphrasing, style transfer, human-AI collaboration, and prompt engineering specifically designed to produce text that passes detection algorithms.

The arms race dynamic between generation and detection technologies means that detection accuracy may degrade over time as generation systems evolve to circumvent existing detection methods. Domain specificity limitations affect the performance of detection systems when applied to specialized academic fields with distinctive linguistic conventions, technical terminology, and rhetorical structures. Detection algorithms trained on general-purpose text may exhibit reduced accuracy when applied to highly technical scientific writing, legal scholarship, or other specialized domains that differ significantly from typical training data (Panter & Sterba, 2011).

Cross-lingual detection challenges become apparent when applying AI detection systems to multilingual academic environments. Most detection systems are primarily trained on English text and may exhibit poor performance when applied to other languages or to text that has been translated between languages, either by humans or by AI systems. The interpretability and explainability of AI detection systems present challenges for institutional decision-making processes that require clear evidence and rationale for misconduct determinations. Many detection systems operate as "black boxes" that provide probability scores without clear explanations of the specific features or patterns that led to their conclusions, making it difficult for institutions to build convincing cases or provide appropriate due process protections. Temporal instability in detection accuracy creates ongoing challenges for institutional policies that rely on these systems. As AI generation technologies evolve rapidly, detection systems may become obsolete or significantly less accurate over relatively short time periods, requiring continuous updating and revalidation that may strain institutional resources and create inconsistencies in enforcement practices (Rosnow & Rosenthal, 2013).

4. PREVENTION STRATEGIES

- **Ethical AI Literacy for Researchers and Students**

The development of comprehensive ethical AI literacy programs represents a fundamental prevention strategy that addresses AI-driven research misconduct through education, awareness-building, and the cultivation of ethical decision-making capabilities among researchers and students. These programs must go beyond technical training to encompass the philosophical, practical, and institutional dimensions of ethical AI use in academic contexts. Foundational AI literacy components should provide researchers and students with essential understanding of how AI systems function, their capabilities and limitations, and the implications of their use for research integrity. This includes education about language model training processes, the role of training data in AI outputs, the stochastic nature of AI generation, and the ways in which AI systems may inadvertently reproduce or synthesize content from their training datasets without explicit citation or attribution. Ethical decision-making frameworks specific to AI use in research contexts should help individuals navigate the complex boundary between appropriate AI assistance and inappropriate AI dependence. These frameworks should address questions such as when AI use requires disclosure, how to maintain intellectual integrity while benefiting from AI capabilities, methods for validating AI-generated content, and approaches for ensuring that human cognitive contribution remains central to the research process (Edwards, 2020).

Practical skills training should equip researchers and students with concrete capabilities for responsible AI integration in their work. This includes techniques for prompt engineering that minimizes plagiarism risks, methods for fact-checking and validating AI-generated content, approaches for appropriately citing and acknowledging AI assistance, and strategies for maintaining transparency about AI use throughout the research process (Karmakar et al., 2025).

Discipline-specific ethical considerations should be addressed through tailored training programs that recognize the unique challenges and opportunities presented by AI use in different academic fields. Scientific disciplines may require focused attention on data integrity and experimental validity, while humanities fields may need emphasis on textual authenticity and interpretive originality. Professional fields such as medicine, law, and engineering may require specialized attention to regulatory compliance and professional responsibility standards. Assessment and competency evaluation components should ensure that ethical AI literacy programs effectively develop the intended capabilities and knowledge among participants. This may include scenario-based evaluations, practical exercises in ethical AI use, and ongoing competency maintenance requirements that keep pace with evolving AI technologies and ethical standards (Rosnow & Rosenthal, 2013).

Continuous learning frameworks should acknowledge that AI technologies and their ethical implications evolve rapidly, requiring ongoing education and skill development rather than one-time training programs. These frameworks should incorporate mechanisms for staying current with technological developments, emerging ethical standards, and evolving institutional policies regarding AI use in research contexts.

- **Guidelines for Legitimate AI Use in Research Writing**

The establishment of clear, practical guidelines for legitimate AI use in research writing represents a crucial prevention strategy that provides researchers and students with concrete boundaries and expectations while preserving the benefits of AI assistance for scholarly productivity and quality. These guidelines must balance the recognition of legitimate AI applications with the preservation of core values such as originality, authenticity, and intellectual contribution (Palanski et al., 2021).

Disclosure requirements should specify when, how, and to what extent researchers must acknowledge AI assistance in their work. These requirements should address different levels of AI involvement, from minor editorial assistance to substantial content generation, with corresponding disclosure expectations. Clear guidance should distinguish between assistance that requires acknowledgment versus assistance that requires explicit disclosure as co-authorship or methodological reporting. Intellectual contribution standards should clarify the expectation that human researchers remain the primary intellectual contributors to their work, with AI serving in supporting rather than generative roles. These standards should address the importance of human-driven conceptualization, critical analysis, synthesis, and interpretation while acknowledging appropriate roles for AI in tasks such as literature searching, initial drafting, and editorial refinement (Rosnow & Rosenthal, 2013).

Quality assurance requirements should specify the responsibility of researchers to validate, verify, and take intellectual ownership of any AI-assisted content in their work. This includes obligations to fact-check AI-generated information, ensure accuracy of citations and references suggested by AI systems, and verify that AI-assisted writing accurately represents the researcher's intended meaning and contribution. Attribution and citation guidelines should address the complex questions surrounding how to appropriately acknowledge AI assistance without treating AI systems as co-authors. These guidelines should provide standardized formats for acknowledging different types of AI assistance while maintaining clarity about human versus artificial contributions to the work. Prohibited uses should be clearly specified to establish boundaries around AI applications that are categorically inappropriate in research contexts. This may include prohibitions on AI-generated data fabrication, AI-assisted citation manipulation, submission of substantially AI-generated work without disclosure, and use of AI to circumvent institutional policies or journal requirements (Edwards, 2020).

- **Developing Transparent AI-Use Policies in Institutions**

The development of transparent, comprehensive AI-use policies at the institutional level provides the foundational framework for preventing AI-driven research misconduct while supporting legitimate innovation and productivity enhancement. These policies must address the diverse needs and contexts within academic institutions while providing clear, enforceable standards that can be consistently applied across different departments and disciplines.

Policy scope and applicability should clearly define which activities, individuals, and contexts fall under AI-use regulations. This includes specification of coverage for student work, faculty research, staff activities, and collaborative projects, as well as distinctions between different types of AI tools and applications that may require different regulatory approaches. Risk assessment frameworks should be incorporated into institutional AI policies to provide structured approaches for evaluating the appropriateness and potential risks of specific AI applications in different contexts. These frameworks should consider factors such as the level of AI involvement, the stakes of the work, the availability of validation mechanisms, and the potential for harm from AI-related errors or misconduct (Palanski et al., 2021).

Governance structures should establish clear lines of responsibility and accountability for AI policy development, implementation, and enforcement within institutional settings. This includes designation of oversight bodies, definition of reporting relationships, establishment of appeal processes, and creation of mechanisms for policy updates in response to technological developments. Training and support requirements should mandate appropriate education and resource provision to ensure that institutional community members have the knowledge and tools necessary for compliant AI use. This includes requirements for faculty development, student training, staff education, and ongoing professional development to maintain currency with evolving technologies and standards (Edwards, 2020).

Monitoring and enforcement mechanisms should provide practical approaches for detecting policy violations, investigating potential misconduct, and implementing appropriate responses while respecting due process protections and academic freedom principles. These mechanisms should balance the need for oversight with recognition of the practical limitations of comprehensive monitoring in academic environments. Integration with existing policies should ensure that AI-use regulations complement and reinforce existing academic integrity, research misconduct, and intellectual property policies rather than creating conflicting or redundant requirements. This integration should address potential gaps or overlaps between different policy domains while maintaining coherent institutional standards (Panter & Sterba, 2011).

- **Promoting Open Science, Reproducibility, and Raw Data Sharing**

Open science practices represent powerful prevention strategies against AI-driven research misconduct by increasing transparency, enabling verification, and creating accountability mechanisms that make fraudulent research more difficult to sustain. The promotion of open science principles specifically adapted to address AI-related challenges can significantly enhance the integrity of research processes and outcomes. Raw data sharing requirements can help prevent AI-driven data fabrication by providing opportunities for independent verification and analysis of research datasets. Open data policies should address the specific challenges posed by AI-generated datasets while establishing standards for data documentation, metadata provision, and accessibility that enable effective validation by other researchers (Resnik, 2014).

Methodological transparency standards should require detailed documentation of research processes, including any AI assistance or automation employed in data collection, analysis, or interpretation. These standards should promote sufficient detail to enable reproducibility while addressing the specific challenges of documenting AI-assisted research processes that may involve complex algorithmic procedures.

Code and algorithm sharing can enhance transparency in AI-assisted research by providing access to the computational tools and procedures used in research processes. This includes sharing of custom AI implementations, data processing pipelines, statistical analysis code, and other computational components that enable independent verification and reproduction of research results. Pre-registration practices adapted for AI-assisted research can help prevent selective reporting, result manipulation, and post-hoc hypothesis generation that may be facilitated by AI tools. Pre-registration standards should address the challenges of documenting intended AI use, specifying analysis plans that incorporate AI assistance, and maintaining accountability for deviations from pre-registered procedures (Edwards, 2020).

Collaborative verification networks can leverage the distributed expertise of research communities to identify potential AI-driven misconduct through peer review, post-publication review, and collaborative validation efforts. These networks should provide mechanisms for reporting concerns, sharing validation results, and coordinating responses to potential misconduct cases. Version control and transparency practices should encourage researchers to maintain detailed records of their research processes, including AI assistance, which can support accountability and reproducibility. This includes recommendations for documentation standards, version control systems, and transparency practices that enable effective oversight and verification (Pellegrina & Helmy, 2025).

- **Role of Peer Reviewers and Editors in Early Prevention**

The peer review process represents a critical front line for preventing AI-driven research misconduct through expert evaluation, validation, and quality control that can identify problematic AI use before publication. However, the effectiveness of peer review for addressing AI-related challenges requires adaptation of traditional review processes and the development of new competencies among reviewers and editors. Reviewer training on AI-related issues should provide peer reviewers with the knowledge and skills necessary to identify potential AI-driven misconduct, evaluate appropriate AI disclosure, and assess the quality and validity of AI-assisted research. This training should address both technical aspects of AI detection and broader questions about appropriate AI use in research contexts (Resnik, 2014).

Enhanced scrutiny protocols should guide reviewers in applying appropriate skepticism and validation procedures when evaluating submissions that may involve AI assistance. These protocols should provide structured approaches for assessing data plausibility, checking citation accuracy, evaluating methodological coherence, and identifying potential indicators of AI-generated content. Red flag identification should help reviewers recognize patterns and characteristics that may indicate inappropriate AI use or AI-driven misconduct. These indicators might include unusual productivity patterns, statistical anomalies, stylistic inconsistencies, citation irregularities, or implausible experimental results that warrant additional scrutiny or investigation (Cunningham & McCrum-Gardner, 2007).

Validation requirements should specify when and how reviewers should request additional documentation, raw data, or methodological details to verify the authenticity and integrity of submitted research. These requirements should balance the need for thorough validation with practical constraints on reviewer time and expertise. Editorial oversight responsibilities should establish clear expectations for editor engagement in AI-related quality control, including the development of editorial policies, oversight of reviewer training, management of misconduct investigations, and coordination with institutional authorities when misconduct is suspected.

Post-publication monitoring should extend prevention efforts beyond initial publication through ongoing surveillance, reader feedback mechanisms, and post-publication peer review that can identify AI-driven misconduct that may have escaped initial detection. These mechanisms should provide practical approaches for addressing misconduct discoveries after publication while maintaining appropriate due process protections (Edwards, 2020).

5. INSTITUTIONAL RESPONSE FRAMEWORK

- **Policies for Addressing AI-Driven Misconduct Cases**

The development of comprehensive institutional policies for addressing AI-driven research misconduct requires careful consideration of the unique characteristics of AI-related violations while maintaining consistency with established principles of academic integrity and due process. These policies must provide clear procedures for investigation, evaluation, and response while recognizing the technical complexity and evolving nature of AI-related misconduct. Case classification frameworks should establish systematic approaches for categorizing different types of AI-driven misconduct based on severity, intent, scope, and impact. These frameworks should distinguish between inadvertent AI misuse resulting from insufficient knowledge or training versus deliberate fraud or deception, with corresponding differences in investigative procedures and potential sanctions (Aoyagi & Portenga, 2010).

Evidence standards should specify the types and quality of evidence required to substantiate allegations of AI-driven misconduct, recognizing the technical challenges involved in proving AI generation or manipulation. These standards should address the use of detection software, expert testimony, statistical analysis, and other forms of evidence while establishing appropriate confidence thresholds for disciplinary action. Investigation procedures should provide structured processes for examining AI-driven misconduct allegations that account for the technical expertise required, the potential need for external consultation, and the importance of maintaining confidentiality and due process protections throughout the investigation. These procedures should address the roles of different institutional actors, timelines for investigation completion, and standards for documentation and record-keeping (Pellegrina & Helmy, 2025).

Burden of proof specifications should clarify the allocation of responsibility for demonstrating misconduct versus innocence in AI-related cases, recognizing the challenges of definitively proving AI generation while protecting individuals against false accusations. These specifications should address the roles of detection technology, expert analysis, and circumstantial evidence in meeting evidentiary standards. Appeal and review mechanisms should provide appropriate opportunities for individuals to challenge misconduct findings, request reconsideration of evidence, and seek review of sanctions imposed for AI-related violations. These mechanisms should ensure access to independent review while maintaining the integrity and efficiency of the institutional response process (Aoyagi & Portenga, 2010).

- **Investigative Committees and Due Process**

The establishment of specialized investigative committees for AI-driven research misconduct cases requires careful attention to expertise requirements, procedural protections, and the unique challenges posed by technologically complex allegations. These committees must possess sufficient technical competence to evaluate AI-related evidence while maintaining adherence to established principles of academic due process and procedural fairness. Committee composition should include members with diverse relevant expertise, including technical knowledge of AI systems, research methodology expertise, disciplinary subject matter knowledge, and procedural and legal competence in academic misconduct cases. The interdisciplinary nature of AI-driven misconduct often requires committees that can integrate technical analysis with disciplinary standards and procedural requirements (Karmakar et al., 2025).

Technical consultation protocols should establish procedures for engaging external experts when committee members lack sufficient technical expertise to evaluate complex AI-related evidence. These protocols should address the selection of qualified consultants, the scope of their engagement, compensation arrangements, and the integration of technical opinions into committee decision-making processes. Due process protections must be rigorously maintained throughout AI misconduct investigations, including rights to notice of charges, access to evidence, opportunities for response and defense, representation by counsel or advisors, and impartial evaluation by qualified decision-makers. The technical complexity of AI cases should not diminish these fundamental protections but may require adaptation of procedures to accommodate technical evidence and expert testimony (Edwards, 2020).

Evidentiary procedures should establish standards for the collection, preservation, and evaluation of digital evidence relevant to AI misconduct allegations. This includes protocols for securing digital files, maintaining chain of custody for electronic evidence, ensuring the reliability of detection software results, and providing opportunities for respondents to challenge technical evidence through expert testimony or independent analysis. Confidentiality protections should balance the need for thorough investigation with protection of individual privacy and reputational interests, particularly given the potential for false positive results from AI detection systems. These protections should address limitations on information sharing, procedures for handling preliminary findings, and protocols for managing public disclosure of investigation results (Aoyagi & Portenga, 2010).

- **Sanctions and Academic Penalties for AI Abuse**

The development of appropriate sanctioning frameworks for AI-driven research misconduct must carefully calibrate penalties to reflect the severity and circumstances of different violations while serving the dual purposes of individual accountability and systemic deterrence. These frameworks must account for the spectrum of AI-related violations from inadvertent misuse to deliberate fraud while maintaining proportionality and educational value in sanctions imposed. Graduated sanction systems should establish tiered penalty structures that correspond to different levels of AI misconduct severity, intent, and impact. Minor violations involving inadequate disclosure or limited inappropriate AI use might warrant educational interventions, warning letters, or mandatory training, while serious violations involving systematic data fabrication or large-scale fraudulent publication might warrant suspension, termination, or permanent exclusion from academic positions (Resnik, 2014).

Restorative justice components should emphasize rehabilitation and education alongside punishment, particularly for cases involving inadvertent misconduct or first-time violations. These components might include mandatory training programs, supervised research periods, mentoring relationships, or community service contributions that help violators understand and internalize appropriate standards while contributing to the academic community's knowledge about AI ethics. Professional development requirements can serve both punitive and educational purposes by mandating participation in ethics training, AI literacy programs, or professional development activities that address the underlying knowledge or skill deficits that contributed to the misconduct. These requirements should be tailored to individual circumstances while ensuring meaningful engagement with relevant learning opportunities. Research supervision restrictions may be appropriate in cases where AI misconduct raises concerns about an individual's capacity to mentor others or maintain research integrity standards. These restrictions might include temporary suspension of supervisory privileges, required co-supervision arrangements, or mandatory oversight of research activities for specified periods.

Publication consequences should address the impact of AI misconduct on the scholarly record through mechanisms such as retraction requirements, correction notices, publication bans, or restrictions on submission to certain venues. These consequences should be coordinated with publishers and professional organizations to ensure consistent application across the broader academic ecosystem. Career and advancement impacts should be proportionate to misconduct severity while recognizing the significant professional consequences of academic integrity violations. Serious misconduct may warrant restrictions on promotion, tenure consideration, grant eligibility, or professional recognition, while minor violations might involve temporary delays or additional requirements for career advancement (Edwards, 2020).

- **Rehabilitation and Education vs. Punitive Approaches**

The institutional response to AI-driven research misconduct should carefully balance punitive measures with rehabilitation and educational interventions that address the underlying causes of misconduct while promoting long-term behaviour change and community protection. This balance requires nuanced understanding of different misconduct contexts and tailored approaches that serve both individual and institutional interests. Root cause analysis should inform institutional responses by identifying the factors that contributed to AI misconduct, including knowledge deficits, skill limitations, environmental pressures, or systemic institutional failures. This analysis should guide the selection of appropriate interventions that address underlying causes rather than merely responding to symptoms of deeper problems (Panter & Sterba, 2011).

Educational intervention design should create meaningful learning experiences that help individuals understand the ethical, professional, and practical implications of appropriate AI use while developing the knowledge and skills necessary for future compliance. These interventions should be evidence-based, engaging, and tailored to individual learning needs and misconduct contexts. Skill development programs should address practical capabilities that individuals need to use AI appropriately in their research contexts. This might include training in prompt engineering, fact-checking techniques, citation practices, disclosure methods, or quality assurance procedures that enable responsible AI integration without compromising research integrity(Karmakar et al., 2025)

Mentoring and supervision enhancements can provide ongoing support and oversight for individuals who have committed AI misconduct, helping them navigate future research challenges while providing accountability and guidance for appropriate practice. These arrangements should be structured to provide meaningful support while maintaining appropriate boundaries and expectations. Community service opportunities within academic settings can help individuals contribute to institutional efforts to address AI-related challenges while demonstrating their commitment to rehabilitation and community welfare. This might include participation in policy development, training program delivery, awareness campaigns, or research on AI ethics and integrity issues (Panter & Sterba, 2011).

Monitoring and accountability systems should provide ongoing oversight and support for individuals undergoing rehabilitation while respecting privacy and autonomy rights. These systems should balance the need for verification and accountability with recognition of individual dignity and the importance of trust-building in rehabilitation processes. Long-term follow-up and support should recognize that rehabilitation is an ongoing process that may require sustained intervention and support over extended periods. This includes mechanisms for checking progress, providing continued education, addressing new challenges, and modifying interventions based on changing circumstances or emerging needs (Cortina, 2020).

- **Building Trust and Transparency in Institutional Governance**

The maintenance of institutional trust and legitimacy in addressing AI-driven research misconduct requires transparent governance processes, consistent policy application, and ongoing community engagement that demonstrates institutional commitment to fairness, integrity, and continuous improvement. These elements are essential for maintaining community support and cooperation in addressing AI-related challenges. Transparency in policy development should involve meaningful community participation in the creation and revision of AI-related policies, including opportunities for input from faculty, students, staff, and other stakeholders who will be affected by these policies. This participation should include public comment periods, community forums, expert consultations, and other mechanisms for gathering diverse perspectives and building consensus.

Process transparency should provide appropriate visibility into institutional procedures for addressing AI misconduct while respecting necessary confidentiality protections for individuals involved in investigations. This might include publication of anonymized case studies, statistical reporting on misconduct cases, procedural guides that explain investigation processes, and regular updates on policy implementation and effectiveness. Decision-making transparency should explain the rationale and standards used in institutional responses to AI misconduct, helping community members understand how policies are applied and ensuring consistency in institutional actions. This might include publication of decision frameworks, explanation of sanctioning principles, and communication about factors considered in different types of cases (Cortina, 2020).

Accountability mechanisms should provide opportunities for community oversight and feedback on institutional performance in addressing AI-related challenges. This might include regular reporting to governance bodies, external review of policies and procedures, community surveys about institutional effectiveness, and mechanisms for raising concerns about institutional responses. Continuous improvement processes should demonstrate institutional commitment to learning and adaptation based on experience, emerging knowledge, and community feedback. This includes regular policy review and revision, incorporation of lessons learned from misconduct cases, adaptation to technological developments, and responsiveness to changing community needs and expectations (Edwards, 2020).

Community education and engagement should promote broader understanding of AI-related challenges and institutional responses while building support for integrity initiatives. This might include public lectures, workshop series, newsletter communications, website resources, and other educational initiatives that help community members understand and engage with AI-related issues. External collaboration and benchmarking should position institutions as participants in broader efforts to address AI-driven research misconduct while learning from other institutions' experiences and contributing to collective knowledge development. This includes participation in professional organizations, research collaborations, policy development initiatives, and information sharing networks that advance understanding of effective approaches to AI-related challenges.

6. LEGAL AND ETHICAL CONSIDERATIONS

- **Intellectual Property Issues in AI-Generated Content**

The intersection of artificial intelligence and intellectual property law presents complex challenges for research integrity that extend beyond traditional concepts of authorship, originality, and ownership to encompass questions about the copyrightability of AI-generated content, the rights of training data owners, and the liability implications of AI-assisted research misconduct. These issues require careful analysis of existing legal frameworks while anticipating likely developments in intellectual property doctrine. Copyright ownership questions surrounding AI-generated content remain largely unsettled in most jurisdictions, with significant implications for research contexts where AI systems may contribute substantially to written outputs, data visualizations, or other creative elements of scholarly work. Current legal uncertainty about whether AI-generated content can be copyrighted, and if so, who owns such copyrights, creates challenges for researchers seeking to understand their rights and obligations regarding AI-assisted work (Panter & Sterba, 2011).

Training data copyright implications present another layer of complexity, as modern AI systems are trained on vast corpora that may include copyrighted academic work, published research papers, and other protected content. The extent to which AI-generated outputs may infringe copyrights in training data remains legally uncertain, creating potential liability risks for researchers who use AI systems without understanding the intellectual property implications of their training datasets. Fair use analysis in academic contexts may provide some protection for AI-assisted research activities, particularly when such use serves educational, research, or commentary purposes that align with traditional fair use principles. However, the application of fair use doctrine to AI-generated content involves novel questions about the nature of derivative works, the commercial impact of AI use, and the transformative character of algorithmic processing that have not been definitively resolved by courts (Powell, 2020).

Attribution and authorship requirements in academic settings may conflict with intellectual property law principles regarding ownership and credit for creative works. While academic integrity standards typically require attribution of sources and assistance, intellectual property law may not recognize AI systems as legitimate authors or rights holders, creating potential inconsistencies between academic and legal requirements. Licensing and permission issues become particularly complex when researchers use AI systems to process, analyze, or synthesize content that may be subject to licensing restrictions or permission requirements. The terms of use for AI systems, academic databases, and research materials may impose conflicting obligations that create legal risks for researchers who fail to navigate these requirements appropriately.

- **Data Privacy and Security Concerns in AI-Assisted Research**

The use of AI systems in research contexts raises significant data privacy and security concerns that extend beyond traditional research ethics protections to encompass questions about data processing by commercial AI providers, cross-border data transfers, and the potential for unauthorized disclosure or misuse of sensitive research information. These concerns require comprehensive risk assessment and mitigation strategies that address both legal compliance and ethical obligations. Personal data protection requirements under regulations such as GDPR, CCPA, and similar privacy frameworks may apply to research activities that involve AI processing of personally identifiable information, creating compliance obligations that researchers may not fully understand or appreciate. These requirements may impose restrictions on data sharing with AI providers, require specific consent procedures, or mandate particular security measures that affect the feasibility of AI-assisted research (Cortina, 2020).

Sensitive data handling becomes particularly challenging when research involves confidential business information, classified research, proprietary datasets, or other sensitive materials that may be subject to contractual or regulatory restrictions on sharing or processing. The use of commercial AI systems for processing such data may violate confidentiality agreements, export control regulations, or institutional policies governing sensitive information management. Third-party data processing concerns arise when researchers use commercial AI services that may store, analyze, or otherwise process research data on remote servers controlled by private companies. These arrangements raise questions about data security, provider access to research information, potential government surveillance, and the long-term availability and control of research datasets (Panter & Sterba, 2011).

Consent and disclosure requirements may apply when research participants' data or information is processed using AI systems, particularly when such processing was not anticipated at the time of initial consent or when AI analysis may reveal information beyond the original scope of research participation. These requirements may necessitate additional consent procedures or disclosure mechanisms that address AI-specific privacy risks. Cross-border data transfer restrictions may limit researchers' ability to use AI services that involve international data processing, particularly when research involves data from jurisdictions with strict data localization requirements or restrictions on transfers to certain countries. These restrictions may limit the available AI tools or require specific legal mechanisms such as adequacy decisions or standard contractual clauses (Wible, 2016).

Data breach notification and response obligations may apply when AI-assisted research activities result in unauthorized access, disclosure, or loss of research data, particularly when such data includes personally identifiable information or other sensitive content. Researchers must understand their obligations to notify affected individuals, institutional authorities, and regulatory agencies in the event of AI-related data security incidents.

- **Cross-Border Ethical Challenges in Global Academia**

The globalized nature of contemporary academic research creates complex cross-border ethical challenges related to AI-driven research misconduct that arise from differences in legal frameworks, cultural norms, ethical standards, and enforcement capabilities across jurisdictions. These challenges require coordinated international approaches that respect jurisdictional sovereignty while promoting consistent standards for research integrity. Jurisdictional conflicts may arise when AI-driven research misconduct involves researchers, institutions, or activities in multiple countries with different legal standards, enforcement mechanisms, or cultural approaches to research integrity. These conflicts may create challenges for investigating misconduct, coordinating responses, or ensuring appropriate sanctions when violations span multiple jurisdictions (Kang & Hwang, 2020).

Cultural and normative differences in research ethics may affect how different academic communities understand and respond to AI-related challenges, particularly regarding issues such as authorship attribution, collaboration disclosure, data sharing practices, and the appropriate role of AI assistance in scholarly work. These differences require careful navigation to maintain international research collaboration while respecting diverse ethical traditions. Regulatory arbitrage concerns may arise when researchers or institutions deliberately exploit differences in AI regulation, research integrity standards, or enforcement capabilities across jurisdictions to evade oversight or engage in misconduct that would be prohibited in more restrictive environments. These concerns require international coordination to prevent the emergence of regulatory havens for AI-driven research misconduct (Panter & Sterba, 2011).

International cooperation mechanisms are needed to facilitate information sharing, coordinate investigations, and ensure consistent enforcement of research integrity standards across borders. These mechanisms must balance the need for effective cooperation with respect for national sovereignty, privacy protections, and due process requirements in different legal systems. Standards harmonization efforts should promote convergence toward common principles and practices for addressing AI-driven research misconduct while recognizing legitimate differences in legal and cultural contexts. These efforts might include development of international guidelines, model policies, best practices sharing, and capacity building initiatives that enhance global capabilities for addressing AI-related challenges. Capacity building considerations recognize that different countries and regions may have varying levels of technical expertise, regulatory infrastructure, and institutional capacity for addressing AI-driven research misconduct. International collaboration should include technical assistance, training programs, resource sharing, and other capacity building initiatives that enhance global capabilities for maintaining research integrity (Wible, 2016).

- **Future of Academic Integrity Codes in the AI Era**

The evolution of academic integrity frameworks to address AI-related challenges requires fundamental reconceptualization of core principles, practices, and enforcement mechanisms while maintaining the essential values and purposes that underlie research integrity requirements. This evolution must anticipate continued technological development while providing stable foundations for ethical research conduct. Conceptual framework evolution should address how traditional concepts such as authorship, originality, collaboration, and intellectual contribution apply in contexts involving AI assistance, generation, and processing. These frameworks must provide clear guidance for distinguishing between appropriate AI assistance and inappropriate AI dependence while preserving core academic values (Kang & Hwang, 2020).

Dynamic policy adaptation mechanisms should enable academic integrity codes to evolve in response to rapid technological development without requiring constant wholesale revision or creating instability in research standards. These mechanisms might include flexible interpretation guidelines, regular review processes, or modular policy structures that can be updated as needed. Technology-neutral principles should provide stable foundations for academic integrity requirements that remain relevant despite technological change while offering sufficient flexibility to address novel AI applications and capabilities as they emerge. These principles should focus on underlying values and purposes rather than specific technological configurations or capabilities (Wible, 2016).

Stakeholder engagement should actively involve faculty, students, administrators, publishers, and technology providers in shaping academic integrity standards. Continuous dialogue and consensus-building are essential to guide appropriate AI use in research. Institutions need strong implementation support, including training, guidance, and technical assistance, to adapt effectively while ensuring consistency. Ongoing assessment mechanisms should monitor effectiveness, identify challenges, and highlight improvements, enabling evidence-based policy development and continuous refinement of academic integrity frameworks in response to evolving AI-related issues (Kang & Hwang, 2020).

7. CONCLUSION

The rise of AI-driven research misconduct marks a transformative challenge to academic integrity, demanding adaptive, collaborative, and proactive responses from all sectors of the research community. This chapter highlighted how AI technologies can facilitate large-scale plagiarism, data fabrication, and content manipulation, posing risks that exceed traditional academic dishonesty. As AI continues to evolve faster than detection tools and institutional policies, the threat to the credibility of scholarly communication intensifies. Addressing this requires a multifaceted approach that integrates technological innovation, ethical education, policy development, and cultural reform. Building a culture of transparency, accountability, and integrity is essential, supported by continuous education, advanced detection systems, and adaptive governance frameworks. Responsibility for safeguarding research integrity must be shared among researchers, institutions, publishers, and policymakers. Sustained vigilance, policy updates, and international collaboration will be crucial as AI capabilities expand globally. Ultimately, the success of these efforts will be reflected not just in preventing misconduct but in preserving public trust, academic freedom, and the ethical pursuit of knowledge. By aligning human judgment with responsible technological use, academia can uphold the principles that define research excellence in the era of artificial intelligence.

REFERENCES

Aoyagi, M. W., & Portenga, S. T. (2010). The role of positive ethics and virtues in the context of sport and performance psychology service delivery. *Professional Psychology, Research and Practice*, *41*(3), 253–259. https://psycnet.apa.org/record/2010-11935-011. DOI: 10.1037/a0019483

Connelly, L. M. (2014). Ethical considerations in research studies. *Medsurg Nursing*, *23*(1), 54–56. https://go.gale.com/ps/i.do?id=GALE%7CA360608990&sid=googleScholar&v=2.1&it=r&linkaccess=abs&iss PMID: 24707669

Cortina, J. M. (2020). On the whys and hows of quantitative research. *Journal of Business Ethics*, *167*(1), 19–29. https://idp.springer.com/authorize/casa?redirect_uri=https://link.springer.com/article/10.1007/s10551-019-04195-8&casa_token=pFPN_pEjrIEAAAAA:a7jsAzcP8Hm4W6wK6-3f6xraknWh930FRFSHrnaqzlPat7_SpNuyxuBIRici2x7ZxIJ86nCVCjJCbUdRvw. DOI: 10.1007/s10551-019-04195-8

Cunningham, J. B., & McCrum-Gardner, E. (2007). Power, effect and sample size using GPower: Practical issues for researchers and members of research ethics committees. *Evidence-Based Midwifery*, *5*(4), 132–137. https://go.gale.com/ps/i.do?p=HRCA&sw=w&issn=14794489&v=2.1&it=r&id=GALE%7CA172050741&sid=googleScholar&linkaccess=abs

Edwards, J. R. (2020). The peaceful coexistence of ethics and quantitative research. *Journal of Business Ethics*, *167*(1), 31–40. https://www.jstor.org/stable/45386639. DOI: 10.1007/s10551-019-04197-6

Kang, E., & Hwang, H.-J. (2020). The Consequences of Data Fabrication and Falsification among Researchers. *Journal of Research and Publication Ethics*, *1*(2), 7–10. DOI: 10.15722/jrpe.1.2.202009.7

Karmakar, D., Das, A., & Khati, A. (2025). Building Ethical Foundations: Educating Researchers for Responsible Use of AI. In Chakraborty, S. (Ed.), (pp. 163–190). Advances in Human and Social Aspects of Technology. IGI Global., DOI: 10.4018/979-8-3693-9035-1.ch008

Palanski, M., Newman, A., Leroy, H., Moore, C., Hannah, S., & Den Hartog, D. (2021). Quantitative research on leadership and business ethics: Examining the state of the field and an agenda for future research. *Journal of Business Ethics*, *168*(1), 109–119. https://idp.springer.com/authorize/casa?redirect_uri=https://link.springer.com/article/10.1007/s10551-019-04267-9&casa_token=3IBckg96A7wAAAAA:Rd7UiM22ZZ3pOkcpXbfXdGRowJWUSeo_8amyATaxHC6BdCxaA_3mwLhgxFvGcQZfY2H3DSxI1q1LA79w_g. DOI: 10.1007/s10551-019-04267-9

Panter, A. T., & Sterba, S. K. (2011). Ethics in quantitative methodology: An introduction. In *Handbook of ethics in quantitative methodology* (pp. 1–11). Routledge., https://api.taylorfrancis.com/content/chapters/edit/download?identifierName=doi&identifierValue=10.4324/9780203840023-1&type=chapterpdf DOI: 10.4324/9780203840023

Pellegrina, D., & Helmy, M. (2025). AI for scientific integrity: Detecting ethical breaches, errors, and misconduct in manuscripts. *Frontiers in Artificial Intelligence*, *8*, 1644098. Advance online publication. DOI: 10.3389/frai.2025.1644098 PMID: 40964145

Pennock, R. T. (2018). Beyond research ethics: How scientific virtue theory reframes and extends responsible conduct of research. In *Cultivating Moral Character and Virtue in Professional Practice*. Routledge. DOI: 10.4324/9781315182414-13

Powell, T. C. (2020). Can Quantitative Research Solve Social Problems? Pragmatism and the Ethics of Social Research. *Journal of Business Ethics*, *167*(1), 41–48. DOI: 10.1007/s10551-019-04196-7

Rani, R., & Sharma, R. K. (2012). Ethical Consideration in Research. *International Journal of Nursing Education*, *4*(1). http://ijone.org/scripts/IJONE%20Jan-June%202012.pdf#page=49

Rao, K. N., Mair, M., Arora, R. D., Dange, P., & Nagarkar, N. M. (2024). Misconducts in research and methods to uphold research integrity. *Indian Journal of Cancer*, *61*(2), 354–359. DOI: 10.4103/ijc.ijc_4_23 PMID: 39016268

Resnik, D. B. (2014). Data Fabrication and Falsification and Empiricist Philosophy of Science. *Science and Engineering Ethics*, *20*(2), 423–431. DOI: 10.1007/s11948-013-9466-z PMID: 23982326

Rhodes, R. (2005). Rethinking Research Ethics. *The American Journal of Bioethics*, *5*(1), 7–28. DOI: 10.1080/15265160590900678 PMID: 16036651

Rosnow, R. L., & Rosenthal, R. (2013). Quantitative methods and ethics. *The Oxford Handbook of Quantitative Methods*, *1*, 32–54. https://books.google.com/books?hl=en&lr=&id=kOqOqVMgfzYC&oi=fnd&pg=PA32&dq=ethics+in+quantitative+research+&ots=-ARaEoQxTr&sig=xLtRbd2OwevYCyzcoFT0Luqo-S0

Rossouw, T. M., van Zyl, C., & Pope, A. (2014). Responsible conduct of research: Global trends, local opportunities. *South African Journal of Science*, *110*(1–2), 1–6. http://www.scielo.org.za/scielo.php?script=sci_abstract&pid=S0038-23532014000100011&lng=en&nrm=iso&tlng=en. DOI: 10.1590/sajs.2014/20130103

Steneck, N. H., & Bulger, R. E. (2007). The History, Purpose, and Future of Instruction in the Responsible Conduct of Research. *Academic Medicine*, *82*(9), 829–834. DOI: 10.1097/ACM.0b013e31812f7d4d PMID: 17726385

Watson, J. C., II, & Etzel, E. F. (2019). *Ethical and legal issues in sport and performance psychology.* https://psycnet.apa.org/record/2019-05400-041

Webster, S., Lewis, J., & Brown, A. (2013). Considerations in qualitative research. *Qualitative Research Practice: A Guide for Social Science Students and Researchers, 1*, 77. https://www.torrossa.com/gs/resourceProxy?an=5017584&publisher=FZ7200#page=102

Wible, J. R. (2016). Scientific misconduct and the responsible conduct of research in science and economics. *Review of Social Economy*, *74*(1), 7–32. DOI: 10.1080/00346764.2016.1135598

Chapter 14
I Think, Therefore I Plagiarize:
The Eros of Authorship in Times of Artificial Intelligence

Nuno Sousa
http://orcid.org/0000-0002-5146-8514
Centro de Estudos Clássicos, Faculdade de Letras, Universidade de Lisboa, Portugal

ABSTRACT

Generative Artificial Intelligence (AI) disrupts not only textual production but also the epistemic foundations of authorship, originality, and academic integrity in higher education. This chapter critically examines the erosion of authorship as an ethical and subjective practice under linguistic automation. Drawing on philosophy of technology, epistemology, and pedagogy, it shows how detection-first responses risk inequity and due-process failures, while international guidance now prioritises assessment redesign and transparency. We introduce the EROS framework (Ethics, Reflexivity, Originality, Situatedness) to re-conceptualise integrity through accountability, process evidence, and contextualised originality. The chapter details a 12-point blueprint, rubrics, and governance mechanisms, illustrating with vignettes and decision trees how integrity can be safeguarded without punitive overreach. Ultimately, it argues for reclaiming authorship as an existential and creative act, fostering critical co-authorship with machines and hermeneutic responsibility in an AI-saturated academy.

DOI: 10.4018/979-8-3373-5586-3.ch014

INTRODUCTION: FROM INNOVATION TO EPISTEMIC DISRUPTION

The mainstreaming of generative AI has precipitated a discursive shift: from isolated concerns about plagiarism detection to a broader interrogation of what counts as authorship and authenticity in knowledge-making. While previous waves of educational technology reshaped delivery and access, Generative AI intervenes in the production of discourse itself, rendering porous the boundary between human and machinic agency. This is not merely another iteration of digital literacy challenges; it is a reconfiguration of the symbolic economy in which higher education trades.

At stake are not only assessment practices but also the ethical architecture of the university. Detection-first responses, however understandable in the short term, risk entrenching coercive governance and reproducing inequities, particularly for multilingual and non-native writers, who have been shown to be disproportionately misclassified by AI-detection systems (Liang et al., 2023). Nor is a technological fix forthcoming: major developers have publicly acknowledged the difficulty of reliable AI-text detection at scale, and sector guidance increasingly cautions against over-reliance on automated indicators (OpenAI, 2023; Turnitin, 2023, 2025; Webb, 2025). If detection is fragile, then the path to integrity must be reconstructed elsewhere: in pedagogy, in institutional design, and in a renewed concept of authorship as an ethical relation to language and knowledge.

To situate the argument that follows, it is useful to visualise how generative AI mediates the relationship between authorship, originality, and academic integrity and how this mediation cascades into assessment, policy, and equity. The schematic below organises these dynamics at a glance, foregrounding the locus of disruption and the downstream domains it reconfigures (see Figure 1).

Figure 1. **Epistemic disruption map: How generative AI reframes authorship, originality, and academic integrity across assessment, policy, and equity domains**

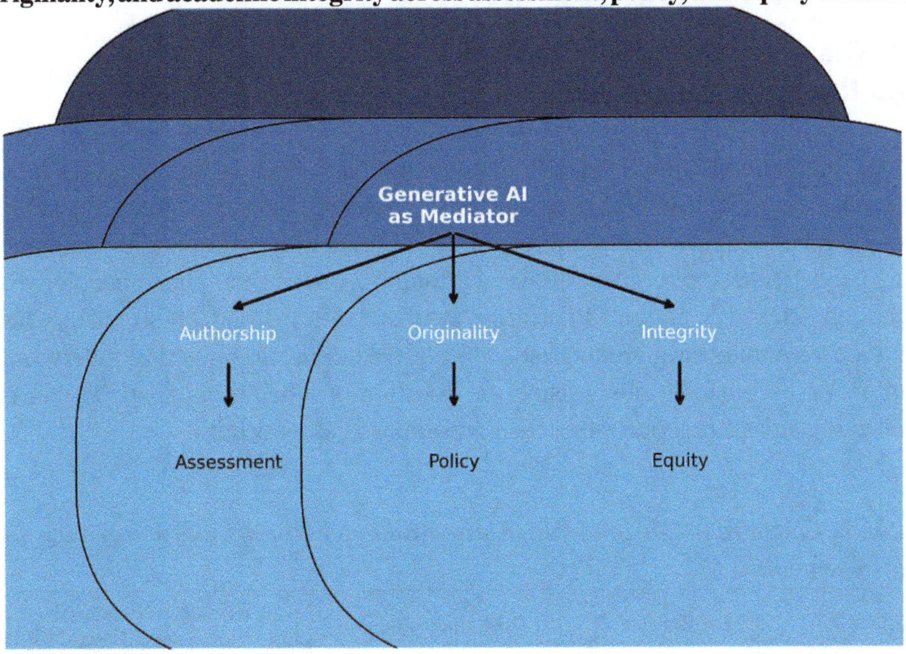

Read as a programmatic overview, Figure 1 clarifies that debates about plagiarism are only a surface symptom of a deeper reconfiguration in meaning-making. The next section therefore turns to the conceptual genealogy of authorship, tracing how classical lenses already anticipate and are challenged by the conditions of AI-mediated writing.

This chapter develops that reconstruction in four moves. First, we situate Generative AI within a genealogy of authorship, from Foucault's author function to Ricoeur's hermeneutics of selfhood and Baudrillard's simulacral condition. Second, we diagnose the limits and risks of detectionism as a governance paradigm, mapping its inequities and epistemic side effects. Third, we introduce the **EROS Framework** (Ethics, Reflexivity, Originality, and Situatedness), as a normative and practical orientation for AI-mediated authorship. Finally, we translate the framework into an actionable redesign of assessment, outlining methods, rubrics, and institutional policies capable of sustaining integrity without defaulting to punitive automation.

2. THEORETICAL LENSES: AUTHORSHIP UNDER AUTOMATION

2.1 The author-function, narrative identity, and the fate of originality

Foucault famously historicized the author as a function that organizes and limits meaning, a dispositif tethering discourse to a sovereign subject (Foucault, 1977). Generative AI exposes the contingency of this function by simulating signature traits, style, cohesion, argumentative scaffolding, without the phenomenology of intention. Ricoeur's notion of narrative identity (1992) is equally strained: when texts are assembled through stochastic models, the diachronic unity that underwrites authorship becomes porous, raising the question of whether authenticity can be reconstructed as a practice rather than presupposed as an origin.

Table 1. Comparative theoretical lenses on authorship, risk, and integrity in the age of generative AI

Author	Key Concept	Risk Diagnosis	Contribution to Integrity/ Assessment Design
Foucalt (1977)	Author-function	Authorship as institutional function	Reframe integrity as discursive governance
Ricoeur (1992)	Narrative identity	Risk of fragmented meaning	Hermeneutic accountability in authorship
Baudrillard (1994)	Simulacra	Collapse of originality into simulation	Critique reliance on detection/ representation
Haraway (1991)	Situated knowledges	Risk of universalizing machine epistemics	Stress contextual integrity and positionality
Daston & Galison (2007)	Objectivity	Tension between mechanical objectivity and judgement	Encourage trained judgment in evaluation
Stiegler (2010)	Technics as prosthesis	Delegation of memory and thought	Co-authorship with technology; care in education
Floridi (2013)	Ethics of information	Diffusion of responsibility in the infosphere	Embed ethical disclosure practices

Before prescribing policy responses, we need a genealogy of the authorial subject. The timeline below aligns pivotal theoretical lenses, from the author function to posthuman co-authorship, to show how each problematises intention, identity, and originality in ways that are amplified by Generative AI (see Figure 2).

Figure 2. **From the "author function" to AI-mediated authorship: A schematic genealogy of concepts shaping academic authorship**

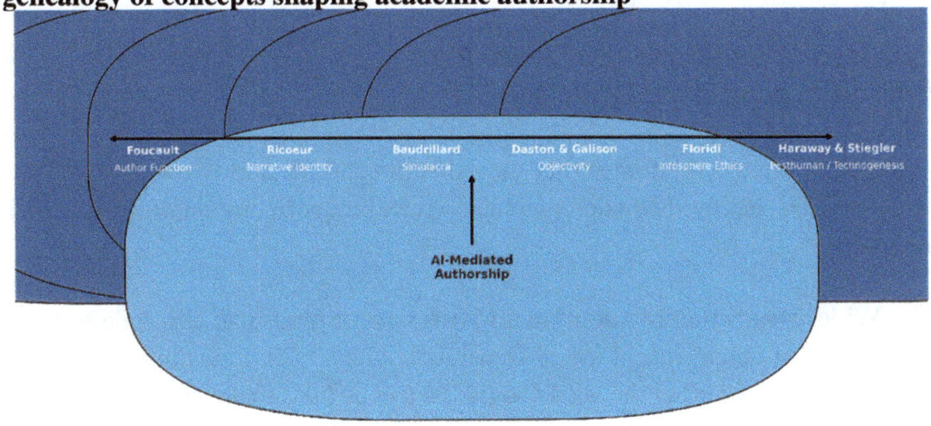

This genealogy motivates a shift from origin-based notions of authenticity to practice-based accountability. Building on this theoretical scaffolding, the chapter next examines how detection-first governance collides with equity, validity, and due-process constraints.

2.2 Simulacra, objectivity, and the digital epistemic regime

Baudrillard's insight that signs can precede and produce the real (1994) finds a technical substrate in Generative AI autoregressive assemblages. What appears a original may be a hyperreal remix within high-dimensional representational spaces. Daston and Galison's (2007) history of objectivity reminds us that scientific ideals mutate with instruments; similarly, ideals of originality must be rethought when instruments write. Floridi's information ethics (2013) provides a pivot: integrity becomes the governance of informational flows and transformations, not merely the policing of origins. The question, then, is how to cultivate authorship as an ethical modulation of informational resources in a socio-technical system.

2.3 Posthuman co-authorship and technics of memory

Haraway's cyborg politics and Stiegler's account of tertiary retention (technical memory) illuminate authorship as always-already distributed across devices, archives, and protocols. Generative AI radicalizes this distribution, rendering co-authorship with non-human systems explicit. If authenticity cannot rest on isolation, it must rest on accountability, a traceable, reflexive relation to sources, prompts, revisions, and decisions constitutive of the text.

2.4 State of Evidence (2023–2025): detection, policy, and practice

Recent literature reinforces that the AI/authorship debate is not resolved by total detection, but by methodological and ethical reconfiguration of writing and assessment:

- **Widespread student adoption and assessment pressure:** UK-wide surveys report very high student use of Generative AI by 2025 (including in assessed tasks), underscoring the need for assessment designs that evidence cognitive agency and hermeneutic accountability (HEPI/Kortext, 2025);
- **Limits, bias, and evasibility of detectors:** While detectors can flag some unedited model text, performance degrades under trivial paraphrase or humanization. False positives disproportionately affect non-native writers (Liang et al., 2023). Research reports incremental robustness advances but persistent trade-offs and validity concerns for high-stakes use (Webb, 2025);
- **Policy pivot toward design and transparency:** International and national bodies converge on rejecting purely punitive responses, recommending responsible-use policies, disclosure, staff development, and assessment redesign (UNESCO, 2025; QAA, 2024/2025; EDUCAUSE, 2025);
- **From student integrity to research integrity:** In 2025 the focus extends to research practices (e.g., opacity, hallucination, privacy), with recommendations for disclosure and accountability across the research lifecycle (Bjelobaba et al., 2025).

Table 2. Risks, evidence (2023–2025), and EROS-aligned implications for integrity governance.

Risk/Claim	Key Evidence (year)	Implication for Policy/ Assessment (EROS link)	Section Cross-ref
Plagiarism vs epistemic disruption	ICAI (2021); Bittle (2025)	Policies must shif from surveillance – epistemic accountability	Sec. 2.4
AI undermines originality	HEPI (2025); QAA (2024-2025)	Redesign assignments toward reasoning/ process-based evidence	Sec. 3
Risk of inequity (bias vs non-native writers)	Liang et al. (2023)	Fairness audits; Multilingual calibration	Sec. 3.1

continued on following page

Table 2. Continued

Risk/Claim	Key Evidence (year)	Implication for Policy/ Assessment (EROS link)	Section Cross-ref
From student integrity to research integrity	Bjelobaba et al. (2025); UNESCO (2025)	Extend EROS to publication ethics, data disclosure	Sec. 7
Institutional fragmentation	EDUCAUSE (2025)	Strategic, system-level alignment required	Sec. 8

3. INTEGRITY UNDER STRAIN: DETECTIONISM, GOVERNANCE, AND EQUITY

3.1 The limits of detection

Institutions have sought assurance in AI detectors. Yet prominent tools have been deprecated or explicitly qualified for low accuracy (OpenAI, 2023), and vendor guidance cautions against over-interpretation, noting false positives and the need to triangulate evidence (Turnitin, 2023, 2025). Empirical studies highlight disparate impacts on non-native English writers (Liang et al., 2023). A detectionist posture risks epistemic injustice and due-process failures. Integrity cannot be reduced to classifier thresholds.

Institutional responses often default to detectionism. Yet the governance pathway that begins with a low or ambiguous detector signal can rapidly escalate to harmful outcomes. The flowchart below contrasts that pathway with a due-process model grounded in triangulated evidence and dialogic defense (see Figure 3).

Figure 3. **Detectionism risk pathway and a due-process alternative based on triangulated evidence and dialogic defense**

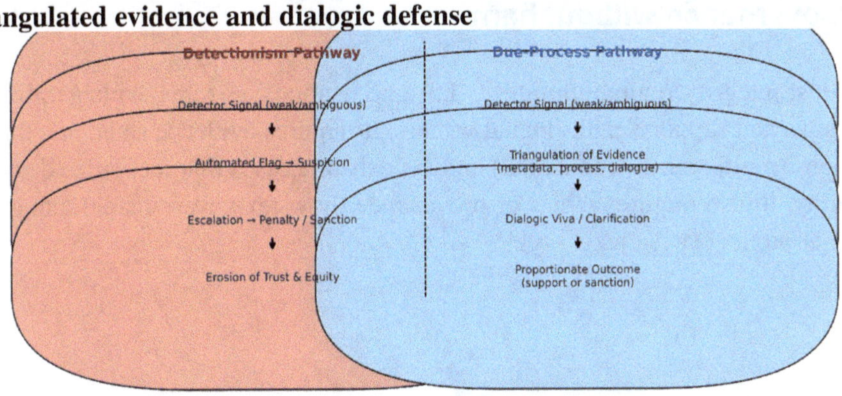

By reframing detector outputs as *weak signals* rather than dispositive evidence, Figure 3 anchors integrity in procedure rather than suspicion. This frames the normative turn of the chapter: a positive account of AI-mediated authorship operationalised in the **EROS** framework.

Table 3. Known limitations and fairness concerns in AI-text detection, with recent sources

Limitation	Reference	Implication
Bias against non-native writers	Liang et al. (2023)	False positives risk inequity
Evasion via paraphrasing/ humanization	Zhou et al. (2025)	Weak reliability under adversarial use
Ambiguity at low probability scores	Turnitin (2023)	Unsuitable for high-stakes decisions
Obsolescence of detectors	Webb (2025); Turnitin (2025)	Tools outdated quickly by model advances
Trade-offs in improve detectors	Zhou et al. (2025)	Gains in precision, losses in fairness

3.2 Values, not scores

The International Center for Academic Integrity anchors integrity in values, honesty, trust, fairness, respect, responsibility, and courage (ICAI, 2021). GenAI makes these not less but more salient. Policies should balance transparent expectations, formative education, and proportionate responses. UNESCO's guidance likewise urges human-centred, capacity-building approaches to GenAI in education (UNESCO, 2025).

3.3 Governance without harm

A just integrity regime minimizes false accusations, ensures explainability of decisions, and supports multilingual writers. It requires evidence standards for allegations (multi-source, contextual) and appeals processes that recognize detector fallibility. It also requires ethics of provenance (how texts were made) alongside ethics of product (what texts say).

4. THE EROS FRAMEWORK FOR AI-MEDIATED AUTHORSHIP

We propose **EROS** (Ethics, Reflexivity, Originality, Situatedness), as a conceptual and practical scaffold for authorship in AI-suffused academia. The acronym is not ornamental: it re-centers the EROS of writing as desire-infused commitment to truth-seeking and shared understanding.

- ✓ **E – Ethics:**
  - o Declare permissible and impermissible AI uses by task type;
  - o Require disclosure statements;
  - o Adopt proportionate, educative responses to misuse;
  - o Align with institutional values and legal norms.
- ✓ **R – Reflexivity:**
  - o Require process artifacts (prompt logs, planning notes, version histories, source trails, revision rationales);
  - o Embed metacognitive reflection on when and why AI was used;
  - o Assess reasoning, not just outcomes.
- ✓ **O – Originality:**
  - o Redefine originality as transformative contribution (conceptual, methodological, or applied) evidenced by argumentation, synthesis, or design choices; emphasize intertextual rigor and critical distance from model outputs.
- ✓ **S — Situatedness:**
  - o Contextualize claims within local data, constraints, and lived experience;
  - o Prioritize tasks that demand place-based analysis, empirical engagement, or domain-specific calibration beyond generic text generation.

The EROS framework translates the foregoing critique into practice. Ethics, Reflexivity, Originality, and Situatedness are not abstract virtues; they specify artefacts, behaviours, and evaluative criteria that make authorship accountable under AI mediation (see Figure 4).

Figure 4. **The EROS framework for AI-mediated authorship: Ethics, Reflexivity, Originality, and Situatedness**

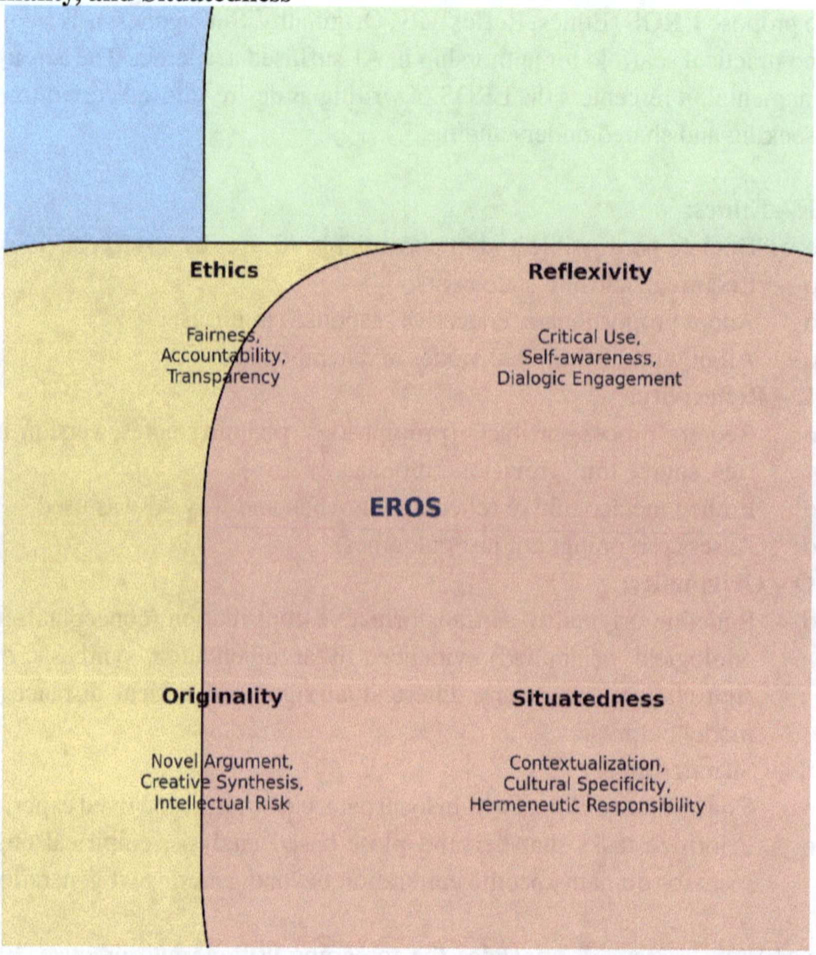

With these four pillars in view, the policy blueprint can be read as an implementation guide: who must do what, when, and with which artefacts, so that authorship becomes traceable and learning demonstrable rather than merely presumed.

Policy Blueprint (12 Points)

1. AI-use taxonomy by assessment type;
2. Syllabus-level AI disclosure;
3. Process portfolios as default;
4. Viva/oral defenses for high-stakes tasks;
5. Staged submissions with feedback loops;
6. Annotated bibliographies and source justification;

7. Local/experimental data integration;
8. Team charters specifying AI roles;
9. Equity safeguards for multilingual writers;
10. Evidence standards for misconduct (multi-modal, contextual);
11. Appeals protocol with human review;
12. Continuous staff development aligned with UNESCO/QAA/Jisc guidance.

Table 4. Operationalizing the EROS blueprint: Stakeholders, artefacts, and evidence

Blueprint Point	Stakeholder(s)	Artefacts	Evidence	Metric (non-punitive)
Disclosure norm	Student, University	Syllabus, disclosure form	Logs, drafts	Transparency index
Process evidence	Student	Portfolio, drafts	Versions, timestamps	Depth of iteration
Viva voce	University, Program	Oral exam, Q&A	Recorded viva	Consistency verification
Research transparency	University; Researcher	Data mgmt; Plan, prereg	Open datasets	FAIR compliance
Institutional framing	University; Services	Integrity policy	Audit reports	Reflexive adoption

5. ASSESSMENT REDESIGN: METHODS AND RUBRICS

5.1 Methods that reward thinking over outsourcing

- ✓ **Dialogic vivas** (10–15 minutes) anchored in submitted work; probes focus on decision paths, counter-arguments, and limitations;
- ✓ **Process portfolios** compiling drafts, prompt histories, reflection memos, and decision logs;
- ✓ **Situated case clinics** using local datasets, institutional policies, or field observations;
- ✓ **Design critiques** where students justify model selection, prompt strategies, and post-editing;
- ✓ **Civic-ethics briefs** requiring normative argumentation grounded in value frameworks (e.g., ICAI) and policy constraints.

Figure 5 depicts an assessment pipeline that privileges reasoning trajectories over product-only evaluation. Each stage generates evidence of learning, from task design to provenance, enabling proportionate decisions and meaningful feedback.

Figure 5. **Assessment pipeline prioritising reasoning and provenance over product-only evaluation**

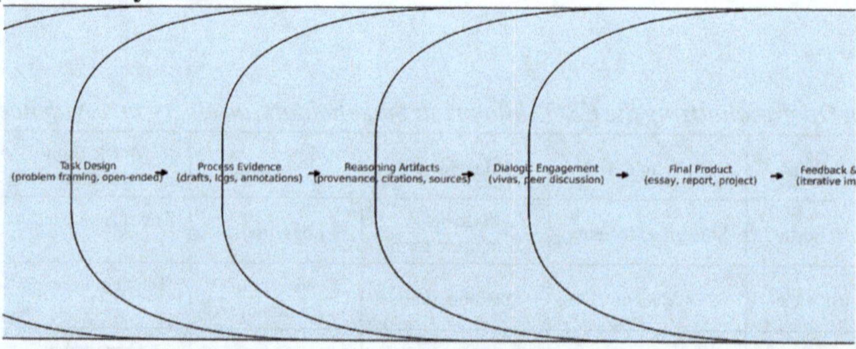

Operationally, the pipeline synchronises with rubric design: criteria assess argumentation, evidence and attribution, reflexivity, originality, and communication. The next tables instantiate these expectations and distribute responsibilities across stakeholders.

5.2 Rubric exemplars (condensed)

- ✓ **Argumentation (30%)**: Clarity, coherence, intellectual risk-taking, counterfactual reasoning;
- ✓ **Evidence & Attribution (25%)**: Depth, diversity, and proper citation; transparent provenance of AI assistance;
- ✓ **Reflexivity (20%)**: Insight into choices, constraints, and ethical trade-offs; quality of reflection artifacts;
- ✓ **Originality (15%)**: Transformative synthesis or contributions; context-sensitive novelty.
- ✓ **Communication (10%)**: Style, structure, audience-appropriate register.

Table 5. Condensed rubric for AI-aware academic writing and argumentation

Criterion	Excelent (30%)	Strong (25%)	Adequate (20%)	Weak (10-15%)
Argument originality	Critical engagement, AI integrated reflexively	Balanced originality e AI	Depedent on AI texto, some reflection	Uncritical reliance
Evidence and citation	Transparent, triangulated	Mostly transparente	Limite disclosure	Opaque use
Process documentation	Drafts, portfolio clear	Partial documentation	Minimal	Absent
Language and coherence	Academic, critical tone	Generally coherent	Some AI hallucinations	Poor fluency
Ethical reflection	Strong ethical awareness (AI limits, risks)	Moderate reflection	Minimal	Absent

5.3 Guardrails and equity

Use plain-language rubrics; provide language-support resources; prohibit sole reliance on detectors; implement blinded second-marking for contested cases; maintain records of evidence review.

6. VIGNETTES: FAILURE MODES AND TRANSFORMATIONS

- **Vignette A - The False Positive:**
    - A multilingual student is flagged at a low AI-indicator percentage. Applying the policy blueprint, staff do not escalate based on score alone; They request process artifacts and hold a dialogic viva. The student demonstrates independent development, and the flag is dismissed. Lesson: evidence standards and appeals protect integrity and equity.
- **Vignette B -The Invisible Co-Author:**
    - A class permits AI brainstorming but not drafting. A student submits fluent prose with shallow argumentation. In a viva, they cannot defend key claims. The case is treated as insufficient learning rather than misconduct, with a redesign plan focusing on argumentation and process evidence.
- **Vignette C - The Productive Partnership:**
    - A capstone cohort uses Generative AI to generate design alternatives, then critically evaluates and integrates them into a prototype using local

stakeholder data. Provenance is documented; originality resides in evaluative judgment and contextual adaptation.

The decision tree below consolidates the vignettes into a single procedure. It shows how weak signals trigger evidence gathering, when a short viva is indicated, and how to distinguish learning needs from misconduct in a proportionate, auditable manner (see Figure 6).

Figure 6. **From suspicion to proportionate outcome: A decision tree operationalising due-process integrity**

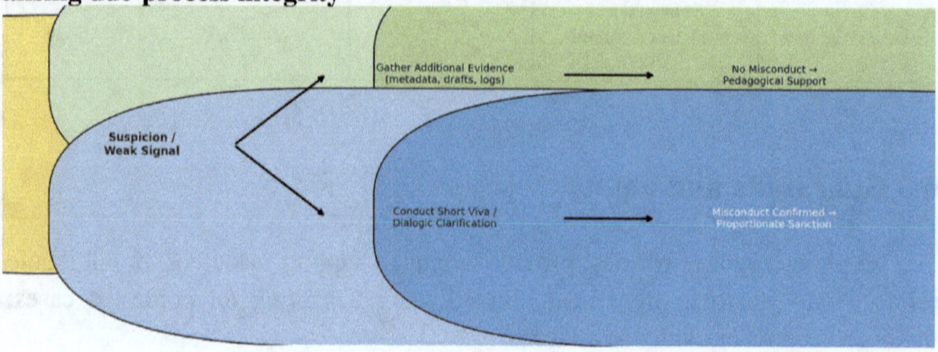

Because the process is evidence-led, it protects both equity and standards. Institutions must, however, resource the workflow, hence the implementation roadmap that follows.

7. OBJECTIONS AND REPLIES

- **Allowing AI corrodes standards**
  - Standards anchored in rote production were always weak proxies for thinking. Redesigning assessments to evidence reasoning strengthens standards;
- **We must detect to deter**
  - Detection may deter some behaviours; it also harms innocents and incentivizes adversarial workarounds. Proportionate use as one input among many can be justified; sole reliance cannot;
- **Generative AI makes originality impossible**
  - Originality is not virginity; it is transformation under constraints. Context, judgment, and synthesis remain humanly accountable, even when tools assist.

8. IMPLEMENTATION ROADMAP (INSTITUTIONAL LEVEL)

- ✓ **Phase 1 - Orientation (0–3 months):** Adopt AI-use taxonomy; publish values-aligned policy; run staff workshops on assessment redesign:
- ✓ **Phase 2 - Pilots (3–9 months):** Select 3–5 courses for pilot rubrics and process portfolios; set up equity safeguards; document outcomes;
- ✓ **Phase 3 - Scale (9–18 months):** Embed EROS-aligned practices in program standards; establish an appeals panel; integrate pilot data into continuous improvement.

The roadmap specifies sequencing and deliverables across three phases. By marking policy, pilots, and scale-up milestones, it aligns academic integrity with programme review cycles and staff development (see Figure 7).

Figure 7. **Institutional implementation roadmap for EROS-aligned integrity governance**

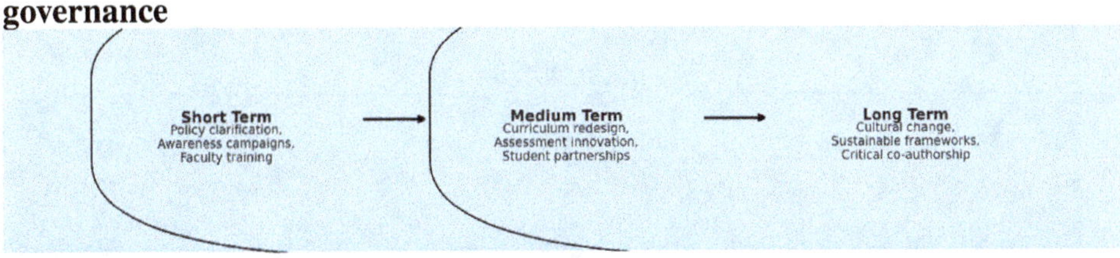

Governance: Create an Academic Integrity & AI Committee; set evidence standards; require detector results to be contextualized and corroborated.

Embedding these practices invites systematic study. The closing section therefore sets a research agenda to evaluate efficacy, equity, and trust over time.

Table 6. Governance Matrix (Responsible, Accountable, Consulted and Informed - RACI)

Task/Area	Programme	Department	Central Services	Students	Integrity Committee
Policy design	R	A	C	I	A
Faculty training	A	R	C	I	C
Evidence standards	C	R	A	I	A
Appeals and fairness	I	C	R	C	A

9. RESEARCH AGENDA

✓ Authorship-provenance protocols (version control, content credentials) versus pedagogical process audits;
✓ Equity impacts across languages and disciplines; mitigation strategies;
✓ Longitudinal effects of EROS-aligned assessment on learning outcomes and trust climates;
✓ Comparative studies of detection-reliant vs. pedagogy-first regimes.

To ensure that practice evolves with evidence, Figure 8 maps priority domains and methods. It links provenance protocols, equity analysis, longitudinal learning outcomes, and comparative governance regimes to appropriate study designs.

Figure 8. **Research agenda map: Methods and domains for studying AI-mediated authorship and integrity**

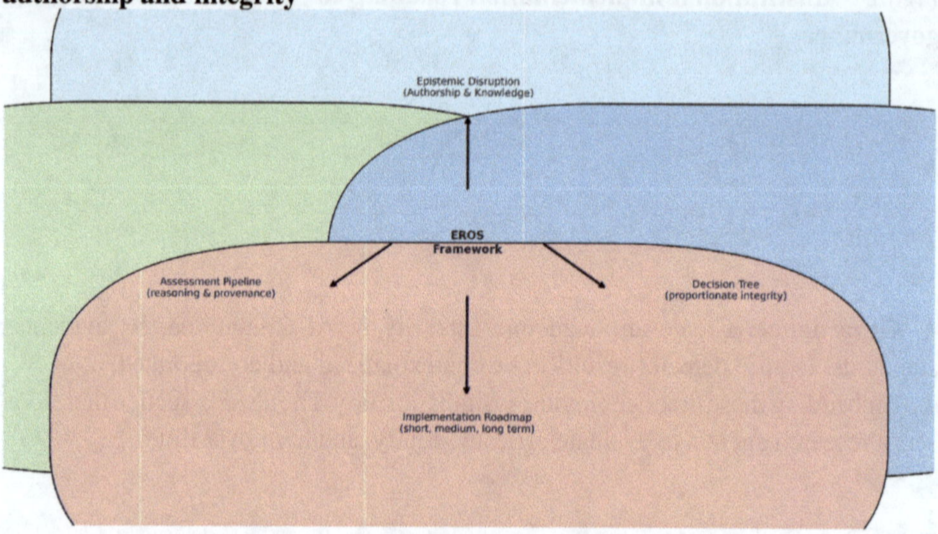

Taken together, these lines of inquiry provide continuous feedback into assessment, policy, and staff development, closing the loop between theory, governance, and pedagogy outlined throughout the chapter.

10. CONCLUSION: RECLAIMING THE DESIRE TO KNOW

If Generative AI unsettles the author as origin, it also invites the author as custodian: one who tends to sources, arguments, and audiences with care. The desire to know, to persuade, to be persuaded, to remake the world with words, survives automation when institutions reward thinking as a trajectory, not merely as a deliverable. The task ahead is not to restore a mythical purity of authorship but to design for accountable, situated, and courageous scholarship. That is the charge of integrity in the age of artificial co-authors.

AUTHOR´S NOTE

This chapter is intentionally ambitious and provocatively argued. It can be expanded or trimmed to meet word-count requirements and adapted to discipline-specific contexts. If the publisher requires structured metadata (e.g., "Key Terms & Definitions" immediately after the References), the section above is already formatted accordingly. We further disclose that ChatGPT was used exclusively for grammatical review, language polishing, and the creation of illustrative figures; all ideas, analyses, and conclusions are the authors own, and any remaining errors are our responsibility.

REFERENCES

Baudrillard, J. (1994). *Simulacra and simulation* (Glaser, S. F., Trans.). University of Michigan Press.

Bittle, R., & El-Gayar, O. (2025). Generative AI and academic integrity in higher education. *Information (Basel)*, *16*(4), 296. DOI: 10.3390/info16040296

Bjelobaba, S., Waddington, D., & Weber-Wulff, D. (2025). Maintaining research integrity in the age of generative AI. *International Journal for Educational Integrity*, *21*(18). Advance online publication. DOI: 10.1007/s40979-025-00191-w

Daston, L., & Galison, P. (2007). *Objectivity*. Zone Books.

EDUCAUSE. (2025). *2025 EDUCAUSE AI Landscape Study: Into the Digital AI Divide*. https://library.educause.edu/resources/2025/2/2025-educause-ai-landscape-study

Floridi, L. (2013). *The ethics of information*. Oxford University Press. DOI: 10.1093/acprof:oso/9780199641321.001.0001

Foucault, M. (1977). What is an author? In Bouchard, D. F. (Ed.), *Language, counter-memory, practice: Selected essays and interviews* (Bouchard, D. F., & Simon, S., Trans.). Cornell University Press., https://monoskop.org/images/1/13/Foucault_Michel_Language_Counter-Memory_Practice_Selected_Essays_and_Interviews_1977.pdf

Haraway, D. (1991). *Simians, cyborgs, and women: The reinvention of nature*. Routledge. https://www.routledge.com/Simians-Cyborgs-and-Women-The-Reinvention-of-Nature/Haraway/p/book/9781856492180

HEPI (Higher Education Policy Institute). (2025). *Student Generative AI Survey 2025* (HEPI). https://www.hepi.ac.uk/wp-content/uploads/2025/02/HEPI-Kortext-Student-Generative-AI-Survey-2025.pdf

ICAI (International Center for Academic Integrity). (2021). *The fundamental values of academic integrity* (3rd ed.). https://www.chapman.edu/academics/academic-integrity/_files/the-fundamental-values-of-academic-integrity.pdf

Liang, W., Yuksekgonul, M., Mao, Y., Wu, E., & Zou, J. (2023). GPT detectors are biased against non-native English writers. *Patterns (New York, N.Y.)*, *4*(7), 100779. DOI: 10.1016/j.patter.2023.100779 PMID: 37521038

Open, A. I. (2023). *New AI classifier for indicating AI-written text (retired)*. https://openai.com/blog/new-ai-classifier-for-indicating-ai-written-text

QAA (Quality Assurance Agency for Higher Education). (2024–2025). *QAA advice and resources on generative AI.* https://www.qaa.ac.uk/sector-resources/generative-artificial-intelligence/qaa-advice-and-resources

Ricoeur, P. (1992). *Oneself as another* (Blamey, K., Trans.). University of Chicago Press.

Stiegler, B. (2010). *Taking care of youth and the generations* (Barker, S., Trans.). Stanford University Press.

Turnitin. (2023). *Understanding the false positive rate for sentences of our AI writing detection capability.* https://www.turnitin.com/blog/understanding-the-false-positive-rate-for-sentences-of-our-ai-writing-detection-capability

Turnitin. (2025). *AI writing detection in the classic report view.* https://guides.turnitin.com/hc/en-us/articles/28457596598925-AI-writing-detection-in-the-classic-report-view

UNESCO. (2025). *Guidance for generative AI in education and research* (updated). https://www.unesco.org/en/articles/guidance-generative-ai-education-and-research

Webb, M. (2025). AI detection and assessment – an update for 2025. https://nationalcentreforai.jiscinvolve.org/wp/2025/06/24/ai-detection-assessment-2025/

Zhou, Z., Dong, Y., Du, G., He, Y., Ma, X., Sanabria, R., Liu, R., He, J., Zhang, Z., Liu, W., Cai, Z., Huang, S., & Wan, X. (2025). Kill two birds with one stone: Dynamic perturbations for robust long-text watermarking and effective detection. In *Proceedings of the 2025 Conference of the North American Chapter of the Association for Computational Linguistics (NAACL)* (Long Papers). DOI: 10.18653/v1/2025.naacl-long.446

KEY TERMS AND DEFINITIONS:

Authorship (AI-mediated): A distributed practice of meaning-making that integrates human judgment with algorithmic affordances under conditions of documented accountability;

Academic integrity: A values-based commitment (honesty, trust, fairness, respect, responsibility, courage) shaping teaching, learning, and research practices;

Detectionism: A governance paradigm that privileges automated detection tools as primary arbiters of integrity, often at the expense of due process and equity;

Eros of authorship: The desire-laden, ethical and creative impulse to speak in one's own voice through accountable engagement with sources, audiences, and tools;

Process portfolio: A curated set of artifacts (drafts, prompts, notes, reflections, logs) evidencing the trajectory of thinking and composition;

Provenance (textual): The documented lineage of a text's production, including sources, tool usage, and revision decisions;

Reflexivity: Methodical self-examination of choices, assumptions, and constraints in the production of knowledge;

Situatedness: Contextual anchoring of arguments in local data, disciplinary norms, and lived experience;

Transformative originality: Novel contribution demonstrated through synthesis, problem-framing, or design decisions rather than mere novelty of phrasing;

Viva (dialogic defense): A structured oral examination used to probe understanding, decision paths, and authorship accountability.

Compilation of References

Abbasi, B. N., Wu, Y., & Luo, Z. (2025). Exploring the impact of artificial intelligence on curriculum development in global higher education institutions. *Education and Information Technologies*, *30*(1), 547–581. DOI: 10.1007/s10639-024-13113-z

Abdullah, A. (2025). Integrating artificial intelligence in higher education: a study on adoption and application of AI by business teachers at Turku University of Applied Sciences.

Abou Adel, M. A., Abouelnour, M. M., Alhourani, M. I., & Awad, A. (2025). Towards intelligent universities enhanced with artificial intelligence (AI). Journal of Infrastructure. *Policy and Development*, *9*(1), 10412. DOI: 10.24294/jipd10412

Abulail, R. N., Badran, O. N., Shkoukani, M. A., & Omeish, F. (2025). Exploring the Factors Influencing AI Adoption Intentions in Higher Education: An Integrated Model of DOI, TOE, and TAM. *Computers*, *14*(6), 230. DOI: 10.3390/computers14060230

Achieng, S. A. (2023). Intercultural competence in foreign language teaching and learning. Strategies and challenges. In *17th International conference for Language, Individual & Society* (Vol. 17, pp. 19-26). International Scientific Publications. DOI: 10.62991/LIS1996073068

Agarwal, P., & Vij, A. (2024). Assessing the challenges and opportunities of artificial intelligence in Indian education. *International Journal for Global Academic & Scientific Research*, *3*(1), 36–44. DOI: 10.55938/ijgasr.v3i1.71

Ahmad, S. F., Han, H., Alam, M. M., Rehmat, M., Irshad, M., Arraño-Muñoz, M., & Ariza-Montes, A. (2023). Impact of artificial intelligence on human loss in decision making, laziness and safety in education. *Humanities & Social Sciences Communications*, *10*(1), 311. DOI: 10.1057/s41599-023-01787-8

Ahmed, Z., Shanto, S. S., & Jony, A. I. (2024). Potentiality of generative AI tools in higher education: Evaluating ChatGPT's viability as a teaching assistant for introductory programming courses. *STEM Education*, *4*(3), 165–182. DOI: 10.3934/steme.2024011

Akinwalere, S. N., & Ivanov, V. (2022). Artificial intelligence in higher education: Challenges and opportunities. *Border Crossing*, *12*(1), 1–15. DOI: 10.33182/bc.v12i1.2015

Al Daraai, S. B., Al Maqrashi, M., Al Zakwani, M., & Al Shaikh, Z. (2024). *Integrating AI in higher education*. IGI Global., DOI: 10.4018/979-8-3693-2145-4.ch008

Al Luhaybi, M. (2021). *Explainable machine learning for educational data* (Doctoral dissertation, Brunel University London).

AL-ALosi. A. (2025). Navigating AI adaptation in organizational operations: Challenges, strategies, and ethical considerations. https://doi.org/DOI: 10.31219/osf.io/z78fu_v1

Alamäki, A., Nyberg, C., Kimberley, A., & Salonen, A. O. (2024). *Artificial intelligence literacy in sustainable development : A learning experiment in higher education*. Issue March., DOI: 10.3389/feduc.2024.1343406

Alasadi, E. A., & Baiz, C. R. (2026). Generative artificial intelligence in higher education: A systematic review of perceptions, implementation and pedagogical transformation. *Education and Information Technologies*, *31*, 1553–1580. DOI: 10.1007/s10639-025-13867-0

Alejandro, A. C. N. (2025). Pedagogical shifts in the age of GenAI : Faculty perspectives from a higher education context. *Journal of Pedagogical Sociology and Psychology*, *7*(3).

Aler Tubella, A., Mora-Cantallops, M., & Nieves, J. C. (2024). How to teach responsible AI in Higher Education: Challenges and opportunities. *Ethics and Information Technology*, *26*(1), 1–14. DOI: 10.1007/s10676-023-09733-7

Alexander, B., Ashford-Rowe, K., Barajas-Murph, N., Dobbin, G., Knott, J., McCormack, M., & Weber, N. (2019). *Horizon report 2019 higher education edition* (pp. 3-41). EDU19.

Ali, M. Y., & Richardson, J. (2025). *AI literacy guidelines and policies for academic libraries : A scoping review*. DOI: 10.1177/03400352251321192

Ali, I., Warraich, N. F., & Butt, K. (2025). Acceptance and use of artificial intelligence and AI-based applications in education: A meta-analysis and future direction. *Information Development*, *41*(3), 859–874. DOI: 10.1177/02666669241257206

Aljemely, Y. (2024). *Challenges and best practices in training teachers to utilize artificial intelligence : a systematic review*. Issue October., DOI: 10.3389/feduc.2024.1470853

Al-Kfairy, M., Mustafa, D., Kshetri, N., Insiew, M., & Alfandi, O. (2024, September). Ethical challenges and solutions of generative AI: An interdisciplinary perspective. In *Informatics* (Vol. 11, No. 3, p. 58). Multidisciplinary Digital Publishing Institute. https://doi.org/DOI: 10.3390/informatics11030058

Allen, B., McGough, A. S., & Devlin, M. (2021). Toward a framework for teaching artificial intelligence to a higher education audience. ACM Transactions on Computing Education (TOCE), 22(2), 1-29.

Almalki, M., Alkhamis, M. A., Khairallah, F. M., & Choukou, M. A. (2025). Perceived artificial intelligence readiness in medical and health sciences education: A survey study of students in Saudi Arabia. *BMC Medical Education*, *25*(1), 439. DOI: 10.1186/s12909-025-06995-1 PMID: 40140763

Al-Mughairi, H., & Bhaskar, P. (2024). Exploring the factors affecting the adoption AI techniques in higher education: insights from teachers' perspectives on ChatGPT. *Journal of Research in Innovative Teaching and Learning*. DOI: 10.1108/JRIT-09-2023-0129

Alnasib, B. N. (2023). Factors affecting faculty members' readiness to integrate artificial intelligence into their teaching practices: A study from the Saudi higher education context. *International Journal of Learning. Teaching and Educational Research*, *22*(8), 465–491. DOI: 10.26803/ijlter.22.8.24

Alqawasmi, A. A., Alsalhi, N. R., Eltahir, M. E., Alakashee, B. A., Al-barakat, A. A., & Al, S. M. (2025). Artificial Intelligence : Faculty Awareness and Impact on Digital Transformation Skills and Technological Trends. *Research Article Cite, 17*.

Altabrawee, H., Ali, O. A. J., & Ajmi, S. Q. (2019). Predicting students' performance using machine learning techniques. *JOURNAL OF UNIVERSITY OF BABYLON for pure and applied sciences, 27*(1), 194-205.

Alvarado, H. A. L. (2026). Redefining Teaching in the Age of AI: A Reflective Autoethnography of Becoming a Mathematics Teacher. In *Redefining the Roles of Educators and Students in the AI Era* (pp. 77-98). IGI Global Scientific Publishing. https://doi.org/DOI: 10.4018/979-8-3373-8027-8.ch004

Al-Zahrani, A. M., & Alasmari, T. M. (2024). Exploring the impact of artificial intelligence on higher education: The dynamics of ethical, social, and educational implications. *Humanities & Social Sciences Communications*, *11*(1), 1–12. DOI: 10.1057/s41599-024-03432-4

Al-Zyoud, H. M. M. (2020). The role of artificial intelligence in teacher professional development. Universal Journal of Educational Research, 8(11B), 6263-6272.

Amaewhule, E. C. (2025). Literacy Level and Attitude of Academics towards the Adoption of Artificial Intelligence (AI) in Public Universities in Rivers State. *International Journal of Educational Management, Rivers State University.*, *1*(1), 73-86.

Anderson, J., Nguyen, C. A., & Ucok Hughes, M. (2025). Mapping theory to practice: AI-enhanced teaching theories for fostering diverse perspectives in business education. *Journal of International Education in Business*. DOI: 10.1108/JIEB-07-2024-0081

Anitha, C. (2025). Applications of Natural Language Processing in Chatbot. *Journal of Information Systems Engineering & Management*, *10*(33s), 1099–1106. Advance online publication. DOI: 10.52783/jisem.v10i33s.5936

An, S., Bates, R., Hammock, J., Rugaber, S., & Goel, A. (2018). VERA: popularizing science through AI. In *International Conference on Artificial Intelligence in Education* (pp. 31-35). Cham: Springer International Publishing.

An, Y., Yu, J. H., & James, S. (2025). Investigating the higher education institutions' guidelines and policies regarding the use of generative AI in teaching, learning, research, and administration. *International Journal of Educational Technology in Higher Education*, *22*(1), 10. DOI: 10.1186/s41239-025-00507-3

Aoyagi, M. W., & Portenga, S. T. (2010). The role of positive ethics and virtues in the context of sport and performance psychology service delivery. *Professional Psychology, Research and Practice*, *41*(3), 253–259. https://psycnet.apa.org/record/2010-11935-011. DOI: 10.1037/a0019483

Asselman, A., Khaldi, M., & Aammou, S. (2023). Enhancing the prediction of student performance based on the machine learning XGBoost algorithm. *Interactive Learning Environments*, *31*(6), 3360–3379. DOI: 10.1080/10494820.2021.1928235

Atlas, S. (2023). *ChatGPT for Higher Education and Professional Development: A Guide*.

Bacalso, F. D., Villamor, F. E., Paclipan, C. P., Orquia, C. J. B., Rendon, I. P., Albiso, A. T., & Himang, C. M. (2026, May). Institutional approaches to generative AI management in higher education: a systematic review. In *Frontiers in Education* (Vol. 11, p. 1814426). Frontiers Media SA. https://doi.org/DOI: 10.3389/feduc.2026.1814426

Baeten, T. (2025). *The Influence of Artificial Intelligence Adoption on Educator Perceptions* (Doctoral dissertation, University of Wisconsin--Stout).

Bajwa, N., Tudor, T., Varela, O., & Leonard, K. (2024). Teaching in Higher Education after COVID-19: Optimizing Faculty Time and Effort Using a Proposed Model. *Education Sciences*, *14*(2), 121. DOI: 10.3390/educsci14020121

Baker, J. A. (2021). Artificial intelligence in education: Bringing it all together. In *OECD digital education outlook 2021: Pushing the frontiers with AI, blockchain, and robotics* (pp. 43–56).

Baker, R. S., & Inventado, P. S. (2014). Educational data mining and learning analytics. In Larusson, J. A., & White, B. (Eds.), *Learning analytics: From research to practice* (pp. 61–75). Springer. DOI: 10.1007/978-1-4614-3305-7_4

Balfour, S. (2013). Assessing Writing in MOOCs: Automated Essay Scoring and Calibrated Peer Review. *Research & Practice in Assessment*, *8*, 40–48.

Baran, E., AlZoubi, D., & Morales, A. S. (2023). Design and implementation of an automated classroom analytics system: Stakeholder engagement and mapping. *TechTrends*, *67*(6), 945–954. DOI: 10.1007/s11528-023-00905-2

Barua, P. D., Vicnesh, J., Gururajan, R., Oh, S. L., Palmer, E., Azizan, M. M., Kadri, N. A., & Acharya, U. R. (2022). Artificial intelligence enabled personalised assistive tools to enhance education of children with neurodevelopmental disorders—A review. *International Journal of Environmental Research and Public Health*, *19*(3), 1192. DOI: 10.3390/ijerph19031192

Barus, O. P., Hidayanto, A. N., Handri, E. Y., Sensuse, D. I., & Yaiprasert, C. (2025). Shaping generative AI governance in higher education: Insights from student perception. *International Journal of Educational Research Open*, *8*, 100452. DOI: 10.1016/j.ijedro.2025.100452

Bates, T., Cobo, C., Mariño, O., & Wheeler, S. (2020). Can artificial intelligence transform higher education? *International Journal of Educational Technology in Higher Education*, *17*(1), 42. DOI: 10.1186/s41239-020-00218-x

Batool, A., Zowghi, D., & Bano, M. (2025). AI governance: A systematic literature review. *AI and Ethics*, *5*(3), 3265–3279. DOI: 10.1007/s43681-024-00653-w

Baudrillard, J. (1994). *Simulacra and simulation* (Glaser, S. F., Trans.). University of Michigan Press.

Bayne, S. (2015). Teacherbot: Interventions in automated teaching. *Teaching in Higher Education*, *20*(4), 455–467. DOI: 10.1080/13562517.2015.1020783

Beardsley, M., Albó, L., Aragón, P., & Hernández-Leo, D. (2021). Emergency education effects on teacher abilities and motivation to use digital technologies. *British Journal of Educational Technology*, *52*(4), 1455–1477. 10.1111/bjet.13101. DOI: 10.1111/bjet.13101

Bearman, M., Ryan, J., & Ajjawi, R. (2023). Discourses of artificial intelligence in higher education: A critical literature review. *Higher Education*, *86*(2), 369–385. DOI: 10.1007/s10734-022-00937-2

Bećirović, S., Polz, E., & Tinkel, I. (2025). Exploring students ' AI literacy and its effects on their AI output quality, self - efficacy, and academic performance. *Smart Learning Environments*, *3*(1), 29. Advance online publication. DOI: 10.1186/s40561-025-00384-3

Beckingham, S., Lawrence, J., Powell, S., & Hartley, P. (2024). Using generative AI effectively in higher education. *London: Routledge*, *10*, 9781003482918.

Behera, A., Trivedi, P., Patra, S. K., & Makeni, C. (2025). Artificial intelligence and higher education: A systematic review. *American Journal of STEM Education*, *11*, 27–52. DOI: 10.32674/0x43s107

Bender, E. M., Gebru, T., McMillan-Major, A., & Shmitchell, S. (2021). On the dangers of stochastic parrots: Can language models be too big? *Proceedings of the 2021 ACM Conference on Fairness, Accountability, and Transparency*, 610–623. DOI: 10.1145/3442188.3445922

Berens, J., Schneider, K., Gortz, S., Oster, S., & Burghoff, J. (2019). Early detection of students at risk—Predicting student dropouts using administrative student data and machine learning methods. *Journal of Educational Data Mining*, *11*(3), 1–41.

Beretta, V., Calandra, D., Cho, C. H., Demartini, C., & Biancone, P. (2021) Sustainability Education: Preparing Future Leaders for a Sustainable Economy.

Bimba, A. T., Idris, N., Al-Hunaiyyan, A., Ibrahim, S. U., Mustafa, N., Supa'at, I., & Ahmad, M. Y. (2021). The effects of adaptive feedback on student's learning gains. *International Journal of Advanced Computer Science and Applications*, *12*(7), 68–80. DOI: 10.14569/IJACSA.2021.0120709

Bird, K. A., Castleman, B. L., & Song, Y. (2025). Are algorithms biased in education? Exploring racial bias in predicting community college student success. *Journal of Policy Analysis and Management*, *44*(2), 379–402. 10.1002/pam.22569. DOI: 10.1002/pam.22569

Birks, D., & Clare, J. (2023). Linking artificial intelligence facilitated academic misconduct to existing prevention frameworks. *International Journal for Educational Integrity, 19*(1), 1–10. DOI: 10.1007/s40979-023-00142-3

Birkstedt, T., Minkkinen, M., Tandon, A., & Mäntymäki, M. (2023). AI governance: Themes, knowledge gaps and future agendas. *Internet Research, 33*(7), 133–167. DOI: 10.1108/INTR-01-2022-0042

Bittle, K., & El-Gayar, O. (2025). Generative AI and academic integrity in higher education: A systematic review and research agenda. *Information (Basel), 16*(4), 296. DOI: 10.3390/info16040296

Bjelobaba, S., Waddington, D., & Weber-Wulff, D. (2025). Maintaining research integrity in the age of generative AI. *International Journal for Educational Integrity, 21*(18). Advance online publication. DOI: 10.1007/s40979-025-00191-w

Bleikher, O., Snegurova, V., Rvanova, A., Gotskaya, I., & Nakonechnaya, O. (2025). *ARTIFICIAL INTELLIGENCE (AI) LITERACY AMONG TEACHERS : THE CASE OF ITMO UNI- VERSITY LA ALFABETIZACIÓN EN INTELIGENCIA ARTIFICIAL (IA) EN LOS DOCEN- TES : EL CASO DE LA UNIVERSIDAD ITMO* (Vol. 21, Issue 106).

Boison, R. B. (2025). Barriers and Enablers to Artificial Intelligence (AI) Adoption in Administrative Functions in Public Universities in Ghana: A Case Study of the University of Education, Winneba. *Canadian Journal of Educational and Social Studies, 5*(4). Advance online publication. DOI: 10.53103/cjess.v5i4.377

Bo, N. S. W. (2025). OECD digital education outlook 2023: Towards an effective education ecosystem. *Hungarian Educational Research Journal, 15*(2), 284–289. DOI: 10.1556/063.2024.00340

Bond, M., Khosravi, H., De Laat, M., Bergdahl, N., Negrea, V., Oxley, E., Pham, P., Chong, S. W., & Siemens, G. (2024). A meta systematic review of artificial intelligence in higher education: A call for increased ethics, collaboration, and rigour. *International Journal of Educational Technology in Higher Education, 21*(1), 4. DOI: 10.1186/s41239-023-00436-z

Bonneton-Botté, N., Miramand, L., Bailly, R., & Pons, C. (2023). Teaching and rehabilitation of handwriting for children in the digital age: Issues and challenges. *Children (Basel, Switzerland), 10*(7), 1096. DOI: 10.3390/children10071096

Bostrom, N. (2017). Strategic implications of openness in AI development. *Global Policy, 8*(2), 135–148. DOI: 10.1111/1758-5899.12403

Bower, M., Torrington, J., Lai, J. W. M., Petocz, P., & Alfano, M. (2024). How should we change teaching and assessment in response to increasingly powerful generative Artificial Intelligence? Outcomes of the ChatGPT teacher survey. In *Education and Information Technologies* (Vol. 29, Issue 12). Springer US. DOI: 10.1007/s10639-023-12405-0

Brown, M, McGreal, R and Peters, M. (2023). A Strategic Institutional Response to Micro-Credentials: Key Questions for Educational Leaders. *Journal of Interactive Media in Education*, 2023(1): 7, pp. 1–17. DOI: DOI: 10.5334/jime.801

Brown, M., Mhichil, M. N. G., Beirne, E., & Mac Lochlainn, C. (2021). The Global Micro-Credential Landscape: Charting a New Credential Ecology for Lifelong Learning. *Journal of Learning for Development*, *8*(2), 228–254. DOI: 10.56059/jl4d.v8i2.525

Brown, M., & Nic-Giolla-Mhichil, M. (2022). Unboxing micro-credentials: an inside, upside and downside view (Descifrando las microcredenciales: en qué consisten, ventajas e inconvenientes). *C&E, Cultura y Educación*, *34*(4), 938–973. DOI: 10.1080/11356405.2022.2102293

Brown, R., Sillence, E., & Branley-bell, D. (2025). *AcademAI : Investigating AI Usage*. Attitudes, and Literacy in Higher Education and Research., DOI: 10.1177/00472395251347304

Brugliera, P. (2024). The Effectiveness of Digital Learning Platforms in Enhancing Student Engagement and Academic Performance - Consensus. *Journal of Education, Humanities, and Social Research*, *1*(1), 26–36. Advance online publication. DOI: 10.70088/xq3gy756

Buabbas, A. J., Miskin, B., Alnaqi, A. A., Ayed, A. K., Shehab, A. A., Syed-Abdul, S., & Uddin, M. (2023). Investigating students' perceptions towards artificial intelligence in medical education. [). MD]. *Health Care*, *11*(9), 1298.

Buckingham Shum, S., & Ferguson, R. (2012). Social learning analytics. *Journal of Educational Technology & Society*, *15*(3), 3–26.

Buele, J., & Llerena-aguirre, L. (2025). *Transformations in academic work and faculty perceptions of artificial intelligence in higher education*. Issue July., DOI: 10.3389/feduc.2025.1603763

Buolamwini, J., & Gebru, T. (2018). *Gender Shades: Intersectional Accuracy Disparities in Commercial Gender Classification* Proceedings of the 1st Conference on Fairness, Accountability and Transparency, Proceedings of Machine Learning Research. https://proceedings.mlr.press/v81/buolamwini18a.html

Burger, B., Kanbach, D. K., Kraus, S., Breier, M., & Corvello, V. (2023). On the use of AI-based tools like ChatGPT to support management research. *European Journal of Innovation Management*, *26*(7), 233–241. DOI: 10.1108/EJIM-02-2023-0156

Cabir, M. N. (n.d.). Artificial intelligence-based digital transformation strategy in higher education institutions. https://doi.org/DOI: 10.34190/eciair.19.014

Car i , A., Leoste, J., Iucu, R., Kikkas, K., Tammemäe, K., & Männik, K. (2022). Conceptualizing micro-credentials in the higher education research landscape. A literature review. In *Conference on Smart Learning Ecosystems and Regional Development* (pp. 191-203). Singapore: Springer Nature Singapore.

Castelli, M., & Manzoni, L. (2022). Generative models in artificial intelligence and their applications. *Applied Sciences (Basel, Switzerland)*, *12*(9), 4127. DOI: 10.3390/app12094127

Castro, G. P. B., Chiappe, A., Ramírez-Montoya, M. S., Nieblas, C. A., Barrera Castro, G. P., Chiappe, A.,…Alcántar Nieblas, C. (2025). Key Barriers to Personalized Learning in Times of Artificial Intelligence: A Literature Review. *Applied Sciences, Vol. 15, Page 3103, 15*(6). DOI: 10.3390/app15063103

Cedefop (2023). *Microcredentials for labor market education and training: microcredentials and evolving qualifications systems*. Luxembourg: Publications Office. Cedefop research paper, No 89. https://data.europa.eu/doi/10.2801/566352

Cedefop, (2024). *Microcredentials: striving to combine credibility and agility*. Publications Office of the European Union. https://data.europa.eu/doi/10.2801/966682

Celik, I., Dindar, M., Muukkonen, H., & Järvelä, S. (2022). The promises and challenges of artificial intelligence for teachers: A systematic review of research. *TechTrends*, *66*(4), 616–630. DOI: 10.1007/s11528-022-00715-y

Chadha, A. (2024). Transforming higher education for the digital age. *Journal of Interdisciplinary Studies in Education*, *13*(S1). Advance online publication. DOI: 10.32674/em2qsn46

Chan, C. K. Y. (2023). A comprehensive AI policy education framework for university teaching and learning. *International Journal of Educational Technology in Higher Education*, *20*(1), 38. DOI: 10.1186/s41239-023-00408-3

Chen, A., Wei, Y., Le, H., & Zhang, Y. (2024). Learning-by-teaching with ChatGPT: The effect of teachable ChatGPT agent on programming education. *ArXiv, abs/2412.15226*.

Chen, Q. (2025). Students' Perceptions of AI-Powered Feedback in English Writing: Benefits and Challenges in Higher Education. *International Journal of Changes in Education*. DOI: 10.47852/bonviewIJCE52025580

Chen, X., Zhou, Y., Chen, X., & Zhou, Y. (2025). Open-Source Collaboration and Technological Innovation in the Industrial Software Industry: A Multi-Case Study. *Systems, Vol. 13, Page 433, 13*(6). DOI: 10.3390/systems13060433

Chen, L., Chen, P., & Lin, Z. (2020). Artificial Intelligence in Education: A Review. *IEEE Access : Practical Innovations, Open Solutions*, *8*, 75264–75278. DOI: 10.1109/ACCESS.2020.2988510

Chen, T., & Guestrin, C. (2016, August). Xgboost: A scalable tree boosting system. In *Proceedings of the 22nd acm sigkdd international conference on knowledge discovery and data mining* (pp. 785-794).

Chen, X., Xie, H., & Hwang, G. J. (2020). A multi-perspective study on artificial intelligence in education: Grants, conferences, journals, software tools, institutions, and researchers. *Computers and Education: Artificial Intelligence*, *1*, 100005. DOI: 10.1016/j.caeai.2020.100005

Chen, Z., Chen, C., Yang, G., He, X., Chi, X., Zeng, Z., & Chen, X. (2024). Research integrity in the era of artificial intelligence: Challenges and responses. *Medicine*, *103*(27), e38811. DOI: 10.1097/MD.0000000000038811

Chew, E., & Chua, X. N. (2020). Robotic Chinese language tutor: Personalising progress assessment and feedback or taking over your job? *On the Horizon*, *28*(3), 113–124. DOI: 10.1108/OTH-04-2020-0015

Chiang, Y. H. V., Chang, M., & Chen, N. S. (2024). Can generative AI help realize the shift from an outcome-oriented to a process-outcome-balanced educational practice? *Journal of Educational Technology & Society*, *27*(2), 347–385. https://www.jstor.org/stable/48766179

Chicioreanu, T. D., & Cosma, I. (2017). I Am a Teacher in the Digital Era. What to Choose: Google Classroom or Moodle?. *eLearning & Software for Education, 2*.

Chigwada, J. (2024). A proposed framework for a digital literacy course for artificial intelligence in academic libraries (Vol. 90, Issue 2). DOI: 10.7553/90-2-2388

Chimbunde, P., & Jakachira, G. (2025). Threading through the needle of digital education in Sub-Saharan Africa: Understanding the concerns of university lecturers. *Interactive Learning Environments*, *33*(1), 39–51. DOI: 10.1080/10494820.2024.2335479

Chimpiri, T. R. (2025). AI-augmented ERP systems in higher education: Pathways to digital transformation (pp. 1–7). DOI: 10.1109/ICCIT65724.2025.11167093

Chiu, T. K., Xia, Q., Zhou, X., Chai, C. S., & Cheng, M. (2023). Systematic literature review on opportunities, challenges, and future research recommendations of artificial intelligence in education. *Computers and Education: Artificial Intelligence*, *4*, 100118. DOI: 10.1016/j.caeai.2022.100118

Chubb, J., Cowling, P., & Reed, D. (2022). Speeding up to keep up: Exploring the use of AI in the research process. *AI & Society*, *37*(4), 1439–1457. DOI: 10.1007/s00146-021-01259-0 PMID: 34667374

Chung, C., & Ackerman, D. (2015). Student reactions to classroom management technology: Learning styles and attitudes toward Moodle. *Journal of Education for Business*, *90*(4), 217–223. DOI: 10.1080/08832323.2015.1019818

Clark, D. (2024). *Artificial intelligence for learning: Using AI and generative AI to support learner development*. Kogan Page Publishers.

Clarke, V., & Braun, V. (2017). Thematic analysis. *The Journal of Positive Psychology*, *12*(3), 297–298. DOI: 10.1080/17439760.2016.1262613

Clouder, L., Karakus, M., Cinotti, A., Ferreyra, M. V., Fierros, G. A., & Rojo, P. (2020). Neurodiversity in higher education: A narrative synthesis. *Higher Education*, *80*(4), 757–778. DOI: 10.1007/s10734-020-00513-6

Colangelo, N., Assouline, S. G., & Gross, M. U. M. (Eds.). (2004). *A nation deceived. How schools hold back America's brightest students* (Vol. 2). University of Iowa.

Connelly, L. M. (2014). Ethical considerations in research studies. *Medsurg Nursing*, *23*(1), 54–56. https://go.gale.com/ps/i.do?id=GALE%7CA360608990&sid=googleScholar&v=2.1&it=r&linkaccess=abs&iss PMID: 24707669

Cortina, J. M. (2020). On the whys and hows of quantitative research. *Journal of Business Ethics*, *167*(1), 19–29. https://idp.springer.com/authorize/casa?redirect_uri=https://link.springer.com/article/10.1007/s10551-019-04195-8&casa_token=pFPN_pEjrIEAAAAA:a7jsAzcP8Hm4W6wK6-3f6xraknWh930FRFSHrnaqzlPat7_SpNuyxuBIRici2x7ZxIJ86nCVCjJCbUdRvw. DOI: 10.1007/s10551-019-04195-8

Cosgrove, J., & Cachia, R. (2025). *DigComp 3.0: European Digital Competence Framework* (5th ed.). Publications Office of the European Union., https://publications.jrc.ec.europa.eu/repository/handle/JRC144121

Cotton, D. R. E., Cotton, P. A., & Shipway, J. R. (2024). Chatting and cheating: Ensuring academic integrity in the era of ChatGPT. *Innovations in Education and Teaching International*, *61*(2), 228–239. DOI: 10.1080/14703297.2023.2190148

Council of Europe. (2024). Framework convention on artificial intelligence and human rights, democracy and the rule of law (CETS No. 225). https://www.coe.int/en/web/conventions/full-list?module=treaty-detail&treatynum=225

Crompton, H., & Burke, D. (2023). Artificial intelligence in higher education: The state of the field. *International Journal of Educational Technology in Higher Education*, *20*(1), 22. DOI: 10.1186/s41239-023-00392-8

Crompton, H., & Burke, D. (2024). The educational affordances and challenges of ChatGPT: State of the field. *TechTrends*, *68*(2), 380–392. DOI: 10.1007/s11528-024-00939-0

Cui, R., Xie, X., Fan, L., & Yang, X. (2024, August). The Application and Challenges of Artificial Intelligence in Supporting Educational Innovation. In *2024 4th International Conference on Big Data Engineering and Education (BDEE)* (pp. 38-42). IEEE. DOI: 10.1109/BDEE63226.2024.00014

Cunningham, J. B., & McCrum-Gardner, E. (2007). Power, effect and sample size using GPower: Practical issues for researchers and members of research ethics committees. *Evidence-Based Midwifery*, *5*(4), 132–137. https://go.gale.com/ps/i.do?p=HRCA&sw=w&issn=14794489&v=2.1&it=r&id=GALE%7CA172050741&sid=googleScholar&linkaccess=abs

Dafoe, A. (2018). *AI governance: A research agenda.* Centre for the Governance of AI, Future of Humanity Institute, University of Oxford. https://www.governance.ai/research-paper/agenda

Dai, K. (2025). The Digital Divide and Rural Education — A Study Based on CFPS Data. *International Theory and Practice in Humanities and Social Sciences*, *2*(9), 42–53. Advance online publication. DOI: 10.70693/itphss.v2i9.754

Danault, R. R. (2025). *University of New Hampshire Scholars Repository Adapting to AI : The Evolving Role of Faculty in Higher Education*. University of New Hampshire Scholars Repository Faculty.

Dandachi, I. E. (2024). AI-powered personalized learning: Toward sustainable education. In *Navigating the intersection of business, sustainability and technology* (pp. 109–118). Springer Nature Singapore.

Daston, L., & Galison, P. (2007). *Objectivity*. Zone Books.

Davis, A. J. (2024). AI rising in higher education: Opportunities, risks and limitations. *Asian Education and Development Studies*, *13*(4), 307–319. DOI: 10.1108/AEDS-01-2024-0017

Davis, C., Bush, T., & Wood, S. (2024). Artificial intelligence in education: Enhancing learning experiences through personalized adaptation. [IJCITSM]. *International Journal of Cyber and IT Service Management*, *4*(1), 26–32. DOI: 10.34306/ijcitsm.v4i1.146

Davis, F. D. (1989). Perceived usefulness, perceived ease of use, and user acceptance of information technology. *Management Information Systems Quarterly*, *13*(3), 319–340. DOI: 10.2307/249008

Delello, J. A., Sung, W., Mokhtari, K., Hebert, J., Bronson, A., & De Giuseppe, T. (2025). AI in the classroom: Insights from educators on usage, challenges, and mental health. *Education Sciences*, *15*(2), 113. DOI: 10.3390/educsci15020113

Denny, P., Prather, J., Becker, B. A., Finnie-Ansley, J., Hellas, A., Leinonen, J., Luxton-Reilly, A., Reeves, B. N., Santos, E. A., & Sarsa, S. (2024). Computing education in the era of generative AI. *Communications of the ACM*, *67*(2), 56–67. DOI: 10.1145/3624720

Doan Erlangga, A. P., & Magdalena, Y. (2025). AI-driven transformation of higher education. *Systematic Reviews*, •••, 1–7. DOI: 10.1109/ICCIT65724.2025.11167254

Doe, J., Smith, J., Brown, R., Green, A., White, M., Johnson, E., & Carter, E. (2025). Leveraging deep and reinforcement learning to optimize academic performance in higher education: A comprehensive scoping review. *AI*, *6*(2), 40. DOI: 10.3390/ai6020040

Dogan, M. E., Goru Dogan, T., & Bozkurt, A. (2023). The use of artificial intelligence (AI) in online learning and distance education processes: A systematic review of empirical studies. *Applied Sciences (Basel, Switzerland)*, *13*(5), 3056. DOI: 10.3390/app13053056

Dong, C., Zhang, F., & Dong, C. (2023, February). F. Z. (2023). Book Review: Machine Learning and Human Intelligence: The Future of Education for the 21st Century. *Policy Futures in Education*, *21*(2), 239–240. Advance online publication. DOI: 10.1177/14782103221117655

Duan, Y., Edwards, J. S., & Dwivedi, Y. K. (2019). Artificial Intelligence for Decision Making in the era of Big Data–Evolution, Challenges and Research Agenda. *International Journal of Information Management*, *48*, 63–71. DOI: 10.1016/j.ijinfomgt.2019.01.021

EDUCAUSE. (2025). *2025 EDUCAUSE AI Landscape Study: Into the Digital AI Divide*. https://library.educause.edu/resources/2025/2/2025-educause-ai-landscape-study

Edwards, J. R. (2020). The peaceful coexistence of ethics and quantitative research. *Journal of Business Ethics, 167*(1), 31–40. https://www.jstor.org/stable/45386639. DOI: 10.1007/s10551-019-04197-6

EHEA (2020), *Rome Ministerial Communiqué,* European Higher Education Area (EHEA).

Eke, E. O. (2024). Assessing the readiness and attitudes of Nigerian teacher educators towards adoption of artificial intelligence in educational settings. *Journal of Educational Technology and Online Learning, 7*(4-ICETOL 2024 Special Issue), 473-487.

Elamrani Elhassani, A., Oulamine, A., & Elbarhoumi, F. (2025). Rethinking the adoption of artificial intelligence in higher education: A bibliometric study of barriers, ethical issues, and governance challenges. *IJDAM: International Journal of Digitalization and Applied Management, 2*(2), 97–116. DOI: 10.23882/ijdam.25216

Elken, M., Maassen, P., Nerland, M., Prøitz, T. S., Stensaker, B., & Vabø, A. (2020). *Quality work in higher education*. Springer International Publishing. DOI: 10.1007/978-3-030-41757-4

Ersoy, C. (2025). Inclusive Transformation with Artificial Intelligence: Ethical Aspects, Policies, and Strategic Approaches for Equitable Education. *Pitfalls of AI Integration in Education: Skill Obsolescence, Misuse, and Bias: Skill Obsolescence, Misuse, and Bias*, 271-292

European Commission. (2020). *A European approach to micro-credentials – Output of the microcredentials higher education consultation group – Final report.* European Commission.

European Commission. (2021). *Commission Staff working document: Accompanying the proposal for a Council Recommendation on a European approach to micro-credentials for lifelong learning and employability (SWD(2021) 367),* Brussels. https://eur-lex.europa.eu/legalcontent/EN/TXT/?uri=CELEX:52021SC0367 (accessed on October 22, 2025).

Evangelista, E. D. L. (2025). Ensuring academic integrity in the age of ChatGPT: Rethinking exam design, assessment strategies, and ethical AI policies in higher education. *Contemporary Educational Technology, 17*(1), 1–19. DOI: 10.30935/cedtech/15775

Facione, P. A. (2020). *Critical thinking: What it is and why it counts*. Insight Assessment.

Faisal, E. (2024). Unlock the potential for Saudi Arabian higher education: A systematic review of the benefits of ChatGPT. []). Frontiers Media SA.]. *Frontiers in Education*, *9*, 1325601. DOI: 10.3389/feduc.2024.1325601

Farid, O. (2025). Strategies for leading institutional change in the age of digital transformation. DOI: 10.20944/preprints202504.1846.v1

Farooq, U., Malik, S., & Syed, A. S. (2024). Revolutionizing higher education: The transformative impact of artificial intelligence on teaching, learning, and career preparation. *ShodhKosh Journal of Visual and Performing Arts*, *5*(3). Advance online publication. DOI: 10.29121/shodhkosh.v5.i3.2024.3239

Federspiel, F., Mitchell, R., Asokan, A., Umana, C., & McCoy, D. (2023). Threats by artificial intelligence to human health and human existence. *BMJ Global Health*, *8*(5), e010435. Advance online publication. DOI: 10.1136/bmjgh-2022-010435 PMID: 37160371

Feng, M., Heffernan, N., Collins, K., Heffernan, C., & Murphy, R. (2023). Implementing and Evaluating ASSISTments Online Math Homework Support At large Scale over Two Years: Findings and Lessons Learned. In (pp. 28-40). DOI: 10.1007/978-3-031-36272-9_3

Feuerriegel, S., Hartmann, J., Janiesch, C., & Zschech, P. (2024). Generative AI. *Business & Information Systems Engineering*, *66*(1), 111–126. DOI: 10.1007/s12599-023-00834-7

Fitas, R. (2025). Inclusive education with AI: Supporting special needs and tackling language barriers. *AI and Ethics*, *5*(6), 5729–5757. DOI: 10.1007/s43681-025-00824-3

Fitria, T. N. (2021, December). Artificial intelligence (AI) in education: Using AI tools for teaching and learning process. In *Prosiding seminar nasional & call for paper STIE AAS* (pp. 134-147).

Floridi, L. (2013). *The ethics of information*. Oxford University Press. DOI: 10.1093/acprof:oso/9780199641321.001.0001

Fossland, T., & Tømte, C. E. (2020). Technology as quality work? educational leaders and teachers' use of digital technology. In *Quality work in higher education: organizational and pedagogical dimensions* (pp. 57–77). Springer International Publishing. DOI: 10.1007/978-3-030-41757-4_4

Foucault, M. (1977). What is an author? In Bouchard, D. F. (Ed.), *Language, counter-memory, practice: Selected essays and interviews* (Bouchard, D. F., & Simon, S., Trans.). Cornell University Press., https://monoskop.org/images/1/13/Foucault_Michel_Language_Counter-Memory_Practice_Selected_Essays_and_Interviews_1977.pdf

Fowler, D. S. (2023). AI in Higher Education. *Journal of Ethics in Higher Education*, *3*(3), 127–143. DOI: 10.26034/fr.jehe.2023.4657

Francis, N. J., Jones, S., & Smith, D. P. (2025). Generative AI in higher education: Balancing innovation and integrity. *British Journal of Biomedical Science*, *81*, 14048. DOI: 10.3389/bjbs.2024.14048

Gamage, K., Dehideniya, S., Zhiheng, X., & Tang, X. (2023). ChatGPT and higher education assessments: More opportunities than concerns? *Journal of Applied Learning & Teaching*, *6*(2). Advance online publication. DOI: 10.37074/jalt.2023.6.2.32

Garcia-Ruiz, M. A., Lin, R., Nam, S., Hu, S., Nasir, M., & Santana-Mancilla, P. C. (2026). Integrating AI and XR for Smarter Learning in Computer Science Education: Teaching in the Age of Intelligence and Immersion. In *New Media Applications in Digital Education* (pp. 33-72). IGI Global Scientific Publishing. https://doi.org/ DOI: 10.4018/979-8-3373-5157-5.ch002

Gârdan, I. P., Manu, M. B., Gârdan, D. A., Negoi ă, L. D. L., Pa tiu, C. A., Ghi ă, E., & Zaharia, A. (2025, February). Adopting AI in education: Optimizing human resource management considering teacher perceptions. [). Frontiers Media SA.]. *Frontiers in Education*, *10*, 1488147. DOI: 10.3389/feduc.2025.1488147

Garzón, J., Patiño, E., & Marulanda, C. (2025). Systematic review of artificial intelligence in education: Trends, Benefits, and challenges. *Multimodal Technologies and Interaction*, *9*(8), 84. DOI: 10.3390/mti9080084

Gauthier, T. (2020). The value of microcredentials: The employer's perspective. *The Journal of Competency-Based Education*, *5*(2), 1–6. DOI: 10.1002/cbe2.1209

George, B., & Wooden, O. (2023). Managing the strategic transformation of higher education through artificial intelligence. *Administrative Sciences*, *13*(9), 196. Advance online publication. DOI: 10.3390/admsci13090196

Ge, Z., & Hu, Y. (2020). Innovative application of artificial intelligence (AI) in the management of higher education and teaching. *Journal of Physics: Conference Series*, *1533*(3), 32089. DOI: 10.1088/1742-6596/1533/3/032089

Ghimire, A., & Edwards, J. (2024). From guidelines to governance: A study of AI policies in education. In Olney, A. M., Chounta, I.-A., Liu, Z., Santos, O. C., & Bittencourt, I. I. (Eds.), *Artificial intelligence in education: Posters and late breaking results, workshops and tutorials, industry and innovation tracks, practitioners, doctoral consortium and blue sky* (pp. 299–307). Springer Nature Switzerland., DOI: 10.1007/978-3-031-64312-5_36

Gligorea, I., Cioca, M., Oancea, R., Gorski, A. T., Gorski, H., & Tudorache, P. (2023). Adaptive learning using artificial intelligence in e-learning: A literature review. *Education Sciences, 13*(12), 1216. DOI: 10.3390/educsci13121216

Gobert, J. D. (2023). Inq-ITS: Creating rigorous assessment and real-time support of science learning. *XRDS: Crossroads. The ACM Magazine for Students, 29*(3), 36–40. DOI: 10.1145/3589647

González-Calatayud, V., Prendes-Espinosa, P., & Roig-Vila, R. (2021). Artificial intelligence for student assessment: A systematic review. *Applied Sciences (Basel, Switzerland), 11*(12), 5467. DOI: 10.3390/app11125467

Grace, E. G., Vidhyavathi, P., & Malathi, P. (2023). A study on" AI in education: Opportunities and challenges for personalized learning. *Industrial Engineering Journal, 52*(05), 750–759. DOI: 10.36893/IEJ.2023.V52I05.750-759

Gruenhagen, J. H., Sinclair, P. M., Carroll, J. A., Baker, P. R., Wilson, A., & Demant, D. (2024). The rapid rise of generative AI and its implications for academic integrity: Students' perceptions and use of chatbots for assistance with assessments. *Computers and Education: Artificial Intelligence, 7*, 100273. DOI: 10.1016/j.caeai.2024.100273

Guan, H., Dong, L., & Zhao, A. (2022). Ethical risk factors and mechanisms in artificial intelligence decision making. *Behavioral Sciences (Basel, Switzerland), 12*(9), 343. DOI: 10.3390/bs12090343 PMID: 36135147

Gumasing, M. J. J., Endozo, E. K., Laingo, J. C. C., & Tapucar, W. H. (2023, March). Usability evaluation of online learning management system: Blackboard, Google Classroom and Canvas. In *2023 11th International Conference on Information and Education Technology (ICIET)* (pp. 92-97). IEEE.

Gunder, A., Vito, M., Ramírez, M., & Ford, C. (2025). Beyond AI awareness: How institutions are strategically and pedagogically embedding AI skills development. *Ubiquity Proceedings, 14*, 14. Advance online publication. DOI: 10.5334/uproc.182

Guo, S., Wang, Y., Yu, J., Wu, X., Ayik, B., Watts, F. M., & Zhai, X. (2025). Artificial Intelligence Bias on English Language Learners in Automatic Scoring. *International Conference on Artificial Intelligence in Education*; pp. 268–275. DOI: 10.1007/978-3-031-98462-4_34

Guo, Y. (2021). University classroom teaching model based on decision tree analysis and machine learning. *Mobile Information Systems*, *2021*(1), 6926013. DOI: 10.1155/2021/6926013

Gustilo, L., Ong, E., & Lapinid, M. R. (2024). Algorithmically-driven writing and academic integrity: Exploring educators' practices, perceptions, and policies in AI era. *International Journal for Educational Integrity*, *20*(1), 3. DOI: 10.1007/s40979-024-00153-8

Hadidi, R., & George, J. F. (2023). Potential Uses of AI-Based Platforms in Teaching and Learning. *Journal of the Midwest Association for Information Systems*, *2023*(2), 1–8. DOI: 10.17705/3jmwa.000081

Hahn, M. G., Navarro, S. M. B., Valentín, L. D. L. F., & Burgos, D. (2021). A systematic review of the effects of automatic scoring and automatic feedback in educational settings. *IEEE Access : Practical Innovations, Open Solutions*, *9*, 108190–108198. DOI: 10.1109/ACCESS.2021.3100890

Hamdy, S. M. (2025). Universities Devoid of Teaching Staff " Can AI Replace the Role of Professors in the Near Future? *Arab Journal of Administration*, *45*(6), 451–464. DOI: 10.21608/aja.2024.308915.1687

Haraway, D. (1991). *Simians, cyborgs, and women: The reinvention of nature*. Routledge. https://www.routledge.com/Simians-Cyborgs-and-Women-The-Reinvention-of-Nature/Haraway/p/book/9781856492180

Hariyanto, Kristianingsih, F. X. D., Maharani, R., Hariyanto, Kristianingsih, F. X. D., & Maharani, R. (2025). Artificial intelligence in adaptive education: a systematic review of techniques for personalized learning. *Discover Education; 4:1*, *4*(1). DOI: 10.1007/s44217-025-00908-6

Haroud, S., & Saqri, N. (2025). Generative AI in higher education: Teachers' and students' perspectives on support, replacement, and digital literacy. *Education Sciences*, *15*(4), 396. DOI: 10.3390/educsci15040396

Harry, A. (2023). Role of AI in education. *Interdiciplinary Journal & Hummanity (INJURITY)*, *2*(3). https://radensa.ru/wp-content/uploads/2024/05/Role_of_AI_in_Education.pdf

Harry, A., & Sayudin, S. (2023). Role of AI in Education. [INJURITY]. *Interdiciplinary Journal and Hummanity*, *2*(3), 260–268.

Hartley, K., Hayak, M., & Ko, U. H. (2024). Artificial intelligence supporting independent student learning: An evaluative case study of ChatGPT and learning to code. *Education Sciences*, *14*(2), 120. DOI: 10.3390/educsci14020120

Hashim, S., Omar, M. K., Ab Jalil, H., & Sharef, N. M. (2022). Trends on technologies and artificial intelligence in education for personalized learning: Systematic literature. *Journal of Academic Research in Progressive Education and Development*, *12*(1), 884–903. DOI: 10.6007/IJARPED/v11-i1/12230

Heffernan, N. T., & Heffernan, C. L. (2014). The ASSISTments Ecosystem: Building a Platform that Brings Scientists and Teachers Together for Minimally Invasive Research on Human Learning and Teaching. *International Journal of Artificial Intelligence in Education*, *24*(4), 470–497. DOI: 10.1007/s40593-014-0024-x

Heidari, E., & Ekström, J. (2025). From Paper to Algorithm: A Qualitative Study on Teachers' Perspectives on AI in English Literature Education. https://urn.kb.se/resolve?urn=urn%3Anbn%3Ase%3Ahv%3Adiva-23341

Hennekeuser, D., Vaziri, D. D., Golchinfar, D., Schreiber, D., & Stevens, G. (2024). Enlarged education—Exploring the use of generative AI to support lecturing in higher education. *International Journal of Artificial Intelligence in Education*, •••, 1–33.

Hennekeuser, D., Vaziri, D. D., Golchinfar, D., Schreiber, D., & Stevens, G. (2024). Enlarged education–exploring the Use of Generative AI to support lecturing in Higher Education. *International Journal of Artificial Intelligence in Education*, •••, 1–33. DOI: 10.1007/s40593-024-00424-y

HEPI (Higher Education Policy Institute). (2025). *Student Generative AI Survey 2025* (HEPI). https://www.hepi.ac.uk/wp-content/uploads/2025/02/HEPI-Kortext-Student-Generative-AI-Survey-2025.pdf

Hirankerd, K., & Kittisunthonphisarn, N. (2020). E-learning management system based on reality technology with AI. *International Journal of Information and Education Technology, 10*(4), 259-264. doi: https://doi.org/DOI: 10.18178/ijiet.2020.10.4.1373

Hojeij, Z. (2025). Strategic leadership for AI integration in higher education. Advances in Computational Intelligence and Robotics Book Series, 329–348. DOI: 10.4018/979-8-3693-7332-3.ch020

Holmes, W., Anastopoulou, S., Schaumburg, H., & Mavrikis, M. (2018). Technology-enhanced personalised learning: Untangling the evidence.

Holmes, W., Bialik, M., & Fadel, C. (2019). *Artificial intelligence in education: Promises and implications for teaching and learning*. Center for Curriculum Redesign.

Holmes, W., & Porayska-Pomsta, K. (2022). *The ethics of artificial intelligence in education: Practices, challenges, and debates*. Routledge., DOI: 10.4324/9780429329067

Holmes, W., Porayska-Pomsta, K., Holstein, K., Sutherland, E., Baker, T., Shum, S. B., Santos, O. C., Rodrigo, M. T., Cukurova, M., Bittencourt, I. I., & Koedinger, K. R. (2022). Ethics of AI in education: Towards a community-wide framework. *International Journal of Artificial Intelligence in Education, 32*(3), 504–526. DOI: 10.1007/s40593-021-00239-1

Holmes, W., & Tuomi, I. (2022). State of the art and practice in AI in education. *European Journal of Education, 57*(4), 542–570. DOI: 10.1111/ejed.12533

Holstein, K., & Doroudi, S. (2021). Equity and artificial intelligence in education: will" aied" amplify or alleviate inequities in education? *arXiv preprint arXiv:2104.12920.*

Holstein, K., Vaughan, J. W., Daumé, H., Dudik, M., & Wallach, H. (2019). Improving Fairness in Machine Learning Systems: What Do Industry Practitioners Need? *Proceedings of the 2019 CHI Conference on Human Factors in Computing Systems*, (pp. 1–16). DOI: 10.1145/3290605.3300830

Hooda, M., Rana, C., Dahiya, O., Rizwan, A., & Hossain, M. S. (2022). Artificial intelligence for assessment and feedback to enhance student success in higher education. *Mathematical Problems in Engineering, 2022*(1), 5215722. DOI: 10.1155/2022/5215722

Hoque, R., Sorwar, G., & Alzoubi, M. (2021). A Comprehensive Review of the Use of Artificial Intelligence in Education: Opportunities and Challenges. *Journal of Educational Technology & Society, 24*(2), 110–123.

Hu, S. (2024). The effect of artificial intelligence-assisted personalized learning on student learning outcomes: A meta-analysis based on 31 empirical research papers. *Science Insights Education Frontiers, 24*(1), 3873–3894. DOI: 10.15354/sief.24.re395

Husayn, E., Alrumayh, S., Kasheem, M., Ibrahim, D., Alouzi, K., Shalghoum, N., & Almajri, S. (2025). The Impact of Artificial Intelligence on Knowledge Management : Faculty Perspectives from the University of Zawia ' s Faculties of Economics, Management, and Law. *Journal of Education and Teacher Training Innovation, 3*(1), 52–66. DOI: 10.61227/jetti.v3i1.163

Huskisson, S., O'Mahony, T., & Lacey, S. (2024). Improving student outcomes using automated feedback in a first-year economics class. *International Review of Economics Education, 47*, 100303–100303. DOI: 10.1016/j.iree.2024.100303

Hwang, G. J., Xie, H., Wah, B. W., & Gašević, D. (2020). Vision, challenges, roles and research issues of Artificial Intelligence in Education. *Computers and Education: Artificial Intelligence, 1*, 100001. DOI: 10.1016/j.caeai.2020.100001

ICAI (International Center for Academic Integrity). (2021). *The fundamental values of academic integrity* (3rd ed.). https://www.chapman.edu/academics/academic-integrity/_files/the-fundamental-values-of-academic-integrity.pdf

ICDE. (2019). *The Present and Future of Alternative Digital Credentials (ADCs),* International Council for Open and Distance Education (ICDE), Oslo.

Ifenthaler, D., & Yau, J. Y.-K. (2020). Utilising learning analytics for study success: Reflections on current empirical findings. *Research and Practice in Technology Enhanced Learning, 15*(1), 1–17.

Irfan, M., & Ali, S. (2023). Integration of Artificial Intelligence in Academia : A Case Study of Critical Teaching and Learning in Higher Education. *Global Social Sciences Review, VIII*(I), 352–364. DOI: 10.31703/gssr.2023(VIII-I).32

Irish, A. L., Gazica, M. W., & Becerra, V. (2025). A qualitative descriptive analysis on generative artificial intelligence: Bridging the gap in pedagogy to prepare students for the workplace. *Discover Education, 4*(1), 48. DOI: 10.1007/s44217-025-00435-4

Islam, N. M., Laughter, L., Sadid-Zadeh, R., Smith, C., Dolan, T. A., Crain, G., & Squarize, C. H. (2022). Adopting artificial intelligence in dental education: A model for academic leadership and innovation. *Journal of Dental Education, 86*(11), 1545–1551. DOI: 10.1002/jdd.13010 PMID: 35781809

Iucu, O., & Car i , A. (2025). Competency Profiles in Administrative Sciences. An Analysis of the Students' Perceptions and Possible Curricular Reshapes Through Micro-Credentials. *Transylvanian Review of Administrative Sciences, 21*(74), 5–29. DOI: 10.24193/tras.74E.1

Jackaria, P. M., Al-adzran, G. S., Alvarado, H. A. L., Jiripa, R. H. M., & Al-sabrie, Y. S. (2026). Students' Learning Math With the Aid of AI and the Need of Shifting Classroom Instructions. In *Generators, Bots, and Tutors: Creative Approaches to Human-AI Synergy in Classroom Instruction* (pp. 31-56). IGI Global Scientific Publishing. https://doi.org/DOI: 10.4018/979-8-3373-0847-0.ch002

Jackaria, P. M., Pon, M. M. R., Eldani, N. A. S., Alvarado, H. A. L., & Iralan, S. A. (2026). Leveraging the Use of AI Tools in Practice Teaching: Insights from Science Pre-Service Teachers. In *Redefining the Roles of Educators and Students in the AI Era* (pp. 99-126). IGI Global Scientific Publishing. https://doi.org/DOI: 10.4018/979-8-3373-8027-8.ch005

Jackaria, P. M., Hajan, B. H., Mastul, A. H., & Sali, F. Z. (2024). Generation AI in a Reimagined Classroom: Challenges, Opportunities and Implications to Education. In Zaremohzzabieh, Z., Abdullah, R., & Ahrari, S. (Eds.), *Exploring Youth Studies in the Age of AI* (pp. 181–192). IGI Global Scientific Publishing., DOI: 10.4018/979-8-3693-3350-1.ch009

Jackman, G. A., Marshall, I. A., & Carrington, T. (2025). Opportunity or Threat: Investigating Faculty Readiness to Adopt Artificial Intelligence in Higher Education. *Caribbean Journal of Education and Development, 1*(2), 4–27. DOI: 10.46425/cjed1201029055

Jacobs-Basadien, M., & Pather, S. (2026). Assessing AI policy and guideline progress within the South African public higher education system: Insights from documented policies. *Universal Access in the Information Society, 25*(2), 71. DOI: 10.1007/s10209-026-01340-9

Jaime-Vargas, J. A. (2025). Generative AI for enhancing accessibility and inclusion in higher education: A systematic review. *HighTech and Innovation Journal, 6*(2), 723–734. DOI: 10.28991/HIJ-2025-06-02-022

Jain, S., & Jain, R. (2019). Role of artificial intelligence in higher education—An empirical investigation. *IJRAR-International Journal of Research and Analytical Reviews, 6*(2), 144–150.

Jaiswal, A., & Arun, C. J. (2021). Potential of artificial intelligence for transformation of the education system in India. *International Journal of Education and Development Using Information and Communication Technology, 17*(1), 142–158.

Jensen, T. W. (2025). AI literacy in the context of working with sources : Pitfalls and possibilities of generative AI models in academic writing. *Journal of Academic Writing, 14*(S2), 1–12. DOI: 10.18552/joaw.v15iS2.1224

Jeyakarthic, M., & Karthic, K. (2025). *Artificial Intelligence and Society* (Issue May).

Jiang, Y., Hao, J., Fauss, M., & Li, C. (2024). Detecting ChatGPT-generated essays in a large-scale writing assessment: Is there a bias against non-native English speakers?, *217*(C %J Comput. Educ.), 14. DOI: 10.1016/j.compedu.2024.105070

Jianzheng, S., & Xuwei, Z. (2023). Integration of AI with Higher Education Innovation : Reforming Future Educational Directions. *International Journal of Science and Research (Raipur, India), 12*(10), 1727–1731. DOI: 10.21275/SR231023183401

Jin, Y., Yan, L., Echeverría, V., Gašević, D., & Martínez-Maldonado, R. (2024). Generative AI in higher education: A global perspective of institutional adoption policies and guidelines. https://doi.org//arxiv.2405.11800DOI: 10.48550

Johnson, J. W., & Kathirvel, K. (2025). Evaluating the effectiveness of ChatGPT in language translation and cross-lingual communication. In *Applications of Mathematics in Science and Technology* (pp. 434–439). CRC Press., DOI: 10.1201/9781003606659-82

Johnston, H., Wells, R. F., Shanks, E. M., Boey, T., & Parsons, B. N. (2024). Student perspectives on the use of generative artificial intelligence technologies in higher education. *International Journal for Educational Integrity*, *20*(1), 2. DOI: 10.1007/s40979-024-00149-4

Jones, B., & Carter, D. (2019). Relationships between students' course perceptions, engagement, and learning. *Social Psychology of Education*, *22*(4), 819–839. DOI: 10.1007/s11218-019-09500-x

Jowi, J. O. (2024). Recent developments in higher education in Africa: Partnerships for knowledge transformations. *Kokusai Kyoiku Kyoryoku Ronshu*, *26*(1), 34–48. DOI: 10.1108/JICE-11-2023-0037

Kaku, M. (2019). 10 Robots, artificial intelligence, and the future of work. *Environmental Health and the US Federal System: Sustainably Managing Health Hazards*, 254.

Kallunki, V., Kinnunen, P., Pyörälä, E., Haarala-muhonen, A., Katajavuori, N., & Myyry, L. (2024). Navigating the Evolving Landscape of Teaching and Learning: University Faculty and Staff Perceptions of the Artificial Intelligence-Altered Terrain. *Education Sciences*, *14*(7), 727. DOI: 10.3390/educsci14070727

Kamak, R., Debo, D., & Saaida, M. (2024). *Challenges of AI in higher education. LVR Center*. Libra Academy.

Kamalov, F., Santandreu Calonge, D., & Gurrib, I. (2023). New era of artificial intelligence in education: Towards a sustainable multifaceted revolution. *Sustainability (Basel)*, *15*(16), 12451. DOI: 10.3390/su151612451

Kang, E., & Hwang, H.-J. (2020). The Consequences of Data Fabrication and Falsification among Researchers. *Journal of Research and Publication Ethics*, *1*(2), 7–10. DOI: 10.15722/jrpe.1.2.202009.7

Karataş, F., Eriçok, B., & Tanrikulu, L. (2025). *Reshaping curriculum adaptation in the age of artificial intelligence : Mapping teachers ' driven curriculum adaptation patterns* (Issue August 2024). DOI: 10.1002/berj.4068

Karimov, A., Saarela, M., & Kärkkäinen, T. (2024, October). Teachers' Adoption of AI Tools: Motivations, Challenges, and Skills Required. In *eLearn: World Conference on EdTech* (pp. 610-615). Association for the Advancement of Computing in Education (AACE).

Karmakar, D., Das, A., & Khati, A. (2025). Building Ethical Foundations: Educating Researchers for Responsible Use of AI. In Chakraborty, S. (Ed.), (pp. 163–190). Advances in Human and Social Aspects of Technology. IGI Global., DOI: 10.4018/979-8-3693-9035-1.ch008

Kashif, H., Alamdar, R., & Naseer, F. (2024). REDEFINING FACULTY ROLES IN AN AI-DRIVEN EDUCATIONAL ECOSYSTEM WITH IMPLICATIONS FOR TEACHING AND CURRICULUM DEVELOPMENT. *Joural of Media Horizons, November*.

Kasneci, E., Seßler, K., Küchemann, S., Bannert, M., Dementieva, D., Fischer, F., Gasser, U., Groh, G., Günnemann, S., Hüllermeier, E., Krusche, S., Kutyniok, G., Michaeli, T., Nerdel, C., Pfeffer, J., Poquet, O., Sailer, M., Schmidt, A., Seidel, T., & Kasneci, G. (2023). ChatGPT for good? On opportunities and challenges of large language models for education. *Learning and Individual Differences*, *103*, 102274. Advance online publication. DOI: 10.1016/j.lindif.2023.102274

Katsamakas, E. (2024). Artificial Intelligence and the Transformation of Higher Education Institutions : A Systems Approach. *Sustainability Article*, 1–21.

Katsamakas, E., Pavlov, O. V., & Saklad, R. (2024). Artificial intelligence and the transformation of higher education institutions: A systems approach. *Sustainability (Basel)*, *16*(14), 6118. DOI: 10.3390/su16146118

Kayyali, M. (2025). AI in higher education. Advances in Educational Technologies and Instructional Design Book Series, 31–62. DOI: 10.4018/979-8-3693-7949-3.ch002

Kazimova, D., Tazhigulova, G. O., Shraimanova, G., Zatyneyko, A. M., & Sharzadin, A. M. (2025). Transforming university education with AI: A systematic review of technologies, applications, and implications. [iJEP]. *International Journal of Engineering Pedagogy*, *15*(1), 4–24. DOI: 10.3991/ijep.v15i1.50773

Kelly, A. E. (2026). AI-Supported Knowledge-Building Action Networks (KBANs) for Education. In *Third International Handbook of Educational Change* (pp. 1–19). Springer Nature Switzerland. DOI: 10.1007/978-3-031-88898-4_13-1

Khan, A. A., Badshah, S., Liang, P., Waseem, M., Khan, B., Ahmad, A., & Akbar, M. A. (2022, June). Ethics of AI: A systematic literature review of principles and challenges. In *Proceedings of the 26th international conference on evaluation and assessment in software engineering* (pp. 383-392). https://doi.org/DOI: 10.1145/3530019.3531329

Khan, A., Jehangir, M., & Wang, X. (2025). The rise of AI in academia: Adaptation strategies for transforming higher education. *American Journal of Smart Technology and Solutions*, *4*(2), 42–48. DOI: 10.54536/ajsts.v4i2.4892

Khan, S., Mazhar, T., Shahzad, T., Khan, M. A., Rehman, A. U., Saeed, M. M., & Hamam, H. (2025). Harnessing AI for sustainable higher education: Ethical considerations, operational efficiency, and future directions. *Discover Sustainability*, *6*(1), 23. DOI: 10.1007/s43621-025-00809-6

Kim, J., Lee, S. S., Detrick, R., Wang, J., & Li, N. (2025). Students-Generative AI interaction patterns and its impact on academic writing. *Journal of Computing in Higher Education*, •••, 1–22. DOI: 10.1007/s12528-025-09444-6

Kim, Y. J., Murai, Y., & Chang, S. (2021). Implementation of embedded assessment in maker classrooms: Challenges and opportunities. *Information and Learning Science*, *122*(3-4), 292–314. DOI: 10.1108/ILS-08-2020-0188

Kohnke, L., Zou, D., Ou, A. W., & Gu, M. M. (2025). Preparing future educators for AI-enhanced classrooms: Insights into AI literacy and integration. *Computers and Education: Artificial Intelligence*, *8*, 100398. Advance online publication. DOI: 10.1016/j.caeai.2025.100398

Kovari, A. (2025). A systematic review of AI-powered collaborative learning in higher education: Trends and outcomes from the last decade. *Social Sciences & Humanities Open*, *11*, 101335. Advance online publication. DOI: 10.1016/j.ssaho.2025.101335

Kumar, D., Haque, A., Mishra, K., Islam, F., Mishra, B. K., & Ahmad, S. (2023). Exploring the transformative role of artificial intelligence and metaverse in education: A comprehensive review. *Metaverse Basic and Applied Research*, *2*, 21. DOI: 10.56294/mr202355

Kunter, M., Baumert, J., & Köller, O. (2007). Effective classroom management and the development of subject-related interest. *Learning and Instruction*, *17*(5), 494–509. DOI: 10.1016/j.learninstruc.2007.09.002

Kurni, M., Mohammed, M. S., & Srinivasa, K. G. (2023). AI-enabled gamification in education. In *A Beginner's Guide to Introduce Artificial Intelligence in Teaching and Learning* (pp. 105–114). Springer International Publishing.

Kušić, S., Vrcelj, S., & Zovko, A. (2022). Micro-credentials–Improvement or Fragmentation in Higher Education? *Journal in Education and New Developments*, *2*, 152–156. DOI: 10.36315/2022v2end033

Kuzilek, J., Hlosta, M., & Zdrahal, Z. (2017). Open university learning analytics dataset. *Scientific Data*, *4*(1), 1–8. DOI: 10.1038/sdata.2017.171 PMID: 29182599

Labadze, L., Grigolia, M., Machaidze, L., Labadze, L., Grigolia, M., & Machaidze, L. (2023). Role of AI chatbots in education: systematic literature review. *International Journal of Educational Technology in Higher Education, 20:1, 20*(1). DOI: 10.1186/s41239-023-00426-1

Lampos, V., Mintz, J., & Qu, X. (2021). An artificial intelligence approach for selecting effective teacher communication strategies in autism education. *npj Science of Learning, 6*(1), 25. https://doi.org/DOI: 10.1038/s41539-021-00102-x

Latif, E., Liu, V., & Zhai, X. (2026). A systematic review of intelligent and robot tutoring systems: Evolution, pedagogical design, and AI-driven classification. *Smart Learning Environments*, *13*(1), 1. DOI: 10.1186/s40561-025-00427-9

LeBlanc, P. (2021). *Students first: Equity, access, and opportunity in higher education*. Harvard Education Press.

Lee, D., & Kwon, H. (2024). Meta-analysis on effects of artificial intelligence education in K-12 South Korean classrooms. *Education and Information Technologies*, *29*(17), 22859–22894. DOI: 10.1007/s10639-024-12738-4

Lee, I., Zhang, H., Moore, K., Zhou, X., Perret, B., Cheng, Y., & Pu, G. (2022, February). AI book club: An innovative professional development model for AI education. In *Proceedings of the 53rd ACM Technical Symposium on Computer Science Education-Volume 1* (pp. 202-208). https://doi.org/DOI: 10.1145/3478431.3499318

Lee, J., Suh, T., Roy, D., & Baucus, M. (2019). Emerging technology and business model innovation: The case of artificial intelligence. *Journal of Open Innovation*, *5*(3), 44. DOI: 10.3390/joitmc5030044

Liang, J., Stephens, J. M., & Brown, G. T. (2025, April). A systematic review of the early impact of artificial intelligence on higher education curriculum, instruction, and assessment. In *Frontiers in Education* (Vol. 10, p. 1522841). Frontiers Media SA. https://doi.org/DOI: 10.3389/feduc.2025.1522841

Liang, W., Yuksekgonul, M., Mao, Y., Wu, E., & Zou, J. (2023). GPT detectors are biased against non-native English writers. *Patterns (New York, N.Y.)*, *4*(7), 100779. DOI: 10.1016/j.patter.2023.100779 PMID: 37521038

Li, F., Ruijs, N., & Lu, Y. (2022). Ethics & AI: A systematic review on ethical concerns and related strategies for designing with AI in healthcare. *AI*, *4*(1), 28–53. DOI: 10.3390/ai4010003

Li, M., & Su, Y. (2020). Evaluation of online teaching quality of basic education based on artificial intelligence. [iJET]. *International Journal of Emerging Technologies in Learning*, *15*(16), 147–161. https://www.learntechlib.org/p/217942/. DOI: 10.3991/ijet.v15i16.15937

Lima, D. A., & Isotani, S. (2021, October). Constraints, effectiveness and solutions in using Google Classroom as a Learning Management System during Covid-19 pandemic: a systematic literature review. In *2021 XVI Latin American Conference on Learning Technologies (LACLO)* (pp. 38-43). IEEE. DOI: 10.1109/LACLO54177.2021.00012

Lin, Y., Luo, Q., & Qian, Y. (2023). Investigation of Artificial Intelligence algorithms in education. *Applied and Computational Engineering*, *16*(1), 180–184. DOI: 10.54254/2755-2721/16/20230886

Litman, D., Zhang, H., Correnti, R., Matsumura, L., & Wang, E. L. (2021). A Fairness Evaluation of Automated Methods for Scoring Text Evidence Usage in Writing. In (pp. 255-267). DOI: 10.1007/978-3-030-78292-4_21

Liu, N. (2025). Exploring the factors influencing the adoption of artificial intelligence technology by university teachers: The mediating role of confidence and AI readiness. *BMC Psychology*, *13*(1), 311. DOI: 10.1186/s40359-025-02620-4 PMID: 40148913

Llerena-Izquierdo, J., & Ayala-Carabajo, R. (2025). Ethics of the Use of Artificial Intelligence in Academia and Research: The Most Relevant Approaches, Challenges and Topics. In *Informatics* (Vol. 12, No. 4, p. 111). MDPI. https://doi.org/DOI: 10.3390/informatics12040111

Lo Leo, S. (2024). *Evaluating AI Literacy in Academic Libraries : A Survey Study with a Focus on U. S. Employees*. Academic Department Resources., DOI: 10.5860/crl.85.5.635.This

Lockley, A., Derryberry, A., & West, D. (2016). Drivers, affordances and challenges of digital badges. In Ifenthaler, D., Bellin-Mularski, N., & Mah, D.-K. (Eds.), *Foundation of digital badges and micro-credentials. Demonstrating and Recognizing Knowledge and Competencies* (pp. 55–70). Springer., DOI: 10.1007/978-3-319-15425-1_4

Loukkola, T., & Cirlan, E. (2020). *Micro-credentials: What is behind all the buzz?* European University Association. https://www.eua.eu/our-work/expert-voices/micro-credentials-what-is-behind-all-the-buzz.html (accessed on December 9, 2025).

Luckin, R., & Holmes, W. (2016). Intelligence unleashed: An argument for AI in education.

Luckin, R., & Holmes, W. (2016). Intelligence Unleashed: An argument for AI in Education.

Luckin, R., Holmes, W., Griffiths, M., & Forcier, L. B. (2016). *Intelligence unleashed: An argument for AI in education*. Pearson Education.

Luo, L., & Yusuf, A. (2026). Bridging AI and pedagogy: How AI-adaptive feedback shapes Chinese EFL students' writing engagement, metacognitive writing strategies, and writing performance. *Assessment & Evaluation in Higher Education*, *51*(3), 508–531. DOI: 10.1080/02602938.2025.2548919

Machumu, H. (2014). Quality Assurance Practices in Higher Education Institutions: Lesson from Africa. *Journal of Education and Practice*, *5*, 144–156.

Magrill, J., & Magrill, B. (2024). Preparing educators and students at higher education institutions for an AI-driven world. *Teaching & Learning Inquiry*, *12*. Advance online publication. DOI: 10.20343/teachlearninqu.12.16

Mah, D. K., & Groß, N. (2024). Artificial intelligence in higher education: Exploring faculty use, self-efficacy, distinct profiles, and professional development needs. *International Journal of Educational Technology in Higher Education*, *21*(1), 58. DOI: 10.1186/s41239-024-00490-1

Mangundu, J. (2025). Navigating artificial intelligence governance: Insights from South African higher education IT decision-makers. *The African Journal of Information Systems*, *17*(1), 1–20.

Manuel, C. C. J. (2025). The impact of AI on inclusivity in higher education: A rapid review. *Education Sciences*, *15*(9), 1255. DOI: 10.3390/educsci15091255

Martin, F., Zhuang, M., & Schaefer, D. (2024). Systematic review of research on artificial intelligence in K-12 education (2017–2022). *Computers and Education: Artificial Intelligence*, *6*, 100195. DOI: 10.1016/j.caeai.2023.100195

Martins, M.Maicon Roberto Martins. (2023). Adapting change management strategies for the AI era: Lessons from large-scale IT integrations. *World Journal of Advanced Research and Reviews*, *19*(3), 1604–1629. DOI: 10.30574/wjarr.2023.19.3.1556

Ma, X., & Jiang, C. (2023). On the ethical risks of artificial intelligence applications in education and its avoidance strategies. *Journal of Education. Humanities and Social Sciences*, *14*, 354–359.

McCalla, G. (2023). The History of Artificial Intelligence in Education – the First Quarter Century. In B. du Boulay, T. Mitrovic, & K. Yacef (Eds.), Handbook of Artificial Intelligence in Education. Edward Elgar Publishing., Retrieved February 13, 2024, from. DOI: 10.4337/9781800375413.00010

McCarthy, C. R. (1999). Dual-Enrollment Programs: Legislation Helps High School Students Enroll in College Courses. *Journal of Secondary Gifted Education*, *11*(1), 24–32. DOI: 10.4219/jsge-1999-610

McCarthy, J. (1956). Measures of the value of information. *Proceedings of the National Academy of Sciences of the United States of America*, *42*(9), 654–655. DOI: 10.1073/pnas.42.9.654

McCartney, M. L., & Rick, H. A. (2021). The adult student/consumer model: Micro-credentials as a solution for adult learners. In *Ensuring Adult and Non-Traditional Learners' Success With Technology, Design, and Structure* (pp. 244-261). IGI Global Scientific Publishing.

McDonald, N., Johri, A., Ali, A., & Collier, A. H. (2025). Generative artificial intelligence in higher education: Evidence from an analysis of institutional policies and guidelines. *Computers in Human Behavior: Artificial Humans*, *3*, 100121. DOI: 10.1016/j.chbah.2025.100121

Mcgrath, C., Cerratto, T., Juth, N., & Palmgren, P. J. (2023). Computers and Education : Artificial Intelligence University teachers ' perceptions of responsibility and artificial intelligence in higher education - An experimental philosophical study. *Computers and Education: Artificial Intelligence*, *4*(April), 100139. DOI: 10.1016/j.caeai.2023.100139

McGreal, R., & Olcott, D.Jr. (2022). A strategic reset: Micro-credentials for higher education leaders. *Smart Learning Environments*, *9*(1), 9. DOI: 10.1186/s40561-022-00190-1

Medina Vásquez, M. L., Campos Ramírez, L. C., Yataco Bernaola, M. L., Yataco Torrealva, J. R., Ramos Torrealva, Z. M., Castro Cárdenas, D. M., & Altamirano, S. F. S. (2025). Inclusive pedagogy and active learning in higher education: Cluster and dimensional insights into teaching competency integration. *Social Sciences & Humanities Open*, *12*, 102060. 10.1016/j.ssaho.2025.102060. DOI: 10.1016/j.ssaho.2025.102060

Mehl, G.. (2020). *The Dual Enrollment Playbook: A Guide to Equitable Acceleration for Students*. Aspen Institute College Excellence Program.

Mehrabi, N., Morstatter, F., Saxena, N., Lerman, K., & Galstyan, A. (2021). A Survey on Bias and Fairness in Machine Learning. *54*(6%J ACM Comput. Surv.). *Article, 115*. Advance online publication. DOI: 10.1145/3457607

Mejía, A., & Garcés-Flórez, M. F. (2025). What do we mean by academic integrity? *International Journal for Educational Integrity*, *21*(1), 1. DOI: 10.1007/s40979-024-00176-1

Memarian, B., & Doleck, T. (2023). ChatGPT in education: Methods, potentials, and limitations. *Computers in Human Behavior: Artificial Humans*, *1*(2), 100022. DOI: 10.1016/j.chbah.2023.100022

Memarian, B., & Doleck, T. (2024). A review of assessment for learning with artificial intelligence. *Computers in Human Behavior: Artificial Humans*, *2*(1), 100040. Advance online publication. DOI: 10.1016/j.chbah.2023.100040

Mhlambi, S. (2020). From rationality to relationality: Ubuntu as an ethical and human rights framework for artificial intelligence governance. *Carr Center for Human Rights Policy Discussion Paper Series*, 2020-009. Harvard Kennedy School. https://carrcenter.hks.harvard.edu/files/cchr/files/ccdp_2020-009_sabelo_b.pdf

Mhlanga, D. (2023). Open AI in education, the responsible and ethical use of ChatGPT towards lifelong learning. In *FinTech and artificial intelligence for sustainable development: The role of smart technologies in achieving development goals* (pp. 387–409). Springer Nature Switzerland., DOI: 10.1007/978-3-031-37776-1_17

Michel-Villarreal, R., Vilalta-Perdomo, E., Salinas-Navarro, D. E., Thierry-Aguilera, R., & Gerardou, F. S. (2023). Challenges and opportunities of generative AI for higher education as explained by ChatGPT. *Education Sciences*, *13*(9), 856. DOI: 10.3390/educsci13090856

Micro, H. E. (2019). Challenges and Opportunities of Micro-Credentials in Europe. Briefing Paper on the Award, Recognition, Portability and Accreditation of Micro-Credentials: an Investigation through Interviews with Key Stakeholders & Decision Makers. MicroHE Consortium. https://microcredentials.eu/wp-content/uploads/sites/20/2021/05/D3.1-Interviews-with-Key-Stakeholders-Decision-Makers-Overall-Summary-Report.pdf. (accessed on October 16, 2025).

Miller, W. (2024). Adapting to AI: Reimagining the Role of Assessment Professionals. *Intersection: A Journal at the Intersection of Assessment and Learning, 5*(4), 99-113. https://aalhe.scholasticahq.com/article/121439-adapting-to-ai-reimagining-the-role-of-assessment-professionals

Miller, T. (2019). Explanation in artificial intelligence: Insights from the social sciences. *Artificial Intelligence, 267*, 1–38. 10.1016/j.artint.2018.07.007. DOI: 10.1016/j.artint.2018.07.007

Milutinović, V., Đorđević, S., & Obradović, I. (2025). Factors shaping the adoption of artificial intelligence in education. *Metodička teorija i praksa, 28*(1).

Mittelstadt, B. D. (2019). Principles alone cannot guarantee ethical AI. *Nature Machine Intelligence, 1*(11), 501–507. DOI: 10.1038/s42256-019-0114-4

Mizumoto, A., & Eguchi, M. (2023). Exploring the potential of using an AI language model for automated essay scoring. *Research Methods in Applied Linguistics, 2*(2), 100050. DOI: 10.1016/j.rmal.2023.100050

Mohamed, A. M., Shaaban, T. S., Bakry, S. H., Guillén-Gámez, F. D., & Strzelecki, A. (2025). Empowering the faculty of education students: Applying AI's potential for motivating and enhancing learning. *Innovative Higher Education, 50*(2), 587–609. DOI: 10.1007/s10755-024-09747-z

Mohamed, S., Png, M. T., & Isaac, W. (2020). Decolonial AI: Decolonial theory as sociotechnical foresight in artificial intelligence. *Philosophy & Technology, 33*(4), 659–684. DOI: 10.1007/s13347-020-00405-8

Mohsen, S. A., & Munassar, N. M. A. (2025). Combining Deep Learning with Edge Computing in Improving Accessibility and Performance of E-Learning. *Journal of Science and Technology, 30*(8), 1–12. Advance online publication. DOI: 10.20428/jst.v30i7.2935

Moorhouse, B. L., Wan, Y., Wu, C., Wu, M., & Ho, T. Y. (2025). Generative AI tools and empowerment in L2 academic writing. *System, 103779*, 103779. Advance online publication. DOI: 10.1016/j.system.2025.103779

Morales-Cevallos, M. B., Alonso-García, S., Martínez-Menéndez, A., & Victoria-Maldonado, J. J. (2025). Artificial Intelligence Adoption Amongst Digitally Proficient Trainee Teachers: A Structural Equation Modelling Approach. *Social Sciences (Basel, Switzerland), 14*(6), 355. DOI: 10.3390/socsci14060355

Morris, M. R. (2020). AI and accessibility. *Communications of the ACM, 63*(6), 35–37. DOI: 10.1145/3356727

Morselli, D., & Schumacher, S. (2025). The Age of AI in faculty development. Survey insights on integration of digital tools and AI. *AI Nel Faculty Development*, *1*, 99–106. DOI: 10.7346/PO-012025-12

Moturu, V. R., & Nethi, S. D. (2022). Artificial intelligence in education. In *Emerging IT/ICT and AI technologies affecting society* (pp. 233–244). Springer Nature Singapore., DOI: 10.1007/978-981-19-2940-3_16

Moubayed, A., Injadat, M., Nassif, A. B., Lutfiyya, H., & Shami, A. (2018). E-learning: Challenges and research opportunities using machine learning & data analytics. *IEEE Access : Practical Innovations, Open Solutions*, *6*, 39117–39138. DOI: 10.1109/ACCESS.2018.2851790

Moya, B., Eaton, S. E., Pethrick, H., Hayden, K. A., Brennan, R., Wiens, J., & Lesage, J. (2023). Academic integrity and artificial intelligence in higher education contexts: A rapid scoping review protocol. *Canadian Perspectives on Academic Integrity, 5*(2), 59-75. https://doi.org/DOI: 10.11575/cpai.75990

Moya, B., Eaton, S., Pethrick, H., Hayden, A., Brennan, R., Wiens, J., & McDermott, B. (2024). Academic Integrity and Artificial Intelligence in Higher Education (HE) Contexts: A Rapid Scoping Review. *Canadian Perspectives on Academic Integrity*, *7*(3), 59–75. DOI: 10.55016/ojs/cpai.v7i3.78123

Muhammad, A. F., Astiana, N., Ardi, H., Nitswat, N., Nur, S. H., Razak, A. Z., Tajuddin, F. N., Aquil, A., Nur, M., Syahbana, S., Padjadjaran, U., Makassar, U. N., & Hasanuddin, U. (2025). *Impact of Artificial Intelligence on Academic Literacy among University Students in Indonesia : A Case Study* (Vol. 5, Issue 1).

Müller, S. D., & Mønsted, T. S. (2025). AI-enhanced learning: Exploring the use of generative AI as a study tutor.

Murgatroyd, S. (2024). *The future of higher education in an age of artificial intelligence*. Ethics International Press.

Murtaza, M., Ahmed, Y., Shamsi, J. A., Sherwani, F., & Usman, M. (2022). AI-based personalized e-learning systems: Issues, challenges, and solutions. *IEEE Access : Practical Innovations, Open Solutions*, *10*, 81323–81342. DOI: 10.1109/ACCESS.2022.3193938

Nailah, W., & Syahiza, A. (2023). Influence of Psychological Well-Being and School Factors on Delinquency, During the Covid-19 Period Among Secondary School Students in Selected Schools in Nakuru County : Kenya. [IJRISS]. *International Journal of Research and Innovation in Social Science*, *VII*(2454), 1175–1189. DOI: 10.47772/IJRISS

Neumann, M., Rauschenberger, M., & Schon, E. M. (2023). "We Need To Talk About ChatGPT": The Future of AI and Higher Education. *Proceedings - 2023 IEEE/ACM 5th International Workshop on Software Engineering Education for the Next Generation, SEENG 2023*, 29–32. DOI: 10.1109/SEENG59157.2023.00010

Ngan, T., & Hastie, D. (2025). Artificial Intelligence for Academic Purposes (AIAP): Integrating AI literacy into an EAP module. *English for Specific Purposes, 77*, 20–38. DOI: 10.1016/j.esp.2024.09.001

Ngarambe, J., Yun, G. Y., & Santamouris, M. (2020). The use of artificial intelligence (AI) methods in the prediction of thermal comfort in buildings: Energy implications of AI-based thermal comfort controls. *Energy and Building, 211*, 109807. DOI: 10.1016/j.enbuild.2020.109807

Nirala, K. K., Singh, N. K., & Purani, V. S. (2022). A survey on providing customer and public administration based services using AI: Chatbot. *Multimedia Tools and Applications, 81*(16), 22215–22246. DOI: 10.1007/s11042-021-11458-y

Nithya, A. (2025). *Faculty readiness and professional development for AI integration.*, DOI: 10.34293/9789361634437.ch.005

Norberg, M. (2025). *PERCEPTIONS OF AI IN HIGHER EDUCATION : AFFORDANCES AND RISKS FOR STUDENTS WITH SWEDISH AS A SECOND* (Issue March).

OECD. (2019). *Recommendation of the Council on Artificial Intelligence.* Organisation for Economic Co-operation and Development.

OECD. (2021a). *"Quality and value of micro-credentials in higher education: Preparing for the future", OECD Education Policy Perspectives, No. 40.* OECD Publishing., DOI: 10.1787/9c4ad26d-

OECD. (2021b). *"Micro-credential innovations in higher education: Who, What and Why?", OECD Education Policy Perspectives, No. 39.* OECD Publishing., DOI: 10.1787/f14ef041-

OECD. (2023). *"Micro-credentials for lifelong learning and employability: Uses and possibilities", OECD Education Policy Perspectives, No. 66.* OECD Publishing., DOI: 10.1787/9c4b7b68-

OECD. (2023). *OECD framework for the classification of AI systems.* OECD Publishing., DOI: 10.1787/cb6d9eca-

Oh, S. H., & Sanfilippo, M. (2024). University Governance for Responsible AI. *Proceedings of the ALISE Annual Conference.* DOI: 10.21900/j.alise.2024.1706

Okumu, G. J., & Kenei, J. K. (2024). Adoption of Artificial Intelligence in Technical and Vocational Education and Training Institutions in Kenya. *THE KENYA JOURNAL OF TECHNICAL AND VOCATIONAL EDUCATION AND TRAINING VOL, 7*, 2.

Okunade, A. I. (2024). The Role of Artificial Intelligence in Teaching of Science Education in Secondary Schools in Nigeria. *European Journal of Computer Science and Information Technology, 12*(1), 57–67. DOI: 10.37745/ejcsit2013/vol12n15767

Oliver, B. (2022). *Towards a common definition of micro-credentials*. UNESCO Publishing., https://unesdoc.unesco.org/ark:/48223/pf0000381668

Olszewski-Kubilius, P. (2009). Special schools and other options for gifted STEM students. *Roeper Review, 32*(1), 61–70. DOI: 10.1080/02783190903386892

Olszewski-Kubilius, P., & Limburg-Weber, L. (2004). *Designs for excellence: A guide to educational programs for academically talented secondary students and their parents*. Northwestern University, Center for Talent Development.

Oncioiu, I., & Bularca, A. R. (2025). Artificial intelligence governance in higher education: The role of knowledge-based strategies in fostering legal awareness and ethical artificial intelligence literacy. *Societies (Basel, Switzerland), 15*(6), 144. DOI: 10.3390/soc15060144

Open, A. I. (2023). *New AI classifier for indicating AI-written text (retired)*. https://openai.com/blog/new-ai-classifier-for-indicating-ai-written-text

Ortega-Ruipérez, B., & Correa-Gorospe, J. M. (2024). Frontiers | Peer assessment to promote self-regulated learning with technology in higher education: Systematic review for improving course design. *Frontiers in Education, 9*, 1376505. Advance online publication. DOI: 10.3389/feduc.2024.1376505

Osman, Z., & Yatam, M. (2024). *Enhancing artificial intelligence-enabled transformation acceptance among employees of higher education institutions*. International Journal of Academic Research in Accounting, Finance and Management Sciences., DOI: 10.6007/IJARAFMS/v14-i2/21322

Oussous, A., Menyani, I., Srifi, M., Lahcen, A. A., Kheraz, S., Benjelloun, F.-Z.,… Benjelloun, F.-Z. (2023). An Evaluation of Open Source Adaptive Learning Solutions. *Information, Vol. 14, Page 57, 14*(2). DOI: 10.3390/info14020057

Ouyang, F., Zheng, L., Jiao, P., & Moore, G. D. (2022). Artificial intelligence in online higher education: A systematic review of empirical research. *Computers and Education: Artificial Intelligence, 3*, 100088.

Owan, V. J., Abang, K. B., Idika, D. O., Etta, E. O., & Bassey, B. A. (2023). Exploring the potential of artificial intelligence tools in educational measurement and assessment. *Eurasia Journal of Mathematics, Science and Technology Education*, *19*(8), em2307. Advance online publication. DOI: 10.29333/ejmste/13428

Owoc, M. L., Sawicka, A., & Weichbroth, P. (2021). Artificial Intelligence Technologies in Education: Benefits, Challenge. *IFIP Advances in Information and Communication Technology*, *599*, 37–58. Advance online publication. DOI: 10.1007/978-3-030-85001-2_4

Oyedokun, G. (2025). *AI and Ethics*. Academic Integrity and the Future of Quality Assurance in Higher Education.

Oyedotun, S. A., Ejenarhome, O. P., & Oise, G. P. (2025). Learning Analytics and Predictive Modeling: Enhancing Student Success through Data-Driven Insights. *Journal of Scientific Research and Reports*, *2*(3), 42–51.

Page, L. C., & Gehlbach, H. (2020). How an artificially intelligent virtual assistant helps students navigate the road to college. *AERA Open*, *6*(4), 1–12.

Page, M. J., McKenzie, J. E., Bossuyt, P. M., Boutron, I., Hoffmann, T. C., Mulrow, C. D., Shamseer, L., Tetzlaff, T., Akl, E., Brennan, S., Chou, D., & Glanville, J. (2021). The PRISMA 2020 statement: An updated guideline for reporting systematic reviews. *BMJ (Clinical Research Ed.)*, *372*(71), 1–9. PMID: 33782057

Palanski, M., Newman, A., Leroy, H., Moore, C., Hannah, S., & Den Hartog, D. (2021). Quantitative research on leadership and business ethics: Examining the state of the field and an agenda for future research. *Journal of Business Ethics*, *168*(1), 109–119. https://idp.springer.com/authorize/casa?redirect_uri=https://link.springer.com/article/10.1007/s10551-019-04267-9&casa_token=3IBckg96A7wAAAAA:Rd7UiM22ZZ3pOkcpXbfXdGRowJWUSeo_8amyATaxHC6BdCxaA_3mwLhgxFvGcQZfY2H3DSxI1q1LA79w_g. DOI: 10.1007/s10551-019-04267-9

Pant, A., Hoda, R., Tantithamthavorn, C., & Turhan, B. (2024). Ethics in AI through the practitioner's view: A grounded theory literature review. *Empirical Software Engineering*, *29*(3), 67. DOI: 10.1007/s10664-024-10465-5

Panter, A. T., & Sterba, S. K. (2011). Ethics in quantitative methodology: An introduction. In *Handbook of ethics in quantitative methodology* (pp. 1–11). Routledge., https://api.taylorfrancis.com/content/chapters/edit/download?identifierName=doi&identifierValue=10.4324/9780203840023-1&type=chapterpdf DOI: 10.4324/9780203840023

Patel, A. (2025). Artificial Intelligence-Driven Personalized Learning: Application, Challenges, and Future Directions in Digital Education. *Digital Education and Future Learning, 1*(1), 1-18. https://journals.cypedia.net/defl/article/view/97

Paul, J., Farhath, O., & Selvan, M. (2024). AI based Proctoring System –. *RE:view*, 1–5. Advance online publication. DOI: 10.1109/ICICT60155.2024.10544779

Pavlik, J. V. (2023). Collaborating with ChatGPT: Considering the implications of generative artificial intelligence for journalism and media education. *Journalism & mass communication educator, 78*(1), 84-93.

Pawilen, G. T., Tomida, E., & Eugenio, D. O. (2024). Quality assurance framework for micro-credentials in Japan and in the Philippines: Micro-credentials in Japan and in the Philippines. *International Journal of Curriculum and Instruction, 16*(2), 401–421.

Peláez-sánchez, I. C., Velarde-camaqui, D., Glasserman-morales, L. D., & Peláez-sánchez, I. C. (2024). *The impact of large language models on higher education : exploring the connection between AI and Education 4. 0*. Issue June., DOI: 10.3389/feduc.2024.1392091

Pellegrina, D., & Helmy, M. (2025). AI for scientific integrity: Detecting ethical breaches, errors, and misconduct in manuscripts. *Frontiers in Artificial Intelligence, 8*, 1644098. Advance online publication. DOI: 10.3389/frai.2025.1644098 PMID: 40964145

Pelletier, K., McCormack, M., Reeves, J., Robert, J., Arbino, N., Al-Freih, M., Dickson-Deane, C., Guevara, C., Koster, L., Sanchez-Mendiola, M., Skallerup Bessette, L., & Stine, J. (2022). *2022 EDUCAUSE Horizon Report Teaching and Learning Edition*. Boulder, CO: EDUC22. https://www.learntechlib.org/p/221033/ . (accessed on January 2, 2026).

Pendidikan, J. T., & Sangadji, K. (2025). AI-Assisted Academic Writing : Evaluating Postgraduate Students ' AI Literacy and Skills. *Journal Teknologi Pendidikan, 27*(April), 45–55.

Peng, C., Zhou, X., & Liu, S. (2022). An introduction to artificial intelligence and machine learning for online education. *Mobile Networks and Applications, 27*(3), 1147–1150. DOI: 10.1007/s11036-022-01953-3

Pennock, R. T. (2018). Beyond research ethics: How scientific virtue theory reframes and extends responsible conduct of research. In *Cultivating Moral Character and Virtue in Professional Practice*. Routledge. DOI: 10.4324/9781315182414-13

Perera, M., & Aboal, D. (2019). The impact of a mathematics computer-assisted learning platform on students' mathematics test scores: The case of the automotive industry in turkey.

Peres, F. (2023). *Health literacy in ChatGPT: exploring the potential of the use of artificial intelligence to produce academic text*. https://doi.org/DOI: 10.1590/1413-81232024291.02412023EN

Perkins, M., Furze, L., Roe, J., & MacVaugh, J. (2024). The AI Assessment Scale (AIAS): A framework for ethical integration of generative AI in educational assessment. *Assessment & Evaluation in Higher Education*, *49*(8), 1223–1237. DOI: 10.1080/02602938.2023.2290283

Pierrès, O., Christen, M., Schmitt-Koopmann, F. M., & Darvishy, A. (2024). Could the use of AI in higher education hinder students with disabilities? A scoping review. *IEEE Access : Practical Innovations, Open Solutions*, *12*, 27810–27828. DOI: 10.1109/ACCESS.2024.3365368

Porter, B., & Grippa, F. (2020). A platform for AI-enabled real-time feedback to promote digital collaboration. *Sustainability (Basel)*, *12*(24), 10243. DOI: 10.3390/su122410243

Portilla, J. E. N., Cedeño, J. K. Z., Jácome, G. O. L., & Gallegos, L. A. M. (2025). Systematic Review: Artificial Intelligence (AI) in Education 4.0. *The Journal of Educators Online*, *22*(3), n3. https://eric.ed.gov/?id=EJ1473947. DOI: 10.9743/JEO.2025.22.3.13

Powell, T. C. (2020). Can Quantitative Research Solve Social Problems? Pragmatism and the Ethics of Social Research. *Journal of Business Ethics*, *167*(1), 41–48. DOI: 10.1007/s10551-019-04196-7

Pratama, M. P., Sampelolo, R., & Lura, H. (2023). Revolutionizing education: harnessing the power of artificial intelligence for personalized learning. *Klasikal: Journal of education, language teaching and science*, *5*(2), 350-357.

QAA (Quality Assurance Agency for Higher Education). (2024–2025). *QAA advice and resources on generative AI*. https://www.qaa.ac.uk/sector-resources/generative-artificial-intelligence/qaa-advice-and-resources

Qadhi, S. M., Alduais, A., Chaaban, Y., & Khraisheh, M. (2024). Generative AI, research ethics, and higher education research: Insights from a scientometric analysis. *Information (Basel)*, *15*(6), 325. DOI: 10.3390/info15060325

Qadir, J. (2023). Engineering education in the era of ChatGPT: Promise and pitfalls of generative AI for education. In *2023 IEEE global engineering education conference (EDUCON)* (pp. 1-9). IEEE.

Qamar, N., Kiran, H. M., Ahmad, F., Saeed, S., & Abid, B. (2020). Software engineering fresh graduates career choices and software industry demands: An empirical analysis. *Int. J. Comput. Sci. Netw. Secur*, *20*(12), 72.

Qiu, R., Xiao, Y., Kong, W. M., & Gao, X. (2023). *Empowering higher education: A comprehensive review of artificial intelligence integration*. Springer Nature., DOI: 10.1007/978-981-99-5961-7_21

Qureshi, I. (2019). The Impact of AI on Teacher Roles : Towards a Collaborative Human-AI Pedagogy. *AI Edify Journal*, 1–11.

Rahayu, S. (2023). The impact of artificial intelligence on education: Opportunities and challenges. *Jurnal Educatio FKIP UNMA*, *9*(4), 2132–2140.

Rahman, M. M., & Watanobe, Y. (2023). ChatGPT for education and research: Opportunities, threats, and strategies. *Applied Sciences (Basel, Switzerland)*, *13*(9), 5783. DOI: 10.3390/app13095783

Raj, N. S., & Renumol, V. G. (2022). A systematic literature review on adaptive content recommenders in personalized learning environments from 2015 to 2020. *Journal of Computers in Education*, *9*(1), 113–148. DOI: 10.1007/s40692-021-00199-4

Ralston, S. J. (2021). Higher Education's Microcredentialing Craze: A Postdigital-Deweyan Critique. *Postdigit Sci Educ*, *3*(1), 83–101. DOI: 10.1007/s42438-020-00121-8 PMID: 40476912

Ramsey, E., Fazio, P., Smith, M., Antoniou, G., Wallberg, W., Migliano, K., Peroni, M., Muckridge, B., Solomon, G., Qian, L., & Wolf, D. (2025). Artificial Intelligence in Higher Education : A Case Study of Faculty Teaching Methodologies at a Private University. [IJASSE]. *International Journal of Academic Studies in Science and Education*, *3*(1), 1–30. DOI: 10.55549/ijasse.43

Rani, R., & Sharma, R. K. (2012). Ethical Consideration in Research. *International Journal of Nursing Education*, *4*(1). http://ijone.org/scripts/IJONE%20Jan-June%20 2012.pdf#page=49

Rao, K. N., Mair, M., Arora, R. D., Dange, P., & Nagarkar, N. M. (2024). Misconducts in research and methods to uphold research integrity. *Indian Journal of Cancer*, *61*(2), 354–359. DOI: 10.4103/ijc.ijc_4_23 PMID: 39016268

Raptopoulou, A. (2025). ChatGPT in Higher Education : Supporting Academic Literacy Through ChatGPT- Based Activities. *European Journal of Education, 60*(2), e70131. Advance online publication. DOI: 10.1111/ejed.70131

Rastrollo-Guerrero, J. L., Gómez-Pulido, J. A., & Durán-Domínguez, A. (2020). Analyzing and Predicting Students' Performance by Means of Machine Learning: A Review. *Applied Sciences (Basel, Switzerland), 10*(3), 1042. DOI: 10.3390/app10031042

Resnik, D. B. (2014). Data Fabrication and Falsification and Empiricist Philosophy of Science. *Science and Engineering Ethics, 20*(2), 423–431. DOI: 10.1007/s11948-013-9466-z PMID: 23982326

Reuben, B., & Kabilan, M. K. (2024). Assessment of university lecturers' readiness to adopt artificial intelligence (AI) technology in North-East of Nigeria. *International Journal of Advanced Research in Education and Society, 6*(2), 482–490.

Revesai, Z. (2025). Generative AI dependency: The emerging academic crisis and its impact on student performance—a case study of a university in Zimbabwe. *Cogent Education, 12*(1), 2549787. DOI: 10.1080/2331186X.2025.2549787

Rhodes, R. (2005). Rethinking Research Ethics. *The American Journal of Bioethics, 5*(1), 7–28. DOI: 10.1080/15265160590900678 PMID: 16036651

Ricoeur, P. (1992). *Oneself as another* (Blamey, K., Trans.). University of Chicago Press.

Robert, J., Muscanell, N., McCormack, M., Pelletier, K., Arnold, K., Arbino, N., Young, K., & Reeves, J. (2025). *2025 EDUCAUSE Horizon Report: Teaching and Learning Edition.* Boulder, CO.

Robinson, L., Schulz, J., Khilnani, A., Ono, H., McClain, N., Levine, L., & Tolentino, N. (2020). Digital inequalities in time of pandemic: COVID-19 exposure risk profiles and new forms of vulnerability.

Robinson, T. (2025). Generative artificial intelligence in higher education: Understanding faculty adoption through the technology acceptance model. *I-Manager's Journal of Education Technology, 22*(1), 18. DOI: 10.26634/jet.22.1.21796

Rogers, E. M. (2003). *Diffusion of innovations* (5th ed.). Free Press., https://teddykw2.wordpress.com/wp-content/uploads/2012/07/everett-m-rogers-diffusion-of-innovations.pdf

Rosnow, R. L., & Rosenthal, R. (2013). Quantitative methods and ethics. *The Oxford Handbook of Quantitative Methods, 1*, 32–54. https://books.google.com/books?hl=en&lr=&id=kOqOqVMgfzYC&oi=fnd&pg=PA32&dq=ethics+in+quantitative+research+&ots=-ARaEoQxTr&sig=xLtRbd2OwevYCyzcoFT0Luqo-S0

Rossouw, T. M., van Zyl, C., & Pope, A. (2014). Responsible conduct of research: Global trends, local opportunities. *South African Journal of Science, 110*(1–2), 1–6. http://www.scielo.org.za/scielo.php?script=sci_abstract&pid=S0038-23532014000100011&lng=en&nrm=iso&tlng=en. DOI: 10.1590/sajs.2014/20130103

Ru, K. C., & Tang, R. (2025). Promoting AI literacy through U. S. academic libraries : An analysis of LibGuides from ARL and Oberlin group libraries using the EDUCAUSE AI literacy framework. *Information Research, 30*(iConf), 847–865. DOI: 10.47989/ir30iConf47182

Russell, S. J. (2010). *Artificial intelligence a modern approach*. Pearson Education, Inc.

Saaida, M. B. E. (2023). AI-Driven transformations in higher education: Opportunities and challenges. *International Journal of Educational Research and Studies, 5*(1), 29–36. www.multidisciplinaryarticle.org

Sajja, R., Sermet, Y., Cikmaz, M., Cwiertny, D., & Demir, I. (2024). Artificial Intelligence-Enabled Intelligent Assistant for Personalized and Adaptive Learning in Higher Education. *Information (Basel), 15*(10), 1–23. DOI: 10.3390/info15100596

Salhab, W., Ameyed, D., Jaafar, F., & Mcheick, H. (2024). *A systematic literature review on ai safety: Identifying trends, challenges and future directions*. IEEE., DOI: 10.1109/ACCESS.2024.3440647

Salmon, I., & Psarras, A. (2024). Facilitating change management of higher education institutions by integrating artificial intelligence tools in their balanced scorecards. DOI: 10.35629/3002-12102026

Sambuli, N. (2016). Challenges and opportunities for advancing Internet access in developing countries while upholding net neutrality. *Journal of Cyber Policy, 1*(1), 61–74. Advance online publication. DOI: 10.1080/23738871.2016.1165715

Sanchez Barrioluengo, M. (2025). *Micro-credentials in higher education,* Biagi, F. and Di Pietro, G. (editors), Publications Office of the European Union, Luxembourg, https://data.europa.eu/doi/10.2760/0157920, JRC142086.

Schaller, N.-J., Ding, Y., Horbach, A., Meyer, J., & Jansen, T. (2024). Fairness in Automated Essay Scoring: A Comparative Analysis of Algorithms on German Learner Essays from Secondary Education. In E. Kochmar, M. Bexte, J. Burstein, A. Horbach, R. Laarmann-Quante, A. Tack, V. Yaneva, & Z. Yuan, *Proceedings of the 19th Workshop on Innovative Use of NLP for Building Educational Applications.*

Schiff, D. (2022). Education for AI, not AI for education: The role of education and ethics in national AI policy strategies. *International Journal of Artificial Intelligence in Education, 32*(3), 527–563. DOI: 10.1007/s40593-021-00270-2

Schwab, K., & Zahidi, S. (2020). The future of jobs report 2020. World Economic Forum, October 2020. https://www3.weforum.org/docs/WEF_Future_of_Jobs_2020.pdf (accessed on October 21, 2025).

Sejdiu, N. P., & Sejdiu, S. (2025). The quiet transformation of higher education in the AI era. *Open Research Europe, 5*, 249. DOI: 10.12688/openreseurope.20715.1 PMID: 40963694

Selvaratnam, R., & Venaruzzo, L. (2024). Human-centered approach to the governance of AI in higher education: Principles of international practice. *Journal of Ethics in Higher Education, 5*(5), 79–102. DOI: 10.26034/fr.jehe.2024.6864

Selwyn, N. (2019). *Should robots replace teachers? AI and the future of education.* Polity Press.

Selwyn, N. (2022). The future of AI and education: Some cautionary notes. *European Journal of Education, 57*(4), 620–631. DOI: 10.1111/ejed.12532

Seo, K., Tang, J., Roll, I., Fels, S., & Yoon, D. (2021). The impact of artificial intelligence on learner–instructor interaction in online learning. *International Journal of Educational Technology in Higher Education, 18*(1), 54. DOI: 10.1186/s41239-021-00292-9

Sharma, A., & Rani, R. (2025). *Artificial Intelligence and Speech Technology.*

Shata, A., & Hartley, K. (2025). Artificial intelligence and communication technologies in academia: Faculty perceptions and the adoption of generative AI. *International Journal of Educational Technology in Higher Education, 22*(1), 14. DOI: 10.1186/s41239-025-00511-7

Sheikh, H., Prins, C., & Schrijvers, E. (2023). Artificial intelligence: Definition and background. In *Mission AI* (pp. 15–41). Springer., DOI: 10.1007/978-3-031-21448-6_2

Siemens, G., & Long, P. (2011). Penetrating the fog: Analytics in learning and education. *EDUCAUSE Review*, *46*(5), 30–40.

Simiyu, D. (2021). Blended Learning: The Post Covid-19 Solution for Higher Education in Kenya (A Case of KCA University). *International Journal of Research and Innovation in Social Science*, *05*(11), 815–819. DOI: 10.47772/IJRISS.2021.51145

Singh, S., & Waoo, A. A. (2024). Exploring the transformative impact of artificial intelligence on higher education. *ShodhKosh Journal of Visual and Performing Arts*, *5*(5). Advance online publication. DOI: 10.29121/shodhkosh.v5.i5.2024.1895

Smith, A. M., & Green, M. (2018). Artificial intelligence and the role of leadership. *Journal of Leadership Studies*, *12*(3), 85–87. DOI: 10.1002/jls.21605

Smith, N., & Vickers, D. (2024). Living well with AI: Virtue, education, and artificial intelligence. *Theory and Research in Education*, 22(1), 19–44. DOI: 10.1177/14778785241231561

Smith, S. J., Rowland, A., Goldman, S., & Carreon, A. (2024). A Guide for Special Education Leaders to Utilize Artificial Intelligence: Students' Perspectives for Future Consideration. *Journal of Special Education Leadership*, *37*(2), 77–92. https://files.eric.ed.gov/fulltext/EJ1441807.pdf

Solanki, M. (2025). Exploring the factors affecting dropout rates in higher education institutions in India. *International journal of applied,* 2(01), 43-49.

Sood, I.. (2020). *Future Impacts of Modularization and Micro-Credentials on European Higher Education and list of validated scenarios*. MicroHE Consortium.

Steel, C., Louder, J., & Drager, Y. (2022). A Global Perspective on the Potential and the Complexities of Micro-credentials. *Anthology White Paper, 3*.

Steinert, Y. (2023). *Faculty Development : Principles and Practices*. Featured Article Faculty.

Steneck, N. H., & Bulger, R. E. (2007). The History, Purpose, and Future of Instruction in the Responsible Conduct of Research. *Academic Medicine*, *82*(9), 829–834. DOI: 10.1097/ACM.0b013e31812f7d4d PMID: 17726385

Sternberg, R. J., Chowkase, A., Parra-Martinez, F. A., & Landy, J. (2022). Criterion-referenced assessment of intelligence as adaptation to the environment: Is it possible, plausible, or practical? *Journal of Intelligence*, *10*(3), 57. DOI: 10.3390/jintelligence10030057

Stes, A., Clement, M., & Van Petegem, P. (2021). The Effectiveness of a Faculty Training Programme: Long-term and institutional impact. *International Journal for Academic Development ISSN, 1324*(November). Advance online publication. DOI: 10.1080/13601440701604898

St-Hilaire, F., Vu, D. D., Frau, A., Burns, N., Faraji, F., Potochny, J., . . . Kochmar, E. (2022). A new era: Intelligent tutoring systems will transform online learning for millions. *arXiv preprint arXiv:2203.03724.*

Stiegler, B. (2010). *Taking care of youth and the generations* (Barker, S., Trans.). Stanford University Press.

Stöhr, C., Ou, A. W., & Malmström, H. (2024). Perceptions and usage of AI chatbots among students in higher education across genders, academic levels and fields of study. *Computers and Education: Artificial Intelligence*, *7*, 100259. DOI: 10.1016/j.caeai.2024.100259

Sutherland-Smith, W., & Dawson, P. (2022). Higher education assessment design. In *Contract cheating in higher education: Global perspectives on theory, practice, and policy* (pp. 91–105). Springer International Publishing., DOI: 10.1007/978-3-031-12680-2_7

Syukri, M., Basri, M., Halim, A., & Maghfirah, S. (2025). Improving Students Ability to Evaluate and Conclude Through a Scientific Approach. *Current STEAM and Education Research*, *3*(1), 1–12. DOI: 10.58797/cser.030101

Takerngsaksiri, W., Warusavitarne, C., Yaacoub, C., Hou, M. H. K., & Tantithamthavorn, C. (2024, July). Students' perspectives on ai code completion: Benefits and challenges. In *2024 IEEE 48th Annual Computers, Software, and Applications Conference (COMPSAC)* (pp. 1606-1611). IEEE. https://doi.org/DOI: 10.1109/COMPSAC61105.2024.00252

Tan, S. (2020). Artificial intelligence in education: Rise of the machines. *Journal of Applied Learning & Teaching*, *3*(1), 129–133. DOI: 10.37074/jalt.2020.3.1.17

Tan, X., Cheng, G., & Ling, M. H. (2025). Artificial intelligence in teaching and teacher professional development: A systematic review. *Computers and Education: Artificial Intelligence*, *8*, 100355. Advance online publication. DOI: 10.1016/j.caeai.2024.100355

Tapalova, O., & Zhiyenbayeva, N. (2022). Artificial intelligence in education: AIEd for personalised learning pathways. *Electronic Journal of e-Learning*, *20*(5), 639–653. DOI: 10.34190/ejel.20.5.2597

Tarisayi, K. S. (2023). Strategic leadership for responsible artificial intelligence adoption in higher education. DOI: 10.55056/cte.616

Taylor, J. E. T., & Taylor, G. W. (2021). Artificial cognition: How experimental psychology can help generate explainable artificial intelligence. *Psychonomic Bulletin & Review, 28*(2), 454–475. DOI: 10.3758/s13423-020-01825-5

Tierens, T., Decuypere, M., & Hartong, S. (2024). Navigating open-source platforms in schools: An inquiry into changing teacher professionality. *Learning, Media and Technology*. Advance online publication. DOI: 10.1080/17439884.2024.2392114

Tlili, A., Shehata, B., Adarkwah, M. A., Bozkurt, A., Hickey, D. T., Huang, R., & Agyemang, B. (2023). What if the devil is my guardian angel? ChatGPT as a case study of using chatbots in education. *Smart Learning Environments, 10*(1), 1–24. DOI: 10.1186/s40561-023-00237-x

Tonbuloğlu, B. (2023). An evaluation of the use of artificial intelligence applications in online education. *Journal of Educational Technology and Online Learning, 6*(4), 866–884. DOI: 10.31681/jetol.1335906

Topping, K. J., Gehringer, E., Khosravi, H., Gudipati, S., Jadhav, K., Susarla, S.,… Susarla, S. (2025). Enhancing peer assessment with artificial intelligence. *International Journal of Educational Technology in Higher Education, 22:1, 22*(1). DOI: 10.1186/s41239-024-00501-1

Torrisi-Steele, G. (2025). AI and the humans in higher education. Advances in Educational Technologies and Instructional Design Book Series, 209–230. DOI: 10.4018/979-8-3373-0502-8.ch009

Torrisi-Steele, G. (2025). AI in higher education. Advances in Computational Intelligence and Robotics Book Series, 171–198. DOI: 10.4018/979-8-3373-2397-8.ch007

Tsai, C. W., Lee, L., Lin, M. Y. C., Cheng, Y. P., Lin, C. H., & Tsai, M. C. (2025). Effects of integrating self-regulation scaffolding supported by chatbot and online collaborative reflection on students' learning in an artificial intelligence course. *Computers & Education, 232*, 105305. DOI: 10.1016/j.compedu.2025.105305

Tsarkos, A. (2024). Navigating change in Education 5.0. Advances in Educational Marketing, Administration, and Leadership Book Series, 256–280. DOI: 10.4018/979-8-3693-3045-6.ch015

Tuomi, I. (2018). *The impact of artificial intelligence on learning, teaching, and education*. Publications Office of the European Union.

Turnitin. (2023). *Understanding the false positive rate for sentences of our AI writing detection capability.* https://www.turnitin.com/blog/understanding-the-false-positive-rate-for-sentences-of-our-ai-writing-detection-capability

Turnitin. (2025). *AI writing detection in the classic report view.* https://guides.turnitin.com/hc/en-us/articles/28457596598925-AI-writing-detection-in-the-classic-report-view

UNESCO. (2018). Digital credentialing: Implications for the recognition of learning across borders. UNESCO Education Sector. https://unesdoc.unesco.org/ark:/48223/pf0000264428

UNESCO. (2021). *Recommendation on the ethics of artificial intelligence.* United Nations Educational, Scientific and Cultural Organization.

UNESCO. (2023). *Guidance for generative AI in education and research.* UNESCO.

UNESCO. (2024). Global report on AI in education: Ethics and governance. UNESCO Publishing. https://www.unesco.org/en/artificial-intelligence/recommendation-ethics

UNESCO. (2025). *Guidance for generative AI in education and research* (updated). https://www.unesco.org/en/articles/guidance-generative-ai-education-and-research

University System of Georgia. (2025). Nexus Degree, https://www.usg.edu/academic_programs/nexus_degree (accessed on October 20, 2025).

US Department of Education. (2023). Artificial intelligence and the future of teaching and learning. *Washington, DC: Office of Educational Technology, U.S. Department of Education* https://files.eric.ed.gov/fulltext/ED631097.pdf

Valiente, O. (2014). The OECD skills strategy and the education agenda for development. *International Journal of Educational Development, 39*, 40–48. DOI: 10.1016/j.ijedudev.2014.08.008

Van Damme, D. (2014). Does lifelong learning perpetuate inequalities in educational opportunities? OECD., https://oecdedutoday.com/does-lifelong-learning-perpetuate-inequalities-in-educational-opportunities/, Retrieved October 20, 2025, from.

Van Noordt, C., & Misuraca, G. (2022). Artificial intelligence for the public sector: Results of landscaping the use of AI in government across the European Union. *Government Information Quarterly, 39*(3), 101714. DOI: 10.1016/j.giq.2022.101714

Vázquez-Cano, E., Mengual-Andrés, S., & López-Meneses, E. (2021). Chatbot to improve learning punctuation in Spanish and to enhance open and flexible learning environments. *International Journal of Educational Technology in Higher Education, 18*(1), 33. DOI: 10.1186/s41239-021-00269-8

Vázquez-Parra, J. C., Henao-Rodríguez, C., Lis-Gutiérrez, J. P., Palomino-Gámez, S., & Suárez-Brito, P. (2024). *Perception of AI tool adoption and training: initial validation using GSEM method*. Applied Computing and Informatics.

Venkatesh, V. (2022). Adoption and use of AI tools: A research agenda grounded in UTAUT. *Annals of Operations Research, 308*(1), 641–652. DOI: 10.1007/s10479-020-03918-9

Vera, I. A. D., Briones, W. L., & Heredia, M. I. V. (2024). Ethical perspectives on the application of Artificial Intelligence in Higher Education. *Sinergias Educativas, 9*(1). Advance online publication. DOI: 10.37954/se.v9i1.438

Vesna, L. (2025). Digital Divide in AI-Powered Education: Challenges and Solutions for Equitable Learning. *Journal of Information Systems Engineering & Management, 10*(21s), 300–308. Advance online publication. DOI: 10.52783/jisem.v10i21s.3327

Vieriu, A. M., & Petrea, G. (2025). The impact of artificial intelligence (AI) on students' academic development. *Education Sciences, 15*(3), 343. DOI: 10.3390/educsci15030343

Virvou, M., Alepis, E., Tsihrintzis, G. A., & Jain, L. C. (2019). Machine learning paradigms: advances in learning analytics. In *Machine learning paradigms: Advances in learning analytics* (pp. 1–5). Springer International Publishing.

Waddington, L. (2022). Supporting faculty adoption of technology and online learning: pandemic inspired possibilities.

Walker, L. (2025). Artificial intelligence in medical education: Potential and pitfalls. *Australian Journal of General Practice, 54*(10), 743–746. https://search.informit.org/doi/10.3316/informit.T2025101800002790791144166. DOI: 10.31128/AJGP-02-25-7559

Walter, Y. (2024). Embracing the future of Artificial Intelligence in the classroom: The relevance of AI literacy, prompt engineering, and critical thinking in modern education. *International Journal of Educational Technology in Higher Education, 21*(1), 15. DOI: 10.1186/s41239-024-00448-3

Wang, S., Wang, F., Zhu, Z., Wang, J., Tran, T., & Du, Z. (2024). Artificial intelligence in education: A systematic literature review. *Expert Systems with Applications, 252*, 124167. DOI: 10.1016/j.eswa.2024.124167

Wang, Y. (2021). Factors Affecting the Adoption of AI-Based Applications in Higher Education: An Analysis of Teachers' Perspectives Using Structural Equation Modeling. *Journal of Educational Technology & Society, 24*, 116–129.

Watson, J. C., II, & Etzel, E. F. (2019). *Ethical and legal issues in sport and performance psychology.* https://psycnet.apa.org/record/2019-05400-041

Webb, M. (2025). AI detection and assessment – an update for 2025. https://nationalcentreforai.jiscinvolve.org/wp/2025/06/24/ai-detection-assessment-2025/

Webster, S., Lewis, J., & Brown, A. (2013). Considerations in qualitative research. *Qualitative Research Practice: A Guide for Social Science Students and Researchers, 1*, 77. https://www.torrossa.com/gs/resourceProxy?an=5017584&publisher=FZ7200#page=102

Westera, W., Prada, R., Mascarenhas, S., Santos, P. A., Dias, J., Guimarães, M., Georgiadis, K., Nyamsuren, E., Bahreini, K., Yumak, Z., Christyowidiasmoro, C., Dascalu, M., Gutu-Robu, G., & Ruseti, S. (2020). Artificial intelligence moving serious gaming: Presenting reusable game AI components. *Education and Information Technologies, 25*(1), 351–380. DOI: 10.1007/s10639-019-09968-2

Westover, J. (2024). Embracing AI in change management. *Human Capital Leadership Review, 13*(1). Advance online publication. DOI: 10.70175/hclreview.2020.13.1.11

Wheelahan, L., & Moodie, G. (2022). Gig qualifications for the gig economy: Micro-credentials and the 'hungry mile'. *Higher Education, 83*(6), 1279–1295. DOI: 10.1007/s10734-021-00742-3 PMID: 34366441

Wheeler, S. (2019). *Digital learning in organizations: Help your workforce capitalize on technology*. Kogan Page Publishers.

Wibawa, A. P., & Kurniawan, F. (2024). Advancements in natural language processing: Implications, challenges, and future directions. *Telematics and Informatics Reports, 16*, 100173. Advance online publication. DOI: 10.1016/j.teler.2024.100173

Wible, J. R. (2016). Scientific misconduct and the responsible conduct of research in science and economics. *Review of Social Economy, 74*(1), 7–32. DOI: 10.1080/00346764.2016.1135598

Williamson, B., Bayne, S., & Shay, S. (2020). The datafication of teaching in Higher Education: Critical issues and perspectives. *Teaching in Higher Education, 25*(4), 351–365. DOI: 10.1080/13562517.2020.1748811

Williamson, B., & Eynon, R. (2020). Historical threads, missing links, and future directions in AI in education. *Learning, Media and Technology, 45*(3), 223–235. DOI: 10.1080/17439884.2020.1798995

Williamson, B., Komljenovic, J., & Gulson, K. (2023). *World Yearbook of Education 2024: Digitalisation of Education in the Era of Algorithms*. Automation and Artificial Intelligence., DOI: 10.4324/9781003359722

Wilson, J., & Huang, Y. (2024). Validity of automated essay scores for elementary-age English language learners: Evidence of bias? *Assessing Writing*, *60*, 100815. Advance online publication. DOI: 10.1016/j.asw.2024.100815

Wimpenny, K., Finardi, K., Orsini-Jones, M., & Jacobs, L. (2022). Knowing, Being, Relating and Expressing Through Third Space Global South-North COIL: Digital Inclusion and Equity in International Higher Education. *Journal of Studies in International Education*, *26*(2), 279–296. DOI: 10.1177/10283153221094085

Woldegiorgis, E. T. Challenges of integrating technology in East African higher education systems in the post-pandemic era: emerging academic cultures. *Technology, Pedagogy and Education*, 1-19. DOI: 10.1080/1475939X.2025.2520589

Woodruff, K., Hutson, J., & Arnone, K. (2023). Perceptions and barriers to adopting artificial intelligence in K-12 education: A survey of educators in fifty states.

World Economic Forum. (2020). *The future of jobs report 2020*. World Economic Forum._https://www.weforum.org/publications/the-future-of-jobs-report-2020/ (accessed on October 18, 2025).

Wu, C., Zhang, H., & Carroll, J. M. (2024). AI governance in higher education: Case studies of guidance at Big Ten universities. *Future Internet*, *16*(10), 354. DOI: 10.3390/fi16100354

Wu, Y. (2023). Integrating generative AI in education: How ChatGPT brings challenges for future learning and teaching. *Journal of Advanced Research in Education*, *2*(4), 6–10. DOI: 10.56397/JARE.2023.07.02

Yang, H., Kim, J., Lee, W., Yang, H., Kim, J., & Lee, W. (2023). Analyzing the Alignment between AI Curriculum and AI Textbooks through Text Mining. *Applied Sciences, Vol. 13, Page 10011, 13*(18). DOI: 10.3390/app131810011

Yavich, R., Davidovitch, N., & Gerkerova, A. (2025). Exploring the Association between AI Tool Use and Academic Self-Efficacy among University Students in Israel. *African Educational Research Journal*, *13*(3), 311–324. https://eric.ed.gov/?id=EJ1484697

Youn, C. H., Salam, A. R., & Rahman, A. A. (2025). AI-Driven Tools in Providing Feedback on Students' Writing. *International Journal of Research and Innovation in Social Science, IX*(IIIS), 58-67. DOI: 10.47772/IJRISS.2025.903SEDU0006

Yuan, Y. (2024). *A study of artificial intelligence-driven change in higher education in the age of digital intelligence*. Contemporary Education and Teaching Research., DOI: 10.61360/BoniCETR242016080306

Yusuf, A., Pervin, N., & Román-González, M. (2024). Generative AI and the future of higher education: A threat to academic integrity or reformation? Evidence from multicultural perspectives. *International Journal of Educational Technology in Higher Education, 21*(1), 21. DOI: 10.1186/s41239-024-00453-6

Zahid, A., & Nawab, A. (2025). Teaching strategies influencing learning strategies: Exploration of teaching and learning practices in a higher education context in Pakistan. *Social Sciences & Humanities Open, 11*, 101442. DOI: 10.1016/j.ssaho.2025.101442

Zakir, H. O. S. S. A. I. N. (2025). Exploring EFL Students ' AI Literacy in Academic Writing : Insights into Familiarity, Knowledge and Ethical Perceptions İngilizceyi Yabancı Dil Olarak Öğrenen Öğrencilerin Akademik Yazımda Yapay Zekâ Okuryazarlığını Keşfetmek : Aşinalık, Bilgi ve In rec. *Journal of Theoretical Educational Science, 18*(January), 157–181.

Zawacki-Richter, O., Marín, V. I., Bond, M., & Gouverneur, F. (2019). Systematic review of research on artificial intelligence applications in higher education — Where are the educators? *International Journal of Educational Technology in Higher Education, 16*(1), 39. Advance online publication. DOI: 10.1186/s41239-019-0171-0

Zekânın, Y., & Öğretim, Ü. (2024, October). S. (2025). The Impact of Artificial Intelligence on University Teaching Processes. *Kastamonu Education Journal, 33*, 448–468. DOI: 10.24106/kefdergi.1748350

Zhai, X., Chu, X., Chai, C. S., Jong, M. S. Y., Istenic, A., Spector, M., Liu, J.-B., Yuan, J., & Li, Y. (2021). A Review of Artificial Intelligence (AI) in Education from 2010 to 2020. *Complexity, 2021*(1), 8812542. DOI: 10.1155/2021/8812542

Zhai, X., & Nehm, R. H. (2023). AI and formative assessment: The train has left the station. *Journal of Research in Science Teaching, 60*(6), 1390–1398. DOI: 10.1002/tea.21885

Zhang, K., & Aslan, A. B. (2021). AI technologies for education: Recent research & future directions. *Computers and education. Artificial Intelligence, 2*, 100025.

Zhang, S., Zhao, X., Zhou, T., & Kim, J. H. (2024). Do you have AI dependency? The roles of academic self-efficacy, academic stress, and performance expectations on problematic AI usage behavior. *International Journal of Educational Technology in Higher Education, 21*(1), 34. DOI: 10.1186/s41239-024-00467-0

Zhao, J., Chapman, E., & Sabet, P. G. (2024). Generative AI and educational assessments: A systematic review. *Education Research and Perspectives*, *51*, 124–155. https://search.informit.org/doi/10.3316/informit.T2025061800005500592641426. DOI: 10.70953/ERPv51.2412006

Zhao, Y., & Watterston, J. (2021). The changes we need: Education post COVID-19 and the opportunities of AI. *Journal of Educational Change*, *22*(1), 3–12. DOI: 10.1007/s10833-021-09417-3

Zhou, W., & Kim, Y. (2024). Innovative music education: An empirical assessment of ChatGPT-4's impact on student learning experiences. *Education and Information Technologies*, *29*(16), 20855–20881. DOI: 10.1007/s10639-024-12705-z

Zhou, X., Fang, L., & Schofield, L. (2023). Assessing AI literacy among academic staff: Insights from a higher education survey. *Research Article*, *18*(1), 138–159.

Zhou, Z., Dong, Y., Du, G., He, Y., Ma, X., Sanabria, R., Liu, R., He, J., Zhang, Z., Liu, W., Cai, Z., Huang, S., & Wan, X. (2025). Kill two birds with one stone: Dynamic perturbations for robust long-text watermarking and effective detection. In *Proceedings of the 2025 Conference of the North American Chapter of the Association for Computational Linguistics (NAACL)* (Long Papers). DOI: 10.18653/v1/2025.naacl-long.446

Zobel, T., Staubitz, T., & Meinel, C. (2023) Introducing a Smart Learning Assistant on a MOOC Platform: Enhancing Personalized Learning Experiences. In *2023 IEEE 2nd German Education Conference (GECon)* (pp. 1-6). IEEE.PI.

Zuiderwijk, A., Chen, Y. C., & Salem, F. (2021). Implications of the use of artificial intelligence in public governance: A systematic literature review and a research agenda. *Government Information Quarterly*, *38*(3), 101577. DOI: 10.1016/j.giq.2021.101577

About the Contributors

Nuzhat Younis is a Lecturer and SFHEA with extensive experience. She is currently affiliated with UWE Bristol and EDA College, delivering undergraduate and postgraduate modules while supervising research projects across multiple domains, including cybersecurity and business analytics. Nuzhat has a diverse academic and technical background, with teaching and leadership roles across the UK, Middle East, and South Asia. She is pursuing a PhD in Management and IT, focusing on the impact of AI tools in higher education. Passionate about inclusive digital education, she actively contributes to curriculum development, quality assurance, and staff training initiatives.

Yasmine Z. Rosunally is a Senior Lecturer in Information Science at the University of the West of England, with over 18 years of experience in higher education. She specialises in Transnational Education (TNE), curriculum design, and international programme management, having led initiatives across China, Nepal, Vietnam, and Hong Kong. Yasmine is a recognised researcher in technology-enhanced learning, gamification, and AI in education, with numerous publications in high-impact journals. She holds a PhD in Applied Computing and is a Senior Fellow of the Higher Education Academy (SFHEA). Yasmine also serves as an external examiner and advisor for several UK universities.

Mazhar Malik is Associate Director/Head of Artificial Intelligence department at UWE Bristol, with extensive expertise in cybersecurity, IoT, digital forensics, and computing education. He has held senior academic leadership roles in the UK and internationally, including at Head of Computing and IT at Global College of Engineering and Technology Oman. Dr. Malik actively contributes to global programme reviews, academic quality assurance, and professional accreditation. His research interests include network and IoT security, digital forensics, data analytics, and technology-enhanced learning. His research portfolio includes over 50 peer-reviewed publications on secure routing in IoT, smart cities, medical data analytics, and AI-enhanced cybersecurity. Notable works include contributions to Vehicular Communications, Computers, IEEE Access, PLOS ONE, and Scientific Reports.

***

Muhammad Ali is an Associate Professor in the Department of Life Sciences at the University of Management and Technology (UMT), Lahore, bringing over a decade of dedicated professional and academic experience in the field of Life Sciences. He holds a PhD in Virology and Immunology from the National University of Sciences and Technology (NUST), Islamabad, complemented by M.Phil. and B.Sc. (Hons) degrees in Biotechnology & Genetic Engineering and Plant Breeding & Genetics, respectively. His international exposure includes a significant tenure as a Visiting Scholar and Researcher at McGill University, Montreal, Quebec, Canada, under an HEC-Pakistan fellowship. Dr. Ali's prolific research contributions are evident in his impressive publication record, which includes over 50 research articles in peer-reviewed journals with a cumulative impact factor of over 200 and over 3000 citations. His scholarly impact is further underscored by an H-index of 15 and an i10-index of 20. He has also authored 3 book chapters with Springer and Elsevier and contributed 22 GenBank submissions. As a resource person, he taught more than 25 different courses in the domain of Biological Sciences with more than 90% student feedback. In research, he mentored more than 50 MS/MPhil research projects. A recognized expert in his field, Dr. Ali is a full member of the World Society for Virology and holds memberships with the American Society for Microbiology and The American Phyto pathological Society. His commitment to academic excellence and scholarly contribution was recognized with the UMT Best Employee of the 1st Quarter & award in 2019, alongside several prestigious HEC-Pakistan, Ministry of Science and Technology (MoST), Pakistan and National Bank of Pakistan (NBP) Scholarships and awards throughout his academic journey. He is founding editor of two journals – BioScientific Reviews (Quarterly) and Current Trends in Omics (Biannual) under the umbrella of KRSS, UMT. With his profound academic background, extensive research output, and supervisory experience, Dr. Muhammad Ali possesses the intellectual depth, leadership qualities, and commitment to scientific rigor essential for an Editor-in-Chief role, poised to advance 'Scientific Inquiry & Review', a quarterly journal, reputation and impact within the global scientific community.

Hana An L. Alvarado is a pre-service mathematics teacher from Mindanao State University–Tawi-Tawi College of Technology and Oceanography (MSU-TCTO), located in Sanga-Sanga, Bongao, Tawi-Tawi, Philippines. She is an early-career researcher specializing in mathematics education, with research interests spanning ethnomathematics, STEM education, multilingual pedagogies, culturally responsive teaching, and artificial intelligence integration. Her work explores how these domains influence students' mathematical reasoning, participation, and learning experiences in linguistically and culturally diverse contexts.

M. Azhagiri completed his Bachelor of Engineering in Information Technology from Vinayaka Missions Kirupananda Variyar Engineering College, affiliated with Vinayaka Missions Research Foundation, deemed to be university located in Salem, Tamil Nadu, India, in 2009, his Master of Engineering in Computer Science and Engineering from Paavai Engineering College at Namakkal, affiliated with Anna University, Tamil Nadu, India, in 2011, and his Doctor of Philosophy in Computer Science and Engineering from St Peters Institute for Higher Education and Research, Tamil Nadu, India, since 2020. Currently, he is working as an Associate Professor in the Department of Computer Science and Engineering at the SRM Institute of Science and Technology, Ramapuram, Chennai, India. He has 12 years of teaching experience with good programming skills. He has been certified in various courses from Coursera and NPTEL. He has published 40 articles in National and International Journals, Conferences, and Symposiums. His area of research is computer networks, network security, and machine learning.

Komal Bhardwaj is currently working at the Maharishi Markandashwar Institute of Management, MMU. She has a rich experience of more than 8 years of teaching in the field of management. She has a research experience in the areas of assets pricing, option pricing, derivatives and study on stock volatility. Her research interest includes consumer behaviour, investments, corporate governance and assets liability management. She also worked as a thesis supervisor for a program called upgrade- LJMU MBA at upgrade education private limited.

Tashi Ongmu Bhutia is a distinguished academician in the field of Physical Education, currently serving at the Government B.Ed. College, Soreng, Sikkim. She began her academic journey at the prestigious Lakshmibai National Institute of Physical Education (LNIPE), Gwalior, where she completed both her Bachelor of Physical Education (B.P.Ed.) and Master of Physical Education (M.P.Ed.) with excellence. Driven by a passion for research and academic growth, she pursued her doctoral studies at the University of Delhi, earning a Ph.D. in Physical Education. Over the years, Dr. Bhutia has contributed significantly to promoting physical education, sports, and wellness through her teaching, mentorship, and scholarly pursuits. Her academic background and professional dedication reflect her commitment to advancing the standards of teacher education in Sikkim. Known for her expertise, discipline, and inspiring approach, she continues to shape the future of aspiring educators while fostering holistic development through physical education.

Anindita Das is an esteemed Associate Professor at the Lakshmibai National Institute of Physical Education (LNIPE), Gwalior, with a distinguished career in teaching, research, and sports. Since joining LNIPE in 2007, she has been actively engaged in teaching core subjects such as Health Education, Physiology, and Football (practical). Dr. Das has made significant academic contributions through her authorship of numerous research papers in Scopus, patents, books and chapters in the field of physical education and sports sciences. She has published over twenty research articles in reputed national and international journals and has presented her work at a wide array of conferences. Notably, she presented papers at the Pre-Olympic Congress in Liverpool, UK (2012) and the World Congress on Kinanthropometry in Santiago, Chile (2018). A recipient of international training, Dr. Das completed a 3-month International Coaching Course (ICC) in General Conditioning at Semmelweis University, Budapest, Hungary, in 2009, further enriching her academic and practical expertise. Beyond academics, Dr. Das is a former athlete who has passionately contributed to women's football. She was a four-time member of her university's intervarsity women's football team and won a bronze medal in the All India Intervarsity Women Football Tournament in 2002. She also represented Madhya Pradesh in the National Women's Football Championship and played a key role when her team participated in the 1st Khelo India University Games (KIUG) held in Bhubaneswar, Odisha, in February 2020. Dr. Das continues to inspire students and peers alike with her commitment to excellence in physical education, research, and sports development.

Beaulah David is currently serving in the Department of Computer Science and Engineering at Nehru Institute of Technology, Kaliyapuram, Coimbatore, Tamil Nadu, India. She holds a Ph.D. in Computer Science and Engineering and has extensive experience in both academic teaching and research. Her primary areas of expertise include artificial intelligence, machine learning, and data analytics. She has published several research papers in reputed international journals and conferences. Dr. Beaulah actively guides students and encourages innovative research in emerging technologies. Her academic vision focuses on bridging theoretical knowledge with practical applications in computing. Through her dedicated efforts, she continues to contribute significantly to the advancement of computer science education and research.

Amandeep Dhaliwal, an Associate Professor at Manav Rachna International Institute of Research & Studies, Faridabad, is an academician and researcher with over 14 years of experience in academia and 5+ years in the corporate sector. With a doctorate from BIMTECH, Greater Noida, her research focuses on entrepreneurship, student engagement, outcome-based education and business analytics with special interests in areas of AI, ML, Meta, and amalgamation of these with ICT technologies. An accomplished researcher, Dr. Dhaliwal has more than 30 publications, Her works are featured in reputed journals, including Scopus and ABDC-listed publications. She has many case studies published to her credit. Her areas of specialization She has presented at 14 national and international conferences and delivered expert talks. Notable awards include the Stough Young Scholar Award and Best Research Paper accolades in MRCON 2020 and 2023.Over the years, she has developed keen interest and expertise in academic systems, and academic accreditation. Passionate about teaching, Dr. Dhaliwal emphasizes fostering creativity and excellence among students while contributing to research and institutional development.

Ceren Ersoy is a researcher and academician at Gazi University, Gazi Faculty of Education, Department of Special Education, where she has served since 2013. Since 2022, she has also been affiliated with the Gazi University Educational Policy Research Center. She completed her undergraduate studies in English Language Teaching at Dokuz Eylül University and pursued graduate studies in the field of giftedness and special education. She earned her first master's degree in Gifted Education from Anadolu University and successfully completed all coursework in the Education of the Mentally Handicapped program at Gazi University. She later obtained her Ph.D. from Gazi University's Institute of Educational Sciences, with a specialization in the identification of gifted students. Throughout her academic career, Dr. Ersoy has actively contributed to various national and international projects focused on inclusive education, special education, gifted education, and digital learning. Her areas of expertise include the identification and assessment of giftedness, cognitive and metacognitive skills, acceleration and enrichment strategies, technology-assisted learning, curriculum development, teacher competencies and professional development, as well as educational gamification, artificial intelligence in education, virtual reality, creativity, and education policy. She continues to make significant scholarly contributions through numerous conference presentations, published book chapters, and collaborative research projects.

Karuppasamy Govindasamy is a dedicated researcher in Physical Education and Sports Sciences at the Department of Sports, Recreation and Wellness, Symbiosis International (Deemed University), Hyderabad Campus, Telangana. He has authored over 108 publications in Scopus and 51 publications in Web of Science journals, along with patents, book chapters, and books. His research focuses on innovative training methodologies and the integration of theory and practice in sports science.

Dr. Govindasamy is UGC-NET and JRF qualified, has received multiple Best Paper Presentation awards, and was honored with a national-level Young Researcher Award. He also serves as a reviewer for 13 top-ranking international journals.

Sherlyn A. Iralan is a pre-service mathematics teacher and an undergraduate student pursuing a Bachelor of Secondary Education major in Mathematics at Mindanao State University–Tawi-Tawi College of Technology and Oceanography (MSU-TCTO), Philippines. Her research interests include mathematics education, and artificial intelligence in education.

Potchong M. Jackaria currently holds a rank of Associate Professor 3 under the Science and Mathematics Department of the College of Education, Mindanao State University Tawi-Tawi, College of Technology and Oceanography in Tawi-Tawi, Philippines. Prior to working at MSU, he had an extensive experience teaching in different public schools handling elementary level mathematics and later as school head. Asst. Prof. Jackaria obtained his master degree in Education in Administration and Supervision from MSU Tawi-Tawi College of Technology and Oceanography and a Master of Science Education Major in Mathematics from MSU-Iligan Institute of Technology. He was involved in teachers' training and is interested in research areas including mathematics teaching, technology in education, teachers professional development, and education policy.

Debajit Karmakar, is a distinguished research scholar and accomplished academic in the field of Physical Education and Sports Science. Currently pursuing his Ph.D. at the prestigious Lakshmibai National Institute of Physical Education (LNIPE), Gwalior, he has established himself as a prolific researcher. Mr. Karmakar completed his educational journey with remarkable academic excellence, earning his B.A./B.Sc. (Hons) in Physical Education from Visva-Bharati University, Santiniketan, followed by his B.P.Ed. from the same institution where he topped in his class. His Master's degree in Physical Education is from LNIPE, and he subsequently qualified UGC NET-JRF & WBSET examinations, demonstrating his academic prowess. A specialist in football and sports psychology, Mr. Karmakar has made significant contributions to academic literature with extensive publications in Scopus & Web of Science indexed journals. His research focuses on mental training, performance psychology, and innovative training methodologies. He has authored multiple books on sports psychology and performance enhancement, while also serving as editor for several academic publications.

Abhishek Kumar is a leading voice in the world of inclusive sports, celebrated for his dual role as a dedicated management professional and a pioneering coach. His work is a testament to the power of sports in transforming lives, particularly for athletes with intellectual disabilities. With a Master's in Physical Education and a Ph.D. from Delhi University, Abhishek's deep academic knowledge is matched by his extensive practical experience. As a two-time Gothia Cup winning coach in 2024 and 2025 for Special Olympics Bharat, he made history by leading India to its first-ever trophy in the special category of the world's largest soccer championship. His expertise in team management and athletic development has been instrumental in preparing athletes for global stages, including the 2023 Berlin World Games and the 2025 World Special Winter Games in Italy. Beyond his work in coaching, Abhishek's background spans managing sports academies and organizing professional boxing events, showcasing his commitment to developing comprehensive sports programs. His passion and leadership have cemented his reputation as a true champion for sports excellence.

Vinod Kumar is an Assistant Professor at Guru Kashi University Talwandi Sabo Punjab. He has completed his M. Com. from Kurukshetra University, Kurukshetra, Haryana. He is a research scholar at Guru Jambheshwar University of Science and Technology, Hisar, Haryana. He has published various research papers/book chapters in different reputed journals and edited books. His specialization area is agricultural marketing.

Muhammad Nouman is a Lecturer at the Sirindhorn School of Prosthetics and Orthotics, Faculty of Medicine, Siriraj Hospital, Mahidol University, Bangkok, Thailand. Trained in Biomedical Engineering with advanced specialization in Prosthetics and Orthotics, his academic and research career integrates biomechanics, rehabilitation engineering, computational modeling, and clinical innovation. Dr. Nouman's primary research focuses on diabetic foot complications, particularly in pressure offloading, finite element analysis, advanced material design, and 3D-printed orthotic technologies. He has contributed pioneering work on insole-based interventions and gait optimization, and his publications appear in leading international journals including Gait & Posture and Foot & Ankle International. He is the author of the comprehensive reference book A Guide to Insole-Based Approaches for Diabetic Foot Complications and has served as a peer reviewer for several indexed journals in the fields of biomechanics, rehabilitation science, and diabetic foot research. His recent projects explore AI-integrated rehabilitation, personalized orthotic systems, and big-data-driven clinical analytics. Dr. Nouman is actively engaged in ASEAN regional collaborations to advance education and translational research in prosthetics and orthotics, bridging clinical insight, computational intelligence, and human-centered design.

Deependra Nath Pathak is an Associate Professor, Amity Law School, Amity University, Patna and Dr. Pathak awarded a Ph.D. from BBA Central University, Lucknow. He holds LL. B from Banaras Hindu University, LL.M. from BBA Central University, Lucknow. He has 8 years' experience in university and 3 years in a judicial coaching. He had qualified for UGC-NET in Law. Dr. Pathak has numerous publication research papers and book chapters in UGC Care and Scopus index journal and has presented at various national and international conference. Dr Pathak is good motivater and his many students has served as a judicial officer, Law officer and other services. Dr Pathak is awarded with Best faculty, Teaching excellence, Best researcher at National and International Level.

Nosheen Qamar received the Ph.D. degree in computer science from the National University of Computer and Emerging Sciences (FAST-NUCES), Lahore, Pakistan. She is currently an Assistant Professor with the Department of Software Engineering, University of Management and Technology, Lahore. Before joining the academia, in 2015, she gained seven years of industry experience as a Software Development Manager. Her research interests include software engineering, design patterns, software project management, software teams, empirical software engineering, and software requirements engineering.

Retna Mony R is an academic and researcher specializing in English Literature. He holds a Ph.D. in English Literature from Manonmaniam Sundaranar University and a Post-Doctoral Fellowship from Christ University, Bangalore. With over 11 years of teaching experience, he has served as Assistant Professor of English at institutions including Manonmaniam Sundaranar University, Mohan Babu University, and currently, K L University, Vijayawada. His expertise spans Indian English literature, sociocultural studies, neurolinguistics programming, qualitative research, and communication skills training. A recognized Ph.D. supervisor, he has guided research in literature, artificial intelligence, and socio-political studies. He has published extensively in Scopus and Web of Science indexed journals, contributed book chapters, and presented at national and international conferences. He is also a patent holder for innovations in language learning frameworks and devices. His career philosophy centers on the integration of literature, technology, and ethical pedagogy, advancing education as both a humanistic and cognitive endeavor. Through his ongoing work, he continues to bridge the gap between literary humanism and AI-driven innovation, contributing to the evolving discourse on education, ethics, and digital humanity. His ongoing projects explore the ethical dimensions of AI through literature and his work reflects a commitment to bridging literature, pedagogy, and contemporary social issues.

Shivendu Kumar Rai is working as a HoD-Dept of Journalism and Mass Communication in the Tecnia Institute of Advanced Studies, Rohini, New Delhi. Before that, he worked as Assistant Professor at Galgotias University, Greater Noida and as Acting Dean and assistant Professor, Faculty of Professional Studies, Department of Journalism and Mass Communication, Rama University, Kanpur (U.P.) He has done Graduation in Mass Media (2011) from Jamia Millia Islamia Central University, and Post-Graduation & M.Phil in Mass Communication (2013 & 2014) from Makhanalal Chaturvedi National University of Journalism and Communication, Bhopal.& Ph.D. (2020) in Mass Communication from Mahatma Gandhi International Hindi University, Wardha (Maharashtra). He has qualified UGC- NET examination twice in 2018 and 2019. He worked as a Doctorate Research Fellow at Indian Council of Social Science Research, New Delhi in PhD Research Topic Project "Changes In the Communication Strategies of Political Parties: Special Reference to tribal areas of Sonbhadra". Dr. Shivendu Kumar Rai has published 25 full-length research papers in reputed UGC Listed/ Peer Review Research Journals. He has attended 50 Seminars/Workshops/Conferences/FDP etc. His area of expertise is Communication for Development, New Media Communication Research, and Political Communication.

Abhijeet Rajan is an Associate Professor, Amity Law School, Amity University, Patna and Dr. Rajan got his PhD awarded from Banaras Hindu University. He holds LL.B from Delhi University, LL.M. from Banaras Hindu University. He has 8 years experience in University and 3 years in a judicial coaching . He had qualified for UGC-JRF in Law. Dr. Rajan has numerous publication research papers and book chapters in UGC Care and Scopus index journal and has presented at various national and international conference. Dr Rajan is a good motivater and his many students has served as a judicial officer, Law officer and other services.

|A RAJESH - Contributing Author|Dr. A.RAJESH, has completed his Ph.D in the Department of Computer Science and Engineering from Dr.MGR Educational and Research Institute, Chennai, Tamil Nadu, India. He obtained his B.E degree in Electronics and Communication Engineering from Govt. College of Engineering, Salem, Tamil Nadu, India. He earned his M.E degree in Computer Science and Engineering from Sathyabama Institute of Science and Technology, Chennai, Tamil Nadu, India. He is currently working as Professor in the Department of Computer Science and Engineering in Jain University, Bangalore, Karnataka, India. He has published around 71 research papers in Peer-reviewed/Scopus/SCIE indexed journals. He has also published 9 books and 5 patents. He has produced 10 Doctorates under his guidance. His research interests include Intelligent Systems, AI, Machine Learning, Deep learning, and Data mining.

Radha Ranjan, Assistant Professor, Amity University, Patna, Bihar. Dr. Radha Ranjan holds a PhD in Law from the Department of Law and Governance, Central University of South Bihar, NAAC Accredited A++ University and UGC Category 1 University.He has obtained the degree of BA (Hons) Spanish language from EFL University, LL. B from Banaras Hindu University, LLM from National Law School of India University, Diploma from University of Catolica Chile and qualified UGC NET in Law and Criminology. Dr. Ranjan has multiple publications in Research Papers, Articles, Blogs, book chapters in edited volumes, Peer reviewed, UGC CARE journals and presented papers in several National and International Seminars/Conferences and actively participated in various national and international workshops, FDP. He is an active editorial member, reviewer and advisory editorial board member of National as well as International Journals respectively and members of reputed society and organisation. Dr. Ranjan has substantial experience of constitution Law, Cyber-Law, Criminal Law and Human Rights.

Junaidy Suparman Rustam, M.N.S. is a nursing educator and Vice Rector for Academic Affairs at Mohammad Natsir University, West Sumatra, Indonesia. He has over two decades of experience in nursing education, clinical practice, and leadership, with previous roles as Head of School at Yarsi Health Science College and Head Nurse at Ibnu Sina Islamic Hospital. His professional and research interests include critical care nursing, patient comfort interventions, and community health. He has presented widely at international conferences in Thailand, Malaysia, Japan, and Indonesia, receiving multiple awards for best oral presentations and academic excellence. Mr. Rustam is an active member of the Indonesia Nurse Organization, the Indonesia Nurse Education Association, and several professional and volunteer networks dedicated to healthcare, disaster response, and education.

Nosheen Sabahat received the Ph.D. degree in computer software engineering from the National University of Sciences and Technology (NUST), Islamabad, Pakistan. She is currently an Assistant Professor with the Forman Christian College (A Chartered University), FCCU, Lahore, Pakistan. She received the Pakistan's Higher Education Commission (HEC) Indigenous Scholarship for M.S. leading to Ph.D. She has authored several research publications in internationally reputed journals and international conferences. Her research interests include software project management, usability evaluation, software sizing, requirements engineering, and empirical software engineering.

Norsaremah is currently a Professor in the Department of Computer Science at the International Islamic University Malaysia. She brings over 20 years of academic experience, preceded by nearly five years in the software industry as a software developer. She earned her PhD in Computer Science from the University of Auckland, New Zealand, and has since built a strong research portfolio in empirical software engineering and evidence-based software engineering. Dr. Norsaremah has published over 80 papers in both local and internationally refereed journals and conferences, including prestigious venues such as: IEEE Transactions on Software Engineering, Empirical Software Engineering, Information & Software Technology, IEEE Software and Journal of Systems and Software.

GarimaSehrawat is working as an Assistant Professor at Maharishi Markandashwar Institute of Management, MMU. She has a rich experience of more than 5 years of teaching in the field of Management. She has interest in the diverse areas of Agribusiness, Finance and consumer behavior. She has published several research papers and presented them at prestigious national and international conferences.

Nuno Miguel Teixeira Sousa completed his Master's degree in Information Science in 2023 from the Faculty of Arts and Humanities of Coimbra University and his Bachelor's degree in Information Science in 2021 from the Faculty of Arts and Humanities of Coimbra University. He is currently studying for a PhD in Information Science at the Faculty of Letters of the University of Lisbon since 2024 and he is investigator of Center for Classical Studies. Actually is a Senior Technician at the Library of the Law Faculty of the Coimbra University. He has received 4 awards. Works in the field(s) of Social Sciences with an emphasis on Communication Sciences with an emphasis on Information Sciences.

Karthik Srinivasan received the Ph.D. degree in information and communication engineering from Anna University, Chennai, India, in 2015. He is currently an Assistant Professor with the Department of Information Technology, Saudi Electronic University, Saudi Arabia. He has 20 years of teaching experience with good programming skills. He has published 40 articles in National and International Journals, Conferences, and Symposiums. He is a Reviewer and an Editorial Board Member of various National and International Journals. He was a chair person in National and International Conferences in various Institutions. He is a life time member of the IAENG, CSTA His research interests include machine learning, network security, and the Internet of Things.

Varadharajan Bhoopathy is a Professor at Sree Rama Engineering College. He holds a Ph.D. in Information and Communication Engineering from Anna University and has over 16 years of academic experience. Specializing in wireless sensor networks and IoT, he has published numerous research papers and holds several international patents. Dr. Bhoopathy is a recipient of prestigious awards for his contributions to education and research. His commitment to academia continues to drive innovation and excellence in the field of computer science.

Index

A

C

D

E

F

G

H

I

M

O

P

R

S

T

X

www.ingramcontent.com/pod-product-compliance
Lightning Source LLC
LaVergne TN
LVHW062332300926
849161LV00007B/1664